Here's what America's top magazines, newspapers and readers are saying about Skiing America — They love it.

"Ski vacationers will want to look at Skiing America and Ski Europe."
—Consumer Reports
Travel Letter

"When Leocha talks about something he finds lacking, there is no sugar coating . . . when he writes about something he likes, you know you're getting the truth."
—Wood River Journal
Sun Valley/Ketchum

"It provides independent evaluation of the ski terrain and offers more extensive information than found in other guides."
—Skier News

"If you're planning a ski vacation . . . this guide should serve you well."
—Ski Magazine

"Up-to-the-minute info, so accurate that even ski resort personnel peruse these pages . . . The only guidebook you'll ever need. The latest edition is packed chockablock with detailed information about the ski experience at every major resort in the United States and Canada."
—Robb Report

"Charlie Leocha is first a skier, then a writer. He shuns the party line of the big ski corporations, preferring instead to talk to locals. Skiing America's perspective is direct, credible, and no-holds-barred."
—Daily Record, NJ

"Detailed information on lift ticket prices, cross-country facilities, nightlife and more."
—Powder Magazine

"The flavor, feel and personality of each resort."
—Boston Globe

"Includes everything needed to make an educated decision about which slopes to hit."

—*PhysiciansFinancial News*

"Let's you know where the action is . . . on and off the slopes."
—KFYI, Phoenix AZ

"I finished reading your book and wanted to tell you how useful and informative I found it to be. In particular, it appears (with great relief) that the information is totally reliable. For those ski resorts of which I have personal knowledge, I found your comments and observations to be *totally* in accord with my own feelings."
—JLC, Toronto, Canada

"Your book made the planning of the trip a breeze and my husband was thrilled with the skiing."   —JSH, Dallas TX

"Your book is, in our experience, unique and we will certainly rely upon it when we next plan a vacation."   —MIG, Burlington VT

"We are enthusiastically looking forward to our trip—mostly because of your book; the gracious responses to the phone calls we made, the wonderful down-to-earth descriptions you gave us of what we should expect and the clear concise information. (The book is going with us to Colorado.)"   —JR, Media PA

"Thanks for a great vacation. I used your book to great advantage with planning a two-week trip . . . keep up the good work."
—KSH, Philadelphia PA

"I hope my comments help one-100th of what yours have helped me. Thanks for the book, It's a wealth of information."
—TR, Sherman Oaks CA

"Packed with information for ski resorts across America."
—Good Morning Houston

"Simply the best ski guide you can buy."
—The Sports Final

Ski Resorts
in Skiing America '95

California
Alpine Meadows
Squaw Valley
Northstar
Heavenly Valley
Kirkwood
Diamond Peak
Sugar Bowl
Mammoth
June Mountain
Snow Summit
Bear Mountain
Snow Valley

Oregon
Mt. Bachelor
Timberline
Mt. Hood Ski Bowl
Mt. Hood Meadows

Idaho
Sun Valley
Brundage/Silver Mt.
Schweitzer Mt.
Bogus Basin

Canada
Mystic Ridge/Norquay
Lake Louise
Sunshine
Jasper
Whistler
Blackcomb
Red Mountain
Gray Rocks
Mount Tremblant
Mont-Sainte-Anne

Colorado
Aspen
Aspen Highlands
Snowmass
Teihack/Buttermilk
Vail
Beaver Creek
Steamboat
Crested Butte
Irwin Lodge
Copper Mountain
Breckenridge
Keystone
Arapahoe Basin
Telluride
Winter Park
Arrowhead

New Mexico
Taos
Angel Fire
Pajarito
Red River
Ski Apache
Sandia Peak
Santa Fe
Sipapu

Arizona
Snowbowl
Apache Sunrise

Montana
Big Sky
Big Mountain

Alaska
Alyeska

Utah
Alta
Snowbird
Solitude/Brighton
Deer Valley
Park City
Wolf Mountain

Wyoming
Jackson Hole
Grand Targhee
Snow King

Vermont
Killington
Mount Snow
Haystack
Stratton
Sugarbush
Mad River Glen
Stowe
Jay Peak
Okemo
Smugglers' Notch

Midwestern
Sugar Loaf
Crystal Mountain
Shanty Creek
Boyne Highlands
Chestnut/Sundown
Giant's Ridge
Big Powderhorn
Indianhead/Whitecap
Lutsen/Spirit
Blackjack/Porcupine
Devil's Head/Rib

New Hampshire
Attitash/Wildcat
Cranmore/Black
Bretton Woods
Cannon Mountain
Waterville Valley
Loon Mountain

Maine
Sunday River
Sugarloaf/USA

New York
Lake Placid
Hunter Mountain
Windham

Mid-Atlantic
Showshoe
Silver Creek
Seven Springs
Hidden Valley
Camelback
Timberline
Canaan Valley
Blue Knob
Whitetail
Wintergreen
Elk/Wisp

Washington
Mt. Baker
Crystal
Alpental
Hyak
Snoqualmie
Stevens Pass
Ski Acres

Contributors to *Skiing America '95*

Charlie Leocha has skied virtually every major international resort. He also is author of *Ski Europe*, a guidebook to the Alps' top ski resorts, and writes about travel and skiing for scores of magazines and newspapers. His most recent books are *Travel Rights*, a pocket guide that explains your rights while traveling, and *Getting To Know You*, 365 questions, activities, observations and ways to get to know another person better.

Steve Giordano is a Pacific Northwest travel and recreation writer and photographer who contributes to the *Bellingham Herald*, *Adventure Northwest* and *Pacific Northwest* magazines. He is first vice-president of the Pacific Northwest region of the North American Ski Journalists Association (NASJA).

Katy Keck worked in France under chefs at Michelin-star restaurants. She owns and runs Savoir Faire Foods, a consulting company in New York specializing in food styling, recipe development and catering. She is co-owner of a hot New York City restaurant, New World Grill at 329 W. 49th Street.

James Kitfield was awarded the Gerald R. Ford prize for distinguished reporting, and the Jesse H. Neal award for excellence in reporting. He was Editor of *Overseas!*, a travel and entertainment magazine in Europe. His articles appeared in *Newsday*, *LA Examiner*, *Penthouse*, *Omni* and others. His first book, *Prodigal Soldiers*, will be published by Simon & Schuster in late 1994.

Diane Slezak Scholfield writes a weekly ski column for *The San Diego Union-Tribune* and broadcasts a daily ski segment on San Diego radio station KFSD. She has written ski and travel stories for *Ski*, *Snow Country*, *Ski Impact*, *Adventure West*, *The Miami Herald*, *The Washington Post* and many other newspapers and magazines, and she was twice named Ski Writer of the Year by NASJA.

Other contributors: **Susan Vreeland**, various chapters; **Peter Rose**, Big Sky and several Idaho resorts; **Mary Jo Tarallo**, mid-Atlantic; **Tom Carter**, Santa Fe and mid-Atlantic; **Mike Terrell**, Midwest; **Cindy Bohl**, changes at New England areas; **Dave Barrell**, Jay Peak, Smugglers' Notch and Okemo; **Paul Todd**, Alyeska.

Skiing
America
'95

by Charles A. Leocha

Diane Slezak Scholfield, executive editor

with
Steve Giordano
Katy Keck
James Kitfield

WORLD LEISURE CORPORATION
Hampstead, NH   Boston, MA

Help us do a better job

Research for this book is an ongoing process. We have been at it for more than a decade. Each year we revisit many of these resorts, and every winter we speak with locals from every resort.

If you find a new restaurant, hotel, bar or disco that you feel we should include, please let us know. If you find anything in these pages that is misleading or has changed, please let us know. If we use your suggestion, we will send you a copy of next year's edition.

Send your suggestions and comments to:
Charlie Leocha, *Skiing America*, World Leisure Corp.
Box 160, Hampstead NH 03841, USA

Distributed to the trade in USA by
Login Publishers Consortium, 1436 West Randolph Street, Chicago, IL 60607; (312) 733-8228, (800)626-4330.

Distributed to the trade in Canada by
General Publishing Co. Ltd., 30 Lesmill Road, Don Mills, Ontario M3B 2T6, Canada, tel. (416) 445-3333.

Distributed to the trade in Europe by Roger Lascelles,
47 York Road, Brentford, Middlesex TW8 0QP Tel. 081-847 0935.

Mail Order, Catalog and Special Sales by
World Leisure Corporation, 177 Paris Street, Boston, MA 02128.
Tel. (617) 569-1966, fax (617) 561-7654

ISBN: 0-915009-34-X

Contents

How to get the most out of Skiing America

How many times have you picked up a guidebook and said, "Thanks for the facts, guys, but what's this place *really* like?"

Well, we're going to tell you. This is a straightforward, honest, opinionated guidebook to North America's top resorts. We know that a ski vacation is made up of much more than the number of chair lifts or ski trails. We describe the personality of each resort, where we found the best skiing, where we liked to eat and where we enjoyed the liveliest off-slope fun. And we give you all the facts you'll need—hotel and restaurant descriptions, lift ticket and lesson prices, day-care programs, nightlife activities, and where to call or write for more information.

Most of the ski areas we describe are destination resorts—ones that can support five to seven days of ski and non-ski activity without becoming repetitive. Smaller areas near major cities are included so skiers may take day trips while in the vicinity.

What's new in this edition

A recent skier survey showed shopping is the most popular non-ski activity. Leading off the "Other Activities" section of each chapter this year is a shopping summary, including nearby factory outlet centers. We expanded the "Getting There" section to include "Getting Around." We point out which resorts require a car and which have reliable public transportation.

We also have added a new chapter on Summit County, Colorado, which details the lodging and dining in Frisco, Dillon and Silverthorne, three towns near the ski resorts of Breckenridge, Keystone/Arapahoe Basin and Copper Mountain.

And as always, each chapter is chock-full of new information and changes from last season.

A note about prices

Many of the prices in this book are from the current 1994/95 ski season. Where we have been unable to obtain current prices we have noted the 93/94 prices in the text. Where there is no notation, assume the prices are from last season. Unfortunately, as of late July many resorts had not announced their new prices.

The prices provided in this guidebook are in no way official and are subject to change at any time; they in fact do change with the seasons. Our intention is to provide you with the best possible information for planning and comparison.

Chapter organization

Each resort chapter has several sections. We begin by sketching the personality of the place—is it old and quaint, or modern and high-rise? Clustered at the base of the slopes, or a few miles down the road? Remote and isolated, or freeway-close? Family-oriented or catering to singles? Filled with friendly faces or an aloof herd of "beautiful" skiers?

The **Mountain Facts** box outlines the basic statistics of each resort. We note the **base and summit altitudes,** a major factor for those with altitude-related medical difficulties and an important consideration for sea-level dwellers who are planning a rigorous week on the slopes. The **vertical drop** provides one indicator of the amount of skiing, top to bottom, at the resort. This, combined with the total **skiable acreage** and **number and types of lifts** will give you a good idea of how much skiing is available. **Uphill lift capacity** is the number of skiers the total lift system can carry up the mountain each hour—a larger uphill lift capacity normally means shorter lift lines. **Bed base** is the approximate number of people who can be accommodated overnight near the resort. Most destination resorts try to keep uphill capacity much bigger than bed base to ensure short lift lines. Resorts with great uphill capacity/bed base ratios may still have long weekend lines if they are near major cities. We try to identify these.

A detailed description of **where to ski** is next, followed by a **mountain rating.** The first section describes various sections of the mountain and how to find your way around. The mountain rating will tell you what the resort has for beginner, intermediate or expert skiers. More important, this section also suggests which resorts might be too tough for the beginner or too mild for the expert. (Where trail maps are included, use them only for reference when planning your trip. Use the official maps provided by the resorts when you ski.)

Cross-country information will tell you which resorts have Nordic trails, as well as significant cross-country and backcountry skiing opportunities near the resort.

The **snowboarding** section outlines special snowboard facilities such as halfpipes, and snowboarding lessons and rentals (and tells you where boarders aren't allowed).

The major **ski school programs** are listed with prices.

Lift ticket prices are listed for adults, children and seniors. We've organized them in a new way this edition: a chart that has one-day, three-day and five-day prices for adults and children, with any additional information listed in paragraph form following the chart. Where possible we list the 94/95 prices, but in cases where no date is noted, assume the prices are from the previous season.

Under **accommodations** we list both the most luxurious places to stay and many of the budget lodges. Where distance to the lifts is a factor, we note which condominiums to book and which to avoid. We also suggest lodging that is particularly suited to families.

The **dining** recommendations always include the best gourmet restaurants in town, but we don't leave out affordable places where a hungry family or a skier on a budget can chow down and relax. We have compiled these suggestions from dozens of interviews with locals and tourists, then combined them with our own dining experiences. For a few resorts—the Aspen area, Crested Butte and Steamboat—Katy Keck visited the top restaurants and wrote a Savoir Faire section.

Après-ski/nightlife describes places to go when the lifts begin to close, and where to find entertainment later in the evening. We tell you which bars are loud, which are quiet, which have live music and what kind. If we know a cover charge is required, we tell you.

Details on resort **child care** facilities are given with prices, times and ages of children accepted. We describe unusual programs and any special procedures to register children.

Non-skiing activities and facilities, such as shopping, tennis, racquetball, fitness clubs, sleigh rides, hot-air ballooning, dog sledding and snowmobiling are included under **other activities**.

Finally, we give detailed **getting there and getting around** instructions and finish with key phone numbers and addresses for **information/reservations**.

Types of accommodations

A hotel is normally located in the resort proper, is relatively large, with 25 rooms or more, and comes without meals. Accommodations with the Modified American Plan (MAP) includes breakfast and dinner.

A country inn, or mountain inn, is more rustic and usually has fewer rooms than a hotel. Many of these inns have packages that include breakfast and dinner.

A bed-and-breakfast (B&B) tends to be even smaller, with just a few rooms. Sometimes guests share a common bath, but not always. Breakfast is included and some B&Bs also offer dinner arrangements.

Motels don't have the amenities of a hotel or the ambiance of a B&B, and often are further from the slopes. Motels are good for families and budget-minded skiers.

Condominiums have become the most affordable group lodging at American ski resorts because of their separate bedrooms and kitchen facilities. Many are ski-in, ski-out, or within easy walking distance of the lifts. They usually have a central check-in facility. Most condominiums have daily maid service for everything but the kitchen.

When you call the resort central reservations number, ask for suggestions. Most of the staff have been on tours of the lodgings and can make honest recommendations based on your needs.

High and low season

Ski resorts have several pricing seasons. The highest prices are during the Christmas-New Year's holidays. The "regular season" usually runs all of February and March. "Value season" is in January after New Year's. "Low season" usually is the first weeks of December and April. These vary from resort to resort, so ask for more information when you call. The most noticeable change is in the cost of accommodations, but some resorts also lower the prices of lift tickets, especially in the pre-season and in the spring.

Skier ability levels

These are the terms we use in the "Where to ski" sections:

Never-evers are just what the name implies. We apply the term to the novice for the first few days on skis.

Beginners have about a week of instruction and can turn and stop (more or less) when they choose, but still rely on the stem christie and wedge turns.

Lower intermediates can link stem christies and are beginning to make parallel turns.

Intermediates can negotiate any blue trail and can parallel ski (more or less) on the smooth stuff. They go back to survival rules on expert trails, and struggle in heavy powder and crud.

Advanced skiers can ski virtually any trail with carved turns, but are still intimidated by deep powder, crud and super steeps.

Experts can always ski anything, anytime, anywhere. They are few and far between.

A warning about ski-area trail ratings: All North American ski areas use what seems to be a universal trail-rating system. Green circles designate the easiest runs, blue squares show the more difficult runs and black diamonds designate the toughest runs. However, the system only shows the relative difficulty of the runs at that particular ski area, not compared to other areas. A black run on the gently rolling hills of Angel Fire, New Mexico will probably be easier to ski than a blue run at nearby Taos.

Ratings are largely determined by steepness, but are also influenced by other things, such as the run's width and whether it is groomed regularly. When you ski at a new area, ALWAYS warm up on a run that is rated one color below what you usually ski. That way you'll avoid nasty surprises.

Skiing for everyone

Skiers come in all abilities, sexes, interests and ages. Better equipment and slope grooming techniques mean that skiing is easier to learn and you never have to give it up as you age. As more people are attracted to the sport, resorts are putting more emphasis on teaching how much fun you can have downhill skiing, cross-country skiing or snowboarding. This is a sport that combines the best of Mother Nature with the best of friendly people out to enjoy themselves.

The first step is learning to ski. We touch on the basics of lessons, equipment and clothing, then explore special programs, now offered at many resorts, for older skiers, disabled skiers, women and advanced skiers.

The experience of beginning to ski

When you ski, you escape from your everyday routine. No matter your level of skiing expertise, you find challenge, beauty and a balance with nature. This is a sport where everyone from beginner to expert can have fun, a sport you do in clean air and stunning scenery, and a sport where you'll easily meet and enjoy other skiers.

Learning to ski is not difficult IF you don't try to teach yourself. We firmly believe that lessons are the only way to go for never-evers, whatever their athletic ability. Natural athletes may quickly develop balance, but they'll also develop bad habits that will hinder later progress. Toddlers can start as young as 2, and you're never too old to learn—really. And learning to ski or snowboard will not break the bank. Many ski areas offer free or heavily discounted lessons for beginners.

After only four or five downhill lessons, most beginners have improved enough to negotiate their way down more than half the marked ski trails in North America. For cross-country you need only a couple of lessons to begin gliding through the forests and across rolling meadows.

How do you get started? Call any of the resorts listed in this book and ask about learn-to-ski packages. Most include lift tickets, rental equipment and lessons. Or visit your local ski shop and ask them about learn-to-ski programs close to home. They can give you tips and set you up with the right equipment.

While learning to ski, rent your equipment. Renting is much less expensive than buying at this point, because as you get better you'll need more advanced gear. Ski shop pros will help you with the correct ski length and type, bindings, and adjustments. As you improve, they can suggest how to upgrade: increasing ski length and stiffness, acquiring higher performance boots, and so forth. The two principal places to rent are ski shops near home or at the ski resorts; the choice will probably be based on the way you get to the resort—flying or driving—and how much time you'll spend there. If possible, rent near home or, at the resort the night before you start skiing. There's a horrible time's-a-wastin' feeling about standing in line to get fitted your first morning there.

Proper clothing also is important. You don't need the latest, most colorful ski fashions—what you can find in your closet should do just fine, provided you can find such basics as a pair of long johns, a sweater, a waterproof or water-resistant jacket, wool or acrylic socks, and a pair of wool trousers or nylon wind pants. One warning: Because your backside will be spending time in contact with the snow at first, don't wear jeans or other cotton pants. In fact, don't wear anything made of cotton next to your skin, such as cotton socks or a T-shirt. Cotton soaks up and holds moisture—either sweat or snow—and you soon will be cold. If you are missing any of the basics, borrow from a friend. The secret to staying just warm enough is layering. A few lightweight garments are better than one heavy one, since layers trap the air. Remove or add layers as temperatures change.

Wear a hat—50 percent of your body heat can escape through your head! Wear gloves—they will keep your hands warm and protected. Ski gloves, as you will note if you inspect a pair in a sports store, are padded and reinforced in ways different from any other gloves you're likely to have on hand—sorry about that—so these may have to be a specific purchase if you can't borrow them. Though you can get by with sunglasses on your first few days (do wear some: high-altitude sun is very nasty to unprotected eyes), amber goggles are *vital* for seeing trail contours on overcast days. Use sunscreen—at high altitudes the sun's rays are stronger and the reflection of rays off the snow increases your total dose.

Your first lessons will teach you how to walk, slide, and—very important—stop. Then the lessons focus on how to get up after falling (you may have already practiced that lesson on your own). You will learn the basic wedge turn, also called a snowplow turn. With this turn you will be able to negotiate almost any groomed slope. Your instructor will show you how to use the lifts, and you'll be on your way. You'll be surprised how much you're enjoying it from the start, and how fast you improve.

You don't have to start with downhill skiing. Many skiers go right to cross-country or to snowboarding. Just pick the sport that suits you best.

Enjoy!

Getting in shape

How important is it to be in shape for skiing? Well, we aren't going to lie to you—the more fit you are, the more fun you'll have and the better you'll ski.

But this doesn't mean you have to devote half your life to jogging and hamstring stretches. We won't lie to you about this, either—most of the contributors to this book would never be mistaken for Jane Fonda or Arnold Schwarzenegger, writing being the sedentary profession it is. But we all have learned—sometimes the hard way—that if we get lax about our exercise programs at home, we pay for it when we're doing our on-slope research.

A moderate exercise program—about an hour three to four times a week—is all it takes. Here are some of the key things to include:

• Aerobics. Get that heart pumping so your whole body will process oxygen more efficiently. A good portion of America's skiers—especially those who buy guidebooks—live at or near sea level. Most of the Rocky Mountain ski areas are at 8,000- to 11,000-foot elevations where the air is thin. Those who lead sedentary lives where the oxygen is plentiful will be exhausted after two or three hours where there's less of it. You've spent big money for your ski trip—why waste a minute?

• Flexibility. Stre-e-e-tch those muscles, particularly the ones down the backs of your legs. Sometimes your skis decide to head in different directions, and sometimes your feet stay attached. If your hamstrings or inner-thigh muscles are tight, a fall like that could put you out of commission for the rest of your vacation.

• Strength. Most skiers, even new ones, know that strong leg muscles make skiing a lot easier. Muscles just as important, but ignored by many skiers, are the ones in your upper body. Have you ever had to push yourself across a long, flat section of the mountain? Have you ever carried 15 pounds of ski equipment from your car or lodge to the chair lift? Have you ever pushed yourself up off the snow after a fall? Sure you have, and you do all those things with your arms and shoulders.

Of course, it's important to consult your doctor before going from a completely chair-bound lifestyle to a regular exercise program. And it's best to get some professional help regarding the best program for you. Fitness centers—especially in cities that have a lot of skiers—often have ski-conditioning classes during the fall months that concentrate on exercises that mimic skiing movements. Such a class can really give you a head start on the season.

If you can't find a ski-conditioning class in your area, you can take one with your VCR. Several ski-conditioning videos are on the market now, such as Patty Wade's "In Shape To Ski." Wade, a fitness instructor in Aspen, teaches a ski-conditioning class each autumn that many of the locals swear by. Her 60-minute video workout offers a thorough and tough workout (even Patty breathes hard during the workout). You can adjust the pace to your level by not doing the exercises as long as she does. Call (800) 925-9754 for ordering information if you can't find it at a local video outlet.

Another way to get in shape for skiing is with a ski-specific exercise machine such as the ones by NordicTrack. You're probably familiar with that company's cross-country trainer, but now they make an Alpine trainer too. Some of our contributors have used the NordicSport™ World Class™ Ski cross-country type trainer and swear by it for great aerobic exercise. The NordicSport™ downhill 450 Alpine trainer gets mixed reviews— one contributor really likes it, the other is lukewarm Both agree that it helps develop on-slope balance. These machines are shown above. Call 1-800-445-2231 for additional information.

Mountain maladies

Even those skiers in the best of shape can find themselves spending their vacation in the condo if they aren't careful. These four "skier maladies" are easily avoidable. Here's how to keep from being a victim:

•**Altitude sickness**. Caused by a too-fast gain in elevation, the symptoms are a bit like the flu—nausea, headaches, insomnia. The best way to avoid it is to go easy the first day or so—ski slow and easy, eat light and drink lots of water but little alcohol. If this is a persistent problem for you, go to ski areas where the base elevation is below 8,000 feet.

•**Snow blindness**. Always wear sunglasses or goggles when you ski, and be sure they protect your eyes from damaging rays. Sun reflecting off bright snow can easily "sunburn" your retinas. Your eyes will feel as if someone has dumped a load of sand in them, and the only cure is resting in a darkened room for a day or two—no reading, no TV and definitely no skiing.

•**Hypothermia**. It's 10 degrees outside, the wind is howling and you don't want to wear a hat because it will flatten your hair? Your vanity could make you sick. When you lose body heat faster than you can replace it, you're risking hypothermia. Wear enough clothes so you're warm, but not so many that you're soaked through with sweat. (Cold weather and wet clothing act as a hypothermia magnet.) If you start to shiver, get inside. Add a layer of clothes. If you still are shivering, quit for the day. Better to lose a few hours than several days.

•**Frostbite**. This is what happens to fingers, toes, cheeks, noses and ears when body tissue starts to freeze. If any of these start to feel cold, check to see if your skin is turning white. If it is, get inside, drink something warm and non-alcoholic, and cover the affected part with extra clothing or warm it with body heat. Don't rub it or hold it near a fireplace, because you could do further damage.

Programs for older skiers

Skiing isn't just for youngsters anymore. One of the fastest growing age groups in skiing is 55 and older. By the year 2010, 37 percent of all skiers are expected to be in that age group.

Some of those skiers learned when they were young and never stopped skiing, but others started late in life. Many ski areas have started programs that cater to the upper age group. Nearly every ski area in North America offers free or heavily discounted lift tickets to skiers when they reach 60, 65 or 70.

And thanks to clubs such as the Over the Hill Gang and the 70+ Club, older skiers always have companionship. The 70+ Club started in 1977 with 34 members. Now, it has more than 10,000 members—all 70 or older—in several countries.

Here is a partial list of clubs and programs for older skiers. New programs are starting every season, so give the ski school at your area a call.

Clubs: Members of the **70+ Ski Club** wear distinctive red-and-white patches that identify them as part of this elite group. A $5 lifetime membership fee, plus a copy of a legal document that clearly shows date of birth (such as a passport, driver's license, etc.), is all it takes to join. Founder Lloyd Lambert was a pioneer in getting discounts for older skiers. About 19 members are still skiing in their 90s. For membership information, write to Lambert at 104 East Side Drive, Ballston Lake NY 12019.

The Over The Hill Gang is for skiers 50 and older. This nationwide group has local chapters all over the country whose members not only ski, but also play volleyball and tennis, go hiking and sailing and enjoy the outdoor life. Contact the Over The Hill Gang at 3310 Cedar Heights Dr., Colorado Springs, CO 80904, (719) 685-4656.

Members of the **Over Eighty Ski Club** get their names inscribed on a Scroll of Distinction at the U.S. Ski Hall of Fame. The club began in 1985, and the list has included kings (the late Olav V of Norway was a member) and commoners. To become a member of this special group, send a minimum donation of $25 to the U.S. Ski Hall of Fame, attention: Ray Leverton, Box 191, Ishpeming MI 49849-0191.

Elderhostel offers learn-to-ski programs several times a year at Sunday River Ski Resort in Maine. The skiing is combined with other academic courses. This is the first Elderhostel campus to offer skiing. For information, call Elderhostel in Boston at (617) 426-8056.

Ski area programs: Special instruction or social programs for seniors are offered at Purgatory-Durango, Colorado; Park City, Utah; Badger Pass, California; Waterville Valley, New Hampshire; Aspen, Colorado; Stratton, Vermont and Sun Valley, Idaho, among other resorts. Some are day programs; others are week-long vacations with big-band dances and wine-and-cheese parties. Resorts keep adding programs every year in order to attract this important age group.

Women's ski instruction

Nearly every major ski resort, and many of the smaller ones, has some sort of program just for women.

Why segregate? Annie Vareille-Savath, Telluride's Ski School Director, observes, "The skill level of women often drops when a man enters their ski class. Even strong, successful women, assertive in their own fields, sometimes feel intimidated and humiliated when they are in a mixed skiing atmosphere. They crumple into self-conscious inability or regress to silliness, stiffness or fear."

The goal of such seminars is not to segregate women from their male friends on the slopes permanently, but to provide a temporary environment geared to eliminating learning barriers so that "women only" instruction ultimately becomes unnecessary.

Because lessons usually are with the same instructor each day, improvement is both dramatic and clearly recognizable.

Discussions address issues particular to women skiers, such as fear of speed, and equipment selection to compensate for a woman's body build. Most programs incorporate video sessions. Some seminars are as heavy on social fun as improving skills; others are directed toward higher-ability skiers who want to learn to race, ski moguls, etc.

Women's programs that have received very high reviews are at Squaw Valley, where instructor Elissa Slanger originated this type of program two decades ago; Telluride, where Vareille-Savath's influence as ski-school director shows through, and Crested Butte, where Kim Reichhelm, a former amateur and professional ski racer who also has been the Women's World Extreme Skiing Champion (for successfully skiing ultra-steep slopes), will operate her Women's Ski Adventures program. Information about the Telluride and Squaw Valley programs are available from those ski areas; for Reichhelm's program at Crested Butte, call (800) 992-7700.

Three of the contributors to *Skiing America* have participated in a women's seminar within the past five years and all three reported vast improvement in their skiing ability. We can recommend these programs wholeheartedly.

Research on helping women ski better is ongoing and extensive. Some of the latest discoveries are included in a new book, *WomenSki,* by award-winning Colorado ski journalist Claudia Carbone and published by World Leisure Corporation, which also publishes this guidebook.

Skiing for the physically challenged

At more and more ski areas, you're likely to see a few empty wheelchairs next to the ski racks in the base area. Skiing is a great sport for physically challenged people, because gravity plays such a major role. Specially designed equipment is available for just about any type of disability. At most resorts that cater to physically challenged skiers, if they don't have the right equipment, they'll invent it. There is no reason why a physically challenged skier can't ski as fast as an able-bodied one; in fact, sometimes they're faster—a real ego boost for those who must proceed a little slower than most on dry land.

Winter Park, Colorado has been the pioneer in this area, and it still has one of the best programs. Hal O'Leary, founder and director of the **National Sports Center for the Disabled,** began with a few sets of borrowed skis and a broom-closet office. Now with a full-time staff of 13 and a volunteer organization of 850, Winter Park handles 2,500 participants with 45 types of disabilities, and gives 14,500 lessons yearly.

Among those who can ski are amputees, wheelchair users, the blind and those with cerebral palsy and multiple sclerosis.

National Handicapped Sports now has chapters and programs in more than 60 cities and resorts, and reports that more than 12,000 individuals are in learning programs each year.

Among the other ski schools for the disabled:

Tahoe Handicapped Ski School at Alpine Meadows; offices at 5926 Illinois Avenue, Orangevale CA 95662; (916) 989-0402. Onsite phone number: (916) 581-4161.

Bear Mountain (two and a half hours east of Los Angeles) Box 6812, Big Bear Lake CA 92315; (909) 585-2519.

Breckenridge Outdoor Education Center, Box 697, Breckenridge CO 80424; (303) 453-6422.

New England Handicapped Sportsmen's Association. The program is at Mt. Snow/Haystack in Vermont; offices are at 26 McFarlin Rd., Chelmsford MA 01824; (508) 256-3240.

Ski Windham; offices at 1A Lincoln Ave., Albany NY 12205; (518) 452-6095.

Park City Handicapped Sports Association, Box 680286, Park City UT 84068; (801) 649-3991.

Hal O'Leary, Director, **National Sports Center for the Disabled**, Box 36, Winter Park CO 80482; (303) 726-5514.

National Handicapped Sports, 451 Hungerford Dr., Suite 100, Rockville, MD 20850, (202) 393-7505. Provides a list of chapters and programs throughout the U.S.

Clinics for advanced skiers

Advanced skiers hardly ever take lessons, and it's no wonder. Until recently, advanced skiers were taught just like beginners: groups of four to six, make a few turns, then listen to the instructor give generalized tips on improvement. That format works well for lower-level skiers, all of whom need to learn the same skills. But while most skiers develop bad habits as they progress, not all develop the same ones. One skier may need to work on pole plants; another may need to keep his shoulders square to the hill and a third may be sitting too far back on her skis. Just like World Cup racers, these skiers need fine-tuning. They need a coach, not an instructor: someone who will observe the way they ski and then give very specific tips on breaking the habits that keep skiers from progressing to the next level.

Resorts are responding to advanced skiers' needs with lessons that are vastly different from the ones offered to lower-level skiers. First of all, they aren't called "lessons"—they are "workshops" or "clinics." Instead of the standard ski-stop-listen format, most of these clinics are heavy on ski, ski, ski and listening to the instructor as you go or while on the lift. Quite a few work on the "condition du jour"—powder, moguls, crud, etc. Many have video feedback.

If you're an intermediate or advanced skier, look into these programs. But when you're at the ski school office, here are a few tips to be sure to get what you want:

• Don't use the word "lesson." Ask what type of "clinics" or "workshops" are offered for upper-level skiers.

• Be specific when asking about the format. How much time is spent skiing? What skills will we work on?

• Insist that the instructor address each students' needs. Some instructors won't target individuals for fear of offending them. That's fine for beginners, but not for better skiers who need fine-tuning.

• If after the clinic you don't feel you got your money's worth, go to the ski school office and politely tell them why. ("I expected to actually ski moguls during the mogul clinic, not practice short turns on groomed slopes.") If the ski school is smart, they'll get you in the right workshop.

One instructional method we can recommend heartily is **Perfect Turn®**, which began at Sunday River, Maine, and has spread to Mt. Bachelor, Oregon; Jiminy Peak, Massachusetts; and Blue Mountain, Ontario. Perfect Turn operates on total positive reinforcement. The ski pros (they aren't called instructors) never tell you what you're doing wrong; only what you're doing right.

Example: a non-Perfect Turn ski instructor would first tell a student, "You're sitting back too far on your skis," then illustrate how to correct that—perhaps by telling the student to push her shin against the tongue of her boot just enough to keep a pretend hundred-dollar bill from flying away. The Perfect Turn ski pro skips the critical comment and goes right to the correctional tip. Additionally, the pro identifies what the skier does very well and compliments those skills lavishly.

Now, didn't your mother ever tell you that you catch more flies with honey than with vinegar? The Perfect Turn pro took that lesson to heart. Because he makes you feel confident about your current skills, you believe that you can take on a bigger challenge and do that well, too. Jump off that cornice into those igloo-sized moguls? Sure, coach, if you say I can do it, I can.

Yeah, yeah, it sounds hokey. But it works. One of our contributors, on the cusp between intermediate and advanced, took one Perfect Turn lesson early last season, then merrily led two *Skiing America* staffers—both advanced skiers—down a slope of cut-up powder. Throughout the season, she skied black diamonds with more confidence than ever before. If you learn faster when you get positive strokes, make a trip to a ski area that offers this program.

Lake Tahoe Area

Alpine Meadows
Squaw Valley USA
Northstar-at-Tahoe
Kirkwood, Heavenly
Diamond Peak, Sugar Bowl
with Reno, Nevada

Few regions on the North American continent have the ski-resort diversity of the Lake Tahoe region. When you consider the elements of a perfect ski vacation—variety of terrain, good snow, comfortable lodging, beautiful scenery, a wide choice of restaurants and nightlife, a myriad of other activities, accessibility—Lake Tahoe would rank near the top in all but a couple of categories (and it would be above the median in the rest).

Lake Tahoe, one of the largest and most stunning mountain lakes in the world, straddles the border of California and Nevada about 200 miles east of San Francisco. The lake is surrounded by five world-class ski areas, plus several smaller resorts (several of these "smaller" resorts have more than 1,000 skiable acres).

Tahoe is best divided into three regions for vacation purposes. Though you can run yourself ragged by trying to ski at every major area in a week, it's better to concentrate on the North Shore, South Shore or northeast Nevada corner. The South Shore is highly developed, lined by high-rise casino-hotels hugging the California-Nevada state line. The Nevada northeast shore is quiet but upscale, with fewer and smaller casinos. The California North Shore has mom-and-pop cabins, some stylish B&Bs and upscale lakefront condos.

Tahoe's ski nightlife is unique. No other ski area has 24-hour casinos and big-name entertainment on a regular basis. Whatever skiing, lodging or nightlife you like, you'll probably find it somewhere around the 72-mile perimeter of Lake Tahoe.

Because this region is so huge, we need two chapters to describe it all. This one will detail everything but the skiing. You'll find descriptions of the seven largest resorts in the next chapter.

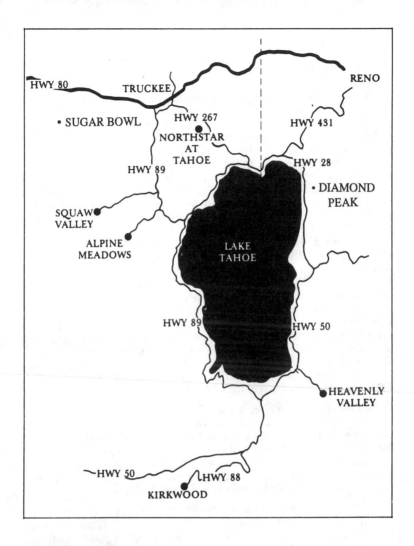

Cross-country

The Lake Tahoe region may have the largest concentration of cross-country ski areas in the U.S.

The largest single area, without question, is in California at **Royal Gorge,** just off I-80, west of Donner Summit at the Soda Springs exit. Royal Gorge has nearly 9,000 acres of terrain, and more than 300 km. of trail with a skating lane inside the tracks. They also make snow and use modern snowcats. (916) 426-3871. Adult trail fees, $17.50, $8.50 for children 7-14; discounts for multiday tickets and skiers 65 and older.

Northstar-at-Tahoe has 65 km. of groomed and marked trails. (916) 587-0273. Trail fees, $15 adults, $8 children 5-12; beginner lessons (one-and-a-half hour) with equipment, $35.

The Tahoe Donner Cross-Country Area is also off I-80 at Donner State Park exit. This area has 65 km. of trails, all double-tracked with wide skating lanes. Tahoe Donner has California's only lighted night cross-country skiing. Call (916) 587-9484 for current trail, lesson and rental fees.

Tahoe Nordic, two miles north of Tahoe City, offers 65 km. of trails at lake level (7,000 feet). (916) 583-9858. Call for fees.

Squaw Valley USA Nordic Center is at the east end of the resort parking area. Trails climb 600 feet and range from back-country, unpatrolled trails to prepared tracks. Trail fees are $12 for adults; $8 for children. (916) 583-6300.

Diamond Peak Cross-Country Area has more than 35 km. of groomed tracks and skating lanes for all levels. Trail fees are $11 for adults all day; $7 half day. Children 6-12 and seniors 60-69 pay $7 and $5 respectively. Older than 69 and younger than 6 ski free. Rentals and lessons are available.

On the South Lake Tahoe end, **Kirkwood** has 80 km. of machine-groomed track, double tracks, skating lanes and three interconnected trail systems with three warming huts, including the 1864 Kirkwood Inn, an old trappers' log cabin chockablock with nostalgia. The White Pine trail has an environmental theme: signs along the trail discuss the flora and wildlife. Trail fees, $13 adult, $5 children, $10 seniors (209) 258-7248.

Accommodations

The Tahoe basin has hundreds of options. Lake Tahoe accommodations can be divided into: 1) at the resorts (listed in the next chapter); 2) North Shore, 3) South Shore; 4) Reno. Skiers concentrating on Squaw, Alpine, Northstar, Diamond Peak and Sugar Bowl will find the North Shore and Reno handiest. Those skiing Heavenly or Kirkwood should head to South Lake Tahoe.

Accommodations—The North Shore

The North Shore of Tahoe is relatively quiet. From bed-and-breakfast inns and cabins on the lake to plush condominiums and medium-sized casino hotels, there is a place for everyone.

The most upscale bed-and-breakfast is the **Rockwood Lodge** (916-525-5273), originally built in the mid-1930s. There are only four bedrooms, two with private bath. The furnishings are antiques, the carpeting so plush you'll be asked to remove your shoes before walking through the house; the baths feature brass and porcelain fixtures, and the beds have down comforters. The lodge is next to the base of the Homewood Ski Area, on the west shore of Tahoe about seven miles south of Tahoe City. Rates: About $100-$150 per night. NOTE: this is a No-Smoking inn and does not accept children.

The Mayfield House (916-583-1001), another B&B, was once a private residence in Tahoe City. The atmosphere is elegant and romantic. Full breakfasts come with the rate, which is $85 to $115. None of the six rooms has a private bath.

Just to the south of Tahoe City is the **Sunnyside Lodge** (916-583-7200, or in California only, 800-822-2754), located directly on the lake. There are 23 rooms, all with a lake view. A few rooms have fireplaces. Room No. 39 makes a great honeymoon suite, but reserve early because there is a four- to six-week waiting list. All rooms are bright and tastefully furnished. This is an excellent property with a lively bar après-ski and a good restaurant, the Chris Craft. Rates: $95 a night for standard rooms; up to $150 for lakefront suites.

Perhaps the most luxury for the money on the North Shore is the **Tahoe Vista Inn & Marina** in Tahoe Vista (916-546-4819). The six units here are spectacular and sited directly on the lake. The Jacuzzi tubs are big and the picture windows looking onto the lake are massive. Rates range from $160 a night for the smallest unit to $225 a night for a one-bedroom suite with a panoramic lake view. A two-bedroom suite goes for $215, but doesn't have quite the view of the other room.

Among the casinos just over the border, the top property is the **Cal-Neva Lodge** (800) 225-6382 (800-CAL-NEVA) of Frank Sinatra and Marilyn Monroe fame. Every room has a lake view, and the best are from the deluxe suites on the top three floors. There are also honeymoon bungalows with heart-shaped tubs, round beds and mirrored ceilings. Standard rooms are $69 midweek, $99 weekends; the deluxe suites run $89 Sunday through Thursday, and $109 the other two nights.

For families or anyone looking for a great deal, **North Lake Lodge** in Kings Beach, a collection of 10 buildings only a few feet from the shore, is one of the oldest hotels on the lake but still in great shape. Continental breakfast is included in the rates and the shuttlebuses stop just across the street. The lodge rates are $40 for a queen with bath or $45 for a king or two doubles with bath. The rates range from $45 a night for a queen with bath to $60 for two queens with kitchen and bath. Call (916) 546-2731.

Two other family properties are the **Charmey Chalet Resort** (916-546-2529) and the **Franciscan Lakeside Lodge** (916-546-7234).

The North Lake Tahoe Visitors Bureau at 800-824-6348 (TA-HOE-4 U) can also suggest a list of private homes and condos.

Away from the lake in Truckee, but convenient to Northstar and Sugar Bowl, is the **Truckee Hotel** (916-587-4444), which has been welcoming guests since 1873. Mostly it housed timber and railroad workers, but one of the residents was a madam who reportedly ran a little business on the side. It has recently been renovated, but you'll still feel like you're sleeping in the Old West. Eight of the rooms have baths, but these feature old-fashioned claw-footed tubs and cost $90 to $115. Others share baths with prices ranging from $70 to $85. Some rooms are large enough to sleep six, and there is a restaurant, The Passage, that serves lunch and dinner.

Accommodations—South Lake Tahoe

These divide into three categories and areas: the casinos just over the border in Nevada for great views, bright lights and nonstop nightlife; at the top of Kingsbury Grade, near the base of the Nevada side of Heavenly, for upscale condominiums and top-quality hotels; and along the California lake shore for moderately priced motels.

For casinos, try **Harvey's** (800-648-3361 from outside Nevada or 702-588-2411 from Nevada) and **Harrah's** (800-648-3353 or 702-588-3515), which has everyone's highest ratings, from AAA to Mobil. Other casino-hotels within walking distance of the state line are **Caesars Tahoe** (800-648-3353) and the **Lake Tahoe Horizon Casino Resort** (800-648-3322).

For the Nevada side of Heavenly accommodations, there are scores of condos at Stagecoach Base and Boulder Base areas.

At the base of Kingsbury Grade on Highway 50 you'll find the **Lakeside Inn & Casino** (800-624-7980), which offers some of the best deals. The rooms are simple and motelish but access to the mountain is excellent. Rates are $55-$65 a night.

The California side of South Lake Tahoe has many small motels lining Lake Tahoe Boulevard for miles. The most luxurious hotel is the **Embassy Suites Resort** (800-362-2779 or 916-544-5400), which appears to be one of the casino-hotels, but is actually on the California side (so, no casino). Rates range from about $129 to $219.

Among the best of the motel bunch are two Best Western properties—**The Timber Cove Lodge** (800-528-1234 or 916-541-6722), located on the beach; and **Station House Inn** (800-822-5922 or 916-542-1101), which is within walking distance of the casino area, just on the California side of the border.

Lakeland Village (800-822-5969) has a hotel and collection of condominiums right on the lake with convenient shuttlebus service to the bases of Heavenly and Kirkwood. Expect to pay $85 for a studio or $130 for a suite with loft in the Lodge. Townhouses cost from $165, for a one-bedroom unit that is not lakefront, to $395 for a four-bedroom, three-bath unit on the lake. **The Tahoe Chalet Inn** (916-541-3311 or 800-821-2656 in California) is three blocks from the casino area and is one of the better Tahoe Boulevard strip establishments. Finally, for those who want a room just across from Heavenly's lifts on the California side, the **Tahoe Seasons Resort** has received acceptable reviews from everyone locally (916-541-6700).

One more, for couples only: The **Fantasy Inn** (800-367-7736, 916-541-6666) opened a couple of years ago with 53 rooms designed for romance. Tahoe had another Fantasy Inn a while back that was a bit tacky in decor, but this one is very tastefully done. Each room has one bed in a choice of several shapes (round, heart-shaped, water or regular mattress, king-size), a private spa for two, an in-room music system with 30 channels for virtually every music genre from classical to heavy metal, adjustable peach-colored lighting and showers with His and Hers shower heads. Eight of the rooms are theme suites, such as Rain Forest (plants and rattan decor), Caesar's Indulgence (a sexy black decor), Penthouse (a subtle teal and peach) and Romeo and Juliet (the honeymoon suite that we didn't see because it was continually booked during our visit). A wedding chapel is on the premises. Per-night rates are $88 Sunday-Thursday and $128 Friday and Saturday for the Princess room, $108/$148 for the Royal room (it's a little bigger), and $148/$198 for the theme rooms. Ask about special ski and/or wedding package rates. If you can swing it financially, take a theme room for a night or two. You won't forget it.

Accommodations—Nevada's Northeast Corner

Reno offers big-time casino atmosphere closer to the North Shore and at lower prices than you'll find at the South Shore. There are special events scheduled throughout the winter and spring. Reno also has a planetarium and two major museums. Reno is about a half hour to 45 minutes by car from the Tahoe Area resorts. Some hotels have ski shuttles; but most visitors here probably will want a car. Call (800) 367-7366 (FOR-RENO) for reservations and a vacation planner.

Incline Village is a quiet upscale community that is home to Diamond Peak ski area. It has several very fine hotels and condo units. Call (800) 468-2463 (GO-TAHOE) for information.

Dining

The North Shore

For those not concerned with price:

Glissandi at the Resort at Squaw Creek (916-583-6300) brings New York or San Francisco class and service, all overlooking Squaw Valley. Reservations suggested.

Captain Jon's (916-546-4819) in Tahoe Vista serves excellent seafood and French country specialties. Closed Mondays.

Le Petit Pier (916-546-4464) in Tahoe Vista presents upscale French cuisine. Reservations needed. Open daily.

Swiss Lakewood Restaurant (916-525-5211), in Homewood, is Lake Tahoe's oldest and one of its finest dining experience. Cuisine is French-Swiss and classic continental. Service impeccable. Closed Mondays, except holidays.

Wolfdales (916-583-5700) in downtown Tahoe City has superb dining. Reservations are suggested. Closed Tuesdays.

Graham's is a new restaurant that locals recommend, located in Squaw Valley at the Christy Inn (916-581-0454).

Katy Keck's recommendation: **Christy Hill** in Tahoe City (115 Grove Street, reservations recommended, 916-583-8551) is a real find. Just on the edge of the Lake Tahoe North Shore, Christy Hill offers superb lake views in an intimate, casually elegant atmosphere. Chef-owner Matt Adams and his wife Debbie are charming hosts, which makes every visit a delight.

The menu, which changes several times each week, is loaded with the freshest fish and specialty produce. Matt's fascination with eastern flavors is evident, but his style is pure California. Start with a fresh Anaheim chile relleño stuffed with house, smoked chicken and Sonoma pepper jack cheese, or fresh Atlantic sea scallops broiled and served with spicy Napa cabbage and a sesame ginger dressing.

Entrées include fresh Atlantic king salmon, sautéed with a coating of fresh ginger and cracked pepper, served with a cabernet sauce. Or try the grilled eggplant stuffed with a sauté of spinach, mushrooms, asparagus and goat cheese with a sauce of roasted tomatoes and oregano. The fresh New Zealand venison with shitakes is cooked to perfection. Save room for the fabulous desserts. The restaurant is open for dinner only from Tuesday through Sunday from 5:30 p.m. Appetizers are $7-$12 and entrées range from $19 to $24.

For more moderate fare try:

Ristorante D'Aosta in Olympic House at Squaw Valley USA (916-583-2614) provides an elegantly casual setting, or ride the cable car to the top of Squaw Valley USA and dine at the **Poolside Café** overlooking Granite Chief and Emigrant Peaks.

The Basque Club Restaurant (619-587-0260) in the Northstar-at-Tahoe Golf Clubhouse serves a family-style five-course meal of traditional Basque cuisine—be sure you're hungry. There are always two entrées, plus many side dishes you think are entrées before the real thing is served. Sleigh rides depart hourly from the clubhouse.

Black Bear Tavern (916-583-8626) is in a historic log building just south of Tahoe City on Highway 89, with gourmet dinners at moderate prices.

Others to try: **The Passage** in the Truckee Hotel has good soups and interesting salads, and a pleasant atmosphere with antiques; **Cottonwood Restaurant** in Truckee; **River Ranch** at the access road to Alpine Meadows; **Grazie** in the Roundhouse Mall for "nouveau" Italian food and great lake views. **The Soule Domain** in Crystal Bay received consistent raves from people at both ends of the lake. **The Steak and Lobster House** in the Crystal Bay Casino also has excellent food for moderate prices. For Mexican with a big dose of margaritas and a shoulder-to-shoulder crowd on weekends, a good choice is the **Hacienda del Lago** in Tahoe City in the Boatworks Mall. **Fast Eddie's** in Tahoe City can rustle up a side of tasty barbecue ribs.

For lots of good food at very reasonable prices:

Bacchi's just outside Tahoe City or **Lanza's** in Kings Beach, both serving good Italian fare. **The Family Tree** in Tahoe City has perhaps the best all-round family food. **Bobby's Rib Place** serves great ribs, while in Tahoe City at the Fanny Bridge, **Willi B's** is known for great Cajun, and **Bridgetender** for burgers and an extensive beer selection.

The casinos on the Nevada/California border all serve inexpensive breakfast, lunch and dinner specials.

For the best pizza, try **Pizza Junction** outside of Truckee, where they make their own Truckee River Beer, or the **Lakehouse Pizza** where you can enjoy a great view of Lake Tahoe, as well as **C.B's Pizza** in Kings Beach.

The best breakfasts are at the **Squeeze In** where the list of omelets requires a speed-reading course. The Squeeze In has all the atmosphere you could want in a breakfast joint—built in a former alley and only 10 feet wide. On weekends expect to wait a while—this place is popular. Down the street is the **Coffee And**, which also serves up a good basic breakfast. Also try **The Fire Sign** about two miles south of Tahoe City, and for those further to the north, try the **Old Post Office** in Carnelian Bay or the **Log Cabin** in Kings Beach. Near Alpine Meadows, try **The Alpine Riverside Cafe** for breakfast and lunch.

South Lake Tahoe

For the best restaurants in the higher priced category:

Evan's American Gourmet Café on 89th Street has become one of the best-liked restaurants on the south shore. The chef prepares California Cuisine with an unusual flair. Expect to pay for his efforts, but they are reported to be well worth it.

For good reasonable restaurants, try:

Fresh Ketch for fish, **Cantina Los Tres Hombres** or **Bueno Rico's** for Mexican, or head to one of the casinos' great buffets or fixed-price dinners. **Harvey's** has a reasonably priced Seafood Grotto with large portions. **Zackary's Restaurant** in Embassy Suites has the best blackened salmon. **Bennigan's** is in Bill's Tahoe Casino across from the High Sierra. Then there's the **Chart House**, with a lake overlook on the Kingsbury Grade.

For great breakfasts head to **The Red Hut**, where you can pack into a small room and listen to the talk of the town. A new branch opened on Kingsbury Grade handy for skiers heading to the Nevada side of Heavenly. At **Heidi's**, you can get anything from dozens of Belgian waffles to chocolate pancakes. The other two locals' spots for morning gossip and breakfast, **Frank's** and **Ernie's**, just about face each other on Route 50 south.

At Heavenly, table linen lunch service is offered at **Top of the Tram** Restaurant.

And just in case you crave a malt "so thick it holds the straw up," head to the **Zephyr Cove Resort**. The banana-chocolate shake is highly recommended.

Après-ski/nightlife

South Shore: Head to **Carlos Murphy's** immediately after skiing or stop in the **California Bar** at Heavenly's Base Lodge, with its famous Grizzly Bear. If you want quieter après-ski with a flickering fireplace, stop in at **Christiana Inn** across from the Heavenly ski area.

Later in the evening, **Turtle's**, a Tahoe institution which relocated to the Embassy Suites, has good dancing. **Wild West**, in the Round Hill Mall, plays a mixture of country, R&B and Top 40.

And of course, the casinos have musical reviews that are extravaganzas of sight and sound, as well as top-name performers.

North Shore: try **River Ranch** on the Alpine Meadows access road, which was voted top après-ski in North Lake Tahoe. Also, **Pete 'n' Peter's** or **Rosie's Café** in the center of Tahoe City or **Pierce Street Annex** behind Safeway near the Boatworks Mall in Tahoe City. Or head to **Sunnyside**, just a couple of miles south of Tahoe City on the lake. **Hacienda del Lago** in the Boatworks has nachos till 6 p.m. or try **Humpty's** across from the Safeway Mall. The bar at the **Olympic Village Inn** has live music every weekend. In Truckee there is occasional music at **The Passage** in the Truckee Hotel and at the **Bar of America**, both at Commercial Row. The **Hilltop Lodge** overlooking Truckee on Highway 267 has country music. The casinos on North Lake Tahoe have entertainment every night. Sure bets are the **Cal-Neva Lodge**, **The Crystal Bay Club**, **Hyatt Lake Tahoe** and the **Tahoe Biltmore**.

A hot new après-ski spot is **Naughty Dawg** on the main road in Tahoe City, where you can get munchies in dog dishes and "shotskis," a ritual drinks served in an unusual way.

Getting there and getting around

By air: Reno is the major airport for the Tahoe area, with more than 90 non-stop flights a day from various parts of the country. The airport is 45 miles from Squaw Valley USA, 50 miles from Alpine Meadows, 38 miles from the Northstar-at-Tahoe, 55 miles from Heavenly and 70 miles from Kirkwood.

The Lake Tahoe Airport, near South Lake Tahoe and 10 minutes from Heavenly, has service from some parts of California. Buses and hotel shuttles take skiers to the major resorts from both airports.

By train: Amtrak serves Truckee and Reno on the California Zephyr line, running Oakland to Chicago. Call (800) 872-7245.

By boat: The Tahoe Queen Ski Shuttle, an authentic Mississippi sternwheeler, double-decked and heated, takes South Shore skiers across Lake Tahoe to and from the big North Shore ski resorts. Buses take skiers from the lake to the major ski areas. A breakfast buffet and dinner are served; price extra. The return trip includes dancing and cocktails. Call (916) 541-3364 for reservations, and confirm a day before, because departures depend on ice conditions on the lake. Cost for transportation only is $18.

By bus: Shuttlebuses run between almost every major hotel on the North or South Shore and from Reno to each of the major ski resorts. Check for schedules when you arrive. Most of the shuttles that cruise around the North or South Shores are free, but when you need to go from one end of the lake to the other, expect to pay about $4 round-trip. Call the ski areas or hotels for more information.

Sierra Nevada Gray Lines (800-822-6009 or 702-329-1147) operates a daily ski shuttle between downtown Reno and Alpine Meadows, Northstar-at-Tahoe (except Saturdays) and Squaw Valley USA from mid-December through the end of March. **Tahoe Casino Express** runs 14 times daily between Reno airport and South Shore for about $15 each way.

By car: Driving time from Reno is about an hour to any major resort except Kirkwood, which is approximately 90 minutes. San Francisco is about four hours away, by I-80 to the North Shore and Highway 50 to South Lake Tahoe. During storms, the police don't let anyone up the mountains without chains or a 4-wheel-drive vehicle, so come prepared.

Sugar Bowl is off I-80 just west of Donner Lake. Alpine Meadows and Squaw Valley are on Highway 89 and Northstar-at-Tahoe is off Highway 267 (both highways run between I-80 and Highway 28, which hugs the North Shore). Diamond Peak is on Highway 28 in Nevada on the lake's east side, Heavenly is right off Highway 50 in South Lake Tahoe and Kirkwood is on Highway 88 (follow signs from South Lake Tahoe).

Though we hate to make this recommendation, (because it adds to the congestion and pollution around this beautiful lake), bring a car if you intend to move frequently from north to south, or if you are staying in North Lake Tahoe. You can get along fine without a car if you station yourself in South Lake Tahoe and use public transportation to get around. Based on extensive personal experience, we also recommend that you concentrate on either the North Shore or South Shore during a trip. Otherwise you'll run yourself ragged.

The Tahoe Area Ski Resorts

Squaw Valley USA

Squaw Valley USA, site of the 1960 Winter Olympic Games, is perhaps the best-known ski resort in the region. Host of the 1960 Winter Olympics, the ski area and the valley have added a lot in the past few years, including a 405-room luxury hotel, high-speed chair lifts and a mountaintop ice skating rink.

The area undoubtedly offers some of the finest skiing in the United States. Opening the trail map of Squaw, you'll notice that there aren't any trail-cut runs, just wide open snow fields—4,000 acres of them. Anything within the boundaries can be skied by anyone daring enough to challenge the mountain. This is big-bowl skiing, and where the bowls end, the chutes and tree skiing begin. Here super skiers test themselves.

Access to most of the ski area, including slopes in the saddle between Broken Arrow Peak at 8,200 feet and the summit ridge at 8,900 feet, starts at the base with a six-person gondola or the 150-skier cable car. Or start with the Squaw One superchair and then connect to others. Six separate peaks, each with every conceivable exposure, overlook Lake Tahoe.

Extreme skiers will be in heaven at Squaw. Two popular spots are the Palisades above Siberia Bowl and Eagle's Nest at the top of KT22, with plenty of vertical air. Locals will take you to where you can ski terrain that resembles an elevator shaft.

Experts who like to keep their skis on the snow will find plenty of challenging terrain. The entire KT22 side of Squaw Valley is expert. Try Chute 75, the Alternates, and the Dead Tree Chute, or the National Chute off the Palisades. At Elevation 8200, on the upper mountain, try the Funnel or the Elevator Shaft, or hike to the top of Granite Chief. These are all true, very black, diamonds.

The intermediate terrain also has challenge and variety. Taking the Headwall Lift, They can opt for Chicken Bowl or drop over the back of the ridge to Sun Bowl. Up Siberia Express, experts turn to the left getting off the lift, intermediates traverse to the right. There, Newport, Mainline, Gold Coast and Emigrant serve wide-open intermediate slopes. Intermediates will like the Shirley Lake area served by a detachable quad and a triple chair. The Mountain Run is a great end-of-the-day cruise: top to bottom, without stopping, a hefty 3.5-mile run. Because of its reputation of being as crowded as the Hollywood Freeway in the late afternoon, a second roughly parallel (and easier) run, Home Run, has been cut.

Though Squaw Valley's well publicized black-diamond terrain has given it a menacing reputation, it has a little-known surprise: This is a great spot for never-evers to learn. Squaw has a gentle bowl at the top of the cable car known as Bailey's Beach, served by two slow-moving lifts. Though Bailey's Beach is not physically separated from the other terrain, better skiers rarely use it. Beginners usually long to head toward the summit just like the big boys and girls, and here, they can. They just ride the cable car up to High Camp (where they'll also find restaurants, shelter and the ice rink), and at the end of the day, ride the cable car back down.

Snowboarding

Snowboarding is permitted on all sections of Squaw Valley USA. Squaw has a halfpipe, lessons, rentals and a terrain park.

Ski school (93/94 prices)

Squaw Valley USA Ski School has more than 150 instructors and special courses for children, women, powder skiing, bump technique, and racing. The specific program prices are available from the school at (916) 583-0119. Never-evers get a **First-Timer Package** for either skiing or snowboarding that includes a beginner lift ticket, equipment rental and a two-hour lesson.

Advanced beginner to intermediate skier levels get instruction through a new **Ski Your Pro** format where instructors are assigned to training areas on the mountain, and skiers can join in at any time for as long as they want for $26. Higher-level skiers get two-hour **workshops** that center on a specific skill, such as moguls, powder or gate training, also for $26.

Private lessons cost $50 an hour and $15 for each additional person. All-day private lessons run $275.

Children aged 3-12 can take an all-day lesson, including lunch, lift ticket, activities and ski instruction for $55. The half-day price is $40 and includes a snack instead of lunch.

Lift tickets (93/94 prices)

	Adult	Child (Up to 12) Senior (65+)
One day	$41	$5
Three days	$114 ($38/day)	$15 ($5/day)
Five days	$180 ($36/day)	$25 ($5/day)

No, that's not a misprint. Children and seniors ski for $5 here, less than the cost of a single cable car or gondola ride, which is $12 for adults; $5 for children.

Squaw has an unusual "No-waiting-in-line-or-your-money-back" program. For $1, skiers register as beginner, intermediate or expert; anyone who waits more than 10 minutes for a lift in his ski category receives a full refund and skis free for the rest of the day. All lifts must be operating for the program to be in effect.

Accommodations

Squaw Valley has several lodging choices. All lodges give easy access to the slopes, but evening activities are limited. Even if you are staying at Squaw, it is best to rent a car if you'd like to explore dining and nightlife in Truckee and Tahoe City.

Resort at Squaw Creek (800-327-3353) is a luxurious hotel that, despite being several stories tall, blends well with the valley. This hotel connects with the ski area by its own lift, and is virtually a self-contained resort. No restaurant problem here: there are five. Squaw Creek also has three pools (one of which is open in winter), several hot tubs, a complete fitness center, cross-country skiing and an ice-skating rink. Rates start at $198 per night midweek, $270 weekends.

Squaw Valley Lodge (800-992-9920; in California, 800-922-9970) is only a few yards' walk from the lifts. The lodge boasts a fully equipped health club, free covered parking and kitchenettes in the units. Cost: $160 a night and up for a studio midweek.

The Olympic Village Inn, (800) 845-5243 (800-VILLAGE) or 916-583-1501, has five hot tubs, and all units have kitchens. Rates: $195 a night on weekends, $165 Sunday-Thursday.

The **Squaw Valley Inn**, (800) 323-7666 or 916-583-5176 is more like a basic hotel, across from the gondola and cable car. Rates start at $145 midweek, $185 on weekends.

Squaw Valley USA also has **central reservations:** (800) 545-4350 or (916) 583-5585.

Child care

Squaw Valley USA's Children's World has licensed infant care for ages 6 months to 2 years. All-day care is $55 with lunch, activities and supervision, while half-day care is $40 (no lunch). Reservations are required; call (916) 583-5585. Children's ski instruction is detailed in the ski school section of this chapter.

Alpine Meadows

Alpine Meadows Facts
Base elevation: 6,835'; **Summit elevation:** 8,637'; **Vertical drop:** 1,802 feet
Number of lifts: 12–2 quad superchairs, 2 triple chairs, 7 double chairs, 1 surface lift
Percent snowmaking: 12 percent, runs from 10 lifts
Total acreage: 2,000 skiable acres
Uphill capacity: 16,000 per hour; **Bed base:** 10,000 (N. Lake Tahoe Area)

For every level of skier, particularly intermediate and advanced, Alpine Meadows has something to offer. It has excellent expert terrain, overwhelming intermediate bowls and trails, and an excellent beginner area. Alpine may seem like a relatively small area until you take the Summit Chair and see the area unfold beneath you.

As you ride up the lift, to the right are the expert Wolverine Bowl, Beaver Bowl and Estelle Bowl; to the left spreads the seemingly endless Alpine Bowl, which is graded as intermediate.

Experts approaching Alpine Meadows have plenty of great bowl skiing and enough steeps to keep their hearts in their throats. Here's a route suggestion: take the expert bowls, to the right ascending the Summit Chair, then take the Summit Chair again and cruise down into the blue territory of Alpine Bowl. Finally, take the Alpine Bowl Chair and traverse to the Sherwood Bowls on the backside of the area or take the High Yellow Traverse to the Saddle Bowl. When you come up the Sherwood Chair, drop down Our Father—and you can say a few enroute—then head to Scott Chair and try out Scott Chute for a direct plunge, or take it easy on tree-lined roundabouts. By then your knees will have earned a cruise. Nearby, the Promised Land has great ski tree skiing for top skiers.

Intermediates, especially those who are better than average, will find this ski area perfect. Stay in the area all day using the Alpine Bowl Chair, or make endless runs off the Roundhouse and Kangaroo Chairs. Beginners will find themselves limited to a small but sheltered area close to the base lodge.

In the Lake Tahoe area, Alpine Meadows has traditionally been the ski area with the longest season. If you are planning a trip early or late in the season, this is your best bet.

Snowboarding

Not allowed.

Ski school (93/94 prices)

Alpine Meadows divides its lessons into those for beginners, and those for everyone else. The **beginner program** includes lifts, equipment and four hours of instruction for $48. Other **group lessons** are $30 for two hours; $40 for four hours. **Private lessons** are $55 an hour. An early bird special (9-10 a.m.) goes for $45. For three or more people, add $20 a person.

Telemark lessons and rentals are offered at the same prices.

Children's lessons: The youngest age accepted by the Alpine Meadows Snow School is 4 years. Snow school for children 4 to 6 costs $57 a full day and $50 for an additional child from the same family; $39 a half day and $36 for additional child. Children must be toilet-trained. Registrations are at the ski school desk.

Lessons for children 6 to 12 are in Kids Ski Kamp. For first-time skiers, an all-day (10 a.m. to 4 p.m.) program with lessons, rentals, lift ticket and lunch is $68; half day is $38, full-day without lunch, $48. For children who already ski, the cost is $60 for lessons and lunch only, $40 for a full day without lunch, or a half day with lunch is $40 and $30 for a half day, no lunch.

Lift tickets (93/94 prices)

	Adult	Child (7-12)
One day	$42	$16
Three days	$114 ($38/day)	$39 ($13/day)
Five days	$180 ($36/day)	$60 ($12/day)

Seniors 65-69 ski for $29; children 6 and younger ski for $6; 70+ ski free.

Accommodations

Alpine Meadows doesn't have lodging at the base, but has lodging-lift packages. Call Alpine Meadows at (800) 441-4423.

Child care

Alpine Meadows has no child care. See ski school section for information on lessons.

Northstar-at-Tahoe

Northstar-at-Tahoe Facts
Base elevation: 6,400'; **Summit elevation:** 8,600'; **Vertical drop:** 2,200 feet
Number of lifts: 11–1 gondola, 4 quad super chairs, 2 triple chairs, 2 double chairs, 2 surface lifts
Percent snowmaking: 50 percent of developed acres
Total acreage: 2,000 total acres, 500 developed acres
Uphill capacity: 18,270 per hour; **Bed Base:** 3,500 at resort

---

Unlike Squaw and Alpine, Northstar is a totally planned ski area designed to make skiing easy. Condos line the lower slopes, and the runs are planned for family skiing. Here an intermediate can feel like a World Cup racer. The grooming is impeccable—you'll have to look hard for bumps—and the entire area management and operations are squeaky clean.

Although Northstar's Mount Pluto is an extinct volcano, you won't find bowls and cornices as at Squaw or that other massive Western volcano, Mammoth. The skiing is all trail-cut.

Advanced skiers or those aspiring to the upper levels of intermediate will find some challenge in the drops off the East Ridge (labeled as black diamonds, but the mapmaker was being generous). Normally at least two of the runs are groomed and the others have moderate bumps. Tonini's is the longest, but The Plunge is the steepest. The only bad part is that it's over too soon. Chute, Crosscut and Powderbowl are also fun—short but sweet. If you're an air skier, you'll be disappointed; these blacks would be blues at Squaw.

Instead of getting your exhilaration by plummeting down some shaft, enjoy the longer rides with moderately steep and sustained pitch off the backside via Lookout Chair and the long traverse called Back Door. This run makes you feel as though you're in another mountain range, far away from any crowds; seven stretched-out swaths provide some of the longest continuous pitches in the West, all served by the Backside Express quad lift. Though they're all labeled as advanced runs, an intermediate will have no difficulty in good conditions.

The gem of Northstar lies between these runs, through the trees. Start down Rail Splitter, then take off into the woods to the right or left. After a storm, Northstar is one of the prime areas where locals can enjoy powder through the trees long after Squaw's powder has been skied off.

Intermediates will enjoy the smooth blues that descend from the two ridges into Main Street, the intermediate run that nearly every other run on the mountain feeds into. Avoid Main Street except when you need to get to a lift.

Northstar is a good never-ever and beginner resort because its gentlest terrain is below the gondola, while all the other runs are above it. Better skiers leave this terrain to the learners except at day's end, when some of them use it to practice tucks. Luckily for everyone, this is fairly flat terrain, so no one can keep up excessive speed.

Snowboarding

Boarding is allowed on all areas of the mountain. There is a halfpipe, snowboard lessons are available and boards may be rented at the Village Ski Rental Shop.

Ski school (93/94 prices)

Beginner group lessons: Intro to Skiing I is a 1.75-hour lesson with beginner lift access and equipment for $40; Intro to Skiing II is the same program but with expanded lifts for $55. Normal 1.75-hour group lessons with all-day lifts for all levels are $25. Three-day programs, with lessons and lifts, are $185.

Skill improvement clinics for higher level skiers are $25 for a 1.75-hour lesson. Specialty clinics for women, older skiers and snowboarders are offered a few weekends each year. A free one-hour seniors' clinic (age 60+) is very Wednesday at 10 a.m. A free one-hour women's clinic is each Tuesday at 10 a.m.

Northstar has a Ski With The Legends clinic program for advanced and expert skiers and snowboarders, taught by well known Olympic and U.S. Team skiers and pro snowboarders. Clinics are twice daily; call for prices and instructor schedule.

Private lessons run $50 per hour with each additional person $20. Take your private lesson at 9 a.m. and you'll save $10.

MT. PLUTO ELEVATION 8610'

● Easiest
■ More Difficult
◆ Most Difficult
□ Snowmaking
✚ First Aid

The **Starkids** all-day program for children 5 to 12 is $53 a day with lifts, lessons and lunch (add $10 for equipment).

Lift tickets (93/94 prices)

	Adult	Child (6-12)
One day	$40	$18
Three days	$108 ($36/day)	$49 ($16.33/day)
Five days	$174 ($34.80/day)	$78 ($15.60/day)

Senior rate is $20 a day for skiers 60 to 69, and $5 for those over 70. A gondola ride costs $5/$3. Children under five with a parent ski free.

NOTE: Northstar limits daily lift pass sales. In event of a sellout, no afternoon passes will be sold. If you get there before noon and they are sold out, you get a lift ticket for another day.

Northstar also has a frequent-skier program called Club Vertical that offers discounted lift tickets, prizes for achieving certain vertical-feet-skied levels, and a separate chair lift entrance to help skiers speed through lift lines.

Accommodations (93/94 prices)

This area was created for condo living. The village has a convenient lodge, with rooms from $129 a night, two-night minimum. The condo rates range from $129 a night for a studio to $240 for a two-bedroom, two-bath unit. Northstar also has full-sized homes for rent, accommodating five to eight people for $300 to $450 a night. Special packages include lifts, rentals and lessons. Reservations: (800) 466-6784.

Child care (93/94 prices)

Minors' Camp accepts toilet-trained children 2-6 years old. The program combines skiing with other activities, including art, snow play, science, drama and language development. Reservations are suggested; call (916) 587-0278. Costs: all day, $39; slightly more for ski instruction. Hours: 8 a.m. to 4:30 p.m. Learn-to-ski classes with lifts, lessons and lunch start at $49.

Heavenly Ski Resort

Heavenly Ski Resort Facts

California Side–Base: 6,540'; Summit: 10,040'; Vertical drop: 3,500 feet
Nevada Side–Base: 7,200'; Summit: 10,040'; Vertical drop: 2,840 feet
Number of lifts: 23–Aerial tram, 3 quad superchairs, 7 triple chairs,
8 double chairs, 4 surface lifts; Percent snowmaking: 66 percent (240 acres)
Total acreage: 4,800 patrolled acres (1,084 skiable trail acres)
Uphill capacity: 33,000 per hour; Bed Base: 22,000 in S. Lake Tahoe

Heavenly is big. It ranks Number One at Lake Tahoe for highest elevation (10,040 feet), greatest vertical rise (3,500 feet) and longest run (5.5 miles). Except for its famous face run—

Gunbarrel—and Mott Canyon, the resort is most appropriate for the giant category of intermediates and advanced skiers; in short, 90 percent of America's skiers.

Heavenly is also the only two-state ski resort. Skiers can start out from either California or Nevada.

The California base, on Ski Run Boulevard from Highway 50, strikes awe in all but the best skiers because its visible face, Gunbarrel, is a straight ladder of bumps 1,700 feet high, often with dangerous-looking rocky protrusions in early winter or late spring. Leap over that by taking either the Gunbarrel Chair or the aerial tram. Then head down Patsy's (a horrible bottleneck on weekends, unfortunately) to the Waterfall Chair, which gives access to superb intermediate and advanced runs off Ridge, Canyon and Sky Express Chairs.

From the top of the Sky Express, the best of the California side opens up. After you have admired the inspiring view of Lake Tahoe, drop down Ellie's if you are looking for bumps—or if you want long smooth cruising, head to the right when you get off the chair and steam down Liz's Canyon, Betty's or Ridge Run.

When you have had enough of California, strike out for Nevada, where 50 percent of the terrain is located. (The connecting trail will have snowmaking coverage this season.) You get to the Nevada side from the top of Sky Express; go left along the Skyline Trail, which requires a bit of pushing. Now here's the trick for advanced intermediates who want the best of the Milky Way Bowl: the Skyline Trail will dip a bit after you get off the Sky Express Chair. You then have to make a small climb and the trail starts down again. Just as you begin dropping, look to your right for tracks leading into the trees and follow them. After a short traverse you will end up at the top of the Milky Way Bowl with about twice the vertical you would have found had you stayed on the trail. The same traverse applies to skiers riding on the Dipper, which is the summit chair on the Nevada side. If you ski from the top of Milky Way to the bottom of Mott Canyon in one long run you will drop over 2,000 vertical feet through black and blacker terrain.

The Nevada side has even better cruises. From the top of the Dipper are the Big Dipper and Orion. Advanced intermediates with moguls on their minds can bump down Big Dipper Bowl or traverse a bit further and try the Little Dipper. Another good advanced run is through the ponderosa pines on either side of Little Dipper. The Galaxy Chair is a good spot for low intermediates to gain confidence. For a cruise that seems to take forever, take Olympic Downhill to Stagecoach Base.

Skiers can also start from the Nevada side by driving on the Kingsbury Grade to either the Stagecoach or Boulder bases. Most skiers start from California, so doing this is often a good way to avoid the crowds.

Super-experts who used to scorn Heavenly now have their own playground, Mott Canyon. This north-facing wall is peppered with pines and has about half-a-dozen advanced expert chutes. This lift-served area can only be entered through designated gates.

Home to California means taking the new Dipper Express (a high-speed quad that replaced a triple chair) back up to the top and traversing right to the California Run. Or take Comet and then cruise the 49er Run. The runs meander into a small depression where the three-mile, winding Roundabout trail down the face gets most of the intermediate traffic at the end of the day (beginners may want to ride the tram back down). Or with a short lift up, mogul maniacs can get to the top of Gunbarrel and East Bowl, two of the longest, steepest bump runs in skidom.

Though Heavenly is exactly that for intermediates and up, never-evers should pick another resort for their skiing baptism. Except for a tiny learning section at the California base, Heavenly's green terrain is smack in the middle of a place where four lifts have their boarding areas. Skiers dart in every direction, making a most intimidating scene.

Snowboarding

Snowboarding is allowed on both sides of the mountain. When there's enough snow, Heavenly constructs a halfpipe. Lessons and rentals are available on the Nevada and California sides. A Shred Ready never-ever snowboard lesson is three hours long and includes a limited-access lift ticket for $35, while an intermediate or advanced Mountain Adventure lesson is $28. This lesson has a You Be The Judge guarantee—if you didn't learn anything new, you can repeat the lesson.

Ski school (93/94 prices)

Group lessons include a never-ever special for $43 that includes a three-hour lesson, rentals and access to the beginner lifts. A two-day introductory special with two three-hour lessons, rentals and beginner lift access is $86.

Group lessons for other levels are in the form of **special workshops.** The Adult Mountain Adventure is two hours for $28; $75 for three lessons and $115 for five. These do not have to be used consecutively, and all have the You Be The Judge guarantee, where you can repeat the class if you didn't learn anything new. Daily Specials. that shows how to master the conditions of the day—powder, crud, moguls and racing. Twenty-minute mini-clinics cost $10.

Heavenly has special three-day **clinics** for $299 (lifts, lessons and some meals) for racing, women, seniors and other topics that are offered at certain times of the season.

Private lessons are $50 an hour per person between 9 and 10 a.m., and $62 per hour at 10 a.m. or after. Each additional person is $25. Two-hour private lessons cost $100 for one, three hours cost $155, and all-day private lessons are $350 for one to five people. Reservations suggested for private lessons. Call (702) 586-7000, Ext. 6244.

Ski Explorers is a **children's program** for all abilities, ages 4-12. Full day ($58) includes instruction, lunch, snacks and limited lift access. Half day ($38) begins at 10 a.m., without lunch. On heavy snow days or for children who can't ski a whole day, Ski Explorers also includes some behind-the-scenes field trips to see a grooming snowcat, how the ski patrol works, or avalanche dog demonstrations.

Lift tickets (94/95 prices)

	Adult	Child (6-12) Senior (65+)
One day	$42	$18
Three days	$123 ($41/day)	$51 ($17/day)
Five days	$190 ($38/day)	$80 ($16/day)

Youth (ages 13-15) ski for $30 a day, $87 for three days, $140 for five days. Children 5 and younger ski free with a paying adult.

Accommodations

Heavenly's base area is in South Lake Tahoe, which means plenty of accommodations. See the South Lake Tahoe accommodations section earlier in this chapter. **Heavenly Central Reservations** can arrange an entire ski vacation including airfare, transfers, lessons, rentals, non-ski activities, skiing and lodging. Midweek packages are a particular good deal. (800) 243-2836 (2-HEAVEN) or (702) 588-4584.

Child care

Heavenly has no child care program for those younger than 4. For children's instruction, see the Ski School section.

Kirkwood

Kirkwood Facts
Base elevation: *7,800'*; **Summit elevation:** *9,800'*; **Vertical drop:** *2,000 feet*
Number of lifts: *11—6 triple chairs, 4 double chairs, 1 surface lift*
Snowmaking: *none* **Total acreage:** *2,300 patrolled acres; 1,500 skiable trail acres*
Uphill capacity: *15,000 per hour;* **Bed Base:** *10,500 in S. Lake Tahoe*

After the glitz of Heavenly and its casino-laced home town, Kirkwood is like taking a trip back into the wilderness. The lovely drive through Hope Valley to Kirkwood from South Lake Tahoe takes only about 45 minutes, but it is light-years away in altitude and ambiance. There are no bright lights, no ringing jackpots, no wide blue lake, no high-rise buildings and no urban noise.

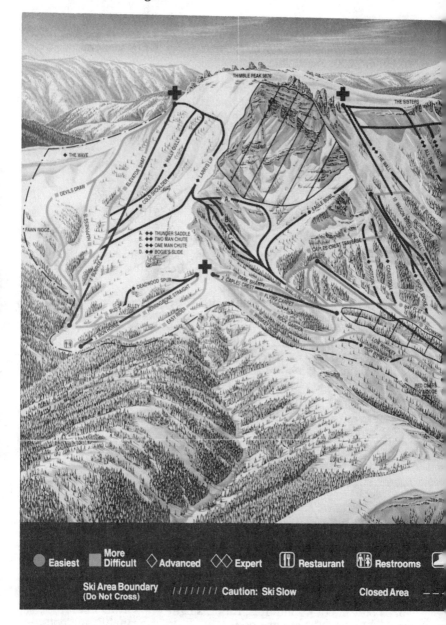

THIMBLE PEAK 9876'

THE SISTERS

♦ THE WAVE

ELEVATOR SHAFT
HOLLY GULLY
COLD SHOULDER
LIGHT'S LIP

■ DEVILS DRAW

THE WALL

EAGLE BOWL

* FAWN RIDGE

HAPPINESS IS

A. ♦♦ THUNDER SADDLE
B. ♦♦ TWO MAN CHUTE
C. ♦♦ ONE MAN CHUTE
D. ♦♦ BOGIE'S SLIDE

CAPLES CREST TRAVERSE

♦ DEADWOOD SPUR

BUD'S VALLEY
HERRINGBONE STRAIGHT
EAST RIDGE

CAPLES CREST

FLYING CAPLES

RED CLIFFS

● **Easiest**   ■ **More
Difficult**   ◇ **Advanced**   ◇◇ **Expert**   🍴 **Restaurant**   🚻 **Restrooms**

Ski Area Boundary
(Do Not Cross)   //////// **Caution: Ski Slow**   **Closed Area**

GLOVE ROCK

PALISADES BOWL

F ◆ JIM'S
G ◆ SENTINEL
H ◆ RABBIT RUNS
◆ CHAMOIX
◆ FIREBALL

TIMBER CREEK LODGE

CONDOMINIUMS

CONDOMINIUMS

CROSS COUNTRY TRACK

RESIDENTIAL AREA

KIRKWOOD MEADOW ELEVATION 7890'

🔋 Ski Shop   ◻ First Aid   ✏ Telephone   🍸 Bar   🔔 Ski School   ⛽ Gas Station

Avalanche Control Boundary
(Do Not Cross When Closed)

Kirkwood operates under special use permit
from U.S.F.S. El Dorado National Forest.

Instead, you have the feeling that you are entering a special secret place, known to only a select few.

Kirkwood is a great area for the skiers who have mastered the stem christie and who are just into paralleling. And it will thrill any expert, even super-expert, with its steeps and dozens of chutes. Kirkwood's northeast exposure in a snow pocket gives light, dry conditions and produces storms that linger and dump more. Last season, Kirkwood stayed open until May 4, so it's a good spot for some sunny, late-season conditions.

Right now, Kirkwood has no snowmaking—the only major California ski area that has none. By the time you read this, however, Kirkwood may be covering some of its popular runs with machine-made snow, including one top-to-bottom run.

Beginners will find a great learning area served by Snowkirk Chair to the east, and the beginner area reached by Bunny Chair at the far west. Intermediates choose to ski either on the lower sections of the face, using the Hole 'n' Wall and Solitude Chairs, or work their way over Caples Crest (Chair Two), then stay high on the trail (far right) and traverse to the Sunrise section. Here is plenty of groomed intermediate terrain to the east of Chair Four (Sunrise). This area is called The Wave because it gets a cornice that looks like a giant rounder. On the right, or west side of the chair, the half dozen runs of Thunder Saddle keep powder for three days after a snowfall because it takes two chairs to get skiers there. Watch your step along the ridge. When you get toward the bottom of the steeps, after dropping down One Man Chute, Bogie's Slide or Corner Chute, tuck and keep your speed up for the flat run back to the Wagonwheel or Cornice chairs.

Chair Ten—Wagonwheel—had a new entry cut to eliminate the leap formerly required to get into the black runs below the Sisters. Some of the best skiing is further west, below False Peak through the chutes and trees that an aggressive intermediate could negotiate with care. But intermediates should first try the Cornice (Chair Six), which is between pure blue and advanced runs. By working the mountain from east to west, as described here, you can keep finding powder as well as new challenges.

The Sentinel Bowl gets groomed about every three days or so and is beautiful for anyone looking for super-smooth steeps (some experts complain that it needs more bumps). If you want bumps, try Olympic, Look-Out Janek, Zack's or Monte Wolfe, which drop to either side of the Cornice Chair. Kirkwood often waits to open the Wall until late morning or early afternoon so that the sun can soften the face to allow a bit of edge. California skiers appreciate the wait; New Englanders, used to real ice, can't understand what all the fuss is about.

Snowboarding

Boarding is permitted on all areas of the mountain; however, it is limited off Chair 10 during hard snow conditions. The area has numerous naturally occurring halfpipes and quarterpipes. Boards may be rented at the Mountain Outfitter ski shop at the base, and the ski school has lessons.

Ski school (93/94 prices)

Kirkwood's Ski School offers **Pro Turn Ski Clinics** for all levels except beginners. These are 90 minutes long and cost $12, and are designed to smooth out rough edges, rather than teach the basics from scratch. **Private lessons** cost $50 for an hour and a half, $20 each additional person.

A **Learn To Ski package** including a lesson, beginner lift ticket and rental equipment costs $25. The ski school guarantees that a never-ever will be able to ski the beginner area by the end of the day, or return for a free lesson. Days 2 and 3 for beginners also cost $25.

Kirkwood runs **special clinics** for women, and skiers aged 40 and older, each day between Friday and Monday inclusive. These two-hour programs cost $15. More intense three-day programs are run several times a season; call for details.

Children's lessons are for ages 4-12 and called Mighty Mountain. The program includes equipment, lessons and lifts. This program is $50 for a full day, with lunch; $35 for a half day.

Lift tickets (93/94 prices)

	Adult	Child (Up to 12)
One day	$39	$5
Three days	$111 ($37/day)	$15 ($5/day)
Five days	$180 ($36/day)	$25 ($5/day)

Ages 60 and older ski for $19; students ages 13-22 ski for $29, but older students will need to present full-time student ID to get the discount.

Accommodations

Many skiers would rather stay here than put up with the nearly one-hour commute from South Lake Tahoe. Of the condo complexes, the top choice is Sun Meadows, which is across from the Solitude and Cornice chairs and about as centrally located as you can get in Kirkwood. The second choice is The Meadows, between Timber Creek and the Cornice Chair. The Whiskey Run condos are a favorite with families because the Mighty Mountain children's ski school is on the ground floor. Rates for all condos are the same. During regular season a studio costs $110 on weekends and $75 midweek. A one-bedroom unit, which sleeps up to four, runs $155 on weekends; $120 midweek. A two-bedroom premium unit will cost $220 on weekends and $160 during the week. Reservations: (209) 258-7000.

Child care

Kirkwood Day Care accepts children 3 to 8 years. All day costs $35 including lunch, half day is $25. Hourly charges are $5. See the ski school section for children's ski instruction.

Tahoe Interchangeable tickets (94/95 prices)

The Ski Lake Tahoe interchangeable lift pass is good at Kirkwood, Heavenly, Northstar, Alpine and Squaw Valley USA. Sierra-at-Tahoe, a ski area about 12 miles from South Lake Tahoe, has been added this season. Five of six consecutive days costs $205, and six of seven, $246. (both $41 per day).

Diamond Peak

Diamond Peak Facts

Base elevation: 6,700'; **Summit elevation:** 8,540'; **Vertical drop:** 1,840 feet
Number of lifts: 7–1 quad superchair, 6 double chairs
Percent snowmaking: 80 percent **Total acreage:** 675 acres
Uphill capacity: 7,500 per hour **Bed Base:** 6,000

Diamond Peak's origins were nearly 25 years ago as a neighborhood ski area serving a family-oriented clientele. Terrain additions have made it a medium-sized resort, but it still maintains the flavor of an intimate neighborhood resort. It is primarily an intermediate mountain, though its Solitude Canyon area has the greatest concentration of advanced terrain.

The rest of the skiing is in two areas: The Ridge, ending at the old octagonal Snowflake Lodge overlooking Lake Tahoe; and Diamond Peak, the recent expansion. The runs off The Ridge, served by Lakeview Chair, are gentle blacks and blues, relatively short, each with only a very short pitch that most advanced skiers would call a genuine black. Crystal Ridge off Diamond Peak is a long blue (with a super view of the lake), while the canyons and gullies off it are considered advanced, with slightly steeper pitches than off the Lakeview Chair. Most of the expert terrain here, however, would be labeled intermediate at Squaw.

This is a great learner's mountain because of its friendly atmosphere and manageable size. Diamond Peak employs about 100 instructors—equal to much larger areas—another indication that Diamond Peak is a good place to learn to ski. For children 6-12, for example, Sierra Scouts mixes ski instruction with the natural history of the Lake Tahoe region. Service clearly is a high priority. A strong point is that even the highest chair, Diamond Peak, is sheltered, so it can run in heavy winds. In fact, when other North Shore resorts shut down because of wind, they send skiers to Diamond Peak.

This is a very friendly area, a good choice for families who might feel lost on a bigger mountain.

Snowboarding

Snowboarding is allowed on all parts of the mountain except on three runs served by the Red Fox lift. Boarders have a mountaintop snowboard park that is off-limits to skiers. Rentals and lessons are available.

Ski school (93/94 prices)

All-day **group lessons** are $36; half day is $23. **Private lessons** are $45 an hour. A **Learn-to-Ski Special**, including beginner lifts, rentals and two-hour lesson is $29. **Children's** programs are for ages 4-7 (all day with lunch is $55) and for ages 7-12 (all day including lunch is $46).

Lift tickets (94/95 prices)

	Adult	Child (6-12) Senior (60-69)
One day	$35	$14
Three days	$99 ($33/day)	$36 ($12/day)
Five days	$165 ($33/day)	$60 ($12/day)

Younger than 6 and older than 69 ski for free. Diamond Peak has a super Family Package, good any day of the season. It starts with a lift ticket good for one adult and one child for $38. Four additional family members may be added at these prices: adult, $30; child/senior, $5; teen (13-17), $25.

Accommodations

Incline Village has several hotels and condo complexes. Two worthy of mention are **Hyatt Regency Lake Tahoe Resort and Casino** and **Inn at Incline Motor Lodge and Condominiums**. The Hyatt is a four-star luxury hotel with rates from $75 to $230 a night, while the Inn at Incline has more modest facilities and rates (starting around $60 a night.)

Child care

Diamond Peak has a small on-site day care center for kids 4-6. Call the resort for more details.

Sugar Bowl

Sugar Bowl Facts
Base elevation: 6,883'; Summit elevation: 8,383'; Vertical drop: 1,500 feet
Number of lifts: 9–1 gondola, 1 quad superchair, 2 quads, 5 double chairs
Percent snowmaking: 8 percent Total acreage: 1,000 acres
Uphill capacity: 8,500 per hour; Bed Base: 460

Sugar Bowl is one of the oldest resorts at Lake Tahoe and the oldest chair lift-served resort in California. From the moment you step out of your car and board the Magic Carpet gondolas to ride *down* across a pristine valley to the lifts, you feel you're stepping back in time. Probably when you descend from the gondola, you'll see a classic red sleigh. You'll see no cars though, the gondola ride is the only access.

Skiing at Sugar Bowl is full of surprises. Runs, especially those off 8,383-foot Mt. Lincoln, are a series of chutes and gullies with twists and bumps and loops and swoops, all giving the advanced skier a terrific roller coaster ride. Confident skiers will love the g-forces unleashed when banking off the sides of narrow drainages. Sugar Bowl is not a put-it-in-neutral-and-glide kind of mountain.

Intermediates can enjoy the peak by heading far to the left when getting off Silver Belt Chair, where they will find runs like Lake View and Bill Klein's Schuss to their liking.

The other mountain, Mt. Disney, has some easier expert runs off either drainage of a ridge, with wide intermediate terrain to the far right for cruising. Beginners will find meandering routes on either side of Christmas Tree Chair, some of which take them through a quaint little neighborhood of chalets. Beginners also will like the runs off the Nob Hill and Meadow lifts.

New this year is a high-speed quad chair that will open up new mostly intermediate terrain on Mt. Judah. This addition will increase Sugar Bowl's acreage and lift capacity, but the numbers were not available at press time.

Sugar Bowl is recommended for a day's change of pace from the larger Tahoe resorts. The feeling of intimacy captured by the unique entry, the highly interesting swoops and gullies of Mt. Lincoln and the friendly attention one usually gets at a medium-sized resort are sheer delights.

Snowboarding

The entire mountain is open to snowboarders and all ski school program offered to skiers also are available to shredders.

Ski school (93/94 prices)

A two-hour group session is $24. Private lessons are $40 an hour, with each additional person $15. The ABC package of lift, lesson and rental for never-evers through intermediates is $45 for adults, $35 for children. PowderKids all-day program for ages 6-12 is $50, which includes lifts, two lessons and lunch.

Lift tickets (93/94 prices)

	Adult	Child (Up to 12)
One day	$35	$8
Two days	$60 ($30/day)	$16 ($8/day)

Other than the two-day ticket, which must be consecutive days, Sugar Bowl does not have multiday discounts. (Most skiers are here for one or two days at a time.) Seniors 60 and older pay $15 on non-holiday weekdays; full price on weekends. Adults who turn in their all-day lift ticket by 12:30 p.m. receive a credit coupon for use another day.

Accommodations

Sugar Bowl has a lodge that is certainly unusual, and possibly unique at American ski resorts: a base lodge that also is a hotel. In addition to the usual services on the ground floor, Sugar Bowl's base lodge also has 28 rooms on the upper two levels. Though the lodge was built in 1939, the rooms have been remodeled for a combination of historic charm and modern convenience. Adding to the charm is that access is only by the four-passenger gondola. The dining room preserves the grace of a former era with its decor and jacket-required dress code. Room rates, based on double occupancy, start at $85 per night.

A limited number of condominiums and private chalets also are available for rental during the ski season. Call (916) 426-3651, Ext. 542, for reservation information.

Child care

Sugar Bears Child Care is a licensed center for ages 3-6 with educational and recreational activities as well as skiing and quiet time. The program includes snacks, lunch and ski equipment. All day is $44, and half day (without lunch) is $32.

Information/reservations

Lodging: South Lake Tahoe: (800) 822-5922; **North Lake Tahoe:** (800) 824-6348 (TAHOE-4U); **Reno:** (800) 367-7366 (FOR-RENO).

Alpine Meadows, Box 5279, Tahoe City CA 95730; Information (800) 441-4423 or (916) 583-4232; snow phone (916) 581-8374.

Squaw Valley USA, Box 2007, Olympic Valley CA 96146; information (916) 583-6985; snow phone (916) 583-6955; reservations (800) 545-4350.

Northstar-at-Tahoe, Box 129, Truckee CA 95734; information and reservations (916) 587-0200 or (800) 533-6787.

Kirkwood, Box 1, Kirkwood CA 95646; information (209) 258-6000; snow phone (209) 258-3000; reservations (209) 258-7247 or (800) 967-7500.

Heavenly, Box 2180, Stateline NV 89449; information (916) 541-1330; ski conditions (916) 541-7544 (541-SKII); reservations (702) 588-4584 or (800) 243-2836 (2-HEAVEN).

Diamond Peak, 1210 Ski Way, Incline Village NV 89451; 24-hour information (702) 831-3249; snow phone: (702) 831-3211; reservations (800) 468-2463 (GO-TAHOE).

Sugar Bowl, Box 5, Norden CA 95724; information and reservations (916) 426-3651; ski conditions (916) 426-3847.

Mammoth Mountain
June Mountain
California

When you stand at the base lodge and scan the mountain you can't even see a quarter of the ski terrain. The encircling ridge, all above treeline, promises dramatic skiing, but what you don't see can be even better. This is what remains of a massive prehistoric volcano. Even now with most of the cone missing, it gives access to half a dozen wide bowls with the largest, once the interior of the cone, a whopping 13,000 feet across. In addition, lower peaks like Lincoln Mountain, Gold Hill and Hemlock Ridge, all with groomed swaths and moguled canyons, stretch six and a half miles in width. Mammoth is one of the nation's largest ski areas in size, and is at times the nation's busiest ski area, with more than 14,000 skiers swooping over its slopes on an average weekend. And yet, outside of California, it is not well known.

When you come to Mammoth Mountain, you come to ski—at the top of the mountain road there's not much to distract you from it. There is a labyrinthine base lodge with ski school, lift ticket windows, rental shops and hundreds of season lockers for locals and coin lockers for visitors. Across the parking lot is the Yodler chalet, brought piece by piece from the Alps and rebuilt to house a restaurant and bar. Nearby is the Mammoth Mountain Inn.

At the bottom of the mountain road lies the small but spread-out town of Mammoth Lakes. Here is just about all you need for a ski vacation short of luxury hotels. Don't expect a cozy, picturesque small-town atmosphere, though. As the town grew to support the ski area's success, newcomers haphazardly transplanted Southern California sprawl and mini-malls to the

Mammoth Mountain Facts
Base elevation: 7,953'; **Summit elevation:** 11,053'; **Vertical drop:** 3,100 feet
Number and types of lifts: 30—1 quad superchair, 4 quads, 7 triple chairs, 14 double chairs, 2 gondolas, 2 surface lifts **Acreage:** 3,500 skiable acres
Percent of snowmaking: 6 percent (200 acres)
Uphill capacity: 43,000 skiers per hour **Bed base:** 30,000

mountains. Most visitors drive from Southern California, but the few who don't may feel the need for wheels—not much is within easy walking distance. However, there is a free town bus that runs day and night.

If size intimidates you, Mammoth's little sister, June Mountain, a half-hour drive from Mammoth Lakes, will appeal. Its Old-World village atmosphere in a sheltered canyon is on a more human scale. That is not to say it's a puny resort. Seven chair lifts and an aerial tram scale a 2,590-foot vertical rise (as opposed to 3,100 feet at Mammoth).

June Mountain Facts

Base elevation: 7,545'; **Summit elevation:** 10,135'; **Vertical drop:** 2,590 feet
Number and types of lifts: 8–2 quad chairs, 5 double chairs, 1 "QMC" tram
Acreage: 500+ skiable acres
Uphill capacity: 12,000 skiers per hour **Bed base:** 30,000 region, 2,000 local

---

Where to ski

First-time visitors cannot help but smile at the size of the mountain. Forget knowing the names of peaks at this resort—everything goes by number. The mountain is crisscrossed with a network of chair lifts numbered in the order they were built. Chair 22, for example, is in a different area than Chair 23. It makes perfect sense to skiers who grew up with the mountain, but it's confusing to the first-timer who hears regulars planning their day football-quarterback style: "Take one to three, then backside to 23, down the ridge to 14, then to 13 and lateral to 19."

With massive weekend crowds the lines at the base lifts can be long, but since the area is so expansive you can easily avoid the crowds if you avoid the main base area. From left to right on the trail map, try Chairs 9, 18, 25, 22, 21, 10, 5, 12, 13 and 14.

Expert yaa-hoo skiers will strike out for the ridge, reachable by the gondola or a series of chairs. There, any chute or path will open into a wide bowl. Mammoth's signature run, a snarling lip of snow called The Cornice, looms large in every expert skier's memory bank. Other runs dropping from the ridge are considered steeper and more treacherous. Reached from the gondola, Hangman's—Mammoth's toughest—is an hour-glass-shaped chute hanging from the summit and bordered by wicked rocks; at its narrow part there's space for only one turn—a perfect one. Other expert shots can be found off Chair 22, and on powder days, you often can find untracked or less-tracked snow on the far east Dragon's Back off Chair 9, or the far west Hemlock Ridge above Chair 14.

One of the most popular advanced areas is the group of bowls available from Chair 3. They're great warm-up runs for experts, but plan to get here early. By 9:30 or 10 a.m. on weekends, the line is outrageous, although it diminishes at lunch time. At busy times, knowing skiers head for Chair 19, which offers half a dozen runs hidden in a glen; these resist crowds and keep their grooming late into the day. Also, Chairs 22 and 25, which provide access to Lincoln Mountain and its intermediate runs and advanced chutes, rarely have lines, a phenomenon that amazes locals who know them.

Chair 1, a high-speed detachable quad, takes off from the Main Lodge. It is especially popular because experts can either plunge down Gravy Chute or weave through The Wall, a panel of bubbly moguls, while their intermediate friends can coast down wide, smooth Broadway and meet them at the bottom.

The mid-to-lower mountain lets the intermediate traverse vast expanses and crisscross runs. Hidden canyons like Lower Dry Creek are full of swoops and surprises, and require tighter turns. For long cruising, head to the eastern edge of the ski area and Chairs 15 and 24. Other intermediate playgrounds are served by the tree-lined runs dropping from Chairs 8, 4, 16, 20, 21, and 10 between Hut 2 and the Chair 2 Outpost. At the other extreme of the area, a local secret when lines are long, is Chair 12 and the drop over to Chairs 13 and 14.

Beginner trails like Hansel and Gretel weave gently through evergreens, and there are sheltered slopes for learning, tucked away from the paths of speed demons shooting down from the top. (Look out for this breed on Stump Alley, a crowded all-out raceway down to Chair 2.) Hidden gullies give variety even to the beginner; the never-ever slopes (off Chair 11 at the Main Lodge and Chair 7 from Hut 2) have terrain as interesting as the more difficult ones.

June Mountain: Beginners and intermediates will find June Mountain challenging, although it has none of the high, broad bowls that make Mammoth Mountain famous. The steepest terrain at June, The Face, is as steep as anything at Mammoth. Because it is on the lower mountain, it unfortunately doesn't keep the snow as long as the upper runs—intermediate cruisers and expert chutes like Dave's Drop and Pro Bowl. Since June is more sheltered than Mammoth and none of its slopes is above the tree line, June tends to hold powder longer than Mammoth's more exposed bowls, and the snow doesn't crust up so quickly.

Mountain rating

Mammoth Mountain has terrain for all levels of skiers—and no matter what yours is you won't be shortchanged. If you are visiting for the first time, take a trail map and if you're with a group, decide where to meet if you get separated. We usually pick a centrally located short chair, such as Chair 20, as a meeting place rather than Mid-Chalet or the base lodge, which are usually loaded with bodies looking for other bodies. We just keep skiing that chair and watching from the lift until we all hook up.)

This is a huge mountain, and because of the crazy lift numbering system, it's hard to figure out how to get back to your starting point without the map.

June doesn't have quite as wide a range of terrain, but most skiers will enjoy it. The pace at June is slower, the crowds considerably fewer and sometimes nonexistent (locals come here on weekends and holidays), and the atmosphere friendly.

Cross-country

Twenty to 25 miles of groomed trails, actually summer roads, wind around four of the dozen or more high Alpine lakes, for which the town is named. **Tamarack Lodge**, a 50-year-old summer hunting and fishing lodge, maintains these trails and charges $14 for access ($10 for those 11-17; free younger than that). The Lakes Basin includes many trail heads into the backcountry, where no fee is charged. Rentals and lessons are available. On weekends it's advisable to reserve: 934-2442.

Just out of town at the 8,000-foot level is **Sierra Meadows Ranch and Equestrian Ski Touring Center**. A 55-km. network of mainly flat, machine groomed trails gives a magnificent view of Sherwin Bowl (now planned as another downhill area). Trail access is $10 for adults, $5 for children. Rentals and lessons available. Make reservations for advanced, telemark and children's lessons. A private lesson is $25 per hour; 934-6161.

The **U. S. Forest Service** gives ski tours of Mono Lake, explaining its bizarre geological formations, at 1 p.m. on Saturdays and Sundays during heavy snow times. Reserve at 934-2505.

Snowboarding

Both Mammoth and June offer snowboarding on all runs. June Mountain is the snowboard center with national competitions, a halfpipe and a snowboard park with steep jumps, a quarter pipe, table jumps, and other treats. Snowboarding lessons and rentals are available at both areas.

Ski school (94/95 prices)

At peak season, Mammoth's ski school has 400 instructors. At either Mammoth or June, an all-day **group lesson,** with six to eight in a group, is $38; half day is $25. A book of five all-day group lessons is $175.

Children's group lessons for ages 4 to 12 called Mammoth Explorers begin at 10 a.m. and include a supervised lunch, as well as four hours of lessons. The cost is $58 per child. Half-day sessions are $25; full day without lunch is $38.

Teens 13 to 17 have specially developed clinics starting at 10 a.m. Cost is $38 for a full day and $25 for either the morning or afternoon.

Private lessons for adults or children cost $60 for one hour, $10 is charged for each additional person. A five-day **Advanced**

Skiing Clinic, conducted from 9 a.m. to 4 p.m. at Mammoth Mountain only, is $210. This clinic is offered just once a month, on the first Monday; reservations required.

All lessons are available at both the Main Lodge and Hut II. Reservations are not necessary, but questions can be answered at 934-0685 for Main Lodge, 934-0787 for Hut II. June Mountain Ski School number is 648-7733.

Lift tickets (94/95 prices)

	Adult	Child (6-12) Senior (65+)
One day	$40	$20
Three days	$114 ($38/day)	$57 ($19/day)
Five days	$180 ($36/day)	$90 ($18/day)

Lift tickets are interchangeable for Mammoth and June Mountains. Children 5 and younger ski free, as do never-evers taking a ski school lesson. The multiday rates listed here are non-holiday rates. During holidays, regular per-day rates apply, though you still can buy a multiday ticket.

Anyone who skis Mammoth more than six days in a season should buy a Mammoth Club Card. It costs $60, but allows skiers to buy lift tickets for $30.

Ticket offices are at the Main Lodge, Warming Hut II and Chair 15 areas, as well as June Mountain. Additional satellite offices at Chairs 4, 10 and 2 are open weekends and holidays.

Accommodations (93/94 prices)

One of the nicest places to stay, **Mammoth Mountain Inn,** is also closest to the slopes—just across the parking lot. Lodging is deluxe to moderate, including hotel units with room service, motel and condominium units. Rates are $95 for rooms to $365 for a condo that sleeps eleven; (800) 228-4947.

Mammoth Lakes has been called Condo City of the Sierras. Just beyond town, **Snowcreek** (934-3333; 800-544-6007) is huge, wooded, spread out and posh, with athletic club including racquetball and basketball. It's actually a neighborhood. Units are spacious one-, two- and three-bedroom loft style, $105-$350.

Closer to the slopes, in fact adjacent to Hut II, two other large condominium complexes have a range of units. **Sierra Megeve** (934-3723; 800-227-7669), **Mountainback** (934-4549; 800-468-6225) **1849 Condominiums** (934-7525) and **Aspen Creek** (934-3933; 800-227-7669) cost between $155 and $495 depending on size and amenities.

In the middle of town, only a walk to restaurants and a shuttle to the lifts, you'll find **Sierra Nevada Inn** (800-824-5132; 934-2515) has hotel rooms starting at $65 and chalet units up to $280. **The Snowgoose Inn** (800-874-7368, California only; 934-2660) is one of three bed-and-breakfast inns in town. Decorated with antiques, breakfast served communally in a friendly atmosphere, approximate rates are $78 to $168.

The least expensive private rooms are at **Motel 6** (934-6660) but it takes no reservations. Three places offer dorm rooms: **Kitzbuhel Lodge** (934-2352) is good for groups and young people, with a huge dining room and group kitchen. Three to 14 beds are in each room. Cost is $20 a night for men and women. Besides motel rooms and large suites, **Alpenhof Lodge** (934-6330) has dorm rooms for $64 for men only, with three beds to a room and the bath at the end of the hall. **Ullr Lodge** (934-2454) is a European-style dorm for men only, mainly share-a-bath rooms, for about $20 a night. They will rent to women if four take one room. The last two are on the shuttle line right in town.

June has two large condominium complexes. **Interlaken** charges from $85 for studios midweek to $185 for three-bedroom units. Weekend prices are $120-$240. **Edgewater** has only one size unit, suitable for six to nine people, for $105 midweek to $165 on weekends. All other lodgings at June are small and quaint, even funky. **The Haven** has studios for $65. Call June Lake Properties Reservation at (800) 648-5863 (648-JUNE) or Century 21 Rainbow Ridge at (800) 462-5589 for condominium reservations.

Fern Creek Lodge (800-621-9146) has cabins for $38 and motel rooms for $59. **Whispering Pines** (800-648-7762) has motel rooms for $59 and cabins for $75. **Boulder Lodge** (648-7533) has motel rooms for $48 and cabins for $85, some of which can sleep 17 people.

A full-service RV park is four miles from the resort.

Dining

Mammoth Lakes has more than 45 dining options, from gourmet French cuisine to delicatessen sandwiches and quick take-out. The top-of-the-line menu is found at **Anything Goes** (934-2424), served daily in a cozy dining room. The choices change each week. Here the focus is on great presentation combined with healthy, generous portions. A bit pricier and a bit more elegant is **Natalie's** (934-3902) where the atmosphere is romantic with lace curtains and a coordinated decor. **O'Kelly and Dunns Restaurant** (934-9316) has prices in the range of Anything Goes, and reeks of American country with dried flowers, grasses and quilts gracing the walls.

For the most romantic (and expensive) dining head out to **Lakefront Restaurant at Tamarack Lodge** (934-3534) where the menu is basic but excellently prepared. The specialties are normally worth the trip. The atmosphere is Old World in a small dining room decorated with photos of movie stars who used to hang out here. After dinner wander into the lodge and have after-dinner drinks in front of the fireplace. On a night with a full moon, make plans to head out to **Convict Lake Restaurant** (934-3803) south of Mammoth Lakes on Route 395. On those nights when the moon reflects on the lake, there is no prettier setting for dining in front of a flickering fire.

Nevados (934-4466) receives good recommendations, but expect to pay handsomely for continental cuisine with unusual dishes. Mammoth Mountain Inn's **Mountainside Grill** (934-0601) is worth the trip up the mountain from town.

For the best steaks and prime rib head to **Whiskey Creek** (934-2555), or try **The Mogul Restaurant** (934-3039) and the **Chart House** (934-4526) which also serves fish dinners.

Families (or anyone with limited funds) will want to stop in at **Berger's** (934-6622) for big, big portions. The tuna salad is massive and you can have not only burgers but also chicken, salad, Canadian stew, and homemade pastries like carrot cake and cheesecake. Another family spot is **Angel's** (934-7427) with great ribs, beans and barbecue.

The **Old Mammoth Pasta House** (934-8088) dishes out huge portions of fresh pasta and friendly service. **Nik-N-Willie's Pizza**, (934-2012) recently added sit-down dining (it was strictly take-out), and locals consider it the best pizza in town. Pizza also is served at **Giovanni's** (934-7563) or **Perry's Italian Cafe** (934-6521). The best Mexican food is at **Roberto's** (934-3667) with homemade tortillas and authentic big portions, but no margaritas. If you can't get a seat at Roberto's or can't live without a margarita, head to **La Sierra** (934-8083), **Gringo's** (934-8595), known for its "almost world famous" Rotisserie Chicken," or **Gomez's** (924-2693).

Grumpy's (934-8587) holds the distinction of the town's best greasy chicken and big steaks, also the best cole slaw, all presented in a big-screen TV, sports bar atmosphere. (Warning: Grumpy's can get very smoke-filled on busy weekends.)

Shogun (934-3970) has Japanese cuisine and a sushi bar. Try **Matsu's**, (934-8277) for inexpensive Chinese-American.

Ocean Harvest (934-8539) is the prime seafood restaurant, offering a nautical atmosphere and fresh fish caught from the owner's boat.

The best breakfast in town is served at **The Stove** (934-2821) with biscuits 3 or 4 inches high. Or head to the **Swiss Cafe** (934-6196) for excellent croissants. Both remain open for excellent lunches as well.

For dining on the mountain for lunch or dinner the best bet by far is at the **Mountainside Grill** (934-0601) in the Mammoth Mountain Inn. Surprisingly, the prices are not much more than the cafeteria. Or head over to the more crowded **Yodler** (934-0636). If you are in town for a quick lunch check out the **Gourmet Grocer** (934-2997) and **Schat's Bakery** (934-6055) for their sheepherder's bread.

Après-ski/nightlife

Lively après-ski gets underway across the parking lot from the Main Lodge at the **Yodler**. It has a large-screen TV and a bartender who will try anything. **Josh Slocum's** in town is the après-ski hangout for ski patrol members and instructors. At **Austria Hof**, singer and guitarist Gayle Louise entertains after skiing. Entertainment also is at the **Ocean Club** and at Mammoth Mountain Inn's **Dry Creek Bar**.

Dancing and general meet markets are at **Whiskey Creek** and **The Rafters**. For a great night out where you are sure to meet someone, try Country & Western dancing on Thursday and Saturday nights at **Annie Rose's,** where Stogie's used to be.

There's plenty of nighttime hoopla at **Grumpy's** and its **Western Saloon and Sports Bar**. Featured are five giant-screen TVs, pool, foosball, inexpensive chili and burgers.

Shogun has follow-the-bouncing-ball karaoke singalong on Saturday nights with a sushi bar, tempura, sukiyaki and teriyaki, which you can wash down with sake and imported beer.

Child care (94/95 prices)

The **Small World Day Care Center** at Mammoth Mountain Inn, just across the street from the Main Lodge and at June Mountain offers these services:

Child care for newborn to 23-month-old children is $45 per day; $30 for a half-day. Care for kids 2 to 12 years is $40 for a full day and $30 for a half-day. Additional children in a family get a $5 reduction. Fees include snacks and lunch, except for infants.

The combined day care/ski school rates at Mammoth Main Lodge for ages 4 to 12 include supervised activity from 8 a.m. to 5 p.m. and a ski lesson from 10 a.m. until noon. Rate is $60, including lunch. Call 934-0646.

Other activities

Shopping: Mammoth's shopping is oriented as much for the local population as for tourists. You won't find many trendy boutiques here, though there is a small factory outlet center on Main Street.

Snowmobiles can be rented from DJs Snowmobile Rentals; 935-4880; Center Street Rentals, 934-4020; or Mammoth Snowmobile Rental, 934-9645. **Bobsledding** down a designated track is available through Sledz, 934-7533. **Sleds** are available at Kittredge Sports; 934-7566. **Dogsled rides** are offered by Dog Sled Adventures, 934-6270.

Sleigh rides with (or without) a cozy ranch-house dinner are offered at Sierra Meadows Ranch; 934-6161. **Hot-air balloon trips** with High Sierra Ballooning Company (934-7188) take off from Mammoth Meadow. **Snowcreek Athletic Club** (934-8511) has a variety of indoor and outdoor facilities.

Mammoth Lakes also has two movie theaters (one with two screens), **Minaret Cinemas** and **Plaza Theater** (both at 934-3131). The *Mammoth Times*, a free weekly newspaper, is a good source for special events listings.

Getting there and getting around

Getting there: By car from Los Angeles, Mammoth is 307 miles north on Highway 395; from Reno it is 168 miles south on Highway 395. It is difficult to reach Mammoth in winter from the San Francisco Bay area, because the shortest route, Highway 120 through Yosemite, is closed in winter. Northern Californians can use either Interstate 80 or Highway 50 to reach Highway 395, but those roads pass by Lake Tahoe and its multitude of fine ski areas, so not many Bay Area skiers make it here.

TW Express (800-421-9353) has daily service to the Mammoth Lakes airport from Burbank, Los Angeles, Orange County and new this year, San Francisco. **United Express** has daily flights from Los Angeles, Sacramento, Ontario and San Diego. **Eastern Sierra Auto Rentals** (935-4471) is available at the airport, or you can catch a bus into town.

Skiers also can get to Mammoth from Southern California via **Greyhound** (800-231-2222), **Hot Doggers Tours** (213-698-6211) or **Mammoth Express** (800) 446-4500.

Getting around: The resort operates a free shuttle that runs throughout the town and to Mammoth's Main Lodge (four miles from town) and to Warming Hut II and Chair 15. A nightly shuttle makes half-hourly loops around town until midnight during the week; 1 a.m. on Friday and Saturday nights (technically, 1 a.m. Saturday and Sunday morning). Mammoth's visitors bureau says having a car is an option; we haven't tried it ourselves. Chances are you'll be driving here, so you'll have one if you need it.

Information/reservations

Central reservations for **Mammoth Lakes Visitors Bureau,** 934-8006 or (800) 367-6572, handles accommodations, car and ski equipment rentals, airline and lift tickets, ski school, child care and even restaurant reservations. **June Mountain** has three booking agencies: 648-5863 (648-JUNE); (800) 648-6835; and (800) 462-5589. The last two numbers are within California only.

Twenty-four-hour **snow report** for Los Angeles is (213) 935-8866; Orange County, (714) 955-0692; San Diego, 231-7785. Road information is 873-6366.

Mammoth Mountain Ski Resort business office is 934-2571. **June Mountain Ski Resort** office is 648-7733.

For a Mammoth/June Mountain Travel Planner call (800) 832-7321.

Unless otherwise noted, all area codes are 619.

Southern California Areas

Bear Mountain, Snow Summit
Snow Valley

Quick: which of the following is *not* found in Southern California: Sun. Palm trees. Golf. Smog. Surfboards. Skiing. Movie stars.

Okay, it's a trick question. You can find *all* of the above in Southern California. When winter rain falls on Southern California's palm trees, snow falls on the mountains that ring the Los Angeles basin.

These mountains are home to nine ski areas, most of which lie between 6,500 and 8,800 feet. Three of them—Bear Mountain, Snow Summit and Snow Valley, all in the San Bernardino mountain range—attract the majority of the skiers, and are the only ones that aren't strictly day areas.

Ask just about any Southern California skier what he or she thinks of the local ski areas, and they'll probably tell you they never ski here—they only ski Utah, Colorado or Mammoth. Well, *someone* is skiing here. Combined, these nine areas record a couple of million skier visits each year.

Southern Californians just don't know how good they have it. On many a sunny winter day, it is entirely possible to spend the

---

Bear Mountain Facts
Base elevation: 7,140'; **Summit elevation:** 8,805'; **Vertical drop:** 1,665 feet. **Number and types of lifts:** 11–1 quad superchair, 1 quad, 3 triples, 4 doubles, 2 surface lifts. **Acreage:** 174 skiable acres **Percent of snowmaking:** 100 percent **Uphill capacity:** 15,000 skiers per hour **Bed Base:** 2,500 within 5 miles

Snow Summit Facts
Base elevation: 7,000'; **Summit elevation:** 8,200'; **Vertical drop:** 1,200 feet. **Number and types of lifts:** 11–1 quad superchair, 2 quad chairs, 3 triple chairs, 5 double chairs **Acreage:** 230 skiable acres **Percent of snowmaking:** 100 percent **Uphill capacity:** 17,650 skiers per hour **Bed Base:** 2,500 within 5 miles

Snow Valley Facts
Base elevation: 6,700'; **Summit elevation:** 7,898'; **Vertical drop:** 1,198 feet. **Number and types of lifts:** 13–5 triple chairs, 8 double chairs **Acreage:** 230 skiable acres **Percent of snowmaking:** 74 percent **Uphill capacity:** 18,550 skiers per hour **Bed Base:** 1,700 within 15 miles

morning skiing in the San Bernardino mountains and the afternoon playing a round of golf in Palm Springs. The few out-of-staters that venture to Big Bear Lake, where the two leading ski areas are, are usually astonished at the skiing that's available.

That's not to imply that skiing here is on a par with skiing in Utah, Colorado or Mammoth. The Southern California areas have much less terrain, and often rely on snowmaking to cover the runs. All three have extensive snowmaking; however, Bear Mountain and Snow Summit have a more reliable water supply. Even if the season has been dry, you'll find surprisingly good snow on the runs. And if the winter has been a wet one, as it was a couple of seasons ago, all of the areas are worth a try.

The Big Three are very similar in that all have 174-250 skiable acres on largely intermediate terrain. The differences are in accessibility and visitor amenities. Snow Valley is a little easier to reach, but its lodges and restaurants are fewer in number and farther from the slopes. Bear Mountain and Snow Summit are farther away, but are in the resort town of Big Bear Lake, where lodging and restaurants are pleasant and plentiful.

Where to ski

Beginners, intermediates and snowboarders will have the most fun at these areas. All have limited amounts of advanced terrain. All allow snowboarding, and all but Bear Mountain have night skiing.

At **Bear Mountain**, beginners have their own area under the Inspiration triple chair. They start with very flat terrain served by a Poma lift, move to an ever-so-slightly steeper slope accessed by a chair lift, then graduate to a long, gentle run.

Lower intermediates will be happiest with runs off the Goldmine or Showdown mountains, while upper intermediates will like Silver Mountain. Advanced skiers should head for the top of Bear Peak, which has the area's only real hair-raising run, Geronimo. When snow conditions permit, advanced skiers may go off-trail within the ski area boundaries for some of the best tree and glade skiing you'll find in Southern California.

Novices at **Snow Summit** also have a private, gentle slope, served by Chairs 4 and 8. Those with at least a few trails under their skis can head for the green runs under Chair 9, which is a Family Ski Park, meaning no snowboarders allowed on busier days. Intermediates will love Miracle Mile, a long cruiser that descends from the summit (8,200 feet) to the base (7,000 feet), and the trails served by Chairs 1, 2, 3, 5, 7 and 10. Upper intermediates will enjoy the runs under Chair 11, a surprisingly underskied section of the mountain.

Advanced skiers have the steep (but short) pitch of The Bowl served by Chair 6. The Bowl is almost always skiable, thanks to snowmaking, but also attracts a lot of hotshots who think they ski better than they can. Snowboarders have a freestyle park on the Westridge run with bumps, jumps and obstacles. Though the park is open to skiers, boarders mostly use it.

Snow Valley has the gentlest overall terrain of the four. Never-evers have several acres of flat runs at the base, strong beginners can handle the blue runs, and strong intermediates can handle most black-diamond trails. Solid intermediates especially should head for Chairs 4, 8 and 9, rated black on the trail map, but often deserted. A nice touch here: The base of each chair has a large vertical sign on it, clearly stating the number of the chair and the symbols for the difficulty of terrain it serves.

Snow Valley's toughest area, Slide Peak, is not visible from the parking lot. It is a wide face with a respectable pitch. Half the face is groomed, while the other half is left alone to build moguls. Lack of snow closes it, off and on, in dry seasons.

• • •

If you have the choice, don't ski on Saturdays or holidays! The parade of cars crawling up the roads combined with the parade of skiers careening down the slopes is not conducive to a relaxing day. Sunday is the much better choice, if weekends are your only option.

During dry winter seasons, chances are that these areas will be operating: all have very good snowmaking systems covering much of their terrain. When the winter has been wet, though, consider some smaller areas that have limited or no snowmaking—all are less crowded than the Big Three and all have lower prices: **Mt. Baldy**, north of Upland; **Ski Sunrise**, next to Mountain High in Wrightwood; **Big Air Green Valley**, near Running Springs (for snowboarders only) and **Kratka Ridge** and **Mt. Waterman**, both on the Angeles Crest Highway north of La Canada-Flintridge.

Mountain High, via Highways 138 and 2 from Interstate 15, is one of the largest Southern California ski areas, with 205 acres, snowmaking and 11 chairs (including a high-speed quad), but it is strictly a day area with few and Spartan restaurants and overnight accommodations.

Mountain ratings

These areas are most suitable for intermediate skiers, although beginners will find them comfortable, unintimidating places to learn on uncrowded days. (On *crowded* days, beginners may find them very intimidating!) Advanced skiers can be entertained if snow conditions cooperate, but experts may be bored after a couple of runs. Those who dislike sharing the slopes with snowboarders may not like these areas—Southern California is a hotbed of snowboard activity.

A tip for upper-level skiers: After a snowfall, head for **Mt. Baldy**, off Interstate 10 north of Upland. This lesser-known area has the steepest slopes and the largest vertical drop (2,100 feet) in Southern California. Its biggest problem is very little snowmaking on the advanced terrain, and one double chair lift that leads from the parking lot to the upper mountain, where much of the skiing is. On super powder days, the line waiting to board that chair is agonizingly slow.

Cross-country

Although drought sometimes makes it tough for Southern California Nordic centers to operate, they do exist. The **Palm Springs Nordic Center,** which is at 8,500 feet on 10,800-foot Mt. San Jacinto, is accessible only by the Palm Springs Aerial Tramway. Skiers with equipment may use the ungroomed trails for free (the tram ticket is $14.95). Ski and snowshoe rental equipment is available. Lessons are given on weekends. Call (619) 327-6002. Note: This is not near any of the downhill ski areas, but it overlooks those great Palm Springs golf courses.

Nearer to downhill skiing is the **Green Valley Lake Cross-Country Center,** just beyond Running Springs in the town of Green Valley Lake. It has about five miles of set tracks, and many more miles of ungroomed trails in the San Bernardino National Forest. The longest trail is 13 miles from Green Valley Lake to Fawnskin. The trail fee is $3. Group lessons and rentals are available. The phone number is 867-7754, but it's seasonal. If you get a recording that says the number is not in service, wait for snow and call again.

Snowboarding

It's not too surprising that the ski areas in the surf and skateboard capital of the U.S. embrace snowboarding. All four major areas not only allow boarders, but they also have excellent snowboard parks, halfpipes, rentals, lessons and many contests and competitions. Most ski and sporting goods shops near the areas also rent snowboards. One of the smaller ski areas, **Big Air Green Valley** 867-2338, is only one of two areas in the entire nation devoted entirely to snowboarders (the other is in Illinois).

A few snowboarders with bad attitudes have caused some problems at Southern California areas, so the areas have developed some very good programs to try to keep both the skier and snowboarder camps happy. Three Southern California areas have skier-only runs. Mountain High East is for skiers only, as are the runs on Bear Mountain's Silver Peak. Snow Summit restricts its Chair 9 area to skiers only at busy times.

Ski school (93/94 prices)

Bear Mountain has some of the most innovative programs, including a New Skier Center, EXCL classes that last 90 minutes and have no more than three students, the only disabled-skier school in Southern California and daily racing clinics. Skiers can see themselves on videotape at the free on-mountain Skier Evaluation Center.

Bear Mountain has an especially good New Skier/Snowboarder Program. It is set up very well, and the director, Aubrey Duncan, is a former pro football player who freely shares with novices his frustrations and eventual triumph of learning to ski as an adult. (As do the other instructors.) The attitude is, "We learned; so can you." The beginner package for skiers or snowboarders (rentals, lifts and lessons) is $29 during the week and $39 on weekends. Each new skier also receives a coupon book good for future discounts at the area on rentals, lessons and lift tickets.

Children's lessons (ages 4-12) are $50 for a full day, with lunch, and $35 for a half day. Equipment rental is $10 extra.

EXCL classes are $21. Racing clinics are $25. Private lessons are $50 per hour; $35 for each additional person. Bear Mountain also teaches telemark lessons, the only Southern California area to do so.

Snow Summit offers a beginner package for $39.75 midweek ($44.75 weekends). Its two-hour group lessons are $20; private lessons are $50 per hour. Children 8-12 can get all-day instruction (four hours) for $30, or a half day (two hours) for $20. Children 5-7 have longer lessons: all-day lessons are six hours and cost $50; $30 for a half-day (three-hour) lesson. Children's prices include lift access during the lesson.

Snow Valley's beginner package costs $29 for ages 6 and older on weekdays ($35 weekends and holidays). Ninety-minute adult or child group lessons are $18 (but just $4 more for three hours). Private lessons are $50 per hour.

Lift tickets (93/94 prices)

	Adult	Child (Up to 12)
Bear Mountain	$38	$21
Snow Summit	$38.75	$19.75
Snow Valley	$37	$22

These are one-day weekend prices. Specific ticket information for each area:

Bear Mountain: Buy a ticket for two or three consecutive days and the price drops $5 per day for adults and $4 for children. Seniors 65 and over ski midweek for $21.

Snow Summit: Seniors (60 and older) and ages 13-18 can ski midweek for $24.75; ages 19-22 pay $29.75 midweek. Night skiing is $23.75 for adults; $12.75 for kids, 3-9:30 p.m. You can ski free on your birthday by showing ID at the ticket window.

Snow Valley: Tickets bought through Ticketmaster are $27, good any day. The day lift ticket is good the same night as well; night skiing alone costs $24. Ages 65-69 ski for children's prices; older than 69 or younger than 6 ski free. Snow Valley also has an Option Pass, a point-ticket system that allows skiers to pay only for what they ski and save the unused points for use on a return visit. This is a great alternative for those who don't ski a full day.

Accommodations

Southern California skiing is overwhelmingly day skiing. Nearly all the skiers drive up from the urban valleys, ski, and drive home. The largest resort town was Big Bear Lake, home of Bear Mountain and Snow Summit. But it had little "resort" aura: most lodging was in time-worn buildings dating back to the '40s and '50s, and the town rolled up the sidewalks about 7 p.m. or so. You'd leave your restaurant and think you had stumbled into the Twilight Zone, the streets were so deserted.

In the past two years, however, downtown Big Bear Lake (called "The Village") has received a much needed and highly successful facelift recently, and is beginning to look like a cozy mountain resort. Old-style streetlights and planter boxes are much more inviting for an evening stroll. Now, if some of the downtown stores would just stay open past 5 p.m. . .

A new hotel, **Northwoods Resort Hotel,** is set to open this season with 155 rooms, lodgepole-style furnishings, a 4,000-square-foot lobby with stone fireplace and a "woodsy" decor. It has an attached dining room and rates are quite reasonable: $89-$129 weekends, with lower rates midweek. The hotel is in Big Bear Village, close to Bear Mountain and Snow Summit. Call (800) 866-3121 for reservations.

No properties here are slopeside; however, **Mountain Vista Resort** (585-7855), has lodging within walking distance of Bear Mountain.

The **Big Bear Inn** is very unusual, a conglomeration of marble floors and walls, ornate statuary, oversize Oriental antiquities, Baroque chandeliers and a lobby ceiling with a painting of a cloud. Rates for its 80 rooms run from about $75 to $250, depending on room size and time of year. Reservations: (800) 232-7466 (BEAR-INN).

For a lake view, try **Marina Riviera** (866-7545), with a pool, spa and Jacuzzi tubs and rates $90-$175, depending on size of room and midweek vs. weekend; or **Forest Shores,** with studios and one, two, and three bedrooms. (866-6551.)

The town has a lot of mom-and-pop motels, small lodges and cottages, some on the lake, others in nicely wooded areas, still others on the single main boulevard. Two groups of cabins that are particularly quaint are **Oak Knoll Lodge** (866-2773) and **Cozy Hollow Lodge** (866-9694).

For B&Bs, try these: **The Inn at Fawnskin,** on the opposite shore of Big Bear Lake, is contemporary and tranquil, but has just four rooms, so booking ahead is important. (866-3200). **Gold Mountain Manor** has a triple diamond rating from AAA and is furnished in antiques and Western artifacts. (585-6997). **Eagle's**

Nest B&B is moderately priced and offers free shuttle service to ski areas. (866-6465).

Several services handle lodging reservations ranging from motels and cabins to condos and luxury homes. Ski packages are available. Call **Big Bear Central Reservation Service,** (866-4601); **Mountain Lodging Unlimited,** (800) 487-3168; or **Sleepy Forest Resorts,** (800) 544-7454. For general recorded information about the Big Bear area, call (909) 866-7000.

A limited number of sites are available at the full-service **Big Bear Shores RV Resort** on the lake's north shore (opposite the town). Call 866-4151.

Lake Arrowhead is a small resort about 30 miles west of Big Bear Lake and about 10 miles from the nearest skiing at Snow Valley. The largest hotel is the **Lake Arrowhead Hilton,** with 261 rooms ranging from $139 to $239. This is a full resort hotel, featuring lakeview rooms, a health club and spa, and meeting and banquet facilities. Reservations: 336-1511 or (800) 800-6792. The next largest lodge is **The Saddleback Inn**, with 34 rooms spread among a central building and outlying cabins. Other properties include B&Bs, cabins and condos.

Call the **Lake Arrowhead accommodations and lodging information** at (800) 545-5784 for more information.

Dining

In **Big Bear Lake:** Dining prices are either moderate ($15-$25 for entrees) or budget. **The Iron Squirrel** (866-9121) is not only considered the finest dining by locals, it is an entirely No-Smoking restaurant. Escargots are a common appetizer, and salmon is a specialty. **Knusperhauschen** (585-8640), known locally as George and Sigi's and open only for dinner, has a continental menu of pheasant, beef Wellington and cioppino.

More moderate, **The Blue Ox** (585-7886) serves up its "Big Swede Ole Dinner," a baked potato stuffed with Hungarian goulash, which is mighty good. **The Old Country Inn** (866-5600) specializes in better-than-average German, Italian and American food at moderate prices. **Mandarin Garden** (585-1818) serves a fine shrimp curry and good Szechwan dishes. **Captain's Anchorage** has steak and seafood (866-3997), and **The Blue Whale** is good for prime rib and seafood (866-5771). The **Log Cabin** (866-3667) has great specials for German and American food, a bakery and a bar with a large assortment of imported beers.

Many places are inexpensive. For Mexican food, try **La Montana** (866-2606) or **Nacho's** (866-6309). **Maggio's Pizza** (866-8815) has full dinners, as well as Italian subs and sandwiches and calzones. **Pong's Place** serves oriental specialties (866-8688). Check out **Paoli's** for Italian food (866-2020). **Boo Bear's Den** (866-2932) has the widest variety—from burgers to Australian lobster. The **Cowboy Steak House** serves up big portions of barbecue and home style food (866-1486).

In or near Lake Arrowhead or Snow Valley:

Snow Valley has been improving its restaurant services, and has a sit-down restaurant, **WR's Eatery**, that serves dishes such as parchment-wrapped tarragon shark and New York steak with peppercorn sauce. Call 867-4160 or 867-2751.

The **Cliffhanger Restaurant** on Highway 18 leading to Lake Arrowhead has Greek and Italian specialties in the $13-$30 range. Lunch runs about $7-$15. Great views of the San Gabriel Valley (if the smog isn't too thick.)

Lake Arrowhead Village has about 20 restaurants ranging in atmosphere and price from **McDonald's** to the lakeside **Candlewood Restaurant**.

Après-ski/nightlife

Because these areas attract many more day skiers than overnighters, après-ski is much more plentiful than night life. Each ski area has a bar at the foot of the slopes where skiers relax before heading down the mountain; live music is standard on weekends, recorded music during the week.

Big Bear Lake has most of the night life that exists. The hottest new spot is **Ron's Sports Pub** on Big Bear Boulevard, 878-2255. It has karaoke, video trivia contests, a big-screen TV, a varied beer selection and nightly appetizers. Other places to try: **Prospector's, The Moonridge Club** at the Big Bear Inn, the **Pine Cone, Chad's,** and **the Sugarloafer.**

Child care

The only area with child care is **Snow Summit,** which has its **Little Bear Care Center** for ages 2-7. Activities include crafts, games, videos for all ages and ski lessons for 4-year-olds (ages 5-7 enroll in regular children's ski school). A telephone hotline at the tops of Chairs 2 and 10 give parents access to the care center. The cost (93/94 prices) is $40 for all day (nine hours with lunch), $25 for four hours. Reserve by calling 866-5766, Ext. 354. On weekends, the center is often booked two weeks in advance; and you should plan on making reservations for your child, even on weekdays.

If your children are too young for ski school and you can't get them into the Snow Summit child care center, leave them at home with a baby sitter. Four is the minimum age for most of these areas' children's learning programs and they enforce it, and there is no place for toddlers to play in the snow where they won't get run down accidentally by skiers.

Other activities

Shopping in Big Bear Lake is a pleasant diversion, but not the reason to come here. Some fun shops in Big Bear Lake include **Adora Bella** and **Room to Room** for some unusual home and kitchen accessories, and nearly everyone's favorite for funky selection and decor, **Bear Mountain Trading Company**, on the road up to Bear Mountain ski area. Unfortunately, many of the stores are open only in the day.

Lake Arrowhead's village has many fine shops in a layout more conducive to strolling and window-shopping.

Getting there and getting around

Getting there: Two options: drive yourself, or take one of the many bus-and-lift-ticket packages. Call the ski areas for information on the latter option. If you drive, carry chains. The California Highway Patrol will not let unchained vehicles past its checkpoints during and even a couple of days after storms.

From Los Angeles:

Bear Mountain and Snow Summit: The least crowded route is to take I-10 east to the Orange Avenue exit. Follow the signs to Highway 38, which leads to Big Bear Lake. The shorter but most crowded route is I-10 east to the Mountain Resorts exit and follow Highways 30, 330 and 18 through Running Springs to Big Bear Lake.

Tip: To avoid bumper-to-bumper traffic in the city of Big Bear Lake, take Highway 38 around the north side of the lake through Fawnskin, and turn right on the Stanfield Cutoff on the east end of the lake.

Snow Valley: Take I-10 east, then take the Mountain Resorts exit and follow Highways 30, 330 and 18 east, just past the town of Running Springs. To reach Lake Arrowhead, take Highway 18 west from Running Springs.

Getting around: Big Bear Lake has a free trolley, from all corners of the town and to both ski areas. Though quite reliable, it is infrequent in winter. Traffic and parking at the two areas can be awful, especially on Saturdays. If you're staying overnight in Lake Arrowhead, you will need a car.

Information/reservations

Bear Mountain: Box 6812, Big Bear Lake, CA 92315, (909) 585-2519. Snow report: (213) 289-0636 (LA number); (619) 238-5555 (San Diego number).

Snow Summit: Box 77, Big Bear Lake, CA 92315, (909) 866-5766. Snow report: (310) 306-0800 (LA number); (619) 294-8786 (San Diego number.)

Snow Valley: Box 2337, Running Springs, CA 92382, (909) 867-2751. Snow report: (800) 680-7669 (680-SNOW).

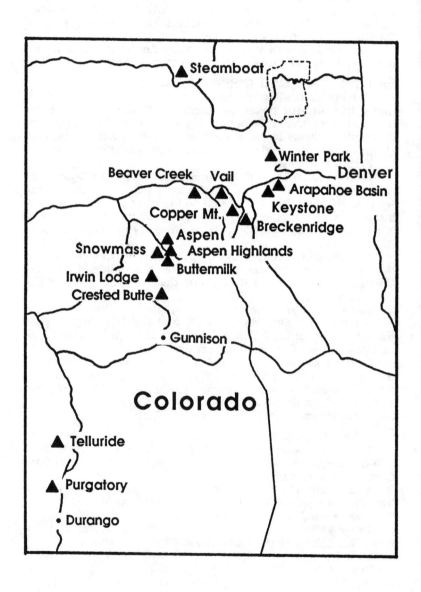

Aspen Area, Colorado

Aspen Mountain, Tiehack Mountain
Aspen Highlands

Ask a crowd of non-skiing Americans to name a ski resort, and you can bet your life savings that Aspen will be one of those they name. Aspen fits a niche unique among North American ski resorts. Sure, other resorts attract wealth, but Aspen's wealth glitters and sparkles with a "look-this-way" flamboyance. Style and sex sparkle. Sophisticated New York and Hollywood fashions shimmer against turn-of-the-century brick façades. Sequined and rhinestoned denim jackets leave Jeep Cherokee limos and parade into discos. Learjet pilots wait patiently for parking spaces on the Aspen Airport tarmac. And America's paparazzi aim their lenses at every celebrity in town so that supermarket tabloids can keep their pages filled each winter.

Yes, Aspen's a town perfectly developed for soap opera excesses. For the nouveau riche, the rising star or a lottery winner with sudden wealth, Aspen is the Promised Land. For dreamers who long to be a part of this crowd, though, it can be Never-Never Land.

Unlike most other resorts, which focus on skiing as the primary activity with all else serving as a support system, Aspen functions in an upside-down world. Skiing, for many, has become a sideline to the glitz, the gourmet dining and the pulsing nightlife. In this sense, Aspen doesn't compete with other ski resorts. But there will always be a place for Aspen, where you can be discovered, make a splash, and rub elbows with those in the middle of the action. Approached with the right attitude, this side of Aspen can be downright fun, especially if you love to watch people who march to a different drummer.

Aspen is also a Victorian mountain town, albeit a large one, with citizens who have escaped one rat race only to find another creeping up on them. Not every Aspen resident aspires to come up with the most original license plate or throw the most spectacular party. There's also a side to Aspen where perfectly painted lips, careful coiffure and cosmopolitan style are not the rule. Aspen also has women and men who exude a natural freshness, whose smiles are spontaneous rather than reserved for photo sessions. Aspen has restaurants where one can eat without taking out a loan and bars that have never seen a fur coat. Children play tag, mothers attend PTA meetings and men go out for a beer after work.

Aspen also draws skiers who couldn't care less about the off-mountain scene. They come for the skiing, which has received rave reviews for decades. The Aspen area has four separate ski areas, all owned by the Aspen Skiing Company. Aspen Mountain, or Ajax as it's often called, challenges intermediate and advanced skiers. Tiehack, in contrast, is just a nub, but serves as the perfect beginner and cruising mountain (this mountain used to be called Buttermilk). Aspen Highlands is the most varied, with skiing for experts and beginners, cruisers and bumpers. Snowmass, larger than the other three areas combined, is several miles farther down the road from the town. Though it is one of the four Aspen Skiing Company areas and included in that lift ticket, it also has its own accommodations, restaurants and shops, and is covered in the next chapter.

Aspen simply has more happening in winter than just about anyplace else. Make no mistake: Money is the fuel that runs this action machine. But Aspen also has places to stay and eat that are no more expensive than any other ski area. So take your choice: If you want glitz and you don't mind paying for it, you can find it here. If you don't, there are ways to avoid it.

Where to ski

Free mountain tours orient skiers Tours last 90 minutes and outline the history and nature of the area, as well as point out different runs. Tiehack and Snowmass tours meet Sundays at 9 a.m. at the ski school meeting place. Aspen Mountain tours are Monday at 9:30 a.m. at the base of the gondola.

Aspen Mountain is one of skidom's best intermediate and expert playgrounds. Beginners shouldn't even think about tackling this terrain, but with Tiehack so close they don't need to. The Silver Queen Gondola whisks skiers to the summit of Ajax. From here, 3,267 feet of uninterrupted vertical drops to the gondola base.

The basic guideline for Aspen Mountain is that intermediate terrain is on the top knob around the summit and in the gullies between the ridges. The expert stuff drops from the ridges into the gullies. The gentlest terrain—Dipsy Doodle, Pussyfoot and

---

Aspen Mountain Facts

Base elevation: 7,945'; **Summit elevation:** 11,212'; **Vertical drop:** 3,267 feet
Number of lifts: 8–1 gondola, 1 quad superchair, 2 quad chairs, 4 double chairs
Snowmaking: 33 percent **Total acreage:** 631 skiable acres
Uphill capacity: 10,775 per hour **Bed Base:** 15,000

Silver Bell—funnels into Spar Gulch. Ruthie's Road along the ski area boundary connects with Ruthie's Run, and Copper Bowl is a long intermediate run, serving a dozen expert trails from the Bell Mountain Ridge and Gentleman's Ridge.

Tiehack Mountain Facts
Base elevation: 7,870'; **Summit elevation:** 9,900'; **Vertical drop:** 2,030 feet
Number of lifts: 7–1 high-speed quad, 5 double chairs, 1 surface lift
Snowmaking: 27 percent **Total acreage:** 410 acres
Uphill capacity: 6,600 per hour **Bed Base:** 15,000

Tiehack Mountain is all that Aspen Mountain isn't. Beginners can experience top-to-bottom runs as soon as they master the wedge turn or halting stem christies. Intermediates will enjoy an ego boost, and wise experts will let their skis go and enjoy no-stress, no-crowd cruising.

The beginner terrain concentrates under the Tiehack West chair. Tom's Thumb, Red's Rover, Larkspur, Westward Ho and Blue Grouse will keep beginners improving. The Homestead Road turns back to the Savio chair and lazily winds its way to the Main Tiehack area.

Intermediates with confident turns will have fun on Jacob's Ladder and Bear, which drop from the Cliff House to the main area. But the real playground is Tiehack, a part of the mountain that lent its name to the whole area. This area is colored black on the trail map, but don't get too excited—the runs are only black on the map. You'll discover good, solid intermediate trails that make inspiring cruisers. In one day you can ride the Upper Tiehack chair a dozen times, taking a different cruise on each run. Buckskin, Ptarmigan, Sterner, the Glades, Tiehack Parkway and Racer's Edge (where the Mahre brothers trained) all offer 1,500 feet of dipping and sweeping curves. Smile in the evening when you overhear others scoffing about what a waste Tiehack is for real skiers, and savor memories of 15,000 feet of vertical—in just one afternoon.

Aspen Highlands Facts
Base elevation: 8,040'; **Summit elevation:** 11,675'; **Vertical drop:** 3,635 feet
Number of lifts: 9–2 quad superchairs, 5 double chairs, 2 surface lifts
Snowmaking: 20 percent **Total acreage by trails:** 597 skiable acres
Uphill capacity: 9,145 per hour **Bed Base:** 15,000

Aspen Highlands, between Aspen Mountain and Tiehack, used to be independent, but last season it became part of the Aspen Skiing Company family. Aspen Highlands is the best-balanced mountain of the three, with slopes for every level of skier, and it's the locals' favorite. No need for fur-trimmed Bogner outfits here; you can be comfortable if you appear for lunch at mid-mountain in jeans and gaiters. The vertical rise is one of the highest in Colorado (Steamboat rises a few feet higher). The Aspen Skiing Company has constructed two high-speed quads this season which dramatically cuts the time needed to reach the summit.

From the top of Loge Peak, the run back to the base is an uneven series of steeps, catwalks and gentle runouts. This mountain has some fantastic long cruises. The ridge, knifing directly to the summit, has thrilling pitches down both sides.

Beginners are best served on the trails accessed by the Exhibition II chair and the Grand Prix Poma—Prospector, Norway, Nugget, Exhibition and Apple Strudel. Intermediates will want to take the next series of lifts: Cloud 9, Olympic and Loge Peak. (The easiest of the intermediates are off Cloud 9.) Experts should head for the steeps at the top of Loge Peak with Kessler's Bowl, Snyder's Ridge, Sodd Buster, Garmisch and St. Moritz. Dropping from Cloud 9 are The Wall and Le Chamonix, which will test any skier. The Olympic Bowl area has expert and intermediate terrain. After short, steep drops you traverse back to Robinson's Run.

Also check out the lower mountain. The Nugget Chair will take you to the top of Bob's Glades or Upper Stein, or you can drop into Thunderbowl and ski virtually anywhere you want. The Thunderbowl area is served by a chair from the base and a Poma for its upper reaches.

The Merry-Go-Round restaurant at the top of the Exhibition II lift is one of the better cafeterias you'll find on a mountain. The apple strudel here is the real thing and an Aspen tradition, made with Gretl Uhl's original recipe. Freestyle competitions are held Fridays at noon on Scarlett's Run facing the Merry-Go-Round.

Mountain rating

Everyone gets something at Aspen. Beginners will have the most fun at Tiehack. Intermediates probably will have a more varied day at Aspen Highlands than on Aspen Mountain, but the longest runs sweep down Ajax, and it's hard to beat the exhilarating cruising on Tiehack. Experts have a tossup between Aspen Highlands and Aspen Mountain.

Snowboarding (94/95 prices)

Unlimited snowboarding is permitted at Aspen Highlands and on Tiehack Mountain. Boarding is not allowed on Aspen Mountain, and is controlled on certain parts of Snowmass.

Snowmass and Tiehack have halfpipes and terrain parks. All areas offer special snowboard lessons following a format similar to their ski lessons. At Snowmass, a one-day lesson is $50; three days costs $135 (lessons only). Tiehack has a three-day learning program for $129 including rentals, lessons and lifts.

Champion professional snowboarder Kevin Delaney runs a learn-to-snowboard two-day camp for adults at Tiehack that is designed to "provide adults with a smooth and safe entry into the sport of snowboarding" with "fewer falls and more fun." Though none of *Skiing America*'s contributors have enrolled in Kevin's camp—yet—we've met and talked with him. Regular haircut, articulate, and he speaks a language that 30-plus adults readily understand. In short, an ideal instructor for anyone who thinks snowboarding looks like a lot of fun, but who can't relate to the snowboard culture.

Aspen Highlands offers two-hour beginner snowboard lessons twice a day for $35 per session which includes lesson and snowboard rental (bring your own boots, or you can rent some, but the number is limited.)

Rentals are available throughout the Aspen area.

Cross-country

Craig Ward organized the most extensive free Nordic trail system in America, 80 km. of groomed trails. The **Aspen Nordic Council's** free system is accessible from Aspen or Snowmass and includes easy golf-course skiing as well as more difficult trails rising up to Snowmass.

In addition to the free trails provided by Aspen's Nordic Council, **Ashcroft Touring Unlimited** has 30 km. of groomed and set trails, and backcountry skiers can use summer hiking trails. Hut systems connect Aspen with Crested Butte over the Pearl Pass, and Aspen with Vail.

Cross-country contacts and centers (R=rentals, L=lessons, G=guides, F=food, T=trail fee, TL=telemark lessons): **Ashcroft Ski Touring** (R,L,T,F)—925-1971; **Aspen Touring Center** (R,L,TL,G)—925-7625; **Snowmass Touring Center** (R,L,F)—923-3148; **Ute Nordic Center** (R,L,F)—925-2849; **Fred Braun Hut** information on trails to Crested Butte—925-7557; **Tenth Mt. Trail Association** (Aspen to Vail hut system)—925-5775.

Ski school (94/95 prices)

The **Aspen Skiing Company ski school** offers an extensive traditional lesson program. Most prices listed here are tentative 94/95 prices. For reservations and information, call 925-1220 or (800) 525-6200.

Group lessons for all levels are taught at Tiehack and Snowmass. (Intermediate and advanced specialty clinics are taught at Aspen Mountain.) Adult group lessons cost $50 a day. Classes meet daily at 10:30 a.m.

All **teen and children's programs** are held at Tiehack or Snowmass. For children first grade through 19 years the fee is $60 a day (four hours). Special kids' and teens' five-day programs include lessons, fun races, a picnic and video at a cost of $275.

All children 3 to 6 are enrolled in either Powder Pandas at Tiehack or Big Burn Bears at Snowmass. Children from 18 months to 4 years are enrolled in Snowcubs at Snowmass. The programs cost $65 a day including lunch and lifts and $325 for five days.

Private lessons start at $105 for 90 minutes for one student; $135 for two to five people. Two hours of lessons cost $130 for one and $170 for two to five. Full-day lessons run $350 for one to five people. A book of coupons for five full-day lessons costs $1,625 for up to five students.

Specialty clinics: Three-hour racing clinics cost $40 a day or $114 for three days. Bump, powder and video clinics all cost $35 for each two-hour session. The Mountain Masters program for intermediate and advanced skiers provides a guide who will run you for four days, until your legs feel weak, for $295. A special women's seminar costs $195 for three days; $260 for four days.

The Magic of Skiing is a one-week program administered separately from the ASC ski school, but using ASC instructors. "Magic" approaches skiing from a mind/body perspective. Theoretically, the approach to skiing should permeate your entire lifestyle. The cost varies from $1,695 to $2,855, which includes lift tickets, lodging, breakfast, instruction, videotaping and training in relaxation, relationships, fitness and health, and mind/body coordination. For reservations and information, call 925-7099 in Aspen or (716) 924-7302 in New York.

Aspen Highlands Ski School (94/95 prices)

Group lessons are $42 for a full day; $30 for half days; $70 for two days; $105 for three days; $175 for five days.

Private lessons are $70 an hour, $130 for two hours, $195 for three hours and $295 full day. There is no limit on the number of students in private groups.

Four-day never-ever packages with lifts, lessons and rentals cost $200. Three-day packages with lifts, lessons and rentals cost $195 or $165 without rentals.

Snowpuppies (3 1/2 to 6 years) is a program that includes lessons, lifts and lunch for $60 a day, $160 for three days or $240 for five days. For reservations, call 544-3025.

Lift tickets (94/95 prices)

	Adult	Child (7-12)
Three days	$144 ($48/day)	$81 ($27/day)
Five days	$220 ($44/day)	$130 ($26/day)
Six days	$248 ($41.33/day)	$156 ($26/day)

The four Aspen-area mountains are close to each other, but far from any other ski areas and far from any metropolitan areas. Consequently, just about all the visitors ski for more than one day. (The one-day ticket exists, but the current price was not available at press time. Expect it to top $50.) These prices are for pre-purchase tickets. You must buy them at least 14 days before your arrival through the Aspen or Snowmass Tour Office. If you don't, you'll pay from $10 to $40 more, depending on the number of days you plan to ski. Tickets are valid at all four mountains.

Ages 65 to 69 can buy these tickets for $99 for three days, $160 for five and $186 for six. Ages 6 and younger and 70 and older ski free. One little-known way for beginner and low-intermediate skiers to save on Aspen's high ticket prices is to buy a one-day lower-lift ticket at Snowmass or Tiehack for $12.

If you ski between Nov. 24 and Dec. 16, or April 1-16, you'll pay less—$105 for a three-day pass, $165 for five days and $192 for six. Call (800) 525-6200 to order lift tickets.

Accommodations

Accommodations in Aspen range from luxurious to inexpensive. Reservations for virtually all properties are available through the **Aspen Chamber Resort Association**, (800) 262-7736 or (303) 925-9000.

Hotel Jerome 330 East Main Street, (800-331-7213 or 920-1000) is a once run-down historic hotel that has been brought back to more elegance than the silver barons ever knew. The lounges are furnished with overstuffed chairs and framed in etched glass. Rooms are filled with antiques, and each has a brass or carved wooden bed. Baths feature Jacuzzis, marble counters and telephones. Rates in regular season are $329-$629.

For those searching out a smaller, more intimate hotel, the **Sardy House** (920-2525) on East Main Street is a restored Victorian mansion. A more modern addition has been tacked onto the rear, but we suggest you attempt to get one of the original rooms in the main house. Rooms in regular season are $270-$290 and relatively small suites range between $350 and $550.

The Little Nell Hotel (800-525-6200) has 92 rooms and suites, only steps from the Silver Queen Gondola at the base of Aspen Mountain. All rooms have fireplaces, down-filled sofas, oversized beds with comforters, and marble bathrooms. There is a spa and heated outdoor pool. Doubles with mountain view run about $325; with town view about $350 a night. Weekend stays require a three-night minimum.

Other top-rated luxury hotels are the **Aspen Club Lodge** (800-882-2582), the small **Hotel Leñado** (800-321-3457), the **Gant** (800-345-1471), **Hotel Aspen** on Main Street (800-527-7369), **Molly Gibson Lodge** (800-356-6559) and the **Ritz Carlton Aspen** (800-241-3333).

Other Aspen room rates drop dramatically from this stratospheric level to $85-$130 a night for a double.

Our favorite place in Aspen, a lodge of a kind that's disappearing all too fast, is **The Mountain Chalet** (925-7797). This place is just plain friendly to everyone, including families. If you can't stand a 3-year-old crawling over a lounge chair in the lobby

ASPEN LODGE LOCATOR MAP

Colorado - Aspen Area

TO INDEPENDENCE PASS
(CLOSED IN WINTER)

FREE PARKING

FREE PARKING

FREE PARKING

ASPEN MOUNTAIN

1. Aspen Alps
2. Aspen Bed & Breakfast
3. Aspen Club Lodge
4. Aspen Square

Coates Reid & Waldron Condominium & Home Rentals

5. Chateaux Roaring Fork and Eau Claire
6. Pomegranate
7. Shadow Mountain

Condominium Rental Management

8. Alpenblick
9. Aspen Mountain
10. Durant
11. Fasching Haus
12. Fifth Avenue
13. Tipple Inn

14. The Gant
15. Hotel Aspen
16. Hotel Jerome
17. Hotel Lenado
18. Independence Square
19. The Inn at Aspen
20. Limelite Lodge
21. Molly Gibson
22. Sardy House

or families howling over a game of Monopoly, then don't stay here. Rates are reasonable and include a hearty breakfast served family-style. Call early for rooms, because folks reserve space here years in advance.

Other places that treat guests very well are the **Alpine Lodge** (925-7351), **Mountain House** (920-2550), and **Crestahaus Lodge** (925-7081).

Also try **Skier's Chalet** (920-2037) across from the finish line of the World Cup (Lift 1A), the **Christiana** (925-3014) at 501 West Main Street and the **St. Moritz Lodge** (925-3220), only five blocks from the center of town.

Good rooms are also available for $59 to $90 each night at the **Little Red Ski Haus** (925-3333), the **Christmas Inn** (925-3822), **Innsbruck Inn** (925-2980), **Ullr Lodge** (925-7696) and budget champion, **Tyrolean Lodge** (925-4595).

Both the **Maroon Creek Lodge** (800-356-8811, ext. 223) and the **Heatherbed Lodge** (925-7077), opposite Aspen Highlands, are great places to stay out of Aspen's bustle. Rates are about $100 per night, depending on season.

Several management companies rent condominiums. For luxury condos right on the slopes, try **Mountain Queen Condominiums** (925-6366); all are three-bedroom units. The **Aspen Club Management** (800-443-2582 in Colorado, 800-882-2582 nationwide) controls two luxurious condominiums, the Aspen Club and the Clarendon. Expect a unit with two bedrooms and two baths to run $170-$490 in the regular season.

Coates, Reid and Waldron, 720 East Hyman Ave. (925-1400 or 800-222-7736), is the largest management company in the area. Chateau Eau Claire and Chateau Roaring Fork are two of their most popular units. Two-bedroom, two-bath units run $270 a night during regular season. Shadow Mountain is not so luxurious, but has a ski-in/ski-out location. Its two-bedroom, two-bath unit is $245 during the regular season. Pomegranate, near the base of Tiehack, is perfect for cross-country skiers who will pay $230 a night during regular season for a two-bedroom, two-bath unit. There are units in every corner of town, but none would be rated luxurious. They also handle home rentals.

Condominiums directly on the slopes with similar prices are the **Fasching Haus** (925-5900), **Fifth Avenue** (925-7397) and **Durant** condominiums (925-7910). They are available through the Aspen Resort Association.

Just outside of town, the **T-Lazy-7** (925-7254) offers apartments. You'll pay $50 for a double bed in a small studio and $175 for five bedrooms and living area that easily sleeps 10. If you can fill these apartments, they are a deal that's hard to beat, and they're on a real working ranch where kids have no end of exploration. A shuttle service takes skiers to town, Tiehack and Ajax.

The nearest RV park is at Basalt KOA, 20 miles away.

Dining

Let's start with *the* place to eat breakfast, **The Wienerstube** at 633 E. Hyman and Spring. Come here for eggs Benedict, Austrian sausages and home-made Viennese pastries. **Pour la France!** at 413 E. Main is good for croissants and pastries, quiches and waffles, with superb coffee in a high-tech coffee-shop atmosphere. **Main Street Bakery** (925-6446) has home-made baked goods, granola, fruit, eggs and great coffee for reasonable prices.

For more detail on the best gourmet-level dining, Katy Keck, who spent a year working with the top chefs in France, visited Aspen. Her observations follow in the next chapter, Aspen Savoir Faire.

A trip to **Krabloonik** (923-3953 in Snowmass) is a real adventure. Although a bit pricey, the trip includes arrival by dogsled and the only wild-game menu in the area. **Chez Grandmère** in Snowmass has splendid French meals in a restored Victorian farmhouse with one seating per evening for a fixed price per person.

Plenty of dining choices are available that require considerably less money. Among them are some of Aspen's excellent specialty restaurants. **Pepi's Hideout** (925-8845) at the corner of First and Cooper is an elegant little place with many European and American dishes. **Smuggler Land Office** (925-8624) at 415 E. Hopkins in the historic Brand Building has tasty Cajun and Creole food, including Cajun popcorn with a spicy rémoulade. **Cache Cache** (925-3835) on the lower level of the Mill Street Plaza is highly recommended by locals for Mediterranean cuisine. The polenta niçoise, wild mushroom cannelloni and perfectly grilled yellowtail were favorites. **The Golden Horn** (920-3373) at 320 S. Mill has good veal and Swiss specialties. **Mezzaluna** at 600 E. Cooper (925-5882) serves highly rated Italian cuisine.

La Cocina (925-9714), 308 E. Hopkins, is a very popular Mexican place with locals, but **The Cantina** (925-3663) at the corner of Mill and Main is a trendier alternative. **Boogie's Diner** at 534 E. Cooper (925-6610) is a real '50s diner with oldies like Elvis' "Hound Dog," blue plate specials and meatloaf as only Mom could make it. **Little Annie's Eating House** (925-1098) at 517 E. Hyman is still the ribs, chicken, hamburger and potato pancake champ. **The Skier's Chalet Steak House** (925-3381) at 710 S. Aspen has been around since 1951 and is a great food institution, and very inexpensive. **The Steak Pit** (925-3459) at the corner of Cooper and Original also has some of the best steaks in Aspen, though its location in the basement of a grocery store makes that hard to believe. **Lauretta's** (925-1986), 333 East Durant in the Mountain Chalet, is the best family restaurant in town. It also a good spot for filling breakfasts. **Asia**, 132 W.

Main Street, was recommended for the best Chinese (Szechwan, Mandarin and Hunan) food. It is in an opulent Victorian setting, but has free delivery if you prefer (925-5433).

For eating experiences, Aspen goes all out. **The Pine Creek Cookhouse** (925-1044) is located on the cross-country trails of Ashcroft. Don a miner's lamp, put on cross-country skis and head out for a great evening meal. Prices include dinner, the cross-country equipment and guides. **The T-Lazy-7 Ranch** (925-7254) organizes a Western night every Wednesday and Thursday. It includes ragtime piano entertainment, cheese and crackers, sleigh rides, cooking your own steak and chicken on an open grill and a Country & Western band cookin' up some footstompin' music.

Après-ski/nightlife

Shlomo's in the Little Nell Hotel, draws a big crowd as the lifts start to close. If you don't find what you want there, the crowd spreads out to **Little Annie's**, **Cooper Street Pier**, the **Ute City Banque**, the **Red Onion** and **O'Leary's**. **Legends of Aspen**, a sports bar; **The Cantina**, with its very happy hour (have a margarita in the compadre size) and the **Hotel Jerome Bar** are all great après-ski meeting places—the Legends filled with locals, the Cantina loud, the Jerome quiet.

At night, well after 10 p.m., the dance beat begins to take over. The high-energy place to find out who's in town is **Mezzaluna**, with its brassy, horseshoe-shaped bar. You have to be a member of the **Caribou Club**, which often is packed with celebrities. On the Mall, head to **Silver Nugget Saloon**, where another nightclub, Tatou, used to be. **Planet Hollywood** is another new night spot, in the place where Ebbe's was. It attracts a lot of tourists looking for celebrities, but few celebs. A slightly lower-keyed dancing place is the **Tippler**. The **Ritz Carlton** has live music in the lounge; usually local bands during the week, and nationally known jazz musicians on weekends and other busy times.

For a good singles bar, head to the **Ute City Banque** for the best in upscale people-watching. A relatively mixed crowd with normal pedestrian tastes congregate in the **Red Onion**, **Little Annie's** and **O'Leary's**. The **Cooper Street Pier** is very much a local and college student hangout. **Shooter's**, down the stairs across Hyman Avenue from the Ute City Banque, is a very dark and smoky Country & Western bar with great deals on shooters and beer and great dancing. For the best "last call," try **Mother Lode**.

Child care (94/95 prices)

Tiehack, Aspen Highlands and Snowmass all have children's instructional programs, which are detailed in the ski school section. Aspen Mountain does not have instruction for children.

Aspen Skiing Company does not run a day-care center as such. Children aged 18 months to 4 years can enroll in Snowcubs at Snowmass, which has snowplay activities and some very basic ski instruction.

A local preschool, the **Aspen Sprouts** (920-1055), accepts children 2 to 5 years and concentrates on typical preschool activities. Call for reservations.

Other private day-care and babysitting services are available in both Aspen and Snowmass through the Aspen or Snowmass reservations offices, **Supersitters** (923-6080), **Night Hawks** (923-0571) or the Chamber of Commerce (925-1940).

Children from fifth through 12th grade can mingle with local kids at the **Aspen Youth Center** in downtown Aspen. The center has games, ping-pong, pool tables, movies and a dance room, plus a diner with bargain prices. The center does special programs depending on the season. Admission is free and a hotline gives weekly activities information, 925-2139.

Other activities

Shopping: Endless opportunities. Two of our favorites are **Gracy's,** a secondhand clothing store that stocks some drop-dead-gorgeous designer outfits for a fraction of what their original owners paid for them; and **Boogie's**, which has many unique clothing and accessories items in a 1950s setting. Part of the decor is a 1955 red Corvette that Elvis Presley bought for $3,500 (you could easily blow that much in this entertaining, but expensive, store).

Arts lovers will enjoy Aspen's 30 art galleries, its three resident theater groups, three movie houses (including art films) and its winter classical concert series. The Aspen Chamber Resort Association has more information, 925-1940.

Krabloonik Kennels in Snowmass (923-3953) has dogsled rides. Two-hour rides cost $175 and include lunch prepared in a tent in the wilderness.

The **Aspen Center for Environmental Studies** (925-5756) has all-day snowshoe adventure tours for $45, including lunch; a Hallam Lake snowshoe tour on Mondays, Wednesdays and Fridays for $15 a person; and snowshoe guided walks atop Aspen Mountain twice a day (10 a.m. and 1 p.m.). Call 925-5756 for more information.

Go for a hot-air balloon ride with **Unicorn Balloon Company** (925-5752). Daily departures, weather permitting, leave from Aspen and Snowmass. Another balloon company is **Adventures Aloft II** (925-9497).

Sleigh rides, part of the Western party night noted in the dining section, take place at the **T-Lazy-7 Ranch.** The ranch also hosts private sleigh rides for $10 a person, with a five-person minimum. Call 925-7040. **The Aspen Carriage Company**

(925-4289) offers one-hour sleigh rides. Adults pay $15 and children pay $8, with a $40 minimum.

The **Aspen Athletic Club** (925-2531) is open to the public from 7 a.m. to 10 p.m. on weekdays and 8 a.m. to 8 p.m. on weekends for a $20 daily fee.

Getting there and getting around

Getting there: United Express offers nonstop connections into **Aspen airport** with service from Chicago, Dallas and Los Angeles. United Express has frequent flights from Denver. Delta, Northwest and American fly into the **Eagle County airport** near Vail, roughly midway between Denver and Aspen. Ground transportation companies, such as High Mountain Taxi (925-8294) take skiers from Eagle to Aspen.

Vans to Vail, Skiers Connection, High Mountain Taxi and **Aspen Limousine** all operate van services to Denver International Airport.

Amtrak has daily service to Glenwood Springs, where skiers can get ground transportation the rest of the way. **Greyhound** offers daily bus service between Glenwood Springs and Denver International Airport.

Getting around: Aspen has a free city shuttle, the RFTA, with several routes in town and to the various ski mountains. A car not only is unnecessary, you'll have a tough time finding a place to park.

Information/reservations

For Aspen area information or transfers, hotel rooms and lift ticket bookings, call **Aspen Chamber Resort Association** at (800) 262-7736 or (303) 925-9000 ext. 1940.

Aspen Skiing Company Reservations: (800) 525-6200.

Unless otherwise noted, all area codes are 303.

Aspen Savoir Faire

This mountain town with Victorian roots has enjoyed an unparalleled culinary revolution that has bypassed sole meunière for a more exotic "beach party" shellfish. There are black trumpets and white truffles, edible nasturtiums, a veal dish called "@*#?&!", and just everybody is into lemon grass. Aspen is a place where you can enjoy the fine restaurants thoroughly, knowing that the next day you'll ski off those calories.

One of Aspen's long-time favorites had a culinary rebirth a few years back. **The Little Nell** at 675 E. Durant (920-4600) specializes in contemporary American cuisine. Chef George Mahaffey recently arrived from Los Angeles' Bel Air and implemented a light, updated menu at the Little Nell. The menu is a delight: lobster-apple chowder, griddled crab cakes on a sweet corn purée with fried pasta; mushroom raviolis with fried leeks and a sun-dried tomato sauce; all original, all perfectly executed.

Mahaffey's approach, using his individual style and creativity in choosing the ingredients, carries throughout the menu. A favorite entrée is the charred tuna steak on a bed of wasabi potatoes and baby greens, served with a warm lime-cilantro sauce. Save room for the crème brûlée tart. The restaurant, in The Little Nell hotel, serves three meals daily. Dinner starters range from $6 to $12.50, and entrées from $22 to $32. For fine dining, it's one of the best values in town.

Like the Little Nell, the Snowmass Lodge & Club is owned and operated by Aspen Skiing Company. Its new bistro, **Sage**, offers food as distinctive and flavorful as Mahaffey's, with a more southwestern flair and at more moderate prices. Start with the hearty black-bean chili with goat-cheese quesadilla or split a southwest pizza with jack cheese and cilantro. The brief but well chosen ranchland specialities (read: entrées) include sage roasted chicken with mashed potatoes, centercut pork chops with fig chutney and beef tenderloin with farmers' beans. Starters are reasonably priced between $3.50 and $8.50, while entrées range from $12 to $20 for the tenderloin. Call 923-5600 for reservations or to inquire about special drink nights, like Monday Dollar Draft or Thursday Dollar Margarita Night.

Syzygy, now in its seventh successful season, is well established as a favorite among locals. Chef Alexander Kim uses his experience to combine French, southwestern, Oriental and Italian cuisines.

Don't be put off by the hard-to-pronounce name (Siz i je) or the obscure explanation of its meaning on the menu (the conjunction or opposition of three or more heavenly bodies—for us earthlings, that's fine food, good service, and elegant atmosphere.) At 520 E. Hyman Avenue on the second floor (925-3700, reservations required); the atmosphere is intimate yet casual. The menu consists largely of specials that change frequently, but a few menu staples continue to sell out. Get there early if you want the Syzygy roll—a roasted lamb loin sliced thin and wrapped in soft rice paper with glass noodles, carrot and mint pesto—it's rarely there by the last seating.

Start with the seared ahi with Korean spinach, baby lettuces and mango-chili oil. For an entrée, try the slash & burn snapper—fresh red snapper filet marinated in coconut milk, then slathered in achiote barbecue sauce and grilled. Game enthusiasts will be happy to sample the mixed grill: tenderloin of buffalo with chipotle ketchup; wild boar ham with black currant glace; and veal sweetbreads with sweet mustard sauce. Plan on spending a stiff, but worthwhile, $12 to $14 for appetizers and $22 to $34 for entrées; it's a meal well worth remembering. Open daily 6 to 10 p.m.

Piñons (second floor at 105 S. Mill; 920-2021), decorated in a cozy western ranch style, with aged stucco walls, a big leather bar and huge brass bowls filled with corn tortillas, specializes in Colorado Cuisine. The wild pheasant quesadillas with sour cream, salsa and guacamole were rivaled only by the lobster strudel, a flaky combination of phyllo dough, morels and chanterelles. While other appetizers are not nearly so inspired in design, they are all perfectly executed.

Try the salmon spring roll with daikon and cucumber salad. Entrées range from a simple grilled chicken with roasted portobello mushrooms to pan-seared local pheasant breast with foie gras and truffles. The ahi is sautéed with a macadamia nut crust and lime butter, and the elk tournedos, served with ginger and pink peppercorn sauce, is perfectly grilled. In fact, all meats and fish are grilled on a mesquite and cherry wood grill, perfectly. Desserts vary daily, but will usually include the white chocolate macadamia nut tart. You may need a chain saw to get through it, but it's worth every effort for its nutty caramel taste. Prices are steep ($23 to $33 for entrées), but you didn't come to Aspen to save money. Open daily 6 to 10 p.m.; reservations recommended.

If you think, at these prices they should entertain you and clean your apartment for a year, one man will at least do the former. Mead Metcalf has been playing to the Crystal Palace's two sellout crowds per evening (6 and 9:15 p.m.; the latter show on Tuesdays, Thursday and Saturdays) for the last 35 years. At 300 East Hyman Avenue (925-1455; reservations may be necessary several weeks in advance), **The Crystal Palace** adds wit and satire to the old notion of barbershop quartets. Amid stained glass and crystal chandeliers, the talented staff not only cranks out a full dinner and bar service, but then belts out a cabaret revue spoofing the media's latest victims. Last year added skits on Madonna and Dr. Jack Kevorkian to hits about Jim and Tammy and Fergy and Di. For $45 per person, you can choose from perfectly pink beef tenderloin with Madeira sauce, roast duckling with sauce bigarade (a piquant sauce flavored with Cointreau and brandy), rack of lamb or prime rib. The food doesn't have to be good, but it is.

On the outside chance there's still a platinum card burning a hole in your parka, try Aspen's latest in exquisite dining: **Renaissance**, 304 East Hopkins (925-2402). Chef/owner Charles Dale claims to be one of three restaurants in the world to have a daily changing degustation or tasting menu (six courses), as well as offering course-by-course wine pairings by the glass. The menu itself is $65, or with wine, $95. Dale's menu offers modern French cuisine, with a touch of Colorado. The wine selection alone offers impressive choices for a by-the-glass listing. A leader in ecological awareness in Aspen, Dale's menu reflects his concerns: all fish are line-caught or farm-raised. Start with tuna carpaccio, then proceed to perfectly cooked-under-a-brick chicken with potato gnocchi. a specialty often available includes roast smoked magret and confit of duck with Szechuan haricots verts and Chinese pickled ginger sauce. Don't miss the Renaissance grand dessert—it has more chocolate than Switzerland! A la carte menu entrées cost $24 to $32. Open daily, 6 to 10:30 p.m. Reservations recommended.

The **Golden Horn Restaurant**, downstairs at the corner of Mill and Cooper (925-3373), dates back to a 1949 nightclub. Klaus Christ, chef/owner since 1972, has always offered savory Swiss specialties with a wine list cited by *The Wine Spectator* for nine consecutive years as one of the top 100 in the country. But recently Christ introduced a new lighter menu, a departure from many other menus in town, in addition to offering the traditional Swiss fare, such as fondue, stroganoff (albeit salmon), and wienerschnitzel. Called Cuisine Minceur, from a style developed in southern France, it offers three full-flavored courses for less than 450 calories. The menu changes daily, but generally begins with a soup, such as fresh tomato basil, followed by an entrée such as grilled veal chop or swordfish, and completed with fresh berries. Open daily and reservations are advised.

The hottest place in Snowmass is **Cowboys** (923-5249) in the Silvertree Complex. Open après-ski from 2:30 p.m. for appetizers, Cowboys also serves dinner daily from 5:30 to 10 p.m. Chef Philip Kendzior has fired up a menu sure to thrill even the boldest cowboy. The Colorado loin of lamb is stuffed with achiote and roast garlic pesto and served with a rosemary tomato cream. The mesquite-grilled T-bone is served cowboy-style, branded with a sweet and mild barbeque sauce. Shrub dusted tournedos is saddled on a cornbread crouton and served with campfire tomatoes. They claim on the menu to be able to meet special dessert needs, but no one could tell me if they serve S'mores.

For a real adventure, head out to the **Ashcroft Pinecreek Cookhouse** (925-1044) for a casual evening and solid fare. At an elevation of 9,725 feet, this rustic log cabin is among the Elk Mountain peaks and towering pines, near the ghost town of Ashcroft, some 12 miles from Aspen. Turn left in front of the church at the Aspen Highlands turnoff and drive to the end of Castle Creek Road. From here at the Ashcroft Ski Touring Center, the Cookhouse is accessible by a one-and-a-half mile cross-country trek, or by a sleigh drawn by a team of Percherons. Reservations are essential (two to four weeks in advance), as the logistics of running a kitchen not reached by road during the winter is no small matter. Between the noon-2:30 luncheon service, featuring a skier's buffet, and the 6:30 dinner service, the Cookhouse feeds several hundred people each day. And all that food must come in by snowmobile. Meals are prepared right in front of you in the open kitchen.

Food will be served by one of your cross-country guides. Dinner is a prix fixe meal for $55 ($15 extra if you are one of the 29 who chose to take the sleigh). The menu changes daily, but includes choices of venison, lamb, fresh trout, or a pasta dish, such as fettucine with sun-dried tomatoes and shrimp. After the 40-minute trek or the nippy sleigh ride, the cozy cabin with tables adorned with deerhorn and candle centerpieces seems perfect. After the meal and a bit of wine, the trip back to the Touring Center doesn't seem nearly so long or cold.

Dining on the mountain

Unlike the majority of U.S. resorts, the Aspen Skiing Company puts restaurant contracts up for public bidding, so real restaurateurs end up with them.

The latest example of this phenomenon is the arrival of Real Restaurants, the famed restaurant group from San Francisco whose crown jewels include Fog City Diner, Mustards, Gordon's and Tra Vigne. They've formed a new start-up called Colorado Culinary Capers and have opened **Bumps** at the Tiehack base area. The menu features foods from a wood-fired rotisserie, brick ovens and a pit smoker. While turning out rustic foccacia pizzas, the owners have not forgotten the 10 children among them. A "no green stuff" pizza is offered, as well as a hip macaroni-and-cheese with apple-wood smoked bacon and cheddar. Stop in for a bowl of buffalo chili with black beans and cilantro gremolata. (This group also has taken over **Shlomo's** at the base of Aspen Mountain and opened the **Ajax Tavern.**)

Cafe Suzanne is at the bottom of Elk Camp Lift 10 at Snowmass and specializes in French Country Cuisine. Although a cafeteria, the food is a pleasant surprise, with a daily assortment of entrée crêpes, such as buckwheat crêpes with spinach, mushroom or chicken, and dessert crêpes. Suzanne McPherson has taken her classical French training and customized it to the fast-food needs of the mountain. There is a daily hot entrée special, generally a Provençal or Norman dish, and a special soup with a homemade sourdough boule. You won't find a Parisian hot dog with gruyère and Dijon in any other area mountain restaurant. Also, some menu items, such as chicken breast marinated in herbes de Provence, are flagged with a heart logo, indicating American Heart Association heart-healthy selections. Open daily 9 a.m. to 3:30 p.m.

Also at Snowmass, try **Gwyn's High Alpine Restaurant**, at the top of Alpine Springs (Lift 8), for fine dining. Gwyn offers a sit-down breakfast daily from 9:30 until 10:30 a.m. Lunch is served from 11:30 a.m. to 2:30 p.m. Reservations are essential (923-5188). If you take the first chair up, but aren't quite ready to brave the cold, you can relax with an orange blossom and enjoy a zucchini frittata, fresh-fruit pancakes, or alpine potatoes with mushrooms, zucchini, green onions, tomatoes and Alouette, Monterey Jack and cheddar cheeses over a cup of Kona coffee. At noon, you can warm up with the special appetizer—Prince Island mussels, steamed and served with a roasted red pepper, a fresh garden vegetable fondue, a pasta special, the catch of the day—perhaps Rocky Mountain ruby red trout, pan-fried in citrus flour and served with a cranberry-orange butter, a variety of buffalo burgers or the warm vegetable strudel, such as zucchini, mushroom, tomato, or smoked cheddar.

While not a sit-down restaurant, **Bonnie's**, just above Lift 3 on Aspen Mountain, feeds some 1,500 hungry skiers per day between 9:30 a.m. and 2:30 p.m. Go before noon or after 2 p.m., unless you love lines. (If you do find yourself there at peak hours, there's a new outdoor fajita express line for $3.85 that will get you on your way in a hurry.) At $3.25 per slice, owner Bonnie Rayburn's gourmet pizza on freshly made crust is a huge crowd pleaser. Choose from smoked chicken with pesto, spinach with goat cheese, or spicy mushroom and eggplant. Homemade soups, such as the Colorado white-bean chili, are served with large, crusty pieces of fresh French bread. The apple strudel, with homemade pastry and local apples, is legendary.

New to the top of Lift 1A on Aspen Mountain is **La Baita** (literally, "mountain eatery"), run by **Farfalla**, one of Aspen's hottest restaurants. The innovative Italian buffet cafeteria features traditional Italian fare with gourmet pizzas, panini and a variety of lasagnas. The sit-down restaurant, with the best views of town, offers relaxed dining over such dishes as polenta with wild mushrooms, grilled pheasant and creative pastas. Stop by on your way down the mountain for a grappa or Farfalla's famous melon-and-peach vodka.

Aspen Area, Colorado
Snowmass

Though it is lumped into the Aspen experience because it's owned by the same corporation, Snowmass can stand on its own as a ski destination. With all the ski areas jostling for first rank in total acreage and lifts, Snowmass is still one of the top five resorts in America in size. It covers more than 2,500 acres, more than Aspen Mountain, Tiehack and Aspen Highlands combined. It has four mountain peaks and a vertical of more than 3,600 feet. The lift system—which includes five high-speed quads—can move more than 21,000 skiers an hour.

Snowmass is a wonderful intermediate and advanced playground. The Big Burn allows you to activate your auto pilot, and the run from the top of Elk Camp to Fanny Hill is a four-mile-plus cruise. But Snowmass has steeps such as Hanging Valley Glades and Hanging Valley Wall that pucker up intermediates and delight advanced skiers.

The village of Snowmass seems to stretch forever. This is a purpose-built ski resort à la Keystone, Copper Mountain and Steamboat. A village mall area has a cluster of shops, restaurants, bars and ski administration facilities. Most of Snowmass, hundreds of condos, is spread out around the lower part of the ski area. At Snowmass about 90 percent of the accommodations are ski-in/ski-out, where skiers only have to wander from their doors to the slope and ski down to the first lift. It doesn't get much more convenient than Snowmass.

Where to ski

Beginners have a wide, gentle area parallel to the village. Fanny Hill eases down by the mall, Wood Run lift opens another easy glide around the Wood Road side of the village, and further to the left, a long straightaway, Funnel, will give the beginner the feeling he's really covering terrain. Beginners who get antsy and want to see more of the mountain can head up to Sam's Knob, eat

---

Snowmass Facts
Base elevation: 8,223'; **Summit elevation:** 11,835'; **Vertical drop:** 3,612 feet
Number of lifts: 15–5 quad superchairs, 1 triple chairs, 7 double chairs, 2 surface lifts
Snowmaking: 3 percent **Total acreage:** 2,500 skiable acres
Uphill capacity: 21,679 per hour **Bed Base:** 6,000 in resort

lunch, enjoy the view and take the easy way down a meandering trail bearing the names Max Park, Lunchline and Dawdler, which softly turns its way back to Fanny Hill. (Make sure you avoid the blue runs on the face of Sam's Knob because they are not for beginners.) The next step up would be Elk Camp, which is labeled blue but is very gentle.

Intermediates will be in their element. The Big Burn is legendary cruiser's fun. It's an entire side of a mountain that was reportedly set aflame by Ute Indians in the 1880s as a warning to advancing white settlers. The pioneers settled anyway, but the trees never grew back thickly, so the run, dotted by a few spruce trees, is a mile wide and a mile and a half long.

If the pitch there is not quite to your liking, head over to High Alpine, which is perhaps five degrees steeper. (Once you're on the mountain, the lift system will keep you at the higher altitudes until you decide to come down.)

Advanced skiers and experts ready to burn up steep-pitched cruising will think they've found nirvana when they make the first descent into the Campground area. A wonderful long run for solid intermediates or advanced skiers is to come off the top of Big Burn on Sneaky's, then schuss to avoid the uphill stretch at Sam's Knob, cut south around the Knob and head into the blacks of Bear Claw, Slot, Wildcat or Zugspitze to the base of the Campground lift. All offer great cruises and patches of moguls normally of the mellow, sand-dune variety.

Advanced skiers will keep their hearts in their throats by dropping through the trees in the Hanging Valley Glades or into steep open-bowl skiing on the Hanging Valley Wall. Both are labeled as double black diamonds. To get there quickly on powder mornings, take Wood Run, Alpine Springs and High Alpine Chairs. No signs gives the Hanging Valley areas a remote feel. The ski school offers guided tours back here. Check at the ski school desk at High Alpine.

Another playground for the extreme skier is the Cirque, a scooped-out place between Sheer Bliss and High Alpine lifts. Don't try this unless you're comfortable on Hanging Valley Wall. You'll have to be deft of foot on Rock Island   and KT Gully. Even more challenging is AMF at the top. It's not on a trail map, but a local resident says it's "awesome" and stands for "Adios, My Friend."

Mountain rating

This is an intermediate mountain even though it has pockets of advanced terrain and beginner smoothies. Skiers who love cruising will think they have arrived in heaven. Few competent skiers who have returned from Snowmass have been heard complaining. That's the best recommendation of all.

Snowboarding

Snowboarding is allowed on the mountain. However, three chutes are controlled based on snow conditions. Just below the Naked Lady chair on the Funnel trail is a 500-foot long, 50-foot wide halfpipe with eight-foot-high sides. The resort added a terrain garden for snowboarders last season. Private and group lessons are available through the ski school. Boards are rented at D&E Snowboards in the village.

Cross-country

See the Aspen chapter.

Ski school

See the Aspen chapter.

Lift tickets

See the Aspen chapter.

Accommodations

Snowmass is a modern condominium village. There are few hotels but thousands of condominium rooms, and the condos are new and luxurious. Their positioning on the slopes cannot be beat, and the modern touches such as soaring cathedral ceilings and wide-open, glassed-in living rooms will make this seem like a vacation in paradise. All rates below are for the regular season with double occupancy. All reservations are through **Snowmass Accommodations** (800-598-2004).

The prices listed here represent a range. The low price is for value season, normally before Christmas, in January and in early April. The high price is the holiday rate, usually valid during the two-week Christmas holiday and sometimes Presidents' Weekend in February. Regular-season rates will be somewhere in the middle.

Hotel accommodations are relatively limited:

The Snowmass Lodge and Club is below and outside the village, but posh. It serves as the Nordic center and has a deluxe athletic club. There are regular shuttles to the slopes. Rates, including lift tickets: $225-$430 a night.

These two are the class acts in Snowmass Village. The **Silvertree** has rates of $130-$355, while **Wildwood's** rates are $103-$245. Both are comfortable, with beautiful rooms, and close to everything in Snowmass.

Mountain Chalet costs $179-$205 during regular season with rooms as inexpensive as $105 during low season. The **Pokolodi** normal season rates are $130-$140 with low season costs as low as $65.

Condominiums are everywhere in Snowmass. The rates given here are per-night, for two-bedroom units designed to accommodate four. Smaller and larger units are available.

The **Woodrun V** units are the most luxurious and roomiest, with multilevel design, private hot tubs and elegant furnishings. Rate: $317-$677. **Shadowbrook** is probably the best in the village area, with rates running $300 to $525.

The **Top of the Village** two-bedroom units run $200-$455. The **Timberline** condos cost $240-$473 during regular season. Both of these are a good 5- to 10-minute climb above the village mall.

The **Stonebridge** in the center of the village has two-bedroom units for $225-$450. The **Terracehouse, Willows** and **Lichenhearth** are clustered together two levels below Village Mall; two-bedroom units range from $200 to $330. The Willows are unusual because they are separate buildings, either cozy studios with kitchenettes ($119-$180 for two) or two bedrooms for $238-$330. Above the village is the **Sonnenblick**, which has only large units, three to five bedrooms ranging from $430-$1,200. For very large families, or for groups of four to five couples, this could be ideal.

Dining

Snowmass mostly attracts a cook-in-the-condo crowd. But the choices for dining in Snowmass are excellent, and remember, Aspen is only 20 minutes away.

Snowmass claims two of the best restaurants in the area. **Krabloonik** (923-3953) has become an institution, even when measured against the more trendy competition in Aspen. It's a formal dining experience featuring wild game and seafood amid spectacular views and the howling of sled dogs in the kennels outside. With a bit of imagination you can imagine yourself in "Doctor Zhivago" country. **Chez Grandmère** (923-2570), has only seven tables and offers a fixed-price meal in a Victorian setting for about $50. Other top quality spots are **Cowboys** on the Village Mall with gourmet Colorado cuisine, **La Boheme, Il Poggio** and **The Conservatory**.

Midrange dining can be found at **The Tower, Hite's** (with unusual breakfasts), **Pippins Steak and Lobster, Moguls, Brothers' Grille** and **Mountain Dragon**, the latter for Chinese.

For the family, **The Stewpot** features soups, tasty and unusual stews and sandwiches. Or try **S'noBeach Café** (featuring "eggs S'noBeach" for breakfast). A popular hangout is **La Piñata** for fair Mexican food at fair prices, where sombreros and wild art line the walls and locals play darts and table shuffleboard.

Snowmass excels with mountaintop cookery. See Katy Keck's recommendations in Aspen Savoir Faire.

Après-ski/nightlife

The **Timber Mill** and the **Brothers' Grille** are the hubs of immediate après-ski with live music. The Timber Mill tends to be more crowded and rowdier. Brothers' has five different draft beers and almost a dozen hot drinks for quick warmups. **Hite's** has jazz for après-ski.

At night Snowmass is quiet. The hottest action in town is in the **Tower**, where Doc Eason performs continuous magic throughout the night. For those with dancin' boots, head to **Cowboy's** where they strike up western music and dance country swing.

Child care

Children aged 3 to 6 years can enroll in **Big Burn Bears** at Snowmass. This program runs 8:30 a.m. to 4:30 p.m. and includes lunch and instruction. Cost is $65 a day; five-day programs are $325. Rental equipment is $12 a day.

A snowplay program for children 18 months to 4 years is called **Snowcubs.** Reservations are suggested for these programs; call 925-1220 or (800) 525-6200.

Little Red School House (923-3756) offers fully licensed day care for children from 2 1/2 to 5 years; the **Little Red School Toddler Center** (923-5020) offers day care for those from 12 months to 3 years. **Kelly's Kids** (923-2809) provides sitters for 1 to 3 year olds.

Other activities

The **Anderson Ranch Arts Center** in Snowmass Village exhibits work by visiting and resident artists throughout the winter. The center also offers a series of workshops in ceramics, woodworking and photography from January through April. Call 923-3181 for current events.

Also see the Aspen section.

Getting there and getting around

See the Aspen section.

Information/reservations

Snowmass runs one of the best reservation systems in the country. Staff members will take care of your entire ski vacation from air transportation and transfer to lodging and lift tickets, lessons and child care. Call (800) 598-2004, or 923-2010.

Unless otherwise noted, all area codes are 303.

Summit County, Colorado

Some winter vacationers aren't satisfied with skiing at just one resort. When they return to the office, they want to drop the names of a few big ski resorts and be able to compare the black-diamond plunges. For these skiers, we suggest Summit County.

Summit County, about a 90-minute drive from downtown Denver, has four well-known ski areas—Breckenridge, Copper Mountain, Keystone and Arapahoe Basin. Each resort has its own village with lodging, shopping and restaurants. (Okay, A-Basin's lodging is a few miles down the road at Keystone. . .)

If you plan to do most of your skiing at just one of the areas, stay nearby. But if you want to experience them all—or if you'd like to save some money—then set up your base camp in Dillon, Frisco or Silverthorne, three small towns that surround Dillon Reservoir and Interstate 70.

This tri-town area is smack in the center of the ski action. Breckenridge is about nine miles in one direction, Copper Mountain five miles in another, and Keystone and A-Basin seven miles away in a third. Having a car is nice, but not really necessary. The reliable Summit Stage, the free bus system subsidized by sales tax revenue, runs between the towns and the ski areas all day.

Summit County deserves its lofty name. Each of the ski areas, and each of the three mountain towns, has a base elevation above 9,000 feet. (If you have problems with high altitudes, take note. If you like spring skiing, also take note. High elevations usually mean a longer ski season. Copper Mountain closed in late April last year, Breckenridge and Keystone closed in early May, and Arapahoe Basin—the base lodge of which is above 10,000 feet—stays open well into June.)

The Ski the Summit lift ticket, which allowed skiing at all four areas, was discontinued this season. (It wasn't selling well, marketing officials said). Keystone, Arapahoe Basin and Breckenridge are owned by the same company. Those areas offer an interchangeable lift ticket. You'll have to buy a separate ticket to ski at Copper Mountain, but skiing there is worth the trip to the ticket window.

Following this chapter are separate chapters detailing the skiing, lodging, dining and nightlife at Breckenridge, Copper Mountain and Keystone/Arapahoe Basin. This chapter lists accommodations, dining, nightlife and non-ski activities in the tri-town area of Frisco and Dillon/Silverthorne. (We list Silverthorne and Dillon together because the town boundaries meet somewhere around the City Market shopping center. Maybe locals can figure out which town is which, but we can't.)

Accommodations

Frisco: This is our first choice for a home base, for several reasons. One, it is the closest town to Breckenridge and Copper Mountain, and Keystone isn't far away. Two, its downtown area along Main Street has lots of funky shops and restaurants, perfect for a late afternoon or evening stroll. And three, we like friendly mountain inns, and we found a couple of good ones.

Twilight Inn is tucked behind a bookstore at 308 Main Street, (800) 262-1002 or (303) 668-5009. Though not as fancy as the Galena Street Mountain Inn, this B&B is down-home friendly, the kind of place where you'll probably get to know all the inhabitants in record time. Its 12 rooms have a variety of bed arrangements. Examples: A first-floor room with one queen bed and private bath costs $100. A third-floor, shared-bath room with a double-sized bunk bed, a regular-sized bunk bed and a sofa sleeper costs $80 for the first two bodies and $15 for each additional. (Squeeze yourself and seven buddies into this room and you'll each pay $21.25 per night—and that includes breakfast and full attention from the house dog, Jackson.) Rooms on the first and second floors have private baths; the four third-floor rooms share two large bathrooms, one for men and one for women. Guests may use the kitchen, hot tub, steam room, laundry room and two common rooms filled with books, games and magazines (plus a TV in one of the rooms).

The **Galena Street Mountain Inn**, First Avenue and Galena Street (one block off Main Street), (800) 248-9138 or (303) 668-3224, was built two years ago. Its 15 rooms have private baths, televisions and phones, and all are nicely furnished. Two large common rooms, a locked ski storage area, a hot tub and sauna are among the amenities. A full breakfast with hot entrée is included, as are après-ski refreshments. No Smoking, no pets. Nightly room rates, based on double occupancy, are $120 during February and March; about $95 in January. Extra people in a room cost $15 each.

Dillon/Silverthorne: The **Best Western Ptarmigan Lodge** in the Dillon town center is one of the best bargains. Rooms are $95 at the height of the season, $75 in January. (800) 842-5939 or (303) 468-2341.

Off the interstate in Silverthorne are side-by-side chain hotels—**Hampton Inn** (800-321-3509 or 303-468-6200) and **Days Inn** (800-329-7466 or 303-468-8661). The Summit Stage stops at their doors, and they are convenient to the Factory

Stores (see Other Activities Section). Rates are about $135 during high season for the Hampton Inn and $120 at Days Inn.

Budget travelers should stay at the **Super 8** motel in Dillon, across from the City Market shopping center. Most of the best cheap restaurants are in this center, and rooms are $80 in February and March, $75 in January.

The towns have many more B&Bs, chain hotels, private homes and condos. The **Summit County Central Reservations**, (800) 365-6365, can help you find them.

Dining

Frisco: The fanciest restaurant in town is the **Blue Spruce Inn** in a historic log cabin at the corner of Madison and Main, 668-5900. Entrées include such dishes as filet bearnaise, vegetables en croûte, grilled venison and scallops dijonaise. Prices are in the $14 to $27 range. The food is good, though a little sauce-heavy, and the atmosphere and service are very good. Reservations recommended.

More moderate fare is found at **Charity's**, 307 Main Street, 668-3644, which features Mexican and Southwestern dishes with pasta, chicken and seafood for variety. Another Southwestern-styled restaurant is **Golden Annie's**, corner of 6th and Main, 668-0345. Prices are $7-$15 at both; the difference is atmosphere. Charity's is historic saloon, while Golden Annie's is yuppie faux-adobe.

Budget eats: The smells coming from **Smithwick's Bar-B-Q Smokehouse Restaurant** at 400 Main St. (668-3729) are divine. The Smithwicks barbecue an incredible variety of meat: beef, pork, turkey, buffalo, venison, etc. The atmosphere is very casual, with vinyl chairs and linoleum floors.

Locals recommended **Ge-Jo's**, upstairs at 409 Main St. (668-3308), for inexpensive Italian fare, **Whiskey Creek**, near Wal-Mart at 908 N. Summit Blvd. (668-5595), for Mexican dishes, **Szechuan Taste** at 310 Main St. (668-5685) for Chinese food and **Barkley's**, downstairs at 620 Main St. (668-3694) for prime rib and Mexican food. Frisco also has many chain fast-food restaurants, most along Summit Boulevard.

Halfway between Frisco and Breckenridge, in an area called Farmer's Korner, are neighboring restaurants that are quite different. **The Blue River Saloon** (453-4068) is a no-frills local hangout with great burgers, $2 draft beers and a 10-ounce sirloin for $7.95. **The Swan Mountain Inn** (453-7903) offers a nightly four-course meal ($22-$25) in a seven-table dining room with a fireplace. The inn also has a weekend brunch.

Dillon/Silverthorne: Locals and visitors alike rave about **Silverheels Southwest Grill**, 81 Buffalo Dr. in Silverthorne. Fine Southwestern fare and a Spanish tapas bar are the specialties here. The restaurant, located in a hacienda-style building in the Wildernest area, is a bit off the main drag, but worth the search. When you call for reservations (468-2926), ask for directions.

Another choice for finer dining is **Ristorante Al Lago** in the Dillon town center (468-6111), which serves Northern Italian meals in the $13 to $19 range.

For slightly more casual dining in Dillon, try **Antonia's** (468-5055) in the same building as Christy's Sports on Highway 6, **Pug Ryan's**, (468-2145) in the Dillon town center, or **Wild Bill's Stone Oven Pizza**, (468-2006) also in the Dillon town center. In Silverthorne, you can cook your own meat over an open grill at **The Historic Mint** (468-5247) or enjoy inexpensive Tex-Mex food at **Old Dillon Inn** (468-2791).

Budget diners: The City Market center on Highway 6 on the Dillon-Silverthorne border has several highly recommended restaurants, including **Sunshine Cafe** (468-6663), jammed with locals; **Roberto's** (468-5878) for the least expensive Mexican food this side of Taco Bell; and **Nick-N-Willys** (262-1111) for very good take-out pizza.

Breakfast: The best breakfast in the tri-town area is **Claimjumper**, on Summit Boulevard in Frisco across the street from Wal-Mart (668-3617). Not only does it have an extensive omelette-and-pancake menu, it has $1.99 breakfast specials that taste great and fill both the plate and stomach.

A close second is the **Arapahoe Cafe** on Lake Dillon Drive in the Dillon town center (468-0873), a huge favorite with locals. The cafe building used to stand in the old town of Dillon, but was moved in the 1960s when the reservoir was created and flooded the old town. The service is great, the menu names are creative (Arapahuevos Rancheros, Hans and Franz Power Breakfast, etc.) and eavesdropping on the neighboring table will educate you about the local politics. Both restaurants also have inexpensive lunch and dinner menus.

Definitely in the running for the "Best Breakfast" title is **Sunshine Cafe** in the City Market center.

For those who prefer a lighter breakfast, head for the **Butterhorn Bakery**, 408 W. Main Street in Frisco (668-3997). Muffins, pastries, bagels and gourmet coffee are the highlights here. Or, try **Java Mountain Summit** (668-1400), another gourmet coffee establishment next to Safeway on Summit Boulevard in Frisco.

Après-ski/nightlife

Frisco: Most locals head to **Barkley's Margaritagrille** on Main Street or **Whiskey Creek** on Summit Boulevard for happy hour. Several of the restaurants on Main Street that are listed in the dining section also have happy hours.

Dillon/Silverthorne: This seems to be the choice for late-night fun. **Tommy C's,** which is behind Antonia's restaurant and Christy Sports in Dillon, is the leading sports bar, with large-screen TVs, darts, pool tables and foosball. The menu is Chicago sandwiches and pizza.

Old Dillon Inn has live Country & Western music on weekends, and the best margaritas in town. Its 120-year-old bar definitely has authentic Old West atmosphere. The building was pieced together from bits and parts of defunct establishments, then the whole thing was moved in 1961 when Dillon was flooded.

Other popular choices are the **Pub Down Under,** underneath the Arapahoe Cafe in Dillon, or the **Corona St. Grill** or **Pug Ryan's,** both in the Dillon Town Center. For a smoky, low-key locals' hangout with pool and darts, try the **Virgin Islands Lounge** in the City Market Plaza on the Dillon-Silverthorne border.

Child care

Services of the Summit, Inc. in Frisco has professional babysitters aged 18-65 who are insured, bonded and child-care trained. The sitters will come to your hotel or condo anywhere in the county. The cost is $10 per hour (two-hour minimum) for one or two children, with a third child costing an extra $2 per hour. For more information, call 668-0255.

Other activities

Shopping and services: Pack an extra suitcase. Better yet, buy one at one of the four luggage stores in the **Silverthorne Factory Stores.** Then starting filling it with bargains at nearly 70 brand-name factory outlets. This is probably the largest factory outlet center in Western ski country. Among the stores are Carole Little, Anne Klein, Liz Claiborne, Guess?, Nike, Great Outdoor Clothing Co., Pfaltzgraff, Dansk, Corning/Revere, Bass Shoes, Capezio Shoes, American Tourister and Samsonite.

Collectibles and antiques lovers will go nuts at **Junk-Tique,** 313 Main St. in Frisco. It has an excellent inventory of collectible housewares, clothing and furniture at very attractive prices. The store also stocks some new items, such as jewelry and knickknacks. Kids will love the huge black locomotive that is the centerpiece of the store, but keep a close eye on them, or you'll be buying more than you thought.

For those items you forgot and don't want to pay resort prices for, try **Wal-Mart** on Summit Boulevard in Frisco. Near-normal grocery prices are at the **City Market** in Silverthorne or **Safeway** in Frisco. Remember: Only 3.2 beer is sold in Colorado grocery stores. If you want the stronger stuff, or wine or hard liquors, go to a liquor store (conveniently, right next to each of the markets). A 24-hour laundromat is at **Cozy Cleaners,** 109 Dillon Mall in Dillon.

Snowmobiling, sleigh rides, dogsled rides: The **Summit Adventure Park**, on Highway 9 between Frisco and Breckenridge, has many family-oriented activities. They offer day and dinner snowmobile trips, day and dinner horse-drawn sleigh rides, a snoscoot track, (snoscoots are kid-sized, motorized snow scooters), a tubing hill and an Old West variety dinner show featuring "gamblers, gunslingers and dancehall gals." Reservations are advised for the latter event, 453-0353.

Other companies in the Breckenridge/Frisco area that offer snowmobiling and/or sleigh and dogsled rides are **Tiger Run Tours**, 453-2231; **Swan River Adventure Center**, 453-7604 or 668-0930; and **Two Below Zero Dinner Sleigh Rides**, 453-1520. In the Dillon/Silverthorne area, call **Eagles Nest Equestrian Center**, 468-0677.

Cross-country skiing is available at the **Frisco Nordic Center** on Highway 9 about one mile out of town toward Breckenridge. Trail passes are $8 for adults and $6 for those 55 and older or 12 and younger. Rentals and instruction are available, and Dad gets a free trail pass when he skis with two or more of his immediate family members. Call 668-0866.

Getting there and getting around

Getting there: Frisco, Dillon and Silverthorne are just off Interstate 70, about 75 miles west of downtown Denver. Resort Express has regular vans connecting the resort with Denver International Airport. Telephone: (800) 334-7433 or 468-7600. Another option is Vans to Breckenridge/Keystone/Copper, (800) 222-2112 or 668-5466.

Getting around: Frisco is laid out nicely for walking along Main Street. Otherwise, take the Summit Stage, the free bus system that links the towns with each other and the ski areas. A car is an option here; most distances are too far for walking, but the Summit Stage is reliable. Call 453-1241 for route info, or pick up a route map and schedule from the chamber of commerce or the stores that carry them. If you really enjoy nightlife and want to do extensive exploration of the restaurants and bars, we recommend having a car.

Information/reservations

Summit County Central Reservations, (800) 365-6365 or (303) 468-6222, can help with lodging reservations and general information.

Summit County Chamber also has information and many helpful brochures and booklets, (303) 668-0376.

The local telephone area code is 303.

Breckenridge
Colorado

Breckenridge is the ski industry's sleeping giant. Its Colorado neighbor, Vail, gets a lot more press, but Breckenridge keeps creeping closer to Vail's nation-leading skier-visit mark. Both areas drew well over a million skiers last season, making them among the top three areas in the country.

Undoubtedly, many are attracted by Breckenridge's vast ski mountain: the numerous white ribbons that descend from its four peaks are readily visible from town (as well as from the slopes of its sister resort, Keystone). Skiers also like the restored Victorian downtown and its close proximity to Denver, about a 90-minute drive.

Breckenridge has a split personality, but it's been that way from conception. It was named for a man who became a Confederate brigadier general, but its streets are named for Union heroes—Lincoln, Grant and Sherman. Townspeople initially welcomed a former slave, Barney Lancelot Ford—who went on to create the most successful saloon between St. Louis and San Francisco—and then unceremoniously ran him out of town. When the town's residents decided Breckenridge should be the county seat, they staged a midnight raid and "borrowed" the county records from neighboring Parkville.

The Victorian buildings lining the streets witnessed wild revelry during gold and silver booms and the discovery of Colorado's largest gold nugget, but they also stood silent over windswept, vacant streets when Breckenridge joined the list of Colorado ghost towns.

Though the closest Breckenridge comes to being a ghost town these days is during the mud season month of May, it still displays its inherited division. Modern architecture around the base area is a stark contrast to the restored Victorian downtown.

Breckenridge Facts
Base elevation: 9,600'; Summit elevation: (lift-served) 12,146';
Vertical drop: 2,546 feet.
Number and types of lifts: 16—4 quad superchairs, 1 triple chair, 8 double chairs and 3 surface lifts Acreage: 1,915 skiable acres Snowmaking: 43 percent
Uphill capacity: 24,430 skiers per hour Bed base: 23,000

The ski industry brought economic life back to Breckenridge, but the locals have preserved the town's Victorian gingerbread soul. Thus, visitors may submerge themselves in glass-fronted condos, pulsating spas, modern fitness facilities and glitzy discos. They also have in Victorian Breckenridge hundreds of boutiques, scores of pubs and dozens of restaurants packed into brightly colored restored buildings.

The wooden gingerbread kingdom and the concrete-and-glass slopeside developments are tethered by an old-time trolley bus, which shuttles visitors from the restored town — where it seems at home—to Beaver Run, the Hilton and the Village at Breckenridge, some of the more popular multi-story, modern-design base lodging.

Because Breckenridge is so close to Denver, weekend skiers stream into the town. High-speed quad chair lifts on Peaks 8, 9 and 10 normally means a wait of less than 10 minutes. And with the skiing now spread over four mountains, there is plenty of room for skiers even on peak days.

Last season, Breckenridge opened Peak 7, the fourth of its peaks numbered 7-10. All of the 14 gladed trails and the 210 acres of open bowl skiing (of 300 acres total) are rated advanced, making the Peak 7 and 8 areas a magnet for upper-level skiers.

You'll find your fellow skiers are a mixed bag. Though the general atmosphere still is more down-to-earth than at some other Colorado resorts, Breckenridge is starting to attract more of society's upper crust. Many shops now carry more upscale goods, and some of the sales personnel have adopted snooty attitudes. (Restaurant and ski-area workers remain as friendly as ever). Happily, though, long-time Breckenridge locals still retain much of the devil-may-care attitude of their 19th-century predecessors, which helps balance the others out. For now, the Breckenridge crowd is not as upscale as that of Aspen or Vail, nor as laid back as Crested Butte. It's a middle-of-the-road, comfortable atmosphere with plenty of great skiing.

Where to ski

Breckenridge, on four peaks covering nearly 2,000 acres, is the largest of the Summit County ski areas. At the main base facility, at the bottom of Peak 9, the Quicksilver high-speed quad chair powers skiers from the village to Peak 9's higher lifts, which will connect skiers with Peak 10's blue and black trails. The Mercury superchair takes skiers from the Beaver Run base area to the heights of Peak 9 or a Peak 8 connection.

Years ago Breckenridge was known as an excellent beginner and intermediate resort, but the opening of the back bowls off Peak 8, the North Face of Peak 9, and Peaks 7 and 10 added hundreds of acres of expert terrain. Today, Breckenridge boasts a very high percentage of black-diamond terrain (55 percent overall) and the highest in-bounds skiing in North America, yet it still maintains its wide-open, well-groomed runs for beginners and intermediates.

Imperial Bowl, crowning Peak 8, tops out at nearly 13,000 feet, creating a total vertical that's only two feet shy of 3,400. If you noticed that our statistic box shows a much smaller vertical, it's because we list the highest *lift-served* terrain. Imperial Bowl is in bounds, but is not lift-served. If you want to ski it, you must hike first. Same with Peak 7. You can ski from the 12,677-foot summit, but only if you hoof it to the top. Locals love it; visitors from sea level often pass up the opportunity.

Beginners probably will stick to the front side of Peak 9 area unless they are enrolled in the Peak 8 ski school, which has the best never-ever terrain. Peak 9's terrain is a good intermediate and beginner mix of runs. The easiest are Silverthorne, Eldorado and Red Rover, all skiable from the top of the Quicksilver lift. For more challenge, intermediates should take Lift B to the summit and ski down Cashier, Bonanza and Upper Columbia. More advanced intermediates enjoy American, Gold King and Peerless, which might be rated black at a smaller resort.

For the best cruising, head to Peak 10 and alternate between Centennial and Crystal. These runs are slightly easier than American and the other blue-square runs off Mercury superchair, but the combination of a high-speed lift with the rest of the mountain being expert terrain makes the crowds lighter. Everything else on Peak 10 is in the expert category, with Mustang, Dark Rider and Blackhawk boasting monstrous bumps. Cimarron, marked black on the map, often is groomed, making for a swift, fun ride. The Burn, dropping to the left of the high-speed lift, offers limited short-but-sweet tree skiing.

The North Face on the back of Peak 9 is expert territory. Plenty of good skiers have begged for a rest after playing with Tom's Baby, and even prayers won't help lower intermediates who accidentally find themselves in Hades, Devil's Crotch or Inferno—once you drop down the face from Chair E, there is no escape or easy traverse.

Peak 8, where skiing at Breckenridge began, is the most varied of the mountains. Beginners practice wedge turns near the base facility; intermediates can ski alongside the high-speed Colorado lift down Springmeier, Crescendo and Swinger; experts and advanced skiers can play in Imperial Bowl or drop down a half dozen runs, such as Spruce and Rounders, to the right of the Colorado lift on the trail map. Experts can take the T-bar up to wide-open Horseshoe Bowl and the smaller, steeper Contest Bowl. (These bowls are wide—solid intermediates can ski them.)

Mountain rating

Breckenridge has many ingredients for the perfect ski vacation: good, and lots of, terrain for all levels, plenty of slopeside lodging and a charming town. It's urban enough to have a good variety of restaurants and shops, yet not so urban that you'll feel as if you never left home. And if you don't find enough here to keep you busy, Copper Mountain and Keystone are nearby.

Cross-country

The Breckenridge Nordic Ski Center, near Peak 8 base on Ski Hill Road, has 28 km. of groomed, double-set trails for all skiing abilities. Trail passes are $10 for adults, $6 for 55 and older and 12 and younger. Equipment rentals, lessons, and guided backcountry tours are available. You can also rent snowshoes. Call (303) 453-6855.

Ski school (94/95 prices)

Group lessons cost $42 for a full day ($72 including lift ticket); $80 for two days of lessons. **Private lessons** are $70 for one hour, $190 for three hours ($165 if you take the lesson in the afternoon) and $325 for six hours; add $25 for extra students.

Special workshops and clinics include three- or four-day women's seminars, early-season ski and racing clinics, telemark lessons, lessons for disabled skiers and several clinics for advanced skiers, such as bumps, racing and powder classes.

The **children's ski school** handles students from its two children's centers at the bases of Peak 8 and Peak 9. Ski instruction starts at age 3 with a special ski-school morning program. Rentals are not included in the $50 charge, but are available nearby. Child care is available beyond ski-school hours at an additional charge.

Junior Ski School is for 4 and 5 year olds, and again, the program is a combination of ski lessons and day care. Half day (no rentals) is $46; all day is $56.

Older children 6-12 have their own classes at the same pricing as adult instruction. Ticket prices are the same as those for the adult program.

NASTAR races are held daily, 10 a.m. to 3 p.m., on Country Boy on Peak 9 and on Freeway on Peak 8. Register at the top of the course. Fees are $6 for two runs and $1 for additional runs. A self-timed course is open on Peak 8 at Freeway (10 a.m. to 3 p.m.) and on Country Boy on Peak 9 (10 a.m. to 3:30 p.m.) for $1 a run.

Lift tickets (94/95 prices)

	Adult	Child (6-12)
One day	$42	$19
Three days	$111 ($37/day)	$45 ($15/day)*
Five of six days	$170 ($34/day)	$75 ($15/day)*

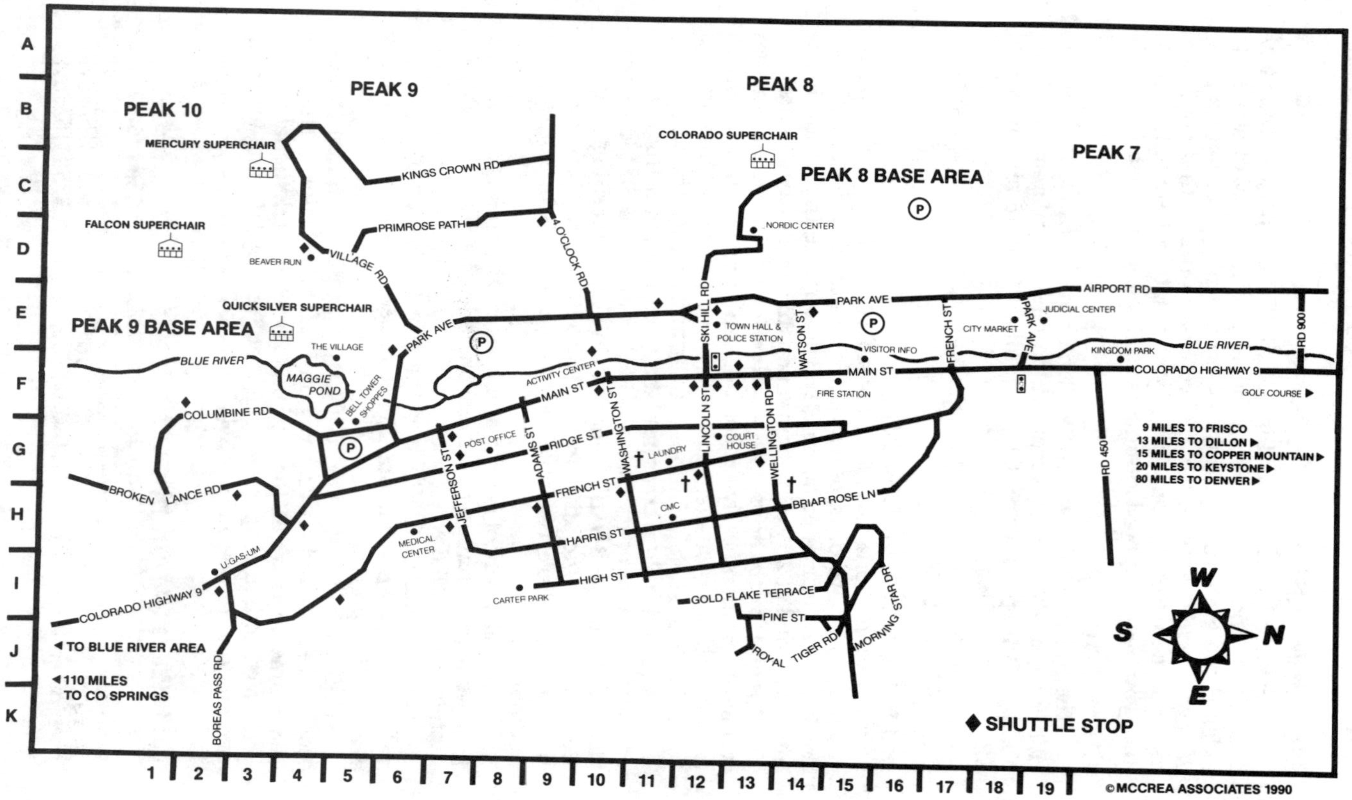
PEAK 10
PEAK 9
PEAK 8
PEAK 7
MERCURY SUPERCHAIR
FALCON SUPERCHAIR
QUICKSILVER SUPERCHAIR
COLORADO SUPERCHAIR
PEAK 9 BASE AREA
PEAK 8 BASE AREA
KINGS CROWN RD
PRIMROSE PATH
4 O'CLOCK RD
VILLAGE RD
BEAVER RUN
NORDIC CENTER
PARK AVE
SKI HILL RD
TOWN HALL & POLICE STATION
WATSON ST
FRENCH ST
CITY MARKET
JUDICIAL CENTER
AIRPORT RD
RD 900
THE VILLAGE
BLUE RIVER
MAGGIE POND
BELL TOWER SHOPPES
ACTIVITY CENTER
VISITOR INFO
KINGDOM PARK
MAIN ST
COLORADO HIGHWAY 9
FIRE STATION
GOLF COURSE
COLUMBINE RD
POST OFFICE
RIDGE ST
ADAMS ST
JEFFERSON ST
WASHINGTON ST
LAUNDRY
LINCOLN ST
COURT HOUSE
WELLINGTON RD
RD 450
9 MILES TO FRISCO
13 MILES TO DILLON
15 MILES TO COPPER MOUNTAIN
20 MILES TO KEYSTONE
80 MILES TO DENVER
BROKEN LANCE RD
CMC
BRIAR ROSE LN
MEDICAL CENTER
HARRIS ST
U-GAS-UM
HIGH ST
CARTER PARK
GOLD FLAKE TERRACE
PINE ST
ROYAL TIGER RD
MORNING STAR DR
TO BLUE RIVER AREA
110 MILES TO CO SPRINGS
BOREAS PASS RD
W
S
N
E
SHUTTLE STOP
A
B
C
D
E
F
G
H
I
J
K
1
2
3
4
5
6
7
8
9
10
11
12
13
14
15
16
17
18
19
©MCCREA ASSOCIATES 1990

The asterisked prices are from last season. Multiday tickets for 2-6 days are available. Ages 65-69 can buy a daily lift ticket for $25; 70 and older for $15; children 5 and younger ski free. All lift tickets are good at Breckenridge, Keystone and Arapahoe Basin.

Accommodations

Breckenridge boasts some of the most extensive ski-in/ski-out lodging of any resort in the U.S. Prices tend to be most expensive at Christmas and from mid-February through the end of March. Early December and all of January are more affordable, as is April. Breckenridge's ski lifts ran until early May last season, but one caveat: Many of the town's shops and restaurants started closing down three weeks earlier.

The Village at Breckenridge (reservations and information: 800-800-7829; local: 453-2000) surrounds the Peak 9 base area. Try to get into Plaza 1, 2 or 3, which are the most spacious units. The three-bedroom units here are giant. Liftside has studios with Murphy beds, and the Hotel Breckenridge rooms are medium-sized, well-appointed studios. All amenities are available: on-site health club facilities, indoor/outdoor pools, hot tubs, racquetball, steam, sauna and exercise room. Rates range from $145-$495 (the latter for four-bedroom units) during regular season; $130-$400, value season.

Beaver Run (reservations and information: 800-525-2253; local: 453-6000). This complex is built alongside Mercury and Quicksilver super chairs serving Peak 9. It is also home to Spencer's Restaurant, Tiffany's disco and the Copper Top for après-ski. It has seven outdoor hot tubs, indoor/outdoor swimming pools, a giant indoor miniature golf course and a great game room for kids tired of skiing. The Kinderhut child-care center, located in the hotel, will take children from the ages of 1 to 3; kids 3 to 6 can take ski lessons. Hotel rooms run about $170 during regular season, while two-bedroom condos go for $385.

The Breckenridge Hilton (reservations and information: 800-321-8444; Denver: 825-3800; local: 453-4500) This hotel is almost but not quite ski-in/ski-out; it's only 50 yards from the slopes. The rooms here are massive, about 40 by 12 feet. There is an indoor swimming pool, whirlpool spas and a fitness and exercise room. Rates per room with two queen beds or a king with sofabed are $145 to $225 during regular season.

The River Mountain Lodge (800-325-2342; 0-800-897-497 United Kingdom direct; local 453-4711.) This collection of studio and one-bedroom suites is in the heart of Breckenridge, only steps away from Main Street. The ski bus stops across the street with excellent access to any area of the slopes. This is one of the most reasonable accommodations in Breckenridge, with studios are $139 to $169; one-bedrooms, $189 to $219; and studios with lofts, $199 to $229. The River Mountain Lodge is building a section of two-, three- and four-bedroom suites targeted to open sometime during the 1994-95 ski season.

In town, try **The Wellington Inn** at 200 N. Main St., (800) 655-7557 or (303) 453-9464. This four-room, bed-and-breakfast inn opened about a year ago in one of Breckenridge's Victorian houses. The rooms are fairly spacious and beautifully decorated. All have outside decks and excellent private bathrooms with spa-jet tubs. Non-holiday winter rates are $139-$169 per room per night, full breakfast included. No Smoking and no pets.

Another attractive mountain inn is the **Allaire Timbers Inn** at 9511 Hwy. 9/South Main St., (800) 624-4904 outside Colorado; (303) 453-7530. This 10-room inn was newly built about three years ago. Each room has a private bathroom (most with the standard tub/shower) and private deck. No Smoking, no pets and no children younger than 12. Prime season rates (mid-February through March) are $130-$190 with breakfast. Christmas holiday rates are $15-$30 higher; regular-season rates are about $15-$30 lower.

For most other lodging, call **Breckenridge Resort Chamber**, (800) 221-1091, (800) 800-BREC or (303) 453-2918. In the United Kingdom, call toll-free 0-800-89-7491. Explain exactly what you want to the reservationist and he or she will attempt to match you to the best property. Remember that the major tradeoff in price is distance to the slopes.

Dining

Breckenridge has not gained a reputation for gourmet dining, and it probably won't in the near future. The best restaurants in town won't set a Michelin taster's tongue to quivering, but they can rustle up acceptable vittles. Our general comment on the top-of-the-line restaurants: too heavy on the sauces and overpriced wine lists.

Our top choices in the expensive category (entrées in the $15-$25 range) are:

The Wellington Inn (formerly Weber's Restaurant), 200 N. Main Street, 453-9464, with the best Victorian ambiance in town and some of the best food. Cuisine is German, featuring sauerbraten and schnitzels, or more traditional fare such as lobster, pasta primavera, steaks and honey dijon chicken. Reservations suggested.

St. Bernard Inn, 103 S. Main Street, 453-2572, has what most consider the best northern Italian food in town. Reservations suggested.

Cafe Alpine, 103 E. Adams St., 453-8218, has an interesting mix of cultural entrées, such as Greek spanekopeta, Thai curried pork, Italian tortelloni, American trout and a Spanish tapas bar. The restored Victorian atmosphere is quiet and intimate

Other recommendations for finer dining: **Pierre's** (French), 453-0989; **Poirrier's Cajun Café**, 453-1877 and **Adams Street Grill** (Southwestern), 453-4700. All are on Main Street. **The Gold Dredge**, on a converted dredge boat sitting in the Blue River behind Le Bon Fondue, has pastas, prime rib, etc.

Best of the moderate ($10-$15) restaurants:

Tillie's, 213 S. Ridge Street, 453-0669, has good basic food. Menu is limited but so are the prices. The hand-carved bar, the tin ceiling and the stained glass provide a good period effect. The Tillie's crowd could often form a quorum for a town meeting.

The Hearthstone, 130 S. Ridge Street, 453-6921, is in a great Victorian house that served as a bordello in the old mining days. Prices are reasonable, food acceptable and ambiance hard to beat.

Other moderate recommendations: **Main St. Bistro**, 453-0514, for mix-and-match pastas and sauces; **Blue River Bistro**, 453-6974, winner of the Annual Taste of Breckenridge contest; and **Le Bon Fondue**, 453-6969, for crêpes and four kinds of fondue.

Some suggestions for good, cheap eats (less than $10):

Beer lovers should try the **Breckenridge Brewery & Pub**, 600 S. Main St., 453-1550. The menu has good variety, and the micro-brewed beer is excellent.

Mi Casa, 600 Park Ave, 453-2071, across from the base of Peak 9, has Tex-Mex food. **Colt's Down Under**, 401 S. Main, 453-6060, has satellite TV for the big sports events and good, inexpensive food 'til late. **The New York Delicatessen**, 110 S. Ridge St., 453-0413, has an extensive Big Apple menu of Coney Island hot dogs, bagels, potato knishes, brisket and more; and **Pasta Jay's**, 326 S. Main St., 453-5800, has pasta, cheap but a bit heavy on the garlic.

Breakfast: For one of the best breakfasts at any ski resort, the hands-down winner is **The Prospector** at 130 S. Main Street (453-6858). The Huevos Ranchero will test your facial sweat glands. Another favorite with the eggs-and-pancake crowd is **The Blue Moose**, 540 S. Main St. (453-4859). For muffins/pastry and gourmet coffee, try **Mountain Java** upstairs at 118 Ridge St. (453-1874) or **Clint's**, 131 S. Main St. (453-1736). The best bargain breakfast is at the **Copper Top** in Beaver Run.

Après-ski/nightlife

Breckenridge's liveliest après-ski bars are **Tiffany's** and **Copper Top** in Beaver Run, the **Village Pub** in the Bell Tower Mall, and **Mi Casa**, with great margaritas by the liter.

Tiffany's at Beaver Run rocks until the wee hours, but after dinner most of the action moves into town. **Downstairs at Eric's** (formerly The Mogul), downstairs at 109 Main Street, has a raucous younger crowd with loud, live music and long lines on weekends. A slightly older group with plenty of locals gathers at **Shamus O'Toole's**, 115 S. Ridge Street, a wide-open roadhouse with live music on most evenings and an eclectic crowd, ranging from absolute blue-collar to those yuppied-up for the evening. Some nights the mix is intoxicating, and on others merely in-toxicated, which often sets off fireworks. **Horseshoe II** on Main Street gets packed and there is dancing at **Johsha's** on Park Avenue across from the Village at Breckenridge. For a non-danc-ing, quieter time, try the **St. Bernard** on Main Street; a cozy bar in the back is often packed with business-class locals. **The Breckenridge Brewery & Pub** has live music and beer specials, and **The Alligator Lounge** on Main Street has touring blues-and-jazz acts, plus local musicians' nights in an unfinished-looking, sheet-rock atmosphere.

The old **Gold Pan**, 103 N. Main Street, is the legacy of Barney Lancelot Ford. It is the oldest continuously operating bar west of the Mississippi. This was once one of the wildest places in the Wild West, with a miner or two known to be thrown through the saloon doors. A long, century-old mahogany bar presides over a now worn, dimly lit room with a pinball machine tucked into the back corner and a couple of well-utilized pool tables. The crowd has shifted to preppie pool players from the group of truckers, pool sharks sporting earrings, and the temporarily unemployed found here four or five years ago.

Child care

The Peak 8 Children's Center accepts children from 2 months to 5 years. Infant care for children up to 2 years is $50 a day, $40 a half day. Parents must provide diapers, formula, food, change of clothes, etc.

Child care for 3 to 5 year olds is $50 a day and $40 for half days. Children of this age can go to either the Peak 8 or Peak 9 children's centers. A Snow Play program allows preschoolers to build snowmen, go sledding and do other outdoor activities. Ski instruction begins at age 3.

Reservations are required; call 453-3258 for Peak 8 Children's Center, 453-3259 for Peak 9 Children's Center. Children's ski instruction programs are detailed in the ski school section of this chapter.

Another possibility for child care and instruction is **Kinderhut,** a privately owned children's ski school and licensed day-care center. It accepts children aged 6 weeks to 8 years. For more information, call (800) 541-8779 or (303) 453-0379.

Other activities

Exploring the old town of Breckenridge is great fun, either with a formal **historical tour** or on your own armed with a free guidesheet.

Shopping: Downtown has scores of boutiques, most of which seem to be T-shirt shops. Some of our non-T-shirt favorites: **Skilled Hands Gallery**, 110 S. Main St., with paintings, jewelry, ceramics and other beautiful items hand-crafted by Colorado artisans; **The Twisted Pine**, two locations on Main Street, for elegant leathers and furs; **Lift Off Sportswear**, 111 S. Main St., for unusual women's clothes with a Southwestern flair; **Mountain Kids**, in Towne Square on Main Street, for children's ski clothing; and **Goods**, near the intersection of Main Street and Lincoln Street, for classic mountain clothing for men and women and funky accessories.

For active types of non-ski activities, see the Summit County chapter.

Getting there and getting around

Getting there: Breckenridge is 98 miles west of Denver International Airport by I-70 to Exit 203, then south on Highway 9. It is a 110-minute drive. Resort Express has regular vans connecting the resort with the airport. Telephone: 468-7600 or (800) 334-7433. Another option is Vans to Breckenridge, 668-5466 or (800) 222-2112.

Getting around: Nearly everything is within walking distance. The town trolley and buses cruise the streets regularly and the Summit Stage links Breckenridge with neighboring Ski the Summit resorts Keystone, Arapahoe Basin and Copper Mountain, as well as the towns of Dillon, Silverthorne and Frisco. Both the town transportation and the Summit Stage are free.

Information/reservations

The Breckenridge Resort Chamber central reservation office handles transfers, lodging and lift tickets. Call (800) 221-1091 or 453-2918.

Breckenridge snow conditions: 453-6118.

Breckenridge Ski Corporation: 453-5000 or (800) 789-7669.

The local telephone area code is 303.

Copper Mountain, Colorado

If ski resorts were people, Copper Mountain Resort would be the ultra-organized type—the kind of guy whose sock drawer has navy dress socks neatly folded on the left side, black dress socks stacked on the right, and white athletic socks nesting in the middle. Copper's trail system and base village are similarly arranged in a logical, easy-to-find manner.

As you face the mountain, the beginner slopes are to the right, the intermediate trails are in the middle and the most difficult runs are on the left. The base village, built from ground up a couple of decades ago, has clusters of restaurants and shops surrounded by multi-story condo buildings, with an efficient free shuttle system connecting the whole thing. Even getting there is a well-organized snap. Drive about an hour and a half west of Denver on I-70, and you'll see the resort and its base village appear on the left side of the freeway.

This is not to imply that Copper Mountain is a dull place for a ski vacation. Heavens, no. The bowls at the top of Copper and Union peaks have plenty of chutes, cornices and powder stashes. Copper's layout makes for a convenient vacation. Just as Mr. Neat doesn't waste time finding a matching pair of socks, you won't waste it consulting the trail map or riding endless lifts to find your type of terrain.

Don't expect to find any old copper mines or even a miner's turn-of-the-century saloon. Copper is strictly a creature of the modern-day master plan. Its condominium villages are divided into three sections. The heartbeat of the resort thumps from the Village Center, where you'll find the high-speed American Eagle and American Flyer quads, as well as most of Copper's dining and nightlife. The condos in this section tend to be more upscale. The East Village, centered at the base of the B lift, offers less expensive accommodations, plus a few bars and restaurants.

Copper Mountain Facts

Base elevation: 9,712'; **Summit elevation:** 12,313'; **Vertical drop:** 2,601 feet.
Number and types of lifts: 19–3 quad superchairs, 6 triple chairs, 6 double chairs, and 4 surface lifts
Acreage: 1,360 skiable acres **Snowmaking:** 20 percent
Uphill capacity: 28,250 skiers per hour **Bed base:** 2,800

The West Village, close to the Union Creek area, is home to Club Med, some upscale properties and the cross-country center.

Copper Mountain will add a third high-speed quad chair this season (it had no name at press time) where the I and J lifts used to be. Those two lifts will be saved for use in a 500-acre expansion, Copper Bowl, which is on the back side of Union Peak and is scheduled to open in 1995-96.

Where to ski

Beginners and intermediates should first hop on the high-speed American Flyer lift, or the H lift in the Union Creek area. Nearly the whole side of the mountain under Union Peak consists of sweeping runs ringed by trees, perfect for the advanced beginner and lower intermediate.

For a long run to the bottom, beginners should bear left when getting off the high-speed quad and take Copper-Tone connection for an easy cruise. Beginners who take the H lift can head right, down Woodwinds to the new high-speed quad chair, ride to the top and ski the equally sweeping Soliloquy to Roundabout connection to the bottom. The K and L lifts, which constitute the far right border of the resort, also are custom-made for the beginner. In fact, this is one of the most extensive networks for the beginner that we've seen.

Intermediates should exit to the right of the American Flyer quad and try the American Flyer, I-Beam and Windsong runs under the new high-speed lift. Better yet, take the American Eagle quad chair from Village Center and dart down any of the runs under this lift. If you're patient enough to continue up the mountain on the E lift, you'll have the best intermediate runs of the resort at your feet. Both Collage and Andy's Encore are worthy challenges for the intermediate, offering good grade without the heavy moguls or tight funnels that can turn a blue run black (and an unwary intermediate black and blue).

Expert skiers need not despair. Powder monkeys can find a virgin slate—and the best views—at the top of Union Peak. It doesn't come without a price, however. Take the S chair after exiting the high-speed American Flyer, then *hike* more than 100 yards up the ridge to whatever spot above Union Bowl strikes your fancy. All three runs that parallel the E lift are short and steep, and Brennan's Grin in particular will bring a smile to a serious bump skier's face. Bear far right off the E lift and you can find serious tree skiing on Enchanted Forest (even more serious tree skiing, albeit unmarked, is available if you bear left about halfway off the Collage run). If you take the Storm King surface lift instead of heading down Enchanted Forest, you'll come to the side of Copper reserved strictly for experts. After you drop into steep Spaulding Bowl (lose a ski here and you'd better hope to have an uphill friend), you can choose from four very worthy expert runs to the bottom of the Resolution lift. Because this lift serves only expert runs, there's rarely a wait.

Mountain rating

This is one of the best ski trail layouts in America. Various skier levels are kept separated so that no one needs to feel intimidated or slowed down by fellow skiers. The beginner area is wonderful and there's plenty of intermediate and expert terrain—51 percent of the mountain is rated advanced.

In the midst of all this order, however, is a fairly confusing lift-naming system. Six of the 19 lifts have names; the others are lettered. But instead of a logical progression through the first 13 alphabet letters, the order goes like this: A, B, B1, C, C1, E, G, and so on, skipping letters at random until finally ending with T, a tiny lift at the Union Creek base area. This may be old hat to locals, but it's baffling for first-time visitors, especially if they use the lifts as meeting places. One of our contributors, a neophyte Copper skier, planned to meet her group at the base of the B lift. She waited 10 minutes at the base of B1 before she finally asked a passing skier if she was in the right location. Adding to the confusion are the American *Eagle* and American *Flyer* chairs. If you're meeting someone at the top of one of those chairs, be very specific: they start in the same general area but unload on different peaks.

Snowboarding

Boarding is permitted on all sections of the mountain. Copper Mountain has an annual snowboard race series. Snowboard lessons and rentals are available.

Cross-country (94/95 prices)

Copper Mountain has created an excellent and varied cross-country trail system. Some 25 km. of set tracks and skating lanes fan out from the Union Creek cross-country center. The center offers rentals, lessons and clinics.

Track fees for adults are $8; children 5 and under and those 70 and older ski free. A package for cross-country first-timers, including half-day lesson, track fee and all-day waxless equipment is $34. The never-ever telemark package includes a half-day lesson, equipment rental and beginner lift ticket for $44.

Group lessons are $26 for a half day. The telemark program costs $46 and includes all lifts. Private lessons are $35 an hour per person; $15 per hour for each person additional.

One innovative twist is that skiers with multiday lift tickets may trade a day of Copper Mountain downhill skiing for the Newcomer Track Package. Overnight hut tours, a gentle ski tour with a four-course progressive meal and various telemark camps are among the special Nordic programs.

The **Copper Mountain Cross-Country Center** phone is 968-2882, ext. 6342.

Ski school (94/95 prices)

Group classes for those 12 and older are 9:30 a.m.-noon and 12:30-3 p.m. Never-evers through skiers working up to easy blue terrain meet at the Union Creek area; upper ability levels meet in front of the Center Building. Costs are $39 a day if you have a lift ticket or $63 including lifts. An introductory package, including a full day of classes, lifts and rentals, is $45.

An excellent package program includes lessons, lifts and rentals for the seasoned skier for $66.

Private lessons lasting 90 minutes cost $75 for one or $90 for two skiers. Half-day private lessons run $145 for one, and all-day lessons for one are $230 and up to four skiers are $300.

Children's classes are for ages 4-6 and 7-12. Both all-day programs include lunch and a lift ticket for $50. Two days is $96 and three days is $135. A half-day afternoon lesson for never-ever skiers, including a half-day lift ticket, is $34. The Kids Value Package (all-day lesson, rental, lift and lunch) is $60.

Lift tickets (94/95 prices)

	Adult	Child (6-12)
One day	$38 (93/94 price)	$17 (93/94 price)
Three days	$105 ($35/day)	$30 ($10/day)
Five days	$175 ($35/day)	$50 ($10/day)

Multiday tickets available for 2-6 days. Skiers aged 60-69 pay $27 per day, those 70 and older and 5 and younger ski free. A ticket for beginner lifts only is $17.

Copper Mountain has Kids Ski Free/Stay Free packages during December, January and April that allow children 12 years and under to ski and stay free when accompanied by parents.

A Seniors Ski Free program allows those 60 and older to ski free when they stay at Copper Mountain during certain periods.

Accommodations

Copper Mountain Lodging Services has one-stop shopping for accommodations. Call (800) 458-8386. The **Copper Mountain Resort Chamber** provides information for the Copper Mountain area at (800) 525-3891, or 968-6477 in Colorado. All Copper Mountain Lodging Services properties include membership in the Athletic Club. (See Other Activities section for more information.)

Lodging is designated according to the village—Village Center, East Village and West Village. All condos are in the same general price range; those managed by Copper Mountain Lodging Services are newer and are concentrated in the Village Center and West Village area. Top condo choice is the **Spruce Lodge** because it's so close to the lifts. The **Telemark Lodge** in

West Village has a small bar and crackling fireplace, and sits equidistant from the downhill lifts and the cross-country area. Next door are the **Beeler Place Townhomes** with glass-enclosed patios (and creaky floors; if you're a light sleeper, pick the bedroom on the top floor). The **Mountain Plaza** has some hotel rooms.

Westlake Lodge and **Bridge End**, both costing the same as Spruce Lodge, are significantly farther from the lifts. The Lodging Services properties are $110-$180 a night for a hotel room, $135-$250 for a one-bedroom condo, $215-$405 for a two-bedroom unit, and $275-$480 for three-bedroom units. These prices are higher during Christmas.

The East Village condominiums are a bit older, slightly less expensive and convenient to the intermediate and expert lifts. However, they will be quite out of the way if your group includes beginners. Of these properties, the **Peregine** is perhaps the most luxurious and **Anaconda** follows. These Carbonate Property Management units start at $99 for a hotel room, $139-$170 for one-bedroom units, $169-$239 for two-bedroom condos, and $230-$300 for three-bedroom units. The **Best Western Foxpine Inn** is the distant poor cousin of Copper Mountain properties.

Excellent packages combine lodging and lifts. From early January through mid-February, packages start around $125 per day per person, double occupancy. Copper Mountain also has one of the few single-occupancy packages, which start at $87 in early December and April, $147 in January/early February and $169 February and March. Call (800) 458-8386 or 968-2882.

Club Méditerranée is the first Club Med built in North America and still its only U.S. winter club. Rooms are small. Programs and activities are nonstop, and everything is included in the price except drinks. There are ski lessons, dancing, and sumptuous spreads for breakfast, lunch and dinner. In fact, Club Med guests rarely venture outside the Club Med world except to ski—even then they are still lesson-wrapped in the Club Med cocoon. For reservations, call (800) 258-2633 (CLUB MED).

Dining

Copper Mountain's range of restaurants is fair for a resort of compact size. **Pesce Fresco** (968-2882, ext. 6505) in Mountain Plaza is the most upscale restaurant. Reservations are suggested. **O'Shea's** in the Copper Junction building has great bargains, especially the dinner buffet, and the best breakfast buffet for miles.

Rackets Restaurant (968-2882, ext. 6386) located in the Racquet and Athletic Club has a southwestern menu and a great salad bar.

The East Village has the best restaurants. Virtually everyone's favorite was **Farley's** in the Snowflake building, which serves up heaping portions of prime rib, steaks and fish. Reservations are a good idea; call 968-2577. (Don't hesitate to ask for the table next to the fireplace.)

Another favorite for light fare and great burgers is the **B-Lift Pub**, which has a breakfast, lunch and dinner menu and is by far the best bar in town.

The **Village Square** shopping area has some specialty choices: **Imperial Palace** for Chinese food and **That Soup Place** for a fair eggs-and-pancake type breakfast and excellent soup-in-a-bread-bowl lunches. **Lizzie's Bagelry**, in the same building but facing toward West Village, has bagels, muffins and other items for those who prefer a light breakfast. The **Corner Grocery** is in Village Square, for those who prefer to dine in their condos. Prices are typical resort; those with rental cars may wish to stop along I-70 to stock up.

Copper Mountain also offers a **Progressive Dinner** on Wednesdays for $39.95 that tours five resort restaurants via horse-drawn wagon. Call 968-2318, ext. 6320 for more information or reservations.

Après-ski/nightlife

This is one of Colorado's better immediate après-ski resorts. The **B-Lift Pub** rocks from 3 p.m. to 5 p.m. It's a great spot to meet avid skiers, because the bar anchors the mountain's expert and intermediate sections. **Kokomo's Bar** in the Copper Commons gets overflow après-ski, and **O'Shea's** hums as well.

Later in the evening, **O'Shea's**, **Farley's** and the **B-Lift Pub** are always a good time. If you like to dance, though, you'll have to head for other parts of Summit County or perhaps to Vail.

Child care (94/95 prices)

The **Belly Button Bakery** and **Belly Button Babies** are two of the most innovative child care programs in Colorado. In-room babysitting services are also available. Sitters require 24-hour advance reservations or cancellations, and cost $7 per hour, plus $1 for each additional child.

Belly Button Babies accepts children 2 months to 2 years. Full day costs $47 and includes lunch. Parents should provide diapers, extra change of clothing, a blanket and a favorite toy.

The Belly Button Bakery, for kids over 2, has "soft ski" play programs and indoor activities. One day with lunch is $47.

Call 968-2318, ext. 6345; or (800) 458-8386. Reservations are required.

Other activities

Shopping: Copper Mountain's shopping opportunities are limited to a few souvenir and limited clothing shops. **The Copper Collection,** in the Village Square center, has some nice upper-end sweatshirts and T-shirts, plus elegant knickknacks, some handcrafted by Colorado artisans. **Turning Point Sports**, a few doors down, also has some nice gift items among its main inventory, which is skiwear.

The **Copper Mountain Racquet and Athletic Club** is the primary nonskiing activity. Membership is included when you stay in Copper Mountain Lodging Services properties. Amenities include a lap pool, Nautilus and free weights, sauna, steamroom, exercise classes and two indoor tennis courts (the latter for an extra fee). Call 968-2882, ext. 6380 for information.

For other activities, see the Summit County chapter.

Getting there and getting around

Getting there: Copper Mountain is about 75 miles west of Denver's airport on I-70. **Resort Express** runs vans between the airport and your lodge, with many daily departures. You can make arrangements when you reserve lodging, or call Resort Express at 468-7600 or (800) 334-7433.

Getting around: A free shuttle runs between the properties and the base area. If the weather is clear, you probably will enjoy the short walk between the outlying condos and the restaurants and shops in the evening. The free Summit Stage bus system can take you to three neighboring ski areas—Breckenridge, Keystone and Arapahoe Basin—as well as to the towns of Dillon, Silverthorne and Frisco. If the bulk of your stay is at Copper, a car is unnecessary. If you plan to head over to Vail or to the other Summit County areas frequently, you'll probably want to rent a car. If you are are not staying at Copper, one warning about parking: Two lots nearest the center lifts cost money ($9 per day last season). There are several free lots; try the B Lift lot for upper-level skiers, or the Union Creek lot for lower-level.

Information/reservations

Call **Copper Mountain Lodging Services** at (800) 458-8386. **Copper Mountain Resort Chamber** provides information only at (800) 525-3891, or 968-6477 in Colorado.

All local area codes are 303.

Keystone/Arapahoe Basin
Colorado

Keystone has no charming 19th-century Victorian town. Most of its restaurants and lodging are spread too far apart for comfortable walking distance. And yet it is one of those resorts where everything works. Keystone is one of the best intermediate playgrounds in Colorado. It also has one of the nation's best summit-to-base beginner runs (Schoolmarm), and advanced skiing on North Peak and the Outback. Add in the Alps-like terrain of nearby Arapahoe Basin, and it meets the needs of every ability level. Its management has created a smoothly humming, homogeneous community with buses shuttling to every corner, foot-of-the-mountain child care, the Rockies' largest snowmaking system, the nation's largest maintained outdoor ice-skating center and one-number central reservations. Keystone's employees also deliver Service—with a capital S and a smile. Even late in the season, when personnel at many resorts get snappy from too many long days, Keystone workers are happy and helpful, including ski-shop technicians, lift attendants, cafeteria workers, hotel staff and instructors.

With no old mining town that the resort could anchor to or build around, Keystone is the product of continuous con-dominium buildup. The closest attempt at a social gathering place is the collection of shops, restaurants and condos grouped around the pond and called Keystone Village. But the "village" has no pulse — it is too far from the base area to be a center for

Keystone/North Peak/Outback Facts
Base: 9,300'; **Summit elevation (lift-served):** 11,980'; **Vertical drop:** 2,680 feet
Number and types of lifts: 19–2 gondolas, 3 quad superchairs, 1 quad chair,
3 triple chairs, 6 double chairs, 4 surface lifts.
Acreage: 1,737 skiable acres **Snowmaking:** 49 percent
Uphill capacity: 26,582 skiers per hour **Bed base:** 5,000

Arapahoe Basin Facts
Base elevation: 10,780'; **Summit elevation:** 13,050'; **Vertical drop:** 2,270 feet
Number and types of lifts: 5–1 triple chair, 4 double chairs
Acreage: 490 skiable acres **Snowmaking:** none
Uphill capacity: 6,066 skiers per hour **Bed base:** 5,000

après-ski activities and too isolated to be much more than a promenade for guests at the Keystone Lodge and the closest condominiums.

Guests don't seem to mind, because Keystone is a phenomenal success. It is a tribute to service, great organization, affordable packaging and proximity to Denver. The resort is perfect for families, couples or small groups of friends who want to spend time with each other. Those searching for nightlife or a singles scene will like Keystone's sister resort, Breckenridge, a little better (but plan to spend a couple of days skiing here—lift tickets are valid at Breckenridge, Keystone or A-Basin).

Where to ski

Unlike other ski areas that have separate peaks side by side, Keystone has three peaks that stack up one behind another. In front is Keystone Mountain, with beginner and intermediate terrain. In back of that is North Peak, and finally, the Outback. Other than one snaking green-circle trail, these latter peaks have just blue and black terrain.

This unusual arrangement lends an exploratory feel to a ski day. As you get farther and farther from the base area, the skiing feels a little wilder, a little off-piste.

Keystone Mountain is one of the better intermediate mountains in Colorado, maybe in America. Snowmaking covers 100 percent of the mountain, and the slope grooming may be surpassed only by Utah's elite Deer Valley. The Mountain House base area has three chair lifts taking skiers up the mountain, and the other base area, River Run, is the lower station of the Skyway Gondola that reaches the Summit House, 2,340 feet higher, in 10 minutes.

The gondola serves the night-skiing area until 10 p.m. This is the largest single-mountain night ski operation in the United States and covers 13 runs.

If you see a trail going up and down the mountain, you can be assured that it is intermediate. These are not pansy-level intermediates—they are great cruises with enough twists, turns and dips to entertain the most jaded skier. Paymaster, the Wild Irishman, Frenchman and Flying Dutchman are runs that play with the mountain's terrain. The bumps, twists and natural steps offered by these cruisers represent nature at its best, and obviously did not have the character bulldozed out of them.

Trails cutting across the mountain are principally for beginners. You can take most of them traversing from the top of the Peru Chair, or take Schoolmarm along the ridge and drop down Silver Spoon or Last Chance.

Advanced intermediates and experts have really only one trail on Keystone Mountain that develops pitch—Go Devil, dropping down the far right edge of the area. Skiers at this level should head for Keystone Mountain's summit, then drop down the super-long groomed Mozart cruise to the base of **North Peak**. The descent to the North Peak base can also be negotiated down **Diamond Back**, which maintains a steeper pitch and is infrequently groomed. (Skiers also can ride the Outpost Gondola to the beautiful restaurant at the top of North Peak.) These North Peak runs are almost all advanced or expert and are a great spot for skiers working on technique and steeps. Starfire is a superb steep, groomed run, and a good warmup for this area. Black diamonds that plunge off this run are Ambush, Powder Cap or Bullet. On the other side of the lift, Cat Dancer and Geronimo offer a challenge, and experts can break their own tracks through the trees directly beneath the lift. Two groomed intermediate runs, Anticipation and Spillway, lead to **The Outback.**

The 663-acre Outback is a mix of open-bowl skiing, natural chutes and tree-lined glades. The quartet of Timberwolf, Bushwacker, Badger and The Grizz are visible from North Peak and allow tree-skiing fans to pick how tight they want their trees. Two black-diamond bowls are accessible by a short uphill hike from the top of the Outback Express high-speed quad chair. (This in-bounds skiing tops out at 12,200 feet, giving Keystone a 2,900-foot vertical descent, slightly more than is listed in the stat box.) Solid intermediates also can enjoy this peak, with four groomed runs under the high-speed quad. Two other trails, Wildfire and Wolverine, are a bridge between blue and black.

Arapahoe Basin, long a legend with die-hard skiers, was folded into the Keystone package about 10 years ago. Though it is not connected physically to Keystone, you'll sometimes see references to Keystone/Arapahoe Basin, as if it were one area. This stark ski area is only a short five-mile shuttlebus ride from Keystone, but it's another world when it comes to skiing. Arapahoe is the highest lift-served skiing in North America, topping off at 13,050 feet. Arapahoe Basin's above-timberline terrain is subjected to howling winds, plummeting temperatures, and white-out conditions. This is the closest thing Colorado has to skiing the high Alps.

For all its gnarly reputation, Arapahoe has excellent beginner terrain. Never-evers start on their own lift, called Molly Hogan, and the flat, nearly separate terrain beneath it. Wrangler is a very wide and flat trail on the far left of the trail map. Chisolm and Sundance are the next steps up the ability ladder. All three wind down from the top of the Exhibition chair lift. Intermediates can test themselves from the top of either the Lenawee or Norway chairs and enjoy this above-timberline bowl skiing. It's a great place for developed intermediates to push their abilities and get a change of pace.

The "Pali" side of Arapahoe was created for the strong, hardy skier who braves bumps, weather, wind and super-steep terrain to push his or her envelope of experience. The entire east wall has chutes, gullies and steeps regularly searched out by experts, and dozens of expert runs drop from the top of the Palivacinni Lift. When all is said and done the heart of Arapahoe for experts is the "Pali," a legendary avalanche chute, a steep stamped in nature.

Thanks to its elevation, Arapahoe doesn't hit stride until late January when the gullies fill in and the rocks have sufficient cover. It's skiable until June, and sometimes into early July.

Mountain rating

These mountains break easily into categories, with some exceptions as noted above. Keystone weighs in as great beginner and cruising terrain. North Peak is for advanced skiers with expert tendencies. The new Outback is for upper intermediates and expert skiers. Arapahoe Basin is for strong intermediates, advanced and very expert experts, but beginners won't be left in the base lodge. The night skiing is for everyone.

Snowboarding

Keystone is not open to snowboarders. Boarding is permitted at Arapahoe Basin without limits. There is a halfpipe at A-Basin, lessons and rentals.

Cross-country

Keystone has also developed one of the most extensive cross-country touring areas in Colorado. The cross-country touring center (468-4275) at the Ski Tip Lodge services 24 km. of groomed trails around the resort and is open from 8 a.m. to 5 p.m. There are an additional 57 km. of extensive backcountry skiing trails to ghost mining towns in the Montezuma area.

Trail fees are $7.50 a day or $5 for a half day. Lesson packages range from $29 to $45. There are special children's classes for $24. Rentals are available from the touring center. Cross-country activities include moonlight tours for $30 and mountain tours. A women's cross-country seminar is held every spring, focusing on total development for the cross-country experience.

Ski school (94/95 prices)

Keystone's ski school is as smooth-running as its shuttle system, and the mountain is perfect for lessons of every type.

Group lessons meet daily at 10:25 a.m. and 1:30 p.m. for a two-and-a-half-hour session at all three locations (base of Keystone, River Run Plaza and Arapahoe Basin). These sessions cost $32 each. Beginners have a lesson that includes lift tickets for $40, or $54 with rentals included. The Advanced Skier Workshop with three days of instruction is $290.

Private lessons are $70 for one hour and $90 for 90 minutes. A private half-day lesson (three hours) for one to three people is $200. Full-day lessons (six hours) are $300.

For ski school, call (800) 255-3715; in Colorado, 468-4170.

For **children** there is a special Minor's Camp Program for ages 5 to 12 with all-day supervision. The daily rate of $62 includes rental equipment, lift ticket, lesson and lunch. The Mini-Minors is a program for kids 3 or 4 years old. Full day with lunch is $62, half day with lunch, $52.

The Mahre Training Centers are held here exclusively. These are five- and three-day sessions conducted in part by either Phil or Steve Mahre, Olympic medal winners. The skiing, for all levels, teaches fundamentals. In the evening there is a classroom session where on-slope activities and techniques are reviewed, and one of the Mahre brothers is available to answer questions. The three-day program costs $390 and the five-day program costs $650. Both include lifts, six hours of instruction daily, video, races and time for fun. Lodging is not included. The Mahre programs run through mid-January.

Lift Tickets (94/95 prices)

	Adult	Child (6-12)
One day	$42	$19
Three days	$111 ($37/day)	$51 ($17/day)
Five of six days	$170 ($34/day)	$85 ($17/day)

Keystone, Arapahoe and nearby Breckenridge are owned by the same company, so the tickets are automatically interchangeable. Keystone has an additional pricing twist because of its night skiing. Day lift tickets are valid until 9 p.m. Children and young seniors get discounted full-day and multi-day lift tickets, but no discounts for afternoon, twilight or night tickets. Ages 65-69 pay $25 per day; 70 and older ski free. Note: lift tickets limited to Arapahoe Basin are $35 a day.

Twilight tickets (2-9 p.m.) are $31; night (4-9 p.m.) $25; and late night (7-9 p.m.) $17.

Accommodations

Keystone, a condominium community, has three hotels. One is the modern **Keystone Lodge**, which also houses the main restaurants and dozens of conference rooms for business meetings. Another is **The Inn**, a 103-room hotel within walking distance of Keystone Mountain.

The other embodies the only "past" that Keystone exhibits, and is a personal favorite of several *Skiing America* staffers. The quaint **Ski Tip Lodge** is a near-perfect ski lodge. Rooms are rustic (in the best sense of the word) with true ski history, the dining room elegant and the sitting room warm and inviting.

The Ski Tip Lodge only rents rooms with breakfast and dinner included. Private rooms have baths, and the dorm rooms share one. The rooms are not huge but are comfortable and the food usually is very good. Private rooms in regular season based on double occupancy are $110 per person a night; dorm rooms cost $84 per person a night. Call (800) 222-0188.

Condo accommodations are broken into ratings of Bronze, Silver, Gold and Slopeside. Each group has a central swimming pool and, except for the slopeside units, all have about equal access to the lifts, thanks to the excellent shuttle system.

Slopeside condominiums are virtually ski-in/ski-out—they are right across the street from the Keystone Mountain Base Area. The **Chateaux d'Mont** condos are spectacular, by far the most luxurious and worth every penny. We strongly recommend trying to get one of these units. Those renting at the **Keystone Mountain Inn** are paying mainly for location.

Gold condominiums seem to be priced in a higher category because of more lavish decoration and because they are closer to the Keystone Village and Keystone Lodge. This is logical because they would be the best locations for any company planning a meeting at Keystone. However, they are not worth a premium to a skier or his family.

The Silver condominium grouping offers the best value for money and are considered more "homelike." **The St.. John** units have spectacular views and were built with just about every amenity. In the Silver category these units are clearly the leader. In the deluxe group we also highly recommend the **Pines** condominiums. Bronze condos are a little older and less expensive.

Kids 12 and under stay free in the same lodge room or condo with their parents, provided minimum occupancy is met and maximum occupancy not exceeded.

Dining

There are three eating experiences visitors to Keystone should try to include during their stay—**The Keystone Ranch**, the **Ski Tip Lodge** and the **Alpenglow Stube**, perched at 11,444 feet at the top of North Peak.

They all require reservations, which you can make before leaving home by calling (800) 222-0188 (outside Colorado). If you're staying at a resort property, dial extension 4130. If you're staying elsewhere in Summit County, call 468-4130. Use these numbers for all the restaurants we list here.

The Keystone Ranch is a restored log ranch house of the 1930s. Reportedly, the only completely original part of the house standing is the original fireplace. The Ski Tip Lodge exudes a homey, rustic flavor.

The Alpenglow Stube is located in The Outpost, which features rough-hewn timbers, massive fireplaces, vaulted ceilings and expansive windows. It is reached by a ride on the Skyway and Outpost gondolas. The restaurant, seemingly inspired by Heidi and decorated by a Victorian Martha Stewart, features a six-course menu (for a fixed price of $68 per person) of such non-traditional skiing fare as wood-grilled salmon, grilled venison chops and roasted boar tenderloin. Ask to sit at the chef's counter; only eight people get to do it each sitting. You'll see the chefs preparing the meal on open grills, get to taste dishes they're working on for future menus, and get a little more attention than the other diners.

Another experience is **Der Fondue Chessel**, also at the Outpost. Ride the gondola to the top of North Peak and then enjoy fondue, raclette and wine by candlelight with music by a Bavarian band.

In the Keystone Lodge, **the Garden Room Steakhouse** offers fanciful gourmet fare and buffalo or beef steaks at hefty prices ($18-$25 for entrées, with side dishes another $4 or so).

For more casual dining, try **Nonnino's Italian Restaurant**, in Keystone Village, where you choose a pasta and a sauce that is then served family-style, or **RazzBerrys**, in the Keystone Inn, serving grilled items and pastas. For truly casual dining, we got a tasty individual-sized pizza and a draft beer sitting at the bar in the **Snake River Saloon**.

Après-ski/nightlife

Keystone's nightlife is limited unless you consider a night curled in front of a fireplace sipping brandy acceptable instead of to leaning on a bar, knocking back a few brews and dancing.

The best bet for a good night out dancing and meeting the other nightlife denizens is at **Bandito's** (formerly the Last Chance Saloon). Across the highway you will find the **Snake River Saloon**, which has good action with a slightly older crowd. **MonteZuma's** in the Village has a huge dance floor with live bands or DJ music, pool and foosball tables and a basketball toss game. **Keysters** in River Run Plaza offers karaoke.

For immediate après-ski activity, try the **Last Lift Bar** in the Mountain House at Keystone Mountain base or the **Snake River Saloon**. **Tenderfoot Lounge**, in Keystone Lodge, has piano entertainment and a 15-foot fireplace. Locals give high marks to après-ski at **China Café**.

Child care (94/95 prices)

Keystone has made major efforts for children's skiing. (Minor's Camp programs are described under Ski School.) The resort has designated Children Only skiing areas, and classes have an average 5:1 student/teacher ratio.

The **Children's Center at Keystone Mountain** base accepts infants as young as 2 months, and the nursery at Arapahoe accepts children from 18 months. Reservations are required; call 468-4182 or (800) 255-3715.

Child care for children 2 months and older is $46 for a full day and $38 for a half day, either morning or afternoon. Both include lunch. The Snowplay Program, designed for children 3 and older, costs $46 for a full day of activities and lunch, and $38 for a half day of fun.

Other activities

Shopping: A few of the standard souvenir and T-shirt shops are in the Village, but nothing memorable. Head for Breckenridge or the Silverthorne Factory Stores. (See the Breckenridge and Summit County chapters for more information.)

Keystone has a good athletic club with two indoor tennis courts. Tennis lessons are available for $45 an hour.

Sleigh rides to the **Soda Creek Homestead,** including a dinner with all the fixins, will cost adults $49.50; children under 12, $30. The sleigh ride without dinner is $11 a person. Call (800) 451-5930 or 468-4130.

Ice skating in the middle of Keystone Village is open each day and night. The rink, which is smoothed twice a day, has a fee of $7; ice skates can be rented for $6.

Getting there and getting around

Getting there: Keystone is 90 miles from Denver International Airport via Interstate 70. Transportation between the airport and the resort can be booked with the central reservations number, (800) 222-0188.

Resort Express has several daily round trips. Call (800) 334-7433 or check in at the counter when arriving in Denver. **Vans to Keystone** is another option; call (800) 222-2112.

Getting around: The **Summit Stage** provides free transportation between Dillon, Silverthorne, Frisco, Breckenridge and Copper Mountain. Call 453-1241 for information. Keystone and Breckenridge also operate a free shuttle, the Ski KAB Express, between those two resorts from 8 a.m. to 11 p.m.

Within Keystone a free shuttle system runs continuously from 7:30 a.m., passing every 15 minutes. In the evenings the shuttles run every 20 minutes until midnight on weeknights, until 2 a.m. on Fridays and Saturdays. Bartenders and hotel doormen will call the shuttle to ensure pickup in the evenings and late at night, 468-4200. If you are staying and skiing mostly at Keystone, you won't need a car.

Information/reservations

For all reservations except air, call **Keystone Condominium Reservations** at (800) 222-0188 or 534-7712 (toll free from Denver); or the **Keystone Lodge** at (800) 541-0346.

General information: 468-2316 or (800) 222-0188.

Current ski conditions: 468-4111.

Denver-direct ski conditions: 733-0191.

Activities/dining information/reservations (800) 451-5930.

Unless otherwise noted, all area codes are 303.

Crested Butte
Colorado

Great skiing—especially for advanced and expert skiers—and down-home western friendliness make Crested Butte one of our favorite resorts.

Many Colorado resorts cater to the well-to-do celebrity or CEO skier, and that's fine. But this is one place you can come if you want to avoid that scene. You won't find flashy ski outfits, you won't hear talk of yesterday's movement in 30-year bonds, you won't be caught in the middle of a disagreement between a movie star and his agent, and you won't hear much griping about slow lifts or cruddy snow. Crested Butte has a laid-back attitude and the locals have a way of looking at the better side of life. After a few days here, it's contagious.

Entering the town, which has been designated a National Historic District, is like stepping back to the turn of the century. A walk down Elk Avenue, the main street, takes you past the old post office, built in 1900; the hardware store, where old cronies still reminisce around a pot-bellied stove; and The Forest Queen, reputed to have once been a brothel. More than 40 historic structures are tucked in and around the town.

In contrast, the ski area, about three miles away, is surrounded by modern condominiums and a couple of hotels, with more in the planning stages. With the shuttlebus system you won't need a car after you arrive.

Crested Butte has also made a major commitment to snowmaking, which has ensured excellent coverage for early season skiing. The snowfall statistics speak for themselves. Crested Butte has one of the highest average snowfalls of any ski town in Colorado.

Crested Butte Facts
Base elevation: 9,100'; **Summit elevation:** 11,875; **Vertical drop:** 3,062 feet
Number of lifts: 13—2 quad superchairs, 3 triple chairs, 4 double chairs, 4 surface lifts
Snowmaking: 35 percent **Acreage:** 1,162 acres
Uphill capacity: 15,960 per hour **Bed Base:** 5,750

Where to ski

The Crested Butte skier seems to like his terrain just as nature left it. There are plenty of groomed trails for intermediates and beginners, but you'll notice that named trails only cover about half the terrain. Looking at a trail map, on the left is a huge area called the North Face with a series of double diamonds punctuating the mountainside; and on the far right is another grouping of double diamonds hard against the area boundary.

Let's make sense of it all. Beginners have extensive terrain, served by the Keystone lift. However, this is not stuff you want to attempt with the skiing ability you learned from a book on the plane. Never-evers should head to the Peachtree lift, take a couple of lessons and practice for a day or two before attempting the Keystone lift. When you're ready for Keystone, get off at the second stop and try Houston and Painter Boy.

Intermediates in search of long cruising runs should go up Keystone or Silver Queen, and head down Treasury, Ruby Chief, Forest Queen, Bushwacker, Gallowich and variations of the same. The Paradise Bowl at the top of the Paradise lift gives intermediates a taste of powder on good days. Advanced intermediates can manage most of the runs down from the Silver Queen superchair. The short and steep Twister and Crystal both have good bail-out routes about halfway down. Tree skiing off the Teocalli and the high-speed quad lifts let skiers test themselves on natural slalom courses.

Upper Forest, Hot Rocks and Forest have always technically been part of Crested Butte's lift-served terrain. But in 1987 the resort linked the huge North Face area with the other lifts by installing a short Poma lift to drag skiers to the crest of the North Face and the Phoenix Bowl. This area offers what experts claim is the best extreme skiing in Colorado, comparable to Utah steeps. The resort has free tours of the North Face daily at 10:45 and 12:45, and will add guides for the new Teocalli Bowl area. The North Face normally opens in mid-January.

Mountain rating

Crested Butte has terrain for every level of skier. It needs it, because there are no alternatives in the near vicinity, with the notable exception of 2,000 acres of snowcat powder skiing at nearby Irwin Lodge, the largest such operation in North America.

Cross-country

Crested Butte is linked with one of the most extensive cross-country networks in Colorado. For those on skinny skis, the adventures are virtually limitless. Crested Butte was the pioneering resort in the rediscovery and popularization of telemark skiing; it has more telemark skiers per capita than any other big-time ski resort.

In April hundreds of free-heel skiers scramble up the North Face and drop 1,200 vertical feet through deep snow competing in the Al Johnson Memorial Uphill/Downhill Race. Johnson used to deliver mail on Nordic skis to 1880s mining camps. Every month the Crested Butte Nordic Center sponsors a different race event, ranging from citizens' races to team relays and the Alley Loop race.

The **Crested Butte Nordic Center** is located at the edge of town, on 2nd Street between Sopris and Whiterock Streets. The town maintains about 20 km. of Nordic tracks, which begin a few yards from the Nordic Center. After skiing, the center also has hot tubs and racquetball courts for après-Nordic activity. There are more than 100 miles of backcountry trails. Call 349-1707 for pricing on lessons, rentals and trail fee. Group lessons, half-day and all-day tours are scheduled several times each week, but private lessons and special tour requests must be made a day in advance.

Snowboarding

Snowboarding is allowed on the entire mountain including the double-diamond Extreme Limits. Snowboard lessons are $28 per two-hour session. A first-timer's package that includes a two-hour lesson and all-day rental equipment is $43.

The resort and Western State College in Gunnison have developed a group of snowboarders who promote proper behavior on the slopes.

Ski school (94/95 prices)

Group lessons: Adult group lessons range from $28 for a half-day (two-hour) lesson to $116 for five half-day lessons. A three-day introduction to skiing package costs $168, and includes three two-hour lessons and lifts.

Private lessons: One and a half hours are $74 for one, with each additional person costing $25; two hours cost $95 per person with additional students costing $35 apiece; three hours are $135 for one; and six hours cost $250 for one.

Special programs for bump and double-diamond powder skiers cost $42 a day. NASTAR races cost $5 for two runs and $1 for each additional run. Race clinics include coaching and a race for $40 for adults; $35 for kids. A two-hour private racing clinic can be arranged for $92, children or adults; additional persons cost $35 for adults; $30 for kids.

Children aged 8-12 enroll in Buttebusters. Half-day lessons are $34; full-day, lunch included, is $44. Miners is the program for children aged 4-7. Half-day lessons are $40; full-day with lunch, $50. The Miners program includes ski rental and supervised play activities and daycare after the lesson. Lesson rates do not include lifts, and more experienced child skiers have classes separate from beginners.

MT. CRESTED BUTTE
Base Area Map

Crested Butte - Colorado

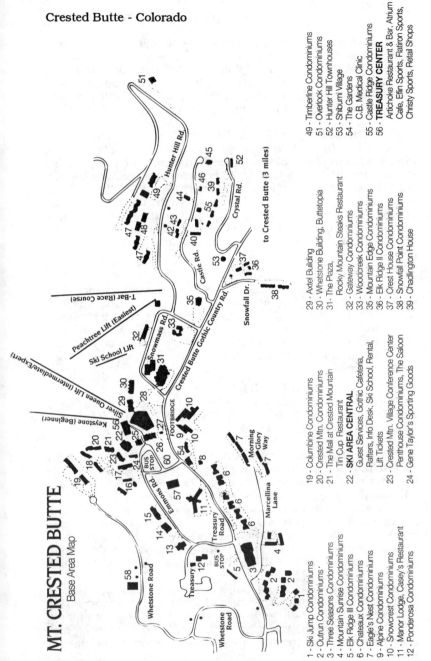

1 - Ski Jump Condominiums
2 - Outrun Condominiums*
3 - Three Seasons Condominiums
4 - Mountain Sunrise Condominiums
5 - Elk Ridge III Condominiums
6 - Chateaux Condominiums
7 - Eagle's Nest Condominiums
9 - Alpine Condominiums
10 - Snowcrest Condominiums
11 - Manor Lodge, Casey's Restaurant
12 - Ponderosa Condominiums

19 - Columbine Condominiums
20 - Crested Mtn. Condominiums
21 - The Mall at Crested Mountain
       Tin Cup Restaurant
22 - **SKI AREA CENTRAL**
       Guest Services, Gothic Cafeteria,
       Rafters, Info Desk, Ski School, Rental,
       Lift Tickets
23 - Crested Mtn. Village Conference Center
       Penthouse Condominiums, The Saloon
24 - Gene Taylor's Sporting Goods

29 - Axtel Building
30 - Whetstone Building, Buttetopia
31 - The Plaza,
       Rocky Mountain Steaks Restaurant
32 - Gateway Condominiums
33 - Woodcreek Condominiums
35 - Mountain Edge Condominiums
36 - Elk Ridge II Condominiums
37 - Crest House Condominiums
38 - Snowfall Point Condominiums
39 - Chadlington House

49 - Timberline Condominiums
51 - Overlook Condominiums
52 - Hunter Hill Townhouses
53 - Shibumi Village
54 - The Gardens
       C.B. Medical Clinic
55 - Castle Ridge Condominiums
56 - **TREASURY CENTER**
       Artichoke Restaurant & Bar, Atrium
       Cafe, Elfin Sports, Flatiron Sports,
       Christy Sports, Retail Shops

13 - Nordic Inn
14 - Evergreen Condominiums
    Crested Butte Sports
15 - Redstone Condominiums
16 - Crested Mtn. North Condominiums
17 - Crested Butte Lodge
    Wong's Chinese Restaurant
18 - The Buttes Condominiums

25 - The Avalanche Restaurant,
    Butte and Company Ski and Dry Goods
26 - Emmons Building, Village Center Rentals
27 - Bakery at Mt. Crested Butte
28 - Grande Butte Hotel - Roaring Elk Rest-
    aurant, The Dugout Sports Bar & Grill,
    Giovanni's Grande Cafe, CBMR Ski
    Rental

40 - West Elk Townhouses
42 - Crystal View Condominiums
43 - Elk Ridge I Condominiums
44 - Solar Sixplex
45 - Snow Castle Condominiums
46 - Edelweiss Condominiums
47 - San Moritz Condominiums
48 - Paradise Condominiums

57 - *NEW IN 1993 - The Mountainlair Hotel
58 - Shenandoah Buttes

HISTORIC CRESTED BUTTE
Town Map

1 - Elk Mountain Lodge
2 - Soupçon
3 - Kochevar's Bar, Karolina's Kitchen
4 - Forest Queen Hotel & Restaurant
5 - Penelope's Restaurant
6 - Slogar Restaurant & Bar
7 - Le Bosquet Restaurant
9 - Post Office
10 - Oscar's Bar & Cafe
11 - Bacchanale Restaurant
12 - Wooden Nickel Bar & Restaurant
13 - Talk of the Town
14 - Gourmet Noodle Restaurant
16 - Paradise Cafe
17 - The Bakery Cafe
18 - Donita's Cantina
19 - Angello's Pizza & Deli
20 - Whiterock Lodge,
    Copper Mine Restaurant
21 - C. B. State Bank
22 - True Value
    Crested Butte Drug Store
23 - McDell's Market
24 - Old Town Inn

25 - C.B. Marketplace
26 - Christina Guesthaus
27 - Purple Mountain Lodge
29 - Claim Jumper Lodge
30 - Tudor Rose
31 - Crested Butte Club
    Crested Butte Nordic Center
32 - Rocky Mountain Rentals
33 - Powerhouse Bar Y Grill
36 - Timberline Restaurant
38 - The Alpineer
39 - Cook Works
40 - Shopping Mall
41 - Idle Spur
42 - Shopping Mall
43 - Gothic Inn
44 - Jimmy's Fish & Grill
45 - Crystal Inn
46 - Crested Beauty
47 - Alpine Lace Bed & Breakfast
48 - Elizabeth Anne
49 - Butte Bagels Feed Shack
50 - Rocky Mountain Chocolate
    Factory

Children aged 2-3 can enroll in the Mites program. Options include 90-minute lessons combined with varying amounts of daycare, ranging in price from $40 to $50. Mites participants must be potty-trained.

Registration and reservations for all programs are at the ski school desk in the Gothic Center, 349-2251.

Lift tickets (94/95 prices)

	Adult	Child (0-12)
One day	$42	$**
Three days (consecutive)	$126 ($42/day)	$**
Five days (of 6)	$185 ($38/day)	$**

For the past few seasons, Crested Butte hasn't charged for lift tickets before Christmas. That's right: **FREE SKIING** November 28 through December 16 this year, and free never-ever lessons for people 7 and older.

Regular-season prices are in effect from the Christmas season through early April. Reduced prices are available November 23-27 and from early March to closing in April. Other multiday tickets also are available.

Skiers 70 and older ski free; 65-69 ski for half-price.

**When children 12 and younger are skiing with one full-paying adult, they pay their age per day. This program has no blackout periods, nor any limits to the number of children, but proof of age may be required.

Accommodations

Most of the accommodations are clustered around the ski area in Mount Crested Butte. The historic town has a handful of lodges, but they are not as modern nor as convenient to the slopes. They are, however, less expensive, closer to the nightlife and offer a taste of more rustic Western atmosphere. A free bus service brings skiers right to the slopes, so the primary inconvenience of in-town lodging is the short bus ride.

Crested Butte Vacations can take care of everything from your plane tickets to hotel room, lift tickets and lessons with one phone call. It also offers some of the best packages available. Before you make any arrangements, call (800) 544-8448 and ask for the best possible deal.

Mountainlair Hotel was brand-new last season and is 200 yards from the Silver Queen superchair. It has 126 large rooms with two king-sized beds in each, two outdoor hot tubs and a coin-operated laundry. Rates are $60-$170 per night.

Grande Butte Hotel (800-341-5437 or 349-7561), has ski-in/ski-out lodging with a tasteful decor and nice-sized rooms. Mountain hotels don't get much better than this, in this price range, at least. Room rates are $99-$600 per night, depending on room size and season.

Crested Mountain Village is perhaps the top luxury group of properties at the mountain. It has a series of spectacular penthouse suites that open onto the slopes.

The Buttes are well-appointed condos 35 yards from the lifts. Rooms range in size from studios to three bedrooms; prices range from $84 to $506 per night.

The Gateway, across from the Peachtree lift and about a two-minute stroll from the Silver Queen, is perhaps the best value of any condo on the mountain when you trade price for space and amenities. One-, two- and three-bedroom units range from $175 to $450 per night. Gateway units are managed by several competing agencies. It is best to book through Crested Butte Vacations, (800) 544-8448.

The Plaza, about 80 yards from the Silver Queen superchair, is one of the most popular condo projects on the mountain. It gives excellent value and is especially popular with groups because special functions can be easily arranged. Two- and three-bedroom units range from $131 to $579 per night.

Wood Creek and **Mountain Edge** are convenient to the lifts, but not particularly well appointed. The **Columbine** is an excellent ski-in/ski-out property. These three properties, together with nine others within shuttlebus distance of the lifts, are managed by Crested Butte Accommodations at (800) 821-3718 or 349-2448.

The Crested Butte Club, on Second Street in town, is the upscale old-world elegance champion of the area. Though the lifts are a bit far, this place is worth the inconvenience. Seven suites have been individually furnished with Victorian furnishings including double sinks and a copper-and-brass tub, as well as beautiful four-poster or canopied beds and a fireplace. The amenities include the fitness club, with heated swimming pool, two steam baths, three hot tubs, weight room, and massage and weight trainer. This is a No-Smoking property. Room rates are $155 to $225. 349-6655.

The Claim Jumper, 704 Whiterock Street; 349-6471, a historic log-home bed-and-breakfast, is the class act in town. Jerry and Robbie Bigelow took it over a couple of years ago and filled it with a collection of memorable antiques. Bedrooms have themes and are furnished with brass or old iron beds. There are only five rooms, four with private bath. Room rates are $69-$109 per night including a full breakfast. Children are not encouraged; No-Smoking. The Claim Jumper can arrange catered, special-occasion wedding ceremonies.

The Cristiana Guesthaus, 621 Maroon Ave.; (800) 824-7899, 349-5326, is only a block from the ski shuttle and a five-minute walk from downtown. This has a mountain inn atmosphere and most of the guests manage to get to know one another. The rooms are small, but most guests spend their time in the hotel's living rooms so the smaller sleeping areas are less of a problem. Let the owners know if you need quiet, because some rooms get quite a bit of traffic from the owner's family and folk using the washers and dryers. Rates are $52 to $85.

The Forest Queen, corner of Elk and 2nd, 349-5336, has a reputation for being inexpensive, with a double with bath for only $40-$70.

The Elk Mountain Lodge around the corner from the Forest Queen on 2nd Street has simple but comfortable rooms, all with private bath, for $98 to $108 per room per night. Call 349-7533. Ask for Room 20 on the third floor with lots of space, a balcony and a great view.

Other B&Bs in town worth a look are **Alpine Lace**, 726 Maroon, 349-9857; and **Whiterock Lodge**, 505 Whiterock Ave. and Route 135, (800) 783-7052 or 349-6669.

Rocky Mountain Rentals at 214 6th Street, 349-5354, offers rentals in private homes in the area as well as in many special condominiums. If you are looking for something out of the ordinary, check with them for help. Another possibility is **Crested Butte Properties**, 349-5780.

Dining

Crested Butte is blessed with more excellent, affordable restaurants than any other resort in the West. You can dine on gourmet French cuisine or chow down on platters of family-style fried chicken and steaks.

The top of the line gourmet restaurants are **Soupçon** (349-5448), located in a tiny old historic building and tucked into an alley off 2nd Street, **Le Bosquet** (349-5808) on Elk and 2nd, and **Timberline** (349-9831) at the end of Elk. Call for reservations at all these during the ski season. **Penelope's** (349-5178) on Elk Avenue has improved its menu dramatically and serves up dinners in a beautiful dining room. For more information on these restaurants, see Katy Keck's Crested Butte Savoir Faire chapter immediately following .

For hard-to-beat group and family dining, head to **The Slogar** (349-5765). It used to be the first bar the miners hit when returning from the mines and is decorated in old bordello decor. Slogar's offers a skillet-fried chicken dinner with mashed potatoes, biscuits, creamed corn, ice cream and even some other extras for a flat price of $11.50 each ($5.95 for children 2-12; kids younger than 2, no charge). It also offers a family-style steak dinner. Reservations recommended.

For other substantial meals, head down Elk Avenue to **Donita's Cantina** (349-6674), where the margaritas are giant and strong and Mexican food comes in heaping portions. Be early or be ready to wait. No reservations.

The Powerhouse Bar and Grill (349-5494) presents Mexican food at Elk Avenue and Second Street. This converted powerhouse offers a unique atmosphere and more Mex than Tex-Mex. For something special try the cabrito, goat cooked with a spicy sauce.

The Idle Spur (349-5026) on Elk Avenue is a restaurant and bar housed in a log barn building with its own micro brewery. The suds are potent and mix with moderate prices and live music on weekends. Cover charges are $3 to $8, depending on the talent, and the food has improved dramatically during the past few years. It's very good for steaks and burgers, served with a family-style salad, sourdough bread and choice of potatoes. For a quick meal, try **Angelo's** for pizza and Italian food.

The best breakfast by far is served in the **Forest Queen**. The atmosphere is Old West and turn of the century. Ask for the *"baggins."* You won't find it on the menu—it has developed as a specialty for most of the locals. The Forest Queen also serves lunch and dinner.

For breakfast on the mountain head to **The Tin Cup** or **The Avalanche.** For a good lunch try **Rafters,** the **Fat Man's Deli** in the Treasury Center, or for a more elegant setting head to **The Artichoke** and start off with artichoke soup. The **Swiss Chalet** serves Alpine fare, such as fondues and raclette, plus a good selection of European beer.

Après-ski/nightlife

Here nightlife means wandering from bar to bar. The immediate après-ski action is centered in **Rafters** at the base of the lifts. Then it begins to move downtown to the **Wooden Nickel**, with some wild drinks, and **The Grubstake**, which has a very happy hour from 10 p.m. to 11:30 p.m. and karaoke. The **Cafe Lobo** (formerly the Eldorado) has dancing, live music and welcome munchies. **Talk of the Town** is a smoky locals' place with video games, shuffleboard and pool tables. **Kochevar's** is another local favorite. The **Idle Spur** has dancing, sometimes even a polka or two.

Rafters has dancing and good singles action most nights in Mount Crested Butte, and on top of that it's within stumbling distance of most of the lodging. Those staying in town can take an inexpensive town taxi service if they miss the last bus of the night.

Child care

The **Buttetopia Children's Programs** care for kids from infants to age 7. Registration and information are in the Whetstone Building; 349-2259. Hours: 8:30 a.m. to 4 p.m.

Care for infants up to six months is $8 per hour, two babies per staffer. Nursery for kids still in diapers costs $44 for a full day; $34 for a half day.

Day care for older preschoolers (potty-trained to age 7) costs $38 per full day and $28 per half day. All day-care programs include crafts, games, snow play and other activities, but no ski lessons. Children's lesson programs are explained in the ski school section of this chapter.

Other activities

Shopping: Lots of great shops at the resort and in town. Among them: **Diamond Tanita Art Gallery**, for jewelry, glass, ceramics, paper, forged iron and other functional art pieces; **Cookworks, Inc.**, a gourmet kitchen shop; **Book Cellar**, with local maps, Western art and collectibles; and **Minor's Closet**, out-of-the-ordinary children's gifts.

Crested Butte has several more active things to do. These include snowmobiling, snowmobile dinner tours to Irwin Lodge, snowcat dinner tours to Paradise Warming House on Crested Butte Mountain, winter horseback riding, sleigh rides with and without dinners, and ballooning—weather permitting. Call Mt. Crested Butte or **Crested Butte Chamber of Commerce** at 349-6438 for brochures and information. For resort activities, call 349-2211.

Getting there and getting around

Getting there: Despite its seemingly isolated location, Crested Butte is one of the most convenient ski resorts to reach in Colorado. United Express and Continental Express offer several flights daily from Denver, plus non-stop jet service from Atlanta, Dallas and Houston into Gunnison, a half-hour from the resort.

Alpine Express meets every arriving flight and takes you direct to your hotel or condo for $32 round-trip ($22 for children; one-way fares available). For reservations, call Crested Butte Vacations, (800) 544-8448.

Getting around: No need for a car. Crested Butte's free town/resort shuttle is reliable and fun to ride, thanks to some free-spirited and friendly drivers.

Information/reservations

Crested Butte Mountain Resort, Box A, 12 Snowmass Road, Mount Crested Butte CO 81225; 349-2333; **Crested Butte Vacations:** (800) 544-8448 or 349-2222. **Snow reports:** 349-2323.

Unless otherwise noted, all area codes are 303.

Crested Butte Savoir Faire

For a town of its size, Crested Butte has an impressive number of fine dining choices, most within steps of one another. At the far end of Elk Avenue is **The Timberline Restaurant**. Chef Tim Egelhoff spent five years as sous chef at Creme Carmel in Carmel, California before opening Timberline a few years ago. He combines seasonal products to create a Café French Cuisine, whose roots are classic French, with a pinch of California and a dash of the Rockies. Served in a quaint old private home, the menu changes often. Start with the warmed goat cheese in puff pastry, layers of crisp pastry stuffed with eggplant, tapanade and creamy goat cheese. Or try the sesame ahi tuna, rolled in sesame seeds, seared rare, and sliced and served with soy and wasabi. I fell in love with the blackened lamb, a boneless loin coated with spicy Cajun seasonings and served with a sweet cassis sauce. Timberline also offers a selection of reasonably priced boutique wines. Open nightly from 6 p.m. For reservations, call 349-9831.

Soupçon Restaurant is hidden in the alley behind Kochevar's Bar. This log cabin started at half its current size in 1916 as a private residence to the Kochevars. While there have been several restaurants over the past 30 years, Soupçon itself dates back almost 20 years. Current owners Maura and Mac Bailey have created an innovative French cuisine, with menu items posted daily on a chalkboard. Reserve two to three days ahead for one of two seatings, 6 and 8:15 p.m. (349-5448.)

A special appetizer often on the menu is oysters aioli, poached in a spicy broth and served with a garlicky aioli on the side. Potato leek soup with tender red bliss potatoes and spicy Andouille sausage is another frequent offering. Entrées range from $16.75 for roast duckling with ginger-orange sauce to $25.50 for Maine lobster with a lemon tarragon beurre blanc.

Le Bosquet, another fine French restaurant, is now in its 18th year in this casually elegant setting. Chef/owner Victor Shepard and his wife Candy offer dishes such as hazelnut chicken in an orange-thyme cream sauce, as well as filet of fresh salmon with a ginger glaze. Tournedos au Bosquet is available in a 4- or an 8-ounce size, with either a black peppercorn or cabernet sauce. Cost is about $30 for three courses, without beverage, tax or tip, although you can lower that tab by ordering from the new lower-priced bistro à la carte menu which offers more casual fare, like lamb shank or pork loin. Open daily, 5:30 to 10 p.m. (349-5808)

Just down the block is **Penelope's**, a restaurant in a greenhouse. Featuring exceptional American cuisine, Penelope's offers a terrific fresh rainbow trout, sauteed and covered with roasted hazelnuts, then laced with an orange honey butter sauce. Start with the smoked loin of venison, wrapped in a buckwheat crêpe and topped with a roasted garlic aioli. Starters range from $4.75 for the gravlax with a dill mustard sauce to $9.50 for the lobster en croûte. Entrées are priced from $13.95 for the trout to $25.95 for rack of lamb. Call 349-5178; open daily 5:30 to 10 p.m.

New last winter was **Cafe Lobo** offering the best in new American food with a southwestern Colorado style, "whatever that means," said my Alpine Express driver. What that means is simple, perfectly prepared, reasonably priced food with a bold use of spices and a heavy hand with chilis—like blue corn trout with a green chili sauce, pork tenderloin with apple and red-chile chutney, stuffed Anaheim peppers, and a grilled cumin chicken. Entrées are priced at $9 to $14.

For the best sushi in town, head to **Jimmy's**, set back in a recess off Elk, between Third and Fourth. Well known as the freshest source of fish from faraway waters, Jimmy's opens at 4 p.m. daily and offers a wide assortment of sushi, mesquite grilled fish (salmon, snapper, tilapia, ahi), shellfish, and a few landlubber specials. Prices are moderate, given the variety and quality this far from the sea.

Those up for serious suds should head to the **Idle Spur Steakhouse and Microbrewery.** Always crowded, always noisy, it offers the finest hand-cut steaks in town. Other choices are burgers (including vegetable and elk—sounds better than it is), Mexican entrées and a selection of fresh fish—all reasonably priced. Six beers are brewed in-house—from the White Buffalo Peace ale to the full-bodied Rodeo Stout. For $3, you can sample four 4-ounce tastes of the home brew. For reservations, call 349-5026. Brewery tours 2 to 5 p.m. daily.

For gourmets with a sense of adventure, join a snowmobile tour to the **Irwin Lodge.** The Irwin Lodge is an immense cedar structure maintained in an 1890s tradition. Start with the toasted raviolis, served with a trio of sauces; and a pesto piñon sauce. Entrées range from elk Wellington stuffed with chanterelles and chilis to grilled halibut with raspberry cream sauce. Four new selections each day of the week come from an eclectic 28-item rotating menu. After one visit, you'll realize that a week's stay is needed to sample all the chef's greats. Entrées are priced from $17 to $26.

Snowmobile tours and the dinner are priced separately, so call (303) 349-2441 to inquire about prices and make arrangements to join a tour. Plan at least one week in advance.

Irwin Lodge, Colorado

Irwin Lodge at Lake Irwin, 12 miles west of Crested Butte, is Colorado's most exclusive and remote ski area. Virtually unlimited skiing stretches over 2,200 acres with an overall 2,100-foot vertical drop, but you won't find a chair lift or a snowmaking gun anywhere, and only 50 or so skiers can use the area at a time. Irwin Lodge specializes in snowcat skiing.

The lodge was built by an eccentric millionaire with a vision of having the perfect ski lodge. The only way in is by snowmobile, snowcat or cross-country skis. There are no phones (the only contact with the outside world is two-way radio), no network television, and only one massive lodge that sleeps about 50.

As you approach the massive wooden building by snowmobile or snowcat, you see the imposing edifice presiding over the frozen lake and an army of rugged pines and spindly aspens. Inside, the lodge is even more impressive. The 120-foot-long living area stretches almost the length of the building and soars two stories to the ceiling. The living area is the most important room; it takes up 60 percent of the structure, with the rest dedicated to the guest rooms.

Mornings begin with breakfast from 8 to 9:30 a.m. Snowcats make their first climb to the ridge at 9:30 a.m. loaded with skiers, and cross-country skiers take off on organized tours a bit later.

Where to ski

Here's a nice surprise: Skiing is available for every level of ability. Naturally, beginners will have their problems but beginner powder skiers will have the time of their life. Two groomed slopes serve the needs of intermediates and beginners, one slope for each. The top of Dan's Delight leads to the advanced areas as well as the groomed slopes. The 70 MPH Basin dropoff opens more difficult terrain.

One run to the left off Dan's Delight starts in a relatively tame bowl. You can choose to continue down through the gladed Central Park area or turn to the left and drop down an expert chute into the wide-open Banzai Bowl. Twenty-five or thirty turns later you enter the trees to begin running nature's slalom gates through the Lumber Yard, where some of the Ponderosa pines are only three to five feet apart. The 70 MPH Basin offers truly advanced terrain which bottoms out at the West Wall, where skiers have a choice of almost a dozen chutes running down the face, starting with open glades and ending through tightening trees.

Normally, skiing starts at 9:30 a.m. and continues until 4:30 p.m. From 12:30 until 1:30 p.m. everything stops for the lunch buffet while the snowcats are serviced and the skiers fuel up for the afternoon.

Irwin also offers snowmobiling and guided cross-country skiing as well as ice fishing and snowshoeing.

Snowboarding

Boarding is permitted but it is difficult if you need to traverse in deep powder: a problem known as postholing occurs when the free leg sinks into the snow. Closest board rentals are available in Crested Butte.

The costs (94/95 rates)

The way to do Irwin is to purchase a package that combines lodging, meals, activities and round-trip transportation from Crested Butte. The three-day/three-night package will run $876, the four-day/three-night package will cost $987, five days and four nights is $1,262 and seven days and six nights will cost $1,813. These packages include snowcat skiing, snowmobiling and/or cross-country skiing.

Folks coming up to ski from Crested Butte pay $175 a day (93/94 price) for the same snowcat skiing, including transportation from Crested Butte and lunch.

Getting there

Round-trip transportation from Crested Butte is included in all packages; see Crested Butte chapter for other transportation information.

Information/reservations

Contact Irwin Lodge, PO Box 457, Crested Butte, CO 81224, (303) 349-5308, or (800) 247-9462 (800-2-IRWIN-2).

Purgatory-Durango, Colorado

If you are ever banished to Purgatory, don't fret—at least if your exile is to this ski area in southwestern Colorado, 25 miles north of the town of Durango.

Purgatory-Durango is a ski area with a sense of humor. It draws heavily from Arizona, New Mexico, Texas, and to a growing extent, Southern California. Its clientele is definitely in the middle-income range of the ski market—heavy on families, college students and anyone looking for a fun time at a lower cost. *USA Today* once designated the town of Durango as the least fashion-conscious town in America, a label the flannel-shirted locals relish. Rather than try to compete with the tonier Colorado resorts for beautiful skiers, P-D boldly proclaimed its uncelebrity status a couple of seasons ago with a refreshing marketing campaign that included magazine ads depicting real skiers, not models, and an Uncelebrities Week where "the list of celebrities not invited and not attending is long and prestigious," according to resort publicity. If you see a stretch limo here, it probably got lost on the way to Telluride.

Not only is Purgatory-Durango a friendly, casual place, but the skiing is fun too, thanks in part to the area's undulating terrain. Millions of years ago glaciers scraped this valley, leaving narrow natural terraces on the mountainside. Purgatory's runs plunge downward for a bit, then level off, then plunge, then level off—all the way to the bottom. The effect is rather like a roller coaster ride. It's super for skiers who love to get air. Those who don't can use the flat spots to rest before the next dropoff.

Like many of Colorado's ski resorts, Purgatory-Durango helped a dying 19th-century town get back on its economic feet. Unfortunately, the ski area is 25 miles away from town. For years skiers stayed in Durango and drove the 50-mile round trip, but that is no longer necessary. Purgatory Village has hotel rooms, condos, restaurants and shops—fewer than Durango, but enough

Purgatory-Durango Facts
Base elevation: 8,793'; **Summit elevation:** 10,822'; **Vertical drop:** 2,029 feet
Number of lifts: 9–4 triple chairs, 5 double chairs **Snowmaking :** 22 percent
Total acreage: 692 acres skiable terrain accessed by lifts
Uphill capacity: 12,700 per hour **Bed base:** 3,120 near resort, 7,000 in Durango

so that the visitors who aren't that wild about nightlife and fine dining can stay close to the slopes.

About that name: it's inspired, along with many trail names, by the Divine Comedy, and since Dante Alighieri's 14th-century epic described an imagined journey through all three realms of the other world—Hell, Purgatory, and Paradise—you'll see runs named Hades, Cherub, Divinity, and No Mercy, as well as an elegant on-mountain restaurant called Dante's. The area founders were thus inspired because Spanish explorers had christened the river that flows through Durango "Rio de las Animas Perdidas," River of Lost Souls.

Where to ski

At Purgatory, skiers enjoy a nice progression from beginner to expert terrain. Never-evers have their own learning area, Columbine Station. An intra-area shuttlebus takes beginners here after they have bought their rentals and lift tickets. After a couple of lessons on the terrain under Lift 9, they are ready to board Lift 7, which takes them back to the base area. Purgatory offers *free* beginner lessons to adults, and over 11,000 skiers take advantage each season. The management figures that if beginners have a good time, they'll be back.

Beginners will like the runs under Lift 4. The easiest of these is Walk-a-Lot, a gently winding catwalk trail. Divinity and Angel's Tread are wide, gentle runs, and Columbine winds through stands of trees, giving beginners a feel of being deep in the woods. As they progress, they may want to head down Salvation toward Lift 3, which goes straight for the summit. From there, they can descend The Bank or Silvertip to Westfork, where they have many choices for getting back down.

The next step is the intermediate runs off Chair 2. Snowmaking on these runs ensures a good surface. After skiers feel comfortable on What, Limbo, and Westfork, they should make for Peace and Boogie, two wide intermediate runs off Chair 3. Still not enough of a challenge? Then head down blue-square The Legends toward Dead Spike, the widest of Purgatory's runs, or continue on The Legends to the mid-loading station on Chair 8. Sally's Run is not so steep as Chet's, but both are challenging blues.

Still not enough to make your heart leap into your throat? Go for Wapiti, a black run under Lift 5. Or try Catharsis or No Mercy, two short black runs under Lifts 1 and 6.

If even this is insufficient challenge, then you're ready for Bull Run, a double-black trail that starts just below Dante's Restaurant off Lift 5. It has a tough pitch as well as funnels and moguls (and once you're on it, you're stuck). Other advanced areas include the short steep runs at the bottom of Lift 8, and Styx and Hades off Chairs 1 and 6.

Purgatory's runs are quite long. Although many stretch from summit to base, they twist and turn, passing islands of trees and picnic tables.

A tip for powder hounds and other natural-terrain fans: the vast majority of P-D's skiers like groomed terrain, so the powder between the trees often is still fresh long into the afternoon after a storm. Tree hounds might like the aspens between Pandemonium and Lower Hades along Lift 6. Beginning adventure skiers can try the easier powder stashes between Peace and Boogie off Lift 3, or Snag for a bit steeper terrain. Paul's Park, below Lift 8, has chutes for gladed skiing. These ungroomed areas are best from January on, but catch them a day or two following a storm. After that the snow will get pretty thick, even if it's trackless.

Mountain rating

Purgatory may be a place where souls suffer before being allowed into Paradise, but that's in Dante's poem. Intermediates get to bypass the limbo stage and head straight for the blessed abodes, such are the variety and plenitude of trails for this level. The resort also offers a lot for beginners and advanced skiers. Only experts looking for extremes may feel that they are somewhat in Purgatory.

Cross-country

The Cross-Country Skiing Center is across Highway 550 from Purgatory. It maintains 16 km. of track, which winds through trees and glades. Rentals are available. Trail fees: $5 a person. Group lessons are $20 for a half-day; with rentals, $25.

Snowboarding

Purgatory has welcomed snowboarders since 1985. Dude Ranch is a half-pipe along the NASTAR race arena and below the Powderhouse, served by Lift 2. Also, the trail called "What" is a natural half-pipe, so snowboarders like to use it. All but the hardiest snowboarders tend to avoid the Legends area, served by Chair 8, because they have to take BD&M Expressway, a long flat run, back to the main area. (Locals say the initials stand for Boring, Dull, and Monotonous; actually, the run is named for three of Purgatory's pioneers.)

The Purgatory Village Center houses the San Juan Snowboard Company, a shop devoted to the sport. It sells equipment and clothing, rents equipment, does tuning and repairs, and arranges backcountry tours led by experienced snowboard guides.

Ski school (94/95 prices)

Purgatory has long been known as a leader in teaching beginners the basics. The **Start 'Em Off Right** program offers two half-day adult beginner lessons FREE with the purchase of two all-day or any multiday adult lift tickets. That means a savings of $60. Purgatory Ski School also offers a free half day of beginner-only adult lessons with the purchase of one adult lift ticket.

Purgatory also has **group lessons** and special workshops for other skier levels. Parallel Performance Courses are daily group lessons for $30 for a half day and $45 for a full day. This program introduces skiers to parallel turns or improves their skills. For intermediate and advanced skiers, the Dante's Performance Workshops are daily two-hour lessons for $24, meeting at 10:30 a.m. and 1:30 p.m., focusing on conditions of the day: powder, crud, cruising, steeps, moguls, etc. These workshops meet outside of Dante's mid-mountain restaurant along Lift 5. Classes are small, and you're already warmed up and on top of the mountain, so you don't spend valuable ski time riding the lift to where the lesson begins.

Private lessons for one skier are $60 for an hour, $110 for two hours and S175 for three hours.. Additional skiers are $25 apiece.

Purgatory also has some innovative **special programs.** For telemark skiers or snowboarders, Sunday Workshops offer two hours of instruction for $15. These specialized afternoon classes are unfortunately offered just a few times each season. Men and women can register for gender-segregated ski workshops, concentrated over three days and offered January 20-22, February 10-12 and March 3-5..

The **Ski Demons program** is for kids aged 3-12. Children are divided by age and by ability or interest. Kids' lessons start with Junior Demons for the youngest skiers and progress to Demons Elite. All kids in Ski Demons receive an all-day lift ticket with their lesson. The full-day program is $49, which includes lunch and morning and afternoon sessions. The half-day program ($40) includes either a morning or afternoon session with no lunch, but an all-day lift ticket.

One of the nation's outstanding instruction programs for disabled skiers is here at Purgatory. For information, call 247-9000, ext. 3217, or 259-0374.

Lift tickets (94/95 prices)

	Adult	Child (Up to 12)
One day	$37	Free
Three days	$102 ($34/day)	
Five days	$155 ($31/day)	

Children ski free here. Parents do not have to buy a ticket, and there is no limit to the number of free child tickets per family. The only block-out dates are Christmas (Dec. 17, 1994-January 1, 1995) and spring break (March 12-19, 1995). Call the area for prices at those times.

Ages 70 and older ski free; seniors 62-69 ski at a discount, usually about half the adult price.

Purgatory-Durango started an unusual program this season called **Total Ticket**. Skiers with four-day or longer multiday tickets may exchange a day of skiing for several major vacation activities in southwest Colorado, such as the Durango & Silverton Narrow Gauge Railroad train (which runs in the early part of winter), Trimble Hot Springs and massage or a Mesa Verde National Park tour. Call for complete details on this program.

Accommodations

Purgatory-Durango has three lodging areas. The condos at the base are the most expensive; hotels and condos within 10 miles of the ski area are a little less so, and lodging in Durango is dirt cheap, but 25 miles away.

Base-area condos at the **Purgatory Village Hotel, Angelhaus Condominiums, Brimstone Condominiums, East Rim, Edelweiss, Sitzmark** and **Twilight View** have full-service units (kitchens, fireplaces, common-area Jacuzzis and laundry facilities) from $85 for a studio $310 for a three-bedroom. Prices vary slightly for similar-size units in the various complexes.

Several other complexes are one to ten miles from the ski area. The prices at **Cascade Village, Needles, Silver Pick, Tamarron** and **Whispering Pines** range from $95 for a Tamarron suite (nine miles south) to $280 for a three-bedroom condo at Cascade Village (one mile north). Most of the outlying condo complexes have free shuttles to and from the ski area. (Even if you brought your own car, leave it behind and take the shuttle: it will get you closer.) And many of them, such as Tamarron, have their own restaurants and sundries shops, so you can get just about anything you need.

Durango may be the only ski town in America where the winter lodging prices are lower than the summer ones. Winter rates are as low as $20 a night for a one-bed unit in a clean, comfortable, but unadorned motel, and several motels have this low-end price. The high end in town is $175 per night for a suite at the **Red Lion Inn**. The average is around $45 a night.

RVs may park in the Purgatory parking lot, but there are no hookups. RV campgrounds are closed in winter.

Dining

Purgatory base area offers **Sterling's, Mesquite Bar and Grill**, and **Farquahrt's** for local eateries. For some of the best fish in Colorado, flown in daily, and for local game, try the **Cafe Cascade**, two miles north of Purgatory (259-3500), elegant dining in a rustic setting with entrées $10-$15; everyone who has eaten here raves about it.

Dante's, midway on Chair 5, offers sit-down gourmet dining at lunch, only for skiers. **The Powderhouse**, also on the mountain, has more mundane fare. Down the hill are the **Tamarron's** three restaurants. In Tamarron's San Juan Dining Room, try the piñon nut waffles with chokecherry syrup. One of our contributors liked them so much she ate them three breakfasts in a row.

Durango is where we find most of the restaurants. **The Palace Grill**, 1 Depot Place (247-2018), has continental cuisine such as honey-glazed duck, with most entrées $14 to $20; it's been one of Durango's top restaurants for years. **Ariano's**, 150 East 6th St. (247-8146), serves north Italian cusine for $8 to $15.

The Ore House, 147 6th St. (247-5707) is an Old West steak house, rustic and casual with entrées in the $10-$15 range; it's become the favorite gift certificate in the weekly Purgatory good-employee gift drawing. **The Red Snapper**, 144 East 9th St. (259-3417) also has fresh seafood in a saltwater aquarium setting. Entrées are about $10-$15, and they have wonderful vegetables and salads.

Pronto Pizza and Pasta, 160 East 6th St. (247-1510) is for families and those looking for a bargain, and features thin-crust pizza and fresh pasta. They feature an all-you-can-eat pasta buffet every weekend and offer deliveries in Durango.

Olde Tymer's Cafe, 1000 Main Ave. (259-2990) in the restored Wall Drug building is one of our top choices, with the best hamburgers in town and huge margaritas. Daily specials include $2.95 burgers Monday nights, $1.25 taco night on Friday—Purgatory employees jam the place these nights. Mexican food on weekends. **The Golden Dragon**, 992 Main Ave. (259-0956) serves Chinese food in huge portions.

Carver's Bakery and Brew Pub, 1022 Main Ave. (259-2545) is the best place in Durango for breakfast; muffins and bagels are fresh daily. It's a hangout for locals. If you prefer the eggs-and-bacon-type breakfast, head for the **Durango Diner**, 957 Main Ave. (247-9889). Sunday brunch at the **Red Lion Inn** is outstanding and a good choice for skiers departing on Sunday, since the inn is between the ski area and the airport.

Après-ski/nightlife

Skiers congregate in three places after the lifts close: **Farquahrt's**, where the music is the liveliest; **Mesquite's**, slightly more sedate; or **Sterling's**, which is the quietest. Nightlife at the ski area is limited to Farquahrt's, which has live bands Thursday through Sunday—they play two sets: 4 to 6 p.m. and 8:30 to 11.

A popular après-ski spot is the **Trimble Hot Springs**, about 20 miles from the ski area toward Durango. Natural mineral springs bubble into two outdoor therapy pools, one heated to 90 degrees and the other to 105. You can swim in the heated outdoor

Olympic-size pool and watch the heavens filled with stars. Private tub rentals and massages are available, too.

If you really want to tango, go to Durango. Catch the Durango Lift from the base area, $5 round trip; everything in town is in walking distance. Depending on the time of year, Durango is either jumping or mildly hopping. Spring Break, which goes on for several weeks in March and April, brings thousands of college students and the bars schedule lots of entertainment.

Durango has quite a variety of musical entertainment. Try **Farquahrt's** downtown for dancing, or the **Sundance Saloon**. Farquahrt's has an eclectic clientele—hippies, neo-hippies and clean-cut college students. The music ranges from reggae to blues, rock'n'roll, and oldies. The dance floor is small and crowded. The Sundance Saloon is a cowboy bar with Country & Western music and dancing.

Carver's Bakery and Brew Pub has strong and tasty locally brewed beers accompanied by fresh rolls from the bakery. To tourists who ask why a bakery is also a brewery, locals quote the sage who once said, "Beer is just a modified form of bread."

The bar on the second floor of **The Pelican's Nest** restaurant (658 Main Ave., 259-2888) has live jazz on the weekends and a jam session on Thursdays—bring your own instrument and join local amateur jazz musicians. On football Sundays, the best big screen in town is **A.J.'s Grill & Sports Bar** (128 E. 6th St., 247-5085), with pool tables, pinball and other games. Live bands play here occasionally, as do stand-up comics.

The other popular hangouts are the **Old Muldoon**, furnished in a dark Victorian style, and the **Solid Muldoon**, which is worth a visit just for the decor. Everything imaginable—typewriter, kayak, bubble gum machine (with gumballs), and the kitchen sink—hang from the ceiling. They spin a wheel of fortune every so often, setting the price of drinks for the next few minutes. Over at the **Diamond Belle Saloon** in the Strater Hotel, a piano player plunks out hit tunes from the Gay 90s—1890s, that is.

Child care

Teddy Bear Camp is for children two months to 3 years old. The nursery-age children (younger than two) receive quality day-care activities for $45 for a full day; $35 half day. Toddlers (2-3) get outdoor snowplay, arts and crafts, games, movies and storytime. Full day is $49, which includes lunch. Half-day, morning or afternoon, is $40 without lunch.

If you're not sure whether to put your child in day care or lessons, Purgatory's new **Kids Central service,** located on the second floor of the Village Center, will help. The staff will assess your child's abilities and interests, then escort him or her to the appropriate spot.

Teddy Bear Camp gets crowded on weekends and holidays, so make reservations. For evening babysitting, call the Teddy Bear Camp for a recommendation of a babysitter who can watch your kids while you enjoy a night out on the town. Call 247-9000.

Other activities

Buck's Livery has evening sleigh rides with dinner. Departures are at 4:30 and 7 p.m., and the cost is $31 for adults, $19 for kids 6 to 12, and $10 for kids under 6. Buck's also has hour-long daytime sleigh rides when enough people sign up, $12 for adults, $8 for kids; prices subject to change, reservations necessary.

High Country Snowmobile Tours offers guided snowmobile trips for $25 per hour, $40 for two riders on the same snowmobile. Call 247-9000, or visit the Purgatory Activities Booth on the second floor of the Village Center for reservations.

Getting there and getting around

Getting there: The Durango-La Plata County Airport, 44 miles south of Purgatory, is served by America West Express, Continental Express, United Express, and Mesa Airlines.

By car, the resort is 25 miles north of Durango, 330 miles southwest of Colorado Springs, 350 miles south of Denver, 232 miles north of Albuquerque, 470 miles northeast of Phoenix, and 825 miles northeast of Los Angeles. There are no major mountain passes from the south or west. Nevertheless, if you don't have four-wheel drive or snow tires, carry chains.

Getting around: The Durango Lift shuttle service runs four to five times a day between town and resort for $5 round trip. If you stay in Durango and use the shuttle just to get to and from skiing, you can get along without a car. But if you stay anywhere beyond a couple of blocks of Durango's main street, rent one.

Information/reservations

With one call you can arrange lodging, transportation, lifts, transfers, ski rentals, and lessons. Call Durango Central Reservations at (800) 525-0892. Ski area information is 247-9000. Telephone area code is 303.

Steamboat, Colorado

Its ad campaign would have you believe that horses outnumber the cars in the ski area parking lot, that cowboy hats and sheep-skin jackets are the preferred ski wear and that you should watch out for tobacco plugs on the dance floors. In reality, this is a big, sleek, modern ski area with few spittoons in sight.

Steamboat Village, the cluster of condos, shops and restaurants next to the ski mountain, is unpretentiously upscale. Boutiques offering elegant high-priced goods are intermixed with T-shirt shops; gourmet restaurants are within steps of ribs-and-hamburger eateries. You will see an occasional socialite swathed in fur, but right behind her will be someone wearing a 15-year-old ski parka. Everyone looks right at home.

In Steamboat Village, the only cowboy hats you're likely to see grace the heads of Steamboat's resident celebrity, Billy Kidd, and the ticket punchers in the gondola building. Venture into downtown Steamboat Springs, though, and you may see cowboys sauntering down Lincoln Avenue. Northwest Colorado still has many cattle ranches, so they'll probably be the real thing.

The downtown area—about 10 minutes by car and about a half hour by shuttlebus—squeezes into its dozen blocks a hodge-podge of old Victorian buildings, 1950s storefronts and a gas station or hardware store here and there. Good restaurants and nightlife havens are at the village, downtown, and on the highway linking the two. A shuttlebus runs between slopes and town every 10 minutes during the day (every 20 minutes at night) making it easy to enjoy the village, town and everything in between.

Steamboat is a particularly great place for non-skiers. In addition to the shopping, Steamboat has many activities that go beyond the usual sleigh rides and snowmobile tours. See Other Activities.

Steamboat Facts
Base elevation: 6,900'; **Summit elevation:** 10,568'; **Vertical drop:** 3,668 feet.
Number and types of lifts: 20—1 gondola, 2 quad superchairs, 1 quad chair, 6 triple chairs, 8 double chairs, 2 surface lifts
Acreage: 2,500 skiable acres **Snowmaking:** 13 percent of groomed trails.
Uphill capacity: 29,941 skiers per hour **Bed base:** 15,500

INSET: BURGESS CREEK AREA
as seen from the base of Burgess Creek Lift, looking toward Thunderhead

VAGABOND
VENEVE
SKYLINE
RAINBOW
HURRICANE
TWISTER
NELSON'S RUN
FOUR POINTS
STORM PEAK EXPRESS
DROP OUT
EGO
VORTEX
SURPRISE
SOWHAT
JAMES
BROWNS RUN
PERKLAND
WHITE OUT
WHY NOT
NORTHER
BLIZZARD
LIGHTNING
HEATHER
TOUR WAY
LON HAM
Top of ELKHEAD
TOWER
RUDI'S RUN
BURGESS CREEK LIFT LINE
VAGABOND
THUNDERHEAD
ARROWHEAD
THUNDERHEAD

◆◆ CHUTE TWO
◆◆ CHUTE THREE
◆◆ CHRISTMAS TREE BOWL
◆◆ EAST FACE
(◆◆ HIKE TO ... EXPERTS ONLY)

MT. WERNER

CHUTE ONE
THE RIDGE
CROWTRACK
BIG MEADOW
FLYING Z
BAR-UE (-UE)
CYCLONE
TYPHOON
TORNADO
DROP OUT
VORTEX
EGO
BURGESS C
VAGABOND
BETWIXT
WHY NOT
VAGABOND
ARROWHEAD
THUNDERHEAD
STORM PEAK
FOUR POINTS
NELSON

0:00

0:00

Steamboat®

Recreation on this public land is provided by a unique partnership between the Steamboat Ski & Resort Corporation and the Routt National Forest.

The Steamboat Ski & Resort Corporation is committed to the wise use of our natural resources, as well as the preservation and enhancement of the Routt National Forest. We hope you will join us in our commitment to preserve our environment by helping to keep your National Forest lands beautiful.

Steamboat Recycles: Please use recycling containers.

STEAMBOAT TOURING CENTER

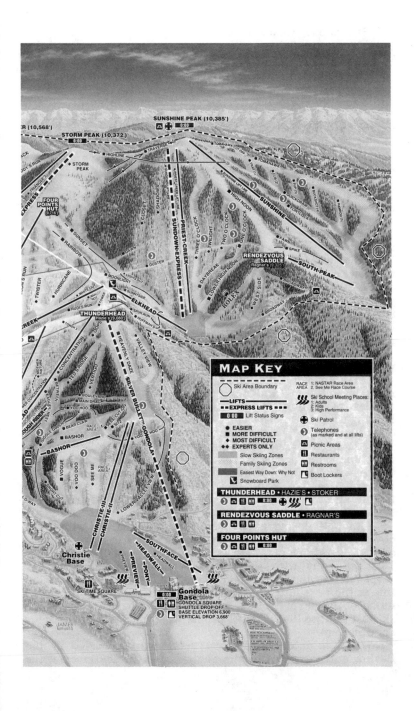

Where to ski

Expert skiing here means trees and lots of them. Steamboat has only a few extreme steeps, but the runs from the Priest Creek and Sundown chairs are tree skiing developed to an art. These trails have been expertly thinned, trees about 50 feet apart along the center, and as close as 10 feet at the edges. That may sound like a lot in the safety of your living room, but when you're gathering speed with not much room to bail out, those trees will seem inches apart.

Such trails produce gallons of adrenaline, even for the best of the best skiers, who now have to cope with a natural slalom course where the poles ain't spring-loaded. To avoid a trip down in a ski patrol sled, skiers must substitute excellent control and technique for simple daring: few skiers wish to repeat an intimate encounter with a silver aspen.

Other good areas for advanced and expert skiers are The Meadows area off to the north of Storm Peak. There, Chutes 1, 2 and 3, the Christmas Tree Bowl, the Ridge and Crowtrack provide great challenges. A favorite locals' area known as the Toutes was incorporated into the ski area boundary last season. This is extreme powder skiing at its best, and the short hike needed to reach it keeps all but the truly dedicated away.

Many of the black-diamond runs aren't as intimidating as you might think. Though the terrain gets steep in spots and the moguls pretty high, the trails are generally wide, allowing ample room for mistakes and recoveries. Westside, a black trail off Rendezvous Saddle, is steep but usually groomed. It's a good starting point for intermediates wondering if they can handle the other black runs.

Among the great cruisers are all the blue trails from the Sunshine Chair (locals scornfully call this area "Wally World"), Sunset and Rainbow off the Four Points lift and Vagabond and Heavenly Daze off Thunderhead Peak. If the crowds build, head for the short intermediate runs reached by the Bashor chair, which often is deserted.

Although Steamboat has plenty of terrain marked with green circles, it is not the best place for never-evers to learn. Novices start on gently sloping terrain at the bottom of the mountain. Two problems with this terrain: the natural fall line is perpendicular to the direction you ski to return to the lifts, and this is the area into which all the skiers on the various slopes funnel at the end of the day. Steamboat gets more than a million skiers a year, so that's a lot of people whizzing by the slow-going snowplowers.

With the exception of some gentle terrain served by the Bashor and the two Christie chairs, most of the green trails higher on the mountain are cat trails. Although they have a gentle grade, they also have some very narrow spots, they intersect advanced runs (where bombers are likely to use the intersection as a launching pad for the next black section), and they have some very intimidating dropoffs on the downhill side. If beginners are part of your group, *insist* that they enroll in ski school so that they will have a pleasant experience.

Mountain rating

Excellent tree skiing for experts, nice mogul runs for advanced intermediates, great cruisers for intermediates. Passable for beginners; not so great for never-evers.

Cross-country

The **Steamboat Ski Touring Center** at 2000 Golf Course Rd. (879-8180) has about 30 km. of groomed, set tracks winding along Fish Creek and the surrounding countryside. The touring center has group and private instruction for all ability levels, rentals at $10 a full day or $8 a half day, a restaurant, and backcountry guided tours. Trail fees are $9 a full day; $7 a half day after 1 p.m.

Track skiing also is available at **Howelsen Hill** in downtown Steamboat (303-879-2043) and at **Vista Verde** and **Home Ranch**, both guest ranches in the town of Clark, about 25 miles from Steamboat.

Rabbit Ears Pass has many marked backcountry ski trails ranging from 1.7 to 7 miles for cross-country skiers, intermediate and above. Call or visit the U.S. Forest Service Ranger Station (57 10th Street in downtown Steamboat, 879-1870) to get current ski conditions and safety tips. Other popular backcountry areas are Buffalo Pass, Pearl Lake State Park, Stagecoach State Recreation Area and Steamboat Lake State Park.

Snowboarding

Snowboarding is allowed on all lifts and trails. Lessons are offered daily and cost $40 for three hours. Steamboat has a new snowboard park, "Dude Ranch," with various jumps, slides and obstacles. Snowboarding has been so popular that the park will be expanded this season and more instructors will be hired.

Ski school (94/95 prices)

In addition to the normal ski-school classes, Steamboat has special classes or clinics for telemark skiing, snowboarding, bumps, powder, skiers 45 and older, women, disabled skiers—even a style clinic to teach those who can parallel how to look more graceful. Group clinics last three hours and cost $38 to $43. New this year are **The Black Diamond Club**, which shows skiers how to ski Steamboat's toughest terrain, and **Steamboat Teens,** for intermediate and advanced skiers aged 13-17.

Steamboat also has the **Billy Kidd Center for Performance Skiing** for intermediate and higher-level skiers. The clinics, which are offered only on specific dates throughout the season, refine the skier's technique in the bumps, through race gates and on tough terrain. The cost is $150 per day for adults; $135 for ages 13-17; $120 for kids.

Adult **group lessons** are $32 for two hours; $48 for all day, with multi-day discounts available. Lift/lesson packages start at $216 for three two-hour lessons and four days of lifts. **Private lessons** are $70 for one hour, $120 for two and $165 for three.

Children have the **Rough Rider program** (ages first grade-15) or **Sundance Kids** (ages 3 1/2-kindergarten). The Rough Rider lessons are $30 for two hours and $52 for all day (no lunch). Sundance Kids is $35 for half day; $52 for full day and lunch.

A special Ski Week package for adults is offered Monday through Friday and costs $137 for five two-hour lessons, an on-mountain barbecue, video analysis, NASTAR racing and a Ski Week pin. A similar children's program is $225, but the lessons are all day and all lunches are included. Lift tickets are extra.

Lift tickets (94/95 prices)

	Adult	Child (Up to 12) Senior (65-69)
One day	$42	$25
Three days	$126 ($42/day)	$75 ($25/day)
Five days	$205 ($41/day)	$125 ($25/day)

Children don't get multi-day discounts, but can qualify for the Kids Ski Free program, which works like this: One child skis free when a parent buys a lift ticket valid for at least five days and stays in a participating Steamboat property. If the parent rents skis, the child gets free rentals. The program is not available during the Christmas vacation period, and only two children per family may ski free, and then only if both parents are skiing.

Seniors 70 and older ski free.

Prices are lower during the value season, from the ski area's opening through mid-December.

Accommodations

The **Sheraton Steamboat Resort**, the only luxury full-service hotel, sits at the center of Steamboat Village and was refurbished to the tune of $2 million last season. The gondola building is about 25 yards from the front door. Nightly rates go from about $159 for a hotel room in January to $549 for a two-bedroom suite at Christmas or February/March.

Nearly all the other lodging at the ski area is in condominiums—hundreds of them surrounding the base area. The quality is quite good in the units that we inspected. Many properties have varying rates based on the time of the season. Before mid-December and after March 31 are the cheapest; January comes next, and Christmas and Presidents' Weekend are most expensive.

Torian Plum (879-8811 or 800-228-2458) is one of the best, with spotless rooms and facilities, an extremely helpful but not overbearing staff, and the ski area out one door and the top bars and restaurants out the other. Prices range from $170 to $480, depending on season. A three-bedroom unit goes for $250 per night early and $835 at Christmas.

Torian Plum's sister properties, **Bronze Tree** and **Trappeur's Crossing,** start at $160 and $135 in early season and top out at $700. Bronze Tree has no one-bedroom units, so the price is for a two-bedroom. Trappeur's Crossing is about two blocks from the lifts.

Generally, prices are based on how close the property is to the lifts. Those in the expensive category ($150 per night and up) include the **Best Western Ptarmigan Inn** (close to lifts, but farther from shopping and night life), **Norwegian Log Condominiums, Storm Meadows Resort** and **Thunderhead Lodge and Condominiums.**

More moderate facilities ($95-$150, generally) include **Timber Run Condominiums** (three outdoor hot tubs of varying sizes), **the Harbor Hotel** in downtown Steamboat (free bus pass is included with your stay), **The Lodge at Steamboat,** and **The Ranch at Steamboat** (great views of the ski hill and the broad Yampa Valley).

Economy lodging includes **the Alpiner Lodge** (downtown), **Shadow Run Condominiums** (500 yards from lifts), **Alpine Meadows Townhomes** (800 yards away) and **The Rockies** (one mile away).

The Steamboat Bed and Breakfast, (879-5724) just a couple of years old, is located at 442 Pine Street. The B&B has rooms filled with antiques. Winter rates are $70-$100 per double room with breakfast. No children, no pets.

Travelers who enjoy elegance will want to know that in the nearby town of Clark is one of only a handful of U.S. Relais and Chateau properties, **The Home Ranch.** Cabins are nestled in the aspens of the Elk River Valley. A stay here includes three gourmet meals per day in the main house and a shuttle to the ski area. Call 879-1700.

Steamboat Central Reservations will make suggestions to match your needs and desires. Let the reservationist know the price range, location and room requirements (quiet location, good for families, laundry or other special amenities). The number is (800) 922-2722.

Dining

Steamboat has a great variety of restaurants—varied menus, varied atmosphere and varied prices. The area has more than 50 restaurants, including one or more Cajun, Chinese, French, Italian, Russian and Scandinavian. Look for the Steamboat Dining Guide in your hotel or condo—it has menus and prices.

Katy Keck covers some of Steamboat's finest dining in detail in her Steamboat Savoir Faire chapter. Here are some that have moderate prices ($15-$20 per meal, including drinks) and a casual atmosphere:

At the ski area or close by:

Dos Amigos (879-4270) serves large portions of Tex-Mex food and sandwiches and is part of the infamous "Steamboat Triangle" après-ski circuit along with **Tugboat** and **Mattie Silks'** bar, and **The Cathouse Cafe.**

La Montaña (879-5800): see Savoir Faire chapter.

Grubstake (879-4448) serves hamburgers, steak sandwiches and the like.

Downtown:

Anderson & Friends, (879-0208), has fresh salads, homemade soups and sandwiches.

Old West Steakhouse (879-1441) is somewhat expensive, but packs in the crowds for steaks and seafood.

Giovanni's (879-4141) has not only Brooklyn-style Italian fare, but also what may be the largest collection of Brooklyn memorabilia this side of the borough.

BW-3 (879-2431) has several flavors of beef and buffalo burgers, and **The Cantina** (879-0826) is downtown's equivalent of Dos Amigos in food and bar. **Mazzola's** (879-2405), between downtown and the ski area, has the best pizza in the region.

You never need to leave the mountain for lunch, because several excellent restaurants are operated by or near the ski area. **Hazie's** and **Ragnar's,** both on the mountain, are wonderful for lunch as well as dinner. **The Grubstake** and **Tugboat** are both good base-area spots to grab lunch, or try **Buddy's Run.**

If you're in town for breakfast or lunch, try the **In-Season Bakery and Deli** (879-1840), which serves homemade soup, sandwiches and salads. Soothing classical music is played on the stereo system, and the pastries are everything you've ever dreamed of.

Good breakfast spots are **Winona's** or **The Shack Cafe** downtown, or **The Tugboat** at the base area. Avid skiers can board the gondola at 8 a.m. and have breakfast at **The Early Bird Breakfast Buffet** at the top of the gondola until the slopes open. Biscuits and gravy are a specialty, with other high-fuel fare also served, cafeteria-style.

Après-ski/nightlife

For immediate, relatively rowdy après-ski, the place to go is the **Inferno**, just behind the base of the Silver Bullet gondola. Skiers pack into the bar where each hour the bartender spins the shot wheel, setting prices anywhere from 35 to 95 cents. When 35 cents comes up, revelers buy shots by the tray.

Dos Amigos, as noted, is one leg of the "Steamboat Triangle." You have margaritas here, then head for the **Cathouse Cafe** and **Tugboat** for beer or mixed drinks. Friday is Zoo Night at the Cathouse, where any beer that has an animal on the label or in the name is $2.

Downtown, the **Old Town Pub** and **The Steamboat Yacht Club** are popular après-ski locations.

Quieter après-ski locations on the mountain include **HB's** in the Sheraton or **Innerlinks**, which had a guitar player singing folk/pop/country tunes the week we were there. Steamboat also has two brew pubs, **Heavenly Daze**, in Ski Time Square at the ski area, and **Steamboat Brewery & Tavern** downtown.

Late-night places include **Inferno, Dos Amigos** and **Tugboat**, all with live music and lots of people.

Downtown, the lively spots include **BW-3, The Steamboat Saloon** (where you'll find many cowboys who drink long-necked beers and dance the two-step) and **The Old Town Pub**. On Wednesdays, head for **the Steamboat Yacht Club** to watch the ski jumping on Howelsen Hill, and anytime, try one of the dozen vodkas at **Gorky Park**, with Russian (and neighboring republics) entertainment.

Steamboat has two movie theaters downtown and one at the mountain, if that's your idea of nightlife. A night trip to Strawberry Park Hot Springs is great fun (See Other Activities). **Buddy's Run** usually has comedy Tuesday through Friday night, and occasionally a big-name artist such as Lyle Lovett will perform at the **Sheraton**.

Child care

Steamboat has a well-deserved reputation for building a family-friendly ski resort with excellent day care.

The **Kiddie Corral** takes children from 6 months to first grade. The Sundance Kids program for children 3 1/2 to first grade is detailed in the ski school section of this chapter. Buckaroos aged 2 1/2 to 3 1/2 get all-day child care and a one-hour ski lesson for $100. Nursery care covers 6 months to 6 years who will not be skiing or playing in the snow. They get games, puppet shows, movies, crafts, rest time and stories for $52 all day or $35 for half day. Three or more days costs $47 per day, lunch included. Parents must bring a lunch for children under 2.

Kids Adventure Club at Night is an evening care program for children 2 1/2 to 12 years every Tuesday through Saturday from 6 to 10:30 p.m. Snacks, games, video and rest time are included for $6 per hour. A second child is an additional $3 per hour, and three or more children are $10 per hour for the group.

Reservations are required for all care programs, plus a deposit of $25 per day is required when reservations are made. That deposit is refundable provided changes are made 24 hours or more in advance. Call Steamboat Central Reservations (800-922-2722) or the Kids Vacation Center, 879-6111, ext. 218.

Other activities

Steamboat has so much to do *off* the mountain, it's tempting to skip the skiing. Here is a mere sampling of what you can do:

• Soak in the natural thermal waters at **Strawberry Park Hot Springs,** about 10 miles north of the ski area, where it comes out of the ground at about 145 degrees. Fortunately it then combines with cold creek water to form three pools of varying temperature. Admission to the hot springs is $7; a tour (transportation and admission) is $18. However, unless you have four-wheel drive or chains, spend the extra for the tour—the road to the springs is narrow, slick and winding. Strawberry Park is open from 10 a.m. to 10 p.m. during the week and stays open a couple of hours later on weekends. Helpful info: After dark, many bathers go without suits (unless it's a clear, moonlit night, you won't see much). The only place to change is an unheated teepee, so wear your swimsuit under your clothes, but take dry clothes. You will also need a large trash bag to put your clothes in; otherwise steam from the pools and the cold air will freeze them. (The tour company will provide you with one.)

• Ride in a hot-air balloon. Four balloon companies offer rides. **Balloons Over Steamboat, Ltd.** (879-3298) is the oldest company in town; others are **Pegasus Balloon Tours** (879-9191), **Eagle Balloon Tours** (879-8687) and **Aero Sports Balloonists** (879-7433). A half-hour balloon ride runs about $75—sounds steep, but the view and experience are spectacular. Winter flights usually go twice in the morning, 8 and 10 a.m. and just before sunset.

• Learn to drive on ice. Now in its 11th season, the **Jean-Paul Luc Winter Driving School** (879-6104) teaches how to drive skillfully and confidently on ice and snow. French race-car driver Jean-Paul Luc and his staff give half-day, full-day and multi-day lessons on a specially constructed course. The school office is in the Torian Plum shopping mall at the ski area.

• **Bobsledding** down a 5,000-foot lighted track is available from 6 to 10 p.m. every night, weather permitting, at Howelsen Hill in downtown Steamboat Springs. Helmets and sleds are provided, and rides cost $7 each, or $50 for a 10-ride punch card.

• **Shopping** opportunities are many and varied, both in the village and downtown.

• The **Steamboat Activity Center**, with a location at 720 Lincoln Avenue and another in Gondola Square at the ski area, is a one-stop information and reservation center. Call 879-2062, or (800) 488-2062 toll-free.

Getting there and getting around

Getting there: Steamboat Springs has two airports. The closer, **Steamboat Springs Airport**, is serviced by Continental Express from Denver. **Yampa Valley Airport** at Hayden, about 20 minutes away, handles jets—American, United, United Express and Northwest have direct flights there from more than 100 North American cities.

Panoramic Coaches' Steamboat Express is available daily from Denver's Stapleton International Airport. For schedule and information, call (800) 525-2628.

Steamboat is 157 miles northwest of Denver via I-70 through the Eisenhower Tunnel, north on Highway 9 to Kremmling, then west on U.S. 40 to Steamboat Springs. Plan on at least three hours by car.

Getting around: A car is optional. Steamboat has an excellent bus system between town and ski area running every 20 minutes. The fare is 50 cents each way. Exact change is necessary, but a buck will pay for two people. If you are going to commute between town and ski area a lot, rent a car; otherwise, take the bus.

Information/reservations

Steamboat Central Reservations is a one-call service that can book airlines, lodging, lifts, transfers and many activities. The number is (800) 922-2722. Telephone area codes are 303 unless otherwise noted.

Steamboat Savoir Faire

Without a doubt, the most impressive evening in Steamboat starts at Gondola Square at the Silver Bullet terminal. Here, you set off on the complimentary journey into the stars on the Silver Bullet. This roomy gondola (in New York, we would call it an apartment with a view) is complete with blankets for the crisp ride to the top of Thunderhead. The view is breathtaking.

Once on top your reservation will be waiting at **Hazie's** (879-6111). Hazie's offers exquisite nouvelle continental cuisine, with unbeatable views. The Steamboat Mountain executive chef, Danish-born Morten Hoj, has created a menu that will intrigue any palate. Choose from one of five delicious appetizers—escargots with garlic herb butter and French brie were delicious, as was the cheese and shittake ravioli. The second course allows the soup du jour or clam chowder, or the Hazie's salad with mixed greens, grapefruit, roasted hazelnuts, peppers and mushrooms.

Try the very popular Châteaubriand Béarnaise or rack of lamb roasted with garlic. Seafood entrées might include charbroiled salmon with fresh pear salsa. There are also several daily specials, which have included grilled swordfish and veal prime ribs, both cooked to perfection. Dessert offerings vary, but are sure to include the ethereal white chocolate mousse. Let the sommelier help you choose from Hazie's list of over 90 wines. Open from Tuesday to Saturday, Hazie's offers this prix fixe four-course dinner, including the gondola ride and an after-dinner drink, for $45 (discounts for children aged 6 to 12, those 5 and younger eat free).

Hazie's also serves lunch (reservations recommended) from 11:30 a.m. to 2:30 p.m., featuring an assortment of soups and salads, and entrées like Maryland crab cakes, lemon pepper chicken breast, or the popular Hazie's burger.

If you find your skiing keeps you over in the Sunshine Peak area, however, try **Ragnar's** at Rendezvous Saddle featuring Scandinavian and continental cuisine in an atmosphere reminiscent of Steamboat's earlier days. Lunch is served from 11:30 a.m. to 2:15 p.m., and reservations are suggested—879-6111. Start with a smorgasbord platter, an assortment of Scandinavian herring, salami, ham, Danish paté and Nordic cheeses. Entrées range from daily specials such as mesquite-grilled chicken Florentine to wienerschnitzel and chicken breast Lillehammer (sautéed to a golden brown and served with a juniper-lingonberry cream sauce). Prices range from $8.25 for a mesquite-grilled hamburger to $12.95 for Norwegian salmon.

At night, five times a week (Tuesday through Saturday), Ragnar's offers a prix fixe Scandinavian menu at $59 for adults. This evening also starts at Gondola Square, but once off the Silver Bullet at the top of Thunderhead, you climb into a sleigh to continue your journey to Rendezvous Saddle. You'll want at least one mug of hot spiced glögg before relaxing to music and enjoying the meal. For reservations, call 879-6111, Ext. 320.

For Steamboat's pinnacle of French dining, try **L'apogee** (911 Lincoln Avenue, 879-1919). Chef/owner Jamie Jenny, along with chef Richard Billingham, has created a casually elegant ambiance where he serves some of the area's finest French food, with an unparalleled wine list. Several specials, often wild game, are offered each day. Menu staples include the center-cut filet of beef, wrapped in applewood-smoked bacon, and topped with parsley-and-parmesan breadcrumbs, capers and roasted red peppers. Appetizers start at $7.75 and entrées range from $18 for roasted chicken with truffle oil to $26.50 for a rack of Colorado lamb with a macadamia-nut stuffing.

While the food cannot be too highly praised, it is the wine list that is truly impressive. There are more than 500 wines, ranging from $12 to $1,000 a bottle, all maintained in three temperature-controlled cellars. L'apogee also features Steamboat's only cruvinet system, serving over 30 wines and ports by the glass.

This talented kitchen crew also services the more casual **Harwig's Grill** (same address, no reservations). Jenny's grill menu reflects his passion for Southeast Asian flavors. Start with the Shu Mei dim sum, chestnut- and pork-filled wontons with a fiery soy dipping sauce, Jamaican jerk chicken, or the madras veggies. The menu offerings range from Hunter's stew to Down Under lamb burgers, but it is the chalkboard that will tell the real story of the day. All fish can be ordered sautéed, poached or grilled. First-time clients are often surprised when they see jackalope on the board, but will take Jenny's humor more seriously after trying the delicious mignonette of rabbit tenderloin and émincée of elk, with a chasseur sauce. Prices range from $3.25 for appetizers to $8-$11 for entrées. The list of 60 wines here is under $21 per bottle. Daily from 5 p.m.

As if Jenny et al weren't busy enough with L'apogee and Harwig's, they also are in the kitchens at **Cipriani's** and **Roccioso's** in the Thunderhead Lodge. These restaurants are open daily, serving fine cuisine in the evenings only, 5:30 to 10:30 p.m. Call 879-8824 for reservations.

Cipriani's offers traditional northern Italian fare, with Jenny's special flair: tender fry-aged Colorado filet is char-grilled to perfection and finished with a Montepulciano wine and roasted garlic; veal marsala is dressed up with earthy morels.

Entrée prices range from $14.50 for pasta primavera to $24.50 for center-cut Colorado lamb chops with a Chianti glaze.

Roccioso's shows the Italian flair, but at more moderate prices. Starters include a cheesy artichoke perfumed with garlic and a colorful medley of vegetables and antipasto. Entrées are under $11. Try the calamari alla diavola.

For more than Mex, don't miss **La Montaña**, (879-5800) located at 2500 Village Drive. Chef Michael Fragola has created an inventive menu that goes way beyond tacos and fajitas. Start with the award-winning grilled braided sausage, a trio of elk, lamb and chorizo sausages, braided together and mesquite-grilled. The chef's keen understanding of southwestern ingredients is reflected well in an ever-changing list of specials. Try mesquite grilled sea scallops on smoked corn salsa with a guajillo prickly pear sauce or the yellowfin tuna steak seared with a pepita crust and served with a margarita beurre blanc. For traditionalists, the fajitas are cooked to sizzling perfection—and not just chicken and beef. They also are available in pork, shrimp and melt-in-your-mouth elk.

Fragola also has a light cuisine menu, with such greats as sweet pepper relleño, stuffed with corn, chilis, mushrooms and low-fat mozzarella. Appetizer prices are about $7 and entrées about $10 for Tex-Mex taco dinners and $16 to $22 for the southwestern specials. Save room for the fried ice cream with three sauces—caramel, chocolate and raspberry.

Now in its fourth season is the **Steamboat Smokehouse** at 912 Lincoln Ave. Here, in a no credit card, no reservations, no-nonsense atmosphere, are some of Colorado's best Texas-style hickory smoked barbecued anything—you name it—brisket, sausage, turkey, chicken, ham and even a daily road kill special (open 11 a.m. to 10 p.m.).

A popular seafood restaurant is the **Steamboat Yacht Club**, at 811 Yampa Avenue on the banks of the river. The dining room overlooking the water is a great place for watching night skiing or Wednesday night ski jumping on Howelson Hill. Offering both lunch (11:30 a.m. to 2:30 p.m.) and dinner (5:30 to 10 p.m.) daily, there is a wide selection of fresh fish. The menu is designed to mix and match fish, cooking techniques and sauces to suit your tastes. Try the yellowfin or mahi mahi, grilled or blackened, then choose from a citrus mango butter, a Szechwan style or Santa Fe style sauce. Prices are a reasonable $15.50. The Yacht Club also has a full selection of meat and poultry. For reservations, call 879-4774.

If you are unable to choose between these excellent dining spots, plan a trip back for the Annual Sizzlin' Chefs Classic, a grilling contest sponsored by the local culinary association.

Telluride, Colorado

Far away from the major skiing hoopla of Colorado, skiers find compact, Victorian, picturesque Telluride. The town, huddled beneath the soaring peaks of the San Juan Mountains in a narrow and spectacularly beautiful valley, is packed with history and legend. Appropriately, surrounding it is some of America's most legendary expert skiing.

You wouldn't imagine anyone sticking a ski resort way out here, starting from scratch—that would be crazy. No, Telluride is the creation of the era of gold and silver mining. The energies poured into digging out precious metals also created the world's first practical alternating-current electrical system for mine equipment, and one of the best town water supplies. But gold meant money, money meant banks, and banks attracted robbers: here Robert Leroy Parker, a.k.a. Butch Cassidy, robbed his first bank. He reportedly practiced his getaway over and over before the robbery, timing his escape down the main street.

Jack Dempsey worked here as a bouncer and dishwasher before becoming famous. Telluride was even witness to politics (of a relatively harmless variety): in 1903 William Jennings Bryan delivered one of his renowned renditions of the "Cross of Gold" speech from the front of the New Sheridan Hotel.

In 1964, Telluride was declared a national historic landmark *in toto*. The main street still appears much as it did when Butch Cassidy began his career, and the original houses around the town have remained unchanged as residents work to restore the old Victorian finishes. And the mountains surrounding the town remain as imposing, beautiful and majestic as ever.

What has changed is the skiing. Telluride will celebrate its 22nd year as a ski resort, changing from a place dedicated to the extremely steep to an all-round area with some of the best beginner terrain in Colorado.

Another change is the emergence of a different face of Telluride, built on the opposite side of the ski mountain and

---

Telluride Facts

Base elevation: 8,725'; **Summit elevation (lift-served):** 11,890'; **Vertical drop:** 3,165'
Number and types of lifts: 10—1 quad superchair, 2 triple chairs, 6 double chairs, and 1 surface lift. **Acreage:** 1,050 skiable acres **Percent of snowmaking:** 15 percent.
Uphill capacity: 10,000 skiers per hour **Bed base:** 4,000

called Mountain Village. This development offers excellent access to the mountain, but it doesn't have the soul of original Telluride. This large, master-planned community is similar to those found at other modern resorts—Beaver Creek, Snowmass, Stratton. It definitely is not part of the legendary historic town of Telluride in feeling, in experience, in shopping, or in nightlife, though both share the same ski area.

Where to ski

Start with what put Telluride on the skiers' map—The Plunge and Spiral Stairs. This duo, where left ungroomed, is as challenging a combination of steep bumps as you can find anywhere. If you manage to get down without too many bruises or sore spots, you can savor some sense of accomplishment. Mammoth is an alternate trail but not any easier. Formerly untamed Bushwacker is just as steep, but these days its massive bumps have succumbed to winch-cat grooming.

Even skiers dropping down below the base of Chair 9 will find a very narrow trail, about two or three moguls wide, which requires better than intermediate skills to negotiate well. For the basic intermediate skier who glides off at the top of Chair 9, the only real alternative is to follow See Forever around to Lookout or to the Gorrono Basin. New trail maps list The Plunge as a double-square advanced run since mountain operations began grooming sections of the run to open it to advanced intermediates. Groomed, this run is a thrill, allowing experts to play on a steep cruise not found on many other mountains in North America, and letting advanced intermediates ski gingerly down.

Perhaps the drive to label The Plunge and its sister super-steep trails as intermediate has been spearheaded by Telluride's limited intermediate terrain. The only true intermediate terrain is in the Gorrono Basin, but Telluride Face with its grooming is now acceptable for advanced intermediates. In fact, even without adding terrain, increased grooming is making more and more runs acceptable for intermediates each year.

At the other extreme, Sunshine Peak is underwhelming, more suitable for advanced beginners than solid intermediates. The most fun for an intermediate, besides a careful exploration of the Plunge and Spiral Stairs face, would be repeated trips up Chair 4, and down Peek a Boo, Humbolt Draw, Pick and Gad and Tomboy. The "expert" runs off Chair 6 are also short and manageable

Telluride strengthened its expert hand with the opening of an additional 400 acres of glade and above-timberline skiing in the Gold Hill area two years ago. These double-diamond runs require a hike to the 12,247-foot mark (if you want to go to the top of in-bounds skiing), which makes Telluride's legal vertical drop 3,522 feet.

Beginners will find this one of the best places in the world to learn to ski. The Meadows has for years been considered a perfect beginners area. With the construction of what is touted as the world's longest quad superchair lift, Telluride has four of the longest and best teaching slopes in skidom.

Mountain rating

Telluride is a rite of passage for experts. It's a chance to test oneself against the most consistent steeps and monstrous bumps most resorts allow to grow. For intermediates, Telluride is making a serious effort to groom more formerly expert slopes, and plenty of challenges exist for anyone trying to graduate to the expert level. If you are an intermediate whose trademark trails are long, mellow cruising terrain, head elsewhere. For beginners, there are few better places to be introduced to skiing.

Telluride does something that more ski areas should do: its trail-rating system incorporates six levels instead of three or four. Intermediate skiers should start with the single-blue-square runs, then graduate to the double-blues before tackling a black diamond run.

Snowboarding

Snowboarding is allowed on the entire mountain. Beginning snowboarding lessons cost $60, including lift and rentals.

Cross-country

Here again the spectacular scenery makes cross-country a joy to experience. For high-mesa cross-country skiing this area is difficult to beat. The **Telluride Nordic Center** offers a 50-km. network of groomed trails around town and the ski area.

Lessons are also available. Track fees are free or $12, depending on what track you use. Adult and children's group lessons are priced at $35. Full day backcountry tours cost $45. Equipment rentals—skis, boots and poles—for a full day are $12 for adults or children. A day on your downhill ski pass can be exchanged for a day of cross-country, including equipment, a two-hour clinic and track fees.

Guided tours wind through the San Juan Mountains and a five-hut, 45-mile network. Huts are approximately six miles apart and each is equipped with padded bunks, propane cooking appliances and a big potbelly stove. The same rates apply to all programs: about $19 per person cabin fee and $25 a day for provisions, which covers breakfast, lunch and dinner. The $100-a-day guide fee is split between the members of the group. Groups are held to a maximum of eight skiers.

Ski school (94/95 prices)

Telluride's 150-instructor ski school, run by Annie Vareille-Savath for the past 15 years, has a good reputation. A successful learning experience usually requires two main ingredients: good instruction and appropriate terrain. Telluride has both.

Group lessons cost $35 for a half day (two and a half hours).

Private lessons are $65 an hour, with each additional skier paying $25. A full day is $350, $75 for each additional skier.

The **Children's Ski Center** (728-4424), takes ages 3 to 12. Lessons and lunch cost $45 per half-day; $60 full-day; $150, three days; $250, five days.

Lift ticket rates for children in Children's Ski School are $12 a day for those from 6 to 12 years and free for those 5 and younger. Rental equipment per day costs $12.

Workshops on powder, bumps, steeps, racing clinics and a video analysis of your skiing, cost the same as normal clinics.

Women's Week is a program that includes lifts, races, video analysis, seminars, and wine and cheese parties. Perhaps because Telluride's ski school is run by a woman, this program is one of the best and longest-running of this type. Two of our contributors have participated in past years, and both made big strides in their skiing ability. Concurrent men's weeks have identical prices to the women's program.

Ski school also offers telemark instruction. NASTAR two-and-a-half hour courses costs $35, or practice on your own for $5 (two runs) and $1 for each additional run.

Lift tickets (94/95 prices)

	Adult	Child (6-12) Senior (65-69)
One day	$43	$24
Three days	$123 ($41/day)	$48 ($24/day)
Five days	$190 ($38/day)	$120 ($24/day)

Telluride's shoulder-season discounted rates, good November 23-December 16 and April 2-10, are $29 per day for adults and $20 for children 6-12 and seniors 65-69.

Other multiday discounts available, as are half-day tickets. Skiers aged 70 and older and children 5 and younger ski free.

Accommodations

In Telluride you can stay down in the old town or in the Mountain Village. We start with accommodations in town; lodging in the mountain village is listed at the end of this section. Most lodging prices include lift tickets.

The San Sofia Bed & Breakfast (800-537-4781) the upscale property in town, is near the Oak Street lift. Rates are $130-$195. This cozy B&B is considered one of Telluride's best, with exceptional service.

The historic **New Sheridan Hotel** (728-4351) is a step back in time. It's on Colorado Avenue close to everything, with a skiers' shuttle stop outside the front door. Rates: $100 to $145.

The Johnstone Inn (728-3316 or 800-752-1901) is a B&B with eight small, quaint rooms with private bath and a full breakfast every morning for $125 to $145 per night, and **Bear Creek Bed & Breakfast** (728-6681 or 800-338-7064) has ten rooms with private bath and TV, roof deck and sauna and steam room for $60 to $155 per night.

The **Manitou Hotel** (800-237-0753 or 800-233-9292 in Colorado) is decorated with country fabrics and antiques. It is near the Oak Street lift and is a two-minute walk from the center of the town. Each room has a double bed, and the price includes continental breakfast. Rates: $145-$197. **The Ice House Lodge,** a block from the Oak Street lift, has been turned into a luxury hotel. You'll get 6-foot tubs, comforters, balconies, and custom furniture. Rates are $120 to $385 a night.

The Riverside Condos are perhaps the nicest in town and located near the base of the Oak Street lift. **The Manitou Riverhouse** is just as near to the lifts but be ready for lots of stairs if you rent here. Around the Coonskin Base check into **Viking Suites Hotel, Etta Place** and **Cimarron Lodge,** where you can almost literally fall out of bed and onto the lifts, and the **Tower House** about two blocks from the lifts. More moderately priced units are **West Willow** and **Coronet Creek**.

In the Mountain Village

This section of Telluride will eventually be connected with the historic downtown by a three-stage gondola that will run morning to evening. For this season, though, access to the historic town is around the base of the mountain by road.

Pennington's (800-543-1437) is the B&B of choice for the utmost in elegance. The rooms are giant and the views magnificent. The only problem is that you are not *really* in Telluride. Prices are $150 to $260 per room with breakfast.

The most luxurious property is the massive **Peaks at Telluride Hotel and Spa,** with 177 rooms and a 42,000-square-foot spa. Rates for deluxe accommodations are $210-$700 per night. Call 728-6800 or (800) 223-6725.

For deluxe accommodations on the mountain, try the **Telemark Condominiums** for $535 to $775 for a group of eight to ten people, **Columbia Place Lodge,** $180-$300 for four persons, or **Kayenta Legend House,** $380-$525 for six people.

Telluride has also organized a **Regional Half-Price Program** with the towns of Cortez, Montrose, Ouray, Rico, Ridgway, Mancos and Dolores. If you stay in one of these spots, you can get half-price lift tickets—$14.50 during bargain season and $21.50 during regular season. **Telluride Central Reservations** can book lodging and more, (800) 525-3455.

Dining

Telluride's upscale dining is found in three downtown restaurants.—all expensive, with entrées in the $15-$24 range. **La Marmotte** located near the Ice House Lodge serves French cuisine; 728-6232. **Silverglade**, 115 W. Colorado; 728-4943, with a menu dedicated to California and a grill. There is plenty of fresh fish, and tasty desserts. A new entry is **221 S. Oak** (it's both the name and address; 728-9507) in a Victorian house with regional American specialties that vary daily in response to the freshest products available.

For more casual and moderate dining: **Leimgruber's** serves German cooking and beer imported from Munich with Gemütlichkeit: 728-4663. **Eddie's** serves up great pizzas. **The Floradora** claims the best burgers in town. **Excelsior Cafe** is known for mid-priced North Italian cuisine. Many say it's the best value in town.

Baked in Telluride does fresh bagels each morning. **The Steaming Bean** serves tempting pastries and the best cup of coffee in town. **The T-ride Country Club** offers cook-your-own steaks and seafood. **Sofio's** serves good Mexican cuisine but be prepared for a long wait—it's worth it. Have a margarita. The **Powderhouse** serves local specialties as well as their secret Powderhouse Cocktail. **The San Juan Brewing Company** provides good basic chicken, fish and beef with local brew.

In the mountain village try a restaurant in the Peaks at Telluride Resort and Spa (728-6800)—**Legend's at the Peaks** with Southwestern cuisine. **Evangeline's** (728-9717) has good Cajun Creole cooking.

If you are staying in a condo you can call for deliveries. Eddie's delivers pizza—728-5335. **Telluride Room Service** (728-4343) delivers gourmet meals from the town's restaurants. **Details** at 728-6048 will even do all your pre-arrival supermarket shopping so your condo shelves are filled before you unpack.

Après ski/nightlife

Telluride makes up in spirit what it lacks in number of bars. For immediate après-ski, stop at **Leimgruber's Bierstube** near the Coonskin Lift for a selection of great beer and a sure shot at meeting folks. For live music the place to be is the **Fly Me to the Moon Saloon** with live entertainment Thursday through Saturday. **The Last Dollar Saloon** has the best selection of imported beer in Telluride, plus pool tables and dart boards. The old Victorian **New Sheridan Bar** is one of the "must sees" in Telluride to experience the essence of the Old West.

Child care

Children's programs for infants through age 12 are in the Village Nursery and Children's Center near the Mountain Village Base Facility. Children's instruction programs are detailed in the Ski School section.

The **Village Nursery** takes children 2 months to 3 years. Cost: infants younger than 12 months, $8 an hour or $45 for a full day; 12 months and older for all day with lunch, $45; half day, $35; call 728-6727 or (800) 544-0507.

Other activities

Shopping: Telluride's main street seems to be populated by T-shirt shops, but you can find some gems, such as **The Bounty Hunter,** 226 W. Colorado, with authentic leather Western wear and handmade cowboy hats; **Mendota,** 129 W. Colorado, with Native American jewelry and artifacts; and **At Home in Telluride**, 137 E. Colorado, a quaint shop with distinctive housewares. They'll ship your purchases home.

Helicopter skiing is run by Helitrax for downhill and cross-country enthusiasts. Box 1560, Telluride CO 81435; 728-4904.

Telluride also has **sleigh rides** from Deep Creek Sleigh Rides, 728-3565; **hot-air ballooning** from San Juan Balloon Adventures, 626-5495; **snowmobile tours** from Telluride Outside, 728-3895 and a town **ice-skating rink.**

Getting there and getting around

Getting there: Telluride has a small, weather-plagued airport five miles from town. United Express has daily flights from Denver; and America West Express has daily flights from Phoenix. Montrose, 65 miles from Telluride, is where most skiers arrive, either by plan or by a diversion from Telluride when weather doesn't permit landing. It is served by United Express from Denver, United from Chicago and Los Angeles, and Continental from Houston.

Ground transport is provided by Telluride Transit (728-6000); Skip's Taxi (728-6667); and Western Express (249-8880). All require 24-hour advance reservation for Montrose pickup.

Getting around: A car is unnecessary. The town is just eight blocks long, so you can walk anywhere. A free bus service runs around town and between town and the Mountain Village.

Information/reservations

Telluride Central Reservations: One call handles everything: (800) 525-3455 (nationwide) or 728-4431.

Telluride Mountain Village Resort Management Company call (800) 544-0507 or (303) 728-8000.

Telluride Resort Accommodations also can help with lifts and lodging: (800) 538-7754 (LETS-SKI) or 728-6621.

The local area code is 303.

Vail
Beaver Creek Resort
Colorado

In skier survey after skier survey, Vail usually is found near the top—never, it seems, lower than two or three. It is a *complete* area, lacking none of the essential ingredients that form the magical stew of a world-class ski resort for the masses. Vail has both an quaint, ersatz Old World village atmosphere and condominum convenience, raucous nightlife and quiet lounges, fine dining and pizzeria snacking. Its off-slope activities are unsurpassed—shopping, skating, movies, museums, sleigh riding and so much more—everything lots of money can buy. Bring lots of money. But, village and expenses aside, there is above all The Mountain.

Vail Mountain is a single stoop-shouldered behemoth so massive that every crease and wrinkle in its cape becomes another entire section to ski or bowl to explore. Though it does not have the ultra-steeps or deeps of some of its Rocky Mountain cousins, what it has is a huge front face of long and very smooth

Vail Facts
Base elevation: 8,200'; **Summit elevation:** 11,450'; **Vertical drop:** 3,250 feet.
Number and types of lifts: 25–8 quad superchairs, 1 gondola, 2 quad chairs, 3 triple chairs, 6 double chairs, 5 surface lifts
Acreage: 4,020 skiable acres **Snowmaking:** 9.75 percent
Uphill capacity: 41,855 skiers per hour **Bed base:** 41,305 within 10 miles

Beaver Creek Resort Facts
Base elevation: 8,100'; **Summit elevation:** 11,440'; **Vertical drop:** 3,340 feet
Number and types of lifts: 10–2 quad superchairs, 4 triple chairs, 4 doubles
Acreage: 1,085 skiable acres **Snowmaking:** 33 percent.
Uphill capacity: 19,075 skiers per hour **Bed base:** 4,700 at resort, 4,000 in Avon

Arrowhead-at-Vail Facts
Base elevation: 7,400'; **Summit elevation:** 9,100'; **Vertical drop:** 1,700 feet
Number and types of lifts: 2–1 quad superchair, 1 surface lift
Acreage: 180 skiable acres **Snowmaking:** 40 percent **Uphill capacity:** 1,707 skiers/hour
Bed base: About 80 at the base; much more nearby

cruisers, and an enormous back-bowl experience of wide-open adventure unlike anything this side of the Atlantic. Vail's network of eight quad superchairs is also the largest in the country. Combined, the mountain and its lift system let you do more skiing and less back-tracking than at almost any other resort you can name.

As important as it is, skiing only constitutes part of the total ski vacation experience. A true world-class resort has to have amenities and atmosphere, and Vail is one of a kind in both areas. You'll find city conveniences such as 24-hour pharmacies (which you don't appreciate until you need medication in a more rural ski resort), but you won't find the typical Colorado mining-town atmosphere: Vail never was a mining town. About 30 years ago, it was a sheep pasture; developers who saw the potential of the mountain built a village styled after an Austrian ski town. Vail gets a lot of ribbing about its Europe-in-the-USA look, but lots of people apparently like it—Vail consistently gets about 1.5 million skier visits each year, more than any other ski area in North America.

Because of its immense size, Vail is ultimately urban skiing—this city-town just doesn't feel rural. It bustles with traffic and people jams in peak periods. You won't see too many stars at night—too many streetlights. And far too many shop personnel are standoffish at their best, and downright rude at worst. Vacationing New Yorkers are astounded at the déja vu.

But for many of Vail's urban dweller customers Vail is enough to make them feel they are getting away from it all. They find the well-lit streets comforting. They don't want to engage in small talk with every shopkeeper in town and they are used to high prices. Vail's bargains are very few and extremely far between—even the parking (in a multistory garage) costs $8 a day.

Beaver Creek Resort

Don't visit Vail without spending a day at Beaver Creek Resort, Vail's sister area 10 miles west on Interstate 70. Beaver Creek Resort is a master-planned complex of condominiums, hotels, a small shopping mall and excellent base facilities. Its purpose, quite simply, is to plop those with a taste for being pampered squarely in the lap of luxury.

Beaver Creek is a monument to the excesses and comfortable decay of the 80s. The initial marketing concept was something like, "If you aren't worth a million dollars, don't even bother coming here." Corporations built extravagant, practically secret, executive hideaways here, callously squandering enough in stockholder funds to pain a compassionate capitalist. It's not all that pretentious any more. Greedy corporate barons have been canned and the companies have been forced to sell off their majestic retreats, but it still leaves a bad aftertaste.

Though one can still search out a few party types listening to live après-ski music in the main lodge, most Beaver Creek skiers disappear into expensive condos or multimillion-dollar homes that dot the golf course on the way up to the resort.

Vail Associates recently purchased a small ski resort, Arrowhead, which has an upscale golf resort at its base. Arrowhead is close enough to Beaver Creek the plan is to connect the ski areas with another Disneyesque Alpine village built in between them.

To get a fix on Beaver Creek Resort, drive up the mountain and pay to park in the underground parking (shuttlebuses to Vail also depart on the half hour for a cost of $2, or you can park free at the Beaver Creek base and take a free shuttle up). As you exit the parking garage directly into the main base-lodge area, stop at the roaring fire pit outside the Hyatt Regency. Order a hot toddy from the waiter and wave to the guests in the outdoor heated swimming pool or bubbling and steaming Jacuzzis. Wonder what the poor slobs back at the office are doing. Now you're in a Beaver Creek state of mind.

Where to ski

Vail Mountain is one of the biggest single ski mountains in North America. But it is segmented: skiers can concentrate on separate bowls and faces for a morning or afternoon, always having the choice of a new path down the mountain. And none of these runs seems intimidating, although there is plenty of challenge for every level of skier.

One suggestion: if you're skiing with a group, arrange a meeting place in case you get separated. This is a big mountain.

Beginners have areas at Golden Peak and Lionshead. A series of crisscrossing catwalks named Cub's Way, Gitalong and so on allow beginners to work their way down the mountain, shifting from trail to trail.

Intermediates will probably run out of vacation time before running out of trails to ski. Few other mountains offer an intermediate the same expansive terrain and seemingly countless trails. Especially worthy cruising areas include the long ride down the mountain under and to the right of the Lionshead gondola; almost any of the runs bordering the Avanti express chair; the Northwoods run; and the relatively short but sweet trio down to Game Creek Bowl—The Woods, Baccarat and Dealer's Choice. Our vote for best run on the mountain, and one available to advanced intermediates (though parts are rated black), is the top-to-bottom, miles-long autobahn named Riva Ridge.

Much of the intermediate skiing on Vail Mountain is good enough that experts won't notice they're not being stretched to their limits. Those who want more challenge, however, should head to the far left of the mountain face to a trio of double black diamonds named Blue Ox, Highline and Rogers Run. The straight-down-the-lift, waist-high, mogul-masher Highline is the stiffest test of the three. Nearby Prima is almost as tough, and the short drop of Pronto down to the Northwoods chair lets you strut your mogul-mauling stuff in front of the lift lines. The only authentic gut-suckers on the front face are the tops of South and North Rim off the Northwoods lift, leading to a tight but nice Gandy Dancer.

Experts can drop down the Northeast Bowl or come off Prima Ridge through tight trees on Gandy Dancer, Prima Cornice or Pronto to the Northwoods area.

Solid skiers, of course, will also want to explore Vail's famous Back Bowls. Stretching seven miles across, they provide more than 2,600 acres of choose-your-own-path skiing. On a sunny day, these bowls are about as good as skiing gets. Confident intermediates also can enjoy the bowls, but should stick close to the swaths in China Bowl and Tea Cup Bowl that the grooming machines make each night. That way, if you get tired or frustrated with the natural conditions, you can bail out easily. The Back Bowls are without a doubt, the best and most extensive bowl skiing in America. Skiers who have skied Vail for years say they now ski the front side only when they come down at the end of the day. The bowls also are an excellent way to escape crowds that may have built up on the front side of the mountain. For complete isolation (a real achievement in Vail, folks), head for the Inner and Outer Mongolia bowls. Let's just leave it at this: they are aptly named.

Beaver Creek Resort

Somehow in its enthusiasm to sell itself as a resort to pamper the well-off, Beaver Creek Resort acquired a reputation as strictly a beginner and intermediate cruiser mountain. Not so. Advanced skiers and experts should spend at least a day here and maybe more. Our advice is to choose a Saturday or Sunday, when the lines at Vail can climb over the 15-20 minute barrier, yet be nonexistent at Beaver Creek Resort.

The mountain is laid out upside down, with the easiest skiing at the top, down the Stump Park lift. Few intermediate or advanced skiers won't get a thrill out of turning their skis loose down one of America's best unheralded cruisers dipping and turning under the Centennial express lift down the lower half of the mountain.

What's most surprising about Beaver Creek Resort is the amount of truly tough stuff. The Birds of Prey runs rival anything Vail offers—all long, steep and mogul-studded. While somewhat shorter, Ripsaw and Cataract in Rose Bowl, and Loco in Larkspur Bowl, are equally challenging. Grouse Mountain provides even more great expert terrain and is being outfitted with snowmaking. The skiing at Grouse Mountain is the steepest you will find. It is for advanced intermediates and above, but adequate width allows uncertain intermediates to traverse their way down.

Arrowhead-at-Vail

This area has just two lifts—one surface tow for beginner lessons, and one high-speed quad that shoots to the top. It also has plenty of wide-open cruising trails, with a winding beginner run (Piece O' Cake) to the left of the trail map, and a couple of isolated advanced plunges (Lone Pine Canyon) to the right. It's a great spot for any group that wants to stick together without having to be within sight of each other at every moment. Lose sight of your friends or family at Vail, and you may not find them again until the end of the day.

Mountain rating

Vail is one of the best ski mountains in the world for all but the extreme fringes of the skier ability chart. Super experts will miss the extreme skiing of a Snowbird, Jackson or Squaw Valley, and frankly, Vail could use a better learning area for adult never-evers, an isolated area with its own lift, separate from the human freeways that Vail's trails can become. Experts have the Back Bowls, with acres of powder skiing. Advanced and intermediate skiers have long cruisers, and beginners have many runs to choose from.

Beaver Creek is the spot for aggressive, bump-hungry experts with the Birds of Prey and Grouse Mountain runs. Lower intermediates will also be happy at Beaver Creek Resort with its long runs and virtually no lift lines. In fact, anyone who does not want to see anything resembling a line should take a trip to Beaver Creek Resort.

Arrowhead is best for families with young children, or any group that wants to stick together. It also is quite good for those who like moderately pitched, groomed trails.

Cross-country

Beaver Creek has created a 30-km. track system at McCoy Park at the top of Chair 12. This area is considered 20 percent advanced, 60 percent intermediate and 20 percent beginner. Because it's at the top of the mountain the track system has beautiful views in every direction. It is open from 9 a.m. to 3 p.m. daily. Adult track fees are $15 for an all-day pass, $12 for a half day beginning at noon; children pay $7 for an all-day pass, $5 for a half day.

There are also a series of backcountry opportunities from Golden Peak base. All-day tours cost $51; afternoon tours are $34; Gourmet Tours, including lunch, cost $65.

Check with the ski school for more information on cross-country, because tours and classes take place on selected days rather than daily. One day on a multiday lift ticket may be exchanged for a half-day cross-country lesson or a half-day cross-country tour and rental equipment at either Vail or Beaver Creek Resort. Rentals are available at Golden Peak or the Beaver Creek Cross-Country Center at the base of Chair 12. Call 476-3239.

Telemark lessons and backcountry Nordic trips can be arranged through Paragon Guides (926-5299) at the Arrowhead Backcountry Center.

Snowboarding (93/94 prices)

Boarders are welcome at all three ski areas. At Vail, snowboarders will want to head for the halfpipe on Golden Peak. There is also a halfpipe in Rose Bowl at Beaver Creek Resort called Boarder Beach. At Vail and Beaver Creek, a full-day Discover Boarding lesson is $55; $75 for lesson and lift ticket. Lessons for levels 2-9 are $100 for the lesson and lift. Half-day lift-and-lesson prices are $60.

Ski school (93/94 prices)

In Vail, the ski school has offices and meeting places at Vail Village near the base of the Vista Bahn Express; at Lionshead next to the gondola; at Golden Peak next to Chairs 6 and 12; at Mid-Vail next to Chairs 3 and 4; at the Eagle's Nest at the top of the gondola; at Cascade Village, near the Westin; and at the Two Elk Restaurant, near China Bowl. Private lessons meet at Vail Village. Call the Vail Ski School at 476-3239.

In Beaver Creek Resort, the school locations are in Village Hall next to Chair 1 and at Spruce Saddle atop the Centennial Express lift. Call the Beaver Creek Ski School at 949-5750.

Skiers watch a video that demonstrates the nine levels of skiing skills the school uses to form classes, then place themselves in classes ranging from never-evers to advanced.

A free Ski Tips program meets at 11 a.m. daily at Mid-Vail, Eagles Nest or Spruce Saddle. The session gives you a chance to ski down a gentle slope alongside an instructor who will provide a critique and suggestions on which ski-school program will offer the best benefits.

Private lessons (for one to five people) cost $90 for an hour; two hours cost $180; half day (three and a half hours) costs $255; full day (8:30 a.m. to 3:30 p.m.) costs $370.

Group lessons are $55 for a full day (10 a.m. to 3:30 p.m.) for any level skier. Packaged full-day lessons that include a lift ticket are $75 for never-evers through level 2, $100 for levels 3-9. Three-day lesson/lift/rental packages run $210 for levels 1-2, and $285 for levels 3-9.

Special workshops concentrate on specific skills or snow conditions, such as skiing parallel or handling bumps. Most are morning or afternoon three-hour workshops; contact the ski school for more details.

Pepi's Wedel Weeks were created in the European tradition, which allows skiers to start off the ski season with an inexpensive lesson package. These are held for three weeks only, in November and early December. It's a seven-day program with breakfast, lessons every morning and afternoon, races, a welcome reception, an evening party, a fashion show and a farewell dinner. Call (800) 445-8245 or (800) 433-8735 in Colorado.

The Children's Ski School is anchored by Sport Goofy, the Ambassador of Children's Skiing. The real adventure for kids, however, starts outside the high walls of Fort Whippersnapper atop the Golden Peak lift. Here, children enter a magical land and follow in the tracks of the little Indians Gitche and Gumee, as they accompany Jackrabbit Joe and Sourdough Pete on a quest to find the treasure of the Lost Silver Mine. This adventure is just part of the program offered by the Golden Peak Children's Ski Center, which has the most extensive facilities at Vail for children of all ages. There are also special Kids Nights Out featuring dinner, theater and special games.

Vail has three children's centers: Golden Peak (479-2040), Lionshead (479-2042) and Small World Playschool at Beaver Creek Resort (949-2304). Registration is from 8 to 9:15 a.m., or preregister the day before.

Children 3 1/2 to 6 years have a supervised playroom and programs when not skiing, and the prices include lunch and snacks. Special children's rental shops are available in the Golden Peak and Beaver Creek Resort centers. Beginner equipment for 3 to 6 year olds is available at Lionshead.

Children between 6 and 12 can spend their day on the mountain, be entertained with videos and have supervised meeting rooms. Lunch is also supervised but not included in the price ($7 is suggested as adequate lunch money). Group lessons are $64 a day for lessons and lifts. Information on Kids' Night Out and Family Night Out dinner theater programs is available by calling the Family Adventure line, 479-2048.

Teens aged 13 to 18 have daily all-day classes with members of their age group. Prices are the same as adult lessons.

Lift tickets (94/95 prices)

	Adult	Child (Up to 12)
One day	$46	$33
Four days	$172 ($43/day)	$124 ($31/day)
Seven days	$252 ($36/day)	$189 ($27/day)

Prices effective Nov. 24-Dec. 23 and Jan. 2-March 31, 1995

We list four- and seven-day prices in this chapter rather than three- and five-day prices for two good reasons: because most Vail skiers are there for a few days to a week, and because

Vail has started a new ticket program called Mountains Plus. Any skier who buys a lift ticket for four or more days may exchange a day for credit toward other Vail Valley activities, such as snowmobile tours or cross-country rentals and trails fees. Discounts under this program top out at $36 per day for adults; $27 per-day for children.

Senior citizens 65 to 69 years usually get a discount equal to the lowest multiday day rate, and those 70 and older ski free.

Arrowhead-at-Vail offers a bargain alternative in this region. Until it is connected with Beaver Creek, which could happen by next season, it will have separate pricing. Adults ski for $30; children 16 and younger ski for $20. An adult three-day pass is $85, while a Family Pass (two adults and up to three children 16 and younger) is a very attractive $90. Ages 65-69 pay $25, and older than that ski free. A ticket for the surface lift alone is $10.

Accommodations
Vail Village and Lionshead

Vail's premier properties are clustered in Vail Village at the base of the Vista Bahn Express. Selecting the best place in town is a virtual tossup between four hotels.

The Lodge at Vail (476-5011 or 800-237-1236) is the original, around which the rest of the resort was built. It is only steps away from the lifts, ski school and main street action. **Gasthof Gramshammer** (476-5626) is located at the crossroads of Vail Village. Our favorite and the most economical within this group of hotels is the **Christiania** (476-5641). **The Sonnenalp Hotel** (476-5656 or 800-654-8312) is a group of buildings that exude Alpine warmth and charm. All are expensive. Regular season seven-night/six-day ground packages cost around $1,700.

At the Lionshead end of town the **Radisson** (476-4444) is the top of the line and has an excellent location only three minutes' walk from the gondola. The seven-night/six-day package will cost about $1,300.

The Westin Hotel (476-7111) in Cascade Village is also luxurious. The Cascade Athletic Club is across the parking lot from the hotel and is available without extra charge to Westin guests. The hotel has a dedicated ski lift, which makes getting to the slopes a pleasure. The seven-night/six-day package costs $1,500-$1,800.

Condominiums are plentiful in the Vail region and the prices are sky-high. The most reasonable for those who want to be on the shuttlebus route are found in Lionshead, clustered around the gondola. Village studio units go for about $200 a night; two-bedroom units for about $500; three-bedroom units for about $700 a night with lifts.

The **Vailglo Lodge** (476-5506) is a 34-room hotel that operates like an elegant B&B. In Lionshead, it has easy access to the slopes and town. Room rates are $108 in low season to a high of $224 at Christmas. For other relatively more affordable lodging, try **West Vail Lodge** (476-3890) in West Vail; **Antlers** (476-2471) in Lionshead; **Manor Vail** (476-5651) in Gold Peak; the **Holiday Inn at Vail** (476-5631) and **Vail Village Inn** (476-5622).

Beaver Creek Resort

In Beaver Creek Resort most properties are clustered around the base area and the Beaver Creek Resort village.

Hyatt Regency Beaver Creek has rates ranging from as low as $215 for a standard room to $285-$480 for a mountain view room. The hotel also features an unusual program which matches up singles who want to take advantage of the double occupancy rates. Call (800) 233-1234 for information about Single Share or reservations. The Hyatt also has organized a fun story-telling program which started out for kids but has gained widespread interest.

The Centennial Lodge (800-845-7060) and **Creekside Lodge** (949-7071) are just about 300 yards from the base of the Centennial Lift. The seven-night/six-day hotel/lifts package will cost about $1,500 based on double occupancy.

The Charter Lodge (949-6660) is a bit more expensive and exclusive. **The Poste Montane** (845-7500) is located directly in Beaver Creek Resort Village as are **The Inn at Beaver Creek**. **Pines Hotel, B.C. Lodge** and **St. James Place**.

The absolute bargain condominiums are in Avon at the beginning of the Beaver Creek Resort access road, about a 20-minute drive from Vail's slopes. The Avon condominiums are served by a shuttlebus system. Prices in Avon are about $170-$220 for a one-bedroom unit.

Comfort Inn (949-5511) has five-night packages with four days of lifts for about $460 per person in value season and seven-night packages with six days of lifts for about $760 per person, double occupancy, regular season. Or try the **Christie Lodge** (949-7700).

Dining
Vail Village and Lionshead

Vail has a collection of acceptable restaurants, but has not developed the gourmet reputation of Aspen, Deer Valley or even Steamboat. After speaking with scores of locals and tourists, we have these recommendations:

If you have deep pockets, this first group of restaurants is worth testing. **The Tyrolean Inn** (476-2204) has fine game and is a favorite among visiting Europeans. **Ambrosia's** (476-1964) and **La Tour** (476-4403) also receive consistent and excellent ratings. **Sweet Basil** (476-0125) was recommended by both upscale and blue-collar folk as a great place for lunch and dinner. **Lancelot** (476-5828) has the best prime rib in town, with prices from expensive to moderate. **Alfredo's** (476-7111) in the Westin has perhaps the best Northern Italian fare. **Windows Restaurant** (476-4444) in the Radisson has great dining and a great view.

In Beaver Creek try dining one night at **Saddle Ridge,** now owned by Vail Associates but first built as a corporate retreat for executives. The price is steep, but the food is wonderful. It's a chance for mere mortals to sample the lifestyle of coddled American corporate executives.

For more moderate prices, stop at the **Ore House** (476-5100) in the village and the **Chart House** (476-1525) in Lionshead for steaks. **Blu's** (476-3113) can be moderate if you choose carefully, and **Bully Pub** (476-5656) in the Sonnenalp's **Bavaria Haus** keeps prices traditionally low. **Garton's Saloon** in the Cross-roads Shopping Center has a Mexican menu.

Those on a budget should try **Pazzo's** (476-9026) across from Crossroads, which offers spaghetti or soup and pizza for less than $4, or head to the **Lionshead Bar and Grill** (476-3060) in Lionshead. **Bart and Yetti's** (476-2754) in Lionshead is a good place to head for lunch or light dinner.

The Jackalope (476-4314) in West Vail is a great spot for inexpensive, basic good eats, and a local atmosphere.

In Beaver Creek Resort, try the **Golden Eagle Inn** on the mall, a restaurant run by Pepi Langegger of the Tyrolean Inn. **Legends** (949-5540) in the Poste Montane has the best fish in the area. **Mirabelle** (949-7728) at the bottom of the Beaver Creek Resort access road serves well-prepared nouvelle cuisine. **Covered Bridge Cafe** in the Park Plaza is the most moderately priced of the resort area restaurants. In Avon try the **The Brass Parrot** and **Cassidy's**.

Visitors who are looking for something special, and have a car or are willing to take a taxi, head to nearby Minturn. Here, you'll find the **Minturn Country Club** where you choose your own T-bone, filet or swordfish steak, and then cook it yourself over open grills. Just across the street, the area's best Mexican food is dished out at the **Saloon** or **Chili Willy's.** Casual to the nth degree, they offer pitchers of margaritas and Mexican food so authentic that both will bring tears to your eyes.

Up on the mountain make it a point to have lunch at the beautiful **Two Elk Restaurant** which is being expanded this season. This is what every on-mountain cafeteria dining experience should be.

A memorable Vail dining experience is a night at **Beano's Cabin** at Beaver Creek Resort. Groups meet at the base of the mountain and are served hot chocolate or coffee. They are bundled onto a 40-person sleigh and pulled up the mountain under under the stars by a snowcat. Unfortunately the ride up isn't the romantic experience it might be: the sled is steel, decorated with plastic evergreens; you'll be forced to listen to loud and bad singing, and stories of marauding black bears, and depending on the wind you may suffer diesel exhaust fumes. All in all, the ride is more appropriate for spring break than romance. Once you get there, though, Beano's Cabin is beautiful, modern and rustic, completed by a roaring stone-hearth fire, log beams, an 11-point buck head, and exciting, well-prepared cuisine. The cost is $69 per person. Reservations, 949-5750.

Another experience of this type, but on a much smaller scale, is an evening at Arrowhead's **Anderson Cabin.** Originally built by John Anderson, one of the bachelors that homesteaded in the Bachelor Gulch area, the cabin was restored in 1985. It has no electricity, so up to 20 can dine by lanternlight and watch the chef cook a five-course gourmet meal on a wood stove. Lunch is $60, including a lift ticket at Arrowhead (diners ski in and out); dinner is $80, including a snowcat ride in and the meal, but without alcohol, taxes and tip. Call 926-3029 or (800) 332-3029 for more details.

Après-ski/nightlife

Après-ski in Vail is centered in the Village or in Lionshead. In the Village, try **Cyrano's; Sarah's** in the Christiania for squeezebox music with Helmut Fricker on Tuesdays, Wednesdays and Fridays; and **Vendetta's,** which normally has live music. **Mickey's** at the Lodge at Vail is the top piano bar après-ski spot. Several restaurants have house entertainers; we liked Mike Moloney's personable mix of ballads and country/rock at **Pepi's.**

In Lionshead, **Sundance Saloon** fills up with locals and probably has the best drink prices in town, especially during happy hour in the late afternoon. There are pool tables, a locals' keg party on Thursdays and live music on the weekends. **The Hong Kong Café** is also a hot locals' bar.

For later nightlife with live music, dancing and such, try **Nick's,** which has rock 'n' roll with a disc jockey. **The Club** normally offers acoustic guitar music. **Garton's Saloon** has live country music. **Cyrano's** has a disco in Vail Village. On weekends the **Sundance Saloon** in Lionshead and the **Jackalope** in the West Vail shopping center have live music. **Bogies** in Marriot's Mark is the class act in Lionshead.

Child care

The child care facility is run by the ski school. Reservations are advised, especially during the holidays. A nursery facility, **Small World Play School,** is in Beaver Creek Resort (949-2306), with another in the Golden Peak base area (479-5044).

Children aged 2 months to 6 years may be enrolled in the program. Costs are $55 a day. Half-day programs are available on a space-available basis for $30, either morning or afternoon. For babysitters call 479-2292 or 476-7400.

Other activities

Shopping: Plenty of boutiques and shops, many of the pricey variety. The better stores are concentrated in Vail Village.

Vail has a number of athletic clubs. **The Cascade Club** across from the Westin has indoor tennis courts, squash courts, racquetball courts, Nautilus and free weights, indoor track, outdoor heated pool and thermal spa.

The **Vail Athletic Club** (476-0700) also has fitness facilities in Vail Village. The **Vail Racquet Club** (476-3267) in East Vail has indoor tennis, squash and racquetball courts, swimming pool, Nautilus and weight room.

Steve Jones Sleigh Rides on the Vail Golf Course can be booked by calling 476-8057.

Vail also has a ski museum worth looking at, a movie theater, ice skating rink and many other things to do.

Getting there and getting around

Getting there: These resorts are right on Interstate 70, 100 miles west of Denver and 140 miles east of Grand Junction.

Flights land at the **Vail/Eagle County airport**, about 35 miles west of Vail, and the Denver International Airport 110 miles east. Eagle County airport is served by American, America West, Delta and Taesa Airlines, the latter from Mexico City.

Ground transportation between Denver and Vail is frequent and convenient. The trip to Vail takes about two and a half hours. Contact **Colorado Mountain Express** at (800) 424-6363; or **Vans to Vail** at (800) 222-2112.

Getting around: If you are staying in Vail Village or Lionshead, a car is a big pain. Vail has a reliable, free town shuttle, and the town is designed for strolling. Parking is a headache, and costly, too. The Vail/Beaver Creek shuttlebus is $2. If you plan to commuting between Vail and Beaver Creek, you may want to rent a car. If you are planning a late-season trip ask about the resort transit systems—schedules are often curtailed.

Information/reservations

Vail/Beaver Creek Reservations at (800) 525-2257 or (800) 824-5737 handles air tickets, transfers and lodging.

All telephone area codes are 303 unless otherwise noted.

Town Map
Winter Park

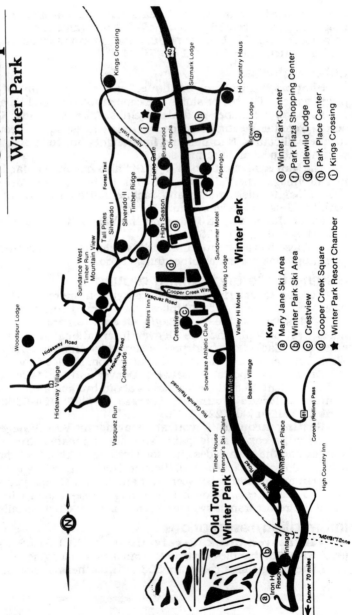

Kings Crossing

Sitzmark Lodge

40

Hi Country Haus

Idlewild Lodge

Forest Trail

Alpine Vista

Love Cafe

Braidwood

Olympia

Alpenglo

Timber Ridge

Silverado II
Silverado I

Tall Pines

Sundance West
Timber Run
Mountain View

High Season

ⓔ

Winter Park

Sundowner Motel

Woodspur Lodge

Hideaway Road

Hideaway Village

Arapahoe Road

Creekside Road

Vasquez Run

Millers Inn

Vasquez Road

ⓓ

Cooper Creek Way

Viking Lodge

Crestview

ⓒ

Snowblaze Athletic Club

Valley Hi Motel

Beaver Village

Rio Grande Railroad

2 Miles

Timber House

Brenner's Ski Chalet

Winter Park Place

John Road

Corona (Rollins) Pass

40

High Country Inn

**Old Town
Winter Park**

Vintage

ⓑ

Iron H
Resort

ⓐ

Moffat Tunnel

◄— Denver: 70 miles

Key

ⓐ Mary Jane Ski Area
ⓑ Winter Park Ski Area
ⓒ Crestview
ⓓ Cooper Creek Square
★ Winter Park Resort Chamber

ⓔ Winter Park Center
ⓕ Park Plaza Shopping Center
ⓖ Idlewild Lodge
ⓗ Park Place Center
ⓘ Kings Crossing

N

Winter Park
Colorado

Winter Park doesn't have the glamour of Aspen or Vail, nor the quaint Victorian charm of Telluride, Breckenridge or Crested Butte. What Winter Park has is a great mountain with a phenomenal variety of terrain and some of the most affordable big-mountain skiing in the United States.

Early this century, when the Moffat Tunnel through the Rockies was completed, Denverites began to ride the train to the area. The shacks first built for the tunnel construction crews made perfect warming huts for hardy skiers who climbed the mountains and schussed down on seven-foot boards. Eventually the ski area became part of the Denver public parks system, which explains its name. Today Winter Park ranks as one of the largest ski areas in Colorado, with 120 trails, 20 lifts and more than 1,300 acres of skiable terrain.

Winter Park has no massive condo complexes lining the roads, and no built-up center of town. Both the ski area and most of the lodgings are tucked into the woods off the main highway. A traveler might well ride through Winter Park and never realize that the town can sleep over 13,200 in some 100 properties.

Lodging is designed with families in mind, the ski school is one of Colorado's most respected and the children's center is one of the biggest and most advanced of any ski resort.

Although Winter Park has maintained a great family reputation, it is surprisingly a good destination for singles. The Mary Jane section of the resort has tough skiing, as difficult as any in Colorado; the town benefits from having only a few, but good, nightlife centers, meaning that you get to meet most of the other skiers in town if that's what you desire; and the mountain inn lodging prevalent here gives singles a great opportunity to meet other vacationers over dinner and drinks, or while enjoying the hot tubs. If you are looking for a solid good time without the fanfare, Winter Park presents you with one of the best.

Winter Park Facts
Base elevation: 9,000'; **Summit elevation:** 12,060' **Vertical drop:** 3,060 feet
Number of lifts: 20—6 quad superchairs; 5 triple chairs, 9 double chairs
Snowmaking: 20 percent **Skiable acreage:** 1,358
Uphill capacity: 32,450 per hour **Bed Base:** 13,200 in Fraser Valley

Where to ski

Visitors who have read most reports about Winter Park arrive expecting a good intermediate resort with plenty of lower-intermediate and beginner trails. Yes, that's all here—what is surprising is the amount of expert terrain.

Though the mountain is completely interconnected by its lifts, it has separate base areas: Mary Jane and Winter Park. The Winter Park base area serves most of the beginner and intermediate trails, with a handful of advanced trails dropping down the left side as you look up. Beginners can ride to the top of the mountain to Sunspot and then ski down Allan Phipps, March Hare and Mad Tea Party, or they can ski all the way back to the base using the Cranmer Cutoff to Parkway. Intermediates starting from the same mountaintop can play down Jabberwocky, White Rabbit and Cheshire Cat.

The Vasquez Ridge area also has an excellent collection of intermediate cruising runs and is served by a quad superchair. (The only drawback to the Vasquez Ridge area is a long runout down the Big Valley trail. The Buckaroo trail lets you avoid the runout.) If you find yourself on the other side of the ridge, keep up your speed and tuck for the run back to the Pioneer Express lift. Gambler and Aces and Eights are two short, steep mogul runs that take you to the Olympia Lift. To change mountains, green-circle Gunbarrel takes skiers to the High Lonesome Express superchair for a drop into the Mary Jane area.

For advanced skiers, the most popular lift on the Winter Park side probably will be the Zephyr Express Superchair. It skirts the far left boundary of the area and allows drops down Bradley's Bash, Balch, Mulligan's Mile and Hughes—all good advanced terrain. From the top of Zephyr, bump fanatics can dance down Outhouse and end up at the base area of Mary Jane.

Now on to the Mary Jane side of the resort: a blast for any solid intermediate or advanced skier, with some chutes that will make the hair stand up on the expert's neck. The Sunnyside lift has excellent runs for intermediates. If you can handle that with no trouble, try Sleeper, one of Winter Park's "blue-black" designated runs that help intermediates advance to blacks. If that doesn't shake you, head for the black runs off the Iron Horse chair, and if you're still standing, then you're ready for the runs off the Challenger chair—all black-diamond, all ungroomed, and all tough as a bag of nails.

For experts who believe in super-steeps, try the chutes accessible only through controlled gates: Hole in the Wall, Awe Chute, Baldy's Chute, Jeff's Chute and Runaway, all reached by the Challenger lift.

The only bowl skiing is in Parsenn Bowl, 200 acres of open space that opened in 1992. Though rated blue on the trail map, it can be a good workout. Winds often close the Timberline lift, which provides the only access. Even if the lift is open, the cold wind can harden a thin surface layer into breakable crust, which makes turning a bit of a chore. If you can hit Parsenn on a good day though, you're in for a treat. The naked upper part is wide open and of medium steepness, while the gladed bottom part is an absolute delight, especially for those just learning to ski between trees. Winter Park will clear additional gladed terrain in this area for 94/95.

Winter Park is one of the best ski areas in the nation for never-evers. Its $2-million Discovery Park is 20 acres of excellent, gentle, isolated learning terrain for adult beginners, children and disabled learners, served by a high-speed detachable chair lift that slows down for loading and unloading. Winter Park will further improve its learning terrain this season with another high-speed quad to replace the double-chair Prospector lift, and a "Magic Carpet," a base-area conveyor belt that transports beginners up the learning slope, eliminating the need for side-stepping. It is very heartening to see a major ski area invest money and planning in the very things that make learning easier for adult beginners.

Mountain rating

Winter Park is one of the few ski areas on the continent that can truly serve the needs of all skier ability and interest levels. Very few mountains have the nearly flat, isolated terrain that never-evers need, while also boasting the precipitous plunges that experts adore. Winter Park is lucky enough to have both, plus plenty at every stage in between.

Snowboarding

Snowboarding is allowed on the entire mountain. Many of the rental shops in the area have boards for hire. Lessons include a 4 1/2 hour first-time lesson for $20 with the purchase of a full-day, all-lifts ticket. There is a series of three-hour workshops for $55. Private lessons are $90 for an hour and a half.

Cross-country

Tour Ski Idlewild (726-5564) has 30 km. of machine-maintained trails for all skier levels. Trail fees are $9 a day for adults and $6 for children and seniors; half days cost $6 adult, and $4 for children; children 6 and under ski free. Private lessons are $30 an hour. A learn-to-ski package costs $25 for lessons, rental and trail fee. Children and seniors: $20.

Devil's Thumb Ranch (726-8231), near Tabernash, connects with Idlewild to form an 85 km. network. The rates for both areas are identical.

Snow Mountain Ranch (726-4628) offers 90 km. of maintained trails for all levels. There is also a lighted 3 km. loop for night cross-country skiing. The trail fee is $8 a day and children younger than 12 pay $4. Group lessons are available for $12 and private lessons are $20 an hour. Snow Mountain Ranch also is a YMCA with inexpensive dorm lodging.

Ski school (94/95 prices)

Regularly rated by experts one of the best in the country, Winter Park ski school has something for everyone from never-evers to hot skiers and snowboarders.

The Winter Park side is the focus of most **group lessons**. Beginners can get a $20 four-and-a-half-hour lesson with the purchase of their first lift ticket, lessons for two days on skis cost $45, and for three days the price will be $75.

Intermediate and advanced skiers can choose from several **workshops,** including four-and-a-half-hour Parallel Breakthrough for $45, Bump Workshop or Style and Technique, both of which are three hours long and $50.

Private lessons are $90 an hour and a half for 1-4 persons. Six hours of private lessons costs $320; three hours, $160.

Children's programs operate out of the children's center. Ute is for 3-4 year olds; $55 gives all-day lessons with rentals. Cheyenne is for kindergarteners, Navajo is for first through third graders, and Arapaho is for fourth grade through 12 years old. All three programs, including lifts and lunch, cost $60 without rentals; $70 with.

National Sports Center for the Disabled

Winter Park operates the leading disabled skiing instruction program in the world. It also has a full-time race training program for disabled skiers. The programs are designed to help such skiers reach their potential for full mountain enjoyment. Basic instruction is available for all levels, and the race program is open to physically disabled skiers of advanced intermediate level or above.

Lift tickets (94/95 prices)

	Adult	Child (6-13) Senior (62-69)
One day	$38 (93/94 price)	$18
Three days	$102 ($34/day)	$54 ($18/day)
Five days	$165 ($33/day)	$90 ($18/day)

Children younger than 6 and seniors 70 and older ski free. The resort also has a limited-lift ticket program called Preference Pricing, a great idea that more ski areas should adopt. The beginner-only lift at Mary Jane costs $5 a day. For $18 a day ($12 for kids), skiers have access to six lifts (Galloping Goose and Pony Express at Mary Jane, and Arrow, Gemini, Endeavor and Discovery at Winter Park) servicing 200 acres of terrain on both sides of the resort with up to 1,000 feet of vertical. These lift tickets should be perfect for parents skiing with children and lower-level skiers who don't need access to all the terrain.

Accommodations

Winter Park has a group of mountain inns unique in Colorado: they are like small bed-and-breakfasts but with dinner thrown in as well. They all serve meals family style, so that guests get a chance to meet one another easily. Most inns have transportation to and from the slopes, making a car unnecessary. The food is usually fantastic and plentiful, and the inn owners go out of their way to please their guests.

There are eight such mountain inns in Winter Park. Perhaps the most upscale is the **Gasthaus Eichler** (726-5133). This inn is very European and the rooms are well decorated with down comforters on the beds. Each bathroom is equipped with a Jacuzzi tub. It's perfect for those wanting quiet, elegant accommodations right in the center of town within walking distance of restaurants and nightlife. Rates based on double occupancy are approximately $70 per person in regular season for bed, breakfast and a massive dinner. This is a quality bargain that is hard to beat.

Arapahoe Ski Lodge (726-8222 or 800-338-2698) also located downtown, is a pleasant, friendly No-Smoking mountain inn that feels like home. The rooms have private baths. It features a large spa and indoor swimming pool. Prices based on double occupancy are $74 per person per night with dinner, breakfast and transport to the slopes. Single skiers pay $98.

The Woodspur Lodge (726-8417 or 800-626-6562) The lodge living room is massive with a fireplace, soaring roof and plenty of space. This central area makes a perfect meeting place for the guests. The rooms here are of two types—newly restored and old style. Ask for one of the updated rooms if you are staying as a couple and one of the older rooms for larger groups. The lodge is served by local buses as well as lodge vans that shuttle skiers to the area and the town. Rates based on double occupancy are $70 per person including breakfast and dinner. The food is great.

The Timber House Ski Lodge (726-5477 or 800-843-3502) is tucked into the woods at the edge of the ski area. A private trail lets you ski directly back to the lodge. The emphasis is on a chance to meet fellow guests either in the giant living room with stone fireplace, sitting at long tables with food served family style, or soaking in the outdoor hot tub. Rates based on double occupancy are $57-$88 per person with breakfast and dinner.

The remaining mountain inns are outside of town toward Tabernash. **The Outpost Inn** (726-5346) is the most comfortable and homey. Here Jerry and Susie Frye serve homecooked meals and nonstop hospitality. Vans shuttle skiers to the ski area each morning and collect guests again when the lifts close. There is a spa attached to the building which becomes a social center in the evenings. A maximum of 20 guests at a time stay at the inn. Rates are $68 per person double occupancy.

High Mountain Lodge at Tally Ho Ranch (726-5958) is a rambling lodge more akin to a motel in its room arrangements, but with a cozy group living room and dining area that are the signature of the mountain inns. It has a swimming pool. The inn overlooks a frozen lake and gives you splendid isolation. Transportation back and forth to the ski area is provided. Rates are about $68 per day with breakfast and dinner.

The next lodges are not part of the Mountain Inn Association, but offer similar accommodations.

Chalet Z (726-5416) is a B&B just around the corner from the Timber House with a personality of its own. It is accessible from the ski area by the Billy Woods Trail, which also ends at the Timber House. Rates based on double occupancy are $67 per night including breakfast.

Beau West B&B (726-5145 or 800-473-5145) is only 500 yards from Winter Park base and features gourmet breakfasts. It has a hot tub and great views. Rates are $60-$75 per person based on double occupancy.

The next two inns are located in cross-country areas in the nearby town of Fraser. **Idlewild Lodge** (726-5562), at the area of the same name, and the **Devil's Thumb Ranch**. Both charge about $55 per person for two sharing a room and include breakfast and dinner.

The condos of Winter Park are the mainstay accommodations for most skiers. The most luxurious is the **Iron Horse Resort** (726-8851), the closest that Winter Park has to a true ski-in/ski-out complex, though that stretches the definition a bit. There is a swimming pool and a fitness center. The condos range from studios to two-bedroom suites. One-bedroom units cost $125-$320 a night, and two bedrooms $185-$395. Iron Horse is located a bit outside of the town center, but there is excellent shuttle service for those who want to strike out for nightlife.

The Vintage (726-8801) is also slightly out of the center of town but right next to the ski areas. It features a restaurant, fitness room, swimming pool and good shuttle service into the town. One of the finest properties in Winter Park, the Vintage has studios from $195, two-room suites for $225-$400; three-room suites for $250-$500.

For some of the best condominiums in the center of town, try either the **Snowblaze** or **Crestview Place**. Both are virtually across the street from Cooper Creek Square. Snowblaze (726-5701) also features a full athletic club with racquetball court, swimming pool and fitness center, which are included in the price of the condo. The units are all equipped with color TVs.

Studio units normally come with a Murphy bed, and two- and three-bedroom units have baths for each bedroom, private saunas and fireplaces. Approximate costs: two-bedroom units cost $130-$237; and three-bedroom units, which sleep up to eight, $187-$316.

Crestview Place (726-9421), just remodeled, does not have an athletic club or private saunas, but has fireplaces and full kitchens. Costs: two-bedroom units, $204-$264 a night; three-bedroom units, $272-$352.

One of the most popularly priced condominiums is the **Hi Country Haus** (726-9421). These condos are spread out in a dozen buildings and share a recreation center with four hot tubs, sauna and heated swimming pool. They are within walking distance of town and are on the shuttlebus routes. Costs: two-bedroom units, $180-$222; three-bedroom units, $240-$296.

For the least expensive lodging we could find, try **The Bunk House** (726-4657) at $15 per night for a dorm room.

Dining

Winter Park isn't packed with high-priced restaurants; instead, the emphasis is on good, solid cooking for hungry skiers and families.

The **Gasthaus Eichler** (726-5133) in the center of Winter Park has an Austrian/German-influenced menu. Locals all raved about **The Last Waltz** (726-4877), which is in the King's Crossing Shopping Center on Highway 40. One resident claims the Last Waltz has the best breakfast in town and the others give unanimous thumbs up to the solid American and Mexican menu, which features homemade dishes with very fresh ingredients. Save room for dessert.

For venison and fondue, head to the **Chalet Lucerne** (726-5402). **The Divide Grill** in the Cooper Creek Square serves up Northern Italian dishes and has a good salad bar. **Deno's** (726-5332) also has excellent pasta dishes as well as chicken, steak and shrimp selections. And surprisingly, **The Stampede Nightclub and Grill** (726-9433) and **The Slope** (726-5727), also known as two of the town's top nightlife spots, get good marks for excellent fare.

For family fare try the **Crooked Creek Saloon** in Fraser, a couple of miles away, for basic steaks and down-home cooking. **Lani's Place** is the spot for basic Mexican food at great prices.

For the best breakfast in town head straight to **The Kitchen** and ask Rosie to rustle up some eggs. You probably won't find Rosie doing much cooking but if she's around she'll liven up the breakfast crowd. **Carver's Bakery & Café** behind Cooper Creek Square serves hearty breakfasts and healthy lunches and dinners.

On the slopes, the best lunch is found in the **Club Car** restaurant at the Mary Jane base area. The new **Lodge at Sunspot** atop the mountain is a spectacular setting for a gourmet lunch. Winter Park has long had a fun way to order a pizza for lunch. Head for the telephone located at the top of the Winter Park section of the mountain, call **Mama Mia's Pizzeria** in Snoasis and your pizza will be waiting when you arrive.

For something different, ride one of the new gondola cars for dinner at the **Lodge at Sunspot**, the spectacular summit mountain restaurant. A six-course menu is $49 inclusive, except for alcohol and gratuity. Winter Park this season modified the Zephyr Express lift with 20 gondola cabins that will be used to transport dinner guests to the Lodge at Sunspot. During the day, it will be a high-speed quad. Call 726-5514 for information and reservations.

Après-ski/nightlife

For après-ski, the **Derailer Bar** in the West Portal of the Winter Park Base area is the place to be. **The Slope**, close to the base area on the road leading out to Highway 40, also gets a good crowd at happy hour, 4-6 p.m. If there are any sports events on tap, the place to go is **Deno's Mountain Bistro**, which has a half-dozen TV sets, plus more than a hundred types of beer and 200 wines. **Lani's Place** in Cooper Creek Square serves up excellent happy-hour 99¢ margaritas and tacos.

The later nightlife centers in two main dancing places. **The Slope** has live music most nights, and **The Stampede** in the Cooper Creek Square has disco and infrequent live bands. For a quiet drink without the loud music head down to **Soufflé's**. The **Iron Horse** often has a guitar player in the bar and a Comedy Club one night a week during ski season.

The Crooked Creek Saloon in downtown Fraser also has food and music. The only problem is transportation.

Child care

Here, Winter Park clearly stands far above the rest of the skiing world. Winter Park has the absolute best children's programs and children's center in American skidom, and its commitment is evident in the multistory center built expressly for the purpose. On some days the program handles more than 600 children—anyone who has organized anything for a group that size (of whatever age) knows what an undertaking this is. The center is open from 8 a.m. to 4 p.m.

Child care for ages 2 months to 5 years, including lunch, costs $45 a day; $30 half day. Instructional programs for older children are detailed in the Ski School section.

Reservations are required for all child care. Reservation forms may be obtained from Winter Park Central Reservations, or write to: Children's Center, Winter Park Resort, Box 36, Winter Park, CO 80482.

Other activities

Shopping: A few shops here and there, but this is not Winter Park's forte.

Jim's Sleigh Rides in Fraser leave daily at 1,7 and 8:30 p.m. You'll ride along a two-and-a-half-mile trail, pass log cabins and make a brief stop for hot refreshments around a roaring campfire. Adults pay $14 and children under 12 pay $11. For reservations, call 726-5527.

Dashing Through the Snow sleigh rides offers bonfire rides at 1, 7 and 8:45 p.m. and a dinner trip at 6 p.m. Call 726-5376.

Snowmobile tours are available with **Trailblazer** (726-8452) or **Sporting Country Guide Services** (726-9247). Snowmobile tours run $35 for one hour, $55 for two hours and $100 for four hours. For dogsled rides call 726-8301.

Snow Scoots are scaled-down snowmobiles that drivers aged 8 and older can operate around a marked, flat track. Snow Scoots is on the highway between Winter Park and Fraser.

One rare, but eminently enjoyable activity at ski resorts is tubing—sliding down a hill upon an inflated innertube. The **Fraser Valley Tubing Hill** (726-5954) has what you'll need for a night of tubing—a hill, rental tubes and two rope tows to pull you back to the top. It's a blast.

Getting there and around

Getting there: Winter Park is 67 miles northwest of Denver on U.S. Highway 40. Take I-70 West to Exit 232, then head toward Granby on Highway 40. **Home James** vans take skiers from the Denver International Airport to Winter Park. The one-way fare is $30 from the airport to Winter Park; $60 round trip. Reserve through central reservations, or contact the van lines directly. Home James: 726-5060 in Colorado; or (800) 525-3304.

Amtrak's California Zephyr, which runs between Chicago and San Francisco, makes a daily stop in Fraser, only a few miles from the ski area. Skiers from Chicago can board the train in the afternoon and arrive in Winter Park the next morning. West Coast skiers board in the morning and arrive by the next afternoon (Los Angeles passengers ride the Desert Wind train and change to the Zephyr in Salt Lake City.)

Sleeper cars are available, but sleeping in the coach seats is not so bad as you might think. There's lots of leg room, and the seats recline nearly all the way. Special packages make the trains very affordable. Call Winter Park Central Reservations for details.

Call Amtrak for information and train-only reservations: (800) 872-7245 (USA-RAIL).

The **Rio Grande Ski Train** is a unique institution in the United States. This special train leaves Denver on weekends mid-December to April.

The ski train, operating for more than 50 years, brings 800 passengers from Denver directly to the Winter Park base area, chugging along 56 miles and climbing 4,000 feet. The 14-car train snakes through the spectacular Rocky Mountains, through 28 tunnels and across canyons, ravines, and ice-crusted rivers. The scenery is as gripping as any I have seen in years of train travel through the Swiss and Austrian Alps. The train leaves Denver at 7:15 a.m. and departs Winter Park at 4:15 p.m.

Two classes of service—club and coach—are available; club car includes après-ski snacks. Rates are $45 club and $30 coach. For information and reservations, call 296-4754.

Getting around: Destination skiers are advised to rent a car for any extensive restaurant and bar-hopping. If you plan to stick close to your lodging at night, you won't need a car if your lodge has transportation to the ski area. In fact, a car is a pain at the ski area. Though both base areas have parking, the spaces fill up, especially on weekends, with heavy traffic from Denver. Even if you bring a car, the efficient shuttlebus or individual lodge shuttle to the ski area are often easier than driving yourself.

Information/reservations

Winter Park Central Reservations, Box 36, Winter Park CO 80482; (800) 453-2525 (nationwide); or 726-5587. All area codes are 303 unless otherwise noted.

Utah skiing
and staying in Salt Lake City

Name a big city with a small-town friendly feel, yet is a major airline hub and is an hour's drive from seven major ski areas. If you said Salt Lake City without hesitation, you must be a skier.

Without a doubt, Utah ranks as the most convenient major skiing in the country. Of course, snow is the most important ingredient for any ski vacation and Utah is blessed with some of the best—light, fluffy and abundant. It billows over your head, temporarily blinds you as you sense your way down a steep incline, and occasionally chokes you when you open your mouth to howl and giggle at the wonderful sensation.

Within an hour's drive of Salt Lake City, you can find one ski resort that pampers guests like no other (Deer Valley); others that help you only if you want it (Alta, Wolf Mountain); still others with a bustling, urban feel (Snowbird, Park City); and the ones that have an isolated, backcountry atmosphere (Sundance, Solitude). Some of Utah's ski towns resound with the deep bass

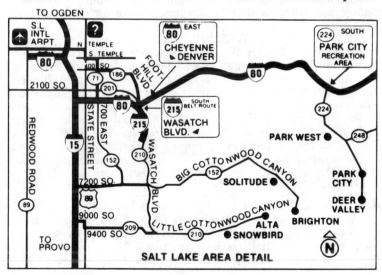

SALT LAKE AREA DETAIL

of live rock bands and the raucous whooping of rowdy skiers; in others, the loudest night noises are the snores of exhausted weekend athletes. Utah has ski areas with frightening precipices, others with gently undulating meadows.

Utah's biggest blessing is its accessibility. No other region has so many major ski areas so close to a major airport (Lake Tahoe comes close, but Reno doesn't have nearly the flights Salt Lake City does). Transportation is well-organized and efficient, so you don't even need a car.

Utah's biggest detriment is a lingering, and largely false, reputation for being a stick-in-the-mud. Utah's liquor laws have changed radically in the last decade, but many skiers still believe that finding a palm tree in Maine is easier than buying a drink in Utah. Not any more. In many places, you won't notice any difference between buying a beer here and at home. And as far as entertainment goes, Salt Lake City is unsurpassed in variety. You can watch a professional basketball or hockey game; see a ballet, symphony or theater performance; laugh 'til your sides ache at a comedy club; and even rock the night away in a rowdy night club, the dance floor packed ear to ear.

Salt Lake City

Salt Lake City is a perfect spot to enjoy the pleasures of Utah skiing, for several reasons. One, you're centrally located to sample all the major ski areas. Two, hotels are very inexpensive, perhaps a result of having more than 10,000 rooms available for nightly use. Three, Salt Lake City has a ton of fun stuff to do at night.

The **Utah Transit Authority (UTA)** has a very efficient ski bus system serving Brighton and Solitude in Big Cottonwood Canyon and Snowbird and Alta in Little Cottonwood Canyon. The buses are clean, pleasant and inexpensive, and go directly from downtown to the ski areas. UTA has a free fare zone downtown, convenient for sightseeing and evening activities. Unlike many other urban areas, downtown Salt Lake City is safe for groups to walk at night. **Lewis Brothers Stages** (800-826-5844 or 359-8677) has a SkiExpress service that picks up skiers from downtown hotels and takes them to one of seven ski areas. Many of the hotels include the service in their rates.

Unless otherwise noted, all area codes are 801.

Accommodations

Although rates are a little higher in the downtown area than in outlying parts of the city, it is worth the extra few bucks to be close to Salt Lake City's major attractions. The convention and visitors bureau has complete lodging lists. Here are some recommendations (all rates are per night, double occupancy; 801 is the area code):

Salt Lake Marriott (800-345-4754 or 531-0800) is across from the Salt Palace Convention Center and is connected to the Crossroads Plaza shopping mall. Rates are $69-$159.

Howard Johnson Hotel (800-366-3684 or 521-0130) also has a great location close to the Marriott. Temple Square is across the street. Rates are $51-$165.

Red Lion Hotel (328-2000) is a few blocks farther south on West Temple, but it's within stumbling distance of the Zephyr nightclub (See Après-ski/nightlife). Rates are $89-$120. A less expensive choice in this area is the **Peery Hotel** (521-4300; $59-$109). A restored building, it is nicely elegant, but its main drawback is street noise.

In the vicinity of West Temple and 500 South are several good hotels. **Little America Hotel and Towers** (363-6781) has some of the largest rooms we've ever seen in a hotel—great for spreading out all the junk that skiers bring. The views are nice—try to get a northeast corner room for vistas of the Wasatch Mountains and downtown. Rates are $59-$108.

Also recommended are **Embassy Suites Hotel** (359-7800; $93-$129) and the **Salt Lake Hilton** (532-3344; $85-$132).

The **University Park Hotel** (581-1000; $94-$104) is near the University of Utah, a little farther from downtown but closer to the resorts. The Nickelodeon Club, a hangout for the university students, is in the hotel, too. Another option, for those looking for the coziness of an inn, is **The Brigham Street Inn** (364-4461), on East South Temple near the university.

For budget downtown accommodations, try the **Salt Lake City Center Travelodge** (531-7100), **Travelodge Temple Square** (533-8200), **Deseret Inn** (532-2900), **Emerald Inn** (533-9300) or **Best Western Olympus Motel** (521-7373). All have rooms between $35 and $80.

For more lodging listings, contact the **Salt Lake City Convention and Visitors Bureau**, 800-541-4955 or 521-2822.

Dining

Downtown Salt Lake City has more than 60 restaurants. While you will feel comfortable in most of them with casual wear, you may want to dress up a bit for the finer establishments.

For a commanding night view of the state capitol and downtown, try **Nino's** (136 E. South Temple, 359-0506) at the top of the University Club Building for elegant Italian dining. More casual Italian dining can be found at **Baci'Trattoria** (134 W. Pierpont Ave., 328-1500), **Ferrantelli Ristorante Italiano** (300 Trolley Square, 531-8228) with its New York atmosphere, and **Della Fontana** (336 S. 400 East, 328-4243), which is in a converted church with stained-glass windows and a waterfall cascading from the ceiling.

For Asian dining: **Charlie Chow** (277 Trolley Square, 575-6700) has the most interesting atmosphere, but **Pagoda** (26 E St., 355-8155) has been around the longest, since 1946. **Mikado** (67 W. 100 South, 328-0929) has private Japanese zashiki rooms.

Cafe Pierpont (122 W. Pierpont Ave., 364-1222) and **Rio Grande Cafe** (270 S. Rio Grande, at the Amtrak Station, 364-3302) are downtown's best bets for Mexican food.

American and steak and seafood restaurants abound. **New Yorker** (60 Post Office Place, 363-0166) has an elegant atmosphere in the dining room. Its more casual neighbors, **Market Street Grill** (322-4668) and **Oyster Bar** (531-6044) emphasize seafood, but also serve steaks and chicken. **Lamb's** (169 S. Main, 364-7166) is Utah's oldest restaurant, dating back to 1919 and still packed today. **The Green Parrot** (155 W. 200 South, 363-3201) plays rock-jazz-blues while serving the renowned cuisine of Chef Glen Austin. Another spectacular night view awaits diners at **Room at the Top** (150 W. 500 South, 532-3344), the Salt Lake Hilton's fine restaurant. **Shenanigan's** (274 S. West Temple, 364-3663) has a fun atmosphere.

Après-ski/nightlife/other activities

Utah's liquor laws: A few years ago, getting a simple glass of wine here was a major effort, requiring a trip to the state liquor store before going to a restaurant, then paying corkage or a set-up fee before you could consume your own brown-bagged bottle. Now, it's much easier. No more brown bags, no more set-ups. Drinking establishments fall under three categories:

Restaurants can serve alcohol from noon to midnight "to customers intending to dine." If you order wine or a cocktail with dinner, for example, you won't notice any difference.

"Bars" don't exist in Utah, at least, not by that name. If you are planning just to drink, not eat, you'll do so at a **private club.** Utah residents buy an annual membership costing $25-$35 for each club. Visitors pay $5 for a two-week membership, valid for the visitor and five guests. Because the annual memberships also allow for five guests, some visitors just approach a local outside the club and ask if they can be a guest. Once inside, they thank their "sponsor" and split for separate tables. If you lack such audacity, just think of the membership as a cover charge.

Taverns are open to the public and may or may not serve food, depending on the establishment. The only alcohol served at taverns is beer.

For a unique happy hour after a day on the slopes, stop by the hole-in-the-wall **Cotton Bottom Inn**, at the base of Big and Little Cottonwood Canyons. This is a raucous, sawdust-on-the-floor tavern with the best garlicburgers in Utah and an earthy crowd. The address is 2320 E. 6200 South, but it's a little hard to find. Ask a local to direct you.

For lively après-ski downtown, try the **Dead Goat Saloon** (Arrow Press Square, 165 S. West Temple). A quieter, pleasant location is **D.B. Cooper's** (19 E. 200 South), which Salt Lake City's career crowd seems to favor.

Salt Lake City has two brew pubs, **Squatter's Pub** (147 W. Broadway, 363-2739) and **Red Rocks Brewery** (254 South 200 West, 521-7446), Both brew their own beers on the premises and serve excellent pub fare.

Music lovers shouldn't miss the Thursday night **rehearsals of the Mormon Tabernacle Choir.** No, it's not your usual ski-town nightlife activity, but the rehearsals are free and absolutely awesome for classical music lovers. You can drop in and leave as you wish.

Bella Vista, the private club next to Nino's Restaurant, has a great penthouse-style view of the state capitol building and downtown's lights. And for high-energy dancing, it's **Zephyr** (301 S. West Temple), which lives up to its billing as "Salt Lake City's premier showcase for local and national entertainment." On the night we stopped, a rock-jazz band called Crazy 8s was playing, the dance floor was jammed, and management had to unweave the dancers and throw them out the door when the club closed.

Other rowdy night spots include **Club Max** at the Red Lion Hotel, **Power Plant** on South Highland Drive and **Nickelodeon Club**, at the University Park Hotel for dancing to DJ music.

You can go shopping at **Trolley Square,** shops and boutiques in a restored trolley barn; attend a **Utah Jazz** basketball game, or attend theater, symphony, dance or opera performances. Now, what other ski town can offer all that?

The Interconnect Adventure Tour

Utah has a unique trek for experienced skiers, which takes them to five different resorts in a single day via backcountry routes. The all-day tours, for six to 14 skiers, are led by experienced mountain guides, and require traversing and walking—you need to be a confident skier and in condition.

The four-area tour (Solitude, Brighton, Alta and Snowbird) is offered three days a week, while the five-area tour (those four and Park City) goes the other four days. Each tour lasts about eight hours and costs $95, including lunch and transportation back to the point of origin. (And a ski pin that shows you did it.) Reservations are necessary. Call (801) 534-1907 and have a credit card.

Park City Area

Park City, Deer Valley, Wolf Mountain

Walk outside the Alamo Saloon on a wintry dusk, just as the lights of Main Street begin to twinkle seductively and the sidewalks fill with après-ski traffic, and you can almost imagine the tinkling sound of spurs. Squint your eyes slightly and the strolling figures become the miners and cowboys who roamed this same street a hundred years ago, swaggering between more than 30 saloons in what was the largest silver mining town in the country. Just as suddenly, the vision is gone, and the strolling figures are once again well-heeled skiers and funseekers. Yet the flamboyant atmosphere of a gold-rush town remains. Park City is one western ski resort whose authenticity runs as deep as the local silver mines.

That unstrained air of originality is evident in the century-old buildings of Main Street, most of which are included in the National Register of Historic Places. It is there in the clapboard houses, which seem to tilt precariously on the mountainsides, and in the old weathered mine buildings, which share the mountains above town with adjacent ski runs. It's there in the very un-Utah-like funkiness and live-and-let-live attitude of the Park City locals.

That attitude of quirky independence is perhaps not surprising in this town in Utah's Wasatch Mountains, which was originally founded by soldiers who had been sent west to discourage Brigham Young from seceding from the Union. After surviving a period between 1930 and 1950 when it was all but a ghost town, Park City now can rest its hat on the stand reserved for world-class ski resorts.

In one category, Park City stands above all competition. This is the most accessible destination resort of its caliber in the country. Lying just 27 miles outside of Salt Lake City by six-lane Interstate 80 and Utah 224, it is a 45-minute drive from the airport, door to door. Skiers from either coast who carefully chart days of actual skiing per vacation time taken can get one and a half extra days on boards per trip because they don't have to devote an entire day to getting here and back.

Park City is home to three ski areas that appeal to quite different crowds, which makes it a versatile ski destination. Park City Ski Area itself is a massive, round-shouldered mountain that will appeal to the skier who demands expanse and skiing diversity. Nearby Deer Valley has built a reputation for pampering at a price, but its slopes include tougher trails than it gets credit for. Wolf Mountain, the new name of ParkWest ski area, is unpretentious and inexpensive, and extends the only welcome mat in the area to snowboarders. With the Main Street of Park City as the spiritual epicenter, this trio combines to form one truly world-class ski destination.

Park City Ski Area—Where to ski

At the base area, the Three Kings and First Time lifts service excellent learning terrain. Beginners, even those just getting into their snowplow turns, can take the gondola to the Summit House and ski a very long run back. This trail starts with Claimjumper, shifts to Bonanza, then finishes at the base area on Sidewinder. And for an adventure and a chance to see a different part of the mountain, take the Webster Run down to the Pioneer Lift, where you can have lunch at the midmountain restaurant and watch experts bouncing down the steep face of Blueslip Bowl.

Intermediates have mind-boggling choices. If you want to start with a worthy cruiser, take Pay Day from the top of the lift by the same name. The views are spectacular on this autobahn run, and at night it becomes one of the longest lighted runs in the Rockies.

Probably the most popular runs for intermediates are the 11 trails served by the King Consolidated quad superchair lift, which replaced a triple chair last season. These runs have a steep (but wide and smooth) pitch, and will be even more popular now that the King Con chair can carry almost twice as many skiers in half the time.

Both intermediates and advanced skiers will enjoy the runs under the Prospector quad chair.

Experts looking for a solid challenge will find Park City most accommodating. Start off with a trip to the top of Blueslip Bowl. Reportedly, when this was the boundary of the ski area, resort workers regularly slipped under the ropes, made tracks down the bowl and then skied back into the resort. The management regularly passed out blue (you're fired) slips to anyone caught float-

---

Park City Ski Area Facts
Base elevation: 6,900'; Summit elevation: 10,000'; Vertical drop: 3,100 feet
Number of lifts: 14—1 gondola, 2 quad superchairs, 1 quad, 6 triple chairs,
4 double chairs Snowmaking: 40 percent Total acreage: 2,200
Uphill capacity: 23,000 per hour Bed base: 12,000

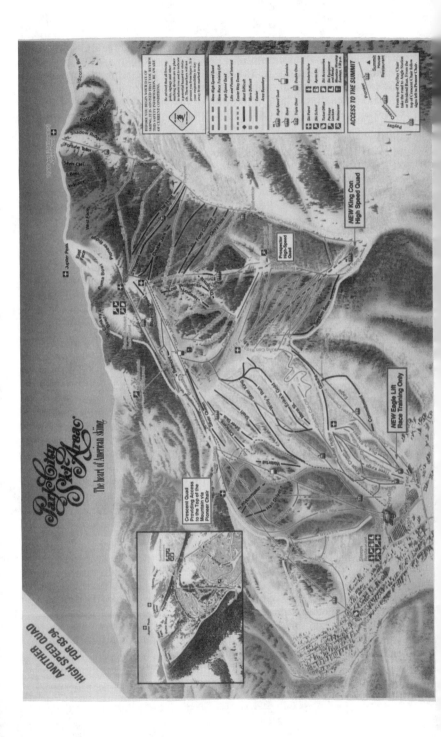

ing through this powder bowl. If you can ski Blueslip with confidence, then try Jupiter Bowl and its neighbors—McConkey's, Puma and Scotts bowls.

Jupiter Bowl has every type of steep expert terrain. To reach the Jupiter lift, take the Jupiter access road from the top of the Pioneer or Thaynes lifts. To the left as you get off the Jupiter lift are wide-open faces, especially on the West Face, which is the easiest way down (a relative term, remember). Narrow gullies and chutes, such as Silver Cliff, 6 Bells and Indicator, drop vertically between tightly packed evergreens. Or head to the right as you get off the chair and try Portuguese Gap, a run more akin to the floor opening below you, or traverse to Scott's Bowl, which is just as steep as Portuguese Gap. The adventurous (and those with parachutes) will find definite thrills in the McConkey Bowl and Puma Bowl areas. When open, these are reached by a long traverse across the West Face ridge and some climbing and hiking over the Pioneer Ridge. We asked Park City officials why they don't put a lift in to access these bowls, but they prefer to keep them the wild and untamed reward for those willing to make the hike. We're of two minds on that philosophy, but it certainly makes sense for those who want to make virgin tracks in a powder bowl. The cornice at the top of both bowls deposits skiers into steep faces and chutes, which empty out into the Pioneer lift area.

A tip to avoid lift lines: the Town triple chair lift brings skiers from the lower part of Main Street to the mid-station of the gondola. Even on holidays or peak periods, the Town lift is usually empty, so those faced with a long line at the bottom of the mountain may want to take the free shuttle here and avoid the crowds. If the gondola has a line—not unusual in peak season—try the Pay Day and Ski Team chairs. From Pay Day, you can ski to the Crescent Chair and then to Pioneer. From Ski Team, ski down Claimjumper or King Con to the Prospector Chair.

Mountain rating

Most reviews of Park City characterize this area as a cruising paradise for intermediates, which is true enough. While it may not have as much of the steep and "gulp!" of Snowbird or Alta, its bowl skiing and chutes are serious—even on the expert scale.

On the other end, Park City has plenty of open and gentle terrain for beginners and lower intermediates. Though the green-circle trails up on the mountain are wide and gentle, they wind in and around tougher stuff. If you're just starting out and concerned about getting in above your head, carry a trail map and pay attention to the signage.

Snowboarding

Snowboarding is not allowed at Park City, but boarders are welcomed at nearby Wolf Mountain (formerly ParkWest).

Park City—Lift tickets (94/95 prices)

	Adult	Child (Up to 12)
One day	$45	$20
Three days	$126 ($42/day)	$60 ($20/day)
Five days	$200 ($40/day)	$90 ($18/day)

Ask about the new "Ski Free" program for stays of four or more days before December 16th.

Multi-area books (coupons good for a day of skiing at Park City, ParkWest, Deer Valley, Alta, Snowbird, Brighton, Solitude or Sundance): five of six days, $220 for adults, $95 for children; six of seven days $264 and $114.

Park City—Ski school (94/95 prices)

Group lessons cost $42 for a full day and $35 for a half-day program. Three consecutive days cost $119 and five consecutive days are $187.

Private lessons cost $74 per hour up to $350 for a day (six hours). An early-bird private lesson, 8:45 to 9:45 a.m. is $45. Prices for a three-skier group are $94 per hour to $400 for the day.

Park City Mountain Experience classes are for upper intermediates and advanced skiers. The classes explore Jupiter Bowl, off-trail skiing and deep powder. These are four-hour classes with an instructor/guide. Classes, 10 a.m. to 2 p.m.: $42.

Kinderschule ski lessons, for children 3 to 6 years, can be combined with a day-care option. The combined day care/ski lessons are $47.25 for a half day, either morning or afternoon, including a snack and a 90-minute lesson. A full day, including lunch and lessons morning and afternoon, costs $65; and a three-day course is $178. There is a modest increase during holiday periods. For lessons only (90 minutes), the cost is $35 for a half day and $40 for a full day. Private lessons are also available for $56 an hour, $61 with two children; $66 for three.

Children aged 7 to 13 can take a two-hour group lesson for the same cost as adults. An all-day lesson that includes a supervised lunch is $67. Three days is $194; five days is $312.

Deer Valley—Where to ski

Deer Valley is renowned for pampering its guests with top-flight gourmet meals, palatial accommodations, attentive service and impeccable slopes. Some of the many amenities include guest service attendants who help get skis off car racks as you pull up to unload, tissues at every lift, a free ski corral service where you can safely leave the best equipment, and grooming crews that comb the snow so pool-table smooth it will make any beginner into an instant intermediate. Experts who sneer at the daily slope manicure can go somewhere else. Deer Valley fills a marvelous niche in the ski world, satisfying those who want to be pampered and are willing to pay a little more for the privilege.

For those who don't get this kind of attention on a daily basis, Deer Valley is a fantasy world of sorts. On-slope phones are perfect for a quick call to your broker or the home office; restaurants make a gourmet salivate; and the skiers are as well groomed as the slopes and as perfectly outfitted as the chalets.

Last season Deer Valley installed a high-speed quad lift and eight north-facing runs on Flagstaff Mountain, an area that had opened with a triple chair just the year before. Flagstaff has both moguls and cruising runs; it's easy to see from the lift which is which. For experts, a short traverse to the left off the top of this lift will open up an entire mountain face of wide-open Ontario Bowl, and challenging tree skiing. Don't miss this experience.

If you want to be seen, and have plenty of company and beautiful scenery, the best runs are Sunset, Birdseye and Success. But if you head for Mayflower Bowl or Perseverance Bowl you'll have these steeper trails virtually to yourself. Run after run down Legal Tender, Wizard, Keno and Nabob are a blast. The Mayflower and Perseverance expert sections are not all groomed, but with so little traffic the bumps never grow monstrous. Orient Express and Stein's Way are perfect cruisers with good advanced pitch, and Perseverance, coupled with the initial steeper sections of Thunderer, Blue Ledge and Grizzly, are just right for advanced intermediates.

Though Deer Valley has a reputation as the land of the smooth cruiser, experts can find some fun terrain in Mayflower Bowl, to the far left of the trail map. The last few years, Deer Valley has been letting the moguls build on Morning Star, Fortune Teller, Paradise and Narrow Gauge. These are long trails bordered by glades you can dart in and out of. You also can request an "experts only" trail map (it has a white cover), which points out advanced runs and several gladed and chute areas.

Though Deer Valley has two short lifts where never-evers can learn, we recommend other resorts for a first ski experience. The novice area is gentle enough, but it's a big step to the next level. Deer Valley's green runs (most on Bald Eagle Mountain) are also access runs that better skiers use to reach the base area. A beginner will feel as though he or she is riding a scooter on a freeway while everyone else is zipping past in Porsches. One beginner run we recommend is Sunset, a gentle scenic route that descends from the top of Bald Mountain. Head back to the base before the end of the day or you'll end up as a human slalom pole.

Deer Valley Facts
Base elevation: 7,200'; **Summit elevation:** 9,400'; **Vertical drop:** 2,200 feet
Number of lifts: 13–2 quad superchairs, 9 triple chairs, 2 double chairs
Snowmaking: 25 percent **Total acreage:** 1,100 acres
Uphill capacity: 22,200 per hour **Bed base:** 12,000

Park City, ParkWest, Deer Valley - Utah

Utah - Deer Valley, ParkWest, Park City

Daily complimentary tours of the mountain leave from the base of the Carpenter Express lift, Snow Park Lodge, at 9:30 a.m. for advanced skiers and 10 a.m. for intermediates.

Mountain rating

On a scale of one to ten, one being a never-ever skier and ten being a top-flight expert, we'd say that Deer Valley is best for levels three through eight and a half. And that's no slam: the vast majority of skiers fit that profile.

Snowboarding

Not allowed. Boarders should head for Wolf Mountain.

Deer Valley—Lift tickets (94/95 prices)

	Adult	Child (Up to 12)
One day	$47	$26
Three days	$135 ($45/day)	$72 ($24/day)
Five days	$220 ($44/day)	$115 ($23/day)

Skiers 65 and older ski for $32 for a single day, $90 for three days and $145 for five days. Deer Valley participates in the Ski Free program through December 16th.

For eight days between Christmas and New Year's, Deer Valley sells a pass for $384 ($48 per day) for adults, $224 ($28/day) for children and $264 ($33/day) for seniors. The single-day rate during that period has been announced at $48/$28/$33, but last year, single-day Christmas rates were a couple of dollars higher than the multiday daily rate. Deer Valley management probably is reluctant to be the first ski area in the nation to break the $50 barrier, even if only for a week.

However, ticket sales are limited to 4,500 skiers, so on holidays the extra few bucks to ski Deer Valley are worth it.

Multi-area books (coupons good for a day of skiing at Park City, ParkWest, Deer Valley, Alta, Snowbird, Brighton, Solitude or Sundance): five of six days, $220 for adults, $95 for children; six of seven days, $264 and $114.

Deer Valley—Ski school (94/95 prices)

This is one area where the number of private lessons far exceeds the number of group lessons.

Private lessons for one or two cost $77 for one hour, $139 for two hours, $215 for a full morning or afternoon and $398 for a full day of instruction.

Group all-day lessons for adults (13 and over) cost $57.

Children's (6 to 12 years) group lessons are $62 for the full day, including lunch. The Reindeer Club program is for ages 4 1/2 through kindergarten for $67 with lunch.

Special clinics include a black diamond workshop for advanced skiers, a style clinic, a ladies only clinic and a mountain extreme class for skiers 18 and older. These all-day classes run from 11 a.m. to 4 p.m. and cost $60.

Wolf Mountain—Where to ski

Wolf Mountain is the new name of ParkWest, a family-oriented, bargain-priced ski area that has had its share of financial troubles during the past few years. New owners recently bought it. As the first step toward revamping the area, the name was changed in a contest that gave the winner a lifetime pass. Big changes are in the works, but unfortunately not many were solidified by the deadline for our book. However, at least for the next season, Wolf Mountain will remain one of the most inexpensive ski areas in the U.S. It doesn't have high-tech lifts or gourmet on-mountain restaurants. It's the only Park City ski area that allows snowboarding. Its runs aren't manicured as meticulously as Deer Valley's, and it's a few miles away from the historic town. With no fluff and no façade, it's an Average Joe's ski resort. In short, Wolf Mountain is a wonderful complement to Park City's other two ski areas.

Wolf Mountain entices skiers to Ski the Hidden Peaks. From the base area only a tiny part of the skiable terrain is visible. Behind the first lifts and the mild terrain of Arrowhead, two massive ridges allow access to more than 50 runs.

Experts will find plenty to keep them busy on the south face of Ironhorse Peak. The chutes and gullies here are as extreme (in fact, impossible to ski without deep powder) as any in Utah. Massacre is the most relentless bump run in Utah, but Renegade, Bad Hombre, Double Barrel, Grizzly and Bear Claw are no picnic either, though Wolf Mountain regularly mows down at least a bump run a week.

For skiers unwilling to be limited by lift-served terrain, Wolf Mountain has Murdock Bowl. You have to earn this trail by hiking the last 600 feet. Once there, you have a three-quarter-mile wide bowl with 120 acres of skiable terrain and views as far as the Great Salt Lake and into the Cottonwood Canyons.

Lookout Peak has a spread of black and blue runs, including the steep Badlands and Slaughterhouse, which occasionally get groomed. The Shortswing Lift serves Ricochet and Haystack, two of the widest cruisers.

Beginners and lower intermediates have the Arrowhead section, visible from the base area, with two dedicated beginner lifts. From the deck of the base lodge, parents can watch their children progress from wedge turns to smooth stem christies. This also is good terrain for first-timers.

Wolf Mountain Facts

Base elevation: 6,800'; **Summit elevation:** 9,000'; **Vertical drop:** 2,200 feet
Number of lifts: 7 double chairs
Snowmaking: 7 percent **Total acreage:** 850 skiable acres
Uphill capacity: 6,700 per hour **Bed base:** 12,000

Wolf Mountain buses connect from the Park City Resort Center and various other Park City stops about every half hour. From Deer Valley, take the Park City bus into Park City and then transfer to the Wolf Mountain bus.

Mountain rating
The only choice in town for snowboarders. Excellent for rugged advanced and expert skiers, for price-conscious intermediates and for lower-level skiers who don't want to pay top dollar for terrain they aren't using.

Snowboarding
Wolf Mountain prides itself as Utah's snowboarding head-quarters, with more certified instructors (30) and more boards in the rental shop (300) than any other Utah ski area. One change for 94/95 is a new snowboard park that will be lit at night. The area also has a few natural halfpipes. Lessons and advanced-skill clinics are available, as is equipment rental.

Wolf Mountain—Lift tickets (94/95 prices)

	Adult	Child (3-12)
One day	$25	$15
Three days	$75 ($25/day)	$45 ($15/day)
Five days	$125 ($25/day)	$75 ($15/day)

Wolf Mountain does not discount tickets for seniors. Children younger than 3 can ski free.

Wolf Mountain—Ski school (94/95 prices)
Two-hour **group lessons** are $30; a four-hour lesson is $40. **Private lessons** are $60 per hour; $45 for each additional hour. Additional people in a private lesson cost $25 each per hour. **Kids Central** is an all-day program with lessons, lifts, day care and supervised lunch for $55. Lessons start at age 4.

Cross-country
White Pine Touring (649-8701 or 649-8710) offers track skiing, lessons and tours at the Park City golf course. Rates are $6 daily ($4 after 3 p.m.), and those 12 and younger and 70+ ski free. A ten-punch pass costs $45 and is completely transferable, so that a family with three teens or a group of friends can use it and save a few dollars. There are 18 km. of set tracks, plus mountain tours and overnight cabins.

The **Norwegian School of Nature Life** (649-5322) offers cross-country lessons and guided backcountry tours.

Accommodations
In and around the Park City Area are bed-and-breakfasts, country inns, hotels and condominiums. At Deer Valley the lodging has a decidedly upscale flavor and tariffs to match.

Park City's accommodations are roughly grouped either in the old town surrounding the Resort Center Complex or in the Prospector Square area. All are served by the free shuttlebus system. In general, low rates reflect early and late season prices in the smallest room or unit; high rates are the holiday rates for the largest unit.

In old Park City the best is the **Washington School Inn**, (800) 824-1672 or 649-3800. This is a very elegant country inn built in a former schoolhouse. Each room's name honors a former Park City teacher and everything is definitely first class. It has a Jacuzzi and steambath, and is steps away from the center of the old town. If you are on your honeymoon, ask for the Miss Urie Room. Room rates range from $75 to $275 and include breakfast and afternoon tea. No children under 12 or pets.

The Blue Church Lodge & Townhouses, 649-8009 or (800) 626-5467, is a unique property, constructed around an old church. It is a block from Main Street and is a grouping of seven condominiums ranging from one to four bedrooms in the church, with four additional townhouses across the street. Again, this is rated as a B&B because breakfast is provided in a common area each morning, though it doesn't fit the category of B&B in the classic sense. It has indoor and outdoor spas and laundry facilities. Rates are $90 to $475.

If the three keys to lodging, as in real estate, are location, location, and location, then **Treasure Mountain Inn** (800-344-2460) at the top of Main Street is a winner. These are studio and one- and two-bedroom condos with full kitchens. Each of the three buildings has a coin-operated laundry, and there is a Jacuzzi in the courtyard. Rates are $82.50-$300.

The bargain-basement accommodations are dormitory digs and rooms in the **Chateau Après Lodge** (649-9372) which has a room rate of $62, with $20 for a dorm bed. Another choice is **Budget Lodging,** 649-2526 or (800) 522-7669, with hotel rooms to four-bedroom units for $50 to $350. It also has a Jacuzzi and laundry facilities.

Near the Resort Center you'll find another cluster of hotels and condos. The best is the **Silver King Hotel,** 649-5500 or (800) 331-8652. This condominium hotel is about 100 yards from the lifts and at the hub of the transportation system. Amenities include an indoor/outdoor swimming pool and underground parking. Some units have private hot tubs. Rates: $135-$510.

The Resort Center Lodge and Inn is the second choice for luxury. It literally surrounds the base area lifts. Call (800) 824-5331 or 649-0800. Lots of amenities: spas, health club, pool, steamroom, concierge, etc. Rates for hotel rooms to four-bedroom units: $99-$1,289.

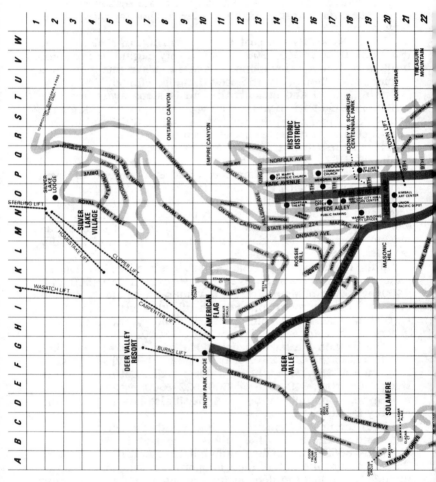

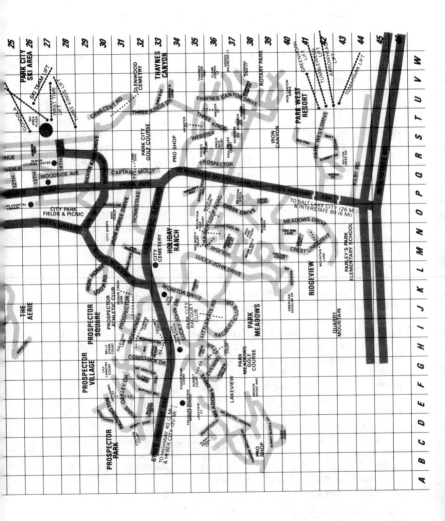

Shadow Ridge is the other top property near the lifts; (800) 451-3031 or 649-4300. It has a sauna, Jacuzzi, laundry and parking. Hotel rooms to three-bedroom condos: $69-$580.

The Snow Flower, at the base of the lifts, is 100 feet from the beginners' area. Call (800) 852-3101 or 649-6400. Single-person jetted hot tubs in each unit, outdoor pools, underground parking, etc. Studios to five-bedroom units go for $55-$645.

For more economical condos, try the renovated **Edelweiss Haus** directly across the street from the lifts and the Silver King Hotel. Call (800) 438-3855 for reservations only or 649-9342 to contact anyone in the hotel. Heated outdoor pool and Jacuzzi; rates for hotel rooms to two-bedroom condos are $75-$345.

The final main cluster of hotels serving Park City is just outside downtown. Here try the **Inn at Prospector Square** (800) 453-3812 or 649-7100. This group of condos includes use of its athletic club in the rates, $69-$479. **The Yarrow Hotel** (800) 327-2332 or 649-7000, is considered a good family accommodation. Children under 12 stay free and the hotel sits in the middle of shopping, movies and restaurants. It is on the shuttlebus route, about a five-minute ride from Park City's Main Street. Rates: $99-$359. The 200-room **Olympia Park Hotel**, (800) 754-3279 (SKI-EASY) or 649-2900, with swimming pool and exercise room, has hotel rooms and suites: $89-$399.

The Homestead is a rambling country resort 25 minutes from Park City in the town of Midway. This 108-year-old restored country inn is charming, with cross-country skiing and snow-mobiling. This is one of the Great Inns of the Rockies, rated Four Diamond by AAA. Ski packages include breakfast and dinner, seven nights lodging, skierized rental car, five days of downhill skiing at any Utah area listed in this book, two hours of snowmobiling or cross-country skiing with pass and rentals for about $870 per adult; and $475 per child based on double occupancy. Non-package rates are $75-$129 for B&B; suites and condos also are available. Call (800) 327-7220 or 654-1102.

For luxury condos and houses at affordable prices as well as a chance to get some last-minute/off-peak bargains in the entire Park City area, call **Affordable Luxury Lodging**, (800) 321-4754. The staff is helpful and will offer suggestions for all aspects of your Utah vacation from skiing to après-ski.

Accommodations—Deer Valley

Top dog is the **Stein Eriksen Lodge**; (800) 453-1302 or 649-3700. Think of any luxury or service and you will probably find it—heated sidewalks between buildings, fireplaces in the rooms, maids twice a day, fresh terrycloth robes, floor-to-ceiling windows. But, these services come at a high price. Room rates start at $265 a night and one-bedroom suites top out at about $1,200.

After Stein's the place to stay on the mountain is the **Stag Lodge**. The **Goldener Hirsch** (800) 252-3373 or 649-7770, offers the elegance and service of a top Austrian hotel at midmountain in Deer Valley.

The **Pinnacle Condominiums** with three- and four-story living rooms are spectacular inside and out. Closer to the lifts—actually ski-in/ski-out properties—are the **Pine Inn** and **La Maçonnerie**. All units have private spas.

The most economical Deer Valley properties are the **Lakeside** units, which do not have private spas but have public Jacuzzis and Deer Valley lodgings' only outdoor heated pool.

For reservations for these properties and others, call **Deer Valley Lodging**, (800) 453-3833 or 649-4040 or Deer Valley Connection at (800) 458-8612 or 645-7700.

Dining—Deer Valley

The best dining is in the Silver Lake part of Deer Valley, but it is difficult to reach in the evenings from Park City unless you have a car or are willing to pay $10+ taxi fare each way. The town bus goes as far as Snow Park Lodge, where you transfer to another bus that will take you up the hill. This latter shuttlebus runs until 10 p.m. To make advance dinner reservations from anywhere in the United States, call (800) 424-3337 (424-DEER).

The Mariposa at Silver Lake Lodge is the gourmets' top choice. Reservations are a must (645-6632).

The Glitretind Restaurant in Stein Eriksen Lodge offers meals with a Norwegian flair. This is not the place to come if pinching pennies. Entrées range from $22 to $27, with pasta weighing in at $17. Don't expect to leave for less than $100 for two. Reservations required: 649-3700.

Glitretind's all-you-can-eat skier's buffet for $19.95, however, rates as an affordable and unforgettable eating experience. There is a chef cooking made-to-order pasta dishes, a carving table, various salads and cold meats, and delectable desserts. Unless you are more disciplined than we were, forget trying to ski for at least an hour after leaving this banquet.

The Seafood Buffet at Snow Park Lodge, spread out Mondays through Saturdays, gets rave reviews from everyone who has had the chance to sample the fare. Adults pay $36 and children pay $17 and it's all you can eat. Reservations: 645-6632.

McHenry's in the Silver Lake Lodge serves moderately priced lunches and dinners.

For breakfast, head to the buffet at the **Snow Park Restaurant** and for lunch choose the **Silver Lake Restaurant**. The food is laid out like a magazine illustration, a spectacular presentation. These cafeteria-style restaurants glisten with shiny brass and sparkling glass, and the cooks decked out in kitchen whites complete with toques add another touch of class.

Dining—Park City

There are nearly 70 restaurants in Park City. After sampling scores of them and conferring with knowledgeable locals about the rest, here's our verdict.

For its inventive southwestern cuisine and funky yet quaint atmosphere, the **Barking Frog** is our favorite, with entrées in the $14-$23 range. This excellent restaurant enjoys stellar word-of-mouth advertising, or call for reservations (649-6222).

The other two restaurants that vie for best-in-town honors are **Alex's** on Main Street, 649-6644, for a French menu, and **Adolph's** just outside town on the golf course, 649-7177, for German and American cuisine. Alex's entrées range between $13 and $20, while Adolph's is a bit pricier, with entrée prices hovering around $20. A bit outside the mainstream is the **Snowed Inn**, which has gourmet food in an elegant old Victorian setting. There are two seatings each night: a four-course meal at 6:30 p.m. and a seven-course dinner at 8:30 p.m. You'll need your own transportation. Reservations required; call 649-6368.

Mileti's on Main Street, 649-8211, serves the town's best Italian food. **Ichiban Sushi** on Main Street, 649-2865, is perhaps unique in the United States, with a Japanese-trained female sushi chef. Even Japanese visitors eat here. Then there's **Scrooge's** on Main Street; 649-XMAS (649-9627). Here Christmas is celebrated the year 'round, and cantankerous Scrooge even comes through the restaurant on occasion. It's great fun for kids of all ages. Expect to spend between $10 and $15 per person. Scrooge also offers the only Dinosaur Steak we've heard of, but this requires a party of 500 or more and depends on the availability of fresh dinosaur at the market. **Cisero's** on Main Street serves great continental Italian food.

Just last year, the **Grill at the Depot** (649-9108) opened in the historic train station at the foot of Main Street and immediately established itself as a worthy addition to this miracle mile of eating establishments. The emphasis is on thick slabs of meat, including wild game, cooked on open grills.

More recommendations are: **Nacho Mama's** in The Inn at Prospector Square for highly recommended southwestern/Mexican food; and **Baja Cantina** at the Resort Center and the **Irish Camel** on Main Street for good drinks and acceptable Tex-Mex food. For very reasonable Tex-Mex in a rowdy atmosphere try **El Cheapo's** at the top of Main Street in the Treasure Mountain Inn (649-0883). **The Eating Establishment** is a locals' cheap-eats favorite, as is the **Park City Pizza Company** on the center of Main Street. **Texas Red's Pit Barbecue** is one of the deals of the century, with 16-ounce T-bone steaks topping off the menu at $10.95. **The Yarrow** offers a family bonanza with all-you-can-eat prime rib buffets every Friday and Saturday. **The Grub Steak** also gets high marks from families. Finally, the

Riverhorse Café on Main Street is a can't-miss choice for anyone who enjoys a no-fuss, low-key-elegant atmosphere.

We do on-mountain lunch alerts only when there is a special experience. In the case of Park City, **Mid-Mountain Restaurant** qualifies because of its setting. Reached on Webster Run near the bottom of Pioneer lift, this beautiful building nestled in the trees was formerly a lodge for miners. It was moved from the Angel Station on the gondola and fully restored. Even though it's a cafeteria, we like the history of the place and the touch of recorded classical music played on the expansive deck.

Après-ski/nightlife

Despite rumors of the Utah party blahs, Park City has some of the best nightlife of any ski town.

Immediate après-ski centers are **Steeps** and the **Baja Cantina**, both located in the Resort Center, and downtown at **Cisero's** where the happy hour can get very lively. **The Coyote Grill** in the Resort Center attracts a quieter crowd.

If you're thirsting for something a little different, try the **Wasatch Brew Pub** at the top of Main Street, where you can watch the brewing process even as you reap its yeasty rewards. The owner grew up in Milwaukee, and he makes beer just the way his grandfather taught him.

The hottest new nightspot is **The Black Pearl,** which features live entertainment nightly. When pop icon Madonna was in Park City during the NBA semi-final matchup between the Utah Jazz and San Antonio Spurs this year, the Material One and beau Dennis Rodman were spotted partying here.

The Club caters to a fairly young crowd and is a good place for singles. The dance floor upstairs, where the motif is velvet bordello, is a place to see and be seen. **The Alamo** next door is your basic saloon, with pool, loud music and louder conversation. Anyone with a serious case of dancing feet should check out **Z Place**, which boasts a ballroom-sized dance floor and very modern music. Z Place often features national bands and on Saturdays everything kicks off with local comedians. **Cisero's** on Main Street is one of the best spots to meet other singles and dance a bit with a mixed crowd ranging from 20s to 40s. **Steeps** in the Resort Center is another main dancing hub of Park City. Here bands often play and there is plenty of room to dance and a great good-time crowd. The age group is similar to Cisero's. **The Down Under** normally has acoustic guitar. **Adolph's**, with piano music, has been recommended for quieter evenings.

When the 60-year-old **Egyptian Vaudeville Theater** has shows, it makes a nice evening's entertainment.

Child care (94/95 prices)

Deer Valley has a licensed facility that handles children 2 to 12 years. Call the ski school for reservations. Full-day child care, including lunch, costs $46. Half-day programs, morning or afternoon, cost $35. Deer Valley also has limited infant care for children as young as 2 months. Be sure to call for reservations. Full-day infant care, including lunch, is $62, and half-day without lunch, either morning or afternoon, is $42.

Designed for 3- to 5-year-old beginners, the Bambi Special program runs from 9 a.m. to 4 p.m. Cost is $84 including lift tickets, a private lesson and children's activities. Child care phone number is 645-6612.

Park City Ski Area has no infant or child care. Children's instructional programs are outlined in the Ski School section.

Another option is **The Children's Chalet** located west of Jeremy Ranch on South Frontage Road off Interstate 80. It is a fully licensed preschool and child-care facility that accepts ages 6 weeks to 12 years. Call 649-5959.

Creative Beginnings Preschool and Child Care and **Guardian Angels** baby sitting service with professional baby sitters are also available in town. The Park City Chamber can get you information about these and other licensed child care facilities in the area as well.

Wolf Mountain's Kids Central facility has day-care facilities for non-skiing children. Call 649-5400 for ages and prices. **Miss Billie's Kid's Campus** welcomes infants and children through age 9. This fully licensed facility is directly across from Wolf Mountain ski area. Call 649-9502 or 649-KIDS.

Other activities

Shopping: For a city-town the size of Park City, the shopping is rather so-so; nice, but nothing exceptional. Among the exceptions: **Hay Charlie's** on Main Street is an unusual store with Western apparel, and **Park City Antiques, Inc.** is worth a look if you like Old West collectibles. Main Street has interesting **art galleries** with differing collections. Deer Valley has several very upscale boutiques. Just off Interstate 80 at the Park City exit is a **factory outlet** center with 48 stores.

Park City's ski calendar has some unusual events. For the past few years, the **World Cup** ski racing tour has opened here over the Thanksgiving weekend. This year, the top women racers in the world will be at the Park City Ski Area. Deer Valley hosts an annual **Tournament of Champions,** showcasing former Olympic or World Cup champions in head-to-head competition each December. The **Sundance Film Festival** is in late January, showcasing new films from around the world.

Old fashioned horse-drawn **sleigh rides** to cozy dinners are available through the Park City Sleigh Company. **Snowmobile tours** are available. Both High Country Tours (645-7533) and Snowwest Snowmobiles (645-7669) have dinner tours.

Several companies give **balloon trips**. Call Adventure Balloon, Park City's Great Balloon Escape, Sunrise Fantasy Balloon, and Balloon Affaire.

Park City Racquet Club (649-8080) has indoor tennis courts, volleyball and aerobic workouts. The **Prospector Square Athletic Club** has health club facilities; 649-6670.

Park City Visitor's Information Center and Museum is open Monday through Saturday, 10 a.m. to 7 p.m., Sundays from noon to 6 p.m. It is packed with history of the Old West and has a self-guided city tour, with background on historical buildings.

Getting there and getting around

Getting there: Park City is 27 miles east of Salt Lake City, by Interstate 80 and Utah 224. The drive from the airport to Park City takes about 45 minutes. **Lewis Brothers Stages,** (800) 826-5844 or 649-2256 in Park City, 359-8677 in Salt Lake City, run airport buses for Park City once an hour for $26 round-trip, half that for children 12 and younger. **Park City Transportation,** (800) 637-3803 or 649-8567, has a series of airport van runs for $36 round-trip. Call ahead to make sure that a van will be waiting. If you arrive without reservations, go to the transportation counter at the Salt Lake City airport and a representative will put you on the next available van. The **All Resort Express** airport service is $34 round-trip. For all services, call 48 hours in advance for Park City-to-airport reservations.

Both Lewis Bros. and Park City Transportation have buses between Park City and Snowbird/Alta. Rate is $19 round trip per person; call for times.

Getting around: To rent a car or not to rent a car? Our recommendation: if you're staying close to the town center or near a stop on the free bus line, do without. The town bus system has four routes with buses that come by about every 20 minutes from 7:40 a.m. to 12:30 a.m. But if you plan to do a lot of skiing at Wolf Mountain or resorts outside Park City, want to make a couple of trips to the factory outlet stores or are staying more than a short walk from the bus stop, you will want wheels.

Information/reservations

Park City has no single central reservations number, but these agencies can book just about every aspect of your trip. Ask about special ski packages.

Park City Holidays; (800) 222-7275 (222-PARK); 649-0493.

Deer Valley Central Reservations (800) 424-3337 (424-DEER); 649-1000.

Information: Park City Area Chamber of Commerce/Convention and Visitors Bureau, 1910 Prospector Avenue, P.O. Box 1630, Park City UT 84060; (800) 453-1360 or 649-6100.

All telephone area codes are 801 unless otherwise noted.

Alta, Utah

It's hard to find a skier who is ambivalent about Alta. They either adore this place, tell all their friends and come back year after year, or they decide, no thanks, this just ain't my cup of tea.

Alta, you see, is as lovably eccentric as your maiden aunt, the one who still has doilies to protect the upholstery on her overstuffed armchairs and who still listens to old Bing Crosby records on her aging turntable—despite your offer to buy her a CD player with remote control (*and* the Crosby CDs). "The music sounds just fine, dear," she says as she feeds you home-baked cookies and real hot chocolate. "I don't want you to spend all your money on me."

Alta, you see, has resisted installing high-speed chair lifts, building high-rise hotels and throwing away money on slick magazine ads. "The snow skis just fine, dear," Alta seems to say as she spoils you with 500-plus inches of fluffy Utah powder spread over 2,200 acres of terrain. "I don't want you to spend all your money on me."

And you won't. The lift ticket is $23, the rock-bottom lowest for a major ski resort (speaking acreage and vertical drop) in North America. If you want more sophisticated facilities, no problem. Head next door to Snowbird—and be ready to pull a few more bills from your wallet.

Alta's low-key attitude is rooted in its history. In half a century of mining, Alta went from obscurity to boom, followed by outrageous scandal when the mines suddenly collapsed in the early 1900s. At a time when glamorous international figures were being courted by the new Sun Valley, Alta was born from the simple desire of Salt Lake residents to have a place where they could ski without having to climb uphill. Beginning in 1939 using its old ore tram, Alta has pulled pretty near four generations of skiers up to its ridges. It still bears the original name, Alta Ski Lifts, without the word "resort" anywhere in sight.

Alta Facts

Base elevation: 8,550'; **Summit elevation:** 10,650'; **Vertical drop:** 2,100 feet
Number of lifts: 12–2 triple chairs, 6 double chairs, 4 surface lifts
Snowmaking: none **Total acreage:** 2,200
Uphill capacity: 9,100 per hour **Bed base:** 1,136

Alta provides a fine contrast to its neighbor Snowbird, just a mile down the road in Little Cottonwood Canyon. Where Snowbird with its high-occupancy tram and multi-story hotel is high-tech, Alta with its serviceable lifts and multitude of mountain inns is homey.

And you probably will forgive Alta like your aunt, for not keeping up with the trends. Of the skiers we know who have been here, the vast majority return or intend to. Must be that no-fuss, home-baked warmth.

Where to ski

Powder is what Alta is all about. Not just because it gets a lot, but because, with its terrain of tree skiing and sheltered gullies, it tends to keep it longer. While most skiers are swishing down groomed runs a couple of days after a storm, the Alta cognoscenti are secretly diving into snow pockets in side canyons and upper elevations.

Alta, like Snowbird, is a what-you-see, you-can-ski resort, with many ways down that aren't named on the trail map. Be individual. Be creative. That's the spirit of Alta.

The ski area has a front and backside, and two base stations. Wildcat Base is the first one you reach. It has basic facilities—ticket office, restrooms, ski patrol. The Albion Base houses the Children's Center, Ski School and retail and rental operations. Albion is where you go to find the beginner slopes, but it has expert terrain at higher elevations. Albion and Wildcat are connected by a long, nearly level, two-way transfer rope tow, the only "lift" of its type we've ever seen. Just grab the rope and let it pull you to the other side.

Uphill from the Wildcat Ticket Office, Wildcat and Collins lifts serve advanced runs on the right side—narrow trails, bump runs, and many glades—with intermediate and more advanced runs on the left. Those to the left are wider, the main intermediate route down being Meadow.

From the left of these two lifts, skiers can access an entirely different ridge, West Rustler, by taking the Germania lift. That means more steep and deep at Eagle's Nest and High Rustler for experts, and intermediate slopes with less intimidating names like Ballroom and Mambo. The line at Germania lift may appear daunting on powder days but rarely averages more than ten minutes, although if there's powder on weekends, it can crank up to twenty.

From the top of Germania Pass the runs down the front side return you to Wildcat base area; runs down the back return you to Albion, or give access to the Sugarloaf and Supreme lifts. Skiers wishing to cross back into the Germania area must do an extensive traverse around the rim of a huge bowl. It has a superb view, and you may be tempted to stop to admire it. Don't: the slope is too gradual to lose what little momentum you have; you won't have to pole, but you will be going mighty slow. The only other Albion-to-Wildcat route is at the base on the transfer tow.

From the Albion base station, Sunnyside and Albion lifts are slow riders across gentle terrain, a wide, rolling beginner's playground. At the top of those lifts, intermediates and experts can take Supreme lift to Point Supreme, the 10,650-foot summit, and from there have plenty of steep tree skiing to the left in an area near the boundary called Spiney Ridge. Some sections are known as Piney Glades and White Squaw. It's all known as steep, and tremendously popular with knowing Salt Lake skiers. Up here you can ski all day without ever going the same way twice.

Also midmountain on the Albion side is Sugarloaf lift, which serves expert bowls as far as the eye can see. Swooping down into a gully to the left of the lift as you descend usually gives you powder pockets. A day or two after a storm, try Devils' Castle, the steeps under the rocks accessible from Sugarloaf.

To follow the sun, start the morning on Sugarloaf, then move to Germania on the front side at midday, and finish on Supreme.

Alta's gate skiing is at the Sunnyside lift and is open Friday and Saturday. The $5 ($7 for unlimited runs) race fee is payable at the race arena.

Mountain rating

Alta is a great place for any level of skier. Experts have powder and steeps. By itself, Alta is an expert's delight, and together with neighbor Snowbird, few other groupings can match it. The major difference is vertical drop. The Snowbird tram opens almost 3,000 feet of continuous expert vertical, versus the maximum expert drop of about 1,000 at Alta.

Intermediates have wonderful slopes here, plus a few very gentle pitches off to one side in the Albion area that don't get groomed—a super place to take your first powder turns. Alta doesn't skimp on grooming—we found the intermediate and beginner runs quite negotiable.

Given the choice between Snowbird and Alta, beginners definitely should start here. Not only are the slopes less intimidating, but so are the skiers (we're talking fashion and attitude here, not ability). The mile-long beginner run serviced by the Albion lift can make a beginner feel like a real skier—and that's what the sport is all about.

Snowboarding

Not permitted. Head over to Snowbird.

Ski school (93/94 prices)

Bearing the name of Alf Engen, the Norwegian ski jumper who came to Utah in 1930, the ski school is bound to have Old World flavor and expertise. More than 100 instructors are quite a sizable squad for a resort this size. **Private lessons** are $50 for an hour, $150 for a morning and $125 for an afternoon, or $250 for all day. Two-hour **group lessons** are $21.

Afternoon workshops focusing on specific skills are called **Bumps Bumps Bumps, Conditions du Jour,** and **Diamond Challenge,** and are $30 for two and a half hours; meet at the blue and white signs below the base of Germania lift.

Lower-level ski lessons meet at the base of the Albion lift, while upper skill levels meet at the base of the Germania lift.

Children's lessons for ages 4-12 are $21 for a two-hour lesson. Packages with lunch are $30 for two hours or $50 for four hours for ability levels 1-2, and $50 and $70 for levels 3-9.

Lift tickets (93/94 prices)

	Adult	Child (Up to 12) Senior (60+)
One day	$23	$23
Three days	$69 ($23/day)	$69 ($23/day)
Five days	$115 ($23/day)	$115 ($23/day)

Yes, we could have skipped the chart in this particular chapter, but we wanted to underscore Alta's sensible approach to pricing: management skips all the discount gimmicks, figures out what it will take to run the place, and charges everyone the same low price. They figure that everyone—adults, children and seniors—occupy one spot on the lifts, so all should be charged the same amount. And just in case you were wondering if a family can still save money here when there is no child discount, a family of four (two adults and two kids between 6 and 12) pays $460 to ski five days at Alta, $550 at Snowbird and $556 at Park City (based on 93/94 prices).

Half-day tickets are available for $17, and Alta accepts Visa and MasterCard (that wasn't the case a couple of years ago).

Accommodations (93/94 prices)

Something very important to know: as a general rule, Alta's lodges do not accept credit cards, though they do accept personal or travelers checks. Hotels will automatically add a 15 percent service charge, as well as local taxes. Always ask if your room has a private bath—some of them do not.

Rustler Lodge (532-2020, 800-451-5223) is midway between the Albion and Rustler/Wildcat base areas. Recent reports say that some of the rooms have seen better days, so make sure to have a clear understanding of your room before you arrive. It has an outdoor pool, saunas and Jacuzzis. Prices include breakfast and dinner, per person double occupancy. Rates start at $99 per night for a room without private bath, $119 and $139 for rooms with bath.

Alta Peruvian (800-453-8488 reservations only; 742-3000) is another option for those who seek fine accommodations. It has similar amenities, features movies each night, and is a short walk from the Wildcat base (or you can take the lodge's free shuttle). The rates include breakfast, lunch, dinner and lift ticket. (Food's great, by the way.) Dorm rooms are $99; double room with private bath ranges from $128 to $165 (per person, double occupancy). One- or two-bedroom suites also are available, as are multiday discounts. No credit cards accepted; personal or travelers checks are fine, as is cash.

The Alta Lodge (800-748-5025, reservations only; 742-3500) is a 57-room mountain inn with saunas, hot tubs, and several common areas, including a library. Skiers grab a rope tow at the end of the day to get back up a small hill to the lodge. Breakfast and dinner are included in the price, and the food is excellent. Daily room rates (based on double occupancy) are $191 for a room with a sink; $243 for a room with private bath. Single-occupancy and dorm rates are available; call for those. No credit cards: use personal or travelers checks, or greenbacks.

Goldminer's Daughter (742-2300 or 800-453-4573 for reservations only), named after a huge mining claim, is closest to the Wildcat lift. You can step out your door into the lift line, and drop by your room between runs for a hat or neck gaiter. All rooms have private bath. Per-person double occupancy rates with breakfast and dinner at $79 to $85. Dorm rooms are $69.

Snow Pine Lodge (742-2000) is Alta's oldest and smallest. It was extensively renovated a few years ago, and has an outdoor hot tub, Scandinavian sauna and a warm and homey atmosphere. Rates (per person, double occupancy) are $98-$106 for a room with private bath, $72-$86 for a shared-bath room, and $66 for a bed in the men's or women's dorm.

Two large condominiums, **Hellgate** (742-2020) and **Blackjack** (742-3200) are located between Alta and Snowbird, with Blackjack better situated for skiing between the two resorts and therefore slightly higher, although Hellgate has van service to the ski areas. Studios range from $132 to $145; one-bedrooms sleeping four, $210 to $230; two-bedrooms sleeping six, $280 to $315; three-bedrooms, $350 to $400. There is no service charge.

Dining

At Alta you eat in your condo or your lodge, and if you're headed for a condo, stop in Salt Lake for groceries.

On the slopes, **Chic's Place** is a fine and unpretentious restaurant with a good view.

Après-ski/nightlife

Bring your own. There's nothing going on but what visitors cook up—either in their condo or the lodge's common rooms. If a little bit of nightlife is all you need, head to Snowbird. But if your ski vacation is not complete without a vigorous night of dancing, stay in Salt Lake City and take the ski bus up here (see the Salt Lake City chapter for details).

Child care

Alta's child care center is a state-licensed facility owned and operated by Redwood Pre-School, Inc. (742-3042). It has programs for children aged 3 months to 12 years that include lunch and play and/or on-snow activities. Children's ski lessons are available from the Alta ski school.

All-day infant care by reservation only is $50; $220 for five days. All-day child care with lunch is $35, $150 for five days.

Other activities

Shopping: A few shops in the Little Cottonwood Canyon area have local handicrafts, artwork and books, but this isn't why skiers come here. You can always take a bus down to Salt Lake City for a day of heavy-duty shopping.

Heliskiing is available in Little Cottonwood Canyon from Wasatch Powder Birds, 742-2800.

Getting there and getting around

Getting there: Salt Lake City is a major airline hub, so flights are numerous from every corner of the continent. Amtrak's California Zephyr and Desert Wind also stop here.

Alta is 25 miles southeast of Salt Lake City in Little Cottonwood Canyon on State Highway 210. Driving time from the city or the airport is one hour, with the most direct route from the airport east on I-80, south on I-215, Exit 6 to Wasatch Blvd., then follow the signs to Alta and Snowbird.

Getting around: Ground transportation from the airport or the city is frequent and plentiful. If you fly in, don't bother renting a car. Most of Alta's lodges have shuttles to get you to the slopes or to visit neighboring restaurants. If you are staying in Salt Lake City, take the Utah Transit Authority bus or a Lewis Brothers SkiExpress van to Alta. (See Salt Lake City chapter).

Bus service links Alta and Snowbird for $1.

Information/reservations

The **Alta Reservations Service** is the central reservations agent for Alta; call 942-0404, or call the individual lodges' 800 numbers if you've decided where to stay. The agency can also arrange rental cars and rooms in Salt Lake City. **Alta Ski Lifts** is at 742-3333. Recorded **snow report** is 572-3939.

All telephone area codes are 801 unless otherwise noted.

Snowbird, Utah

Big-time skiing, deep powder and fast ascents and descents are the hallmarks of Snowbird skiing. If you're a powder devotee, Snowbird is Mecca: every powder skier should make at least one pilgrimage. An eight-minute tram ride takes you to the summit to experience what has earned Snowbird its reputation as the top powder-skiing resort. (You can ski Snowbird's entire 3,100-foot vertical drop in one continuous, thigh-burning run, too.) Nearby ski areas get nearly as much snow (500-plus inches) and it is equally dry, but frequent visitors here would probably bet their North Face powder suits that Snowbird's snow is a droplet or two drier and a flake or three deeper. We've heard Canadian heli-skiing guides measure their powder by Snowbird standards, as in, "Ayuh, it's good, but it's not quite Snowbird powder." It's hard to imagine a more flattering comparison.

Snowbird's look and atmosphere is quite distinctive among American ski resorts. There is no town here, just a shopping center, a skyscraper hotel and a couple of condo complexes. Here, facilities are sleek and high-tech.

Where to ski

To get the lay of the land at Snowbird, understand first the function of the tram. Mounting one lower peak, hanging across a cirque and rising to the 11,000-foot summit, it brings 125 skiers at a time to Hidden Peak, unseen from the base lodge. On powder days, when the first tram arrives, there's a dash for the slopes. Skiers hurl their equipment and then themselves over the railings to make the first tracks. After this thrill, things calm down a bit. Now decisions can be made whether to get equipment on quickly and be the first of the 125-person group down the cirque or wait a bit, let others dash, and then go where they don't.

The choices are to drop under the tram into Peruvian Gulch, with intermediate, advanced and expert routes down, or to head left into the Little Cloud area.

Snowbird Facts
Base elevation: 7,900'; **Summit elevation:** 11,000'; **Vertical drop:** 3,100 feet
Number of lifts: 8–1 aerial tram, 7 double chairs **Snowmaking:** none
Total acreage: 2,000 **Uphill capacity:** 9,000 per hour **Bed base:** 900+

Most tram riders opt for Peruvian. Intermediates peel off the upper ridge at Chip's Run, often marked with large orange balls to indicate the easiest way down. Chip's offers a few expert options en route. Experts tackle The Cirque, a plunge that drops into almost 3,000 vertical feet of expert slopes. You can choose a run about as steep as you want, some with chutes that hold only powder enough to slow your virtual freefall. Anyone who has dropped down upper Silver Fox, Great Scott or Upper Cirque deserves to be treated with reverence—they're using up the extra lives they were blessed with.

From the tram ridge, Primrose Path is an unrelenting black diamond, normally the choice of those who think twice about tiptoeing around The Cirque. The lower section of the Peruvian side of the ridge offers five trails marked expert, but here at Snowbird what you can see, you can ski. So pick your own way.

Should you decide to drop over to the Little Cloud side of Hidden Peak from the tram terminal, the skiing is somewhat tamer—tamer by Snowbird standards. It's a wide scoop carved out of the side of the mountain, with cliffs above and swoops below. Little Cloud, the highest black run, skirts along the top of the bowl and then drops down a third of the resort's distance to Little Cloud lift for a quick ride up the bowl again, or halfway down to the Mid Gad Restaurant. Entering the bowl a bit lower than Little Cloud run, Regulator Johnson charts a steeper, more direct route to either destination.

Five lifts stretch out of Gad Valley. Wilbere is short and serves primarily beginners and intermediates. Mid Gad and Gad I lifts rise higher and primarily serve wide intermediate slopes. Mid Gad serves a run called Big Emma, which though very wide, will give beginners a good test, as its pitch might rate it blue at any other area. You get more vertical for your ride on Gad I and can access some mid-mountain expert runs.

A good starter for upper intermediates is Bassackwards. When that's as smooth as silk, they can stretch themselves on a black run called Carbonate, where they'll get the feel of a steeper, but not terrifying, pitch. The expert terrain is up higher at Gad II lift, which opens narrower trails through the trees and over megabumps. Two trail names tell the story—Gadzooks and Tiger Tail, but Black Forest and Organ Grinder are equal challenges.

Never-evers and unconfident beginners shouldn't tackle the Wilbere lift until they've learned a modicum of control on Chickadee, purely a first-timer's slope in back of the Cliff Lodge.

A coin-operated mechanical race course is set up between Wilbere lift and Mid Gad lift, accessible from either.

Note: we recommend that first-time visitors explore the mountain with the Host and Hostess Program., a free introductory tours of the mountain, taking skiers to the part best suited to their abilities. Tours meet at the Free Guided Tour sign, plaza level of the Snowbird Center. They leave daily at 9 and 10 a.m. and 1 p.m. This is not the normal meet-the-mountain tour some resorts offer, often sticking to intermediate and beginner terrain and moving at a snail's pace: the hosts sort out the groups skillfully and then move to appropriate terrain. It's also a great way to meet people.

Two areas are designated as Family Ski Zones. One begins at the top of the tram and heads down Chip's Run through Peruvian Gulch to Whodunit, then back to the tram base. The other begins at the top of Gad II chair, following Election and Middle-Lower Bassackwards to the base of Gad Valley.

If you want to avoid crowds, start at 9 a.m. and ski Gad II and Little Cloud until 11. Then for the next hour and a half, work the Gad Valley chairs. Between 12:30 and 1:30 the lines lighten up and you can go back to the top. Remember, however, that even a 20-minute wait for the tram is equivalent to two lifts; you get more skiing for your wait. If you want to ski in the sun, the Gad Valley lifts are more protected and get morning sun. In the afternoon, head up to Little Cloud.

Mountain rating

Experts, you have arrived. A healthy half of Snowbird terrain is for you. These are not public-relations black diamonds, either. They are tough, you will leave exhilarated or frustrated, depending on whether you attacked them or they attacked you.

Intermediates, expect to be pushed. Owner Dick Bass, who has climbed the highest mountain on every continent, affirms, "What we gain too easily, we esteem too lightly." Let that be your rallying cry. You will improve, a phenomenon you may not recognize until you go back to ski those home slopes you thought were a challenge. Intermediates will be comfortable on both blues and greens here. If Snowbird exhausts you or you're here for a week and know all the routes in your comfort zone by heart, go up the valley to Alta, which has more mellow intermediate trails.

Beginners, you can learn here, but it will be a challenge. Chickadee is gentle enough, but it's a big jump after that (although the Baby Thunder lift promises to open more beginner terrain). This mountain isn't built for beginners and we want you to ski a second time, so go to Alta or Solitude for your baptism.

Snowboarding

Snowboarding is permitted on most of the mountain. The one place they can't go is Gad II. A snowboard park has been added off the Little Cloud chair lift. Snowbird has some flat stretches, which snowboarders hate because they must unbuckle to push themselves across. Ask a mountain host how to avoid them. Instruction is $45 for a half-day class.

Ski school (93/94 prices)

The instructional menu is varied. Group lessons are offered but there are also many specialty clinics. The **Mountain Experience** is a Snowbird marquee, letting a skier of advanced or expert class join a member of the Snowbird ski family and launch an assault on the entire mountain for $65 for a day or $290 for five days. **Silver Wings** presents skiers over 50 with the opportunity to ski with people of the same ability and age group for $55 a day, $144 for three days, or $240 for five days. Adult **Super Classes** are the same price as Silver Wings. **Adult specialty workshops,** which include Style, Bumps and Diamonds, Race or Snowboard Workshops, are $45 per half day. A three-day women's seminar also is offered.

(Snowbird last season announced a policy of "Eight is Enough," meaning that they guarantee you'll have no more than eight people in a lesson. They note this doesn't apply at Christmas and President's Weekend. We think five or six is enough.)

The **Chickadee Program** has 90-minute lessons for ages 3-4 and skier levels 1-2 for $45. A full-day child or teen Super Class can be arranged through Camp Snowbird for $65 for a full day.

Private lessons in skiing, telemarking or snowboarding are $65 per hour; two to five people can split a $90 charge. A three-hour lesson is $180; $240 for two to five skiers. Also available are Early Bird Specials ($40 for a 9 to 10 a.m. lesson) and Powder Plus lessons, use wide skis designed to float through powder.

Snowbird Ski School has three one-stop registration locations for ski school and purchasing lift tickets. (Tickets are not included in the lesson price, but the Chickadee chair for never-evers and children does not require tickets.) The offices are on Level 1 of the Cliff Lodge, the Plaza Deck of the Snowbird Center and the Alpine Room, Level 2 of the Snowbird Center. For more information or reservations, call 742-2222, ext. 5170.

Lift tickets (94/95 prices)

	Adult	Child (6-12) Senior (62-69)
One day	$40	$26
Three days	$99 ($35/day)	$66 ($21/day)
Five days	$165 ($35/day)	$110 ($21/day)

These are the prices with tram access. For chairs only, the one-day price is $33 and $21, respectively.

Children under 12 staying at Snowbird ski free when an accompanying adult purchases a lift ticket. Seniors 70+ ski free.

Accommodations

Lodgings at Snowbird consist of the Cliff Lodge plus three condominium lodges, all within walking distance of the base lifts. Additional accommodations, accessible by shuttlebus, are plentiful in Salt Lake City. Call (800) 453-3000 or (801) 742-2222. Winter season is mid-December through March; value season is late November through mid-December and April.

The Cliff Lodge spreads like eagle's wings at the base of Snowbird. Inside, there's an 11-story atrium, a glassed-in rooftop and snow-level dining. The views are spectacular, the three restaurants and clubs tastefully decorated, the food wonderfully prepared, the service extraordinary, the rooms comfortable—and so accessible to the slopes.

Rooms with picture windows opening from the shower into the sleeping area add a touch of whimsy as well as a view. The pool, fitness center and spa on top of the hotel offer every variety of body rejuvenation, active and passive. Rates based on double occupancy are $178 a night in winter season, and $103 in value season. One-bedroom deluxe suites start at $480 a night in peak season or $253 in value season. Two-bedroom deluxe suites start at $756 a night in peak season or $400 in value season. Children under 12 stay and ski free with adults.

The Lodge at Snowbird, The Inn, and **The Iron Blosam** are three condominium complexes with similar layouts. They are not as elegant as the Cliff Lodge, but the condos are well maintained, roomy and comfortable. Amenities include outdoor swimming pools, indoor hot tubs, saunas. Rates in winter season are $183 a night for an efficiency or studio, $344 for a one-bedroom unit; and $504 for one-bedroom with loft. In value season, rates are $93, $176 and $259 respectively.

Dormitory space costs $35-$50 a night at the Cliff Lodge.

Dining

The Aerie on top of the Cliff Lodge is the most elegant for exquisite dining and dancing. The **Atrium** at lobby level serves cocktails and hefty buffet breakfasts and lunches. **The Mexican Keyhole,** also in the Lodge, offers Mexican and American fare.

Other restaurants are in the base facility, Snowbird Center. **The Steak Pit** serves steak and seafood in generous portions for hungry skiers. There's normally a wait to get in, but it's worth it. **The Forklift** is a breakfast and lunch spot with easy access back up the slopes yet with a carpeted restaurant atmosphere rather than a burger-and-chili cafeteria. For that you need to go downstairs—**The Rendezvous** has a well-stocked salad island in the center. It also serves breakfast. **Pier 49 San Francisco Sourdough Pizza** has pizza with lots of toppings, and **Suzy's Coffee Cart** has gourmet coffees, cappuccino and espresso.

The Lodge Club in the Lodge at Snowbird has a good light dinner, and **Wildflower** in the Iron Blosam serves up good pasta.

Après-ski/nightlife

Snowbird's nightlife is on the very quiet side.

For immediate après-ski, The **Forklift** and the **Wildflower Lounge** are best. In the evening, **The Aerie** has a bar with quiet piano music and a great sushi bar.

Child care

Snowbird offers its lodge guests licensed day care at the **Camp Snowbird Children's Center** at the Cliff Lodge. Charges for the 93/94 season were $50 a day, with lunch, for ages 6 weeks to 2 years; $48 for ages 2 and 3, and $36 for ages 4-12.

Babysitting is $9 an hour, a little more for an additional child. Friday night activities are scheduled for children.

Reservations are required up to a month in advance for some age groups and time periods. Call the Children's Center at 742-2222, Ext. 5026. The Ski School handles programs that combine ski instruction with day care.

Other activities

Shopping: The Snowbird Center has about a dozen shops. A champion browser will finish them off in an hour or so.

There is no cross country skiing or snowmobiling in Little Cottonwood Canyon, but spectacular **helicopter skiing** is available from Wasatch Powderbird Guides; 742-2222, Ext. 4190.

The **Cliff Spa** Program offers treatments include facials, massage and herbal wraps, as well as a full exercise facility. It is open 6 a.m. to 11 p.m. daily, and the salon is open 9 a.m. to 9 p.m. Half-day and full-day packages are available. Call 742-2222, Ext. 5900 for spa, Ext. 5960 for the salon.

Getting there and getting around

Getting there: Salt Lake City is a major airline hub, so flights are numerous from every corner of the continent. Amtrak's California Zephyr and Desert Wind lines also stop here (at 4 a.m., but the fare is quite inexpensive).

Snowbird is 25 miles southeast of Salt Lake City in Little Cottonwood Canyon. Driving time from the city or the airport is one hour, with the most direct route from the airport east on I-80, south on I-215, Exit 6 to Wasatch Blvd., then follow the signs

Getting around: Ground transportation from the airport or the city is frequent. If you fly in, don't bother renting a car. Everything you need to reach at Snowbird is within walking distance. If you plan to ski a lot of other Utah areas, stay in Salt Lake City and take the Utah Transit Authority bus or a Lewis Brothers SkiExpress van. (See Salt Lake City chapter).

Bus service links Alta and Snowbird for $1.

Information/reservations

Central reservations number is (800) 453-3000. The resort address is Snowbird Ski and Summer Resort, PO Box 929000, Snowbird UT 84092-9000; 742-2222.

Telephone area code is 801.

Big Cottonwood Canyon

Solitude Ski Resort and Brighton Ski Resort

Of any 10 skiers waiting at a bus stop in downtown Salt Lake City for the Utah Transit Authority ski express, it's a sure bet that seven will board the Snowbird/Alta bus to Little Cottonwood Canyon. The other three will board the Brighton/Solitude bus to Big Cottonwood Canyon.

If you're one of the three, be prepared for a silent judgment of your skiing ability by the Snowbird/Alta seven.

One will start the waiting-for-the-bus small talk. "Where are you headed?" he'll ask with a jaunty smile, perhaps with the thought that his group may invite you along on their search for the Steep and Deep.

"Solitude," you answer with an equally jaunty smile.

Your questioner's smile fades as his eyes take in your clothing, how far above your head your skis extend, and whether there is a tell-tale rental-shop sticker at the binding. He's too polite to ask, "If you can't handle Snowbird or Alta, then what are you doing on *those* skis?"

Big Cottonwood Canyon's reputation as the place where the locals learn to ski has more to do with prices than terrain. Snowbird charges $40 a day to use its lifts, Solitude's ticket is $28 and Brighton's is a mere $25.

Neither area is as vast as its neighbors in the next canyon. But to dismiss these two areas as a playground where beginners whet their appetites for the real thing is to woefully underestimate the terrain. Solitude's Honeycomb Canyon has slopes that will bring out the adrenaline in the best of skiers. Brighton's expert offerings are fewer, but have been increasing every year.

Solitude Ski Resort

Solitude has been making changes that will bring it into the Utah big leagues very soon. A redesign of its runs and lift system brought it the 1990 *Snow Country* magazine award for slope and trail design. It restored a 33-year-old building, the Roundhouse, into an elegant on-mountain restaurant. The resort also plans a new base village with an Alpine design, including a much-needed 60-room hotel.

```
┌─────────────────────────────────────────────────────────────┐
│                      Solitude Facts                           │
│ Base elevation: 8,000'; Summit elevation: 10,030'; Vertical drop: 2,030 feet │
│  Number of lifts: 7–1 quad superchair, 2 triple chairs, 4 double chairs      │
│          Snowmaking: none Total acreage: 1,100                │
│  Uphill capacity: 10,750 per hour Bed base: 12,000 in Salt Lake City         │
└─────────────────────────────────────────────────────────────┘
```

Solitude's lift layout is excellent, with a logical progression from beginner to expert areas. Beginners start on the Link chair, a slow-moving lift that accesses a nearly flat, very wide, completely isolated run, Easy Street.

When Link is conquered, on to the Moonbeam II chair, where Little Dollie, Pokey Pine and Same Street will take them back down for another run. The next step is either the Apex or Sunrise chairs, where one green trail is surrounded by lots of blue.

The next level is the Powderhorn or Eagle Express chairs, where there are no green runs, just blue with a few black. If you can handle that, then you're ready for the Summit chair. From the top of the Summit chair, you can go one of three ways.

The first takes you back down to the Summit chair on upper intermediate runs like Dynamite and Liberty. Eventually you'll meet the runs off the Sunrise chair, which head back to the base.

Way Number Two heads toward Brighton on the intermediate SolBright trail. You could go all the way over to Brighton, or you could head down Courageous, a cleared but steep black-diamond run clearly visible from the Summit chair; into Headwall Forest, where you pick your own line through the trees; or jump into a couple of long, steep, narrow chutes.

The third option will take you into Honeycomb Canyon, a wonderful playground for advanced intermediates to experts. Woodlawn is a marked run that follows the canyon floor. On the map it's a blue line, a black line overlapping it. Solitude should skip the blue line on the next printing: Woodlawn has some surprises that only a confident skier can handle. Chief among them are a couple of gigantic mogul fields and an extremely steep section that looks like it might be a small waterfall in the summer. Though covered with snow, not ice, it was a huge, sudden dropoff.

The canyon sides are an expert skier's delight. From the top, traverse until you find a line you like, then go for it. Honeycomb Canyon also can be reached from the Eagle Ridge run in the main part of the ski area, but this entry is strictly double-diamond through trees.

Mountain rating

Solitude is one of the few ski areas in the United States that has excellent terrain for all skier levels.

Snowboarding

Not permitted.

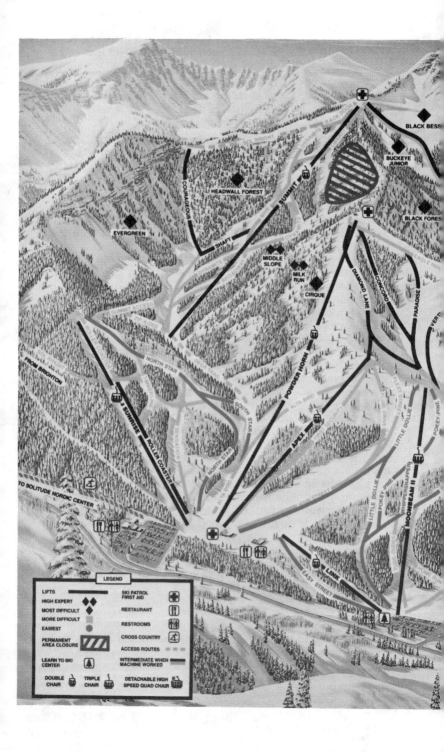

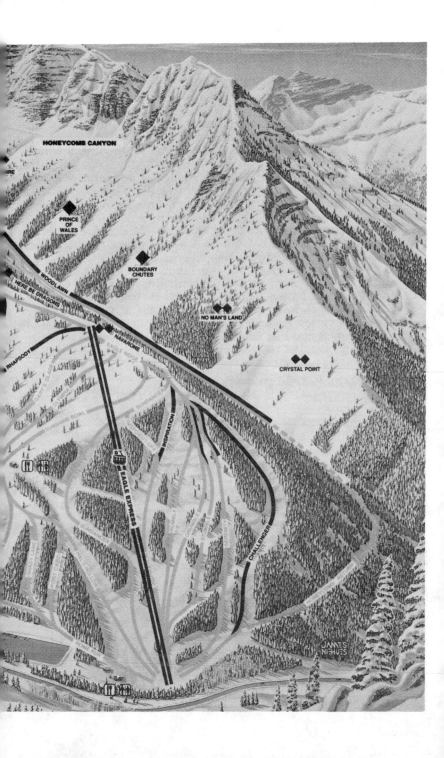

HONEYCOMB CANYON

PRINCE
OF
WALES

BOUNDARY
CHUTES

NO MAN'S LAND

CRYSTAL POINT

WOODLAWN

HERE BE DRAGONS

NAVARONE

RHAPSODY

EAGLE RIDGE

INSPIRATION

EAGLE EXPRESS

CHALLENGER

JAMES
NIEHUES

Cross-country (93/94 prices)

Nordic and Alpine skiing are beautifully integrated at Solitude. Right at the base of the mountain is the Solitude Nordic Center with 18 km. of machine-set track, including an intermediate trail to Silver Lake, which starts at the top of the Sunrise lift (your Nordic pass will get you on the lift). Solitude plans to open its 2,300-square-foot Nordic day lodge at Silver Lake for the 94/95 season. The lodge, a cooperative effort between the ski resort, the U.S. Forest Service and the Utah Department of Transportation, will have rentals and accessories, limited food service and a Forest Service information center.

Trail passes are $8 for those aged 11 to 64, and free for those older or younger. A half-day pass is $6. Rentals and lessons are available. Call 272-7613 for more information.

A very popular program is yurt dining. You ski to a yurt, a round tent-like building popular with the nomads of Central Asia. There you have a gourmet meal and ski back (it's a beginner trail both ways). Reservations are a must for this, and don't be too disappointed if you can't get in. Salt Lake City residents really enjoy it and hog many of the available spaces. The cost is $50 per person, but no children younger than 8 are allowed. Call 534-1400 for reservations.

Lift tickets (93/94 prices)

	Adult	Child (Up to 12)
One day	$28	$16
2 of 5 days	$52 ($26/day)	$32 ($16/day)
3 of 5 days	$78 ($26/day)	$48 ($16/day)

Skiers aged 65 to 74 pay $14, a couple of bucks less than the kids. Older than that, and you ski free. A beginner-lift ticket is $16, and a Big Cottonwood Canyon interconnect ticket, valid at Solitude and neighboring Brighton, is $36.

Ski school (93/94 prices)

A **beginner package** including rentals, lift ticket and a lesson is $34. **Group lessons** are $25 for 90 minutes. **Private instruction** is $50 per hour, with each additional person $20.

SKIwee is for **children** 4 to 7 years old. Quad Squad is for kids 8 to 12. A full-day lesson with lunch is $50; a half-day without lunch is $35

Brighton Ski Resort

Most of the cabins you'll see in Big Cottonwood Canyon have been in Utah families for generations. Families came here to rough it on winter holidays and Brighton is where they came to ski. Brighton has retained that hardy pioneer atmosphere, even though recent improvements, such as two high-speed detachable quad chairs and a brand-new base lodge, have brought it into the

> ## Brighton Ski Resort Facts
> **Base elevation:** 8,755'; **Summit elevation:** 10,500'; **Vertical drop:** 1,745 feet
> **Number of lifts:** 7—2 quad superchairs; 2 triple chairs, 3 double chairs
> **Snowmaking:** 25 percent **Total acreage:** 850
> **Uphill capacity:** 10,500 per hour **Ski area bed base:** 12,000 in Salt Lake City

modern ski world. Despite those high-priced improvements, its $25 per day lift ticket is the second-lowest in Utah—just two dollars more than Alta (which has no speedy lifts).

Brighton's new base lodge replaces an older building that was getting a bit decrepit. The 22,000-square-foot building is finished in tongue-and-groove cedar with vertical log accents and houses a number of skier services.

Good beginner runs descend from the Majestic chair, and from the Snake Creek chair, which goes to the top of the mountain. Beginners should keep an eye out so they don't get onto an intermediate trail: greens and blues do a lot of intertwining here.

Intermediates have the run of practically the whole area. The Snake Creek chair is a little less crowded than the Crest Express high-speed quad and the Majestic chairs. On this side of the area you'll find heavily wooded, fairly narrow runs. On the other side of the parking lot is the Millicent Chair and its wide-open terrain underneath. It's a little steeper over here, but with fewer trees.

Experts should try a short but heart-stopping run called Hard Coin off the Snake Creek chair. The trees are so thick you can hardly pick a line, but it's a marked trail. The Millicent side of the ski area is steeper and has some nice terrain.

Intermediates and advanced skiers also have an area served by the Great Western chair, Brighton's second high-speed quad. The longest run, Elk Park Ridge, is an intermediate cruiser that descends 1,745 vertical feet.

Mountain rating

Good for beginners and intermediates, and getting better for advanced and expert skiing, although not quite up to the level of the other Cottonwood Canyons resorts.

Snowboarding

Allowed on the entire mountain. Rentals are available. Lessons cost $16.

Lift tickets (93/94 prices)

Skiers aged 11 to 69 ski for $25. Ages 10 and younger ski free, two children per paying adult with no restrictions or blackout dates. Skiers 70 and older ski free. Brighton does not sell multiday tickets, but half-day tickets are available.

Brighton also has about 175 acres of beginner and intermediate night skiing from 4 to 9 p.m. every day except Sunday. A pass good at both Brighton and Solitude is $36.

Ski school (93/94 prices)

A **beginner package** including rentals, beginner lift ticket and a lesson is $26. **Group lessons** are $16.

Private instruction is $40 per hour, with each additional person $20. Parallel Pursuits is a clinic program for intermediate or higher skiers to teach skills such as moguls, black-diamond terrain and parallel elegance.

Kinderski is for children 4 to 6 years old. Lessons are one hour and 45 minutes, and cost $20 without equipment, $28 with.

Child care

Neither area has child care.

Accommodations

Most skiers stay in Salt Lake City (see that chapter). The **Brighton Lodge** is a small, cozy lodge at the base of the lifts with heated outdoor pool, Jacuzzi and bar. Rates are $75 per night for a room, $99 for a suite and $45 for an economy hostel. Call (800) 873-5512 or (801) 532-4731.

Last season saw the opening of **Das Alpen Haus** (649-0565) a charming B&B near the foot of Brighton. Four suites each are named after a Swiss ski resort, and the atmosphere is decidedly Swiss Alpine. Prices range from $110 to $180 for two.

Getting there and getting around

Getting there: Solitude and Brighton are about 23 miles southeast of Salt Lake City in Big Cottonwood Canyon on State Highway 190. The most direct route from the airport is east on Interstate 80, south on Interstate 215, Exit 6 to Wasatch Blvd., then follow the signs to Solitude and Brighton.

Salt Lake City is a major transportation hub, so flights are numerous from every corner of the continent. and Amtrak also serves the city.

Getting around: The Utah Transit Authority has excellent, inexpensive bus service from downtown Salt Lake City hotels. If you stay at one of the Brighton lodges, you'll need a car for evening. Dining options in the canyon are slim, so your best bet will be to drive into Salt Lake City.

Information

Solitude, Big Cottonwood Canyon, Box 21350, Salt Lake City, UT 84121 (801-534-1400; sales office 800-748-4754.)

Brighton Ski Resort, Brighton, UT 84121 (800-873-5512 outside Utah, 801-532-4731 in the state).

Sun Valley
Ketchum, Idaho

Sun Valley may provide America's perfect ski vacation. It has a European accent mixed with the Wild West. It is isolated, yet comfortable; rough in texture, but also refined; Austrian in tone, cowboy in spirit.

Ageless would be the one word to describe Sun Valley Village, America's first ski resort, built in 1936 by Union Pacific tycoon Averell Harriman. It exudes restrained elegance with the traditional Sun Valley Lodge, walking village, steeple, horse-drawn sleighs and steaming pools.

In contrast, the town of Ketchum is all-American West, a flash of red brick, a slab of prime rib, a rustic cluster of small restaurants, shops, homes, condos and lodges. It's the town of Ketchum that actually curls around the broad-shouldered ever-green rise of Bald Mountain, known as Baldy to locals. Each snow ribbon dropping from the summit into the valley leads to the streets of Ketchum.

This is Hemingway country. When he wasn't hobnobbing with Ingrid Bergman, Gary Cooper and Howard Hawks, he wrote most of *For Whom The Bell Tolls* in the Sun Valley Lodge, where the photos on display show Darryl Zanuck and other Hollywood celebrities who first made the place famous. Sun Valley has developed or trained many famous winter-sport athletes: skiers Gretchen Fraser, who was the first American Winter Olympic medalist in 1948; Christin Cooper, a 1984 silver Olympic medalist; and Picabo Street, who won a silver at the 1994 Olympics; and ice skaters Peggy Fleming, Dorothy Hamill and Scott Hamilton, Olympic champions all.

The Sun Valley Company keeps the skiing as up-to-date as any in America. They have put $16 million into what they claim is

---

Sun Valley Facts
BALDY: Base: 5,740'; Summit elevation: 9,140'; Vertical drop: 3,400 feet
DOLLAR: Base: 6,010'; Summit elevation: 6,638'; Vertical drop: 628 feet
Number of lifts: 16–6 super quad chairs, 5 triple chairs, 5 doubles
Snowmaking: 30 percent **Total acreage:** 2,000 skiable acres
Uphill capacity: 26,380 per hour **Bed Base:** 6,000

the world's largest automated and computerized snowmaking system, which covers more than half of Bald Mountain's groomed terrain, ensuring Thanksgiving and Christmas skiing. The area that put up the world's first chair lift, designed by railroad engineers to take skiers up Dollar Mountain one at a time, now has six quad superchairs, including one that rises a whopping 3,144 vertical feet in 10 minutes. In the past few years Sun Valley has built new lodges at the base of Warm Springs and one atop Seattle Ridge overlooking the bowls. This season, a new day lodge will open at the River Run base area.

Places like Elkhorn, on the opposite side of Dollar Mountain, are strewn with condo projects, but the community as a whole has maintained its dreamy, hilly, tucked-away atmosphere. Sun Valley, 58 years old, has managed to age gracefully without losing any of the magic it had in its youth.

Where to ski

The main drawback to Sun Valley is the split in the ski areas. Baldy is a mountain for intermediates and advanced skiers. Never-evers, beginners and lower intermediates can't really enjoy this mountain and will end up skiing at Dollar/Elkhorn on the other side of town, so there is no easy way or convenient place for lower-level skiers to meet with their upper-level friends for lunch or après-ski.

Baldy's terrain is best known for its long runs with a consistent pitch that keeps skiers concentrating on turns from top to bottom, rather than dozing off on a flat or bailing out on a cliff or wall. Mile-long ridge runs lead to a clutch of advanced and intermediate bowls. There are short and long black-diamond challenges, and plenty of cruising territory.

Trails are not apt to be quite so wide as at other Rocky Mountain resorts, but they're a lot wider than the ones in New England, and these trails are for the most part long, very long. Many skiers note, after skiing at Baldy for a day, that intermediate on this mountain would be rated expert at most other areas they've skied.

Limelight is a long, excellent bump run for skiers with strong knees and elastic spinal columns. Of the other black descents, the Exhibition plunge is one of the best known. Fire Trail, on the ski area boundary, is a darting, tree-covered descent for those who can make quick, flowing turns. The Seattle Ridge trail curves around the bowls with hypnotic views. The bowl area below, rarely mentioned by most ski writers, is a joy. It has something for every level of skier (except beginners and lower intermediates) and portions catch the sun throughout the day. The Warm Springs side has some marvelous intermediate and advanced cruisers such as Warm Springs, Greyhawk, and Flying Squirrel.

If you want to follow the sun, start your day in the River Run area, then shift to the runs dropping off Seattle Ridge and finish up cruising the Warm Springs face.

Beginners have a whole mountain across the valley, Dollar/Elkhorn. The terrain here is perfect for teaching skiing and good for intermediates perfecting technique or starting out in powder. Skiing on the Dollar side of this mountain is shorter and more limited than on the Elkhorn face, which offers a small bowl with greater pitch and more challenging runs.

Cross-country (93/94 prices)

The Sun Valley/Ketchum area has about 160 km. of trails overall. The most extensive facilities are provided by the **Sun Valley Nordic Center** (622-2250 or 622-2251). Here near the Sun Valley Lodge, 40 km. of cross-country ski trails are groomed and marked for difficulty. They range from easy to isolated forest escapes. There is a half-track width for children as well as a terrain garden. The daily trail fee is $11, with discounts for half day, children and seniors. Group and private lessons are available, as are ski rentals.

There are two other cross-country centers in the immediate region—**Elkhorn Nordic** at Radisson Elkhorn Resort (622-4511) and **Warm Springs Nordic Center** (726-3322) at the Warm Springs Ranch. Elkhorn and Warm Springs each have 10 km. of trails. Warm Springs is groomed daily, but Elkhorn is not.

The Blaine County Recreation District grooms the **North Valley Trails**, which consist of 100 km. of groomed trails in the Sawtooth National Recreation Area and are supported by set trail fees or donations. The largest is the **Wood River Trails** featuring 30 km. of trails winding around Dollar Mountain and from Ketchum to Hailey and Bellevue. When the snow is good the skiing is good, but these trails also serve walkers and bicyclists when the snow melts. **Galena Lodge** has 25 km. and **Lake Creek** has 15.5 km. of trails, and three other areas have less than 10 km. each. The **Boulder Mountain Trail** stretches 30 km. from the Sawtooth National Recreation Area headquarters eight miles north of Ketchum to Easley Hot Springs and Galena, and is groomed all winter, snow conditions permitting.

Avalanche and snow conditions are available 24 hours a day from the Ketchum Ranger District at 622-8027, while North Valley Trails maintains a grooming hotline, 726-6662.

For backcountry tours through the largest wilderness area outside Alaska, contact either **Sun Valley Trekking** (788-9585) or **Sawtooth Mountain Guides** (774-3324). Both feature hut-to-hut skiing and the opportunity to stay in yurts as well.

Snowboarding

Baldy has a halfpipe and snowboarding events. Private lessons for all abilities are available on Dollar and Baldy

Mountains, with reservations required and made through the Sun Valley Ski School. Snowboard clinics cost $31 for two hours.

Ski school (93/94 prices)

Adult **group lesson** prices are $41 for one day (3 hours), $109 for three days and $166 for five days (15 hours). **Children's lessons** run four hours each day and include a supervised ski break. They cost $55 for one day, $147 for three days, and $226 for five days. SKIwee programs are available for children.

The Sun Valley Ski School (622-2248 or 622-2231) has several **specialized clinics**. Racing clinics run three hours per day. Cost is $47 for one day, $90 for two days, $130 for three days, and $195 for five days. A women's clinic for upper intermediates is held five times during the season—call for exact dates. **Private lessons** cost $66 per person for one hour to $175 for three hours in the morning ($160 for three hours in the afternoon). An all-day private lesson costs $305.

Lift tickets (93/94 prices)

	Adult	Child (Up to 11)
One day	$45	$25
Three days	$126* ($42/day)	$65 ($21.66/day)
Five days	$205* ($41/day)	$100 ($20/day)

These are the prices for Baldy's lifts (asterisks indicate 94/95 prices). Tickets are valid both at Baldy and Dollar. If you ski only at Dollar Mountain, prices are: One-day adult $24; three-day adult $60; one-day child $17; three-day child $45.

Skiers 65 and older enjoy a discount. Children 17 and younger ski and stay free when they are with a parent in a Sun Valley Resort hotel or condo or any participating property in Ketchum, Elkhorn or Warm Springs. Unfortunately, blackout periods for this offer are the Christmas/New Year holiday, most of February and half of March.

Accommodations (93/94 prices)

The **Sun Valley Lodge** is the heart of the resort, a place to relax on terrace overlooks and in grand sitting rooms beneath coppery chandeliers. Gleaming outside is a skating rink once ruled by ice queen Sonja Henie. *Sun Valley Serenade*, the '40s movie romance starring Henie and John Payne and featuring music by Glenn Miller, is still shown in the village Opera House. The village is a 3,000-acre Alpine enclave of archways, wall paintings, snow sculptures, and spruce foliage.

Standard rooms at the **Sun Valley Lodge** begin at $125 per night and go up to $285 for parlor suites. Four-night ski packages, including three-day lift tickets, are $359-$679 per person, double occupancy. Longer packages also are available. Because the Lodge was built well before the time of group tourism, each room is unique and pricing depends on room size and such added factors as view and balcony. **The Sun Valley Inn** runs $100 for a standard room to $190 for a family suite. Packages are available. Condos run $110 to $280; condo suites $100 to $345. Call (800) 786-8259 (800-SUN-VALY).

The Radisson Elkhorn Resort, near the base of Dollar Mountain, provides its own resort hotel world away from Ketchum and Sun Valley. Name performers play during the winter season and the health club is well outfitted. Rates range from $88 to $368. Call 622-4511 or (800) 333-3333.

Knob Hill Inn is one of the Ketchum area's most luxurious inns. The building is so Austrian you feel as if you've stepped out of your car into the Tyrol. The indoor swimming pool allows you to swim against waterjets; there is a workout room, all suites have fireplaces, and the in-house restaurant, Felix, is one of the best in Ketchum. The inn is No Smoking throughout. Room rates, with full breakfast, start at $150 for plenty of space and a king bed and range up to $250 for the Penthouse Suite. Call 726-8010 or (800) 526-8010.

The Idaho Country Inn is set on a knoll halfway between Ketchum and Sun Valley. Each of the ten rooms is individually decorated to reflect the Idaho heritage, as the Shoshone Room, Wagon Days Room, and Whitewater Room. Breakfasts here are fabulously healthy and the hot tub sits on a hill behind the inn with a wonderful view. Rooms start at $125 and top out at $185 in high season. Call Terry or Julie Heneghan at 726-1019.

River Street Inn is more of what someone from New England might picture as a charming B&B. It is within walking distance of the center of town. Rooms feature Japanese soaking tubs. Rates including breakfast range from $115 to $155. Call 726-3611.

Pinnacle Inn, located across the street from Warm Springs base, is one of Ketchum's most convenient properties to skiing. This is a collection of studio, one- and two-bedroom apartments with a complimentary breakfast in the restaurant in ski season. Rates range from $150 to $350 per night, with the more expensive apartments accommodating at least two couples. Call 726-5700 or (800) 255-3391.

The Tyrolean Lodge, a Best Western only 400 yards away from the River Run lift, has an Alpine atmosphere with wood-paneled ceilings and downy comforters dressing the beds. A champagne continental breakfast is served. Regular rooms are about $90. Call 726-5336 or (800) 333-7912.

Clarion Inn (formerly the Boulder Mountain Hotel) is a basic hotel with motel flashes, a large outdoor Jacuzzi and full breakfasts. Room doors open to outdoor walkways and the decor is simple. Prices are $90-$175. Call 726-5900 or (800) 262-4833.

Christophe Condominiums and Hotel features roomy condominiums with underground parking. A fire truck races guests back and forth to the lifts as well as the town bus. If you are hunting for budgets ask about discounts on the rooms that are still not remodeled. Rates for simple rooms for two are $75-$90; one-bedroom deluxe condos are $155-$200, with two bedrooms $205-$270. Call 726-5601 or (800) 521-2515.

Tamarack Lodge is smack in the middle of town with a hot tub and indoor pool. Good for families, with microwaves, refrigerators and coffee makers. It doesn't get any more convenient than this for nightlife and dining. Rooms with fireplaces cost more. Rates are $89-119. Call 726-3344 or (800) 521-5379.

Condominiums:

River Run Lodge is a cluster of family-perfect condos within walking distance of River Run lifts. There is a big outdoor hot tub and units have washer/dryers and VCRs. Rates for one-bedroom units with bunks and sleep sofa are $125; for two-bedroom units you'll pay $165-$300. Call 726-9086 or (800) 736-7503.

Premiere Properties has top-of-the-line rentals. They represent million-plus dollar homes within walking distance of the lifts starting at $700 per night as well as condos for mere mortals. Call 726-1569 or (800) 374-1569.

Warm Springs Resorts rents a cluster of condos nestled near Warm Springs Base. Rates are $125 for a studio room for two to $455 for a four-bedroom unit sleeping eight. Call 726-8274 or (800) 635-4404.

Sun Valley Resort has a collection of condominiums surrounding the Sun Valley Village. Studios start at $110 per night; four bedrooms go for $280-$385, and one-, two- and three-bedroom units are in the $160-240 range. Call 622-4111 or (800) 786-8259 (800-SUN VALY).

Dining

In Sun Valley Village

The **Sun Valley Lodge** dining room has old-time elegance and is the only spot in the community with live music and dancing with meals. Specialties include Steak Diane, Chateaubriand Béarnaise Bouquetière, and fresh Idaho trout or poached salmon, all at about $22-$25.

The Ram attached to the Sun Valley Inn serves basic fare ranging from pasta to chops and steaks. The **Ore House** also serves steaks, chicken and fish, filling and well-prepared but nothing to write home about. **Gretchen's** in the Lodge has a fine dinner menu. The **Konditorei** has an Austrian flavor and excellent lunches such as hearty soups served in a bread bowl next to a mountain of fruit.

In Ketchum

Sun Valley has some of the best restaurants in any ski resort in America; anyone with fine dining on his or her mind will not be disappointed. The region's real gourmet action takes place here. The price ranges we give here are a rough guide.

Entrees in the $15-$25 range:

Chez Michel (726-3032) run by Michel Rodigoz, former coach of the U.S. Olympic team, serves fine French cuisine in a cozy series of three rustic rooms. The most romantic setting is in front of the flickering fireplace.

Evergreen (726-3888) has an elegant setting of wood, crystal and glass for what many claim is Ketchum's best food and unarguably the town's best wine list. **Soupçon** (726-5034) has a boldly creative cuisine prepared in a tiny rustic house.

Felix (726-1166) in the Knob Hill Inn has an excellent continental menu and fine service in a very Austrian setting. **Mango** (726-8911), run by a former chef from Chez Michel in a clean well-lighted place with French/California cooking. The tiramisu is to die for.

Entrees from $10-$15:

Salvatore's (726-3111) serves Italian food the way it's supposed to be prepared. Atmosphere is a bit L.A. but the food is perfecto. **The Sawtooth Club** (726-5233) has a great bar with cozy couches in front of a roaring fireplace and a series of small dining rooms tucked above and behind the bar. The food is excellent and very reasonable.

The Pioneer Saloon, (726-3139) a local hangout going back into Ketchum history, is known for its prime rib. **Ketchum Grill** (726-4660) has a daring, innovative menu with flavor mixtures that will keep your tastebuds tingling, and **China Pepper** (726-0959) is the place to head for spicy Thai and Chinese food.

Most entrees less than $10:

Globus Noodle (726-1301) has Chinese/Thai fare. All reports are good from locals and tourists alike.

Louie's (726-7775), in an old church, is a favorite family Italian place with a wide-ranging menu and super pizza. The Eggplant Parmesan is also excellent. Though Louie's has a longer history, locals rave about **Smoky Mountain Pizza** for great, very affordable Italian fare and massive salads. **Piccolo Pasta** (726-9251) has slightly more expensive Italian cooking in a cozy dining room, with fine light home-made pastas.

The **Warm Springs Ranch Restaurant** (726-2609) serves a wide-ranging menu and features mountain trout which you can see swimming in pools near the cozy cabin. This restaurant sits in as pretty a spot you as you can find in Ketchum and its meals are very affordable.

The spot for excellent and inexpensive Mexican food is **Mama Inez** (726-4213) at the start of Warm Springs Road, or head to **Desperado's** (726-3068) just behind the visitor's center on Fourth Street. For slightly more expensive Mexican that is more Tex than Mex try **Tequila Joe's** (622-4511) in the Radisson Elkhorn Resort.

Breakfast is an important institution with most skiers. At the Sun Valley Lodge **Gretchen's** (622-2144) has plentiful fare with moderate prices and **Konditorei** (622-2235) in the Sun Valley Village has good breakfasts. The **Lodge Dining Room** (726-2150) serves an excellent Sunday brunch.

The best, however, are downtown in Ketchum. Locals seem split on the question, but they center on **The Kitchen**, the **Buffalo Café** and the **Kneadery**. All three are open for lunch as well. **The Kitchen** (726-3856) has a dozen varieties of omelets, with pancakes, waffles and a selection of specials served in an airy southwestern pale-colored room. Don't expect any bargains here—prices just about match Sun Valley Lodge. **The Kneadery** (726-9462) is a touch less expensive with a much cozier woodsy atmosphere. The champion bargain breakfast is found at the **Buffalo Café** (726-9795) with its Baldy Breakfast Special featuring pancakes, eggs, bacon and sausage for $3.95.

One more eatery we should mention: Directly across the street from the new Warm Springs Lodge at the base of Baldy is a Ketchum institution, **Irving's Red Hot** stand, where you can get great hotdogs. "The Works" (a dog smothered in fixings and chips) for only $2 is a lunch bargain that can't be beat.

Special Dining Experiences

One evening dining adventure that should not be missed is the horse-drawn sleigh ride to, and dinner at, **Trail Creek Cabin**. The cozy rough-hewn cabin dates from 1937 and seems even cozier after the brisk half-hour sleigh ride from the Sun Valley Inn. The cabin can be reached by sleigh, car or cross-country skis. Check with the Sun Valley Nordic Center to set up a guided cross-country tour. For the sleigh ride, reservations should be made 72 hours in advance, but you can always check later for open space. Call 622-4111. The sleigh ride costs $13. Dinners range from $16 to $22, more or less.

A Winter's Feast is an evening of gourmet dining in an authentic Mongolian yurt (726-5775). You can ski to the yurt along a trail lit by torches or ride in on a sleigh drawn by horses (the sleigh ride is extra). Choose from four menus—salmon, beef, tuna, or lamb—each costing $55, plus wine and gratuity.

Après-ski/nightlife

Ketchum and Sun Valley have highly unusual après-ski, with major comedy and cabaret shows beginning at 5 p.m. and playing to 7 or 8. Sun Valley's historic landmark, the **Ram Bar**, has the **Mike Murphy** comedy show for a $7 cover. A free jazz concert is every Friday at the **Galleria**. Check the schedule for *Sun Valley Serenade* and Warren Miller movies at the **Opera**

House in Sun Valley starting at 5 p.m. And the **Duchin Room** in the Lodge has music starting at 5 p.m.

The **Elkhorn Village Saloon** has occasional concerts, featuring groups such as The Drifters and Bonnie Raitt.

Whiskey Jacque's in Ketchum is the center of downtown action, with live music and a mixed crowd. Good lively Ketchum bars are the **Casino** and **X's**. If you are staying in Warm Springs, or wander over to the **Baldy Base Club** or **Apples** for good immediate après-ski crowds. For more sedate and elegant night action try the **Duchin Room** at the Lodge, which features the Joe Foss Trio until 1 a.m.

Two new spots are **Slavey's Bar** in Ketchum, located where the Saltwater Grill used to be, with great music, a dance floor and a tasty bar-food menu, and **The Sun Valley Wine Company**, with reportedly the largest wine selection in Idaho and a light dinner menu, located above the liquor store on Leadville Street in Ketchum.

Remember—if you are staying in Sun Valley or Warm Springs and plan on partying in Ketchum, the KART bus system stops running at midnight, but A-1 Taxi is available until closing.

Child care

Sun Valley's Playschool, located on the Sun Valley Mall, offers supervised activities, hot lunches and ice skating. Reservations are required. Call 622-2288.

Elkhorn Youth Activity Center at the Radisson takes children from 6 months to 12 years. A full day of care (8 a.m.-6 p.m.) is $40 for ages 3 and older; $50 for younger children. Call (800) 355-4676 (800-ELKHORN) or 622-4511.

Lil'Annie's Day School (726-1411) is geared for ages 2 1/2 to 5 years. Call for reservations and programs.

Other activities

Shopping opportunities are extensive in this long-time resort community. A couple of shops worth highlighting: **The Toy Store**, for unique and educational toys from around the globe; **Wild Willows**, a fun gift store; and **Angel Wings**, a gift store that specializes in angel paraphernalia.

Art galleries are another center of Ketchum's cultural life. Fourteen galleries are members of the Sun Valley Art Gallery Association (726-2602). They provide a beautiful brochure with a gallery map and offer guided evening gallery walks about a dozen times during the year.

Ballooning and **snowmobiling** are available through Mike Mulligan (726-9137). **The Sun Valley Athletic Club** (726-3664) is open to visitors with daily, weekly and monthly rates. It is a full club with child care, massage, aerobics, weights circuit training and swimming. You may even have the chance to work out with Arnold Schwarzenegger, who often hangs out here in his sweats.

Sun Valley Heli-Ski (622-3108) offers backcountry ski adventures for all levels of skiers. **Soaring** or winter glider rides are available through Sun Valley Soaring (726-3054).

The Community Library (788-3054 and 726-3493) is a wonderful resource in Ketchum. The special collections on the history of skiing in Sun Valley make it a perfect stop for anyone interested in the history of the area. It also has the normal library collections, as well as Mac and IBM computers that can be rented.

Sun Valley Center For Arts and Humanities has performances and showings during the ski season. Call 726-9491 for a schedule or the Chamber of Commerce, 726-3423.

Getting there and getting around

Getting around: Sun Valley is not easy to reach. Almost all air connections require another hour or more of bus transfer. The closest airport is Friedman Memorial, 12 miles south of the resort in Hailey, served by Horizon Air and Delta's SkyWest Airlines. When it is open everything works well, but weather often closes it and it cannot handle big jets. Several properties provide complimentary transportation, or use A-1 Taxi, 726-9351. Most guests arrive by jet at Twin Falls, about an hour away, with some also arriving in Boise, about three hours away.

Sun Valley Stages (800) 821-9064, or locally 383-3085 in Boise or 622-4200 in Sun Valley, runs one bus a day between Boise and Sun Valley, which takes about three hours. It runs Boise to Sun Valley at 1 p.m. and Sun Valley to Boise at 7:30 a.m., with extra buses during holidays. Cost is $35 each way or $60 round trip.

Mike Mulligan Luxury Limo (726-5466) provides service serving Hailey, Twin Falls and Boise Airports. **Town and Country Tours** (788-2012) provides private transfers to Twin Falls, Hailey and Boise.

Charter bus service is available to Sun Valley from Boise, Idaho Falls, Twin Falls, and Salt Lake City. Call **Teton Stages** at 529-8036 or (800) 285-8036, or check with Sun Valley Stages.

Getting around: Get around the town and the ski areas with the free KART shuttlebus linking Sun Valley, Ketchum and Baldy about every 20 minutes.

Information/reservations

For **information and reservations** call (800) 786-8259 (800-SUN VALY). For the **snow report** call (800) 635-4150. The address is Sun Valley Resort, Sun Valley, ID 83353.

You can also book Sun Valley and Ketchum lodging through **Chamber of Commerce central reservations.** Call (800) 634-3347, fax (208) 726-4533, or write to Sun Valley-Ketchum Chamber of Commerce, PO Box 2420, Sun Valley, ID 83353

Local telephone area code is 208.

Other Idaho ski areas

Bogus Basin Boise ID (800) 367-4397;
6 lifts, 46 trails, 1,800 vertical feet

Bogus Basin, where counterfeit gold was manufactured in the Western gold rush days, has no counterfeit ski slopes. Sixteen miles north of Boise and 168 miles west of Sun Valley, it is an area known to skiers who go beyond the big-name resorts in search of excellent sleepers. Bogus has first-rate glade skiing and its night skiing is up there with any in the country. Several black runs as well as intermediates and beginners are lighted, twelve in all. They take a skier through enchanted forests to the backside and flanks of a low but wide mountain crown (7,590 feet at Shafer Butte, the summit), offering scintillating city, valley and mountain views. Bogus Basin is open from 10 a.m. to 10 p.m. seven days a week, so that a skier hot for vertical feet can find true exhaustion. An impressive 2,600 skiable acres (Sun Valley has 2,067) offers a great variety of terrain. The ski school, with 130 instructors, is one of the largest in the Northwest. The mountain has two restaurants and the 70-unit Pioneer Inn halfway up the slopes; lift lines are rare.

Schweitzer Mountain Resort Sandpoint ID (208) 263-9555; 6 lifts with superchair, 48 trails, 2,400 vertical feet

This is Idaho's second largest ski area (with 2,350 acres), and first when it comes to snow. The mountain presents challenges, with almost a third of its slopes advanced to expert, and has two large bowls and trails cut through old cedar forests. Terrain is handsome and far-flung. The 82-room Green Gables Lodge at the base is Idaho's No. 1 ski hotel, a smaller version of Canada's chateau-style Canadian Pacific hotels. Schweitzer, in fact, is by design becoming a smaller version of Canada's Whistler/Blackcomb, with hotels above commercial shops, brick paved plazas, and underground parking.

Eight miles down the road is the pretty lakeside village of Sandpoint, frequented in summer by residents of Spokane, 72 miles southwest. Pend Oreille, Idaho's largest lake, is a marvelous water picture beneath the slopes.

Silver Mountain Kellogg ID (208) 783-1111;
7 lifts with gondola, 50 trails, 2,200 vertical feet

Kellogg is trying to go the route of Crested Butte, Telluride, Park City and other boom-to-bust Western mining towns that came back with skiing. As the silver lodes play out here, the skiing plays in. A single-stage gondola offers a 19-minute ride above part of the old town to the ski area, rising from 2,300 feet to 5,700 feet. Three forested, north-facing bowls present intermediate trails and challenging walls and glades. If you took all the trails you'd ski 15 miles and enjoy many handsome views. There is a feeling of seclusion, of getting away from it all, on this mountain. Kellogg has only 150 beds, but the Coeur d'Alene resort, situated on one of the West's most beautiful lakes, has packages including lodging, lifts and transportation to and from the slopes at some very reasonable prices.

Brundage Ski Mountain   McCall, ID; (208) 634-4151;
6 lifts, 36 trails, 1,800 foot vertical

Payette Lake, which Brundage overlooks, is an unknown Lake Tahoe. It is beautiful and sparsely populated, with many outdoor activities including good intermediate downhill skiing. Numerous local skiers have been in the Winter Olympics, and every February the town has a Winter Carnival. From the top of the mountain you can see the Salmon River Mountains, Payette Lakes, Oregon's Eagle Cap Wilderness and the Seven Devils towering over Hells Canyon, America's deepest river gorge. The skiing on 1,300 acres is pleasant and uncrowded, with occasional challenging drops, but mostly cruisers.

The Big Mountain
Whitefish, Montana

True ski-resort discoveries are getting harder to find. If you live in a state or province along the U.S.-Canadian border west of the Great Lakes, you probably already know about this friendly, low-key spot with skiing that stretches on forever. You probably don't want us to tell anyone in the rest of either country about it. We understand. Of course, we'll carefully keep your secret. Not!

If you are a skier who wants lots of terrain to explore and an on- and off-slope atmosphere totally devoid of glitz, you need to head for this aptly named ski resort tucked into the far northwest corner of Montana.

This is an area very popular with Seattle, Calgary and northern Midwest skiers. Many hop on Amtrak's Empire Builder, which on its daily run from Seattle to Chicago and back dumps a load of eager skiers in the town of Whitefish within sight of The Big Mountain's trails.

Though sometimes the resort and the community business leaders long to see their name in the various annual listings of top ski resorts (acreage-wise, this ranks in the top ten, maybe even top five, depending on how one counts), most other times, they'd rather just keep it the Northwest's little secret. Many folks here are expatriates from other ski areas that were once as laid-back and unpretentious as The Big Mountain is now.

The best way in and out of the area is still by train and the most popular nightlife event is the weekly Frabert award party at the Bierstube. (More on that later.) Everything is clean and comfortable, but you won't find concierges and valet parking. This is a down-home, comfortable place where a fur coat would look out of place except on a grizzly-bearded mountain man.

The ski area is eight miles from the town of Whitefish, up a winding access road that can be a bit scary in bad weather. At

---

Big Mountain Facts
Base elevation: 4,800'; *Summit elevation:* 7,000'; *Vertical drop:* 2,300 feet.
Number and types of lifts: 9,—1 quad superchair, 1 quad, 4 triples, 1 double and 2 surface lifts *Acreage:* 3,000 skiable acres, 56 marked trails
Snowmaking: 1 percent three trails, top to bottom
Uphill capacity: 12,000 skiers per hour *Bed base:* 1,500 on mountain

the ski area base is a cluster of five hotels, a circle of condos and a few restaurants and bars. Down the mountain in Whitefish you'll find more hotels, the best restaurants in the area, shopping and the biggest variety of nightlife.

The weather here is a mix of the Rockies and Pacific Northwest maritime. They call it "inland maritime." The climate creates spectacular snow ghosts at the summit, trees encased in many layers of frost. The climate also means plenty of snow. Somehow it produces fantastic light powder, but without the sunshine you'll find in the southern Rockies. If you forget your sunscreen you'll probably survive, but don't forget your goggles. On second thought, pack your sunglasses—sunny days do occur, and when they do, the skiing is spectacular.

Where to ski

Ski anywhere you dare. This is not a resort limited to cut trails and in-bounds bowls. Within the marked boundaries are 3,000 acres of sprawling terrain; another 1,000 acres is in the permit area. The Big Mountain has a mountain host program with free tours of the mountain daily.

The main access to The Big Mountain is the high-speed superchair, The Glacier Chaser, which moves skiers up 2,200 feet of vertical to the summit and serves almost all The Big Mountain's terrain. The front side of the mountain is entirely accessible from The Glacier Chaser. If you ski straight ahead when you get off the superchair you'll drop down the north slope, a mostly intermediate series of runs alternating with tree-studded steeps. The return to the summit is by Chair 7.

If you make a U-turn when you get off the Glacier Chaser you'll reach wide and well-groomed intermediate trails that drop from the summit. Toni Matt, The Big Ravine or North Bowl are all perfect for power cruising with wide GS turns. Toni Matt, Inspiration and the Big Ravine provide top-to-bottom cruising with 2,200 feet of vertical. On the backside of the mountain, the North Slope has a good group of long blue-square trails.

All of these groomed runs are surrounded by fields of powder and thousands of trees beckoning to advanced and expert skiers. Good Medicine defines The Big Mountain experience. This is more an area of the mountain than a defined run through the trees. Through the entire Good Medicine area skiers can choose how tight they want their trees, and they have plenty of opportunities to bail out onto the groomed trails. Locals also can direct you to Movie Land, which starts with dense trees and then opens for great steep tree skiing before ending on Easy Street.

For big-air fans, The Big Mountain has a cornice next to the Summit House. Runs from this cornice, and almost all skiing to the left of the superchair, end up on Easy Street.

Advanced beginners will spend most of their time on Chair 3, but they should make a few runs off Chair 2 or the T-bar before they try The Glacier Chaser. Chair 2's runs are equivalent in pitch to the blue runs off the front of the summit, but much shorter. This lower-mountain area is also lighted for night skiing.

Lower intermediates who want to head for the summit should ski the Chair 7 trails first. The toughest part will be the short upper portion of the North Bowl run, which builds up some formidable moguls by midafternoon.

Never-evers and beginners have an excellent learning area, separate from other skiers, on the gentle trails under Chair 6.

Mountain rating

A friend described Big Mountain as an intermediate Jackson Hole. This is a wide-open, ski-anywhere-you-can mountain with consistent pitch and the added intrigue of nature's own slalom course through acres of frosty pines. It is the tree skiing that makes this a delight for good skiers. Advanced skiers can dance between wide cut trails and the trees, testing their ability. Intermediates have long runs they'll dream about for days. Chair 6 now serves a good beginner area. In short, this is a big enough mountain to satisfy the needs of every ability of skier.

Cross-country

The Big Mountain has excellent cross-country for all levels. Next to the ski area, **The Big Mountain Nordic Center** has 10 km. of trails just below Chair 6. Lessons and rentals are available (862-3511). Trail fees are $5 for adults, $2 for juniors (13-18), $1 for children (7-12) and free for anyone younger when accompanied by an adult. Downhill ski pass holders can use the cross-country trails for $2 a day.

Grouse Mountain Lodge (862-3000) in Whitefish has 15 km. of groomed cross-country trails and the town's only night skiing with 2.4 km. lighted.

The **Izaak Walton Inn** (888-5700), 62 miles east on Highway 2, has 30 km. of groomed trails as well as guides who take skiers into the Glacier National Park wilderness. Guides for groups of two or three cost $75 per person and $60 each for groups of four or more.

Glacier National Park provides a natural cross-country skier's paradise. Here the unplowed park roads and trails provide kilometer after kilometer of ungroomed passages into the heart of the mountains. Check with the communications center (888-5441) or the park rangers for weather and snow conditions.

Snowboarding

The entire mountain is open for snowboarding. The rental shop has equipment and the ski school offers a two-hour group lesson for $22. Under Chair 7 on the north side of the mountain is a natural halfpipe.

WATERCOLOR BY BARBARA MELLBLOM

Montana - The Big Mountain

CHAIR 7
NORTH SLOPE

SUMMIT
HOUSE

EASY STREET

EASY STREET

SCHMIDT'S
CHUTE

GLACIER VIEW

BIG
FACE

CORNICE

NORTH
BOWL
FACE

NORTH BOWL

EAST RIM

EVAN'S
HEAVEN

MOOSE

EASY STREET

PTARMIGAN
BOWL

CHAIR 5

NO NAME

FAULT 1

FAULT 2

NORTH BOWL

BENCH RUN
POWDER
BOWL

ARCH STEP

CHEAP TRAP

HASKILL
SLIDE

CORK SCREW

POWDER TRAP

CHAIR 6 AREA NORTHERN

LANGLEY

INSPIRATION

HOGANS EAST

HOGAN'S

EASY STREET

EASY STREET

LEGEND:

R	= Race Course
●	= Beginner Run
■	= Intermediate Run
◆	= Advanced Run
✚	= First Aid Hut
◉	= Ticket Office
P	= Parking
⌂	= Ski School
- - - -	= Slow Skiing Areas
———	= Night Skiing Area
★	= Info Booth

VILLAGE AREA GUIDE

A Alpinsnack
B Kiddie Korner
C Chocolate Factory
D Moguls Bar & Grille
E Mountain Photography
F Moose's on the Mountain
G Ski School Office ⌂
H Race Dept.
I Ski & Rental Shop
J Chalet & Hell Roaring Saloon
K Alpinglow
L Edelweiss
M Bierstube
★ Info Booth

HUT

The Big Mountain Ski and Summer
Resort is partially located in the USFS
Flathead National Forest

THE BIG MOUNTAIN
Ski & Summer Resort
P.O. Box 1400
Whitefish, MT 59937

© WINTER SPORTS, INC., 1992

Ski school (94/95 prices)

Group lessons for a half day cost $22 and for a full day $34. Lesson packages for three half-day lessons are $60; three full days, $96. Five half-day lessons are $100; full days, $160. Seniors receive a 50 percent discount on group lessons.

Workshops for bumps, steeps and powder are from 1:30 to 3:30 p.m. for $22. Special beginner lessons including lifts and lessons cost $22 for a two-hour session.

Private lessons require reservations (862-3511). Rates are $50 for an hour ($15 for each additional person), $70 for one and a half hours ($20 each additional), $115 for a half day ($30 each additional), and $250 for a full six-hour day ($50 each additional). Beginner private lessons are $90 for two hours.

Children's lessons start at 3-4 years of age. For those 4-6, one- or two-hour Platter Lift Lessons cost $12 per hour. The program for younger children is in conjunction with the Kiddie Korner Day Care Center, and teaches basic skiing lessons and snow fun.

The full-day ski school program for older children includes five-hour lessons for $36 and half-day lessons for $18. Lift tickets are extra. Lunch is optional and will cost an additional $6.

Lift tickets (94/95 prices)

	Adult	Child (7-12)
One day	$35	$19
Three days	$105 ($35/day)	$57 ($19/day)
Five days	$165 ($33/day)	$95 ($19/day)

Because The Big Mountain has night skiing, lift tickets are offered at a day rate, 9 a.m. to 4:30 p.m., and what the resort calls a swing-shift rate from 1 to 10 p.m., good Wednesday to Sunday.

Ages 13-18, college students and 62 and older pay $27 per day, $81 for a three-day ticket and $135 for five days. (The per-day rate stays the same.) Children 6 and younger ski free. Night skiing costs $10 for everyone.

Skiers may ride the platter lift and Chair 6, which service the most gentle terrain, without charge. Also, day ticket holders may ski until 6 p.m. Wednesday through Sunday, and multiday ticket holders may ski at night or ride the Glacier Chaser to the Summit House for dinner. (By the way, the Glacier Chaser turns into a gondola for night riding.) Other foot passengers headed for the summit at night pay $6.

Accommodations

The properties located at The Big Mountain village may all be reserved by calling 862-1960 or (800) 858-5439. Rates here are for regular season, January 22 through April 1. Lower rates are available before Christmas, in January and in April; higher rate apply during the last two weeks in December.

The Kandahar Lodge (862-6095) at the ski area looks like a mountain lodge should—wooden beams, spacious public areas and a soaring stone fireplace. The rooms are large, the food good and the location right on the slopes. A shuttle takes guests to the base area and at the end of the day skiers can glide right to the door. Rates vary from $124 to $184 per night.

In the center of the ski area village is the **Alpinglow Inn** (862-6966). This lodging has beautiful views from the restaurant and perhaps the most convenient location for skiers. Several of the rooms are packed with beds and most sport simple paneling, but you can't beat the location. Rates are $83-$158, based on number of people per room.

The Hibernation House (862-3511) is the economy bed-and-breakfast. Here rooms will house as many as five guests and there is also an indoor hot tub. Rates are $64-$94, depending on number of people per room.

Anapurna Properties and **Big Mountain Alpine Homes** are the two main condo and home management companies. Anapurna guests have access to the only indoor pool on the mountain. Rates start at $120 per night for a studio up to $410 for the larger units and larger private homes.

The **Edelweiss** in the base area (862-5252), has hotel rooms for $115 up to two-bedroom, two-bath condos for $290.

In Whitefish, the **Grouse Mountain Lodge** (862-3000 or 800-321-8822) is the most comfortable and convenient hotel. Its rooms are spacious and a shuttlebus takes guests to the mountain every morning. Cross-country skiing is right out the back door and downtown is only a short walk or ride away. Regular season double room rates are $60-$119.

The Log House on the Hill (862-1071) is a four-bedroom, two-bath home that sleeps 12 and has a hot tub. Rates start at $150 per night.

The Pine Lodge-Quality Inn (862-7600) boasts an indoor-outdoor pool with connecting swim channel, hot tub and free continental breakfast. Rates are $69-$139.

Good Medicine Lodge is built of cedar timbers and has a rustic and informal atmosphere. Rooms are decorated in a Western/Native American motif with fireplaces and solid-wood furnishings. Rates are $75-$85, including breakfast.

The Garden Wall (862-3440) is an antique-filled B&B only a block from the city shuttle. This home is perfect for couples. Rates are $95-$105 per night per double with breakfast.

The Castle Bed and Breakfast (862-1257), in the National Register of Historic Places, is one of Montana's most unusual buildings. The living room is massive with a great fireplace. The house has three guest rooms, one with private bath, two with shared bath. Double rooms with breakfast are $52 to $95 a night.

Dining

This is a town where you find good honest American cooking that includes American-Italian, American-Chinese and Tex-Mex.

The **Summit House** serves dinners with a Glacier Park peak view on Wednesday and Saturday nights from 5:30 to 9 p.m. The Glacier Chaser chairs are replaced by gondola cars to whisk diners up the mountain. Call 862-3511 for reservations.

At the base of the ski area the best food can be found at the **Hellroaring, Moose's** or **Mogul's Bar and Grill**. Though all are casual eateries, Mogul's Bar and Grill makes the most effort to be upscale. Other base area restaurants include the **Café Kandahar, Alpinglow Restaurant** with a great view, and the **Bierstube** for Back Door Burgers.

The bulk of restaurants are found down in Whitefish. The finest dining in the area is at **Logan's Bar and Grill** in the Grouse Mountain Lodge (862-3000) or across the street in the **Whitefish Lake Restaurant** (862-5285) at the golf course. **The End Cafe** (862-4640) is filled with antiques and serves excellent vegetarian and fish entrées. **The Glacier Grande** (862-9400) combines nightlife with Southwest dinners.

Dos Amigos (862-9994) is a basic Tex-Mex spot with a good selection of imported beers. At **Rocco's** (756-5834) you'll find good Italian seafood dishes as well as traditional Italian pastas and chicken, steak and veal Florentine and pizziola-ed. **The Coyote Roadhouse** (837-4250) is the spot to head for Cajun cooking and super-fresh fish. **Stumptown Station** (862-4979) grills up great steaks. **Jimmy Lee's** (862-5303) is the recommended Chinese restaurant if you have a craving for a stir-fry, straw mushrooms or Szechwan duck.

For breakfast, the place to see and be seen is **The Buffalo Café** (862-2833) in Whitefish. If you can get a seat and listen a bit you'll hear about everything happening in town. Try the Buffalo Pie, layers of hashbrowns, ham, cheese and poached eggs, or order the Cinnamon Swirl French Toast; get a side order of chorizo if you decide to stick with basic eggs. It's open for lunch as well. If you can't get a seat there, try the new **"Out of the Blue" Bakery** with great huevos rancheros and baked goods.

Après-ski/nightlife

The Big Mountain has some of the wackiest après-ski and nightlife of any ski town. Tops in junior-high-style fun is **The Bierstube** at the ski area base. Hundreds of ski-club T-shirts (some quite risqué) hang from the rafters; owner Gary Elliott has boxes of 'em and rotates them every so often. Among the various pranks and ceremonies is the Frabert Award, presented each week to the employee or visitor who does the biggest goof-up. (A couple of private pilots won it a few years ago for flying their plane here, then asking the transport van to take them to the

Huntley Lodge—the main hotel at Big Sky, Montana's other big ski resort.) When ski clubs are in town and The Bierstube has a live band, the dancing goes full-blast until closing.

Other après-ski choices at the base are **Moose's on the Mountain** or **Hellroaring Saloon**.

Nightlife, for the most part, is centered downtown along Central Avenue in Whitefish. Having all the bars lined up makes it easy to check out the scene and decide where you want to set up camp. Choose from **The Great Northern, Glacier Grande, The Palace, The Remington, Bulldog Saloon, Casey's** or **Stumptown**. Each is notable in its own way, and a good time for those cruising for rock or country music and drinks. One unique event that ended last season was the mouse races at the Palace Bar. The bar added a casual Tex-Mex restaurant and the health department, which had never been overly fond of pet mice in a drinking establishment, gave Two Thumbs Down to pet mice in an eatery.

For more mellow evenings try drinks and the band at **Logans Bar at the Grouse Mountain Lodge.** For a real cowboy evening, complete with live foot-stomping music and longneck beer bottles you can slip in your back pockets, head to the **Blue Moon Nite Club** in Columbia Falls at the intersection of Highways 2 and 40.

Child care

The main day care facility on the mountain is the **Kiddie Korner Child Care Center** (862-1999). Care for those younger than 12 months or for any non-walking infant costs $4.25 an hour. All other children are charged $3.25 per hour. Reservations are recommended for all children and required for infants under 12 months and non-walkers. Lunches are provided for a nominal fee, or parents provide them or take their children out to lunch. Evening care also is available; call for details.

The ski school has children's programs detailed in the Ski School section of this chapter.

Other activities

Shopping: Quite limited at the base area. Whitefish's Central Avenue has many art galleries and stores that stock Western clothing, jewelry and crafts. **Montana Coffee Traders,** on Highway 93 south of town, has many Montana food gift items, such as huckleberry syrup.

Near the ski area, Old West Adventures has **sleigh rides** through the forests to an Old West roadhouse where hot drinks are served. On Thursday night the ride includes dinner and singing as well as a historical narrative about opening the West. Call 862-2900 for reservations.

Downtown in Whitefish sleigh rides leave the Grouse Mountain Lodge for a 20-minute ride to a camp near Lost Coon Lake. Call 862-3000 for reservations.

Snowmobiling is well organized in this part of the country. Groomed trails are maintained and a guide is available from the Flathead Convention and Visitors Association at (800) 543-3105. Several trails climb to the summit of The Big Mountain.

Snowcat powder skiing is also offered in areas of the mountain eventually will be developed for lift-served skiing. Snowcats cost $35 for four hours of skiing.

Dog sledding adventures provide a fun 12-mile tour of the wilderness. Call 881-2275 for more information.

Getting there and getting around

Getting there: The nearest airport, **Glacier Park International** in Kalispell, is 19 miles south of the resort. However, service in and out of this airport is limited to twice-a-day service on Delta from Salt Lake City and to several Horizon Air commuter flights from nearby Northwest area airports. Glacier Park International is the nearest airport for private pilots.

Train transportation via Amtrak's Empire Builder stops once each morning eastward from Seattle and Portland and once each night westward from Chicago and Minneapolis.

Driving to The Big Mountain is along some of North America's most scenic highways. Access from Banff, Canada or Missoula is Highway 93. Highway 2 runs east and west through Kalispell. Whitefish RV Park is on Highway 93 south.

Getting around: If you stay and play at the mountain, you won't need a car. To get between the mountain and town, you can take **Whitefish Area Rapid Transit** (WART), which has six to seven daily runs. In winter, the schedule works well for those staying in Whitefish and riding the bus to ski, but it's very inconvenient for the mountain lodgers who want to party late at night in town (the last run back to the mountain is about 9:30 p.m.). Taxi service also is available.

Information/reservations

The Big Mountain maintains a central reservations system for all lodging on the mountain. Call 862-1960 or (800) 858-5439.

For information about activities in Kalispell and Whitefish contact the **Flathead Convention and Visitors Association** at (800) 543-3105 or 756-9091. The **Whitefish Chamber of Commerce** provides information at 862-3501.

The telephone area code is 406 unless otherwise noted.

Big Sky, Montana

Lone Mountain's glacial horn juts up there by itself at 11,166 feet, cutting the heavens above Big Sky Resort north of Yellowstone. Beneath is the seven-floor Shoshone Condominium Hotel, and beside that a shopping mall. Wide-open beginner and intermediate terrain create a 360-degree scenic wrap for a village with both traditional European and ultramodern architecture.

The resort has the feel of a mountain enclave plugged into big-city convenience. Sixty percent of the visitors fly in from Alabama and New Jersey and Minnesota. Everything is available in the considerable space of a village that changes in appearance and attitude from rowdy and crowded in one section to stately and reserved in another. But it also has a European feel. Ski school director Robert Kirchschlager is from Salzburg, Austria, and each year brings in English-speaking Europeans to teach. And each skier feeds a ski pass into machines that open gates for lift rides, like the computer systems found in the Alps.

Big Sky opened in 1973, founded by TV announcer Chet Huntley and other investors. Everett Kircher, owner of Boyne Mountain in Michigan, bought Big Sky in 1976. John Kircher, Everett's son, has transformed the place with new equipment, lifts and runs. Big Sky now attracts nearly a quarter of a million skier visits, twice the number of eight years ago. However, they are all swallowed by the 2,400-acre terrain. A big daily turnout is 3,000, meaning short lines for the gondolas.

Nearly everyone who visits spends at least a day in Yellowstone, only an hour away. Snowmobiling and wildlife viewing there are spectacular.

Where to ski

Two gondolas carry skiers up Lone Mountain, which has beginner, cruiser, mildly challenging and hair-raising descents. The Challenger lift provides 400 to 450 acres of bowl, glade and

---

Big Sky Facts
Base elevation: 6,970'; **Summit elevation:** 10,000'; **Vertical drop:** 3,030 feet.
Number and types of lifts: 11–2 gondolas, 2 quad superchairs, 2 triples, 2 doubles and 3 surface lifts
Acreage: 2,402 skiable acres, 50 marked trails **Snowmaking:** 20 percent of trails
Uphill capacity: 12,030 skiers per hour **Bed base:** 3,492

tree skiing on steep inclines and endless seas of bumps that grizzlies as far away as Yellowstone may see. Surface tows serve the A-Z chutes, The Pinnacles and Parachute, the names of which speak for themselves.

The resort averages more than 33 feet of snow a year, and most of this falls on gentle walls extending east to Andesite Mountain. Open Alpine meadows, groomed widths, occasional mogul fields, a challenging cornice and long sweeping descents are featured on Andesite. Sixty-five miles of skiing stretch over 50 slopes, with the longest run three miles long.

Mountain rating

The mountain is rated 16 percent beginner, 44 percent intermediate, 40 percent advanced.

Cross-country

Nationally renowned **Lone Mountain Guest Ranch** offers more than 45 miles of groomed trails. Five miles from Mountain Village, the terrain is set in gently rolling hills, forested areas, wide-open meadows and high Alpine terrain. Lessons, rental equipment and guided tours are available. A favorite trip is a guided tour into Yellowstone National Park. Call 995-4644.

Snowboarding

No restrictions, and the resort has lessons, rentals and two natural halfpipes.

Ski school (94/95 prices)

Group lessons cost $22 for half-day; $70 for four half-day sessions. Seven different clinics cost $22 each. The Learn to Ski package costs $32.

Private lessons cost $53 for an hour, $240 for a full-day lesson, with additional skiers paying extra.

Children's lessons are arranged through Ski Day Camp for Kids for those 6-14. Ski Mini Camp is a program for ages 4-6. Lunch is included with the full-day program. A five-day program with a race on the final day and awards program also is offered.

For information call 995-4211, Ext. 2189.

Lift tickets (94/95 prices)

	Adult	Child (Up to 10)
One day	$38	Free**
Three days	$111 ($37/day)	
Five days	$175 ($35/day)	

Half-day tickets are sold, but are just $4 less. Other multiday rates also available. Skiers 70 and older ski for half price.

**Up to two children ski free per paying adult, good every day of the season.

Accommodations

Big Sky is divided into three areas—the Mountain Village, the Meadow Village and the Canyon. Each area features lodge rooms, suites and one- to five-bedroom condos.

New this season is **River Rock Lodge**, described as a "boutique-style European hotel" with stone and log construction. Its 24 rooms have rates of $95 to $120, including continental breakfast. It is seven miles from the ski area, but free shuttles will get you to the mountain. (800) 995-9966.

In Mountain Village, **Stillwater, Arrowhead, Bighorn, Skycrest** and **Beaverhead** offer a full range of condos. Beaverhead, Bighorn and Arrowhead are ski-in/ski-out, and Bighorn added 17 more units in the summer of 1994. Condo rates start at $103 per night in low season and top out at about $600 for the largest units during the regular season.

In Meadow Village, **Yellowstone** and **Glacier** feature indoor swimming pools. **Golden Eagle Lodge** is recently renovated and offers suites, a restaurant and bar.

In the Mountain Village are the 204-room **Huntley Lodge** and 92-suite **Shoshone Condominium Hotel**, with many luxuries and amenities. The lodge runs $104 for a small room in low season to $222 for a larger room at Christmas. The Shoshone rates run $220-$466. It also includes the Yellowstone Conference Center with a ballroom, amphitheater and breakout rooms. Call (800) 548-4486 or 995-4211.

Dining

Huntley Lodge is known for its fine dining and one of Montana's largest wine selections. In the Mountain Mall, **Whiskey Jack** and **M.R. Hummers** are known for their house specialties. Newcomers in the Mountain Village are **Buckskin Charlie's,** a casual spot for breakfast, lunch or dinner, and **Twin Panda**, with Chinese food.

In the Meadow Village, **First Place** is known for fresh seafood. **Cafe Edelweiss** has excellent Austrian and German food. **Rocco's** has Mexican and Italian. **Allgoods** has an extensive beer and wine list and a grille menu.

In the Gallatin Canyon, **Buck's T-4** is the traditional spot for Montana beef, seafood specialties and wild game.

The **Lone Mountain Guest Ranch** features a gourmet dining room and a sleigh-ride dinner served in a log cabin where your meal is prepared on a 100-year-old wood stove to the melodic accompaniment of local folk singers.

Après-ski/nightlife

First check Big Sky's local newspaper, *The Lone Peak Lookout*, which has current entertainment listings.

The **Whiskey Jack** frequently features recording artists such as The Guess Who and Nicolette Larson, and local bands including Sgt. Rock, Sawmill Creek, Montana Rose and Art Hooker Band. **Buckskin Charlie's** has live blues performers on Monday nights.

Local talent also performs at the **Corral, Chet's Bar** and **The Half Moon Saloon**. Happy hour at **Chet's Bar** often features live entertainment. Warren Miller ski movies and feature films are shown in the amphitheater.

Poker, which is legal in Montana, is available, as are quarter electronic keno machines. Video games are in the lodge's recreation room.

Other activities

Shopping: The resort has several boutiques with the usual gifts and souvenirs, as well as western-style home furnishings, jewelry and clothing, and art galleries that feature western artists. The **Lone Spur** is a good spot for high-quality western clothing, jewelry and gifts.

Snowmobiling in Yellowstone National Park is a major attraction. You can travel to Old Faithful in two or three hours and see buffalo, bald eagles, wild geese and moose. Snowmobilers leave from West Yellowstone, with bus service provided between the ski resort and West Yellowstone snowmobile rental shops. For information, Rendezvous Snowmobile Rentals, 800-426-7669 or 646-9564; Snowmobile Yellowstone, 800-221-1151; Yellowstone Adventures, 800-231-5991 or 646-7735; West Yellowstone, 800-541-7354 or 646-9695.

Getting there and getting around

Getting there: Northwest, Horizon Air, SkyWest and Delta fly into **Bozeman Gallatin Field Airport,** about an hour from the resort. The easiest transit is the **Karst Stage** 42-passenger skier shuttle that runs between the airport, Big Sky and West Yellowstone. Call 586-8567.

The resort is 43 miles south of Interstate 90. The turn-off is just west of Bozeman. It is 50 miles north of West Yellowstone on U.S. 191.

Getting around: A car won't get in the way, but it really isn't necessary. Within the resort, the SnowExpress free shuttle service runs from 7 a.m. to 11 p.m. throughout the winter. If you want to go to West Yellowstone, catch the Karst Stage.

Information/reservations

Big Sky Ski & Summer Resort, 800-548-4486 nationwide; 995-4211 in Montana. For group reservations and conferences, call (800) 548-8096.

The area code for telephone numbers is 406 unless otherwise noted.

Taos, New Mexico

Taos Ski Valley is like no other ski resort in North America. The ski area is a little piece of the Alps, founded by a Swiss and surrounded by hotels and restaurants built by Frenchmen and Austrians. The ski area is nestled near a town, Taos, which is the nucleus of a rich mix of Spanish and Indian cultures, melded over the centuries to produce a style called Southwestern. The style, seen in art, cuisine and architecture, isn't trendy here; it's the way things have always been. Everywhere you look—except right at the ski area—you see brown adobe buildings with pastel-painted window frames and doors and strings of bright-red chiles hanging from the eaves. At the ski area, you see peaked roofs and wooden shutters, so typical of Alpine chalets. It is this exotic blend of European-Southwestern culture that makes Taos Ski Valley unique in the ski world.

Taos Ski Valley holds another distinction among ski areas. While many resorts walk a delicate marketing tightrope, touting whatever expert terrain they possess while at the same time trying not to scare anyone off, Taos Ski Valley seems to enjoy its tough reputation. Its marketers don't play up that image (word gets around among skiers quite efficiently, thank you), but they make no effort to refute it either. Instead they wisely advise skiers to meet the challenge by enrolling in Ski-Better-Week, a package of lessons, accommodations, meals and lift tickets.

Just about everybody at Taos enrolls in ski school. If you aren't part of a class, you will feel like the kid that didn't get chosen for a sandlot baseball team. Après-ski talk centers on Ski-Better-Week anecdotes, and independents will sit at the bar with little to add.

Taos is one of a few remaining large ski resorts still run by a family, in this case, the Blake clan, now headed by Mickey, son of the late founder, Ernie. In the four decades since Taos opened, certain traditions have developed. One is the quest for hidden

---

Taos Facts
Base elevation: 9,207; Summit elevation: 11,819; Vertical drop: 2,612 feet
Number of lifts: 11–3 quad chairs, 1 triple chair, 6 double chairs, 1 surface lift
Percent snowmaking: 34 percent
Total acreage: 1,096 acres terrain, 687 acres of trails
Uphill capacity: 13,500 per hour Bed Base: 3,705 in Ski Valley and town

porrons, hand-blown Mexican glass flasks filled with martinis and buried in the snow under trees for classes to discover. Another tradition is free hot chocolate in winter or lemonade in spring in lift lines if they get too long (this happens most often at the base, where two non-high-speed quad lifts must transport everybody in the morning). Ski classes make up little families within this big family, so generally everyone feels right at home.

Where to ski

Two factors make Taos' intimidating topography approachable: a staff eager to help the newcomer and the outstanding instruction program. Every morning, a crew of blue-jacketed hosts is stationed at ticket area, base, and the tops of all lifts to answer questions about lift lines and appropriate trails. Remember: an intermediate run like Lower Stauffenberg or Porcupine might be considered advanced elsewhere. Here, it is no disgrace to warm up on a green run—it's a good idea.

Taos' skiing is on two sides of a ridge marked by blue-square Bambi at the top and black-diamond Al's Run at the bottom. To the left of the ridge, as you look at the mountain, are wider, gentler runs such as Shalako Bowl, Honeysuckle, and Upper and Lower Totemoff. To the right of the ridge are narrower, steeper runs like dense, tree-filled Castor and Pollux, and intermediate trails such as Lower Stauffenberg and Powderhorn Bowl.

Smooth intermediate bowls can be found off the Kachina quad chair, the widest being Shalako. The least crowded bowl is Hunziker, named after a Swiss lift engineer, kept isolated by a short climb to its entrance. The Hunziker Bowl entices you with a mild concave slope, but just when you feel confident and relaxed, it drops off with the steepness of a waterfall and narrows down to force you into precision skiing in short turns.

For tree skiers, Taos has a special challenge, the twin runs Castor and Pollux. They hardly look like runs, just steep, wooded parts of the mountain, unskiable, where some joker put a sign that looks just like a trail marker. The trees are from two to 15 feet apart, and advanced classes regularly train here.

Powder skiing lasts on Highline Ridge and Kachina Peak. These are not for the faint of heart, for two reasons: they are double black diamonds and Kachina Peak is reachable only after an hour-and-fifteen-minute hike from the top chair at 11,800 feet to the ridge at 12,500 feet. You can, however, ski off Highline Ridge and West Basin Ridge after only a 15-minute hike. Skiers are advised to go with an instructor or a patrolman; at the very least, they must check in with the patrol at the top of Chair 6. The ski patrol will give you a rough screening to see if you can handle the double-diamond terrain. In any case you must ski the ridge with a partner.

Taos is rarely crowded: ticket sales are cut off at 4,800 and the mountain can accommodate many more. If you're looking for no people at all, the farthest run west, Lower Stauffenberg running into Don't Tell, probably will be empty. You definitely will find crowds twice a day: once in the morning as you board the two base lifts, and again in the afternoon. The only ways off the mountain are straight down the infamous Al's Run or a couple of other tough black-diamond routes, or on one of two green-circle cat trails, Whitefeather on the right and Rubezahl on the left. There's usually plenty of room on Al's Run, but not on Whitefeather and Rubezahl. Despite the slow-down efforts of ski hosts stationed every 20 feet or so, both runs resemble the Hollywood Freeway at rush hour, except that the faster skiers aren't stalled in traffic. They zip around the slower skiers, who gingerly wedge their way home. On busy days it's a mess.

Mountain rating

The name Taos Ski Valley is almost too genteel. It implies a softness to the slopes. Less appealing—but more accurate—would be Taos Ski Gorge. A whopping 51 percent of the runs are rated expert, but that doesn't mention that 19 of those 36 runs are double black diamonds.

While experts will adore Taos for its challenge, intermediates may be frustrated and beginners may be downright terrified. Most of the green-circle trails are narrow, high-traffic access runs to more challenging terrain. Many of the blue-square runs start off wide, but then get quite narrow in spots. Those narrow portions can build some menacing bumps.

We strongly recommend that advancing beginners and lower intermediates take a lesson—not only to improve their skills but also to find the best part of the mountain for them. However, only athletic novices should attempt to learn here. Despite a tiny learning area at the base and the highly regarded ski school, the jump from the learning area to the mountain is enormous. Better terrain to learn to ski is at nearby Angel Fire (see New Mexico chapter for more information).

Skiers who are solid intermediate and above: rise up to meet Taos' challenge. If you normally ski blue runs at other resorts, you can ski Taos. It may be tough at first, but persist. You'll catch on. Taos can be an extremely rewarding ski experience *because* of its challenge. If you ski well here, you deserve to strut into the bar at the end of the day. There are few highs in skiing that top the successful conquest of this mountain. And if you don't, the mountain provides a convenient excuse.

Last suggestion: Take a trail map and consult it often.

Cross-country

The nearest Nordic area is Enchanted Forest Cross-Country Ski Area, 40 miles northeast of Taos by Highways 522 and 38.

Just below Bobcat Pass, 3 miles east of Red River, it has 34 km. of backcountry trails, some groomed, and an elevation of 10,300 feet. Trail rates are $9 for adults, with discounts for teens, seniors and children. At the headquarters at Miller's Crossing in downtown Red River, you can rent equipment (including pulks, which are sleds that allow adults to pull small children as they ski) and pick up trail maps. Call 754-2374.

Snowboarding

Not permitted. Monoskis and telemark skis are allowed.

Ski school (94/95 prices)

Ski-Better-Weeks are the core of the Taos ski experience, developed by former French junior Alpine champion and ski school technical director Jean Mayer. Participants are matched for six mornings of intensive lessons, and they ski with the same instructor all week. Sixty-five percent of the participants are intermediate level or higher.

Ski Week costs $348, lifts and lessons, for adults and teens. Juniors 6 to 12 can enroll for $324, and further discounts are available to children and those over 65. Many lodging properties offer this program as a package with meals and accommodations; indeed, you can't stay at Jean Mayer's Hotel St. Bernard unless you're signed up for the ski week.

A variation on Ski-Better-Week is the Masters Ski Week, for those 50 and older who "want a challenging mountain adventure without competing with some 20-year-old on the bumps." Masters Ski Week will start Dec. 18, Jan. 15, Feb. 5 and Feb. 26 during the 94/95 season and costs $348.

Single **group lessons** (two hours, morning or afternoon) cost $28; three or more days cost $24.

Private lessons are $65 a person for the first hour; $45 each additional person or hour. An all-day private lesson is $325, with a maximum of three skiers; half-day private lesson is $210.

The Yellowbird Special for **never-ever skiers** includes novice lift ticket, morning and afternoon lessons for $44; $50 includes equipment rental.

The Junior Elite program for **children** 6 to 12 is detailed in the Child Care section of this chapter. Teenagers are grouped together by skill level and attitude in the Ski-Better-Week program.

Super Ski Week is an intense ski week for adults who wish to focus seriously on improving their skiing. Skiers are analyzed, videotaped and put through what amounts to a mini ski-racing camp every morning and afternoon for a total of five hours. The emphasis is on the fundamentals. This is not a program for the timid or late-night party types. Most skiers have no energy left for anything other than a quick bite to eat and then to bed. But most skiers intermediate level and higher will find their skiing much improved by the end of the week. It's offered at selected times and has varying costs, depending on the season.

The Ski School also has **special programs** in mogul introduction, mountain cruising, steep and deep, and telemark with a guide. The three-day programs cost $72.

Lift tickets (94/95 prices)

	Adult	Child (Up to 12)
One day	$37	$22
Three days	$102 ($34/day)	$57 ($19/day)
Five days	$170 ($34/day)	$95 ($19/day)

Seniors 65-69 ski for $15; 70 years and older ski free. Taos also reduces its lift ticket price in January value season and the early and late season.

Accommodations

What gives Taos its European atmosphere is the emphasis on the complete week-long experience of lessons. The **Ski-Better-Week** packages include up to seven nights lodging (Saturday to Saturday), 20 meals, six lift tickets and six morning lessons. Prices listed here vary by accommodation. At the Village they range from $1,300 per person, double occupancy, at **Hotel St. Bernard** with three meals a day, to about $520 without meals at **Alpine Village**. Between these price extremes the Village has eight other establishments.

The **Hotel St. Bernard Condos** managed by Jean Mayer, Taos ski school technical director, offer the flavor of a European retreat. Dinner is in the famed Hotel St. Bernard, circa 1957, where the cuisine and ambiance are both legendary—and French. Breakfast is buffet.

Kandahar Condominiums on the slopes has hotel rooms as well as two-bedroom condos, which can also be booked with the Ski Week program (no meals).

The Inn at Snakedance has 60 ski-in, ski-out rooms from $115 to $230 per night. Amenities include a spa with hot tub, sauna, exercise and massage facility; a slopeside library with stone fireplace, a glass-walled bar and a restaurants serving continental cuisine with a Southwest flair. Ski-Better-Week packages start at $1,276 per person.

The least expensive is the skiers' hostel, **The Abominable Snowmansion** in Arroyo Seco, nine miles from the Village, where the rates are under $20 for a dorm bed. Contact: Box 3271, Taos NM 87571; 776-8298.

Between the ski area and town is a bed-and-breakfast inn, the **Salsa del Salto**. Formerly the residence of Hotel St. Bernard owner Jean Mayer, it's now run by Jean's brother Dadou, a French-trained chef who cooks Salsa del Salto's gourmet breakfasts. Prices range from $100 to about $175 per room per night. B&Bs can be booked through the Taos B&B Association, (800) 876-7857.

The town of Taos offers a wide range of accommodations, many of them including the Ski-Better-Week package, and most of them less expensive than staying at Taos Ski Valley. (Rates of $60 to $300, depending on the luxury factor.) At the northern edge of town, **Quail Ridge Inn** is a fully appointed condominium complex of 110 units at a tennis ranch, including indoor and outdoor courts. Looking much like a pueblo, it exudes the Southwestern atmosphere. More information from Box 707, Taos NM 87571; 776-2211 or (800) 624-4448. Rooms at **El Pueblo Lodge** (Box 92, Taos 87571; 800-433-9612) and the **Indian Hills Inn** (Box 1229; 800-444-2346) are closer to the bottom of the price range.

The historic **Taos Inn** is the cultural center of Taos. The lobby, built around the old town well, is a gathering place for artists, and the Adobe Bar has a gentle après-ski atmosphere. Rooms feature adobe fireplaces, antiques, Taos-style furniture built by local artisans. Call (800) 826-7466 (800-TAOS-INN).

The **Sagebrush Inn** is an historic inn with a priceless collection of Southwestern art in the lobby and the best nightlife in town. Call (800) 428-3626 or 758-2254.

Taos Valley Resort Association, (800) 776-1111, or locally, 776-2233, can make all reservations and organizes all-inclusive three- to seven-day packages including air, transfers to Taos, lodging, lifts and lessons.

Dining

Because so many properties at Taos Ski Valley offer the Ski-Better-Week packages, which include meals, most restaurants have been operated by the lodges for the needs of their guests. It's still that way at the Hotel St. Bernard and Thunderbird Lodge. The best independent eateries in the village are **Rhoda's Restaurant** and **Tim's Stray Dog Cantina.** Rhoda's, named for Ernie Blake's wife, has many New Mexican specialties. At Tim's Stray Dog (an inevitable name: owner Tim Harter used to work at the Hotel St. Bernard, a.k.a. The Dog), try the Tequila Shrimp. For breakfast and lunch, the Hotel Edelweiss' **La Croissanterie** is excellent.

On the road into the valley, the **Casa Cordova** (776-2500) specializes in European cuisine (entrées are $14-$20). The **Chili Connection** (776-8787) is known for its chicken chimichanga and pollo boracho. Entrées run $7-$11. **The Brett House**, at the junction of Highways 64 and 150, serves continental cuisine in the $10-$18 range. Call 776-8545. **Carl's French Quarter** at the Quail Ridge Inn (776-8319) cooks Cajun.

The town has a lot to offer in ambiance, culture and cuisine. The menu at the intimate **Apple Tree Restaurant** (758-1900) lists Southwestern dishes and continental cuisine. On the historic plaza, **The Garden Restaurant** offers New Mexican as well as American, Italian and French entrées; call 758-9483. **Doc Martin's,** in the Taos Inn, has creative Southwestern cuisine. **Michael's Kitchen**, 304C Paseo de Pueblo Norte (the main drag), gets raves from locals for its breakfasts. Another restaurant that gets high marks for dinner is **Roberto's,** which serves exceptional New Mexican dishes. Call ahead: 758-2434.

Après-ski/nightlife

Yawn. That is the sound of Taos' bone-tired skiers headed off to dreamland soon after dinner. The nightlife will never make any Top 10 lists in the ski magazines.

After the lifts close, skiers will be found on the deck of the **Hotel St. Bernard**, the **Martini Tree Bar** at the Resort Center, or the **Twining Tavern** at the Thunderbird Lodge, sometimes with live music. The St. Bernard has live music every night—an eclectic mix of reggae, country, jazz, and acoustic guitar. The Thunderbird Lodge has live music in spurts. The Martini Tree has live music on Saturdays.

Things are a little more lively in town. **The Sagebrush Inn**, at the south end, has Country & Western dances every Friday and Saturday night, plus C & W music the rest of the week. **Ramona's Dance Hall**, a new addition to the nightlife scene, has the largest dance floor in town, which relegated the floor at The Kachina Lodge's **Cabaret Room** to second-place status (but it's pretty big, too). **Ogelvie's Bar and Grill** in Taos Plaza is also hopping.

Skiers and local artists mix at the **Adobe Bar** of the Taos Inn, which has been called the living room for artsy locals.

The *Taos News* has a weekly entertainment guide.

Child care

Taos Ski Valley will debut a new Children's Center for the 94/95 season that will combine all of these programs for children into one convenient location:

The Junior Elite program, aged 6 to 12, includes a two-hour morning lesson, lunch and afternoon ski session for $55 a day, $270 for five days, and $324 for six days.

Junior Elite for ages 3-5 has a little bit of ski instruction, supervised snowplay and games as well as lunch, for $55 per day. Reservations are recommended, and parents must rent children's skis before coming to the center.

Kinderkare is for little ones (between 1 and 2 years) who are not yet skiing. These toddlers enjoy directed play, lunch and naps. Rates including lunch and snacks are $45 a day. Six days cost $264. The program operates daily from 8:30 a.m. to 4 p.m.

Bebekare is for infants—even newborns. Parents must bring diapers and formula. Rates: $10 per hour, $30 a half day, $45 a full day, $264 for six days; 8:30 a.m. to 4 p.m.

Other activities

Shopping: Georgia O'Keeffe and R.C. Gorman have made Taos legendary among art lovers. About 80 galleries are tucked in Taos's side streets, and the Quast Gallery has a Meet the Artist series at the ski area in winter. A list is available from Taos Chamber of Commerce, Drawer 1, Taos NM 87571; 758-3873 or (800) 732-TAOS.

Fly fishing tours are offered in winter on the Red River by Los Rios Anglers, 223B Paseo del Pueblo Norte, Taos, NM 87571; 758-2798.

Another unusual non-ski activity is a visit to **Taos Pueblo,** the 700-year-old home of the Tiwa Indians. In addition to the two massive adobe structures, the mission church of St. Francis of Assisi remains from the Spanish colonial era. The Tiwa Indians welcome visitors to their pueblo, their workshops, their ceremonies and sacred dances. It is open from 9 a.m. to 4:30 p.m.

Getting there and getting around

Getting there: Taos Ski Valley is 135 miles—about three hours—north of Albuquerque, the nearest major airport. Rent a car—the drive is scenic, and public transportation between Taos and the ski area is spotty. Rental agencies are at the airport. If you choose to leave the driving to someone else, contact Faust's Transportation, 758-3410 in Taos or 843-9042 in Albuquerque; or Pride of Taos, 758-8340.

AMTRAK's Southwest Chief rolls from Chicago and Los Angeles. The Chicago train stops in Raton and the L.A. train stops in Albuquerque. Amtrak has ski packages, which we recommend because they provide connecting transportation, which is difficult to book on your own. Call American Rail Magic Tours at (800) 533-0363.

Overnight **RV parking**, without hookups, is permitted in the Taos Ski Valley parking lot. Two other RV parks: Taos Motel and RV Park, (800) 323-6009 or 758-1667, and Kit Carson Campgrounds and RV Park, 758-3660.

Getting around: If you are enrolled in a hotel-and-meals Ski Better Week package in Taos Ski Valley village and have no desire to go into the town of Taos 18 miles away, you won't need a car. If you want to visit the town, or aren't staying at the ski area, you'll need one.

Information/reservations

Address and phone: Taos Ski Valley, Box 90, Taos Ski Valley NM 87525; 776-2291.

Lodging reservations: Taos Valley Resort Association, (800) 776-1111 or 776-2233.

Snow report number: 776-2916. Local area code is 505.

Ski Santa Fe
New Mexico

Take the brilliant sunlight of the high desert and a seemingly unlimited supply of fresh powder days. Add pre-Columbian Indian Pueblos, Spanish architecture and about 170 art galleries. Mix well with spicy cuisine, a western frontier abandon and a skier-friendly mountain that will satisfy just about any taste, and you get Santa Fe.

It is a land of enchanting contradiction. It is old and new, high mountain and flat desert, with cool winters that surprise out-of-staters who think of New Mexico as hot and dry. Skiing here is unlike anywhere else on the continent. To get a more foreign-feeling ski vacation, you'd need a passport.

While Taos (about 150 miles from Albuquerque) has an international reputation among the ski-'til-you-drop crowd, Santa Fe (just an hour north of Albuquerque) is the ski destination for those looking more for a balanced ski-and-sightseeing vacation than for racking up vertical feet.

Founded by Spanish conquistadors in 1610, 10 years before the pilgrims landed in Plymouth, Santa Fe is North America's oldest capital city. It is rich in history and culture, but of a different kind from mining-town ski areas.

When the Spanish arrived, the area was already populated with an estimated 100,000 Native Americans, who spoke nine languages and lived in some 70 multi-storied adobe pueblos, some still inhabited today.

For the next 150 years, Santa Fe grew as a frontier military base and trading center, where Spanish soldiers and missionaries, Anglo mountain men and Native Americans mixed. In 1846, during the Mexican War, New Mexico was ceded to the United States and Santa Fe, at the end of the Santa Fe Trail, be-

Ski Santa Fe Facts
Base elevation: 10,350'; **Summit elevation:** 12,000'; **Vertical drop:** 1,650 feet.
Number and types of lifts: 7–1 quad superchair, 1 triple chair, 2 double chairs and 3 surface lifts
Acreage: 600 skiable acres **Snowmaking:** 30 percent
Uphill capacity: 7,800 skiers per hour **Bed base:** 4,000 in Santa Fe

came the quintessential frontier town, hosting the likes of Billy the Kid and Kit Carson.

In the early part of this century, Santa Fe took on a new flavor. The Pueblo Indians had known the area as the "dancing ground of the sun" for centuries. With its 7,000-foot elevation and mild climate, Santa Fe became a magnet for men and women of the arts and literature. D.H. Lawrence, Ezra Pound, Willa Cather, Jack London and H.L. Mencken either lived or vacationed here. Artists Edward Hopper and Marsden Hartley spent time here, and Santa Fe was home to Robert Henri, George Bellows, Randall Davey, and Aaron Copland. Today this town of just 60,000 is home to one of the world's premier art colonies. Santa Fe also boasts an renowned opera company.

Where to ski

Ski Santa Fe sits 16 miles above the city. Though the mountain is known as a day-area destination for Santa Fe and Albuquerque skiers, out-of-town visitors will find a surprising amount of terrain.

All the mountain amenities, restaurants, ski rentals, child care, ski school and ticket sales are at the base of the mountain, just a few steps from the parking lot.

Beginners will be happiest on the lower part of the mountain, learning the basics on the wide boulevard of Easy Street. Lower intermediates will find more challenges and a slightly steeper pitch on Open Slope and Upper and Lower Midland.

On a fresh powder day (average once a week), local intermediates and advanced skiers head straight for the Tesuque Peak triple chair, to 12,000 feet and the top of the mountain. To the right (facing the mountain) of the lift is Gayway, a glorious groomed pitch with several spicy turns, that gives new meaning to the term spectacular scenery. On a clear day, skiers can see for 150 miles from this intermediate's delight. Parachute, which parallels Gayway, is a groomed black diamond with a somewhat steeper pitch.

For the most part, the mountain's expert terrain is to the left of the Tesuque Peak chair. With fresh snow, locals go first to Columbine, Big Rocks and Wizard. These runs all check in as very steep, for advanced skiers only.

Roadrunner is the expert bump run directly under the Tesuque chair. Tequila Sunrise and Easter Bowl have the best glade skiing.

On the far side of the mountain, reached by the Santa Fe Super Chief quad, Muerte and Defasio offer narrow, isolated tree skiing for the intermediate.

While there are hopes to overcome some environmental objections and put in a lift in the Big Tesuque Bowl, for the moment the intrepid ski into this area via Cornice (itself a taste of the bowl). Big Tesuque skiers find natural powder, bowl skiing and trees. The bowls empty onto the area's entrance road. Skiers then hitchhike back up to the base area. First timers should go with a local who knows the area: it's genuine wilderness, it's big and people occasionally get lost.

Mountain rating

We had pre-judged Ski Santa Fe to be a typical small, gentle day area. It's not. It definitely has enough terrain to keep any level of skier happy for three to four days. Its gladed runs are great, though short; and Big Tesuque Bowl when skiable, is an adventure. Santa Fe could use an isolated beginner area; its green-circle trails are gentle enough, but right in the line of traffic coming back to the base.

Combined with Santa Fe's outstanding sightseeing opportunities, this is an excellent destination for skiers who don't want to be on the mountain every day. One warning: Ski Santa Fe has one of the highest lift-served elevations in the nation—12,000 feet on top, 10,350 at the base. Those susceptible to altitude problems should take note.

Cross-country

There are maintained backcountry trails in the surrounding Santa Fe National Forest. Maps and specific information are available from the National Forest Service: (505) 988-6940. For trail and snow conditions in the Santa Fe National Forest call (505) 984-0606.

Snowboarding

Boarding is allowed. Depending on conditions, Santa Fe opens its halfpipe.

Ski school (94/95 prices)

Group lessons: Adult skiing or snowboarding (all day) $40; adult (half day) $25. A never-ever skier package with all-day lesson, beginner lift and rentals is $50. **Private lessons:** $55 per hour, each additional person is $25; two-hour are $94, additional skiers, $50; half-day lessons are $135, additional person, $65.

Special clinics include a women's program, racing classes, segregated classes for those 50 and older, mogul clinics, telemark lessons and powder workshops. Prices vary, and not all are offered every week. Check with the ski school, 982-4429.

Children's ski school: Ages 3-4, all-day supervision, including lunch and two-hour lesson $50 (add $11 for rental equipment); ages 5-6, all-day supervision, lunch and four hours of lessons, $52 (rentals $11 extra); (ages 7-9) all day supervision, lunch and four hours of lessons, $56 (rentals are $14 extra). Half-day programs are available.

Lift tickets (94/95 prices)

	Adult	Child (6-12) Senior (62-71)
One day	$35	$22
Three days	$98 ($32.66/day)	$62 ($20.66/day)
Five days	$158 ($31.60/day)	$99 ($19.80/day)

A ticket valid only on the beginner lift is $19. Skiers 72 and older and kids shorter than 46 inches in ski boots ski free.

Accommodations

Ski Santa Fe has no base lodging, but even if it did, you'd want to be in Santa Fe for dining, shopping and the museums. More than 70 hotels, motels, inns, condominiums and B&Bs serve Santa Fe visitors. Winter is low season, so bargains abound. Expect to pay about $45 a night for a hotel located on the Cerrillos Road strip.

A downtown hotel on or near the Plaza will run about $120 a night. These prices can be cut considerably if bought as a package that includes lift tickets. Downtown is where you'll find most of the best restaurants, sights, shopping and nightlife.

La Fonda Hotel is the historic place to stay in Santa Fe. An inn of one sort or another has been on this site for 300 years (Billy the Kid worked in the kitchen here washing dishes). The current La Fonda incarnation was built in the 1920s. This local landmark is an elegant old-style reminder of what Santa Fe once was. Rooms are about $120 a night. Even if you don't stay here, go inside and take a look. They don't make them like this anymore.

The way they make them now is across the Plaza from La Fonda. **The Inn of the Anasazi** is the politically correct place to stay in Santa Fe. Before building, the owner consulted with Native American holy men and received their blessings. The wrought iron, Navajo weavings, and wood carvings were all done by local artisans. Even the vegetables served in the Anasazi restaurants were grown by local Native Americans. Leftovers are given to a homeless shelter and everything is recycled.

Excellent B&Bs are **Adobe Abode, Alexander's Inn**, the spacious **Dancing Ground of the Sun**, the quilt-filled **Grant Corner Inn**, and the classy **Water Street Inn**.

Other accommodations to consider are the new **Hotel Plaza Real**, the historic **Hotel St. Francis** and the adobe **Inn on the Alameda**. For families try the **El Rey Inn**, the **Fort Marcy Compound Condominiums,** and the **Otra Vez** condos.

For information on any of the lodging and ski packages available in Santa Fe call (800) 776-7669 (800-776-SNOW) or the Santa Fe Visitors Bureau at (800) 777-2489 (800-777-CITY).

Dining

On the mountain, skiers have two choices. **La Casa Cafeteria** in the base lodge called La Casa Mall, and **Totemoff's Bar and Grill** at the base of the Tesuque Peak Chair. La Casa offers standard ski fare—chili, burgers, fries and so forth. Its breakfast burrito is awesome, but only for brave palates. Totemoff's features burgers, and cocktails.

While ski cuisine may be fine, back in the city, Santa Fe cooks. If you include fast food, Santa Fe has nearly 200 places to strap on the feed bag. From traditional New Mexican cuisine (move over, Tex-Mex) to steaks and seafood, Santa Fe has more food variety than you could consume in a year.

The Pink Adobe, 406 Old Santa Fe Trail (983-7712) is a local favorite dining spot and is therefore sometimes difficult to get in. They specialize in New Mexican and Creole foods, and reservations are necessary. Prices are moderate to expensive.

Tomasita's Cafe, 500 S. Guadaloupe (983-5721) is fast food with a twist. It's good. Portions are large. The service is friendly. It is a favorite of Santa Fe families, so prepare to wait. It is in-expensive, and has some of the best New Mexican fare in town.

If you are in town at lunch time, do what locals do and go stand in line at **Josie's Casa de Comida**, 225 E. Marcy (983-5311). The regional dishes, created by a real Josie, are excellent. Despite its linoleum tables and homey appearance, you'll find yourself seated next to backpackers, artists, politicians and wealthy matrons. The homemade desserts are legendary in Santa Fe. Josie's is very inexpensive, but closed on weekends.

Après-ski/nightlife

If it is night life you are looking for, Santa Fe has the usual live bands, bars and places to dance.

One of the more wonderful ways to work out the kinks of a fresh powder day is to stop at **Ten Thousand Waves** (988-1047, 982-9304) for a relaxing hot tub under the stars. Between Santa Fe and the ski basin, (about three miles from the Plaza) Ten Thousand Waves is a Japanese-style hot tub resort. Featuring kimonos, sandals, massage and sexually segregated dressing rooms, a soak under the brilliant New Mexican sky is heavenly. There are seven private tubs and one communal tub.

For a completely different hot tub experience, locals like to drive out to **Ojo Caliente** (583-2233). About an hour out of Santa Fe there is a funky (i.e. somewhat run-down) old soaking pool built over a natural hot spring. It is not open in the evening.

In Santa Fe, a wonderful place to mix dinner with entertain-ment is at **La Casa Sena** (988-9232) in the historic Sena Plaza. This stately adobe was built as a family home in the 1860's. Today, it's home to offices and shops. La Casa Sena restaurant features a full menu of New Mexican specialties—and singing waiters and waitresses. For about $20, you can eat, drink and hear what amounts to an exceptional dinner theater show, belted out between courses. Children are welcome, reservations a must.

Child care

The ski area's Chipmunk Corner takes children aged 2 months to 3 years. All-day supervision and activities costs $42. Call 988-9636 for reservations and information.

Other activities

Shopping: It is easy to spend your entire ski vacation in Santa Fe's many shops and galleries. More than 100 **galleries** feature everything from Native American jewelry, blankets and fine art to cutting-edge sculpture, pottery and paintings, normally seen only in places like New York, Florence or Paris. For lazy, romantic, artistic meandering, there is no place on earth like the old adobe galleries on Canyon Road.

The **museums** in Santa Fe are first rate. Must-sees are the Museum of International Folk Art (strong in area Spanish art) and the Museum of Indian Arts and Culture. Skiers with an interest in art should take time to visit the Museum of Fine Arts (with several Georgia O'Keeffe paintings) and the Center for Contemporary Arts.

After having done the museums, galleries and shops, one particularly nice place to visit is the Shidoni Forge in Tesuque. It features five acres of bronze sculpture and a working forge. Saturdays, visitors can watch while workmen pour molten bronze—an unforgettable experience.

Every Indian pueblo holds a festival dance each year to honor its patron saint. Most are held in the summer, but skiers in Santa Fe in late January can attend the festival at San Ildefonso. This celebration, where the Indians wear traditional clothing and dance traditional dances.

Call the Santa Fe Visitors Bureau (505-984-6760; 800-777-2489) for up-to-date information on Pueblo festivals.

Getting there and getting around

Getting there: Santa Fe is 80 miles from Albuquerque (the nearest major airport) on Interstate 25. The ski area is 16 miles from town on Highway 475.

Getting around: Getting to and from Santa Fe and the ski area is difficult without a car. The airport in Albuquerque has the leading rental agencies.

Information/reservations

Ski Santa Fe: 982-4429 or (800) 982-7669.

Santa Fe Convention and Visitors Bureau: 984-6760 or (800) 777-2489.

The local telephone area code is 505.

Other New Mexico ski areas

Angel Fire, Angel Fire, NM (800) 633-7463
6 lifts, 67 trails, 2,180 vertical feet

This four-season resort 22 miles east of Taos is well suited for beginner and intermediate skiers. With a peak elevation of 10,680 feet and a vertical drop of 2,180, this is definitely a destination resort. Its relatively gentle terrain attracts many multi-generational families, who cruise down the three-and-a-half mile, green-circle Headin' Home from the summit to the base as if they had been skiing all their lives. Angel Fire has challenging runs too, but it will make lower-level skiers feel like champs.

If you are planning to spend the night check into the Legends Hotel (800-633-7463) right at the base of the ski area.

Pajarito Mountain, Los Alamos, NM (505) 662-5725
6 lifts, 34 trails, 1,241 vertical feet

This is a day area about 90 minutes south of Taos and an hour north of Santa Fe. Privately owned by the Los Alamos Ski Club, Pajarito has mostly intermediate to expert terrain—especially bumps. It's a little hard to find, partly because New Mexicans guard their "private" enclave and partly because the club's nonprofit status doesn't permit it to market itself—or even to put up directional signs—but it is open to the public.

Red River, Red River, NM (505) 754-2382
7 lifts, 53 trails, 1,600 vertical feet

This is another family-oriented area, 37 miles northeast of Taos. Terrain leans toward beginner and intermediate. Lodging is within a mile of the slopes, offering rustic cabins to luxurious condos. For accommodations information, call (800) 348-6444.

Sandia Peak Ski Area, Albuquerque, NM (505) 242-9133
7 lifts, 26 trails, 1,700 vertical feet

Sandia Peak is Albuquerque's playground. Just east of New Mexico's largest city, it has runs for all levels. Take the Sandia Peak Aerial Tramway, a tourist attraction the year round. For accommodations information call (800) 733-9918.

Sipapu Ski Area, Vadito, NM (505) 587-2240
3 lifts, 19 trails, 865 vertical feet

This was the first New Mexico area to welcome snowboards and has since added a halfpipe. Sipapu, 30 miles southeast of Taos, has lodging close to the lifts, and terrain for all levels.

Ski Apache, Ruidoso, NM (505) 336-4356
10 lifts, 52 trails, 1,900 vertical feet

Located in south-central New Mexico, 200 miles from Albuquerque, this resort is owned and operated by the Mescalero Apache Indian tribe. The ski area has no lodging, but there is plenty in Ruidoso, 16 miles away. Ski Apache's terrain is 45 percent advanced, but the beginner and intermediate trails have a good reputation for being well groomed. The view from the 11,500-foot peak is reportedly spectacular. Ski Apache also has the state's largest and oldest program for disabled skiers. For accommodations information call (800) 545-9011.

StoryBook Cabins (505-257-2115) or the Best Western Swiss Chalet Inn (505-258-3333 or 800-477-9477) are recommended.

Arizona Resorts

Apache Sunrise, McNary AZ
(800) 772-7669, 800-554-6835, (602) 735-7600
9 lifts, 60 trails, 1,800 vertical feet

The drive east of Phoenix takes you into Zane Grey country, where he wrote his Western novels in a cabin. Farther on is a town called Show Low, where early settlers decided on a ranch ownership with a card game won with a deuce of clubs, the low draw. In Whiteriver, U.S. troops and Apache scouts subdued rebellious Apaches a little more than a century ago.

Today the White Mountain Apache Tribe owns and operates Apache Sunrise, by far the state's largest ski area. It is located 215 miles east of Phoenix, about a five-hour drive. Three ski mountains feature wide-open runs and lifts than can take 15,000 skiers per hour. The base area at 9,200 feet rises to an 11,000-foot summit. Much of the terrain is intermediate, with a few challenging, advanced drops. Weather this far south is often good, and snowfall averages 250 inches a year.

Fairfield Snowbowl, Flagstaff AZ (602) 779-4577
4 lifts, 32 trails, 2,300 vertical feet

The San Francisco Peaks rise abruptly above Flagstaff, 140 miles north of Phoenix. They provide the most challenging skiing in Arizona and some of the best views anywhere. Ridge Run, more than a mile long, as well as Casino and Tiger bump runs, could be at top Colorado or Utah resorts. Terrain is rated 30 percent beginner, 40 percent intermediate, 30 percent advanced. The altitude is surprising for a state known for its deserts and canyons—the base area is 9,000 feet and climbs to 11,500 feet. From the top of Mount Agassiz the view includes the Grand Canyon slash, red rocks of Sedona, and mountains outside Kingman. The Earth's curvature is visible from this lofty perch. Snowbowl has 196 skiable acres, with 65 of those acres at Hart Prairie, a beginner's slope just down the road from lifts. Hart Prairie has a modern lodge with room for 500 people; the Agassiz Lodge, at the base of the higher lifts, is nearly four decades old and tight on space.

For general Arizona information, write or call the **Arizona Office of Tourism**, 1480 E. Bethany Home #180, Phoenix AZ 85014, (602) 542-8687. **The Phoenix and Valley of the Sun Convention and Visitors' Bureau** is at 505 N. 2nd Street, Suite 300, Phoenix AZ 85004, (602) 254-6500.

Mt. Bachelor, Oregon

Mt. Bachelor is not your typical mountain. Many peaks are difficult to distinguish from neighboring summits, which may be just a few feet higher or lower. But Mt. Bachelor, a stately volcanic cone that is part of the Cascades mountain range, rises from Oregon's high desert, visible for miles in every direction.

Located on the eastern side of the Cascades, where snow falls lighter and drier than at other northwestern resorts, Mt. Bachelor has become a popular destination for western skiers. Despite no on-mountain lodging and little hot nightlife, Mt. Bachelor attracts skiers with a dependable 16-foot snowpack, clear, dry air, average daytime winter temperatures of 26 degrees and fine skiing from early November to July.

Visitors should keep in mind that all that snow results from a lot of storms, and that winds often close the Summit Express chair, a high-speed quad that zips skiers to the 9,065-foot, treeless summit. An average stormy day brings winds of 60 to 70 miles per hour (the record is more than 200 mph), and those summit winds can kick up "ground blizzards" where the snow swirls into a whiteout six feet high. (Visibility is usually better lower on the mountain, where the ski trails are protected by trees.) But when the weather is clear and you're standing on top, you can see California's Mt. Shasta 180 miles to the south. That view, most commonly seen in spring, is worth a lot.

Though the volcano is extinct, the thinking of Mt. Bachelor's management is anything but. This is a resort that has been quick to embrace new concepts in the ski industry, such as electronic ticketing, a revolutionary ski school and high-speed quad chairs.

Although it is on the cutting edge of ski industry trends, Mt. Bachelor manages to keep its atmosphere very untrendy. No one notices or cares whether your ski clothes match, or even how hot a skier you are.

Mt. Bachelor Facts
Base elevation: 5,800; **Summit elevation:** 9,065'; **Vertical drop:** 3,265 feet
Number of lifts: 12–6 quad superchairs, 3 triple chairs, 1 double chair, 2 surface lifts
Snowmaking: none **Acreage:** 3,200 lift-accessed skiable acres
Uphill capacity: 21,000 per hour **Bed base:** 7,500

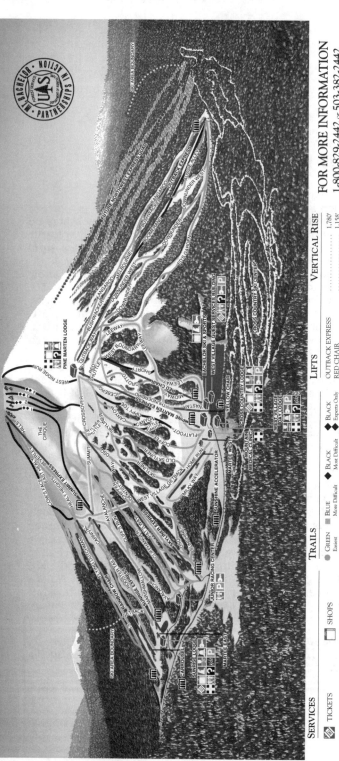

SERVICES

🎿 TICKETS	🏠 SHOPS		
🎿 SKI SCHOOL	👶 DAY CARE		
🍴 FOOD	➕ FIRST AID		
🚻 RESTROOMS	❓ INFORMATION		
🔧 RENTALS/REPAIR	🔒 LOCKERS		
SLOW/FAMILY AREA	P PARKING		

TRAILS

● GREEN
Easiest
■ BLUE
More Difficult
◆ BLACK
Most Difficult
◆◆ BLACK
Experts Only

EASIEST DESCENTS

Outback—Kangaroo/Bushwacker
Yellow—Flatfoot
Pine Marten—Skyliner
Sunrise—Marshmallow
Rainbow—Carnival

Red—Last Chance
Sunshine—Home Run
Skyliner—Avalanche
Summit—Beverley Hills
Carrousel—Carnival

LIFTS	VERTICAL RISE
OUTBACK EXPRESS	1,780'
RED CHAIR	1,158'
YELLOW CHAIR	357'
PINE MARTEN EXPRESS	1,360'
SKYLINER EXPRESS	1,316'
SUNRISE EXPRESS	808'
SUMMIT EXPRESS	1,725'
RAINBOW CHAIR	1,215'
MARTEE EAST	50'
MARTEE WEST	50'
CARROUSEL	171'
SUNSHINE ACCELERATOR	357'

EXPRESS QUAD	TRIPLE	DOUBLE	

FOR MORE INFORMATION

1-800-829-2442 or **503-382-2442**
On-mountain service information and
reservations including Skier Development
Center, Day Care, Banquet/Group Events.

503-382-7888
Ski report and summer events.

1-800-800-8334
Vacation planning assistance and reservations

Where to ski

Mt. Bachelor is best suited to intermediates. The Outback Express, the longest chair lift on the mountain with a 1,780-foot vertical rise, serves excellent intermediate runs. Over here, Boomerang is the only run rated black, and it parallels the lift. One blue-square run, Down Under, often is left ungroomed for mogul enthusiasts.

Other popular chairs for intermediates are the Pine Marten Express, which heads up from the base lodge, and the Skyliner Express, a little to the left on the trail map. Old Skyliner, off the Pine Marten chair, has some marvelous dips and rolls—far more fun than the usual freeway design of many intermediate trails.

Most of the lower mountain is sheltered by trees, but some runs, such as Flying Dutchman and Tippytoe, give the exuberance of upper-mountain skiing. You usually can find moguls on Grotto, Canyon and Coffee Run, all off the Pine Marten chair.

When the Summit Express is open, experts should head for it. The steepest descent is through The Pinnacles, a jagged rock formation reached by a 150-foot hike from the top of the lift, then across the broad, ungroomed expanse of Cirque Bowl. Next might well be Cow's Face, far to the left of Summit Chair, steep but smooth. Because it's unknown to many skiers, it doesn't get carved into moguls, but wind packs it hard.

The longest continuous vertical (3,100 feet) can be had by taking the Summit chair off the backside, occasionally traversing right and ending up at the bottom of the Outback chair.

Intermediates can experience the heady sensation of being on the summit and still get down safely using the broad Healy Heights and Beverly Hills, which are always groomed. In fact, intermediates can't get into trouble at Mt. Bachelor: anything beyond their skill requires a knowledgeable decision to get into it—for example, the hike up to The Pinnacles.

Between the Outback and Red chairs is an unusual geologic feature, a lone cinder cone. It's not served by a lift, so powder lasts there until it becomes wind-packed. By getting up a head of steam from Leeway, skiers can swoop up nearly two-thirds of the way and climb the rest.

Never-evers get a treat at Mt. Bachelor: a high-speed quad chair, Sunshine Accelerator. High-speed quads move very slowly for loading and unloading, which makes them ideal for those learning the tricks of riding chair lifts. But these are expensive pieces of equipment, so it is very rare for a ski area to spend that kind of money for learners. Green-circle trails descend from every lift except the Summit and Outback chairs. More difficult trails are on either side, funneling the faster skiers away from those who are still learning to control their turns.

Mountain rating

Most of the terrain is ideal for intermediates. Expert skiers probably will feel restless after a weekend—they'll have to discover the pleasures of the backside and Cinder Cone.

Cross-country (93/94 prices)

The Mt. Bachelor Rossignol Cross-Country Center, across the parking lot from the West Village base lodge, has 56 km. of machine-set trails. There are 12 loops, from the easy, 1-km. First Time Around to the challenging 12-km. Oli's Alley. The 6-km. intermediate trail, called Zigzag, leads to a heated shelter with good views. The center has equipment rental, clothing and accessories, repairs, trail and lesson information and lunch.

All-day passes are $9.50 for adults, $4.50 for children 7 to 12. Half-day rates start at noon—$8 for adults, $3.50 for children. Ages 65 and older pay $5.75 all day, or $4.25 half day. Children younger than 7 ski free.

Mt. Bachelor also operates 20 km. of groomed tracks at Sunriver Resort, about 14 miles from the downhill area. All-day tickets purchased here can be used at the Mt. Bachelor Nordic facilities in the afternoon, and vice-versa. Tickets at Sunriver are $8 for adults, $3.50 for kids.

Snowboarding

No restrictions. The resort offers lessons based on its Perfect Turn® learning program. A never-ever lesson is $50, including a two-hour clinic and full-day lift ticket and rental board.

Ski school (93/94 prices)

Mt. Bachelor is one of only a handful of ski resorts to offer a revolutionary ski-teaching philosophy called Perfect Turn®. Learning is based on total positive reinforcement, and based on our firsthand experience, it works.

This is what makes Perfect Turn different: A Perfect Turn ski pro never tells you what you're doing wrong (e.g., "You're sitting too far back on your skis. You're letting your hands drop). Instead, the pro picks out something you do very well and compliments you on that skill. Instead of feeling that you're a terrible skier because you do so many things wrong, your subconscious mind tells you that you're a good skier. When it's time for some corrective tips, your mind isn't holding you back.

Perfect Turn sessions for levels 4-9 (low intermediate to expert) cost $24, $20 with a dated performance card from your previous Perfect Turn lesson. Levels 1-3 are $30 for a lesson only; $40 for lesson, ski rental and lift pass.

Private lessons are $40 per hour; $10 for additional skiers. A private lesson with video analysis is $50.

Children's programs are for ages 4-12, based on the same positive approach taken in the adult Perfect Turn sessions.

Learning groups are formed according to age, ability and maturity in the skiing environment. Rates are $60 for lesson, rentals, lifts and lunch; $47 for half-day without lunch. Brand-new skiers can get the half-day package for $40. You must have your child registered by 9:45 a.m. at either the West Village or Sunrise Skier Development Centers.

Special programs include women's clinics, NASTAR, and coin-operated race courses.

Lift tickets (93/94 prices)

	Adult	Child (7-12)
One day	$33	$18
Three days	$90 ($30/day)	$41 ($13.66/day)
Five days	$143 ($28.60/day)	$63.50 ($12.70/day)

Students can buy a daily pass for $25. Ages 65 and older ski for $19 a day; 6 and younger ski for free. Other multiday tickets are available.

If you usually ski fewer than ten runs per day, Mt. Bachelor's SkiData lift system could prove more economical. It tallies your points with each lift ride, until the points you paid for are gone. Use unused points the next day—or even the next season. The tickets are fully transferable and are good for three years. The 200-point ticket is $35, while a 400-point ticket sells for $69. Currently, 16 percent of Bachelor's skiers use the point system. Those who ski all day long should stick to the all-day ticket.

Accommodations

Mt. Bachelor's nearest accommodations are several miles away in or near Bend.

The most extensive lodging complex is **Sunriver**, a resort community 18 miles from Mt. Bachelor and 15 miles south of Bend. The complex has a private airport, many activities, restaurants and stores. A shuttle runs throughout the expansive resort complex, and another shuttle runs between Sunriver and Mt. Bachelor (and costs $7, though this fee is included in some packages). This may be enough for some people, but it's tough to get to Bend. Rates run from $85 to $260 for rooms, private homes and condos. Call (800) 547-3922; in Oregon, (800) 452-6874.

Inn of the Seventh Mountain is Mt. Bachelor's closest lodging, with restaurants, a grocery store that stocks nearly 99 brands of beer, a skating rink, hot tub, snowmobile and sleigh rides, as well as a shuttle to the mountain. Economy rooms are $58, three-bedroom condos are $268, with many offerings and ski packages in between. Call (800) 452-6810 in the U.S.; (800) 874-9402 from Canada.

Bend's most deluxe accommodations are **River House**, nestled along the river close to restaurants and entertainment. Pool, indoor and outdoor spas and a Nautilus exercise room make this a mini-resort in the heart of town. Nightly rates range from $52 for two people to $92 for a river-view suite with three queen beds, two rooms and kitchen. (800) 547-3928; or 381-3111.

Bend has many more places to stay, plus five RV parks, and several more within 25 miles. Phone the Bend Visitors' Information Center for more information, 382-3221.

Dining

A team of three searched diligently for great food at this resort without success. Overall, the cooking is basic and prices are based more on atmosphere rather than the chef's creativity.

Although you'll pay more at elegant **The Riverhouse Restaurant** (389-8810), good seafood is moderately priced at **McGrath's Publick Fish House** (388-4555), which has several unusual entrées, especially those from Northwestern waters.

Pine Tavern Restaurant (382-5581), with the twin pine trees shooting out of the dining room roof, serves great steak, ribs, lamb and prime rib. **Rosette** (383-2780) rustles up a Mediterranean/Northwest cuisine and more lamb dishes than most restaurants. It's quiet and sophisticated.

For ethnic food, try **Chan's** (389-1725) for Szechwan, Hunan and Cantonese; **Murrieta's** (389-1800) in Sunriver for Mexican food; or **Giuseppe's** (389-8899), *Pacific Northwest* magazine's "best ethnic" restaurant, for Italian. **Stuft Pizza** (382-4022) gets raves for its pizza, calzone and sandwiches.

Deschutes Brewery & Public House (382-9242), in the center of downtown Bend, has four to six of its handcrafted brews on tap. The beer is great; the meals are so-so.

For breakfast, try **The West Side Bakery & Cafe** on Galveston for its eggs-and-pancake menu and its fun decor (amusing knickknacks on the walls and ceiling, and a model train that runs through its three dining rooms at just below ceiling level), or **Café Paradiso** on Bond Street, which opens at 8 a.m. with the best smelling coffee in town and pastries.

Après-ski/nightlife

Mt. Bachelor is not known for an exciting après-ski atmosphere, nor is Bend noted for its dynamic nightlife, though both can be found. The **Castle Keep Lounge** in the lower level of the West Village lodge, offers lively après-ski with occasional live music. Also check **The Riverhouse** and **E.L. Bender's** in town.

Later, you'll find dancing at **Willie D's, The Shilo Restaurant and Lounge, Pasha's** and **The Riverhouse,** all in Bend; **Owl's Nest Lounge** at the Sunriver Resort and **Josiah's** at Inn of the Seventh Mountain. Most of the live music is weekends only, but Willie D's rocks all week long. For quieter evenings, try **Café Paradiso** in Bend, a European-style coffee house with acoustic music. **Pine Tavern Restaurant** has a mature adult atmosphere overlooking Mirror Pond. **Stuft Pizza** in Bend has comedy on Saturdays, and big-screen sports other nights.

Child care

A state-licensed day care center for children 6 weeks to 7 years operates at both West Village and Sunrise Lodges. Rates are $30 per day for all ages; a box lunch is $5 more. Reservations are recommended. Call 382-2442 or (800) 829-2442.

Other activities

Shopping: Bend Factory Outlets, a 27-store outlet mall on Highway 97 south of Powers Road, has name brands such as Carter's Childrenswear, London Fog, Eddie Bauer and Bass Shoes. The real draw, though, are two **Columbia Outfitters** skiwear factory outlets, one downtown on Bond Street and the other at 55 N.W. Wall Street. Columbia makes a very practical ski clothing component system with zip-in fleece jacket liners that can be worn separately. Here, they are bargain priced.

Sunriver and Inn of the Seventh Mountain have **ice skating, horseback riding, sleigh rides** and **snowmobiling**.

The Oregon Trail of Dreams Training Camp offers **dogsled rides** by dogs that are training for Alaska's famed Iditarod race. Rates are $60 for adults; $30 for children less than 80 pounds. Call 382-2442 or (800) 829-2442.

The U.S. Forest Service, with a desk on the lower floor of Mt. Bachelor's West Village lodge, has several interpretive programs, including a **snowshoe tour** with a USFS naturalist.

Getting there and getting around

Getting there: Mt. Bachelor is 21 miles southwest of Bend, Oregon, on the scenic Cascade Lakes Highway. Take Highways 26 and 97 from Portland, 162 miles away. State Highway 126 comes from Eugene (132 miles).

United Express and **Horizon Air** have flights into Redmond/Bend Airport (16 miles from Bend) from many West Coast cities. **Amtrak** (800-872-7245, 800-USA-RAIL) provides daily service on the Coast Starlight, which runs from Los Angeles to Seattle. The closest stop is Chemult, 60 miles south of Bend. Arrange ahead for taxi pickup.

Getting around: A car is helpful. If you don't have one, be sure to stay in lodgings with some kind of shuttle service. Mt. Bachelor operates a free park-and-ride operation during the height of the season from its office on 14th Street in Bend, but you'll need a way to reach it.

Information/reservations

Central Oregon Recreation Association (800-800-8334) will assist with lodging, ground transportation and ski packages. In Oregon call 382-8334, or write Central Oregon Recreation Association, P.O. Box 230-97709, Bend, OR 97709.

The ski report phone is 382-7888.

All telephone area codes are 503 unless otherwise noted.

Mt. Hood Region, Oregon

Portland skiers jokingly call these "our little day areas," but the three ski areas within 15 miles of each other on the shanks of Oregon's most beautiful mountain, Mt. Hood, offer a fine range of skiing experiences for destination skiers too.

Most skiers come for the day or an overnight visit. Consequently lodging, dining and nightlife are limited. But the skiing is quite varied and abundant. Best of all, it's within an hour's drive of a major airport, Portland International.

Too bad the region doesn't market interchangeable lift tickets, because it has promise as a no-frills location for destination skiers. Mt. Hood doesn't have much lodging, dining or nightlife, but when you strip away those amenities, what stands out? The skiing; specifically, ski conditions that keep up the enthusiasm of advanced skiers for days at a time. That requires plenty of naturally rugged terrain that hasn't been dynamited to a freeway finish. We found plenty of what we like to ski, as well as some great terrain for the lower ability levels at Timberline and Mt. Hood Meadows.

Timberline

Timberline is known for its historic lodge and summer skiing. The lodge is a beauty, and we offer more detail in the accommodations section of this chapter. Timberline was the continent's first ski area to offer lift-served summer skiing, and now more than 50,000 skiers come each summer. The Palmer Snowfield has a steady pitch at the advanced intermediate level. It's challenging enough for you to find World Cup ski racers from several countries practicing technique. During winter, though, the Palmer chair is closed (too much snow) and Timberline becomes a great beginner/intermediate area.

Timberline Facts

Base elevation: 5,000'; **Summit elevation:** 8,500' summer, 7,000' winter; **Vertical drop:** 2,000 feet winter, about 1,500 feet summer (varies)

Number and types of lifts: 6 - 1 quad superchair, 1 triple chair and 3 double chairs. A fourth double chair and the superchair are used in summer.

Acreage: 1,000 (31 trails) **Percent of snowmaking:** None

Uphill capacity: 6,500 skiers per hour in winter; 8,000 in summer

Bed base: 71 rooms on mountain

Where to ski

Most Timberline skiing is below the main lodge, but few experiences in the skiing world match a ride up the Magic Mile Super Express to the bottom of the Palmer Snowfield. The original Magic Mile lift was the second ski lift in the country, after Sun Valley's. Silcox Hut, which served as the original top terminus and warming hut, was recently restored and serves again as a warming hut and group lodging. Below the Timberline Lodge are plenty of blue and green runs lined by trees, with a few short black-diamond runs. The webbed trail system between the trees makes each run feel like a wilderness excursion.

Snowboarding

Timberline has gone all-out for snowboarders. In winter, the ski area has a Bone Zone, a snow park to challenge the best riders. The base of Paint Brush Glade has a halfpipe. Lessons and rentals are available. Timberline is well known for its summer camps on the snowfield. The U.S. Snowboard Training Center is there eight hours a day for six-day sessions during the summer. Call (800) 325-4430 for more information.

Ski school (93/94 prices)

Timberline embraces the SKIwee program for kids, and charges $58 per day. Adult group lessons cost $16 for 90 minutes. Private lessons are $34 for an hour.

Lift tickets (93/94 prices)

Adults $26, children (7-12) $16, valid 9 a.m. to 5 p.m. Other adult ticket prices range from $8 to $28, depending on the time of day and day of week. Timberline has night skiing until 10 p.m.

Mt. Hood Meadows

Mt. Hood Meadows is the big guy in the area, actually the largest "day" hill in the country. Its ski school is highly regarded in mountain circles, and the terrain has the most variety of the three Mt. Hood areas.

Mt. Hood Meadows Facts

Base elevation: 4,523'; **Summit elevation:** 7,300'; **Vertical drop:** 2,777 feet
Number and types of lifts: 11 - 1 quad superchair, 1 quad, 1 triple chair, 6 double chairs, 2 surface lifts **Acreage:** 2,150 skiable acres (142 acres of night skiing)
Percent of snowmaking: None **Uphill capacity:** 12,345 skiers per hour
Bed base: None on mountain; closest 10 miles away in town of Government Camp

---

Where to ski

Mt. Hood Meadows is the farthest from the lodging centered in Government Camp, but it has by far the most varied terrain. This is a huge ski area, as big as all but the biggest Western destination resorts. Adventurous skiers enjoy the chain of chutes and bowls into Heather Canyon, reached from either the

Cascade Express superchair or the Shooting Star quad chair. The favorite intermediate area is under the Hood River Meadows chair, affectionately called "Herm" for its initials, HRM. Beginners have the runs under the Red and Buttercup chairs, adjacent to the snowboard halfpipe. Night skiing is in the vicinity of the main lodge.

Snowboarding

Mt. Hood Meadows has a groomed halfpipe and 125 rental boards in the High Performance Ski and Snowboard Center. Lessons also are available. Random fact: the average age of weekday snowboarders is 37.

Ski school (93/94 prices)

Mt. Hood Meadows charges $20 for a 90-minute group lesson. Private lessons are $35 an hour, $20 for each additional person. A full-day program for kids 4-6, called Kidski, costs $60, includes lift ticket, lesson, rentals and lunch, and is available weekends and holidays only. Half-day children's lifts-lessons-rental package is $40 for ages 4-6; $48 for first through eighth grades. First-Timer packages (all-inclusive) cost $30 for Alpine, $25 for Nordic, and $40 for snowboarding.

Lift tickets (93/94 prices)

Tickets are $31 per shift for adults. Shifts are 9 a.m.–4 p.m., 11 a.m.–7 p.m., and 1–10 p.m.) Ages 65 and older ski for $20 per shift, while ages 7-12 ski for $20 any time during the day/night. Children 6 and younger ski for $6. Night tickets (4-10 p.m.) cost $10 no matter what age. Half-day and midweek price breaks available.

Mt. Hood Ski Bowl

Mt. Hood Ski Bowl claims to be America's largest night-skiing area. It certainly offers quite a bit under the lights, including some truly steep black-diamond runs. It also emphasizes ski racing, with programs for a variety of age groups.

Mt. Hood Ski Bowl Facts

Base elevation: 3,600'; **Summit elevation:** 5,056'; **Vertical drop:** 1,456 feet
Number and types of lifts: 9 - 4 double chairs, 5 surface lifts
Acreage: 620 skiable acres **Percent of snowmaking:** 25 percent
Uphill capacity: 4,600 skiers per hour
Bed base: Several inns and lodges in Government Camp

Where to ski

Mt. Hood Ski Bowl is gaining a reputation for challenging ski runs with the addition of its outback area and 1,500 feet of vertical reached from Upper Bowl. The mountain is now rated at 40 percent expert terrain, but the 60 runs have enough variety for all skills. Though beginners have some nice terrain, Ski Bowl's lift unloading ramps are strictly black-diamond affairs, with steep pitches and some sharp turns.

Snowboarding

At Ski Bowl, the Multopor side and the Outback are favorites. Ski Bowl sells a $10 snowboard lift ticket good on a surface lift that services a halfpipe and obstacle course. Lessons are by appointment.

Ski school (93/94 prices)

Ski Bowl, with 100 ski instructors, has classes in racing, freestyle, cross-country and snowboarding. Group lessons cost $14, private lessons $28 for an hour. Ski Bowl also teaches lessons at night by appointment.

Lift tickets (93/94 prices)

Adults $22 ($12 nights); children (11 and younger) $15 ($10 nights). Like Mt. Hood Meadows, Ski Bowl sells shift tickets: Opening to 4:30 p.m., 11 a.m. to 7 p.m., 1 p.m. to close.

Cross-country

Timberline has telemark lessons, weekends only, but no groomed cross-country trails. **Mt. Hood Meadows** has no telemark equipment, but it does have 15 km. of groomed Nordic track at the base of the Hood River Meadows lift, with rental equipment and instruction. Trail passes are $7, and the cross-country center is open Wednesdays through Sundays.

The **Mt. Hood National Forest** has nearly 200 km. of cross-country trails. The Trillium Lake Trail is normally groomed and tracked weekly. Maps are available at any ranger station.

Accommodations

The only slopeside lodging in the region is **Timberline Lodge**, 6,000 feet in the middle of the ski area and a National Historic Landmark. Built by the Works Progress Administration in 1937, it is filled with stunning artistic details, such as carved stairway banisters, colored linoleum wall murals and wrought-iron fireplace decor made from old railroad tracks. Rates range from $90 to $150 for rooms with private baths. Eleven chalet rooms with a shared bathroom and shower across the hall go for $52. Though Christmas season is sold out 15 months in advance, try to book a few days the week before the traditional Christmas vacation when the decorations are in place. And one more thing: Timberline Lodge visitors get a courtesy windshield scraper with the usual soap and shampoo—a testament to the 15 feet of snow that falls here. (800) 547-1406; 231-5400 from Portland.

Also at Timberline is a unique group lodging opportunity: **Silcox Hut.** The 45-year-old, newly restored hut was the terminus for the original Magic Mile chair lift. Now, bunkrooms accommodate up to 24 guests (minimum 13, $130 per person, including meals). Call (503) 295-1827 for reservations.

Other lodging is in the town of Government Camp, across Highway 26 from Ski Bowl. Our favorite is **Falcon's Crest Inn**, a delightful bed-and-breakfast run by Melody and Bob (BJ) Johnson. Its five rooms ($85 to $139) all have private baths and varying decor (safari, 1920s, etc.). In December, every room of the inn has a uniquely decorated Christmas tree. Call 272-3403 or (800) 624-7384.

Those who prefer a little more privacy than a B&B affords can go across the street to the **Mt. Hood Inn**. This modern hotel has rooms with two queen beds and continental breakfast starting at $90 per night. King Spa rooms, with Jacuzzi tubs, are $135. Midweek one-night/one-day ski packages start at $99 per couple. 272-3205 or (800) 443-7777.

Other lodging at Government Camp includes **Huckleberry Inn**, with rooms for $45 to $100 and a dorm for $15 per person, 272-3325; or **Thunderhead Lodge Condominiums**, 272-3368.

The Resort at the Mountain, 20 minutes down-mountain from Timberline (and 45 minutes from the Portland airport), sits at 1,500 feet of elevation in the town of Welches. Thus the resort can promote golfing in the morning (27 holes) and skiing in the afternoon. It borders the Salmon River. Ski packages rates at the resort start at $128 per couple. 622-3101 or (800) 669–7666.

Central Oregon Reservations (800) 443-7777 can help with accommodations in the region.

Dining

Timberline Lodge has an elegant restaurant, the **Cascade Dining Room**, that serves breakfast, lunch and dinner at set times. Entrée prices are usually in the high teens. The salmon and lamb are excellent. The **Blue Ox Deli** downstairs delights the senses. It's sort of a theme bar of Paul Bunyan proportions, decorated with murals and original glass work by Virginia Vance. **Wy'East**, across the street, has a cafeteria.

Mt. Hood Meadows has two lodges, each with several eateries. North Lodge has the **Finish Line** for a great lunch, après-ski nibbles and drinks, and a view of the whole area. South Lodge has **Micro Pub & Sausage Haus**, with a good variety of microbrewed beer. You also can buy pizza cooked to order, espresso or latté, or pasta in the various restaurants.

Ski Bowl has more typical ski-cafeteria food in the East and West Lodges, and warm food at the mid-mountain warming hut. Beer and wine are available at the **T–Bar** in the East Lodge, and there's a full bar, the **Beerstube**, in the West Lodge.

In Government Camp, **Falcon's Crest Inn** serves a fixed-price gourmet dinner ($26.95 to $28.95), and frequently does mystery dinners for parties of eight for $96.50 per couple. Call

272-3403 or (800) 624-7384. **Huckleberry Inn** has a coffee shop open 24 hours a day, and is the place for a hearty breakfast. **Mt. Hood Brew Pub**, next to the Mt. Hood Inn, has microbrewed beer, espresso bar, local wines and a pub menu.

Après-ski/nightlife

This is the Pacific Northwest, where hard-working, hard-skiing people can barely stay awake to watch "Northern Exposure." Generally, the choices are night skiing and sleeping. Exceptions are the **Augusta Lounge** in the Resort at the Mountain, which has live music, and the **Mt. Hood Brew Pub.**

Other activities

Not much, at least up on the mountain. A sledding/tubing hill is nearby, but most people come to ski.

Getting there and getting around

Getting there: U.S. Highway 26 east from Portland gets you first to Mt. Hood Ski Bowl, 53 miles from Portland. For Timberline, turn left and continue for six miles. To get to Mt. Hood Meadows, go through Government Camp to Oregon Rte. 35, then turn left. It's 68 miles from Portland. An alternate route to Meadows is to take I-84 east from Portland, following the Columbia River to the town of Hood River, where you turn south on 35. Hood River to the Mt. Hood Meadows turnoff is 36 miles.

Getting around: A car is vital; however, those trying to rent may find themselves in a Catch-22 situation. Tire chains are a necessity, because the snow is wet and slippery. You can get a $50 fine if you're caught without them (or four-wheel-drive) when "Traction Devices Required" signs are posted. The Portland airport has five rental-car agencies. National doesn't allow you to install chains; the rest permit them as long as you pay for any damage to the car. You must buy the chains, but the agencies will not reimburse you for the cost. (And just what are you going to do with a set of used tire chains?) Better to rent a four-wheel-drive car. Hertz, Dollar, National and Budget have them; Avis does not.

All the Mt. Hood ski areas are in Sno-Parks, which require parking permits. They cost $1.50 per day, $2.50 for three days, $9 for the year, and are available at the ski areas and at many stores on the way to the mountains.

Information/reservations

Mt. Hood Meadows, P.O. Box 470, Hwy. 35, Mt. Hood, OR 97041-0470. Office: (503) 337-2222; snow phone: (503) 227-7669.

Timberline, Government Camp, OR 97028. Office: (503) 272-3311; snow phone: (503) 222-2211. Timberline Lodge reservations: (800) 547-1406.

Mt. Hood Ski Bowl, P.O. Box 280, Government Camp, OR 97028. Office: (503) 272-3206; snow phone: (503) 222-2695.

Crystal Mountain, Washington

When the weather is right, the snow is deep, and avalanche danger is not too great, hardcore skiers from all over the West Coast beam themselves to Crystal for unparalleled skiing. The terrain is steep and thrilling, and there's enough of it to keep the adrenaline rushing all day. There's enough snow too, often 12 feet deep at the top.

It's Washington state's only destination Alpine ski resort, just 90 minutes from Seattle. The on-mountain condos, lodges and restaurants delight local skiers who would otherwise have to leave the state for a ski vacation.

Crystal Mountain is a favorite vacation spot for some Canadian ski-hill employees. They don't want their names used, but whole groups of British Columbia liftees and front office personnel can't wait for their annual midwinter ski vacations to Crystal. Their reasoning: Snow conditions at Crystal, near Mount Rainier, are consistently drier and more stable than in British Columbia, and they prefer Crystal's ambiance.

As befitting its Seattle ties, Crystal operates an espresso sled—a portable coffee cart to which skiers can schuss for a caffeine jolt. Another service is Crystal's plainclothes' skiers who keep an eye on decoy skis they plant in public racks in an effort to catch thieves. Lock your skis, nonetheless.

Where to ski

The beginner lift at Crystal, called Discovery, inspires confidence. Blue runs make up another 37 percent of Crystal's 2,300 acres, and black-diamond runs are a whopping 43 percent. That high expert percentage is partly because of the 1,000 skiable acres in the back-country areas, both north and south. It's the kind of terrain that is out of bounds at most ski areas—woods, chutes and steep bowls. The backcountry isn't always open, nor is it patrolled regularly, but it's a major attraction for expert skiers when the ski patrol opens the gates.

Crystal Mountain Facts

Base elevation: 4,400' **Summit elevation:** 7,002' **Vertical drop:** 3,102 feet
Number of lifts: 10—1 quad superchair, 1 quad, 3 triple chairs, 5 double chairs
Snowmaking: 1.3 percent (30 acres near the base)
Acreage: 2,300 **Uphill capacity:** 15,600 skiers per hour **Bed base:** 720

Crystal Mountain offers the highest lift–served skiing and the most variety in Washington. The mountain boasts 3,100 vertical feet and 307 inches of annual snowfall. Crystal also has the only high-speed quad chair in the state. Skiers can get to the top—7,000 feet—in 13 minutes. By skiing connecting trails, you can take a three-mile nonstop run to the bottom.

Cross-country

There are no cross-country trails, rentals or lessons, but $5 will buy a one-time lift ticket to access a backcountry lake trail.

Snowboarding

Crystal is snowboard heaven for sure, dude. Pacific Northwest snowboarders have gravitated to freeriding, as opposed to contest-oriented technical boarding, and Crystal has the deep woods, ridges and carving slopes that keep them coming back for more. Boarder Zone, next to the Quicksilver Chair, has banks, rails, obstacles and a double halfpipe.

Ski school

Crystal's PSIA-certified ski school, with 110 full-time and 40 part-time instructors, gets beginners past the green runs fast.

The **Kids' Club** lesson program is divided by ages 4-6 and 7-11, half day or full day. Rates include all-day lift ticket but not rentals. Half day, ages 4-6, costs $25; all day, $41. Half day, ages 7-11, costs $31; all day, $47. For children aged 2-4, the Lil' Otter special, $39 for all day, combines snow play and skiing, ski equipment, all-day supervision and lunch.

Adult group lessons cost $20 for one two-hour session; $32 for four hours. **Private lessons** (one hour, one or two people) are $36 at 9 a.m. or 3:30 p.m.; $45 at all other times. Two-hour private sessions cost $85 and three hours cost $120.

Inquire at the Summit House for Quick Tips, which are one-run ski consultations at $5 for one to four persons.

Lift tickets (93/94 prices)

	Adult	Child (7-11)
Weekend day	$31	$19
Monday/Tuesday	$15	$15
Wednesday-Friday	$19	$19

Holidays are priced at the weekend rates. Ages 65-69 ski for $20. Night skiing (4-10 p.m.) is $14. Skiers age 70 and older ski free; 5 and younger pay $5. With a Friday lift ticket, Friday night skiing until 10 p.m. is free.

Accommodations

All lodging at Crystal is within walking distance of the slopes. The three hotels and 96 condominiums vary widely in styles and prices, from $40 for two with a shower down the hall in the Alpine Inn Hotel, to $143 for a Crystal Chalet condo.

Lodging can match most budgets. Packages are available for two to five days. For reservations and information: **Alpine Inn Hotel**, 663-2262; **all other lodging**, 663-2558.

The parking lot has 21 RV hookups, $10 per night each.

Dining

Restaurants cater to both the white-linen and take-out crowds, with rustic dining, a cafeteria and après-ski hors d'oeuvres lounges in between. A favorite of the play-hard crowd is the **Snorting Elk Cellar** in the Alpine Inn.

Summit House, a rustic dining lodge at 6,872 feet, serves a passable version of the now-famous Northwest cuisine, but the main attraction is the view of Mount Rainier. It's more than 14,000 feet up, but looks like you could reach out and touch it.

The base has a cafeteria and **Rafters Restaurant.** They're open before the lifts start in the morning, and Rafters stays open to 10 p.m. Friday through Sunday. **Crystal Inn** serves until 9 p.m.

Après-ski/nightlife

The Saloon brings in live bands to appease powder hounds that still have energy at day's end. Tuesday is comedy night.

Other activities

It's not widely known, but a Crystal lift ticket entitles the bearer to enjoy the swimming pool, hot tub, sauna and showers for $2. In the Crystal Inn, these facilities are open seven days a week, noon to 10 p.m. Massages are available but extra.

Child care

Crystal has programs for children aged 8 weeks to 7 years. Programs for ages 2-7 are daily; programs for infants are on non-holiday weekdays only. Full-day care costs $29 for toddlers, $33 for infants. The child care phone number is 663–2265.

Getting there and getting around

Crystal is 76 miles southeast of Seattle, bordering the east side of Mount Rainier National Park. Drive south on I–5 from Seattle, take Exit 142 east to Auburn, Highway 164 to Enumclaw, and Highway 410 east through Snoqualmie National Forest to the Crystal Road.

Bus service from Puget Sound to Crystal Mountain is available on the Crystal Mountain Express. Call (206) 455–5505 for information and reservations.

Information/reservations

Snow condition hot line: 634–3771; **Crystal Mountain office and** ski school, 663-2265; rental shop: 663–2264. **Lodging reservations:** 663–2558. The local area code is 206.

Mt. Baker, Washington

Tucked onto the side of a mountain in the northwest corner of Washington state is a ski area with possibly the deepest snow of any ski hill in the country. At Mt. Baker, any amount of snow less than 100 inches at the lodge is considered slight. The ski area is not actually the 10,778-foot volcano of the same name. It's on an arm of 9,127-foot Mt. Shuksan, one of the most photographed mountains in the world, also one of the most listened to, since its careening chunks of steep glacier avalanche can be seen and heard for miles around (they're well out of the ski area, so no worries, mate). But imagine the thrill of witnessing one from a chair lift.

In an era when smaller ski hills and non-destination resort ski areas are disappearing—there are 35 percent fewer ski resorts than ten years ago—Mt. Baker's success is an exception. Location, location and location, between Seattle and Vancouver, B.C., have a lot to do with it, but the main ingredient is the average annual 750-inch snowfall.

World champion snowboarders practice regularly at Mt. Baker and live in the nearby town of Glacier. Aside from the abundant snow, a main attraction for snowboarders is the half-pipe, the only natural one in the region. Starting from the top of the Shuksan Chairs, it follows a creek bed for a few hundred yards and is normally buried under 20 feet of snow. The halfpipe is the site of the annual Mt. Baker Legendary Halfpipe Banked Slalom Snowboard Competition. The January event has earned a national reputation, attracting riders from all over the U.S., Canada and Europe.

Mt. Baker's two quad lifts in three years and its expanded intermediate terrain are meeting skier hopes. Now, even during record skier days (more than 4,000 skiers is always a record) lift lines never top five minutes.

Mt. Baker Facts
Base elevation: 3,750' **Summit elevation:** 5,250'
Vertical drop: 1,500 feet **Number and types of lifts:** 9 - 2 fixed-grip quads, 6 double chairs, 1 rope tow **Acreage:** 1000 skiable acres **No snowmaking**
Uphill capacity: 6,000 skiers per hour
Bed Base: none at ski area, 300 in Glacier, 17 miles down-mountain

Its terrain helps too. It offers all-day possibilities to beginners, intermediates, and advanced skiers and snowboarders alike, with plenty of gentle groomed slopes, steeps, chutes, and woods that bring out the pioneer spirit. Mt. Baker is in the process of completing the White Salmon Base Area, three miles closer to Glacier than the old base area. Everything is completed but the lodge, which is due for construction in the summer of 1994. For now, parking, ticketing, rest rooms, snacks and chair lifts are all built. It's much closer to the Shuksan side of the ski area than loading from the older parking lot and day lodge.

One drawback to the low elevation of the ski area is that the freezing level can yo–yo, and marginally cold days can turn snow to rain without notice. Some ski patrollers keep a few sets of dry clothes in the aid shacks.

Where to ski

Newcomers sometimes have a tough time figuring how to get back to the lodge, because everywhere they ski takes them farther away. With 1,000 acres to play with, that doesn't sound likely, but the ski area is laid out over two mountains, the Pan Dome side and the Shuksan side. Four chairs serve each side. Shuksan is by far the more popular. It has the heaviest-duty terrain for snowboarders under the double Shuksan chairs and the gentlest groomed slopes for beginners and intermediates.

Chairs 7 and 8 now expand the Shuksan possibilities, but beginners may want to avoid Chair 8 for the time being—its terrain is mostly intermediate. The ride, however, rivals Blackcomb's Jersey Cream Express Chair for the majestic view of its mountain ridges to the left, past the ski area boundary at Rumble Gully.

The Pan Dome side, served by Chairs 1, 2, 3 and 6, is for the mogul bashers and chute shooters, but beginners can easily get back to the lodge on the Austin and Blueberry runs. The signage is good, but don't follow tracks or other skiers if you don't know where they're going. You may end up on steep Pan Face or unmapped places called Rattrap and Gunbarrel. The ski patrol performs award-winning rescues on icy crags that are best avoided.

Mountain rating

"Of my 100 deepest powder days in the last 20 years, 80 of them have been at the Mt. Baker Ski Area," said a local powderhound and heli-skier. The challenge is to pick your days carefully and finish your skiing by 10:30 in the morning, when the runs are skied out.

Mt. Baker's 1,000 acres of skiable terrain are rated at seven percent expert, 21 percent advanced, 42 percent intermediate and 30 percent novice.

Cross-country

Mt. Baker grooms a short Nordic trail loop to the north and west of the main upper parking lot. Elevation is about 4,000 feet and the trail is gentle. There is a $3 charge. The road ends at the ski area, so touring opportunities are all down-mountain on logging roads.

Snowboarding

In the old days of snowboarding, about ten years ago, Mt. Baker snowboarders were carving turns where even the ski patrol would rather not go. In effect, they opened new terrain within the boundaries and so helped skiers improve their skills. There were only a handful of boarders then; now they're a quarter of the mountain's business.

"No chute too steep, no powder too deep," is the motto of the Mt. Baker Hardcore, a group of local snowboarding enthusiasts headed by extreme shredmaster Carter Turk. He co–produced "Baked," a 45-minute video of serious and not-so-serious snowboarding that challenges Warren Miller for astounding feats and offbeat humor. It's one of many snowboarding videos that attract snowboarders to the Mt. Baker region.

The annual Mt. Baker Legendary Banked Slalom takes place in late January every year. Billed as not for the squeamish, the race is a luge-like run with 10- to 20-foot banked walls. The 29 gates are positioned on the walls. It's not hard to figure how a Mt. Baker snowboarder won the extreme championship in Alaska.

Ski school (93/94 prices)

The Komo Kulshan Ski Club is starting its 42nd year of ski instruction at the Mt. Baker Ski Area. Komo Kids, as the learners are called, beef up their skills in what may be the best **children's ski program** in the Northwest. It's an eight-week series of weekend lessons that runs in January and February every year. Lessons are given by PSIA-certified instructors of the Mt. Baker Ski School. Cost is $120 for the season, plus lift tickets.

Adult **group lessons** start daily at 10:30 a.m. and 1 p.m. and cost $18 for each person ($14 for age 12 and younger). Semi-private lessons, for two people, cost $27.50 each for one hour and $30 each for one and a half hours. **Private lessons,** available any time, cost $45 for one hour and $50 for one and a half hours, all ages.

Nordic and snowboard lessons, similarly priced, are available weekends and holidays only.

Lift tickets (93/94 prices)

	Adult	Child (7-15) Senior (60-69)
Weekend day	$26	$19
Midweek day	$17	$12

People 70 and older, or 6 and younger, ski free.

Mt. Baker is open daily into early January, then it closes Tuesdays and Wednesdays through March. (It stays open daily through both U.S. and Canadian spring breaks, which are usually at different times.) In April it's open Fridays and weekends only.

Accommodations

Self-contained campers are welcome to spend the night in the parking lot (no hook–ups, no charge), but the nearest accommodations are 17 miles down the Mt. Baker highway in Glacier.

The **Mt. Baker Chalet**, at mile post 33 on the Mt. Baker Highway at the west end of Glacier, has 20 cabins and condos ranging in price from $50 to $225 per night. Call (800) 258-2405.

The **Snowline Inn**, sort of a two-story condo/hotel, rents studio units for two people for $65. Condo loft units for two rent for $85. Call (800) 228-0119.

Mt. Baker Lodging and Travel (599-2453), in Glacier, has 20 cabins and chalets with kitchens that range in price from $75 to $225.

Bellingham, 56 miles from the ski area on Interstate 5, has a wider range of accommodations, including Best Westerns and B&Bs. **The Hampton Inn**, near the Bellingham Airport, has fitness and business centers, free shuttles and tasteful rooms starting at $64 for two or more people. Those older than 50 pay $59 for any room. Call (800) 426-7866 (800-HAMPTON). The **Bellingham-Whatcom Visitors and Convention Bureau** can be reached for more information at (800) 487-2032.

Dining

The mountain day lodge has a brown-bag room, a cafeteria-style restaurant and a taproom. Fast foods are available at the **Razor Hone Cafe**, at the foot of the Shuksan Chairs.

For dinner, you can't beat **Milano's Cafe & Deli** in Glacier. Milano's specialty is fresh-made pasta at very reasonable prices. The salmon ravioli and tomato sauces regularly draw raves, and the Caesar salad may be the best in the region. There's an excellent selection of Italian wines and regional micro beers. The atmosphere is excitedly post-ski, but most of the staff are snowboarders. Milano's is at 9990 Mt. Baker Highway, Glacier, WA 98244. Call 599-2863.

For a calmer environment, with equally good but pricier dishes, try **Innisfree** just down the highway. Innisfree treats Northwest cuisine as an art form, and grows most of its own organic vegetables. Its address is 9393 Mt. Baker Hwy., Glacier, WA 98244. Call 599-2373.

Après-ski/nightlife

All evening excitement takes place in the town of Glacier, 17 miles down the mountain. The **Chandelier Restaurant** has an active party lounge. Because of all the Canadians, you'll learn to say "give me a beers" and "eh" a lot. One mile west in Glacier proper, just across the street from Milano's, **Graham's** restaurant will give you experiences to talk about for years to come. Glacier is home to the annual June Bigfoot Festival, and off-piste humor abounds. No one does it better than Graham's, from the double bed in the dining room for breakfast, lunch or dinner in bed to the rat-toss game. There's also a horizontal exercise machine of Graham's own invention. Oh, the food: it's totally edible.

Other activities

Anything you can do in a national forest you can do here, but you have to bring your own gear—snowmobiles, for example. Groomed trails leave Glacier in all directions, but no place rents the equipment. Ice skaters even hike up to Alpine lakes, and backcountry tourers go everywhere.

Child care

Day care is available in the lodge at the upper base area for children older than 2 who are toilet trained. Cost is $4 per hour. Ski lessons are offered for children older than 4. All-day supervision includes ski lessons, lift tickets and lunch.

Getting there and getting around

The Mt. Baker Ski Area is at the end of the Mt. Baker highway, 56 miles east of Bellingham, I-5 Exit 255. No public transportation serves the ski area. The drive from Bellingham takes one and a half hours, from Seattle three hours and from Vancouver, B.C., two hours.

Bellingham International Airport is served by Horizon and United Express. Rental cars are available at the airport.

Information/reservations

Mt. Baker offices are in Bellingham, at 1017 Iowa St., Bellingham, WA 98226; call 734-6771. The recorded ski report number is 671-0211. Mt. Baker's on-mountain office at the upper base has a cellular phone for public use.

The **Bellingham-Whatcom Visitors and Convention Bureau** can be reached for information on lodging, travel and entertainment at (800) 487-2032.

The local area code is 206.

Seattle Day Areas
Alpental/Snoqualmie/Ski Acres/Hyak
Stevens Pass

Only 50 miles of interstate highway lies between The Pass (Alpental/Snoqualmie/Ski Acres/Hyak) and Seattle. No wonder *Ski* rated these areas Number One for accessibility. Seattle is one hour away on I–90, which slices through Snoqualmie Pass revealing the Snoqualmie, Ski Acres and Hyak ski areas all in a row on the right. Alpental is a mile off the highway to the left. When Ski Lifts Inc. of Seattle bought 70-acre Hyak in 1990, its dream of owning four ski areas in one mountain pass became real. (Collectively, the four-area group is called The Pass.) It's the largest skiing complex in the state and claims to offer more night skiing than anywhere in the country. All four are open at night, but not all on the same nights. That's true for days too, but the schedule is impossible to memorize. Remember—any two or three of The Pass are open at any given time, and one lift ticket plus the free shuttle will get you anywhere that's open.

One drawback, though. You've heard about the rain in Seattle? Snoqualmie Pass base elevation of 3,200 feet isn't all that high, and the freezing level yo-yos up and down. There's plenty of snow—about 170 inches of snow each winter—but sometimes it's wetter than you'd like.

Stevens Pass is 78 miles from Seattle on Highway 2. Though young skiers get tired of hearing about the good old days, how the first lift was a rope tow powered by a V-8, so skiers

---

The Pass Facts
Base elevation: 3,200'; *Summit elevation:* 5,400';
Vertical: 2,200' Alpental, 1,040' Ski Acres, 900' Snoqualmie, 1,080' Hyak.
Number and types of lifts: 33 total for all 4 areas - 1 quad chair, 4 triple chairs, 18 double chairs, 10 surface lifts. *Acreage:* 1,916 downhill acres, 2,000 Nordic-skiing acres.
Snowmaking: None *Uphill capacity:* 30,140 skiers per hour.
Bed base: 80 units at Snoqualmie Pass

Stevens Pass Facts
Base elevation: 4,061'; *Summit elevation:* 5,800'; *Vertical drop:* 1,979 feet *Number and types of lifts:* 11–1 fixed-grip quad, 4 triples, 6 doubles
Acreage: 1,125 acres. *Snowmaking:* None *Uphill capacity:* 14,350 per hour

wouldn't have to hike uphill any more, that's just how **Stevens Pass** began, back in 1937. Now it has 11 lifts. Stevens is a bit of heaven that's very popular with Seattle area skiers.

Heading up toward Stevens Pass in the winter gives rise to thoughts of skiing the constellation of runs served by the Southern Cross and Jupiter chairs. Polaris Bowl, Andromeda Face and Pegasus Gulch beckon with their own siren songs of snow heaven.

Where to ski

Alpental (closed non-holiday Mondays) is for teenagers-at-heart. It's steep, undisciplined and encourages you beyond its northern boundaries to the Great Scott Traverse. It's unpatrolled, and it's not always advisable to ski there, but big bowls, ridges, bluffs and couloirs all dump you eventually into Trash Can, the safest route out. But wait—it's just as treacherous within the boundaries. Alpental's Internationale run is considered by most Washington skiers to be the steepest, longest (2,200 feet), most exciting, and best run in the state. Luckily, it's wide; even so, the ski patrol closes it on icy days. To the right is an even steeper run, Adrenaline. To the left is Widow Maker, a jump. Then there's Lower Internationale, which opens into a wide bowl with tree skiing on the right side, moguls in the middle and a short chute on the left.

Snoqualmie (closed non-holiday Mondays) features gentle runs with names like Over Easy and Easy Rider, but there are plenty of blue runs over most of the north-looking face. Beaver Lake Chair, near the top, serves the expert terrain. The weekend crowds following backward-skiing uniformed leaders would make you think everybody in Seattle is taking a lesson. They are, but not all at the same time.

Ski Acres (closed non-holiday Tuesdays) is mostly very gentle terrain where Seattle's beginners learn to ski. There are several serious black diamond runs from the very top of the ridge, reached by the Triple 60 Chair, but a cat track to the base lets nervous types off the hook.

Hyak (only open Friday nights, weekends and holidays, between Christmas and the Ides of March) has a regular following that likes the 1,000-foot continuous vertical drop reached by the no-name chair, Chair 23. Most of that following is snowboarders, who also like the halfpipe at the top. They work on improving their turnaround times by speeding down Roz's.

At **Stevens Pass** the favorite areas for venturesome skiers are Mill Valley, with its new black-diamond Borealis run, and the chutes reached by the 7th Heaven Chair. The Southern Cross Chair is 1,000 feet shy of a mile long, but if you swerve back and forth between the trees, you can easily double the distance back down to the bottom. Southern Cross and Jupiter lines are the shortest during lunch. The Way Back trail, above Mill Valley's Corona bowl, is part of the gentle intermediate route to the valley floor. It's called the Way Back because beginners and intermediates can turn right onto Skid Road and descend gracefully to the base area. The Double Diamond run leading to the base area is in fact a double diamond. Adjacent woods make for some good off-piste skiing when the snow is fresh.

Mountain ratings

The Pass has enough terrain variety to keep most skiers happy for a day or two. The three on the south side of the highway have connecting trails, and there's something to be said for skiing more than one hill in a day. Try a variety on the mile-long face and stick with what you like. Clearly, Alpental is for the high-intermediate to expert skier. Only 10 percent of the terrain is rated beginner.

At Stevens Pass, the 26 major runs are about one-third advanced, but the only chair for beginners to avoid is 7th Heaven. All others have easy, or at least intermediate, ways down.

Cross-country

The Ski Acres and Hyak Cross Country Center is located at the base of Ski Acres Silver Fir Chair, the closest one to Hyak. A $9 lift/trail ticket buys two round trips on the Silver Fir Chair to access the 50-km. trail system in the Ollalie Meadows and Rockdale Lake areas. Night fees on the lower 5-km. trail system are $4. Children 5 and younger ski free day or night.

Stevens Pass has a Nordic center with rentals and lessons, open 9 a.m. to 4 p.m. Friday through Sunday plus holidays, and more than 27 km. of groomed trails for both striding and skating. Regional biathlons are held here. The newly enlarged center is five miles east of the Stevens Pass parking lot. Trail passes cost $6 for adults, $5 for seniors and children aged 7-12. It's free for children 6 and younger and seniors 70 and older.

Snowboarding

No inverted aerials allowed. Sorry dudes, but there are plenty of other things to do at The Pass. Snowboards are welcome everywhere. In fact, Northwesterners feel they own the sport because so many champions train in the region.

Stevens Pass is a regional favorite, especially on powder days. Plenty of trees challenge technical turning skills and lots of open terrain and bowls supply the fun.

Ski school

The Skiforall Foundation is the state's premier ski school for people with disabilities. It was once named the Most Outstanding Therapeutic Recreation Program by the Washington Parks and Recreation Department. The foundation's position is that no human handicap can prevent you from enjoying some variety of snow sport. For more information, call 462-0979.

In addition, there are 34 ski schools on The Pass, including race camps, gate running and instructor training, as well as snowboarding lessons. Call: Alpental, 434-6364; Snoqualmie, 434-6363; Ski Acres, 434-6400; Ski Acres/Hyak Cross-Country Center, 434-6646.

Stevens Pass has lessons in all ski and snowboard disciplines in its 24 adult and 13 children's ski schools. Two entry-level specials for skiers and snowboarders, daily at 9:30 a.m. for skiers and 11:30 a.m. for snowboarders, include all equipment, a one-hour group lesson and a Daisy Lift (vertical rise is 308 feet) ticket. Non-holiday weekdays cost $24 for skiers and $30 for snowboarders. Weekend and holiday costs are $32 for skiers or $36 for snowboarders. Specials are available at the ski rental desk in the West Lodge.

Lift tickets (93/94 prices)

The Pass

	Adult/Child (7+)	Senior (62-69)
Weekend day	$26	$18
Monday/Tuesday	$12	$12
Wednesday-Friday	$16	$12

Add $2 if you also want to extend your ticket to nights. Night tickets alone are $16; Sundays, $13. Children 6 and younger pay $5. Skiers 70 and older always ski free.

Stevens Pass

	Adult	Child (7-12)
Weekend day + night	$30	$24
Monday/Tuesday	$12	$12
Wednesday-Friday	$18	$18

Stevens Pass is open daily 9 a.m. to 10 p.m. Subtract $3 for weekend afternoon + night skiing; subtract another $3 for weekend night skiing. Those 62-69 pay $26 for the weekend day + night ticket, then the $3 discount applies for other times. Skiing is free for children 6 and younger and seniors 70 and older.

Accommodations

Best Western Summit Inn has the only lodging in **Snoqualmie Pass**. The inn has a Jacuzzi, sauna, heated pool and restaurant. The 80 rooms range in price from $59 for one person to $102 for four. Call 434-6300 or Best Western's toll-free number, (800) 528-1234. RV parking in the pass is allowed, but there are no hookups.

Stevens Pass has no lodging, but self-contained RVs are welcome in the designated parking lot. Leavenworth, 37 miles east on Route 2, is a full-blown tourist town with lodging galore, mostly in the Alps tradition. Authentic Austrian atmosphere is offered by the **Hotel Pension Anna,** a No Smoking lodging at 926 Commercial St. It has 11 rooms of elegant Austrian furnishings. Rates are $65 and up. Call (509) 548-5807 for information or reservations. For information on other Leavenworth lodgings, call Bavarian Bedfinders at (800) 323-2920.

Skykomish, in the other direction, 16 miles west on Route 2, has the **Skyriver Inn** on the Skykomish River. It's an AAA-rated Two Diamond lodging facility whose rates start at $47.50 for a queen bedroom on the parking lot. A queen overlooking the river is $52.50. There are also some king suites on the river. All units have a little refrigerator and coffee maker, and some have kitchenettes ($5 extra) with campground-quality cookware and utensils. A complete apartment that sleeps six adults comfortably costs $77.50. The Skyriver Inn's address is P.O. Box 280, Skykomish, WA 98288-0280; 677–2261.

Dining

Webb's Bar & Grill in **Snoqualmie's** Alpenhaus Lodge is the place for healthy food. The same lodge also has a cafeteria. **Alpental** has a food service and lounge in each lodge, Alpental Lodge and Denny Mountain Lodge. **Ski Acres** has a deli in the cross-country center, Bonanza Snack Bar at the Bonanza Chair, and a tavern and lounge in the Main Lodge. **Hyak** has a cafeteria and lounge in the Day Lodge.

There are three lodges at Stevens Pass. The Short Run Deli in West Lodge has good made-to-order sandwiches, nachos, soups and baked potatoes. The T-Bar Restaurant, in the T-Bar Lodge, is a rustic full-service restaurant with a soup-and-salad bar. It specializes in ribs and chicken. The Mountain Express Restaurant, in the East Lodge, offers day-skier food: burgers, fries and chili.

Après-ski/nightlife

The Pass is an overgrown day area. It's only an hour's drive to Seattle.

At Stevens Pass, with the night lights on, skiing itself is the nightlife. But there is a sports TV bar, Cloud Nine in the East Lodge. The Soft Landing Lounge, in the West Lodge, features live band entertainment and comedy shows.

Other activities

Shopping: On the way to The Pass is **Great Northwest Factory Stores,** a 40-store, name-brand outlet center that includes Great Outdoor Clothing Co., Bass Shoe, B.U.M. Equipment and others. Take Exit 30 from Interstate 90.

Snowflake Tubing and Snow Play, just across the street from Ski Acres, has a groomed tubing hill. Two double rope tows slide you back up the hill for a $6.50 ticket (5 and younger free). It's open Friday through Sunday, and holidays; night tubing until

10 p.m. Fridays and Saturdays. Bring your own tube (free air) or rent one on site for $5.50.

Stevens Pass has only skiing to offer.

Child care

Snoqualmie and **Ski Acres** both offer child care. The cost for toddlers aged 12 to 30 months is $30 for the day or $4 an hour. For pre-schoolers it's $25 a day or $3.50 an hour. During the week (non-holiday), a day or night lift ticket and child care together cost $30. Add $5 for toddlers. You must register at the child care office in Ski Acres' Main Lodge (at the Holiday Chair) or at Snoqualmie's child care center in the USFS Visitors Information Center near Alpenhaus Lodge. Call 434-7669 (434-SNOW) for information or to make reservations.

Stevens Pass child care, weekends and holidays only, accepts toilet-trained children between the ages of 30 months and 7 years. Call 973-2441 for information.

Getting there and getting around

The Pass: Take I–90 east from Seattle. For Alpental and Snoqualmie, take Exit 52. For Ski Acres, take Exit 53. For Hyak, take Exit 54. Some problems every so often with slick roads. A free shuttle runs between the various ski areas at The Pass.

Stevens Pass: On U.S. Route 2, 78 miles northeast of Seattle, or 64 miles east of I–5 at Everett. It's not served by public transportation. Ninety school and ski club buses in the parking lot might suggest otherwise, but you've got to drive yourself there. The crowds are astounding on sunny holiday weekends. Stevens Pass has become so popular for its quality skiing through varied terrain that the parking lot sometimes fills before late skiers leave home. The road itself has improved dramatically in recent years, to the point where some truckers prefer it to I-90 for winter travel over the Cascades. A highway reader board in Monroe, where Everett and Seattle traffic join, alerts drivers about road and parking conditions ahead.

Information/reservations

The Pass expanded snowline: 236-1600, for conditions, rates and special events. The Pass office: 232-8182.

Alpental Lodge: 434-6112; Snoqualmie Lodge: 434-6161; Ski Acres Lodge: 434-6671; Hyak Lodge: 434-7600.

Stevens Pass: Snow conditions recording, from Seattle 634-1645. Offices and information, 973-2441. Address is P.O. Box 98, Leavenworth, WA 98826.

Local telephone area code is 206, unless otherwise noted.

Jackson Hole, Wyoming

Some ski areas dress up the models for their ads in cowboy hats and chaps so you think you'll be skiing smack in the middle of the authentic Wild West. When you get there, you find that the cowpoke sashaying next to you on the saloon dance floor learned his two-step in a Manhattan Country & Western bar.

Some ski areas claim terrain steep enough to scare the teeth out of the Jurassic Park T-Rex. But when you arrive, you discover it wouldn't even scare the teeth out of Grandpa.

Some ski areas brag about extra-friendly employees and townspeople. You arrive only to learn that friendly greetings seem proportional to the money they think you'll spend.

Jackson Hole lives up to everything it claims.

It has real cowboys, lots of elk, moose and cows. If its herds could be counted in the U.S. Census, Congress would have a lot more representatives wearing big silver belt buckles and boots.

It has gnarly slopes. They don't sell "I Survived the Tram" ski pins here for nothing.

And it has friendly people.

Jackson Hole doesn't *quite* live up to its advertising. Its marketing brochure shows skiers in brand-new colorful matching outfits. If it wanted to be absolutely truthful, it would show some of them wearing mismatched, well-worn ski clothes patched here and there with duct tape. At Jackson Hole, skiers would rather make a statement with their ability, not their attire.

Where to ski

Jackson Hole's 4,139-foot vertical drop is the largest in the United States. Fully half of its 2,000 acres is marked with a black diamond. With stats like that, it's no wonder the area has a reputation for steep, exciting skiing.

But remember that fully half of the 2,000 acres is *not* black diamond. Even better, most of the tough stuff is completely sepa-

---

Jackson Hole Facts
Base elevation: 6,311'; **Summit elevation:** 10,450'; **Vertical drop:** 4,139 feet
Number and types of lifts: 10—1 aerial tram, 2 quad chairs, 1 triple chair, 4 double chairs, and 2 surface lifts
Acreage: 2,500 acres of terrain **Percent of snowmaking:** 10 percent
Uphill capacity: 8,896 skiers per hour **Bed base:** 5,000

rate from the easier runs—intermediates seldom have to worry about getting in over their heads.

Skiing is spread across three areas. Rendezvous Mountain is where you'll find Jackson Hole's tram and a lot of chutes, cliffs, bumps and steep faces. Apres Vous Mountain has 2,170 vertical feet of beginner and intermediate terrain, and Casper Bowl has wide intermediate runs, sprinkled with a few advanced runs.

One surprising feature of Jackson Hole is its excellent beginner terrain. The base of Apres Vous mountain has several long, wide, gentle green runs, perfect for learning and served by the Teewinot and Eagle's Rest chairs. Think ahead: in later life, when you're comparing learn-to-ski stories, won't it be more impressive to say you learned to ski here rather than Powder Puff Valley Ski Area?

Though Jackson Hole is a marvelous place for beginners, it's tough for advancing beginners and lower intermediates. It's a big step from those gently undulating green-circle slopes to Jackson Hole's blues. Although the upper parts of Apres Vous and all of Casper Bowl are wide and groomed, they have a much steeper pitch than blues at other resorts, enough to intimidate some lower-level skiers.

Good intermediates will have a ball. Follow the solid blue lines for groomed terrain and the broken blue lines for ungroomed powder or bumps. You'll run out of gas before you run out of terrain.

Still too tame for you? Then board the big red tram for the 4,139-foot, 12-minute rise to the top of Rendezvous Mountain. This is where the big boys and girls go to play. Because area management charges an extra $2 for each tram ride, on top of your lift ticket, you really have to want to be here. And be forewarned: The "easiest" way down from the summit is Rendezvous Bowl, a huge, treeless face littered with gigantic moguls. Head the opposite direction and you'll face one of the most famous runs in North America, Corbet's Couloir. The most famous of Jackson Hole's many chutes, Corbet's is a narrow, rocky passage that requires a 10- to 20-foot airborne entry.

Further down the mountain are the Hobacks, a spacious area that offers some of the best lift-served powder skiing in America. Experts looking for a warmup should try Rendezvous' longest run, Gros Ventre, which starts out in Rendezvous Bowl, winds across the tops of Cheyenne and Laramie bowls, then mellows just enough the rest of the way down to earn a blue rating on the trail map. It may be bright blue on the map; it's navy blue under your skis.

Mountain rating

Color Rendezvous Mountain and the Hobacks jet black, with occasional slashes of navy-blue advanced intermediate. Casper

JACKSON HOLE™
TETON VILLAGE™

America's world-class resort

RENDEZVOUS MOUNTAIN 10,450' (3185 Meters)
VERTICAL RISE 4,139' (1261 Meters)

APRES VOUS MOUNTAIN
8,481' (2585 Meters)

TETON VILLAGE
ELEVATION 6,311' (1924 Meters)

ROCK SPRINGS
BOWL

COLY
BOWL

RENDEZVOUS
BOWL

CORBET'S
COULOIR

TENSLEEP
BOWL

CHEYENNE
BOWL

LARAMIE
BOWL

CIRQUE

AMPHITHEATRE

HEADWALL

CASPER BOWL

CRAGS

MORAN
FACE

RESIDENTIAL AREA

CONDOMINIUM AREA

MAP COVERS
IES
E MILES)

TRAIL DIFFICULTY SYMBOLS

● EASIEST

■ MODERATELY
DIFFICULT

■ MORE DIFFICULT—
VARIED TERRAIN PLUS
SNOW CONDITIONS
FOR THE BETTER THAN
AVERAGE SKIER

◆ MOST DIFFICULT—
EXPERT

◆◆ MOST DIFFICULT—
EXPERT USE EXTRA
CAUTION

TRAIL NAMES

1. Union Pass Traverse
2. Way Home
3. North Colter Ridge
4. Buffalo Bowl
5. South Colter Ridge
6. Rawlins Bowl
7. Lower Sublette Ridge
8. Rendezvous Trail
9. Bivouac
10. Bird In The Hand
11. Pepi's Run
12. Alta Chutes
13. Grand
14. South Pass Traverse
15. Garnett
16. Lower Tram Line
17. Riverton Bowl
18. Thunder
19. East Ridge Traverse
20. Expert Chutes

21. Gros Ventre
22. Nez Perce Traverse
23. Amphitheatre Traverse
24. Solitude Traverse
25. Avalanche
26. Downhill
27. Slalom
28. Sundance Gully
29. Eagle's Rest Cutoff
30. Eagle's Rest
31. Poch Bergen
32. Rendezvous Flats
33. St. Johns
34. Lower Teewinot
35. Cross Country Ski Trail
36. Solitude Cutoff
37. Ashley Ridge
38. Beaver Tooth
39. Jackson Face
40. Nez Perce
41. Blacktail

42. Surprise
43. Camp Ground
44. Timbered Island
45. Easy Does It
46. Lift Line
47. Sleeping Indian
48. Wide Open
49. Togwotee Pass Traverse
50. Moran
51. Upper Werner
52. Upper Teewinot
53. St. Johns
54. Teewinot Gully
55. Secret Slope
56. North Hoback
57. South Hoback
58. Tower Three Chute
59. Paint Brush
60. Lander Bowl
61. Hanging Rock
62. U.P. Connection

LIFTS

AERIAL TRAM	2.4 Miles Long
12 Minutes	4,139' Vertical Rise
1. EAGLE'S REST DOUBLE CHAIR	2,260' Long
5 Minutes	330' Vertical Rise
2. TEEWINOT DOUBLE CHAIR	3,060' Long
7 Minutes	425' Vertical Rise
3. APRES VOUS DOUBLE CHAIR	5,000' Long
10 Minutes	1,745' Vertical Rise
4. THUNDER DOUBLE CHAIR	3,770' Long
9 Minutes	1,466' Vertical Rise
5. CASPER BOWL TRIPLE CHAIR	3,450' Long
8 Minutes	1,046' Vertical Rise
6. CRYSTAL SPRINGS DOUBLE CHAIR	4,113' Long
9 Minutes	1,196' Vertical Rise
7. UPPER SUBLETTE RIDGE QUAD CHAIR	4,108' Long
8 Minutes	1,630' Vertical Rise
*8. RENDEZVOUS BOWL SURFACE LIFT	2,714' Long
5 Minutes	824' Vertical Rise
9. UNION PASS SURFACE LIFT	1,360' Long
2 Minutes	150' Vertical Rise

* This lift does not operate during periods of adverse wind,
weather or snow conditions.

Bowl is for intermediates up to experts, depending on the grooming. When groomed, Casper's runs can be a cruising delight. Ungroomed, they are just plain hard work, worthy of advanced skiers. Apres Vous is fantastic for advanced intermediates and so-so for advancing beginners.

Snowboarding

Snowboarding is permitted on all areas of the mountain.
A couple of natural halfpipes are Sundance Gully and Dick's Ditch. The ski school gives snowboard lessons and local shops rent boards.

Nearby skiing

The **Snow King Ski Area** is in downtown Jackson, about 12 miles from Jackson Hole. Sixty percent of its 400 acres is rated advanced, thanks to a north-facing slope that plunges sharply above the streets of the town. Its only green-rated terrain is a catwalk that traverses the mountain from the summit to the base. Because it is so steep, always shaded and often icy, locals call it "Eastern skiing out West." Lift tickets are $25 for adults; kids 14 and younger and seniors 60 and older, $16. The hill is open for night skiing Tuesday through Saturday, and tickets are $12 after 5:30 p.m.

Grand Targhee is a 45-minute drive from Jackson. Known for superb powder runs, its 1,500 acres also have excellent groomed trails for intermediates and a separate learning area. If you like ungroomed powder, this is the place.

Cross country

Jackson Hole has some of the most beautiful natural surroundings in the United States. Nordic skiers can strike out for marked trails in Grand Teton or Yellowstone National Parks, or try one of the six touring centers in Jackson and Grand Targhee.

The **Jackson Hole Touring Center** (307-733-2292, Ext. 129) serves as the hub of the Nordic systems in Teton Village with 22 km. of groomed track. Because it is next to the downhill ski area, it has telemark lessons as an option. Full-day beginner group lessons, half-day lessons for other levels and private instruction are available, as are guided excursions into the back country of Grand Teton National Park. Rentals also are available.

Other touring centers are **Grand Targhee** (353-2304 or 800-443-8146), **Spring Creek** (733-8833), **Teton Pines** (733-1005) **Togwotee Mountain Lodge** (543-2847 or 800-543-2847) and **Trails End Ranch** (733-1616).

Ski school (94/95 prices)

Given Jackson Hole's extreme terrain, it's good that the ski school is headed by a three-time Olympic skiing medalist Pepe Stiegler, who has one medal of each metal. The school not only helps the skier make major improvements in his abilities, but is also the place to engage a knowledgeable mountain guide. Jackson Hole's nooks and crannies can best be enjoyed with someone who knows how to reach them.

Four-hour and two-hour adult **group lessons** are $45 and $35 respectively. Three-day morning group-lesson packages are $80. **Private lessons** are given most commonly in a two-hour lesson for $115 for one skier, $145 for two to three skiers and $180 for four to six people. (If you want Stiegler to teach you, it's $100 per 90 minutes; $25 for each additional person, by reservation only).

The SKIwee program for **children** ages 6 to 14 has four-hour group lessons running $37 and two-hour lessons for $29. A three-day, all-day SKIwee package is $95, with lunch an additional cost (or kids can pack a lunch and stay with the supervised group).

Lift tickets (94/95 prices)

	Adult	Child (Up to 14) Senior (65+)
One day	$44	$23
Three days	$132 ($44/day)	$69 ($22/day)
Five days	$205 ($41/day)	$105 ($21/day)

These prices include unlimited tram access. Chair lift-only tickets are about $4 less per day for adults, and about $3 less for kids and seniors. As noted above, each tram ride is $2 additional, and for many people, one run down from the tram will be plenty of excitement. If in doubt, buy a chair lift ticket. You can always upgrade it later.

Accommodations

You have three locations to choose from: Teton Village at the base of the slopes, with fewer restaurants and nightlife options; the town of Jackson, with lots of eating, shopping and partying, but 12 miles from skiing; or a few condo developments and a major butte-top resort in between the two. Bus transportation between town and ski area is readily available.

Teton Village: The following hotels are all within steps of the slopes and each other, so make your choice on facilities rather than location. The seven-day package is per person double occupancy; the daily rate is per room.

Alpenhof (733-3242; 800-732-3244) is the most luxurious of the hotels. Built in peaked-roof Alpine style with lots of exposed wood, it has an excellent restaurant and a large lounge that is a center of relaxed après-ski activity. It has a heated outdoor pool, Jacuzzi, sauna and game room. Rooms generally are rented in a seven-day package that includes a five-day lift pass and round-trip transportation from the airport. Double occupancy cost ranges from $488 to $1,188 based on time of year. Daily rates, when rooms are available, are about $95-$289.

The Best Western Inn at Jackson Hole (733-2311 or 800-842-7666) has the most spacious rooms available (short of condos). It has a heated outdoor pool and Jacuzzi. Rates for the seven-day package based on double occupancy in a standard room are $352 to $1,034. Daily rates are $65-$245.

Sojourner Inn (733-3657 or 800-445-4655) started out as a European lodge but additions have turned it into a rambling hotel with pool, sauna and Jacuzzi. The Main Lodge has the cozier rooms; the one in the Mountain Lodge are larger and more modern. Seven-day package rate is $439 to $964; daily rate is $80 to $225.

Hostel (733-3415) has some of the most inexpensive slopeside lodging in the United States—$316 for the seven-day package and $41 per night per room with one or two skiers; $54 per room for three or four (that's $13 per night!)

Crystal Springs Inn (733-4423) is motel-like—clean and unluxurious. The seven-day package rate is $408-$471; daily rates are $66-$84 per double room.

Condominiums are available through Jackson Hole Vacation Rentals (800-443-6840; 733-4610) and Jackson Hole Realty Property Management (800-443-8613; 733-7945). A two-bedroom unit ranges from about $628 to $1,927 for the seven-day package; $129 to $500 per night.

Town of Jackson: Probably the best hotel in terms of facilities and location is the **Wort Hotel**, an 1880s-style, four-diamond AAA-rated hotel that is just off the main square. The seven-day package runs $525 to $893; single nights are $105-$210.

Snow King Resort is another popular vacationers' choice, although it has more of a Holiday Inn atmosphere. Also, it's a little further from downtown, but right next to the Snow King Ski Area, which has night skiing. Seven-day package is $473-$1,313; single nights, $90-$330.

The **Antler Motel** and the **Parkway Inn** have medium-priced lodging, about $48-$96 per night. The least expensive place in town is the **Western Motel** at $36-$52 per night and $299-$355 for the seven-day package. The Western even has a hot tub and cable TV.

Between town and the ski area: One of the most impressive sights in this area is the ragged peak of Grand Teton Mountain. Unfortunately, you can't see it from the ski area (too close) or from town (the East Gros Ventre Butte blocks the way). The solution? Stay on top of the offending butte at the **Spring Creek Resort**. The resort has luxurious hotel rooms, condominiums and a couple of houses for rent, a marvelous gourmet restaurant and unsurpassed views of the Jackson Valley, Grand Teton and the ski area. Rates start about $120-$500 per couple per night, and the package range is $578-$1,980. Shuttles to town and the ski area are provided.

Dining

Jackson has a lot of excellent eating places, most of which you'll find in town. But you won't starve in Teton Village either. At one end of the spectrum is the **Alpenhof Hotel Restaurant** (733-3462), a quiet, genteel place that serves German and Austrian specialties. At the other extreme is **The Mangy Moose** (733-4913), beloved for its salad bar, down-home steak-and-seafood menu, and lively atmosphere. Somewhere between is **The Sojourner Inn's Pasta House,** (733-3657) where steaming plates of pasta warm a crisp winter night. Seems the proprietors of these Teton Village restaurants got together for a price-setting session—all are in the $7-$15 range for dinner.

In town, you have many choices. For casual, fun, inexpensive dining, it's **Bubba's** heaping plates of "bubbacued" ribs, chicken, beef and pork. No sense in giving you the phone number, because Bubba's doesn't take reservations. Be prepared to wait, and don't expect any favors. Local legend says that Maria Shriver and Arnold Schwarzenegger wanted to be seated immediately upon arrival and Bubba's told them to wait or walk. (Never did find out which they chose, but they should have waited.) And while you wait, send a member of your party across the street to the conveniently located liquor store—Bubba's is BYOB.

Other casual places are the **Calico Pizza Parlor** (733-2460), where Harrison Ford celebrates his birthday; and **Mountain High Pizza Pie** (733-3646).

For excellent dining, **the Granary** (733-8833) at Spring Creek Resort is hard to beat. Entrées range from $15 to $25 and include such local delicacies as medallions of elk. Other good choices are **The Blue Lion** (733-3912), known for its roast rack of lamb; **Gouloff's** (733-1886), with several interesting game bird dishes on its menu; and **Sweetwater Restaurant** (733-3553), with a variety of upscale beef, chicken and fish selections. **Cadillac** (733-3279) is trendy—sometimes fantastic, sometimes so-so. **Lame Duck** (733-4311) has the best reputation of the two Chinese restaurants in town. For Mexican food, go to **Vista Grande** (744-6964), and for pasta, head for **Nani's Genuine Pasta House** (733-3888).

For breakfast, try **Bubba's**, **The Bunnery** (733-5474), which has excellent omelets, whole-grain waffles and bakery items; or **Jedediah's** for great sourdough specialties.

Après ski/nightlife

In Teton Village the rowdiest spot by far is **The Mangy Moose**. In town, **The Million Dollar Cowboy Bar** attracts tourists who love the authentic saddle bar stools and the silver dollars encased in the bar's surface, and locals who like to two-step to the live Country & Western bands and watch the tourists take pictures of each other on the saddle stools. As corny as it sounds, you gotta go, once. **The Silver Dollar Bar** is similar, but has more silver dollars in the bar and less kitsch. **The Shady Lady Saloon** at the Snow King Resort has live entertainment several nights a week.

Child care

Day care for ages 2 months to 5 years is $52 for a full day; $37 for half day. Parents must provide formula or food for infants; toddlers get lunch and a snack in the price. Ski lessons are available for ages 3 to 5.

Other activities

One of the more unusual activities is a sleigh ride through **Jackson's elk refuge.** Thousands of elk winter in the valley, eating the hay provided by their human friends and going calmly about their business as the sleigh passes. The cost is about $15, including transportation from your hotel. Reservations required; call 733-3135 or 733-2888.

There's another fun **sleigh ride** along the East Gros Ventre Butte at night to see the sparkling lights of Jackson below. Rides leave from the Granary restaurant at Spring Creek Resort; ride and dinner cost $45. Call 733-8833 for reservations.

Other activities include **dog-sled rides,** snowmobile excursions to **Granite Hot Springs, helicopter touring and skiing,** and of course, nearby **Grand Teton and Yellowstone National Parks.**

Jackson has many **art galleries** and excellent shopping.

Getting there and getting around

Getting there: American, Delta, Continental, United and United Express serve the Jackson Hole airport.

Getting around: Whether to rent a car is a toss-up. Skiers can get along fine without one, though if you plan to do a lot of nightlife or skiing at Grand Targhee or Snow King, you'll probably want one. Southern Teton Area Rapid Transit (START) buses run frequently between Jackson and Teton Village at a cost of $2 each way. Jackson Hole Transportation runs airport shuttles.

Information/reservations

Jackson Hole Central Reservations, 800-443-6931, for lodging, lifts and transfers.

Jackson Hole Ski Corporation: P.O. Box 290, Teton Village, WY 83025; 733-2292.

Snow conditions: 733-2291.

Local telephone area code is 307.

Grand Targhee, Wyoming

Grand Targhee never thinks about putting in snowmaking equipment. It boasts "Snow from heaven, not hoses." Regulars get concerned when they have to share their 500 inches a year with visitors busing in from other less blessed areas. They're friendly enough at Targhee—it's just that they like to have their snow and ski it too. They fret at waiting a couple of minutes in a lift line.

Grand comes from the backdrop of 13,700-foot Grand Teton Mountain, and Targhee from a local peacekeeping Indian in the mid-1800's. When Averell Harriman was scouting for his dream resort in the early part of the century, he narrowed it down to Targhee and the site that became Sun Valley. Local ranchers and farmers opened Targhee as a ski resort more than 20 years ago.

The lift attendants are ranchers who have been at the area forever. Their working attire includes 10-gallon hats, and they'll lasso your skis if you edge ahead in the lift line. In fact, they chute waiting skiers like cattle, holding them back with ropes and sporting with them. A back rub for women is common. Gloria Steinem wouldn't like it.

Any kind of village would seem crowded on this far-flung terrain. The resort buildings are a hodgepodge of shape and color, quaint and modern at the same time. A fire destroyed the base lodge, retail building and administrative offices in March of 1990. Rebuilt in time for the winter season, the resort won a *Snow Country* award for the best day lodge design in North America.

Expansion is coming, with three lifts planned for Peaked Mountain to the south, where snowcat skiing is now offered. One of the existing three lifts is to be replaced with a high-speed quad in the next couple of years, and a new hotel is planned.

Where to ski

Three chair lifts open high, broad descents mostly above treeline. However, 1,500 acres are more than you expect from three chairs, and most of the terrain is skiable. The gentle, con-

---

Grand Targhee Facts
Base: 8,000'; **Summit elevation:** 10,250'; **Vertical drop:** 2,200 feet
Number of lifts: 4–3 double chairs, 1 surface lift
Snowmaking: none   **Total acreage:** 1,500 skiable acres   **Bed Base:** 432

sistent fall lines are good for learning how to powder ski. Most of the skiing is for families and intermediates, with few narrow trails. Lifts can take up 3,600 skiers an hour, but on a big day at Targhee the crowd is 1,600.

Fred's Mountain, where most of the skiing is done, has excellent cruiser runs and good bump slopes. Tree skiing can be found here and there. The resort grooms about 300 acres of runs; the rest is left to accumulate powder.

Peaked Mountain, just south, has another 1,500 acres reserved for snowcat skiing. Ten skiers per snowcat, and two guides, head out to enjoy this snowy playground. Targhee runs a half-day trip for intermediate or better skiers who want to learn to ski powder that includes a lesson and a snack for $130.

Snowboarding

The area has a gradual, groomed halfpipe. Snowboarding is allowed on all of Fred's Mountain.

Cross-country

The Targhee Nordic Center has 15 km. of track groomed for touring and skating. The track courses through varied terrain, offering vistas of the Greater Yellowstone area as well as meadows and aspen glades.

The Nordic Education Center teaches telemarking as well as touring and skating techniques.

Group lessons are $18 and private lessons $42 an hour.

Guided tours are offered through meadows and along streams. Telemarkers are taken to the powder bowls of Teton Pass. Snowshoe tours and rentals also are offered.

Trail pass rates are $6 a day, $3 for a senior or child, children under 5 ski free.

Ski school (94/95 prices)

Many instructors have stayed on at the Ski School and Training Center dating back to 1969. The training center is noted for its teaching of lessons with a coaching approach.

Adult group lessons are $18.

Children's lessons are $30 for a half-day; $60 for a full day, and include lesson(s), lift ticket and lunch.

Private lessons run $45 an hour.

In addition to the learn to ski powder class outlined in the Where to Ski section, Grand Targhee also has several **special clinics** such as Skiing Steeper and Looking Better.

Lift tickets (94/95 prices)

Full day lift tickets cost $30 for adults and $16 for children 6 to 14 as well as seniors 60 to 69.

Those who ski more than one day at Grand Targhee probably are staying there, too. In those cases, Targhee's lodging-lift packages are the most economical and practical. Children 5 and younger, and seniors 70 and older, ski free.

Snowcat Skiing: 2,400-foot vertical, 1,500 acres, gourmet lunch provided for full-day skiers. Full-day $155 for Targhee package lodging guests, $175 everyone else, $105 half-day. For reservations call (800) 827-4433 (800-TARGHEE) or 353-2300.

Accommodations

The village sleeps 432 people at a hotel, motel and 32 condos. Nightly rates per room at the lodges run from $76 to $172, at the condos $134 to $408.

Packages that include ski tickets and two group lessons are offered for seven nights and six days, five nights and four days, and three nights and three days.

For the hotel and motel rooms, regular season packages per person for two people range from $192 to $317 for three days, $286 to $488 for five nights and four days, $402 to $681 for seven nights and six days.

For the Sioux Lodge condo lofts, regular season packages per person for two people range from $276 to $634 for three days and three nights, $424 to $1,007 for five nights and four days, and $590 to $1,392 for seven nights and six days.

Call (800) 827-4433 (800-TARGHEE) for information.

Dining

In the village, **Cicero's Bistro** has homebaked croissants and pastries and many kinds of coffee.

Skadi's is Targhee's finest restaurant, with entrées such as rack of lamb, whiskey chicken, shrimp scampi and filet mignon, all in the $11-$18 price range. Skadi's also serves breakfast and lunch. **Cactus Kitchen** is Targhee's Mexican-Italian choice, with basic pastas and Tex-Mex dishes, plus a few down-home American choices, such as chicken-fried steak. **Wild Bill's Grille** in the Rendezvous Lodge has pizza, a soup and salad bar, sandwiches and Mexican food for breakfast and lunch, while the **World Famous Trap Bar** serves basic grilled sandwiches, T-bone steak, salmon and chicken, plus après-ski snacks, all until 8 p.m.

Après ski/nightlife/other activities

Grandly isolated, Targhee's strength isn't this. However, there is music nightly at the **World Famous Trap Bar**, an outdoor heated swimming pool, and complimentary movies. Jackson is an hour away.

Child care

Baby's Club takes ages 2 months to 2 years for $36 per day, $24 per half day. Kid's Club takes ages 3 to 9. Day care only is $32 per day; $20 per half day. Day care plus a ski lesson, lunch and lift ticket is $55 per day, $35 half day. The program includes two snacks and lunch in the full day, a snack for half day.

Getting there and getting around

Getting there: Targhee is served by jetports in Jackson, WY and Idaho Falls, ID.   Resort shuttles pick up guests at both airports by reservation. Cars can be rented at both airports and at Grand Targhee.

Targhee is just inside the Wyoming border on the west side of the Tetons, accessible only from Idaho. It is 42 miles northwest of Jackson, 87 miles northeast of Idaho Falls, 290 miles north of Salt Lake City.

Getting around: If you are spending your entire vacation at Grand Targhee, you won't need a car. If you plan to ski at Jackson Hole (or try the nightlife), you will want one.

Information/reservations

Write Grand Targhee Ski & Summer Resort, Box Ski, Alta, WY 83422. (800) 827-4433 (800-TARGHEE). The local telephone area code is 307.

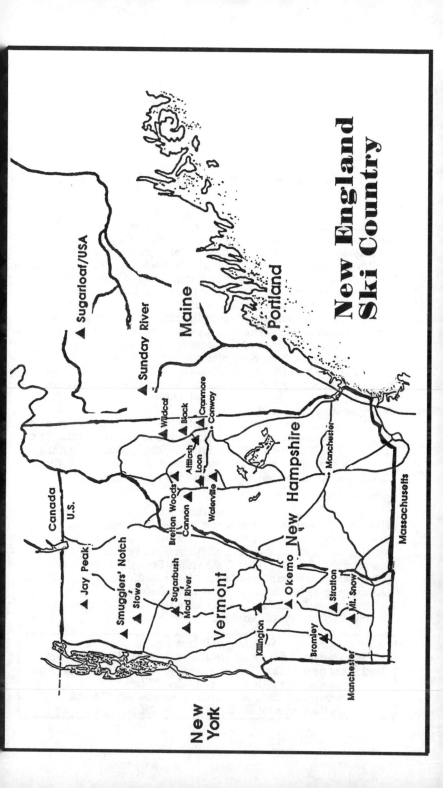

New England
Ski Country

Sugarloaf/USA, Maine

Nestled in the Carrabassett River Valley in western Maine, Sugarloaf/USA is a condo-studded ski resort near the small town of Kingfield. This is a major mountain, more than 2,800 feet of continuous skiable vertical. Sugarloaf's slogan is "Size, Snow and Service"—according to our researchers, The Loaf lives up to it.

First-time visitors get a jaw-dropping first impression of Sugarloaf at one particular curve of Route 27, called "Omigosh!" corner. This unobstructed look at the mountain shows a very big, very well utilized Berg. Runs snake down from the crown in every direction. Because each of these many runs has its own unique twists and turns, Sugarloaf offers a variety of skiing that goes beyond its already impressive size. As one guide put it, "Sugarloaf not only has good uphill capacity, it has exceptional downhill capacity too." The resort claims to have the lowest skier-per-acre ratio in the East.

Because it faces north toward the nearby Canadian border, Sugarloaf does not have an overabundance of sunshine. This, combined with its high latitude and elevation, means big natural snowfalls that come early and stay late. When sunshine comes in March and April, Sugarloaf is a favorite spring skiing spot.

Where to ski

This is a good all-around mountain for any level of skier, but what sets it apart from more run-of-the-mill areas is that it has enough steep and challenging runs to keep experts happily banging the boards all day. In addition to more than 400 acres of classic wooded New England ski trails, Sugarloaf also has 80 to 100 acres of treeless snowfields at the summit, where experts can experience Western-style, open-bowl skiing.

Experts will need little assistance to figure out where to ski. Double-diamond on the trail map is the honest truth.

Sugarloaf/USA Facts
Base elevation: 1,400'; **Summit elevation:** 4,237'; **Vertical drop:** 2,837 feet.
Number and types of lifts: 15–1 four-passenger gondola, 1 quad superchair, 2 quad chairs, 1 triple chair, 8 double chairs, 2 surface lifts
Acreage: 525 skiable acres; **Percent of snowmaking:** 90 percent.
Uphill capacity: 20,035 skiers per hour **Bed base:** 6,000

Steep black runs beckon from the summit on both sides of the main gondola, though the ones on the left are more difficult. The blacks down to the King Pine high-speed quad are all sweet and steep, if a little short. Bump monkeys should head for Choker on this side of the mountain, or to Skidder on the west side; groomers are under orders not to touch these trails, nor Ripsaw, Bubblecuffer and Winter's Way.

Advanced intermediates will find that they can handle most of the single-diamond blacks on this mountain. The Narrow Gauge run from the Spillway East chair is particularly worthy, and because it is officially rated for World Cup racing, in early season you may find yourself skiing next to the U.S. Ski Team.

This is also the closest an intermediate should get to the top. The entire section served by the Wiffletree high-speed quad is an intermediate skiers' playground. On the other side of the mountain the Tote Road stretches from the top of the gondola and winds down three miles to the village area.

At the base of the mountain, beginners will find the very broad and very gentle Boardwalk run, or West Mountain, under the chair by that name. Those looking for a little more challenge graduate to the paths from the top of Bucksaw chair, which is more than a mile long. Try skiing the trails served by the Bucksaw chair for end-of-the-day cruising. This is particularly enjoyable on sunny days when these trails catch the last rays.

S-K-I, the company that owns Killington and Mount Snow/Haystack in Vermont and Bear Mountain in California, bought Sugarloaf last summer and immediately announced plans for a new high-speed quad to service 60 new acres of blue and black terrain for the 94/95 season. Sugarloaf's base area is planned to double in size in a westerly direction, toward the Bucksaw lift. The expansion will allow for new skier services, restaurants, shopping and lodging.

Snowboarding

Allowed on the entire mountain. Sugarloaf has a 500-foot halfpipe and a three-acre snowboard park with 20- to 30-foot snow mounds, guard rails, staircases and barrels for bonking and sliding. Rentals and lessons are available. Maine does not require leashes on snowboards.

Cross-country

Sugarloaf has 85 km. (groomed, double-track) of trails. The Sugarloaf Ski Touring Center is the largest and most complete in Maine. The center is off Route 27, south of the Sugarloaf access road. Three trails offer access from the resort's lodging facilities and the village area. The center also has a lighted, Olympic-sized outdoor skating rink and a 6,000-square-foot lodge with a giant fireplace, a south-facing deck, and food and drink at the Klister Kitchen, which gets high ratings from locals.

sugarloaf/usa
TRAIL GUIDE

SUMMIT 4,237'

A. SPILLWAY X-CUT
B. OLD WINTER'S WAY
C. MIDSTATION X-CUT
D. SLUICE CHUTE

LEGEND

◆◆ EXPERTS ONLY
◆ MOST DIFFICULT
☐ MORE DIFFICULT
● EASIEST
☐ SLOW SKIING
☐ FAMILY SKIING
⌁ SKI AREA BOUNDARY
⌁ CROSS COUNTRY TRAIL NETWORK

✚ FIRST AID CLINIC
P PARKING
✆ PHONE
🅰 RENTAL
Ⓜ MID-STATION

◯ HALFPIPE
🍴 FOOD
🚌 SHUTTLE
🚻 RESTROOMS
🅰 SKI SCHOOL

✹ VERYFINE RACE ARENA

SKIERS AND SNOWBOARDERS RESPONSIBILITY CODE

There are elements of risk in skiing that common sense and personal awareness can reduce.

1. Ski under control or in such a manner that you can stop or avoid other skiers or objects.
2. When skiing downhill or overtaking another skier you must avoid the skier below you.
3. You must not stop where you obstruct a trail or are not visible from above.
4. When entering a trail or starting downhill, yield to other skiers.
5. All skiers shall wear retention straps or ski brakes to prevent runaway skis.
6. You shall keep off closed trails and posted areas and observe all posted signs.
7. You shall not ski while under the influence of alcohol or drugs.
8. If you are involved in a collision with another skier resulting in injury, it is your responsibility to remain at the scene until the ski patrol arrives.
9. You shall observe all posted slow skiing trails and areas.
10. Do not ski trails that are too difficult for your ability.

ANY VIOLATION OF THIS CODE CAN RESULT IN THE LOSS OF LIFT TICKET WITHOUT WARNING AND WITHOUT REFUND.

E. CRIBWORKS
F. BIRCH HOOK
G. WINDROW EXT.
H. BUCKSAW X-CUT

SUGARLOAF GOLF CLUB

LIFTS

⑤ GONDOLA

HIGH CAPACITY QUADS:
① KING PINE ② WHIFFLETREE

TRIPLE CHAIR:
④ SNUBBER

DOUBLE CHAIRS:
⑥ SKIDWAY ⑦ SAWDUSTER ⑧ DOUBLE CHAIR EAST ⑨ DOUBLE CHAIR WEST ⑩ SPILLWAY EAST ⑪ SPILLWAY WEST ⑬ BUCKSAW ⑭ WEST MOUNTAIN

T-BARS:
③ KING PINE ⑫ BATEAU

Group lessons are $12 an hour. Private lessons are $20 an hour. The all-day trail fee is $10 for adults, $7 for junior/senior citizens. Equipment rentals are $12 a day for adults and $8 for juniors and seniors. Call (207) 237-2000.

Multiday ticket holders may exchange a day of downhill for a day of cross-country including trail fee, lesson and equipment. Exchange tickets at the guest services desk in the base lodge.

Ski school (93/94 prices)

Group lessons are free in all lodging packages arranged through (800) 843-5623 (800-THE LOAF). Otherwise, they cost $25 per two-hour course for adults and teens. Sugarloaf has two learn-to-ski packages that include rental equipment, lessons and a beginner-lift ticket. The never-ever level gives access to three lifts for $30, while the next level adds one more lift for $45.

Private lessons are $45 an hour, or $50 per day per person for five or more people.

Children's lessons include the Mountain Adventure program for kids 7 to 12, costing $58 a day, including lunch, lifts and rentals. Ages 4 to 6 are in Mountain Magic, which costs $48 for a full day including lunch. Half days cost $47 for Mountain Adventure and $30 for Mountain Magic. Register at the ski school desk or in the Mountain Magic room in the base lodge.

Special programs concentrate on skills such as bumps, telemarking, powder or hard carving. Peak Performance workshops are scheduled for the second weekend in December and the last week in February, and feature Skiing For Women, Ski Challenge and Snowboard Challenge.

Lift tickets (93/94 prices)

	Adult	Child (6-12) Senior (65+)
One day	$41	$22
Three days	$108 ($36/day)	$57 ($19/day)
Five days	$160 ($32/day)	$80 ($16/day)

Midweek, the single-day adult price drops to $38. Teen prices (ages 13-18) are $33 for a weekend day ($29 midweek), $84 for three days and $130 for five. Two- and seven-day tickets, and half-day tickets are available. Children 5 and younger ski free.

Accommodations

Sugarloaf is a planned condominium community in the mold of Keystone or Copper Mountain. That said, it is one of the more tasteful layouts we've seen, with the central village blending in well with the overall environment. **The Sugarloaf Mountain Hotel** is the centerpiece of the Alpine village. Most unit rates are $80-$260 with the most luxurious suites at $500. The slightly more modest **Sugarloaf Inn** has a quaint New England inn feel. The Sugarloaf Inn offers packages that include ski lessons and use of the Sugarloaf Sports & Fitness Club, with pool, spas, message therapy, tanning beds, exercise equipment and indoor racquetball/squash courts.

More than 900 condo units are spread throughout the resort, all designed so skiers can ski back to their lodging. (Not all have lift access, but a shuttle runs from the lodging to the lifts.) The **Timberwind** and **Gondola Village** units are dorm-style. Families like the latter complex because it's close to the state-licensed child-care facility. The **Bigelow, Snowflower** and **Commons** units are more luxurious, and the **Sugartree** units offer easy access to the health club.

The resort has an RV parking area serviced by lifts.

Dining

Sugarloaf is a compact resort, but has no fewer than 18 eateries. The **Truffle Hound** (235-2355; reservations suggested) has elegant, continental dining. Prize for the best piece of meat goes to **Gepetto's,** 1993 Maine Restaurant Association's Restaurant of the Year, for its teriyaki steak. Our favorite for fine dining and atmosphere was the **Seasons** at the Sugarloaf Inn (237-2000). For pizza or burgers in a homey, noisy atmosphere, try **The Bag and Kettle** (locals call it The Bag.). You can rate the local talent on Blues Monday while eating a Bag-burger and get the lore of Sugarloaf from the locals. The deck at **Arabella's at the Gladstone** is a major lunch spot and the place to mingle with the ski school. For an English pub experience, try **Theo's Restaurant,** where the Sugarloaf Brewing Company peddles its wares.

No trip to a Northeast ski area is complete without a visit to an authentic New England inn, and the **The Inn on Winter's Hill** in Kingfield is worth the 15-mile drive. Sitting on the hill named after Sugarloaf's founder, Amos Winter, the inn has an excellent restaurant, **Julia's** (265-5426). Proprietors Richard and Carolyn Winnick will gladly conduct tours of this fully renovated inn. **One Stanley Avenue** features a unique menu full of Maine-grown fare, and the **Herbert Hotel** is also worth a visit.

In Eustis, 11 minutes north of Sugarloaf, two additional restaurants are worth checking out: **The Trail's End** for steaks and the **Porter House** for home cooking with big portions. **Tufulio's** and **Hugs** in the Carrabassett Valley span the gamut of Italian dishes served in a casual atmosphere.

Après-ski/nightlife

On sunny days, the après-ski crowd gathers on the decks of **Arabella's at the Gladstone** or at **The Bag. Gringo's** has good Tex-Mex bar munchies and frequent live music in its **Widow-maker Lounge.**

The hottest spot for live music and dancing at night is the aforementioned **Widowmaker Lounge.** For a more subdued atmosphere, try the **Sugarloaf Inn** or **The Double Diamond** in the Sugarloaf Mountain Hotel.

On Route 27 in the valley, you'll find the locals at **Carrabassett Yacht Club** or at **Judson's Motel**, the latter a favorite with UMaine and Colby College students.

Teenagers can head to **Rascals**, an alcohol-free teen spot with a DJ and dance floor. Younger teens have **Pinocchio's**, with video games, pinball and board games to keep them entertained.

Child care

Moose Alley is a special kids-and-instructors-only section of the mountain where kids can do some controlled tree skiing.

There are children's activities every night except Sunday in the Mountain Magic Room in the base lodge. Ages 5-12 have one type of activity, while teens do something else. Examples include games and G- or PG-rated movies for the young set, and skating, dances, Wallyball games (a volleyball-type game played on a racquetball court) and PG-13 movies for the teens.

Other activities

Shopping: The village has several shops, including **Pat Buck's Emporium**, a gift store that features handcrafted items by Maine artisans (including beautiful knitted sweaters); and **Gold/Smith Gallery**, with gold and silver jewelry, photo frames, and similar items. In Kingfield you'll find **Scent-sations** in the Herbert Hotel, where you choose your favorite scent and the store will put it into lotions, shampoos and body oils.

Dog sledding, horse-drawn sleigh rides, snowmobiling, snowshoeing, ice fishing and skating are among the activities that Sugarloaf Guest Services can arrange (237-2000).

Getting there and getting around

Getting there: By car, take I-95 north to Augusta, Route 27 through Farmington and Kingfield. Or take the Maine Turnpike to the Auburn exit, Route 4 to Farmington and Route 27 through Kingfield. The drive is about two and a half hours from Portland.

The closest major airport with nationwide service is the Portland International Jetport. Sugarloaf has a shuttle, Riverbend Express, that runs twice daily to and from the jetport. The closest private airport is Sugarloaf Regional, six miles away.

Getting around: A car is optional—most everything in the resort is within walking distance. A shuttle runs on weekends, and is on call during the week.

Information/reservations

Lodging reservations: (800) 843-5623 (800-THE-LOAF); or (207) 237-2000. Snow report: (207) 237-2000. Write: Sugarloaf USA, RR 1 Box 5000, Carrabassett Valley, ME 04947.

Sunday River, Maine

Sunday River, just outside of Bethel and tucked against the New Hampshire border, is a pleasant blend of old New England tradition with modern ski condominiums. Bethel is a typically picturesque New England town, complete with white-steepled church and ivy-covered prep school. The main street is lined with historic buildings, and the village common is anchored by the 75-year-old Bethel Inn.

The Sunday River Ski Resort rises six miles to the north, an hour and a half drive from the Portland airport and about three and a half hours from Boston. As you drive up the access road to the base area, you see condominium complexes right and left, but they don't assault you; they blend with the trees and hills.

The resort doesn't have a main center packed with restaurants, shops and bars. Three separate base lodges—South Ridge, Barker Mountain, and White Cap—provide basic cafeteria and sports shop facilities. South Ridge Lodge is the hub, housing the ski school, the corporate offices and a grocery store. The condominium complexes are small centers to themselves with most boasting an indoor or heated outdoor pool, Jacuzzis and saunas. The Summit Hotel provides upscale accommodations and amenities for those who prefer non-condo lodging. A sense of quiet results: the bustle of people created by a town or central hub is dispersed into the condominiums.

It may be quiet, but Sunday River isn't dull. Something always seems to be happening here—ski terrain expansions, new lifts, a new hotel and conference center, a new way of teaching skiing, and a new ski train from Portland. This season, the resort will open new terrain, Jordan Bowl, and has some big plans for a development in Bethel, which include a 140-room hotel and a Victorian-style station for its Silver Bullet Express ski train.

Sunday River Facts
Base elevation: *782'*; **Summit elevation:** *3,100*; **Vertical drop:** *2,300 feet*
Number of lifts: *14—3 high-speed quads, 4 quads, 5 triple chairs, 2 double chair*
Percent of snowmaking: *90 percent* **Snowmaking (total acreage):** *470 acres*
Total acreage: *570 skiable acres*
Uphill capacity: *27,000 per hour* **Bed base:** *5,200 on mountain; 2,000 nearby*

Where to ski

The original base area was Barker Mountain. But since 1985 Sunday River has opened five new mountain peaks. The resort's seventh peak, Jordan Bowl, opened for the 94/95 season it's a huge cirque to the west of the Aurora Peak area. The Jordan Bowl will have up to six lifts and 250 acres of trails when finally built out. This season, it will feature a high-speed quad chair lift (Sunday River's third), a double chair lift and five new trails covering approximately 65 acres. The trails cover the spectrum of ability levels, including a 1.2 mile-long black-diamond cruiser. A trail underneath the quad will have classic New England black-diamond skiing on natural snow.

Beginners start on Sundance and then have the entire South Ridge area to practice linking their turns. Twelve beginner runs in the South Ridge area are serviced by a detachable quad, a triple and a double chair. Advanced beginners can also head to the White Cap quad and enjoy the relatively mellow Moonstruck, Starburst and Starlight runs.

Once a skier is past the basic snowplow and into stem christies, the rest of Sunday River beckons. The North Peak triple chair opens long practice runs like Dream Maker and Escapade. One of the runs in the new Jordan Bowl area will be "kind of like Dream Maker on steroids," said our inside source.

The Aurora area, served by a fixed quad chair and a triple chair, provides experts with plenty of challenge. This area, once the exclusive province of expert and advanced skiers, now is accessible to lower level skiers because of an extension of Sirius from the top of Spruce Peak across Vortex to Lights Out. Also, a green route goes from North Peak to the Aurora Peak base area.

But Aurora is still the spot to find tough skiing. Aurora also has a double-diamond glade that runs from Lights Out to the base of Vortex. And Northern Lights offers an easier way down the mountain, though it's no stroll through the park. Celestial, accessed from Lights Out, may be the nicest of the four gladed trails Sunday River opened last season. It starts out steep and wide, but mellows and narrows as you go down.

From the top of Barker Mountain a steep trio—Right Stuff, Top Gun and Agony—provide advanced skiers long sustained pitches. Agony and Top Gun are premier bump runs. Right Stuff is a cruiser early in the day after it's been groomed, but normally develops moguls by afternoon. Tree skiing fans will find a new gladed area—Last Tango—between Right Stuff and Risky Business. This black-diamond natural slalom area is the gentlest and most spacious of the resort's four mapped glades. Though it's not particularly steep, it's tight. A work road about two-thirds of the way down allows skiers to bail out onto Right Stuff. Those who continue through the trees will find the terrain getting steeper and tighter. If you're less than an expert, you won't have much fun on Last Tango's lower third.

From the top of Locke Mountain, T-2 plunges down the tracks of an old T-bar providing a direct fall-line drop and a spectacular view of Bethel, the valley and Mt. Washington.

Halfway down Cascades, skiers can take a right turn onto Tempest (this trail is a steep intermediate in the morning, but bumped by afternoon), which together with Wildfire and the short Jibe, is served by the Little White Cap quad (Lift 9). Another advanced intermediate trail is Monday Mourning, which starts out steep and wide but mellows near the end, where the NASTAR course is located.

In the morning the sun shines on upper intermediate and advanced skiers heading up the White Heat quad. The White Heat run is a wide swath straight down the mountain from the peak of White Cap. When you put all the superlatives together, this run is the steepest, longest and widest lift-served expert trail in the East. Double-diamond Shockwave offers 975 vertical feet of big bumps and steep pitches. On the opposite side of White Heat, Obsession is a regulation GS trail. New last season: two gladed areas called Hardball (skier right) and Chutzpah (skier left). They start out deceptively mellow and open-spaced, but watch out. Technically, they are the most demanding on the mountain.

Mountain rating

Sunday River is perfect for beginners, with one of the most extensive lift-served beginner areas in New England. The ski school here guarantees you learn to ski in a day, or your money back—last year out of 7,000 beginners only a handful failed.

Intermediates get a mountain full of terrain. Experts will find super steeps and monster bumps on Aurora Peak, Barker Mountain and White Cap.

Sunday River's snowmaking system is one of the best and biggest anywhere. Better yet, the resort is not subject to water restrictions as is the case in much of the East.

Cross-country

Though Sunday River does not have a dedicated cross-country center, this area of Maine is known for some of the best Nordic skiing in New England. The **Bethel Inn Cross-Country Ski Center** behind the hotel links up with 40 km. of marked and groomed trials. They have rentals, lessons and evening sleigh rides. The Bethel Inn also has facilities for instructing in telemark. Call 824-2175.

Trail fees are $11. Midweek, the trail fee is also good for entrance to the recreation center, with outdoor heated pool, sauna and fitness center, until 2 p.m.

The **Sunday River Ski Touring Center** (824-2410) is run by the Sunday River Inn on the Sunday River access road. It has 40 km. of groomed and tracked trails.

Carter's Cross-Country Ski Center (539-4848) off Route 26 in Oxford provides another alternative for skinny skis.

Forty-five minutes from Bethel is the **Jackson Ski Touring Center.** See the Mt. Washington Valley chapter for details of their ski touring programs.

Snowboarding

Snowboarders are allowed anywhere at Sunday River. A 110-meter-long halfpipe is on the Starlight trail, which was converted to a snowboard park in 93/94. The ski school offers Learn-to-Shred and Shred Better clinics which meet at the White Cap Lodge Shred Center. The Learn-to-Shred program, including board, boots and limited lifts, costs $50. The Shred Better clinic lasts one-and-a-half hours and costs $26.

Ski school (94/95 prices)

The Sunday River Ski School teaches **group lessons** using a program it created. Called Perfect Turn®, it combines state-of-the-art ski technique with state-of-the-art educational theory. Sunday River has no lessons or teachers, but rather clinics and ski pros (like golf or tennis pros). This is not just a semantics change: Perfect Turn is so revolutionary that other ski areas are buying the rights to use it in their ski schools. It has spread to Mt. Bachelor, Oregon; Blue Mountain, Ontario; and Jiminy Peak, Massachusetts; two other areas are considering it. We have experienced it and recommend it highly; more details are in the Everybody Skis chapter at the front of the book.

Perfect Turn has 10 levels of clinics. Levels 1-3, for never-evers to advanced beginners, are 90 minutes to two hours. The package includes the clinic, a lift ticket for the South Ridge and North Peak and rental equipment, costing $39 for Level 1. Sunday River guarantees Level 1 skiers that they will be able to ride a lift, turn and stop by the end of the clinic, or they can repeat it free, or get their money back.

Clinics for other levels normally last 75 minutes with a maximum of six skiers. Skiers head for the North Peak lodge, where they watch a short video that demonstrates various levels of skiing ability. Once they see a skier on the video who skis as they do, they know what level clinic to take. The video eliminates the "ski-off," which usually takes up about 40 minutes of a two-hour lesson, and starting on the mountain eliminates the lift ride to where the teaching begins. Clinics run about every half hour throughout the day and cost $22.

Private clinic prices are $50 an hour for one ($20 for each additional student).

Sunday River also has **special workshops** for specific groups, all lasting about two hours and costing $30. The Black Diamond Club, for advanced to expert skiers, is offered four times per week and claims to allow skiers to get in as much as 10,000 vertical feet per session. Other programs are an adult racing program and a Prime Time ski program for adults 50 and older.

A Woman's Turn program, offered on weekends and a couple of times during holiday weeks, gives intermediate and advanced skiers a chance to perfect their turns. Also, Janet Spangler conducts a week-long women's program about four times per season.

Sunday River's **children's lessons** start with the Tiny Turns program, an hour of private instruction for ages 3 and 4 with a half- or full-day session in day care. The private clinic is $28 if the child is registered in day care; otherwise, the clinic cost is the regular private rate.

SKIwee is for youngsters 4 to 6 years of age. Mogul Meisters is for those 7 to 12 years of age. All day in either program, including lunch, lifts and equipment, costs $58. The morning or afternoon programs, without lunch, cost $46.

Lift tickets (94/95 prices)

	Adult	Child (6-12)
One day	$41 (93/94 prices)	$24 (93/94 prices)
Three days	$118 ($39.33/day)	$71 ($23.66/day)
Five days	$196 ($39.20/day)	$117 ($23.40/day)

Children 5 and younger ski free with parent. Seniors 65 and older ski for half the adult price of the day.

Accommodations

The Summit Hotel and condominiums are the most convenient to the slopes. But Bethel also has a group of excellent bed-and-breakfasts and old country inns. If you are planning a Sunday River vacation call the central reservations number, which will handle everything from air travel to day care.

The resort has built a ski dorm, within walking distance of the slopes, designed primarily for groups.

The **Summit Hotel and Conference Center** is a trailside oasis with a 25-meter heated outdoor pool, athletic club, fine dining. and conference and banquet facilities in five meeting rooms and two ballrooms. Rates here start at $108 midweek and $179 weekend for a standard room. The **Snow Cap Inn** provides less luxury a short walk from the slopes (rates $88 midweek, $120 weekend) and the **Ski Dorm** next door offers affordable digs ($22 midweek, $32 weekends/holidays) for single skiers.

Locke Mountain Townhouses are the most upscale, but hard to get, with the ideally located **Merrill Brook** condominiums not far behind. Condominium units are all convenient to the slopes and all have trolley service. Expect to pay $102-$150 for studios that sleep up to three, $272 to $400 for three-bedroom units that sleep up to eight. Additional beds in units are available for $15 per person per night.

In Bethel the **Bethel Inn** (824-2175) has old stylish atmosphere and first-rate rooms. The rates include breakfast and dinner. Double rates run $60 to $125 per person. The inn also has a cross-country center and health club; see Cross-Country section for more details.

The **Douglass Place** is Bethel's original bed-and-breakfast (824-2229). The proprietor has many tales to tell. **The Four Seasons** is in an old elegant building with excellent French cuisine (824-2755 or 800-227-7458). **The Sudbury Inn** is one of the best restaurants in town and a favorite watering hole (824-2174). **The Holidae House** in Bethel has drawn praise for its beautiful decor (824-3400). These B&Bs cost about $45 to $65 per person per night.

Less than a mile from the base of the mountain, the **Sunday River Inn** (824-2410) offers a relaxed setting reminiscent of the great ski lodges of the '60s. It also operates the closest cross-country center. All rates include breakfast and dinner and are $60 per person, double occupancy for a shared-bath room, $73 for a private-bath suite and $39 for a dorm bed where you bring your own sleeping bag.

Additional lodging can be arranged through Sunday River's reservation line (800) 543-2754 (543-2SKI) or the Bethel Area Chamber of Commerce, (207) 824-3585.

Dining

Legends in the Summit Hotel is the best restaurant in the area with a great menu and wine list. The **Fall Line** in the Fall Line Condominiums is convenient, consistent and serves good food. **Rosetto's Italian Restaurant** in the White Cap Lodge is open for dinner daily and for lunch on weekends and holidays.

Saturday's in the South Ridge base is packed for lunch and dinners with good reason. **The Peak Lodge and Skiing Center**, at the summit of North Peak, is a popular lunch spot with a giant deck. **BUMPS! Pub**, in the White Cap Lodge, serves a pub menu which should be avoided unless you're starving.

In Bethel try the **Sudbury Inn** and the **Bethel Inn**. For French cuisine head to **L'Auberge**. **Mother's** on Upper Main Street is a favorite of students from the Gould Academy as well as skiers. **Cisco and Poncho's** offers Mexican food. The **Moose's Tale** at the brew pub at the end of the access road serves an eclectic menu of basic fare. **Skidders**, tucked in a tiny storefront on Main Street, makes fantastic deli take-out. The best pizza is reportedly in West Bethel at **The Only Place**, and the best breakfasts in the **Red Top Truck Stop**, which opens at 5 a.m. for local loggers.

For a memorable meal a bit out of the way try the **Old Rawley Inn** at the junction of Route 35 and 118 in North Waterford (583-4143). Heaping portions are served in this 1790s stagecoach stop filled with Early American and Shaker furniture.

Après-ski/nightlife

If you strike it rich you may find lively action midweek at Sunday River and in Bethel. The area has made a good attempt at booking comedy acts into **BUMPS!**, having torchlight parades and fireworks, and adding to the live entertainment in the bars around the resort. But the real action heats up on weekends.

Immediate après-ski, when found, is at the base of the slopes. Try the **Barker Mountain Base Area**, which has mellow acoustic guitar on weekends, or **BUMPS!** at the White Cap Lodge for libations. **Saturday's** is the liveliest of the mountain spots. In town head to the **Sunday River Brewery** or **Sudbury's.**

At night, **BUMPS!** has bands plucking tunes on weekends and comedy nights planned for Tuesdays. The crowd tends toward young. At the end of the access road the **Sunday River Brewery** has live music and most excellent homemade brew. Downtown, the **Backstage** usually has karaoke during the week, with Country & Western and early rock'n'roll bands on weekends. It also has the only pool tables in town. **Sudbury's** has bands ranging from blues to bluegrass on most nights. A more sedate crowd fills **Legends** at the Summit Hotel for its acoustic music.

Child care

The nursery and day-care facilities are located in the Merrill Brook Village Building II with a new facility at the Summit Hotel. A new child center opens this season at South Ridge for skier development.

The nursery is for infants from 6 weeks to 2 1/2 years. The hourly rate is $7, with additional children in the same family costing $4 per hour. Bring diapers, formula and food for infants. All-day programs cost $37 including lunch for older toddlers ($18.50 for additional toddlers from the same family). Call for reservations, especially on weekends (207-824-3000).

Other activities

Shopping: Bethel has some unusual shops, such as **Bonnema Potters**, with highly distinctive pottery with glazing that depicts the Maine landscape; and **Mt. Mann,** a native gemstone shop. On Church Street, **Samuel Timberlake** produces fine reproductions of Shaker furniture.

At the ski area, **swimming pools and saunas** are in virtually every condominium complex. Guests staying at the few condos that don't have them have use privileges at nearby complexes. The ski dorm has video games and pool tables.

Other activities include **horse-drawn sleigh rides** (make reservations at the Guest Services Desk) and **ice skating** at the White Cap Base Lodge. Skating hours vary; rental skates are available. On weekends and holidays, teens can enjoy their own night club called **MVP's** and kids aged 6-12 can attend **Camp Sunday River**, an evening of supervised activities.

Getting there and getting around

Getting there: Sunday River is in western Maine an hour and a half from Portland and three and a half hours from Boston. From Interstate 95, Exit 11 in Maine to Route 26 north, continue to Bethel, then take Route 2 six miles north to Sunday River.

RV parking is allowed in designated parking areas at the resort. No hookups are available. An RV park is also located at White Birch Camping, in Shelburne, on Route 2.

The most convenient airport is Portland International Jetport, 75 miles from Sunday River and served by Continental, Delta, United and USAir. Private pilots can land in Bethel, five miles away. **SkiBurban Transportation** will pick up from either airport by reservation (824-4646).

Perhaps the most fun way to Sunday River is by train. Last season, the **Sunday River Silver Bullet Ski Express** started runs between Portland and Bethel. A bus transports skiers from Bethel to the slopes. Schedule and fares for 94/95 were not ready by press time; call the ski area for more information.

Getting around: During the main part of the season, on-mountain transportation between the base areas is quite good on shuttlebuses that look like old trolley cars. The shuttle loop expands to include the condos at night. SkiBurban Transport is about the only way to get into Bethel. In shoulder season, the mountain shuttles are by request only. Several off-mountain properties, such as the Sunday River Inn and the Bethel Inn, have shuttle service to and from the slopes. Midwinter, you can get along without a car, but they're nice to have, especially if you want to go to Bethel. Early or late season, you'll need one.

Information/reservations

Sunday River Resort Reservations: (800) 543-2754 (543-2SKI).

Ski Report and Information: (207) 824-6400; (617) 666-4200; (508) 580-0666.

Address: Sunday River Ski Resort, PO Box 450, Bethel, ME 04217. Administration phone: (207) 824-3000.

Local telephone area code is 207.

Mt. Washington Valley
New Hampshire

Wildcat, Cranmore, Attitash
Black Mountain, King Pine
Jackson Touring

These five relatively small ski areas, set into spectacular White Mountain terrain, with the Jackson Ski Touring Foundation (one of the world's best cross-country trail systems), the wild skiing on Mt. Washington, and the year-round resort attractions of Mt. Washington Valley, combine to make a multifaceted destination resort.

This was a destination resort long before anyone came here to ski. A quarter century before the Civil War, fashionable northeasterners started coming here for the summer, first by stage line and then by railroad and carriage, to meet Hawthorne and Emerson, enjoy the scenery with Bierstadt, beat the heat, and find suitable husbands for their daughters. Many of the grand old hotels they visited have been brought up to date to add their charm to the mix of condos, motels, country inns, and B&Bs.

Legends of the early days of skiing—the late Thirties—surround you. Ride up the Wildcat gondola and look back at the fantastic bulk of Mt. Washington with its huge scooped-out ravines. This is hallowed ground, where Toni Matt on his wooden boards schussed over the Tuckerman headwall in one long arc to win the 1939 Inferno race, summit to base in six and a half minutes.

Most of all, what makes this area one of the pioneers of downhill skiing in America is the Eastern Slope Ski School, founded by Carroll Reed. This is where the Arlberg method of ski instruction was introduced to North America by Benno Rybizka, and by his Austrian teacher, the famous Hannes Schneider, who was released by the Nazis in return for banking concessions. His son Herbert Schneider is still active at Cranmore, one of many who were there at the beginning of the modern era.

If anyone wants a break from downhill skiing, this is the place. The prime summer activities of hiking, climbing, and

Auto Rd.
Auto Road

↑ TO
GORHAM

Appalachian Trail

Mt. Washington

Wildcat Mtn.

AMC Headquarters

Scenic Gondola
Glen Ellis Falls

Mt. Washington Valley
New Hampshire
White Mountains

Carter Notch Rd.

16

NORTH

16B

Black Mtn.

Jackson Falls

JACKSON

Ski Touring

?

GLEN

to Crawford Notch →

2

Scenic Vista (State Rest Area)

River Rd.

16 A

Ski Touring

BARTLETT

302

Diana's Bath

INTERVALE

?

Attitash Mtn.

Cathedral Ledge

Mt. Cranmore

Alpine Slide

Echo Lake State Pk.

Skimobile

Conway Scenic Railroad

West Side Rd.

NORTH CONWAY

?

Bear Notch Rd.

Passaconway Rd.

Lower Falls

16

302

to Maine →

Sabbaday Falls

112

302

Kancamagus Highway

CONWAY

■ Attractions

ALBANY

?

□ Points of Interest

16

? Information Booths

153

🚐 Covered Bridges

⛳ Golf Course

△ Ski Touring

EATON

SNOWVILLE

camping out are pursued in the snow-and-ice season by local and visiting fanatics. You can even practice your rock-climbing skills on an indoor wall.

Restaurants, many of them tucked into the tiny country inns or restored barns in the valley, are world class and have acknowledged gourmet reputations. In fact, this valley is home to one of the most famous cooking schools in the country.

Besides the skiing, picturesque inns and tempting restaurants, there are more tax-free factory outlet stores concentrated in Conway and North Conway than in any other area of the United States, making the region a top shopping destination.

Where to ski

Wildcat: For more than a decade, Wildcat has been voted the ski area with the most spectacular scenery in the Northeast, with beautiful views across Pinkham Notch to towering Mt. Washington and Tuckerman Ravine. Wildcat is known as an untamed resort, but in the past few years, Wildcat has tamed some of the bumpy runs. Now the groomers roll all but two of the trails. The trails themselves have also been widened and straightened extensively. However, this resort is still best for strong intermediate to expert skiers.

The skiing is tempered by three factors: the cold, the wind and the pitch of the slopes. The cold, wind and capricious weather changes of nearby Mt. Washington are among the most extreme in North America, so Wildcat skiers need to be dressed properly for changing conditions. The plus side to inclement weather, of course, is a lot of natural snow; Wildcat often is the last New Hampshire ski area to close. Though Wildcat's slopes are wider than they used to be, the area still has a reputation for steep and narrow—in short, classic New England skiing.

> ### Wildcat Facts
> **Base elevation:** 1,950'; **Summit elevation:** 4,050'; **Vertical drop:** 2,100 feet.
> **Number and types of lifts:** 6—1 gondola, 4 triple chairs, 1 double chair
> **Acreage:** 120 acres, 15 miles of trails **Percent of snowmaking:** 98 percent
> **Uphill capacity:** 8,500 skiers per hour **Bed base:** 6,500+

Intermediates should be able to handle the groomed trails covered by snowmaking. For the best intermediate way down the slopes, head to the Polecat side of the gondola; for a descent where it is prudent to pay attention to the details of skiing, loop to the opposite side. Intermediate and beginner trails exist, but skiers at Wildcat are probably there for the challenge. (Wildcat allows novices free skiing on the Snowcat Novice Area served by its own triple chair.)

Attitash: Just west of Glen on Route 302 in Bartlett, Attitash is a great intermediate mountain. It's not too big and not too steep, and has great snowmaking. This season, Attitash will open up 30 more acres on Bear Peak, install a new fixed-grip quad chair, and cut a new easy trail off Attitash Peak.

Attitash has a protected learning slope with triple chair, and there are several beginner trails around the Borvig lifts. Ptarmigan is supposed to be one of the steepest trails in New England, but it is manageable for good intermediates because of the elbow room on the run. The rest of the mountain is enough to keep 80 percent of skiers perfectly satisfied, with Northwest Passage serving up great cruising. The grooming fleet smoothes out almost all the steep pitches nightly, but a couple of trails are allowed to bump up when temperatures and snow conditions allow.

Attitash is one of the few ski areas in the country that supplements its traditional all-day lift ticket with a computerized point ticket that allows skiers to pay by the vertical foot. Called the Smart Ticket®, it's transferable and is good for two years from purchase date. It's an excellent choice for those who only want to ski a few hours.

Attitash Facts
Base elevation: 550'; *Summit elevation:* 2,300'; *Vertical drop:* 1,750 feet.
Number and types of lifts: 7–1 quad chair, 2 triple chairs, 4 double chairs
Acreage: 170 skiable acres *Percent of snowmaking:* 98 percent
Uphill capacity: 5,500 skiers per hour *Bed base:* 6,500+

Cranmore: Now in its 56th year of operation, Cranmore is one of the oldest resorts in America, one that features good balanced terrain. If you arrive in North Conway in the evening, you can't miss it: The lights for night skiing, which lasts until 9 p.m., are visible from a long way off and add one more festive ingredient to the town. Because it's right in North Conway, it has the potential to attain a European-style relationship with the town. Over the past five seasons, Cranmore has invested more than $11 million in various lift, terrain, base lodge and lodging facilities, plus a snowboarding halfpipe.

Cranmore Facts
Base elevation: 497'; *Summit elevation:* 1,697'; *Vertical drop:* 1,200 feet.
Number and types of lifts: 5–1 triple chair, 4 double chairs
Acreage: 185 skiable acres *Percent of snowmaking:* 100 percent
Uphill capacity: 3,500 skiers per hour *Bed base:* 6,500+

Black Mountain: This ski area on Route 16B may be the best place in the valley for beginner lessons and family skiing. From the front side of the mountain, facing Whitneys' Inn, the area is reminiscent of a country club, but behind the ridge accessed by the double chair are 18 sunny and sheltered south-facing trails ranging from beginner to advanced intermediate skiing. Adjacent to the Jackson Ski Touring area, Black Mountain has also become a center for cross-country skiers interested in trying out telemark skiing. Finally, Black Mountain's southern exposure provides a warmer place to ski when it's just too cold at other areas.

Snowboarding isn't allowed on Black Beauty or Lower Black Beauty trails, but the area has a 350-foot halfpipe.

Black Mountain's Family Passport allows two adults and two children 15 and younger to ski for $69 per day, some holiday periods excluded.

Black Mountain Facts
Base elevation: 1,300'; *Summit elevation:* 2,350'; *Vertical drop:* 1,050 feet.
Number and types of lifts: 3–1 triple chair, 1 double chair, 1 surface lift.
Acreage: 85 trail acres *Percent snowmaking:* 98 percent
Uphill capacity: 3,700 skiers per hour *Bed base:* 1,500+

Mt. Washington: If you like to get to the top the old-fashioned way (you *climb* it) try the famous spring skiing in Tuckerman Ravine; all winter, there's the Sherburne Trail and several other areas. Start from Pinkham Notch Camp (see Other Activities). (Note: please heed all information about weather and avalanche conditions. Mt. Washington has a reputation for some of the most vicious weather and quick changes anywhere.)

King Pine: This small area has a modest vertical drop, but for those just starting out and parents who want to keep an eye on young children, an unintimidating area is preferable. King Pine does have one steep trail—reportedly one of the steepest in the state—but top-level skiers are better off somewhere else. King Pine is adjacent to the Purity Spring Resort, which has slopeside lodging and ski packages.

King Pine Facts
Base elevation: 500; *Summit elevation:* 850; *Vertical drop:* 350 feet.
Number and types of lifts: 4–1 triple chair, 1 double chair; 2 J-bars
Acreage: 60 skiable acres *Percent of snowmaking:* 95 percent
Uphill capacity: 4,000 skiers per hour *Bed base:* 6,500+

Snowboarding

New Hampshire law requires snowboarders to have some sort of leash or strap tethering the board to their leg.

Cross-country

Jackson Ski Touring Foundation, Box 216, Jackson, NH 03846, on Route 16A (383-9355) is a mecca for Nordic skiers. It has more than 154 km. of groomed and backcountry trails, country inns are spaced throughout the region, and Mt. Washington towers above.

Mt. Washington Valley Ski Touring Association, Box 646, Intervale NH 03845 has over 60 km. of trails. For ski school, rentals, or snow conditions, call (800) 282-5220.

The Appalachian Mountain Club maintains a network of ski touring trails radiating from the AMC Camp at Pinkham Notch; about 7 km. are rated Easiest or More Difficult (requiring skills up to a strong snowplow and step turn), but about 40 km. are rated Most Difficult, with long challenging hills and narrow trails. AMC also has unusual dining; see that section for more details. Call: 466-2721.

The Nestlenook Inn (383-9443), also in Jackson, offers 35 km. of touring winding through its 65-acre farm.

Purity Spring Resort, home of the King Pine ski area, has 15 km. of groomed and tracked trails near Madison. Rentals and lessons available. Call (800) 367-8897 or (603) 367-8896.

Ski school

All the areas have extensive ski schools. Lessons are naturally slanted to the terrain available at each resort. Some of the prices are from last season; as always, use them as a guideline.

Group lessons are $20 per session at Wildcat, $19 at Attitash, $18 at Cranmore, $15 at Black and $13 at King Pine.

Private lessons are $45 per 90 minutes for one student at Wildcat; $40 an hour at Attitash, $35 at Cranmore, $30 at Black and $28 at King Pine.

Children's lessons (all include lessons, lift ticket and rentals; lower price range is for half day) are $25-$50 at Wildcat's SKIwee program, $35-$50 at Attitash (lunch included, but rentals are $10 extra), $30-$50 at Cranmore, $35-$38 at Black, $20-$39 at King Pine.

Learn-to-ski packages (rentals, lifts and lessons) are $36 at Wildcat and $33 at Cranmore.

Lift tickets (93/94 prices unless noted)

Attitash: Adults, $36, weekend/holidays ($29 midweek); children (12 and younger); $21 ($19 midweek). On Sunday, children 12 and younger pay their age to ski. Attitash also sells an electronic ticket that allows skiers to pay by the run; a good choice for those who don't get full value from an all-day ticket.

Wildcat (94/95 prices): Adults, $36, weekends/holidays; Children (6-12) and seniors (65 and older), $20 weekends. Midweek, everyone 6 and older skis for $19. Children 5 and younger ski free with a ticket-holding parent, and skiers 70 and older can ski free midweek. Two-day weekend tickets are $60 for adults ($30 per day) and $32 for kids/seniors ($16 per day). On Wednesdays two can ski for $30.

Cranmore (94/95 prices): Saturday tickets are $35 for adults and $18 for children 6-14 (younger than that ski free). Sunday, the price is $28 for adults, $15 for kids, but it doesn't include night skiing as Saturday's ticket does. Midweek, $19 for adults, $12 for children.

Black Mountain charges $29.50 for adults on weekends and $14 midweek. Ages 5-15 pay $18 on weekends; $12 midweek. They have a family ticket for $69 which includes two adults and two juniors.

King Pine (94/95 prices): Lift rates are $25 for adults on weekends, $15 weekdays. Kids (12 and younger) ski for $10 a day midweek. Night skiing (Tuesday, Friday, Saturday and holidays): $12 adults, $8 children. Midweek and twilight tickets available; call the ski area.

The **Ski New Hampshire** five-day midweek ticket is valid at 16 New Hampshire resorts and costs $159 for adults. One child 12 and younger may ski free with each paying adult. Additional junior passes are $80.

Accommodations

Accommodations in the Mt. Washington Valley are among the best in skidom if you like rustic, romantic and tiny country inns and bed-and-breakfast establishments. You won't find high-rises, but larger historic inns accommodate those who prefer a large-hotel resort feel. Also, the valley has moderately priced motels suitable for families. Condominiums exist, but for the most part are concentrated at a few base areas. For lodging information, call the **Mt. Washington Valley Chamber of Commerce Lodging Bureau;** the same number is good for reservations: (800) 367-3364.

Stonehurst Manor, North Conway NH; 356-3271 or (800) 525-9100, is created from a turn-of-the-century mansion that belonged to the Bigelow family of carpet fame. It is still manorial. The setting, rooms and restaurant are absolute elegance. A room is $95; master bedroom with balcony or the suite is $135. Make sure you are staying in the manor; there is also a motel nearby with some lodging. Ask about the winter packages.

Sheraton White Mountain Inn at Settlers' Green in downtown North Conway, with 200 rooms and suites, is handy to all the best outlet stores as well as the rest of North Conway. It has its own fitness facility, swimming pool, fitness center and ice skating. Children stay and eat free. Call for details: (800) 648-4397; in NH 356-9300.

White Mountain Hotel and Resort, brand new, at the foot of Cathedral Ledges (the enormous sculptured granite cliffs you see from everywhere in North Conway) is reached by taking River Road off Rte. 16, then West Side Road to Hale's Location. The views back across the valley toward Cranmore are unmatched. Call: 356-7100 or (800) 533-6301.

The Eastern Slope Inn Resort in the heart of North Conway is a palatial New England Inn. This establishment has a bit of everything needed in a hotel. Rooms, suites and town-houses in winter range from $86 to $200 a night per room. Call 356-6321 or (800) 258-4708.

The Eagle Mountain Resort, Jackson; 383-9111; for reservations, (800) 777-1700, is one of those lovingly restored classic 19th-century resort hotels; weekend, $95-$140; slightly lower midweek. Children 17 and under free, sleeping in existing beds; additional adults, $15 per person daily. MAP available.

The Wentworth Resort Hotel, Jackson Village; 383-9700 or (800) 637-0013, is a grand old hotel in the elegant tradition. Rooms are spacious, furnished with antiques and equipped with period baths. Room rates in the hotel range from $95 to $130 a night. Ask about the three- and five-day midweek cross-country packages that include lodging, breakfast and dinner.

The Christmas Farm Inn, Jackson Village; 383-4313, is a cluster of buildings around the main inn, each as quaint as the next. The main inn has 10 rooms, and the other buildings house larger rooms and small apartments. This is as convenient as you can find for the Jackson Ski Touring trails. All rates include breakfast and dinner. A 15 percent service charge and taxes will be added to your bill. Double-occupancy room rates vary from about $135 to $180, depending on location.

The Wildcat Inn and Tavern, Jackson Village NH; 383-4245, was built a hundred years ago, was once the original Carroll Reed Ski Shop, is now old-shoe comfortable and delightful. Right across the street are the Jackson Touring Foundation and Jack Frost Ski Shop. Rates per room, double occupancy: $64-$84. Numerous multiday packages available.

Eastern Inns, North Conway, 356-5447 or (800) 628-3750, is a very handy family-oriented motel at the northern end of North Conway Village with an enormous parking lot, fireplace in the lobby, heated swimming pool, video game room, and sauna. Room rates range from $58 to $120.

For smaller, cozier bed-and-breakfast establishments, **The Buttonwood Inn**, North Conway; 356-2625, is tucked in the woods with cross-country skiing from the back door, or any door for that matter. Room rates are in the $45-$90 range.

The Eastman Inn, just south of the North Conway village on the main road, is a B&B with 14 rooms in one of the oldest houses in town, newly restored with antique charm. Rates per room are $60-$80. Breakfast with waffle irons practically at your table is superb. Call 356-6707 or (800) 626-5855.

The Cabernet Inn is a charming 1842 Victorian cottage that now is a nine-bedroom B&B. Each room has a private bath, and the inn has a Finnish sauna and full country breakfast. Located on Route 16 just north of Conway Village the midweek rates are $89-$119. Call 356-4704 or (800) 866-4704.

The Scottish Lion is on the main drag in North Conway; 356-6381. Bed-and-breakfast rates: $65-$75 per couple per room. Cross-country is right out the back door.

Ellis River House in Jackson, 383-9339 or (800) 233-8309, overlooks the Ellis River, has 20 rooms, some with whirlpool tubs and/or fireplaces, and also has some of Jackson's most popular touring outside the door. Rates: $89-$199.

Riverside Country Inn has been called the most romantic of the country inns. It has seven rooms and doesn't mind kids or dogs. It's on Route 16A in Intervale; 356-9060. Rates: $45-$95.

For larger resort lodges, try the **Best Western Fox Ridge** in North Conway; 356-3151 or (800) 343-1804. This hotel is a rambling, low, motel-like building overlooking the town and the White Mountains. It has a giant pool. The rooms are perfect for children, with lofts and separate bunk rooms available. Rates: $95-$140 per room.

Red Jacket, 356-5411 or (800) 752-2538 (R-JACKET), seems to be almost identical to Fox Ridge, except for the room locations. Rates: $88-$148.

For slopeside condos, **Mt. Cranmore Condominiums** is right at the base and room rental includes guest privileges at the Cranmore Recreation Center (see Other Activities). Representative winter rates are: two bedrooms and loft $175 weekday, $225 weekend, $1,025 per week (based on four people per unit); three bedrooms, and loft $255 weekday, $350 weekend, $1,625 weekly (based on eight). Call: 356-6851 or (800) 543-9206; in New England, (800) 786-6754 (SUN N SKI).

Attitash Mountain Village has a generous mix of amenities, including an indoor pool, hot tubs, sauna, a pond for skating, restaurant and lounge. Sample rates from a wide selection: one-bedroom unit sleeping 6-8, $119 midweek, $179 weekend; three-bedroom unit sleeping 10-14, $219 midweek, $309 weekend. Call 374-6500 or (800) 862-1600.

To be really close to Mt. Washington, and for a head start if you're climbing, skiing, or using its cross-country trails, there's the **Joe Dodge Lodge** at Pinkham Notch, run by the Appalachian Mountain Club, with room for 106. The two-, three- and four-bunk rooms are simple, and rates include either one or two meals. Lodging and breakfast on a weekend, for example, are about $35. The public room has a fireplace, board games, and a well-used piano. Write: Reservations, Pinkham Notch Camp, Box 298-FG, Gorham NH 03581.

Dining

Mt. Washington Valley is home to some of the best restaurants in the nation. Competition between restaurants is so intense that locals refer to these battles as the War of the Chefs.

The Bernerhof, 383-4414, has its own nationally famous cooking school and serves some of the best gourmet meals in the country, let alone the valley.

In Jackson, **The Christmas Farm Inn** (383-4313), **The Inn at Thorn Hill** (383-4242), **Wentworth Resort Hotel** (383-9700), and **Wildcat Inn and Tavern** (383-4245), as well as **Stonehurst** (356-3271) and **The 1785 Inn** in North Conway (356-9025) are all major "War of the Chefs" combatants.

For more down-to-earth meals, try the **Scottish Lion** or the **Red Parka** for great barbecued spare ribs (no reservations; expect up to a two-hour wait on Saturday nights). **Bellini's** and **Merlino's** are best for Italian food, **Horsefeathers** in North Conway for basic American and the **Shannon Door Pub** for Irish entertainment and pizzas.

The best pizza is probably found at **Elvio's** on Main Street. **Peaches** on Main Street has a good breakfast. Other recommended breakfast spots: **The Big Pickle** and **Sugar House Eatery,** both in North Conway.

The **Appalachian Mountain Club** (466-2721) at the base of Mt. Washington in Pinkham Notch gets rave reviews for a slightly different dining experience. Meals are served family-style—a great way to meet some new friends. Wednesdays are International Dinner Series, featuring a different country's cuisine and a slide show and talk from area residents who have traveled abroad. Available spots fill up days in advance, perhaps partly because of the price: $10 for adults, $5 for children 12 and younger.

Another combination of dinner and entertainment is at **Mystery Café** (800-752-2538) at the Red Jacket Inn in North Conway. Diners can eat, drink and be Perry (Mason, that is) for a comedic murder-mystery dinner show.

Après-ski/nightlife

One of the best ski bars in the country is the **Red Parka**, which offers lively immediate après-ski and then into the wee hours. Something is happening every night, and its informality is clearly evident by the beers served in Mason jars and the signs, license plates, and vintage skis plastered over the walls. On nights when there is no live music, live comedy or a movie is featured. (Live comedy may be Bucky Lewis, a piece of live ammunition with guitar or microphone.) **Barnaby's Restaurant** in its new dance club, Club Picasso, has live music daily until 1 a.m. and is normally packed with a just-over-21 crowd and loud rock music. The place to be in Jackson is the **Wildcat Tavern** where folk rock is served up on weekends. On Friday and Saturday nights, **Horsefeathers** at North Conway hops, and the **Up Country Saloon** has live dance music. Locals hang out in **Hooligans** and **Horsefeathers** in North Conway.

Child care

Prices for child care range from $15 to $30 per day; call for more information. Children's instruction programs start at age 4 or 5 at these areas (call for specifics). Prices are listed in the Ski School section.

Attitash has the Attitots nursery that accepts children from 6 months to 5 years. A snow-play program for ages 1-3 is designed to introduce children to skiing. Reservations recommended: 374-2368.

Wildcat's Kitten Club nursery has child care for 18 months to 12 years (younger with advance notice).

Cranmore has a nursery for children of walking age or older, with lunch and snacks.

Black Mountain also has nursery facilities for infants 6 months or older. Facilities are limited, so reservations are suggested.

Other activities

Shopping: Probably the best at any ski area in the nation because of more than 150 factory outlets and New Hampshire's sales-taxless status. The area also has many unusual boutiques with creative gift items. Stop by the chamber of commerce in North Conway and pick up a shopping guide; there are far too many stores to list here.

The **Mt. Cranmore Sports & Fitness Center,** (800) 786-6754 (SUN-N-SKI) at Cranmore base, is a huge all-season facility, with indoor and outdoor tennis courts, pool, aerobics classes, steamroom and sauna. It is also home to the largest (30 x 40 feet) indoor climbing wall in the Northeast. Classes are available through International Mountain Climbing School (356-6316).

Eastern Mountain Sports in The Eastern Slope Inn also has a range of winter climbing and hiking programs, including ice-climbing instruction, ascents of Mt. Washington, and traverses of the Presidential Range; 356-5543.

The Appalachian Mountain Club has a very active, wide-ranging winter schedule of courses and workshops on ski touring, snowshoeing, avalanches, and much more. Their maps and guidebooks to these mountains are an unrivaled gold mine of indispensable information. Headquarters in the area is at Pinkham Notch, almost across the road from Wildcat. Write: AMC Pinkham Notch Camp, Box 289, Gorham NH 03581 (466-2721).

Take a sleigh ride in the valley. Try **Nestlenook's horse-drawn sleigh** (383-0845). **Ice skating rinks** are in Jackson, North Conway and Conway, and at several resorts. King Pine ski area has **dog sled rides.**

Getting there and getting around

Getting there: The Mt. Washington Valley is about 130 miles north of Boston. The closest airports are Portland, Maine, with major airline service from all over the country and Pease Airport in Portsmouth, NH, served by Business Express and Delta Connection. Each is about a 90-minute drive from North Conway. Manchester Airport, further south in New Hampshire, is served by US Air, United and Business Express, and is about a two-hour drive.

The best route from Boston is up Interstate 95 to Route 16, then north on 16/302. An alternate route is to come north on I-93 and take Route 104 to Route 25 to Route 16, and on to North Conway. From Portland, follow 302.

North Conway is notorious for its weekend traffic jams going through town. Most visitors approach from the southern side, and most of the ski areas are on the northern side. It can take an hour to get through town. Try to drive during minimal traffic—at night or midday.

Getting around: Bring a car. Though shuttle transportation has been tested and promised, you can't count on it. At night there is no alternative to having an automobile.

Information/reservations

The **Mt. Washington Valley Chamber of Commerce** can make reservations at local hotels and inns. Call: (800) 367-3364.

Attitash Travel and Lodging Bureau: 374-2368 or (800) 223-7669 (SNOW).

Wildcat reservations: 466-3326 or (800) 255-6439.

Cranmore Ski and Stay: 356-5543 or (800) 543-9206.

Black Mountain information: 383-4490.

King Pine/Purity Spring Resort: 367-8896 or (800) 367-8897.

Jackson Lodging Bureau: (800) 866-3334.

Local telephone area code is 603.

Ski 93
New Hampshire
Waterville Valley, Loon,
Cannon, Bretton Woods

Waterville Valley, Loon Mountain, Cannon Mountain and Bretton Woods are all within 30 to 45 minutes of one another, accessible via Interstate 93—hence their group marketing umbrella, Ski 93. Waterville is the most self-contained, while Loon has almost too much condo development. Cannon is the most historic and untamed area; and Bretton Woods is tame but elegant.

You can ski them all with a five-day midweek lift ticket called the Family Pass, interchangeable at most of the New Hampshire resorts. It allows skiing at 16 resorts, guaranteeing that a skier will never have to ski the same trail twice in one week or even two. The cost is $159 for adults, and free for one child skiing with a paying adult. (Additional child passes are $80.) You can buy the pass on any midweek day; it is then valid for five consecutive midweek days. Blackout periods are Dec. 27-31 and Feb. 20-24.

Waterville Valley

Waterville Valley is one of the best known mountains in New England, largely because of the publicity from staging more than 30 World Cup ski races in the past quarter century. (Ski area creator Tom Corcoran finished fourth in the 1960 Olympic giant slalom.) Though the area is well suited for racing, it isn't what we would want for an entire week of skiing. For an extended weekend, though, it can be a lot of fun. Waterville Valley is sufficiently self-contained that most visitors, once they enter, do not venture any farther than the slopes, just a short shuttlebus ride away. There are a lot of other things to do, too, such as cross-country skiing, shopping and a huge sports complex, with indoor and outdoor swimming pools, tennis, squash and racquetball courts, and indoor track. There is also an indoor skating rink.

Look for changes this year, the ski area has just been purchased by the owners of Killington and Sugarloaf. In the past, one of Waterville Valley's main efforts has been in the area of family skiing. These efforts continue. Facilities for children, such as the sports center with children's pool, the skating rink, video arcade, affordable children's menus, and sleighrides all are important ingredients when young children are considered. When combined with its renowned ski school and the compact village, this resort shines for kids and families.

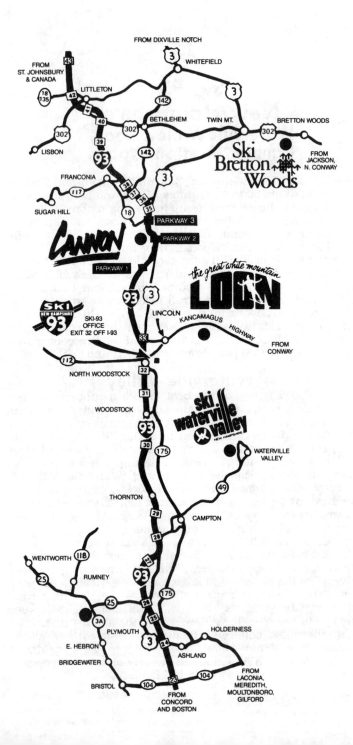

```
┌─────────────────────────────────────────────────────────┐
│                  Waterville Valley Facts                  │
│  Base elevation: 1,984'; Summit elevation: 4,004' Vertical drop: 2,020 feet. │
│    Number and types of lifts: 13—1 quad superchair, 3 triple chairs │
│                   5 double chairs, 4 surface lifts        │
│      Acreage: 255 skiable acres Percent snowmaking: 96 percent │
│      Uphill capacity: 15,660 skiers per hour  Bed base: 6,500 │
└─────────────────────────────────────────────────────────┘
```

Where to ski

Skiing is solid intermediate. These trails were cut more recently than the Front Four at Stowe or the trails down Cannon, so they are not New England's typical steep and narrow—there's elbow room and a chance to check out the slope before committing to the fall line again.

The Valley Run is a beginner/lower intermediate heaven with enough width to allow skiing for a couple of days down different sections. Beginners have a small area with a separate chair lift. One of the toughest runs, True Grit, develops major moguls and drops down the Sunnyside face. Two former tough mogul runs, Ciao and Gema, now are groomed daily. The trails such as White Caps, Sel's Choice, Old Tecumseh and Tippecanoe are intermediate and advanced playthings.

Snowboarding

Snowboarders have a large park, the Boneyard, on the Lower Periphery trail (to the right of the trail map). It features terrain and objects for sliding, bonking and the other things freestyle boarders enjoy. New Hampshire law requires snowboarders to have a board leash or strap.

Cross-country

Waterville has 105 km. of trails, 70 of which are groomed and tracked for skating as well as traditional skiing through the White Mountain National Forest.

Rentals and lessons are available. Trail fees: weekends, $11 for adults, $8 for children 12 and under; midweek, $8 and $5. Reduced prices are in effect for multiday fees, with the fifth day free. A one-day beginner package, including pass, lessons and equipment, costs $28 for adults, $21 for children.

Ski school (93/94 prices)

Regular one-and-a-half-hour **group lessons** cost $20 per session. **Private instruction** costs $49 an hour for one skier, $79 for two to five skiers. Vacation option packages, including three full days of lessons (two sessions per midweek day), cost $59; five full days (two sessions per midweek day) of lessons cost $85.

For **children,** the SKIwee program costs $55 a day for ages 3 to 5, including lunch; and $60 a day for Mountain Scouts and Mountain Cadets, including lunch.

Lift tickets (93/94 prices)

	Adult	Child (6-12)
One day	$39	$24
Three days	$110 ($36.66/day)	$66 ($22/day)
Five days	$159 ($31.80/day)	$80 ($16/day)

Teen (13-19) and college student (ID required) prices are $34 for one-day, $96 for three days, $159 for five days. The one- and three-day prices are for weekends; midweek prices are about $5 per day lower across the age board. The five-day price is for a midweek New Hampshire Family Pass. A child can ski free during non-holiday periods with any parent buying a two-day or more lift-and-lodging package. Kids 5 and younger ski free anytime.

Child care (93/94 prices)

Two nurseries, one at the base area and another in the resort village, are available for children from 6 weeks to 4 years. Rates are $38 a day on weekends and $32 a day midweek. Two days cost $60 weekends and $48 weekdays; three days cost $86 on weekends and $68 midweek; five days, $128 weekends and $99 midweek. Rates are slightly higher for children younger than 2. Nursery care is free for skiers who purchase five-day lift-and-lodging packages. Space is guaranteed only with a reservation. Call 236-8311, Ext. 3196 or 3197.

Loon Mountain

This resort seemingly grew out of nowhere in the late 1970s but become a behemoth—at least in lodging. This is one of the few resorts where the bed base is almost double the lift capacity, which created crowded conditions at times. Fortunately, Loon Mountain and the U.S. Forest Service last March signed an expansion permit that will pave the way for new lifts, snowmaking and trails to be phased in during the next few years, ending a decade-long planning and discussion period.

Loon is a wonderful ski area and has some of the most convenient accommodations to be found in New Hampshire. The area limits lift ticket sales to keep the mountain experience positive. With the addition of a gondola several seasons back, the sold-out signs quit coming out every weekend; now, it's about seven days per season, with perhaps ten near-sellout days. The area's Unconditional Conditions Guarantee™ ensures you'll like the ski conditions or you'll ski free on your next visit.

Loon Mountain Facts

Base elevation: 950'; Summit elevation: 3,050'; Vertical drop: 2,100 feet.
Number and types of lifts: 9—1 gondola, 2 triple chairs, 5 double chairs,
1 surface lift Acreage: 234 trail acres Percent snowmaking: 85 percent
Uphill capacity: 10,200 skiers per hour Bed base: 13,000

Where to ski

The intermediate runs are good and solid, with no expert surprises around the next clump of trees. Advanced North Peak runs are challenging and well removed from lower intermediate traffic. The steeps are there, but half the bumps are groomed out.

The upper trails are a bit twisted, narrow and seemingly undirected at the summit, but they open onto a series of wide intermediate pistes. A favorite is Flying Fox, a delightful cruise. Depending on snow conditions, skiers can link up with the West Basin via Upper Speakeasy, or they can drop down to the parking lot and take the 100-yard-long steam train ride to the adjacent base area. The West Basin area has another collection of intermediate trails.

The central portion of the mountain, serviced by the Seven Brothers triple chair, offers good intermediate-marked trails that advanced beginners can handle.

Beginners have their own area to the right of the West Basin served by the Kissin' Cousin double chair.

Though this could change once Loon's expansion is complete, there isn't enough now to keep a good skier busy for more than three days. However, the proximity of skiing at Bretton Woods, Cannon and Waterville Valley solves this problem.

Snowboarding

Snowboarding is allowed on the entire mountain, and last year the area added a halfpipe. Lessons and rentals are also available. New Hampshire law requires snowboarders to have some sort of leash or strap tethering the board to their leg.

Cross-country

The Loon Mountain Cross Country Center has 35 km. of groomed and tracked trails 745-8111, Ext. 5568. Children 5 and younger and seniors 70 and older ski free on Loon's cross-country trails.

Ski school (94/95 prices)

Loon's Ski School offers **group lessons** in one-and-a-half-hour chunks for $23. Five sessions, $100.

Children 3 to 8 are enrolled in the SKIwee program. There is also a Mountain Explorers class for ages 9 to 12, which includes lunch. This program groups children by ability level. Price is $60 a day.

A **beginner special** for both skiers and snowboarders that includes equipment, one lesson and a limited lift ticket costs $40 per day. Enroll at either rental shop.

The **Hard Core Ski Week** is reserved for skiers with truly advanced skills who want to fine-tune their tactics on all terrain and in all conditions. The five-day midweek program includes five hours of coaching each day, and is scheduled for various weeks throughout the season. Cost is $250.

Private lessons are $55 an hour; $80 for one-and-a-half hours.

Lift tickets (94/95 prices)

	Adult	Child (6-12)
One day	$41	$27
Three days	$105 ($36.66/day)	$70 ($23.33/day)
Five days	$159 ($31.80/day)	$80 ($16/day)

Ticket sales are cut off after approximately 6,000 have been sold. Unfortunately, Loon no longer is using Ticketmaster to sell advance-purchase tickets. If you are serious about weekend tickets, you'll need to buy the tickets the night before you ski, or plan to arrive early.

Skiers aged 65-69 and 13-19 can ski for $29 midweek, non-holiday, but ski for adult prices on weekends. Loon has a popular Saturday/Sunday ticket for $75 for adults, $48 for children, and midweek discounts and other multiday rates are available. Children 5 and younger and 70 and older ski free.

The five-day price is for the New Hampshire Family Pass.

Child care (94/95 prices)

The new Honeybear Nursery is located in the Mountain Club and welcomes kids 6 weeks to 6 years from 8:30 a.m. to 4 p.m. Reservations are required (745-8111). Rates are as follows: half day, $30; one day, $40; each additional day is $35.

Cannon Mountain

Cannon Mountain is state-owned and has long been known by experts as one of the most challenging mountains in the East. It has a 2,146-foot vertical served by an 80-passenger tram. When skiing here you see no signs of civilization except for the ski lodge and lifts. Though once known as a mountain where grooming consisted of shoveling some snow under the lifts, Cannon now takes mountain preparation to heart. Of Cannon's 150 acres, 95 percent are covered by snowmaking. The trails are narrower in legend than they are in reality and the mountain can actually be skied by most intermediate skiers. This is a place for advanced skiers to play and intermediates to push themselves.

Cannon Mountain Facts
Base elevation: *2,000';* **Summit elevation:** *4,146';* **Vertical drop:** *2,146 feet*
Number and types of lifts: *6—1 aerial tram, 1 quad chair, 1 triple chair,*
2 double chairs, 1 surface lift
Acreage: *150 trail acres* **Percent snowmaking:** *95 percent*
Uphill capacity: *6,000 skiers per hour* **Bed base:** *13,000 nearby*

A relatively new fixed-grip quad services the summit and exposes the skier to beautiful scenic vistas of the White Mountain National Forest. The Profile Trail presents the advanced intermediate with a well-groomed, 2,400-foot thrill. The Upper Cannon, Tramway and Vista Way are all intermediate trails that are challenging but certainly negotiable, the steepest being Upper Cannon which offers New England-style steeps. Once down those trails, long, wide cruisers take you to the base.

The Front Five, as known to locals, are the intimidating trails seen from the highway. Three of them, Avalanche, Paulie's Folly and Zoomer, are marked black diamond and rightfully so, especially for Zoomer's bumps. The other two, Rocket and Gary's, have less pitch without the bumps.

Lift tickets (93/94 prices)

	Adult	Junior (6-12) Senior (65+)
One day	$36	$26
Two days	$62 ($31/day)	$45 ($22.50/day)
Three days	$85 ($28.66/day)	$62 ($20.66)

These are weekend prices; midweek discounts are available.

Bretton Woods

Bretton Woods has been linked with the grand old Mount Washington Hotel and international monetary meetings more than skiing, which is relatively new at the resort. The skiing is mild and good for cruising. The resort also has a halfpipe for snowboarders. This mountain, like Waterville, is perfect for families and make special efforts to ensure great family vacations.

Downhill variety is mixed with one of the best cross-country networks (outside of Jackson and Stowe) in New England, boasting 90 km. of prepared trails past dozens of country inns. The Nordic area is centered on the grounds of the Mount Washington Hotel, which provides a spectacular setting.

A beginner special costs $30 including trail pass, lessons and equipment; children 5 and younger ski free and seniors 70+ ski free on non-holiday midweek days. Bretton Woods' nursery takes children aged 2 months to 5 years, $20 a half day and $30 a full day including lunch.

Bretton Woods
Base elevation: 1,600'; Summit elevation: 3,100'; Vertical drop: 1,500 feet
Number and types of lifts: 5–1 quad superchair, 1 triple chair,
2 double chairs, 1 surface lift
Acreage: 175 trail acres Percent snowmaking: 98 percent
Uphill capacity: 7,300 skiers per hour Bed base: 3,000+

Lift tickets (94/95 prices)

	Adult	Junior (6-15)
One day	$35	$22
Two days	$65 ($32.50/day)	$41 ($20.50/day)
Three days	$86 ($28.66/day)	$*

These are weekend prices; Bretton Woods has lower rates for midweek, and even lower rates for men, women and two-skiers-for-one on certain days.

*Juniors pay $41 plus their age for a three-day ticket.

Ski 93 area accommodations

At the resorts

Waterville Valley: The **Golden Eagle Lodge** with 139 condominium suites features a distinctive design reminiscent of the turn-of-the-century grand hotels at the White Mountain resorts.

Additionally, Waterville has three hotel properties and four groups of condominiums all located in the valley. **The Snowy Owl** is perhaps the most charming and something of a modern country inn with breakfast. The **Black Bear Lodge** is slightly larger and more hotel-like, and the **Valley Inn and Tavern** operates as a country inn with rates that can include meals. All are in the same price range with weekend packages offering two nights lodging and lift tickets for $129 (per person, double occupancy) and five-day packages, including the Family Pass interchangeable ticket, for $309, per person, double occupancy. On stays of two nights or more (non-holiday) at the Golden Eagle Lodges or Black Bear Lodge, kids stay and ski free.

Prices include entrance to the sports center and shuttle service. **Condominiums** are available and include access to the sports center.

Loon Mountain: The Mountain Club on Loon; (800) 229-7829 or (603) 745-8111. This ski-in/ski-out property has everything under one roof—from parking to swimming pool, fitness club to restaurants. One problem: many of its rooms have a double Murphy bed with two small day beds along the windows. This arrangement is fine for couples, or for a family with young children, but it is awkward for two unrelated adults who don't want to sleep in the same bed. Package prices start at $79 per person, double occupancy.

Loon also has condominiums. Make reservations through the Mountain Club.

Bretton Woods: The premier property here is the restored 1896 **Bretton Arms Country Inn,** which is a National Historic Landmark adjacent to the cross-country area and has been called one of the most elegant and romantic inns in the state.

Rates are about $115 per night. The **Bretton Woods Motor Inn** features less expensive accommodations between the downhill and cross-country areas. Bretton Woods also has a grouping of **townhouses.** All Bretton Woods properties can be reached through (800) 258-0330 or 278-1000. In winter the ski area provides shuttlebuses to and from the slopes.

In the region

Three motelish properties along Route 3 in Lincoln only minutes from Loon and Cannon join for advertising and offer similar accommodation with identical prices for the most part. Each offers slightly different amenities. **Indian Head Motel Resort** off I-93, Exit 33 on Route 3 in Lincoln; (800-343-8000, 745-8000). This is one of the centers of après-ski action with live bands and a great ice-skating pond and attached cross-country trails. Room rates start at $89. **The Beacon,** (800-258-8934, 745-8118) on the same road as Indian Head, also offers indoor tennis and the large indoor pools. Rates per person, double occupancy: $55, which includes lifts midweek and $60 per night with a two-night minimum and no lift ticket on weekends. **Woodward's Motor Inn** (800-635-8968, 745-8141) is the most family oriented. It has the area's only racquetball court and the best steaks in the region.

Just north of Franconia Notch and Cannon Mountain you'll find the **Red Coach Inn** (800-262-2493 (COACH-93), 823-7422) a modern hotel built behind a gabled cedar façade, a snowball's throw from the unspoiled New England town of Franconia (careful on the speed limit in this town). There is a large indoor pool and exercise room. Resorts most accessible from this hotel are Bretton Woods and Cannon, with Loon only a few minutes down I-93. Room rates are $70-$100.

The Woodstock Inn B&B (800-321-3985, 745-3951) A typical quaint New England lodge, the main building of which is more than 100 years old with no two rooms alike. You'll find rooms in three well-seasoned buildings; tucked under the rafters; some with private bath, some shared bath; all with casual charm. The restaurant in the front of the inn is one of Woodstock's most elegant and the one in the station at the rear is one of the town's most lively. You'll be right in the middle of the action for food and entertainment. Rates per couple with breakfast: $55-$135. A Jacuzzi room, with tub at the foot of your bed, is a bit more.

Amber Lights Inn (726-4077) between Loon and Waterville has five relatively small rooms (four with shared bath) with big hospitality. Carola prides herself on providing one of the area's breakfast experiences with secret egg and cheese creations, homemade muffins and breads slathered with home-preserved jellies and jams. Children younger than 7 are discouraged. Room rates are $45-$60 with a continental breakfast and $55-$70 with the full breakfast. (Go for the full breakfast.)

Wilderness Inn B&B (745-3890) is run by the Yarnells, a couple with small children, who makes other families with youngsters welcome in their house. Parents note: this place has laundry facilities! The B&B is only steps from the center of Woodstock, filled with shops and restaurants.

The Inn at Forest Hills (823-9550; fax 823-5555) is a newly restored English Tudor-style B&B built into a house which was once part of the grand Forest Hills Hotel. It provides a great New England tradition with fine breakfasts just about a mile from the village of Franconia on Route 142 heading towards Bethlehem. Room rates start at $60, double occupancy.

The Mulburn Inn (869-3389) is another B&B in a great Tudor-style setting with oak staircase and stained glass windows. Located in Bethlehem, once considered one of the fresh-air centers of New England, this home provides hospitality in the midst of a tiny New Hampshire town at the northern edge of Ski 93 only about 10 minutes from Bretton Woods. Rooms are in the $60-$90 range.

Dining

The most elegant dining experiences in the southern Ski 93 region can be found at the **William Tell** (726-3618) on Route 49 just outside Waterville Valley or at the **Woodstock Inn's Clement Room** (745-3951). The William Tell has a strong Swiss-German accent with excellent wines. The Clement Room is more eclectic with meals ranging from Jamaican Chicken to Veal Oscar. Both restaurants feature entrées in the $12-$19 range. The Woodstock Inn also serves great daily breakfasts as well as a fabulous weekend brunch; the William Tell is also known for its weekend brunch. For equally adventurous gourmet cuisine at the Bretton Woods end of Ski 93 try the **Bretton Arms Restaurant** (278-3000) in an elegant century-old atmosphere.

At Loon Mountain, try **Rachael's** (745-8111) or **The Granite Grille,** both at the Mountain Club. **The Common Man** (745-3463) offers good basic American dining with a roaring fireplace and rustic surroundings. For the place many locals claim have the best steaks, head to the **Open Hearth Steak House** at Woodward's Motor Inn. **Gordi's Fish and Steak House** (745-6635) is family-oriented and features Maine lobster and steaks. The **Tavern at the Mill** (745-3603) is set in a modernesque barn-like building, which is also one of the nightlife centers just outside Loon. **Truant's Tavern** (745-2239) serves clever dinner entrées in a mock schoolhouse atmosphere—drinking in class was never so much fun. The bar hops on weekends. **Woodstock Station** (745-3951), built in an old train station on Main Street, offers a creative menu of reasonable meals from meatloaf to Mexican. **The Tavern Sports Bar** in the Millfront Marketplace is the spot for pizza (Pizzeria Uno), large-screen TV, pool tables and beer. **The Eagle Cliff Restaurant** in Lincoln (745-8742) serves great pizza or Italian food for sit-down or take-out.

In Waterville Valley village the dining is headed by **Brookside Bistro** (236-4309) at Town Square serving Northern Italian and American meals. On the other side of the Town Square is the **Common Man** with its American menu. Or head to **Chili Peppers** which has the area's best Mexican food. For pizza call **Alpine Pizza** at 236-4173. **Valley Inn** also offers good dining.

At Bretton Woods the **Top o' the Quad Restaurant** serves casual American lunches and dinners Wednesday through Saturday with views of Mt. Washington's summit. Back down the mountain, try **Darby's Tavern** for hearty family dining, only a quarter-mile from the slopes. **Fabyans Station** is a good eatery in an old railroad station. In Franconia head to **Hillwinds**.

For breakfast head to **Jay's Sweetheart Diner, Pegs Place** or **The Country Mile** around North Woodstock. **Jasmann's Pastry Café and Bistro** in the Millfront Marketplace serves authentic New York bagels—with and without eggs—and gourmet coffee. Closer to Waterville try the **Spillway Café** in Campton on Route 49 or test out the Belgian waffles and pastries at the tiny **Coffee Emporium** in Town Square.

Après-ski/nightlife

At Loon after skiing head to the **Granite Bar in the Mountain Club** for good weekend entertainment and a decent, quiet après-ski spot. The **Paul Bunyan Lounge** at the Octagon base has a young, rowdy crowd for après-ski.

Waterville now has a collection of bars in Town Square, each with slightly different après-ski. They are all within a few steps of each other. **Legends 1291**, the **Common Man**, plus the **Brookside Bar and Bistro** all serve up a good time for après-ski, and later in the evening they stand in the same order, ranging from loud disco and rock to quieter moments. **Zoo Station** is an under-21 night club with dancing, video games and a juice bar. The **World Cup Bar and Grill** at the mountain has the normal collection of skiers for après-ski until 5:30 p.m.

Just down the road from Waterville on the way back to the interstate try the **William Tell** for a cozy quiet après-ski or the **Mad River Tavern** for a more raucous setting. Both have popular dinner menus.

The Woodstock area locals set up après-ski camp at **Truant's Tavern** and **Woodstock Station** in Woodstock. **Gordi's Fish and Steak** in Lincoln serves up great après-ski munchies. **Indian Head Resort** in Lincoln offers good après-ski. From Wednesday through Sunday, live bands rock the joint. The **Tavern Sports Bar** is a low-keyed darts, video game and pool hall. Downstairs the **Tavern at the Mill** has the area's best singles action with bands on weekends. **Donny G's** in the Millfront Marketplace has occasional bands as well.

Other activities

Shopping: Waterville Valley's Town Square has several specialty shops worth a look. Lincoln, home of Loon Mountain, has some factory outlet stores, including New England's only North Face outlet, where we picked up some incredible buys on skiwear. The factory outlet bonanza of North Conway is 30 miles east of Bretton Woods. No sales tax makes buying all the sweeter.

Waterville Valley has **sleigh rides** and an **indoor fitness center**. Cannon is the home of the **New England Ski Museum**, a collection of ski memorabilia well worth a brief visit. Though it's closed in winter, drive by **The Mount Washington Hotel & Resort** just east of the Bretton Woods ski area. Its architecture and setting against the towering Presidential Range make a spectacular scene, especially at sunset when the snow-covered mountains turn pink.

Getting there and getting around

Getting there: Boston's Logan Airport is 130 miles away from the Ski 93 areas. Manchester Airport, 70 miles south, is serviced by Delta's Business Express, USAir, and United. It's just over a two-hour drive from Logan and an hour from Manchester airport.

From Interstate 93 heading north, Waterville Valley is 11 miles up Route 49 at Exit 28. Loon Mountain is on the Kancamagus Highway (Route 112) at Exit 32 in Lincoln. Cannon is visible from I-93 just north of Franconia Notch State Park, and Bretton Woods is on Route 302: take Exit 35 to Route 3, which meets Route 302 at Twin Mountain.

Getting around: A car is a necessity unless you stay close to the slopes at one resort and just ski there.

Information/reservations

Ski 93 Central Reservations handles 80 properties in the region and can arrange airline tickets, car rental, lift tickets and ski rentals, (800) 937-5493 (WE-SKI-93); in NH call 745-2409.

Waterville Valley Lodging Bureau handles information and reservations: (800) 468-2553 (GO-VALLEY). Resort offices: 236-8311; ski reports: 236-4144.

Loon Mountain Lodging Bureau at (800) 229-7829 for slopeside lodging or (800) 227-4191 for area accommodation. Resort offices: 745-8111; snow phone: 745-8100.

Bretton Woods Lodging Bureau at (800) 258-0330 or 278-1000; snow phone: 278-5051.

Cannon snowphone: (800) 552-1234 or 823-7771.

Twin Mountain Lodging Bureau: (800) 245-8946 (TWIN).

New Hampshire telephone area code is 603.

Hunter Mountain & Ski Windham
New York

These are the two closest large ski areas to New York City, only a two and a half hours' drive north. These resorts are in the midst of the rugged and rocky Catskills—home to legends such as Rip Van Winkle and the headless horseman of Sleepy Hollow. As far as skiing goes, the area woke with a vengeance almost thirty years ago. Trails were dynamited and dozed through rugged mountains, and snowmaking became an integral part of Eastern ski resorts.

The villages surrounding the mountains reflect the personalities of the local resort. The Villages of Hunter and Tannersville are basic rough Adirondack towns with supermarkets, bars, pubs, hotels and homes. Windham has a manicured look to it with pretty houses, no bars, delis rather than supermarkets and country inns instead of hotels. On the slopes weekend crowds at Hunter reflect a rush-hour subway heritage. Windham skiers are far more sedate. At Hunter you may hear late-night beer-drinking songs and other sounds of merriment. In Windham the loudest midnight sound may be the snow guns, a passing car or water gurgling downstream.

Both Hunter Mountain and Ski Windham have the same amount of vertical and they are only ten miles apart. Hunter is by far the bigger operation—it is major league. It has become the snowmaking champion in the Northeast, shooting out mountains of snow and continually upgrading the system. Ski Windham offers good skiing but doesn't have the difficult terrain found at Hunter. Each area has a high-speed quad pumping skiers up the mountain keeping lines manageable.

Hunter Mountain Facts

Base elevation: 1,600'; *Summit elevation:* 3,200'; *Vertical drop:* 1,600 feet
Number of lifts: 15–1 quad superchair, 2 triple chairs, 8 double chairs, 4 surface lifts
Percent snowmaking: 100 percent *Uphill capacity:* 18,000 per hour

Ski Windham Facts

Base elevation: 1,500'; *Summit elevation:* 3,100'; *Vertical drop:* 1,600 feet
Number of lifts: 7–1 quad superchair, 4 triple chairs, 1 double chair, 1 surface lift
Percent snowmaking: 97 percent *Total acreage:* 220 skiable acres
Uphill capacity: 11,800 per hour

Hunter's skiing is primarily solid intermediate with an advanced flair. Its toughest runs drop off its summit in the East. Hunter One is a mellow beginner paradise.

Ski Windham has a strong intermediate flavor but without the twists and turns and changing scenery provided by Hunter. Its advanced trails are not as tough as Hunter's but will keep skiers happy for a few days and may be better for intermediates focused on technique.

Both resorts are packed on weekends. If you can find any way to come at midweek the skiing is less crowded and everything's a bigger bargain.

Snowboarding

Snowboarding is allowed on the entire mountain at both Hunter and Ski Windham. Windham has just doubled the size of its snowboard park. There are lessons including packages for never-evers, and Small Class Sessions that meet three times a day. Rentals are also available at the mountain.

Ski school (94/95 prices)

Hunter: The Ski with a Pro Free program offers several runs with a pro every day (weather permitting) except Christmas and New Year's at 11:45 a.m. at the top of Snowlite Express.

Hunter has **beginner packages** that include everything one needs to learn to ski or snowboard for $48.

Private lessons cost $55 per hour for one, with each additional skier paying $19. A two-hour private lesson costs $95. All-day (six hours) private lessons are $245 for one and $310 for two.

Children's ski school is open to children 5-12 and includes lifts, lessons, rentals, box lunch and supervision. Rates for the full day are $68; half day, $57. Open 9:30 a.m. to 3:30 p.m.

Pee Wee School is for those 3 and 4. It meets for morning and afternoon sessions for games on skis. Each costs $17, or take two for $28. Rentals and babysitting fee is not included.

Ski Windham: This resort has a full ski school program as well. **Private lessons** run $43 an hour for one person; $75 for two; $95 for three. **Group lessons** are $19 per 1 3/4-hour session, or $85 for a book of five sessions, $170 for a book of ten lessons. The resort also has a full range of **programs for children** 4 to 13.

Lift tickets (94/95 prices)

Hunter: Full-day weekend/holiday lift tickets cost $40 adult; $27 junior (12 and younger); two days cost $74/$52; five days are $173/$118; and ten days, $334/$224. These lift tickets are good anytime during this season.

Midweek non-holiday lift tickets cost is $34/22 for one day; $62/$42 for two days; $145/$95 for five days; and $280/$180 for ten days. There are special rates for Seniors (65 and older), teens (13-18) and students with valid college ID.

Ski Windham: A full-day ticket costs $37 adult/$32 junior (7-12) on weekends, and $30/$27 on weekdays. You can build your own ski week. The first day costs full price and each subsequent day can be purchased at a $2 discount.

On non-holiday weekdays, juniors ski free when accompanied by a paying adult (one child per adult). Children 6 and younger ski free anytime when accompanied by a ticketed adult.

Accommodations

Hunter pioneered a bed-and-breakfast program which now has about 30 country inns participating. These B&Bs have prices starting at about $25. The program includes lift tickets and combined with the Kids Ski Free program is a money-saver.

Ski Windham also has a reservation service with packages that include lifts, lodging and many discounts.

Hunter: call (800) 775-4641. My advice is to try and stay near the resorts. Even Palenville, considered nearby by reservation agents, is at the bottom of a steep grade. Though they are "nearby," they are not very convenient.

We recommend these in the Hunter area: The **Scribner Hollow Lodge** with several upscale suites is perhaps the most luxurious. **Villa Vosilla** and the **Deer Mountain Inn** round out the top three. The **Liftside Condos** are very well appointed and convenient. There is a collection of excellent B&Bs such as the **Kennedy House** and **Washington Irving Lodge** or head to the **Hunter Village Inn** for more of a party atmosphere.

In Windham, the ski area now owns the **Windham Arms Hotel** which offers country inn hospitality with regular shuttles to the ski area. Other accommodations within three miles of Ski Windham (call 800-729-SKIW for reservations and information) range from sprawling inns to B&Bs. **Antonio's Resort, Evergreen at The Thompson House, Christman's Windham House** and **Hotel Vienna** are good hotels in roughly descending order of luxury. B&Bs to try include **Albergo Allegria, Danske Hus** and **the Country Suite**. Rates start at $70 per double room per night weekends; $50 per room weeknights.

Dining

Scores of restaurants are in this region. Around Hunter the **Chateau Belleview** (589-5525) prepares fine continental cooking; **Swiss Chalet** has excellent cooking; and **Deer Mountain Inn** gets recommended by all the locals. For slightly less expensive fare try **P.J. Larkins** (589-5568), **Fireside** (263-4216), and **Pete's Place** (589-9840), all favorites with virtually everyone. Try the Crooked Cafe in Tannersville for breakfast.

Near Windham try **Brandywine** (734-3838) for well-prepared, affordable meals (Wednesday's pasta special is a real bargain) and **The Frog's House** (734-9817). These two spots got the nod from most locals. **Theo's** (734-4455) has tasty Greek food and **Thetford's** (734-3322) has great steaks and seafood.. **Captain's Quarters** (734-3055) is the place to head for fish. **Temptations** (734-3000) serves a '50s evening menu (tuna melt, grill cheese, BLTs and clubs) in a pink, purple and chrome period decor. **Vesuvio** (734-3663) reputedly has the best Italian food in the area. **Chalet Fondue** (734-4650) has the best German menu in town, but locals from both areas recommended a trip to **Marie's Dream House** in Westkill (989-6565) for Austrian/German cooking that is worth the 20-minute drive. The best burger is charcoal grilled at **Jimmy O'Connor's** (734-4270). Try **Seeley's** (734-9892) daily specials for good-food bargains.

For breakfast try **Kountry Kitchen** in Hensonville or to the **Four Stars** (734-4600) or **Starlight Cafe** (734-9862).

Child care

Hunter: The child-sitting program can handle about 50 children. This service is for children who have not yet begun to ski. It costs $25 for a full day (8:30 a.m. to 4 p.m.) or $4.50 per hour. A book of five days will cost $85. Lunch is not included. It can be purchased for $3 per day per child.

Ski Windham: The Children's Learning Center offers non-skiers and skiers a variety of activities, and for those who like to sprawl out on the floor when they draw or read, the floors are heated. Full-day/half-day programs: $44/$27 for non-skiers; $62/$40 for skiers without rentals; and $74/52 with rentals.

Getting there

The best access is up I-87 120 miles north of New York City. For Hunter Mountain, take Exit 20 at Saugerties and follow Rte. 32 to Rte. 32A then to the area. To reach Ski Windham turn north on Rte. 296 off of Rte. 23A or if coming on the New York Thruway, take Exit 21 in Catskill and go west on Rte. 23 for 25 miles.

Both resorts provide busses from the New York City area. Hunter's bus leaves Mondays, Wednesdays, Fridays and Saturdays. Call (800) 552-6262 for information. Ski Windham's bus leaves Monday, Wednesday and Sunday. Call (516) 360-0369 or (718) 343-4444.

At these resorts a car is virtually a must to get around at night to restaurants and nightlife.

Information/reservations

Hunter has a central reservation system which handles thousands of rooms in the region from B&Bs to modern motels and condominiums. Call (518) 263-4641 or (800) 775-4641.

For the Windham lodging service call (800) 729-SKIW.

Lake Placid/Whiteface
New York

As an area that would sit somewhere in the middle of the pack of northeast resorts based on its skiing alone, Lake Placid stands apart as a winter sports magnet. There's no doubt that the 1980 Winter Olympics were instrumental in establishing that reputation; nonetheless, plenty of past Olympic host sites have retreated into relative obscurity. At Lake Placid, the folks have taken the flame, so to speak, and run with it. To fulfill the promise of Lake Placid so evident during the Olympics, the Olympic Regional Development Authority (ORDA) was formed to operate the multi-facility recreational area.

Because probably more world-class winter sports athletes still train and compete here than anywhere else in the free world (more than 8,000 a year) Lake Placid still has something of the feel of an Olympic village. Groups of young athletes are everywhere, and there always seems to be one championship or another underway. Even the athletes themselves revel in watching the daring, if demented, souls who soar off the Olympic jumps.

Lake Placid urges you at every turn to *participate*. In addition to the bobsled run and one of the most extensive and well-prepared cross-country ski circuits anywhere, you can experience the luge run at the Mt. Van Hoevenberg Olympic sports complex about eight miles away (this was the site of the 1983 World Cup Luge Finals). For the uninitiated, bouncing off the walls of a luge track is not unlike being in a pinball game played by unseen Nordic giants, with you as the ball. You have to experience it at least once. Of course, no one in their right mind would *want* to experience firsthand the thrill of being launched off a 120-meter ski ramp, but you can get a breathtaking perspective on that madness by taking the glass elevator 26 stories to the top. The $6 ticket, thankfully, is round-trip.

Lake Placid Facts
Base elevation: 1,200'; **Summit elevation:** 4,416'; **Vertical drop:** 3,216 feet
Number and types of lifts: 10—2 triple chairs, 7 double chairs , 1 rope tow
Acreage: about 158 acres of terrain **Snowmaking:** 93 percent
Uphill capacity: 10,115 skiers per hour **Bed base:** 5,000

Back on Main Street, the town itself is dominated by the arena where the America watched its Cinderella hockey team enter the history books in 1980. Wonderfully situated on Mirror Lake, the town is full of charm, if standing just one standard motel away from being truly quaint. For a relaxing afternoon away from the slopes, take a dogsled ride across the lake for the sheer novelty of it. At night many visitors will find both relaxation and exercise on the Olympic Oval (where Eric Heiden won five gold medals), lulled into an easy rhythm by the sharp scrape of their skates in the crisp night air. My personal favorite, however, is the nighttime toboggan runs. As many as six of your entourage can ride clutching, and yes, yelping together as you shoot down the lighted ramp and spill suddenly out onto the darkness of frozen Mirror Lake with a giddy sense of both fear and elation. It's another one of those winter sports that had always *looked* or *sounded* like a lot of fun, but which you never quite got around to doing. Like so many other visitors, you'll find yourself running out of excuses at Lake Placid. "Come on," this area seems to beckon, "Just do it."

Where to ski

With the greatest vertical drop of any mountain in the East (3,216 feet), Whiteface Mountain has some of the most worthy expert runs this side of the Mississippi. There's also a Medusa's head of excellent advanced and advanced-intermediate runs snaking down the forested slopes of Little Whiteface (a shoulder of the same mountain), and nearly all the bottom third of the mountain is wide-open and gentle—good for advanced beginners.

Like many Eastern mountains, Whiteface stands unshielded, lording it over a vast valley of forests and frozen lakes. That makes for some of the most spectacular views in the world, but winter winds do seem to whip across that valley and climb up the walls of Whiteface with predictable regularity. For many veteran Eastern skiers, the complaint about Whiteface has been that it's too often wind-blown, cold and icy. Having been there three times now, I would say that from my own experience Whiteface is, well, frequently wind-blown, cold and icy. You can't fault any area for unpredictable weather, and on an ideal day Whiteface comes close to being as good as it gets in the East. The local officials have also made a good-faith effort at countering icy slopes with increased snowmaking.

Beginners on Whiteface have a secluded area—off to the right looking up from the base, above Kids Kampus—reserved in their honor. The wide-open runs down to the bottom from the mid-station are all suitable for lower intermediates, giving you a free run of half the mountain.

Intermediates should take the G-lift from the midstation up to the top of Little Whiteface. An observation platform just off to the left at the top of this double chair gives you an unparalleled view of the lakes and valley. Then try the snaking Excelsior run, which twists back down to the mid-station. You can cut the rounded corners of this baby like a bobsled, choosing your own pace. After that warmup, tackle Paron's Run from the tip-top of Whiteface (Lift F—Summit Triple). Before this run was added four years ago, intermediates had no way to enjoy either the awe-inspiring view or best-in-the-East vertical available from the top of the mountain. Advanced skiers should also not miss the Empire and MacKenzie runs from the top of Little Whiteface. They're officially black, but under good conditions manageable.

Experts will want to spend their time on Cloudspin and Skyward, the men's and women's downhill Olympic runs respectively, at the top of Whiteface. These are sweethearts with plenty of pitch and moguls even for the hotdogs. Most of the runs down from Little Whiteface are also black, and they all have good grade.

Mountain rating

Whiteface is one of those rare mountains that has more to offer experts and beginners, with less in the middle range for true intermediates. Experts will find much of the upper half of the mountain challenging, though anything below the mid-station is generally a wide-open cruise with very gentle grade. Beginners will thus find anything below midstation much to their liking. Intermediates will probably feel bored by most of the lower half of the mountain, and stretched by much of the upper. If you are ready to push yourself into the advanced stage, try Little Whiteface.

Cross-country

Here again, the folks at Lake Placid have built strongly on the foundation laid by the 1980 Winter Olympics, and the Mt. Van Hoevenberg complex offers cross-country skiing you are unlikely to find elsewhere—50 km. of marked trails that average 15 ft. wide, regularly groomed and patrolled; bridges built especially for cross-country skiers so you don't have to worry about traffic; snowmaking (5 km.), and emergency phones.

Within the 50-km. complex are ten specially marked loops offering three novice, six intermediate and one expert tour. Additional expert skiing is on the Porter Mountain racing loops. The start/finish stadium at the sports complex also features a ski shop, waxing room, a small snack bar and a warming room. Trail fees are $9 for adults, and $7 for juniors 12 and under, and seniors over 62. Children younger than 6 ski free.

Snowboarding

Snowboarding is permitted on all trails and lifts of the mountain. Complete ski school services are available to boarders, and rentals are found in the base area.

Ski school (93/94 prices)

The Whiteface Mountain Ski School staffs over 75 instructors, and is affiliated with the Professional Ski Instructors of America (PSIA). They will tailor instruction to your particular needs, ranging from race packages, ski weeks and individual lessons, to special programs for juniors and children.

Group lessons cost $18 for 90 minutes. Multiple lessons can be purchased at discounts with five lessons costing $65. Ski week packages begin with a wine-and-cheese party, and end with a race and party. Classes are limited to eight students.

Private lessons are $40 an hour, with $25 for one extra person (limit of two). A half-day private lesson costs $100 (three hours), with $50 for one extra person (limit of two).

Race programs are offered through the Whiteface Alpine Training Center, and operated through the New York Ski Educational Foundation (NYSEF). They include electronic timing, bibs and printed results. You have to book at least two weeks in advance, however, by calling the NYSEF at 946-7001. The resort also has a coin-operated race program.

Children's programs include the Play & Ski packages offered at the Kids Kampus (just to the right of the main lodge area). The supervised program for children 3-6 includes indoor and outdoor activities, with instruction and regular nursery services. There's an easy drop-off area with adjacent parking. Half-day programs are $20. A full-day program costs $40 (including lunch). Children 6 and younger who can already ski can ride free on Whiteface's three lower lifts (for more about the children's program, 946-2223).

Lift tickets (93/94 prices)

	Adult	Child (Up to 12) Senior (62+)
One day	$35	$20
Three days	$85 ($28.33/day)	$56 ($18.66/day)
Five days	$136 ($27.20/day)	$85 ($17/day)

These are weekends and holiday prices; midweek prices are about $7 per day lower for adults and $3 per day for kids and seniors.

Early season specials run until December 23, with adults paying $20 per day and juniors $14. In early March prices drop again, to $23 for adults and $15 for juniors.

Accommodations

Some of the larger hotels centered around the town of Lake Placid tend to be of the more modern, franchise variety. Not so, however, the singular **Mirror Lake Inn** (523-2544), a traditional lodge right on the lake shore, and probably the finest overnight in the area. (It's rated Four Diamond by AAA.) The quaint New England-style exterior continues inside with antiques, chandeliers and mahogany walls. The inn also offers such modern amenities as indoor pool, whirlpool, sauna, health spa, and game room. The two restaurants include one of the best in town, with candlelight dining overlooking the lake. Room rates range from $86-$306, the latter for a suite.

The **Holiday Inn Sunspree Resort** (523-2556 or 800-874-1980) in the center of Lake Placid is the largest hotel in town (209 rooms). It features great views over the lake, rooms with refrigerators and microwaves, a large indoor pool with two-story ceiling, a game room for kids and adjacent fitness center; and two restaurants, one of which becomes a nightclub on weekends. Rooms are in the $49 to $99 range; ask about ski packages.

The **Best Western Golden Arrow** (523-3353 or 800-582-5540) is on the lake with spectacular views and has indoor pool, Jacuzzi, as well as sauna, weight room, and racquetball courts. Room-with-view rates are as low as $60 midweek, and $118-$148 per room on weekends. Also boasting similar amenities is the **Lake Placid Hilton** (523-4411 or 800-755-5598), with two indoor pools and private balconies for each room with a view of the lake. The hotel's bed-and-breakfast package is quite popular, costing $86 for two, midweek. There is also a **Howard Johnson** (523-9555) in town.

The **Lake Placid Lodge** (523-2573, formerly Lake Placid Manor), is a classic Adirondack lodge with rustic rooms, fireplaces and exceptional French-American cuisine. The restaurant is open to the public.

Skiers on a budget should try the **Edge of the Lake Motor Inn** (523-9430), **Town House Motor Inn** (523-2532), **Alpine Air Motel** (523-2180), the **Econo Lodge** (523-2750), and the **Wildwood** on the Lake (523-2750), all of which have rooms for less than $100; some as low as $50.

The nearest RV park is KOA in Wilmington, NY.

Dining

Considered the best restaurant in the area, **Lake Placid Lodge** (523-2573, serves continental cuisine. Also upscale and excellent is the **Hungry Trout** (946-2217), specializing in, you guessed it, fish (entrées $12.95 and up). If your taste runs to the rich and continental, with plenty of sauces, try **Lindsay's at the Woodshed** (523-9470). This cozy, woodsy restaurant with its fireplace in the entrance alcove next to the bar offers excellent atmosphere and a central location. **The Charcoal Pit** (523-3050), open for about 30 years, charbroils lots of steaks and chops.

Solid German fare is available at slightly more moderate prices at the **Alpine Cellar** (523-2180). A full menu of schnitzels, sauerbraten and Rippchen (smoked pork) are available starting around $10.95 per entrée. **Villa Vespa** (523-9959) features authentic Italian fare in the same price category. A personal favorite is the **Artist's Café** (523-9493) which features a prime location overlooking Mirror Lake, as well as steak and fish at reasonable prices: after a chilled dog sled ride on the lake, take a break with a bowl of their excellent onion soup. And no skiing town is complete, of course, without an inexpensive Italian restaurant featuring pizza—**Mr. Mike's Pizza** (523-9770) takes care of that craving.

Après-ski/nightlife

Lake Placid is large enough to generate its own heat as a nightlife center, drawing not only the gypsy moths from the out-of-town vacationers, but also the local variety from the surrounding countryside. Because Whiteface lies separated from the town, however, most of the après-ski action is in the base lodge. **Steinhoff's** and **R.J. McDougall's**, just down the road from Whiteface are also good for an après-ski drink.

At night, the young and hot of foot head to **Mud Puddles**, on the side street next to the speed skating oval. High-tech disco gear is on full display around the dance floor. Most of the other nightlife action centers around the main hotels. **Cristy's** at the Holiday Inn features a large bar and even more generous dance floor, with music spun by a DJ (drink specials on Wednesday nights). **Roomers** at the Best Western also offers dancing to a DJ, or for a live band, try **Dancing Bears Lounge** at the Hilton.

Couples looking for a kinder, gentler nightspot should head for **The Cottage,** across the street from the Mirror Lake Inn. The fire's always going, and at sunset there's an excellent view of Mirror Lake and the surrounding mountains.

Child care

The Bunny Hutch gives children their own lodge and congregating area on the mountain, complete with a children's drop-off, adjacent parking for parents with children, a large nursery, children's rentals and an outdoor terrain garden.

The nursery is open daily for children aged 1 to 6, and the cost is $4 an hour per child, with lunch extra (supervisors can arrange for a variety of hot meals). Nursery service is offered daily 8 a.m.-4.30 p.m. If your child is ready for the slopes, you can enroll him or her in the Play & Ski programs, detailed in the Ski School section.

Other activities

Lake Placid is nothing *but* other activities. The **bobsled rides** at Mt. Van Hoevenberg Olympic Sports Complex are Tuesday through Sunday, 1-3 p.m., and cost $15 (including commemorative Olympic Bobsled Run pin).

Luge rides are offered on Saturdays and Sundays, 1 p.m.-3 p.m., and cost $10 (for more information on both, 523-4436).

Tours of the **Olympic Jumping Complex,** with chair lift and elevator ride, cost $5 for adults, $4 for children and seniors.

The **Olympic Speed Skating Oval** is open 7 p.m.-9 p. m. daily, and 1-3 p.m. on weekends (523-1655).

Operating hours for the **toboggan run** on Mirror Lake are Wednesday, 7-9 p.m.; Friday, 7-9 p.m.; Saturday, noon-4 p.m. and 7-9 p.m., and Sunday noon-4 p.m. The charge is $3 for adults, $2 for children, and $3 for the toboggan rental.

Getting there and getting around

Getting there: Commuter flights from several northeast cities serve Adirondack Airport, 16 miles away on Route 86 in Saranac Lake. Private planes can use Lake Placid Airport.

There's a local rail stop at Westport on the New York City to Montreal line, and then shuttlebus service for the 40-minute ride to Lake Placid (523-4431 for the bus). There are special Amtrak Ski Packages, including rail fare, hotel accommodations, lift tickets and all transfers.

Getting around: It's about a ten-mile drive to both Whiteface (downhill) and Mt. Hoevenberg (cross-country) from the center of Lake Placid. Though regularly scheduled buses exist, it's best to have a car.

From the south, take Exit 24 (Albany) off the New York State Thruway (Interstate 87). Take Northway (still I-87) to Exit 30, follow Route 9 north two miles to Route 73 and continue 28 miles to Lake Placid. From the west, take Interstate 90 (NY State Thruway) to Exit 36 (Syracuse) for Interstate 81. Follow I-81 north to Watertown, then east on Route 3 to Saranac Lake. Then take Route 86 east to Lake Placid.

Information/reservations

For reservations contact the **Lake Placid Commerce and Visitors Bureau,** Lake Placid NY 12946; (800) 447-5224 (44-PLACID) or 523-2445.

The Olympic Regional Development Authority, Olympic Center, Lake Placid NY 12946; 523-1655, 800-462-6236.

Local telephone area code is 518.

Jay Peak, Vermont

Some skiers believe that the farther north they venture, the better the skiing will be. Jay Peak, a mere eight miles from the Canadian border in Vermont, fits that sense of logic.

Ski Jay if you like adventure, spectacular scenery and an international flair. Ski somewhere else if you can't stand a long drive from big cities or you need to be pampered on the slopes.

Jay is a big mountain by Eastern standards, almost 4,000 feet high with a vertical drop of 2,150 feet and a cornucopia of skiing terrain. But, because it is a stand-alone mountain peak, Jay gets weather—all kinds and lots of snow; an average of more than 300 inches.

Jay Peak has Vermont's only tram, a 60-passenger vehicle that quickly whisks skiers from the base to the summit. If you are staying at the Hotel Jay, the tram is just outside your room.

Because of Jay's proximity to French-speaking Québec, 52 percent of its skiers hail from Canada and about half of those are French speaking. You definitely will hear a lot of French.

Jay Peak management encourages the Canadian business with special weeks such as Ontario Week, capped off with spectacular fireworks.

Where to ski

Jay has a low bed count; thus it is a day tripper's resort, with late-arriving crowds on weekends. Be smart and arrive early; try to catch the 8:30 a.m. tram to the summit. Enjoy the views of four states and Canada for a few moments (don't forget your camera) and head over to Stateside area on the blue Vermonter trail. At Stateside you can ski some of Jay's most popular trails without any congestion or lift lines. Lines do form at the tram when all the late arrivals queue up, but Jay's trails are seldom congested thanks to being spread out.

Jay Peak Facts
Base elevation: *1,815'; **Summit elevation:** 3,968'; **Vertical drop:** 2,153 feet*
Number and types of lifts: *6–1 tram, 1 quad chair, 1 triple chair,*
1 double chair, 2 surface lifts
Acreage: *About 325 trail acres* **Snowmaking:** *80 percent*
Uphill capacity: *7,200 per hour* **Bed base:** *800 at resort; another 800 nearby*

The most challenging trails at Jay are mostly here at Stateside and serviced by the Jet Triple chair. The Jet Trail is a black diamond popular with locals. If you need more challenge and spice in your life, try the U.N., a gnarly, narrow, steep son-of-a-gun with hostile moguls. Catch it with good snow and you'll smile all day; catch it with tough Eastern conditions and you'll head for the base lodge for a couple of shooters. Next to the U.N. is Haynes, a black diamond similar to the Jet, but with more terrain changes at the top and wider and a tad easier at the bottom. Two other blacks off the Jet triple are somewhat similar. Both Derrick Hot Shot and Kitzbühel are old-style narrow trails.

Skiers who want a more mellow descent should opt for the Montrealer connecting with Angel's Wiggle or the Northway. By now the latecomers will have formed a line at the Jet Triple and it's time to head to the Bonaventure chair for some great cruising on the Can Am. Or tackle the black-diamond River Quai under the tram into the milder Interstate to the tram base and perhaps a bite to eat, either upstairs in the International Restaurant, with European-style lunches, or the full-service cafeteria, pizza bar, barbecue on the deck, or Golden Eagle Lounge.

If your timing is right, the surge of early lunch skiers will have already ascended the tram and your wait should be short. Your best bet following lunch is to take the Northway to Ullr's Dream, an intermediate trail that becomes a nice glade area halfway down. An alternative is the more difficult Beaver Pond Glade. Don't be surprised at the scarcity of skiers on this flank.

Jay is proud of its tree-skiing opportunities and even posts bilingual warning signs that explain the dangers and rules of skiing in the woods. Management reports that few accidents occur and that the skiers love the ski-anywhere policy. Jay will add about 30 acres of gladed trails for the 94/95 season.

Mountain rating
Jay is a good choice for solid intermediate to advanced skiers, particularly with the woods skiing available. Though management shows 20 percent novice, 55 percent intermediate and 25 percent advanced, we feel that the mountain is a bit more difficult than these percentages suggest.

Snowboarding
Jay encourages snowboarding and was one of the first to offer lessons by certified instructors. A halfpipe is featured, a Burton Demo Center and rentals.

Cross-country
Jay Peak has 20 km. of cross-country skiing on the mountain and another 200 km. locally. Telemarking is permitted at Jay and both instruction and rentals are available. A bonus for cross-country skiers at Jay is the vistas at most bends in the trail.

Ski school (94/95 prices)

Ski School Director Mickey Doheny and his assistant Dana Kennison have been at Jay for 20 years and have assembled a quality group of professionals with a high return rate. On weekends as many as 100 instructors are available for all skiing or snowboarding ability levels. A private lesson costs $36 per hour and a two-hour group lesson is $20.

Lift tickets (94/95 prices)

	Adult	Child (6-12)
One day	$37	$26
Three days	$99 ($33/day)	$69 ($23/day)
Five days	$150 ($30/day)	$105 ($21/day)

These prices include the tram. Older than 65 and younger than 6 pay $5.

Accommodations

The 48-room **Hotel Jay** is convenience personified; it is the center of the base complex and houses guest services and the tram. Packages include lodging, lift tickets, breakfast and dinner, and children younger than 14 stay free. Free child care is offered to Hotel Jay and Jay Peak Condo guests, 9 a.m.-9 p.m. including supervised dinner for children. Two-day package is $219, per person, double occupancy; three days, $319; five days, $519.

Ski-in, ski-out convenience is in the **Slopeside Condominiums,** which have more space than the Hotel Jay, with equipped kitchens and fireplaces. Packages include lift tickets and lodging, but no meals. Two days, four persons per unit, $219 per person; three days, $289; five days, $419.

The **Black Lantern Inn** (326-4507, 800-255-8661) in Montgomery Village, nine miles from Jay on Route 118, was an old stagecoach stop in the early 1800s. It's now a traditional country inn with some new suites complete with Jacuzzi and fireplaces that range from $65 to $85 per person, double occupancy with breakfast and dinner.

The **Inglenook Lodge** (988-2880) on Route 242 less than a mile from Jay, is an 18-room lodge featuring Norwegian hospitality and the area's only indoor swimming pool. Rates range from $39 to $90 per person double occupancy and always include breakfast and sometimes lift tickets.

The **Schnee Hutte Inne** (988-4020), also on Route 242 about a mile from the mountain, features a family atmosphere that centers around a wood stove. Package rates for the 13 rooms are $35-$45 per person double occupancy, including a private room, private bath and breakfast. Ask about their ski packages, the conditions and prices of which vary. The proprietors also handle the adjacent **Trillium Woods Townhouses,** eight units, tri-level with Jacuzzi, sauna and fireplace. Prices vary.

The **Jay Village Inn** (988-2643) in Jay is under new ownership and offers 15 private rooms with private bath in an authentic Vermont country inn. Package rates include a full country breakfast and are $85 per night for a room for two and $100 a night for a three-person room.

Dining/après-ski

Entrées at the **Hotel Jay** dining room include Steak Forestiere sautéed with mushrooms and shallots and Pork Tenderloin Madeira. Fresh fish specials are featured daily.

The **Black Lantern** is known for its moderately priced but extraordinary fare, especially the Lamb Marguerite, which is marinated and broiled. A cozy bar attracts locals and guests.

The Belfry is a converted one-room schoolhouse five miles from the mountain that has excellent seafood and inexpensive blackboard-style menus daily. Very casual—locals love it.

On the mountain, **après-ski** frivolities usually begin at the Golden Eagle Lounge in the base lodge, in the Hotel Jay or in the International Dining Room. The Inglenook Lodge usually features a guitar player around the big open hearth area.

Other activities

Shopping: Bogner, the upscale skiwear company, has one of its few factory outlets 20 miles away in Newport. Montgomery, nine miles away, has several shops with regional handicrafts.

Snowcat rides are available every Thursday, trips to a working farm on Wednesdays, welcome parties all the time, bonfire party and Ski School party at the end of the week.

Getting there and getting around

Getting there: Jay Peak, located on Route 242, is approximately 65 miles northeast of Burlington, 90 miles southeast of Montreal and 210 miles north of Boston.

By air: Burlington International Airport has more than 60 daily flights on USAir, Continental, United, and Delta's Business Connection. Van service is available for hotel and condo guests for about $10. By train: Amtrak's Montrealer to St. Albans, Vt. Ground transportation for the 45-minute trip to Jay is available.

Getting around: If you're staying at the Jay Hotel or one of the slopeside condos and have no intention of exploring the area, you can get by without a car. Otherwise, bring one.

Information/reservations

Address: Jay Peak Resort, Jay, VT 05859. Phone: (800) 451-4449; (802) 988-2611. Note: Canadian dollars are accepted at American face value for lift tickets only.

The local telephone area code is 802.

Killington, Vermont

Killington is one ski area where it's a good idea to carry a trail map. Not only is it the largest of the Eastern resorts, it is also one of the biggest in the United States. Superlatives are its specialty, and the resort lays claim to the biggest, highest, fastest, steepest and largest in various categories as a key component of its marketing strategy. It leads the East, for example, in vertical drop (3,150 feet), lift capacity (36,627 skiers per hour) and longest ski season. (Killington strives to be the first ski area in the country to open—usually aiming for mid-October—and stays open until late May, sometimes June.) Its 158 trails cover six mountain peaks. Juggernaut, the longest ski trail in the U.S., meanders for 10 miles (granted, it's mostly suited to beginners and cross-country skiers). A mostly intermediate run, called the Four-Mile Trail, drops from the top of the gondola at Killington Peak to the base, down more than 3,000 feet of mellow vertical.

Killington is big, and it trumpets its size proudly. But it also does so much so well. Its vast snowmaking operation is the reason its ski season lasts seven months. Its all-inclusive ski packages offer some of the best deals in the country, with substantial savings over buying the components individually. Killington also has developed one of the best central reservations systems, which allows you to book everything from air transportation to car rental, lodging, child care and ski rental with one call: (800) 372-2007. And that trail map? One of the best, small enough to carry easily, but packed with info, even numbers to call if you lock your keys in your car.

The resort will replace its four-passenger gondola this season with a new eight-passenger model. Though the distance it covers will be reduced from 3.5 miles to 2.54 miles, it will be 60 percent faster. Killington also plans to add up to 25 acres of new terrain in the Needle's Eye/Skye Peak area.

Killington Facts
Base elevation: 1,091'; **Summit elevation:** 4,221'; **Vertical drop:** 3,150 feet
Number and types of lifts: 19–1 gondola, 2 quad superchairs, 5 quad chairs,
4 triple chairs, 5 double chairs, 2 surface lifts
Acreage: 852 trail acres **Snowmaking:** 75 percent
Uphill capacity: 36,627 skiers per hour **Bed base:** 4,800 (base), 19,000 (region)

Where to ski

The terrain is almost too sprawling to describe and make any sense of it. We'd suggest that you take the Meet the Mountains Tour, which leaves at 9:45 a.m. from the tour sign in front of the Resort Center at Snowshed. Guides will familiarize you with the area, and you'll pick up historical tidbits as you ski. The groups are assembled as much as possible by ability levels.

Killington has six separate base areas. Three of them are clustered within striking distance of the end of the access road. Snowshed and Rams Head are across the street from one another, and Killington base is just a bit up the access road. Bear Mountain, home of the famed Outer Limits bump run, is up Bear Mountain Road off Route 4. The other two base areas are right off Route 4: the Gondola Area, the terminus for the long Juggernaut and Four-Mile trails and the spot to catch the gondola; and Sunrise Mountain, which has mostly beginner trails.

Never-evers should start at the Snowshed learning area, where four lifts serve a very long, very wide and nicely isolated slope that has an excellent pitch for those just starting out.

The Rams Head double chair covers mainly beginner and intermediate terrain. Vagabond, off to the left of Rams Head chair, is an advanced run connecting with the Snowdon area. The Snowdon area is another cruiser's delight, and is served by two chairs from the base area and a Poma lift serving Bunny Buster, often used by the ski school. Highline and Conclusion are good advanced cruising runs with excellent pitch. Bunny Buster and Chute are similar but with a more mellow slope.

Between Snowdon Mountain and Killington Peak is some of the toughest terrain. The Canyon quad chair services this area for access to double-diamond Cascade, Downdraft, Double Dipper and Big Dipper.

Skye Peak, where Killington will add new terrain this season, has proved to be one of the most popular sections of the mountain. Experts and advanced intermediates can play on Ovation, Superstar and Skye Lark.

From the top of Skye Peak advanced skiers can drop down Skye Burst by following the Skye Peak quad. This connection is not recommended for lower intermediates because it leads to the Bear Mountain quad, which services good advanced and expert terrain. From the top of the Bear Mountain quad, skiers can descend Devil's Fiddle or loop in the opposite direction down Wildfire. For bumpers the real thrill is to drop directly under the chair lift and challenge Outer Limits.

Upon returning from Bear Mountain over to Skye Peak, intermediates may want to try the Needle's Eye, which drops beneath the second section of the gondola. A trip back up the Needle's Eye will put skiers back on Skye Lark or Bittersweet for a smooth cruise to the Killington Base Lodge or to Snowshed.

Beginner trails lead from all six interconnected peaks, which allows starting skiers the panoramic vistas and thrill of skiing from the summit, not possible at most areas where the upper-mountain trails are reserved for seasoned skiers.

Mountain rating

Overall, Killington rates as an excellent choice for beginner and intermediate. Advanced skiers will have a lot of fun in select areas such as Skye Peak and Killington Peak. Though experts will find no extreme skiing, they can find trails that will test them.

Snowboarding

Boarding is allowed on all sections of Killington. Lessons and rentals are available at Snowshed and Killington base lodges. Killington hosts a snowboard mogul competition on Outer Limits in the spring.

Ski school (93/94 prices)

The Killington Ski School has several innovative systems: Mountain Training Stations have specially contoured snow and a ski drill set up at each one to improve certain skills, such as weight distribution and short-radius turns. As you progress from station to station, you actually teach yourself, based on the changing character of the snow. An instructor is available to coach students over the terrain. These stations are an integral part of the Killington learning method.

Learners have many alternatives, such as ski weeks, daily classes, individual lessons, advanced workshops, racing clinics and video workshops.

For the ski week packages, ask a representative at central reservations to send a brochure.

Group lessons cost $22 per person. **Private lessons** cost $58 an hour and each additional person is $26. Three hours of private instruction will cost $152 for one and $205 for two to five students. The full day costs $278 for one and $331 for two to five students.

For **children**, Superstars programs provide a full day of instruction, with lunch, for kids 6 to 12 years. The cost is $72 a day with lunch and $87 with rentals. The two-day program is $130, $154 with rentals. A five-day program costs $288, $339 with rentals.

Call the Killington Lodging Bureau at (802) 773-1330 to make reservations.

Lift tickets (93/94 prices)

	Adult	Child (6-12) Senior (65+)
One day	$44	$25
Two days	$77 ($38.50/day)	$38.50 ($19.25/day)
Five days	$172 ($34.40/day)	$86 ($17.20/day)

Lift ticket prices are normally packaged with lodging and lessons. Half-day and seven-day tickets also are available. Children 5 and younger ski free on Snowshed slope with a paying adult. These free tickets are available at the ski vacation center.

Cross-country

Mountain Top Inn has an extensive cross-country trail system. There are more than 110 km. of trails; 40 km. are groomed daily. Snowmaking here ensures season-long skiing to match the trails at Killington. Mountain Top Inn also has sleigh rides, a great restaurant and its own sugarhouse where they make maple syrup. Call (800) 445-2100 or 483-2311 for more information. **Mountain Meadows Ski Touring Center** (775-7077) has 56 km. of trails, 32 km. groomed and 32 km. tracked. **Trailhead Ski Touring Center in Stockbridge** (746-8038) offers 60 km. of trails, with 35 km. groomed and 35 km. tracked. In Woodstock, the **Ski Touring Center** (457-2114) has 75 km. of trails, with 58 km. of groomed trails and 50 km. of tracked.

Accommodations (93/94 rates)

Killington has no quaint village. An access road lined with hotels, restaurants, ski shops and discos winds up the mountain from Route 4 to the main condominium complexes. None of the accommodations on the road are particularly glitzy—some are just the opposite. The most luxurious nearby property is on Route 4 on the way to Rutland. Consequently, Killington could never lay claim to being Vermont's best or most luxurious in this department. If you want a bargain, call the Killington Lodging Bureau and describe exactly what you want. The tradeoff is usually a longer distance to the lifts. You may make reservations for all these properties by calling (800) 372-2007.

The top hotel on the mountain road at Killington is **The Inn of the Six Mountains** (800-228-4676 or 802-422-4302). There is a 65-foot indoor lap pool, exercise room and frequent shuttles to the slopes. Rates for the five-day, five-night plan are $269 per person, double occupancy, breakfast included.

Killington Village has good values and it may have the best location, with nearby athletic club facilities, some nightlife and an excellent shuttlebus system. Of the Village condominiums, the **High Ridge** units are by far the most desirable. The **Sunrise** condos at the base of Bear Mountain are also at the top end of the Killington condo scale. At the far end of the Killington road is **The Woods at Killington Resort and Spa**, which boasts private Jacuzzis and saunas, and a shuttle to the Snowshed Base.

Both the **Mountain Inn** and the **Cascades Lodge** are very convenient, located in Killington Village, but they are also basic. The Cascades does have a nice indoor pool and the Mountain Inn has some of the best nightlife when the bar is hopping.

The Cortina Inn (773-3331), on Route 4 just past the Pico ski area, is the perhaps the top upscale property in the area. It has a health club, pool, spa, two restaurants, children's activities on weekend nights, and coffee and cookies in the library each afternoon, and many large suites. Rates, per person double occupancy with breakfast: three nights, $177; five nights, $295.

The Vermont Inn (800-541-7795 or 775-0708), with only 16 rooms and fireside dining, everything homemade, is a charming New England country inn. Breakfast and dinner are included. Costs, based on double occupancy for two days and nights, are $150 to $160 per person; five nights of lodging and meals run from $275 to $300 per person.

Another favorite is **The Summit Lodge**. The food is excellent, the casual and friendly atmosphere is infectious and the staff is among the most helpful in the area. Double-occupancy rates, with breakfast only: two nights, $141; three nights, $197; five nights, $278.

Of the other properties on Killington Road, **The Red Rob**, **Killington Village Inn** and **Chalet Killington** rate in that order. The food is reportedly best at the Red Rob, and both the Killington Village Inn and the Chalet offer a casual atmosphere. Rate per person, based on double occupancy with breakfast, for the Red Rob is $231 for a three-night stay. The Chalet for three nights is $195.

Near the base of the Killington Road is the **Northstar Lodge** (422-4040), which offers excellent modern accommodations. It has a pool and shuttle service, and is surrounded by good restaurants. Rates per person, double occupancy, are three nights, $147; five nights, $189.

The Grey Bonnet (775-2537) on Route 100 north received numerous recommendations. There is a nice indoor pool, sauna and pub. Room with breakfast and dinner costs $215 per person for three nights and $269 per person for five nights. You will need your car to get back and forth to the ski area.

For real luxury try an out-of-the-way, but fabulous place, the **Woodstock Inn and Resort** in Woodstock, about 17 miles east of Killington. The inn was extensively renovated about four years ago. Rooms are cozy and beautifully decorated, with hand-stitched Vermont quilts on each bed. The main dining room wine list has 184 selections, both foreign and domestic. Midweek, the inn has a very attractive package plan that includes downhill skiing at nearby Suicide Six or cross-country skiing at the Woodstock Ski Touring Center. Call (800) 448-7900.

Dining

The Killington area has more than 60 restaurants. The best restaurant in the area—ranked among the top restaurants in the nation by *Food and Wine* and *Conde Nast Traveler*—is **Hemingway's** (422-3886).

Our favorites are **The Summit** (422-3535, reservations suggested), an award-winning restaurant with a menu that changes nightly and a great wine list; **Jason's** (422-3303, reservations suggested) in the Red Rob for excellent Northern Italian food; the **Cortina** (773-3331) has excellent New England fare; and **The Vermont Inn** (800-541-7795 or 775-0708) has won awards for its fine formal dining. **Churchill's House of Beef and Seafood** on Route 4 between Killington and Rutland is worth the drive for great food and an extensive wine list.

Claude's and **Choices** (422-4030) on the Killington Road were recommended by more than half-a-dozen locals. They are both in the same building and owned by the same chef. Claude's is the more elegant with entrées that include escargots, scallops and beef Wellington.

For restaurants a bit kinder to the budget: The **Wobbly Barn** is known for steaks and a great salad bar (no reservations); **Mrs. Brady's** and **The Grist Mill** are consistent; **Charity's** has specials every night for those hanging out after happy hour; and **The Back Behind Saloon** is inexpensive and getting more popular every year. All except the Back Behind Saloon are on the Killington Road—you'll find the saloon at the junction of Routes 4 and 100 at the foot of the Northeast Passage.

Après-ski/nightlife

Immediate après-ski action can be found in **Charity's**, where happy hour is 4 to 6 p.m. The **Nightspot** features a happy hour as well. It is a favorite locals' hangout on weekdays, with entertainment and dancing tourists packed in on weekends. At the mountain, the Killington **Base Lodge** and the Snowshed **Pogonips** have some action immediately after skiing.

The Pickle Barrel has a lively happy hour with dancing later in the evening and is frequented by a young college crowd. Après-ski keeps going strong at **The Grist Mill** with karaoke music and more dancing tourists, this time singing as well. **Casey's Caboose** is a favorite locals' haunt with killer spicy buffalo wings. An older, quieter set meets at the **Summit** for happy hour.

For rowdy après-ski and then dancing to loud music, head to the **Wobbly Barn**. When the bar at the **Mountain Inn** has live entertainment, it's great fun. **The Nightspot**, on Killington Road, has good dancing when it's cranking, and it's less expensive than the Wobbly Barn.

Child care (93/94 prices)

The Children's Center is located in the Snowshed Lodge. Killington takes children from 6 weeks to 12 years in the daycare program. The center is fully licensed.

Day-care costs $43 per day and $29 per half day. Two-day rates: $54 for half days (no lunch), $82 for full days with lunch; $115 for five half-days, $172 for five full days.

First Tracks is an introduction to skiing program for children 3 to 8, which consists of two one-hour lessons in the terrain garden, rental equipment and snacks. The program costs $57 for a full day and $38 for a half day. Two-day weekend rates are $73 for half days (no lunch) and $108 for full days with lunch. The five-day program is $152 for half days, $228 for full days.

Reservations are required for the children's center. Call 422-6222. All-day programs run from 8 a.m. to 4 p.m. Add $5 for lunch to half-day programs. Parents must supply food and beverage for children 23 months and younger.

Other activities

Shopping: In Killington, stop at the **Greenbrier Gift Shop** for handcrafted items and gourmet ware. Woodstock, about 17 miles east of Killington on Route 4, is considered one of Vermont's most beautiful villages and is packed with art galleries and shops. Nearby Bridgewater has a 60-outlet mall, the Marketplace at Bridgewater.

The Killington Village Health Spa has a complete fitness center, pool, racquetball courts, steam rooms and Jacuzzis. Call 422-9370. An **outdoor skating rink** is below the Summit Lodge on the Killington Road. **Snowmobiling** is available in Rutland and Killington; call the Cortina Inn, 773-4735. **Sleigh rides** and **horseback riding** are available in Chittendon, 483-6089.

Getting there and getting around

Getting there: Killington is at the intersection of Routes 4 and 100 in central Vermont near the city of Rutland, about three hours from Boston and about 90 minutes south of Burlington. Green Mountain Limousine Service runs transfers from Burlington for $50 per person round-trip, and meets most flights.

Air transportation is available into Rutland by Mountain Aviation (775-5591). Thrifty Rental Cars has an office at the Inn of the Six Mountains. Hertz and Avis have small offices at the Rutland airport.

Getting around: Bring or rent a car. Though you may not use it between your lodging and the slopes, Killington itself is very spread out, and you may want to visit one of the quaint Vermont towns nearby.

Information/reservations

For all information, reservations, and ski packages call (800) 372-2007 from 8 a.m. to 9 p.m. daily.

Address: Killington Ski Area, Killington VT 05751; 422-3333. Snow phone: 422-3261.

Local telephone area code is 802.

Mount Snow/Haystack Vermont

Mount Snow/Haystack has the snowmaking efficiency of Killington, is closer to major cities than Stratton, and has just as careful grooming, but somehow this resort has remained about as down-home, folksy and unpretentious as all Vermont resorts should be. This mountain certainly has the makings to flirt with acquiring glitz or overcrowding the access roads, but thank heaven someone has kept a New England feel to the entire area. West Dover and Wilmington are true Vermont villages, without boutique-filled commercialism.

With the addition of Haystack Mountain a couple of seasons ago, Mount Snow now has 127 trails and 25 lifts—more than any area in the East. The two mountains are not interconnected by lifts, but a shuttlebus plies the route between the two bases.

Mount Snow is a big New England area that works about as perfectly as any area in the country at making snow and moving skiers around on the mountain. It also has 84 trails, and quite uncharacteristic of New England, they are about 100 yards wide. As you look up at the mountain, the terrain is almost perfectly divided from right to left into expert, intermediate and beginner sections. Snowmaking blankets more than 80 percent of the mountain, providing snow from November through early May. Haystack has 1,400 vertical feet with 43 trails and six lifts.

Mount Snow has about 4,000 beds clustered in condos and lodges at the base of the mountain. There are another 3,000 within 10 miles of the resort. While the mountain base has no village complex, West Dover (three miles away) and Wilmington (nine miles away) are traditionally quaint Vermont towns with shops, white-steepled churches, etc.

Mount Snow/Haystack Facts

Base elevation: 1,900'; **Summit elevation:** 3,600'; **Vertical drop:** 1,700 feet
Number of lifts: 24—1 quad superchair, 1 quad chair, 9 triple chairs, 10 double chairs, 3 surface lifts
Snowmaking: 82 percent **Total acreage by trails:** 603 acres
Uphill capacity: 33,830 per hour **Bed Base:** 8,000-9,000

Where to ski

Just about any level of skier can ski Mount Snow anywhere. Solid intermediates can head to the North Face area, which is a grouping of isolated steeper runs, some of which are left to bump up. All the runs covering the face of the mountain and dropping to the village area are great cruisers. The names give you an idea of what to expect—Ego Alley, Sundance and Snowdance. This is the perfect place to dance on the snow.

The Sunbrook area, which catches the sun, is an ideal spot for lower intermediates. The one expert trail in Sunbrook, Beartrap, with its south-facing exposure and snowmaking, is a haven for bump skiers.

To the far south of the resort is Carinthia, which offers long mellow runs for advanced beginners, lower intermediates and anyone who want to have a playful cruise. There are enough zigs and zags and small drops to keep a skier awake.

Haystack's upper mountain has intermediate terrain and the recently developed Witches area for experts. The lower mountain, segregated from the upper trails, is great for beginners.

Mountain rating

The emphasis is definitely on the intermediate. Experts can try some of relatively tough runs on the North Face of the resort, but if you are an expert, don't plan on coming out of your way to ski these runs. They're not that tough. Beginners and never-evers, get ready to improve—this mountain has just your kind of terrain.

Snowboarding

Snowboarding is allowed on both mountains. Mount Snow has a snowboard park, Un Blanco Gulch, located on the Canyon Trail, featuring side hits, a halfpipe, spines and plenty of jumps. Lessons are available through the ski school. Rentals are available at the Mount Snow Rental Shop, Cupola Ski Shop in West Dover and the Timing House in Wilmington. No leash is required in the state of Vermont.

Cross-country

Four major ski touring centers are near Mount Snow. The largest is **Hermitage Cross-Country Touring Center** on Coldbrook Road in Wilmington; 464-3511. It has 50 km. of trails that form a circle from the warming hut out to Mount Snow and back. **Sitzmark Ski Touring Center** (464-5498), **Timber Creek** (464-0999) and the **White House Touring Center** (464-2135) are others offering more than 60 km. of trails skewed toward the intermediate Nordic skier.

Ski school (93/94 prices)

Group lessons at Mount Snow take the form of 45-minute workshops for intermediate and advanced skiers called EXpress Customized Learning (EXCL). Each workshop has a maximum of three students and concentrates on two or three tips to help you improve. EXCL workshops are $22 ($25 on holidays). The price per lesson goes down the more lessons you take. Novices take traditional two-hour class lessons at the same price.

A two-hour **introduction to skiing** program is $62 including beginner lifts and equipment ($69 on holidays).

Private instruction costs $50 an hour for one student; additional students pay $30.

Children have the SKIwee program for ages 4-12, which offers a six-hour daily lesson, including lunch, for $67 for one day ($75 on holidays), $123 for two days, $176 for three days and $282 for five days.

Mount Snow has an unusual twist to children's skiing: Teddy Bear Weeks, four weeks of the season when children 12 and younger ski free for the week if they bring along a teddy bear. The activities include a forest safety talk by Smokey Bear, rides on a snow-grooming machine, a teddy bear ski race and an après-ski ice cream party. (Good luck getting your 11-year-old to take a teddy bear so you can save money on the lift ticket.)

Lift tickets (93/94 prices)

	Adult	Child (Up to 12) Senior (65+)
One day	$43	$24
Three days	$106 ($35.33/day)	$57 ($19/day)
Five days	$168 ($33.60/day)	$87 ($17.40/day)*

*Children ski free when their parents purchase a five- to seven-day vacation package and when they are enrolled in SKIWee.

Holiday prices are a little higher. Adults ski for $39 midweek, while college students with ID ski for $26 midweek. Those with Mount Snow multiday tickets can ski at Killington, Mount Snow's sister resort, or at Haystack. Tickets to ski Haystack alone are $37 for adults on weekends, $27 midweek and $23 for juniors and seniors, $17 midweek.

Accommodations (93/94 prices)

At the immediate base of the mountain are a group of condo projects and a luxury lodge that have shuttle service to the slopes. Most of the other accommodations line Route 100 between the slopes and the town of Wilmington, with some tucked on side roads back into the foothills.

All rates listed here are per person, non-holiday, based on double occupancy. The five-day Ski Week rate is Sunday through Thursday.

The Inn at Sawmill Farm, on Route 100 in West Dover, 464-8131. One of the nation's top country inns, it is in a class by itself. Entry is through a portion of the former barn. The rooms are spacious and feature dressing rooms off the baths. Small fireplace cottages have a sitting room and bedroom. The inn's sitting room provides a panoramic view, and the dining room serves some of the best meals in the valley.

The atmosphere is quite formal, with men required to wear jackets in the public areas and restaurant after 6 p.m. Children younger than 10 are not allowed. Weekend rates: doubles $270 including breakfast and dinner for two; cottages, $290 including breakfast and dinner for two. The Inn at Sawmill Farm does not take credit cards.

Snow Lake Lodge, (800) 451-4211, or 464-7788. This sprawling 92-room mountain lodge is at the base of the main skiing area and has recently been renovated. The lodge has a fitness center, sauna, indoor hot tub, outdoor Jacuzzi, and après-ski entertainment each evening. The Sundance lift is 300 yards away or skiers can ride the free shuttle. The Snow Lake Lodge is excellent with children as well. Rates include breakfast and dinner. Two-day weekend , $159; five-day ski week, $260.

Andirons Lodge, Route 100, West Dover; 464-2114, or (800) 445-7669. This lodge is just two miles from the lifts. These are simple paneled rooms with double beds; some have additional twin beds. There is an indoor pool, a sauna and game room. The attached Dover Forge restaurant serves affordable meals. Rates: two-day weekend package, $88; five-day package, $160.

Matterhorn of Dover, on Route 100, West Dover, 464-8011 or (800) 497-1085. This has been lodging skiers for more than 20 years. The lobby has a two-story stone fireplace and the rooms are simple paneled rooms, with cable TV, most with two double beds. Rates include breakfast and dinner. Two-day weekend, $118; five-day ski week, $199.

Nordic Hills Lodge, 179 Coldbrook Road, Wilmington; 464-5130 or (800) 326-5130. All rooms have cable TV. Rates include breakfast and dinner. Two-day weekend is $115; five-day ski week is $199.

Gray Ghost Inn, on Route 100, West Dover; 464-2474 or (800) 745-3615. This large country inn is operated by a British couple who have decorated some rooms with a country touch and others with mountain wood paneling. Many rooms have smaller or bunk beds for children. Rates include breakfast. Two-day weekend, $90; five-day ski week, $150.

Trail's End, Smith Road, Wilmington; 464-2727 or (800) 859-2585. This inn has 15 country-style rooms. Meals are served family style at three round tables, which means visitors likely will return home with new friends. Rates include breakfast. Two-day weekend, $110; five-day ski week, $220.

Old Red Mill, Route 100 in the town of Wilmington about 15 minutes from the slopes; 464-3700 or (800) 843-8483. This inn, created from a former sawmill, is one of the bargains in the region. The rooms are small, most only about 7 by 12 feet with a double bed, toilet and shower, but all have TV. Larger rooms are available for families. The common areas, bar and dining rooms are rustic Vermont. Rates: two-day weekend, $90 room only; five-day ski week, $99.

Horizon Inn, 464-2131 or (800) 336-5513, Route 9 in Wilmington has an indoor heated pool, whirlpool, sauna and game room. The two-day weekend is $80 and five-day ski week, $100. No meals, but a bargain any way you look at it.

Best Western—The Lodge at Mount Snow, (800) 451-4289 or 464-5112, at the base of Mount Snow, has two-day weekend rates of $132; five-day ski package is $199, both with breakfast and dinner. Kids 12 and under stay and eat free midweek, excluding holidays.

Bed & Breakfasts

Mount Snow also has a group of charming and elegant bed and breakfast establishments. These B&Bs are smaller, most with fewer than 15 rooms.

The Doveberry Inn, on Route 100, West Dover; 464-5652 or (800) 722-3204. This eight-room inn is run by the Rossi sisters, graduates of the New England Culinary Institute, who lavish attention on visitors. No children younger than 8 permitted. TVs and VCRs are in each room with a free video library. Two-day weekend B&B is $110; five-day ski week is $225 with breakfast.

West Dover Inn, Route 100, West Dover; 464-5207 or (800) 732-0745. A historic country inn built in 1846 with 12 elegant rooms furnished with antiques, hand-sewn quilts, and color TVs. There are also two suites with fireplaces and whirlpool tubs. B&B rates: two-day weekend is $110; five-day ski week is $193.

The Red Shutter Inn, Route 9, Wilmington; 464-3768 or (800) 845-7548. This 1894 country home has been converted into an elegant country inn. There are only nine guestrooms. B&B rates: two-day weekend $95; five-day ski week is $190.

The Nutmeg Inn, Route 9W, Wilmington; 464-3351. Built in a 1770s home in the town and decorated with country accents and quilts, this B&B has ten rooms and three fireplace suites. B&B rates: two-day weekend is $105; five-day ski week is $245.

The White House of Wilmington, Route 9, Wilmington; 464-2135. This is an upscale 23-room inn serving breakfast and dinner. Rates: two-day weekend is $190; five day ski week, $350. Prices include breakfast and dinner; breakfast only packages also available.

Condominiums

Condo rates are per person, based on four people in a two-bedroom, two-bath unit, unless noted.

The Mount Snow Condominiums, 464-7788 or (800) 451-4211, are at the base of the lifts; only the Seasons complex is actually ski-in/ski-out and is the most highly recommended. These condos have an excellent athletic center with indoor pools, saunas and Jacuzzis. A two-night weekend is $140; five-day ski week runs $124. The Seasons complex prices are slightly higher.

Timber Creek Townhomes, 464-1222 or (800) 982-8922, are luxury condos located across Route 100 from the ski area. They have an excellent athletic center and 18 km. of cross-country trails just outside. Shuttlebuses run between the complex and the ski area. The two-day weekend rate is $169; the five-day ski week costs $190.

Greenspring at Mount Snow, (800) 247-7833 or 464-7111, are upscale condos a mile from the slopes. This complex has the best athletic center in the area. Two-day weekend rate is $141; the five-day ski week costs $154.

Mount Snow has several packages that include lodging and skiing. For a **complete vacation planner** with descriptions of most area properties, write: Mount Snow, 105 Mountain Road, Mount Snow VT 05356, or call (800) 245-7669 (245-SNOW).

Dining

The top dining experience (and the most expensive) is the **Inn at Sawmill Farm** (464-1130) which has 21,000 bottles in its wine cellar and gourmet continental dining with appetizers ranging from $6 to $14, and entrées $22 to $30. As noted above, dining here is formal and jackets are required on all male guests (if you didn't bring one they do have a selection of blue blazers which may be borrowed). No credit cards.

The Hermitage (464-3511) serves excellent meals at less stratospheric prices. This country inn has a very large dining room with some tables surrounded by overstuffed chairs. The walls are covered with the world's largest collection of hanging Delacroix prints. The wine cellar claims 40,000 bottles of 2,000 different labels. All game birds and venison are raised on the premises and jams, jellies and maple syrup are homemade. Entrées run from $14 to $25.

For other fine dining try **Betty Hillman's Le Petit Chef** (464-8437), **Two Tannery Road** (464-2707), and **Capstones** (464-5207), adjacent to the West Dover Inn. **Doveberry Restaurant** (464-5652) is small and intimate with a chef who is a graduate of the New England Culinary Institute.

The Deerhill Inn and Restaurant, (800) 626-5674 or 464-3100, on Valley View Road in West Dover features American cuisine. One dining room has a mountain view, the other a fireplace.

Fennessey's Parlor (464-9361) according to locals serves up consistently good food at reasonable prices. Decor is turn of the century.

For economical eats, try **Poncho's Wreck** (464-9320) with an eclectic dining room serving Mexican food, steaks, lobsters and fresh fish. Poncho's is a local institution. **B.A.'s Red Anchor** (464-5616), under the same ownership, serves its famous ribs and seafood specialties.

The Vermont House (464-9360) on Wilmington's main street, serves good food for cheap prices and is one of the locals' favorites. **Deacon's Den** (464-9361) is a good place for pizza, burgers and sandwiches right after skiing. **TC's Tavern** (464-9316) serves up good Italian food. **Giuseppe's** (464-2022) across from Poncho's in Wilmington cooks the best pizza in town. And for sandwiches and deli fare try **Julie's Cafe** (formerly Elsa's; 464-8624) on Route 100 in West Dover.

Après-ski/nightlife

Après-ski conversation opener: Did you know that Mount Snow was named for Reuben Snow, a farmer who used to own the land where the resort now sits?

Now that you know that, try it out at the **Cuzzins** at the Mount Snow main base lodge, where Bruce Jacques and the Invisible Band get the crowd jumping between 3 and 7 p.m. each Friday and Saturday. (Cuzzins is fairly rowdy on other days as well.) If you prefer something quieter, try **Snow Lake Lodge.**

At night, the hot spots are **Snow Barn** on Mount Snow, or **Deacon's Den,** both with live music and dancing. For a quiet drink, head for any of the finer restaurants listed in the dining section.

Every Saturday is Club Sundown for teens and young adults to age 20. A DJ spins the hot hits from 8 p.m. to midnight in the Carinthia base lodge. There is a nominal admission charge.

Child care

The Pumkin Patch is one of New England's largest day-care centers. It provides care for children from 6 weeks to 8 years. There are separate rooms for infants and toddlers. Reservations are required; call 464-8501. Prices are $45 all day with lunch, or $185 for five days. Rates are higher during holidays.

The Pumkin Patch also is open Wednesday and Saturday nights for Kid's Night Out from 5:30 to 9 p.m. for pizza, movies and games for ages 3 to 12.

Other activities

Shopping: Though Wilmington has a few quaint shops, this is not a major activity at Mount Snow.

Adams Farm (464-3762), on Route 100 about five miles south of Mount Snow, is the place for **horse-drawn sleigh rides**. The farm has its own trail system with an old cabin where you stop for hot chocolate.

For **snowmobiling**, try High Country Snowmobile Tours (464-2108). Mount Snow has an **ice skating** rink for day and evening skating, and the Carinthia bunny slope is lit at night for **sledding**. You hike to the top and it's BYOS, though you may also use inner tubes and toboggans.

Getting there and getting around

Getting there: Mount Snow is the closest major Vermont ski resort to New York and Boston. It is on Route 100, nine miles north of Wilmington. Mileage from major cities is: Boston, 127; New York City, 213; and Albany, 68.

The closest airports are Albany and Hartford's Bradley International, both about a 90-minute drive.

Getting around: Bring a car. If you stay close to the mountain, you won't need it during the day (shuttlebuses take you to and from the lifts), but you will want it at night.

Information/reservations

Contact the **Mount Snow Vacation Services** for one-stop reservations for everything from airline tickets to car rentals and lifts—(800) 245-7669 (245-SNOW).

For snow conditions, call 464-2151.

Local telephone area code is 802.

Okemo Mountain, Vermont

Okemo Mountain deserves an award for the greatest makeover of an under-utilized mountain and almost forgotten ski town. At one time, Okemo had long, long surface lifts that often lifted skiers above the snow's surface. Today, however, Okemo proudly boasts 10 new lifts in as many years, mostly comfortable high-speed quads. Okemo's natural terrain has been enhanced to provide entertainment and joy for all levels of skiers. Its commitment to improvements have garnered it high rankings in several ski publications for snowmaking, grooming and customer service. Early and late each season, skiers remark how great the conditions are at Okemo, even when other eastern ski areas are struggling to put out a decent snow product. This is the key to Okemo's success.

Okemo has big plans for 1994-95. A $4.5-million capital improvement plan will bring the new South Face area, two high-speed quad chairs, a snowboard park with its own surface lift and an 80-million-gallon snowmaking water-storage pond. The South Face area will have five new trails of intermediate to expert difficulty and a new high-speed quad. Okemo also will replace its Solitude Peak fixed quad with a high-speed chair.

Where to ski

If there is a knock on Okemo it comes from the super-expert skiers who need more steeps and challenge than Okemo has to offer. The trails are all very accessible and the lifts flow the skiers conveniently around the mountain. Two quads rise from the base lodge to provide gentle skiing and access to the NASTAR Trail and to several clusters of condos and townhouses slopeside. There can be a slight logjam at these two lifts, but once up on the mountain, you can ski to a triple chair or two other quads that access the upper trails.

The Northstar Express high-speed quad draws the biggest crowd, but moves skiers up-mountain in a hurry. A less crowded

---

Okemo Facts
Base elevation: 1,150'; *Summit elevation:* 3,300'; *Vertical drop:* 2,150 feet *Number of lifts:* 11–2 quad superchairs, 5 quads, 2 triple chairs, 2 surface lifts *Snowmaking:* 95% *Total acreage:* 400 skiable acres *Uphill capacity:* 21,900 per hour

option is to ski down another 100 yards to the seldom used Sachem quad, which serves as a good tune-up run down Ledges, a wide black-diamond mogul trail that can be skied by most upper intermediates. For a gentler descent, take the Upper and Lower Sachem or Easy Street.

Another ride on the Sachem chair allows a check on the Glades Summit quad chair. Occasionally it does not operate because of strong winds, but when it is running, prepare for a treat. Rimrock is a fine black-diamond run that is wide and varied in terrain. You can cruise it flat-out or enjoy the many subtle terrain changes characteristic of old Vermont trails. The only true double-black trails on the mountain are off this lift: Outrage and Double Black Diamond. Both are gladed, not particularly precipitous, but enjoyable and challenging with proper snow conditions. Two short trails off this lift, Triplesec and Challenger, add variety and usually have good snow cover.

Easily the most popular trail is World Cup, reasonably wide, constantly undulating and sheer pleasure. The Chief is one of Okemo's venerable runs that was widened with the makeover. Still popular, it usually has more moguls than World Cup. The Chief, as most Okemo trails, is divided into upper and lower sections, with the lower part usually less challenging.

The Black Ridge triple chair often has short lines and great snow, because most skiers use the longer trails. Black Out and Sel's Choice are fine black-diamond trails and the Lower Wardance is a good race trail. At the bottom of Sel's is a snowboard halfpipe, off-limits to skiers. The Green Ridge triple and the Solitude Peak high-speed chair have many runs for lower intermediates, especially Easy Rider, Heaven's Gate and Timberline.

Mountain rating

Experts enjoy Okemo at high speeds, intermediates and advanced skiers enjoy it at any speed, and beginners find that the great snow conditions help them advance more quickly. Okemo has been hugely successful providing a quality product for most skiers and it would be a waste to toughen up the trails for the sake of the few who need extremes to be satiated.

Snowboarding

Okemo has a large snowboarding community not confined to the young and restless. Grey-haired ski patrollers and instructors foster a pro-boarding attitude. Boards, gear and rentals are available on the mountain, at the board center in Ludlow at Sport Odyssey and at Dunnett's Ski Rentals. An Introduction To Snowboarding package is $50 for adults and $40 for juniors. It includes a beginner group lesson, rental equipment, and the use of Okemo's three lower-mountain lifts for the full day.

Cross-country

Fox Run Resort, just across from the Okemo entrance, has fine facilities with of 32 km. of trails and a rental and repair shop.

Ski school

Okemo's ski school has become recognized as a leader in ski teaching and varied programs for all ability levels. Its director heads the children's committee of the Professional Ski Instructors of America and her involvement is reflected in the high marks accorded the SKIwee program at Okemo for kids 4-8 years old. There are also **group classes for children** aged 7 and up, and the Young Mountain Explorers half- or full-day program is available for children 8-12.

Okemo has several adult **specialized courses**. Mid-week Cruisers (age 55 and older) meets every Wednesday morning for social skiing and low-key lessons from senior instructors. The Bump Series is a morning lesson on Saturdays and Sundays for two consecutive weekends for competent skiers who would like to be more proficient in the bumps.

Women's Ski Spree is a five-day indulgence for women of all ability levels. Jennifer Speck supervises this program that includes three hours of daily instruction, a welcome party breakfast and lunch daily, guest speakers, video analysis, a farewell banquet and all female instructors.

Group lessons are $22 and **private lessons** are $50 per hour.

Lift tickets (93/94 prices)

	Adult	Child (7-12)
One day	$43	$27
Three days	$114 ($38/day)	$72 ($24/day)
Five days	$180 ($36/day)	$115 ($23/day)

Midweek adult prices are $40; children ski for $24 midweek. The Sunday Solution ticket allows morning skiing on Sunday, $34 for adults, $21 for children. Multiday tickets for two to seven days are available. Children 6 and younger ski free.

Accommodations

Okemo has many slopeside condos and townhouses. Per-person rates vary widely depending on proximity to the slopes and size, but a range would be $120-$185, off-mountain, to $210-$360 slopeside for a five-night ski week with breakfast and dinner included. The Okemo/Ludlow area, which includes Weston, Plymouth and Proctorsville, has 23 country inns and 16 bed-and-breakfast facilities, and 10 motels/motor lodges.

The Castle Inn on Route 131 in Proctorsville is an eye-catching edifice, having served as the Governor's mansion in days gone by. Weekend daily rate per room, double occupancy, breakfast and dinner, is about $180. The dining is truly gourmet and the 11 rooms quite elegant. Call 226-7222 for reservations.

The Echo Lake Inn, north on Route 100, is a charming New England inn with weekend rates of $110-$140 including breakfast and dinner or $90-$120 with breakfast. Presidents Coolidge and McKinley were guests here and the Coolidge family grounds are nearby. Call (800) 356-6844 or 824-6700.

The **Black River Inn** in Ludlow has a 1794 walnut four-poster bed in which Lincoln rested his 6-foot 4-inch frame. Weekend rates are $130-$160 with breakfast and dinner, and $85-$115 with breakfast. Call 228-5585 for reservations.

The **Cavendish Pointe Hotel** offers the full service of a 70-room country-style hotel, restaurant, lounge and game room. Daily weekend rate is $65-$85 per room, no meals. The hotel is on Route 103, two miles from Okemo. Call 226-7688.

The Hawk Inn and Mountain Resort has luxury country inn, home and townhouse facilities. This complex offers a resort feel and features indoor pool, sauna, Jacuzzis and find dining. Bed and breakfast rates are $95-175 midweek and $125-$200 on weekends. Call 672-3811 or (800) 685-4295.

Dining

Priority's in the Village Center not only is a convenient spot for those staying on the mountain, but also has superb, economical fare. The Pasta Diablo, with scallops and shrimp in a spicy red sauce, is a killer.

Nikki's at the foot of Okemo Mountain not only has a primo location, but a very good reputation. Nikki's is moderately expensive, but its Osso Bucco con Orechiette or steamed whole Maine lobster are favorites of the loyal repeat clientele. Nikki's desserts and extensive wine list add to its popularity.

Michael's Steak & Seafood restaurant on Route 103 just east of Ludlow is in a ramshackle sort of place that belies its true character. Many specials and the excellent cuts of steak bring back patrons for good dining at moderate prices.

North of Ludlow on Route 103 is **Harry's,** an understated place that has a high repeat business because of the moderate pricing ($9-$13) and an emphasis on international cuisine.

Après-ski/nightlife

For après-ski, try **Sitting Bull Lounge,** with a wide-screen TV and live music on weekends; **Priority's,** also with wide-screen TV and ski flicks; or **Dadds.**

Later in the evening, **Dadds** features reggae; **The Pot Belly** has country rock, '60s and '70s classics and karaoke on weekends; **Christopher's Sports and Spirits** for skill games and big-screen sports viewing; or **Northern Lights,** Ludlow's Western nightclub with live music on Fridays and Saturdays and a DJ/dance instructor on Sundays. Another hot spot is

Savannah's, with live bands running the musical gamut from blues to rock. Savannah's has karaoke on select Friday nights, and unplugged musicians on Sundays. **Chuckles** is a favorite couples' spot because of its dance floor. **Old Farm House Inn** has rock and country groups, as well as a resident keyboard comic, Bob Emaa. **Cappuccino's** is a bistro with coffees and an occasional acoustic musician.

In February, the dance floor at **The Pot Belly** becomes a cabaret theater Wednesday and Saturday nights, featuring the Weston Playhouse troupe's summer nightclub comedy routines.

Child care

Okemo provides child care for ages 6 weeks to 8 years. Kids 4 and older get an introduction to skiing through the SKIwee program and the use of mini terrain gardens adjacent to the base lodge. You can peek in on your little one when you stop for lunch. Reservations for all children's programs are recommended.

Other activities

Shopping: One of the best browsing stores in the Northeast, the **Vermont Country Store,** is in nearby Weston on Route 100. It's full of interesting and useful little items that are hard to find elsewhere, such as pant stretchers, wire frames that help natural-fiber pants dry without wrinkles; and Vermont Bag Balm, which helps heal sore cow udders and chapped hands. The store is closed on Sundays, but open 9 a.m. to 5 p.m. the other days of the week.

Getting there and getting around

Getting there: Okemo is in south central Vermont on Route 103 in Ludlow. The closest airports are Hartford, CT, Albany, NY, Burlington, VT or Boston. Burlington is the closest airport, about 90 minutes away; while Boston, the farthest, is about a three-hour drive.

Getting around: We recommend a car, either your own or a rental. Though the immediate resort area is compact and easily walkable, you will probably want to try some restaurants, nightlife or activities nearby.

Information/reservations

Address and phone: Okemo Mountain Resort, Ludlow, VT 05149; 228-4041.

Lodging: (800) 786-5366 (800-78-OKEMO).

Snow reports: 226-5222.

Local area code is 802.

Smugglers' Notch, Vermont

Big mountain skiing is the specialty of Smugglers' Notch. Its 2,610 vertical feet places second behind Killington for Vermont's longest vertical descent. Smugglers' has three mountains, one of which, Madonna Mountain, gives a 2,100-foot drop off one chair.

Smugglers' Notch was named in dubious honor of smugglers and bootleggers who brought in forbidden English goods in the War of 1812 and booze during Prohibition, storing the items in a cave between Madonna Mountain and Spruce Peak, the latter one of the peaks at Stowe. Though Route 108 passes Smugglers' and continues through the notch to Stowe three seasons of the year, it closes in winter. That has meant Smugglers' has been overshadowed by its better known neighbor.

Smugglers' was a town-run area with two Poma lifts from 1954 until 1964. For the past 30 years, Smugglers' was led by men who envisioned the resort becoming an Eastern version of Vail. It is now a premier four-season resort with a strong reputation for families. Both *Family Circle* and *Better Homes and Gardens* chose Smugglers' in their separate listings as a top family vacation resort—the only ski resort to make both lists.

One feature that makes Smugglers' so great for families is its pedestrian-friendly village with stores, restaurants, an outdoor ice rink, sledding hill, indoor pool, saunas, steam baths, indoor and outdoor tennis, massage, crafts classes, sleigh rides, movies, parties for kids and adults and the largest licensed day-care facility in New England.

Where to ski

If you are a day visitor, resist the temptation to turn in at the main Village. Instead, continue up the hill to the top parking lot. Here, you'll find fewer cars and a short walk to a point where you can ski right to the Sterling lift. This lift accesses 20 trails and a variety of runs in the mellow category. Best of all, you can ski back to your car at day's end.

Smugglers' Notch Facts

Base elevation: 1,030'; **Summit elevation:** 3,640'; **Vertical drop:** 2,610 feet
Number and types of lifts: 7—5 double chairs, 2 surface lifts
Acreage: 233 acres **Percent of snowmaking:** 61 percent
Uphill capacity: 5,200 per hour **Bed base:** 2,000

When you are sufficiently warmed up, seek out some real challenge from the top of Madonna Mountain where endless panoramas await. Three legitimate double-black-diamond trails beckon the true expert. Freefall is just that; the turns come quickly and you drop 10 to 15 feet with each turn. The F.I.S. trail sports a 41 percent gradient, and with the addition of top-to-bottom snowmaking has become a tad more civilized than in the past. Upper Liftline is typical of Smugglers' approach to grooming: some are, some ain't. Management swears that many Mad River types ski Smugglers' for that very reason and the trails are posted as such. If you're hooked on glades, it's tough to find a better glade run than Doc Dempsey's. We just wish it were longer. Madonna has several other glade areas that aren't specified trails. The best bump runs are F.I.S., the middle portion of Upper Liftline and Exhibition on Sterling Mountain.

Last season, Smugglers' and Stowe cooperated on a Ski-Over-The-Mountains lift ticket. For $33 on weekends/holidays and $26 weekdays, skiers on certain multiday packages at the two resorts could ski to the other resort via an intermediate trail, Snuffy's, and ski all day there. The connection is between Smugglers' Sterling Mountain and Stowe's Spruce Peak.

The third mountain at Smugglers' is Morse, with five trails ranging from beginner to upper intermediate. It is the primary area for ski schoolers who want to avoid the hot-shot skiers. If you are staying in the village, you'll need to ride to the top of Morse and ski down the green-circle Midway trail to access the upper-mountain lifts.

Morse also is home to Mogul Mouse's Magic Lift, a half-speed double chair especially kind to beginners and young children. From the top of the lift winds the Magic Learning Trail, with skiing nature stations, exploration paths and a couple of "caves" that kids can ski through.

Smugglers' has no high-speed quads or triple chairs, which sometimes contributes to moderate waits at the lift loading area. The tradeoff is that the trails are not congested.

Mountain rating

Smugglers' is good for all types of skiers. Only 20 percent of the trails are rated for beginners, but of the 46 percent rated intermediate many are well suited to recent ski school grads. Advanced skiers tune in to the 34 percent at their level, especially the ungroomed and gladed runs. Kids are all over the place here—a magnet for skiers who revel in a family atmosphere, but something to consider for single adults or couples who would rather have quieter surroundings.

Snowboarding

Snowboarding is permitted on all of Smugglers' trails. Lessons and rentals are available.

Cross country

More than 14 miles of scenic cross country skiing on groomed and tracked trails are accessible from the main Smugglers' area. The Nordic Ski Center offers rentals, lessons, skate skiing, backcountry and night tours, and snowshoe rentals and tours.

Ski school (94/95 prices)

Ski School Director Peter Ingvoldstad has been acclaimed as one of the most innovative ski teachers in the country. He believes strongly that the body is more important than the brain and he uses extensive terrain gardens for child instruction.

Lessons are included with several lodging-and-lift packages at Smugglers'. **Children's programs** are divided into the following age groups: 3-6, 7-12 and 13-18. The teen program allows that age group to meet some new friends they can hang out with at the supervised evening teen activities.

Smugglers' has an innovative program called "Mom & Me/Dad & Me" that teaches parents how to teach their youngsters to ski. These lessons, essentially specialized private lessons, are for children aged 2 or older and a parent of at least intermediate skiing ability. Parents are taught games that make learning fun, and safety tips such as how to ride the chair lift.

Group lessons (just short of two hours) are $21 and a one-hour **private lesson** is $36. **Special programs** include classes on style, terrain tactics, women's programs and programs for skiers 55 and older.

Lift tickets (94/95 prices)

	Adult	Child (7-12)
Weekend day	$37	$24
Midweek day	$34	$24
Multiday	**	**

Children 6 and younger ski for free; those 65 and older ski for $28 on weekends and holidays, $26 on weekdays. The seniors' prices are also the adult half-day rate, morning or afternoon. (Children's half-day rate is $20.)

**If you're staying for more than one day here, the wise move is to buy a lodging package that includes tickets and lessons. See the next section for more information.

Accommodations

At Smugglers' the primary and desirable place to stay is in the Resort Village. More than 2,000 beds are within walking distance of the lifts. Prices start at $399 per person (and $1,249 for a family of four) for a five-day Club Smugglers' package, including lifts and lessons. Packages include a welcome party, use of the pool and hot tub, family games nights, bonfires with hot cocoa, outdoor ice skating, family sledding parties, a weekly torchlight parade with fireworks finale, and a Thursday afternoon Showtime and farewell party.

Condos at Smugglers' are spacious, clean and family-furnished—the furniture is sturdy and comfortable, without expensive bric-a-brac items on the tables or walls at risk of being knocked over accidentally. Our condo was well stocked with family-style board games.

Smugglers' has a central check-in area that can get a bit backed up during busy school vacations. Allow some time for checking in. It might be a good idea for one parent to stand in line while the other takes fidgety kids for a walk or window-shopping in the Resort Village. The payoff comes later—once you check in, you won't have to wait in line for tickets or lessons.

Dining

You never have to leave the Village to eat. The **Notch Above Pizzeria** offers pizza, salads, snacks and assorted pasta specialties. The **Club Cafe** offers a Taste of New Orleans buffet, prime rib and lobster bake. Prices are moderate, but even less expensive on Wednesday when families can enjoy the all-you-can-eat spaghetti party. Families really enjoy the **Village Restaurant**, where kids on the FamilyFest® Package dine free when they are with their parents. The menu features American-style dishes listed in a novel manner: for beginner, intermediate and advanced appetites, all indicated by the familiar ski-trail symbols.

Across from the entrance to the Village Center is the ever funky **Banditos Cantina** with low-cost Mexican fare and occasional Chinese or Italian specialties, succulent hickory smoked chicken and ribs and a special children's menu.

Down the road a mile is the **Three Mountain Lodge**, eclectic dining in a hand-hewn post-and-beam atmosphere. Steaks, seafood, veal, rack-of-lamb, Vermont turkey and a special light-fare menu are all moderately priced.

Le Cheval D'Or, on Main Street in Jeffersonville, eight miles from the Village Center, has been named one of 50 distinguished restaurants in the U.S. by *Conde Nast Traveler*, which praised it for its "woodsy, intimate dining room" and "lusty French food." Fresh salmon is cured and smoked on the premises. The cuisine combines French flair with Vermont ingredients, such as pan-roasted twin quail served with red cabbage and braised with Vermont maple syrup. Reservations are suggested (802-644-5556) and casual elegance is the suggested attire. Priciest place in town, but excellent value.

Après-ski/nightlife

Smugglers' has great nightlife, but it's not of the typical "meet market" variety. Organized activities each night provide entertainment for all ages. Examples—a family sledding party on

Wednesday nights at the lighted sled-and-tubing hill, called Sir Henry's Hill; and Monday's Pictionary Family Tournament, featuring the popular draw-and-guess game.

For more traditional fun, try **The Club Cafe** for après-ski and nighttime entertainment such as karaoke on Wednesdays and dancing to DJ music on Saturday nights. Saturday is also comedy night with the best comedians from the Northeast. **Banditos Cantina** turns into the liveliest spot at Smugglers' after dining. Choose from sports and music videos on a giant screen, pool table or live bands on Friday and Saturday. Teens have their own nightly Outer Limits Teen Center with music videos, snacks, and Wednesday and Saturday dance parties.

Child care

Alice's Wonderland Child Care is the largest licensed care center in New England and a major reason why *Family Circle* magazine has chosen Smugglers' as the top family resort for three years running. The facility accepts children 6 weeks to 6 years old and is staffed with professional care-givers who may also be hired for evening babysitting. Twice a week, the center has Parent's Night Out, with dinner and activities for ages 3-12 so Mom and Dad can have some fun on their own.

Other activities

Shopping: The Village Center has a few shops, but they are stocked with necessities and typical T-shirt/hat/pin souvenirs. But if you want handmade Vermont crafts, you can make your own! Smugglers' has an unusual activity, **Artists in the Mountains**. Local artisans teach classes in several traditional New England crafts, such as Colonial Tin Punching, Basket Weaving, Country Stenciling and Dried Flower Arranging. One of our contributors, laid up with a bum knee, took a Bronze Powder Stenciling class, in which she stenciled a country design on a maple-sugar sap bucket using finely ground metallic powders. The classes include all materials and cost $25-$35.

Getting there and getting around

Getting there: Smugglers' Notch is on Route 108 near Jeffersonville in northwest Vermont. Van pickup is available (24-hour notice required; book it when you book lodging) from the Burlington International Airport, 40 minutes away.

Getting around: Everything is within walking distance.

Information/reservations

Address and phone: Smugglers' Notch Resort, Smugglers' Notch, VT 05464; (802) 644-8851.

For lodging reservations call (800) 451-8752 in the U.S. and Canada. In the United Kingdom, call toll-free 0800-89-7159. You can book everything, including airfare and transfers, with one phone call.

Stowe, Vermont

For most of the 1980s, Stowe seemed intent to live off its reputation as a titled member of the New England skiing aristocracy. It displayed an undeniable blue-blood lineage as one of the oldest and most distinguished East Coast ski resorts, and perhaps also a touch of arrogance. As is often the case with royalty in these modern times, however, the castle and surrounding estate began to look a little timeworn when compared to its *nouveau riche* neighbors. The lifts seemed a little old, and the lift lines were not just a little too long. The slopeside facilities had crossed that invisible line separating quaint from antiquated. Those of us who have always appreciated the unique atmosphere of Stowe could only stand by and watch, hoping that someone would reverse its fortunes before Stowe fell into disrepute, a once proud emperor with threadbare regalia.

Well, the emperor really does have new clothes. During the past few years, Stowe has made many improvements, with the idea of ironing out some of the wrinkles of old age without sacrificing the regal bearing and atmosphere—a job well done.

Heading the improvement list was a sparkling red, fastest-of-its-type-in-the-world gondola that whisks skiers up the right side of Mt. Mansfield, at 4,393 feet the highest peak in Vermont. This eight-passenger, high-speed gondola has been nicknamed The Vortex by locals for its ability to suck in hordes of skiers and transport them up the mountain at the rate of 2,400 an hour (up from 900 for the previous lift). That has cut average waiting time at peak periods from 50 minutes to between 8 and 12, and that's at the busiest times. During non-peak periods, skiers usually have no wait at all.

Besides the new gondola, the first phase of renovation also included the recontouring of 30 acres of trails to lessen bottlenecks, eliminate double fall lines, and generally speed the flow.

Stowe Facts

Base elevation: 1,390'; Summit elevation: 3,750'; Vertical drop: 2,360 feet.
Number and types of lifts: 11—1 quad superchair, 1 eight-passenger gondola;
1 triple chair, 6 double chairs, and 2 surface lifts
Acreage: 480 skiable acres Snowmaking: 73 percent
Uphill capacity: 11,465 skiers per hour Bed base: 5,000+

However, Stowe retained its long, narrow, twisting runs cut close into the surrounding forests—runs that are an important part of making Stowe a classic New England ski experience.

Other improvements were in snowmaking, grooming equipment and a new Midway Lodge in the old four-passenger gondola terminal. The lodge includes a pizzeria, bar and grill, and has helped considerably to lighten the overcrowding at the Mansfield Base Lodge.

For those of you who are only familiar with the resort through photographs, Stowe appears to be a New England village nestled at the foot of a large ski mountain, with pubs and restaurants and boutique shopping clustered around a village square. Almost. The 200-year-old village of Stowe is typical New England in its look, with a charming white steepled church and a main street lined with historic buildings as its anchor. But the town lies about seven miles away from the skiing at Mt. Mansfield and adjacent Spruce Peak. To truly enjoy all this area has to offer, you really need a car. We realize that recommendation only contributes to increased street congestion, but the alternative is the Town Trolley, which runs the seven miles between the village of Stowe and Mt. Mansfield. It provides, in the understated words of a British journalist friend who begged a ride back into town with us, "an epic voyage." The trolley. Makes. A lot. Of stops. Between town. And the mountain.

Where to ski

Part of the legend of Stowe revolves around its Front Face, and the fact that it features some of the steepest and most difficult runs in skidom. Having skied the Front Four is a badge of honor for northeast skiers, and deservedly so, given the nature of Goat, Starr, Liftline and National. Besides being steep, the headwalls are frequently draped with vintage New England ice and the trails are liberally moguled.

Experts who are gunning for all four should begin with National and Liftline. The resort's winch cats allow groomers to prepare these two from time to time. Thus, this is a good place to get used to the considerable steepness of the Front Four. Starr is not groomed, and the view from the top of this run, as it disappears in a steep dive toward the base lodge area far below, is one you won't forget. If you haven't met your match by this time, then you're ready for Goat, a moguled gut-sucker no more than three to five bumps wide.

Another suggestion for the experts, who will find roughly 25 percent of the mountain catering to their desires, is a short but lovely little moguled path through tight trees called Centerline, just to the right of Hayride. Centerline was one of the runs that was widened and smoothed to remove the double fall line.

Snowmaking also was added here, making it one of the early-season options for high-level skiers.

A very nice section of glade skiing through well-spaced trees is just off of the top section of Nosedive. Chin Clip from the top of the gondola is long, moguled, and moderately narrow, but it does not have quite the steep grade that the Front Four boast.

Intermediates will find that 59 percent of trails at Stowe are marked for their maximum enjoyment, including much of Spruce Peak. At Mt. Mansfield, ski to the right or left of the Front Four. Advanced intermediates will probably want to chance the tricky top part of Nosedive for the pleasure of skiing the long, sweeping cruiser that beckons further down. Going left from the top of the Forerunner Quad, take Upper Lord until it leads you to a handful of long, excellent intermediate runs all the way to the bottom in Lower Lord, North Slope, Standard and Gulch.

From the quad, reaching the intermediate skiing under the gondola presents a small problem. The connection between these two parts of the mountain is not convenient unless you are an advanced intermediate willing to take a run down Nosedive, rated double-black at its top. (Yes it's narrow and the moguls get pretty big up there, but there's enough room to pick your way down. We got our advanced intermediate staff member down it before she realized its rating.) If you don't want to chance Nosedive, it's a hike from the quad area over to the gondola, or you can take the green-circle Crossover trail toward the bottom of the mountain, which allows skiers to traverse directly across the Front Four to the gondola base. If you want to work your way back from the gondola to the quad, take the Cliff Trail, which eventually hooks up with Lower Nosedive and dumps you at the base of the high-speed chair.

Across the parking lot is Spruce Peak with a small network of intermediate trails and Stowe's best beginner terrain. If you feel as though you need a little elbow room after too many tight New England trails, try Perry Merrill or Gondolier from the gondola, or cut turns about as wide as you want down Main Street on Spruce Peak.

The Big Spruce double is perhaps the coldest chair lift on the mountain, and certainly the oldest. The runs face south, so they lose snow earliest in the spring, and there is no snowmaking at the top of the mountain or on the long intermediate Sterling trail. Skiing upper Spruce Peak is like all skiing was in the old days—no snow from heaven, no skiing. When the snow is good and the wind isn't blowing, though, the mountain can be a cruiser's delight, and powder days are a real treat. From the top of Spruce Peak, skiers can cross over to Smuggler's Notch See that chapter for more details on this interchangeable ticket.

Intermediates may also enjoy Stowe's night skiing, new since 92/93. The upper portion of Perry Merrill and all of Gondolier are lit Wednesday through Sunday (seven nights during holidays) until 10 p.m. The ride up is in the warm gondola.

Beginners should start at the base area of Spruce Peak, then work up to the easy runs off the Toll House chair (Chair 5), then advance to Chair 4.

One route we would recommend to all levels is the four-mile-long, green-circle Toll Road, which starts at the top of the Forerunner quad and winds gently through forested slopes to the bottom. This is a marvelous trail for lower-level skiers, but more proficient skiers probably will enjoy it, too—not for its challenge but for its beauty and intimacy. At a couple of points, you will ski through a tunnel formed by a canopy of trees. Stop for a minute. Listen to the chirping of the birds and the soft plop as small globs of snow depart the naked branches and drop into the pillowy mounds at ground level. A little later, you'll ski by the small wood-and-stone Mountain Chapel, where on Sundays you can attend an informal church service accessible only to skiers. You just won't find this experience out West.

Snowboarding

While snowboarding has not yet caught on as much at Stowe as at some western resorts, board riders are welcome. As a welcome mat, Stowe has built a 600-foot halfpipe on Spruce Peak and offers professional instruction. A never-ever program is $48 for lift ticket and lesson; $68 with equipment rental. Snowboard clinics concentrate on halfpipe maneuvers, carving and pushing the outer limits.

Cross-country

Stowe has one of the best cross-country networks in the country. Four touring areas all interconnect to provide 132 groomed km. of trails, and an additional 107 km. in backcountry.

The Trapp Family Lodge (253-8511) organized America's first touring center and has 58 km. groomed and 48 km. tracked trails. The fee is $10 a day.

The Edson Hill Touring Center (253-7371) has 42 km. of trails with 20 km. trails groomed. Elevation varies from 1,400 feet to 2,100 feet. The fee is $6 a day.

Stowe Mountain Resort (253-3000) has 75 km. of trails, 35 km. of which are groomed. The daily fee is $10.

The Topnotch Resort (253-8585) has 40 km. of trails. Trail fee is $8.

Ski school (93/94 prices)

Need a little guidance getting down the Front Four? A **special workshop** concentrates on Goat, Starr, National and Liftline and costs $35 for three hours. Other clinics are a Breakthrough To Carving workshop for advanced intermediates for $35 and a Mountain Experience Week that works on mastering varying snow conditions and terrain while getting to know the mountain. The Mountain Experience Week is Monday through Friday afternoons, three hours daily, for $104.

Private instruction is available for $45 an hour, with $15 for each additional person. A full day of private instruction costs $210, and for two to five people, $310. **Group lessons** are $24 for one lesson, with each additional lesson $20.

The ski school has **children's programs** for those 3 to 12 years, headquartered at Spruce Peak. Full-day programs with lunch are $62, with each additional day $52.

Teens (13-16) at the intermediate or higher level have a program for $75 for the first day; $65 each additional day.

Telephone extension for the ski school is 2222.

Lift tickets (93/94 prices)

	Adult	Child (6-12) Senior (65+)
One day	$42	$24
Three days	$110 ($36.66/day)	$62 ($20.66/day)
Five days	$170 ($34/day)	$100 ($20/day)

These prices are valid in February and March. Early and late season prices are about $14 per day lower, January prices are about $6 per day lower and Christmas prices are a few dollars per day higher. Children 5 and younger ski free with paid parent or guardian.

Night skiing is $16 for adults and $14 for children. A twilight ticket, valid from 1 to 10 p.m., is $38 for adults, $22 for children.

Accommodations

Stowe features a Build Your Own vacation plan, where you start with a lodging rate and add on various ski lift and lesson packages or individual lift or Nordic trail tickets. Lodging ranges from small country inns and large resorts to hotels in the old New England tradition.

Ye Olde England Inne, on the Mountain Road; 253-7558 or (800) 477-3771. This is a favorite because it is bigger than a country inn and smaller than a full-fledged hotel. Recently restored, Ye Olde England is now considered one of the best lodgings in Stowe. It has been redone with an English country motif and lavish Laura Ashley touches. Because every room is decorated differently, call for specific differences. Room rates include breakfast. Just off the lobby is Mr. Pickwick's Polo Pub with a selection of more than 100 beers, eight available on tap. The pub also has a full selection of pub grub ranging from steak-and-kidney pie to haggis. Rates (all with private bath): $116-$150 per room, double occupancy.

Green Mountain Inn, Main Street; 253-7301 or (800) 445-6629. A charming old inn with a super location in the middle of town. The wide-planked floors are pine, as is the furniture, with many old four-poster canopied beds. Rooms that front on the street are a little too noisy for light sleepers; big delivery trucks rev their engines at the nearby stop sign starting at about 6 a.m. The hotel also has an annex that is not quite so quaint, but is off the main road. Room rates with breakfast are $100 to $205.

Butternut Inn, Mountain Road; 253-4277. A country inn in the classic sense. Of those we visited, the Butternut was our favorite in Stowe. It reflects the eccentricities of the owners, transplanted from Texas. The inn is No Smoking and no children are allowed. Every aspect of the inn is done nicely: its rooms are all different, guests are pampered, dinners are prepared only for the inn guests and include Angus beef and Tex-Mex, which alternate with more traditional New England fare. Anyone who wants everything done beautifully will appreciate the Butternut. Room rates: $95-$160 double occupancy with breakfast and après-ski snacks.

Ten Acres Lodge, Luce Hill Road; (800) 327-7357, or in Vermont, 253-7638. This country inn was converted from an 1840s farm house. As with all country inns, rooms vary in size. Rooms in the main lodge are relatively simple, but the common areas on the first floor are beautiful. Ten Acres Lodge also has a group of eight modern units, called the Hill House, tucked into the woods behind the old farmhouse. These units all have fire-places in the rooms and share an outdoor hot tub. Room rates, including breakfast: $75-$140 per room double occupancy.

The Gables Inn, on Mountain Road; 253-7730 or (800) 422-5371 (GABLES-1). Gables is what all friendly country inns should be. Not a quiet, stuffy place with antiques and Mozart playing, where you're afraid of breaking something. This is a real lived-in house, which helps everyone have a good time. The breakfasts are among the best in Stowe and guests wouldn't think of eating anywhere else—for dinner either. Room rates, based on double occupancy, $120-$200 per person with breakfast and dinner.

The Resorts

When the Trapp Family's life was dramatized in *The Sound of Music*, their everlasting fame was guaranteed. **The Trapp Family Lodge** (253-8511 or 800-826-7000), they established near Stowe upon arriving in the United States is a legend in its own right. Unfortunately, the original building burned down in the late 1970s, and was completely rebuilt from 1980 to 1983. It is still the most popular and upscale place to stay in the area, and is still in the family—it's now run by a granddaughter.

This is virtually a self-contained resort with an excellent cross-country center. The collection of restaurants is among the best in the area, and a modern pool and fitness center provide excellent amenities. Make reservations early because this lodge is normally full throughout the season (Christmas reservations should be made about a year in advance). Rates, with breakfast and dinner: $110-$139 per person, based on double occupancy.

In a category just below the Trapp Family Lodge, but much closer to the lifts and the town, is **Topnotch at Stowe** (253-8585 or 800-451-8686; in Canada 800-228-8686), which proudly boasts the most extensive fitness center and spa in the area. Topnotch has rooms and condos, along with excellent meeting facilities. It also has the only four covered tennis courts in Stowe. Room rates: $154-$224 per person. Condos are higher prices.

The Inn at the Mountain, part of the Stowe Mountain Resort, is four-diamond rated by AAA, and we have no argument with that accolade (800-253-4754). This beautiful inn and the surrounding condominiums (available through the same telephone number) comprise the only ski-in/ski-out facility in Stowe. The flavor is old-world New England warmth. The name of the Broken Ski Tavern in the Inn commemorates the founding of the first steel ski, which was introduced here. An early prototype is sitting in pieces above the fireplace. At breakfast, guests create their own omelets to order, and enjoy bread from the Inn's own bakery.

While the ambiance in the Inn may be old-world, the Fitness Center (free to all guests) across the parking lot is ultra-modern. There's universal weight training, free weights, workout rooms, aerobic classes, Stairmaster, Lifecycle and rowing machines, as well as a sauna and hot tub. Room and condo unit rates, based on double occupancy and including breakfast and dinner range from $195 to $385.

The best family accommodations in Stowe are at the **Golden Eagle Resort Motor Inn**; 253-4811 or (800) 626-1010. This sprawling complex has more than a dozen buildings and facilities, from motel rooms with kitchenettes to apartments. Along with an excellent restaurant, The Alpine, the complex has an excellent fitness center with pool and hot tub facilities. It is all unpretentious and affordable. Because there are dozens of pricing options, the best bet is to contact the property and explain what you are looking for. In general, though, room rates are $110-$170.

The Stoweflake, (253-7355 or 800-253-2232) down the road a bit from the Golden Eagle, is more upscale and has a pool and fitness center. Rates with breakfast and dinner based on double occupancy are $138-$186 a night. (Without meals, $78-$138.) A nice group of townhouse condominiums has studios to three-bedroom units for $150-$370.

The Vermont Ski Dormitory at the foot of Mount Mansfield offers bunk-style sleeping with shared bathroom facilities. Rates are about $35 a night with breakfast and dinner. Call (800) 866-8749 or 253-4010.

Dining

Stowe has long been famous for its cuisine. **Ten Acres** (253-7638) and **Isle de France** (253-7751) are considered by most to be the top gourmet spots in the area. Entrées at both restaurants range between $17 and $24. An up-and-coming restaurant is the **Blue Moon Café** (253-7006) with innovative fine dining. **Stubb's Restaurant** (253-7110) also gets good reviews.

The **Trapp Family Lodge** (253-8511) puts on an excellent Austrian-style meal for a fixed price of about $25. There normally is a choice of about a dozen entrées.

For a total dining experience, try the **Cliff House Restaurant** (253-3000) at the top of Stowe's gondola. A gourmet four-course meal awaits at $35 per person, plus tax and tip.

For alternatives that aren't budget-busters, try **Miguel's Stowe-Away** (253-7574) or the **Cactus Cafe** (253-7770) for Mexican food, **Restaurant Swisspot** (253-4622) for fondues and decadent Swiss chocolate pie, and **Gracie's** (253-8741) for great burgers and meat loaf. **The Shed** burned down last season, but plans to rebuild to serve its great prime rib and steaks for this one. **Foxfire** (253-4887) has good Italian food, as does **Trattoria La Festa** (253-8480). **The Whip** (253-7301) in the basement of the Green Mountain Inn is a good place for a light dinner or sandwiches. And **Mr. Pickwick's Polo Pub** (253-7064) is excellent. When your steak sandwich almost melts in your mouth, they're doing something right.

H.H. Bingham's (253-3000) in the Inn at the Mountain at the base of the Toll House lift, serves moderate continental cuisine with entrées in the $12 to $18 range. Hearty lunches, too.

On-mountain, there are several choices for lunch and snacks. The **Midway Café and Bakery** in the Midway Lodge has fresh-baked pastries and muffins and gourmet coffee, the **Cliff House Café** at the gondola top is a nice atmosphere, and the **Broken Ski Tavern** at the Inn near the Toll House lift is quite relaxing and a little more upscale.

A breakfast favorite is **McCarthy's,** next to the movie theater, adjacent to the Baggy Knees complex. Also the breakfast at **The Gables** shouldn't be missed, especially on weekends.

Après-ski/nightlife

It's difficult to say exactly what ingredients go into making the perfect après-ski bar, but for our money they are all there in just the right measure at the **Matterhorn Bar**. Located a few miles from the ski area on the mountain road, this raucous little roadhouse is packed and rollicking after the slopes close. There's a dance floor, a disc jockey, loud music, a rectangular bar that makes for easy circulation, pool tables, big-screen TV—all the ingredients. There's a more low-key après-ski meeting place at the mountain in the rustic **Broken Ski Tavern** at the Inn at the Mountain.

You can count the hot spots on one hand, and still have fingers left over. Stowe's college-crowd hangout, **Rusty Nail**, burned down last season; so far, no plans to rebuild. For a slightly older group and dancing, the place to be seen is **B.K. Clarkes**. **Mr. Pickwick's Polo Pub** at the Olde England Inne gets a good pub crowd with its 120 different beers, and the bar at **Miguel's Stowe-Away** seems to be a singles meeting place.

Child care

The day-care program, Kanga's Pocket, takes children from 2 months through 6 years. A full day costs $48 ($42 for each additional day) and a half day is $32. Reservations are required; call 253-3000, ext. 2262. The children's center is at the Spruce Peak area.

Other activities

Shopping: Stowe has many fun shops and art galleries for browsing, most in town. **Shaw's General Store** is a century old and was the town's first ski shop. Other unusual shops are **Moriarty Hats & Sweaters** for custom knitted goods, and **Exclusively Vermont**, for various Vermont-made products.

Indoor tennis can be played at the Topnotch Racquet Club on the Mountain Road. Four Deco Turf courts are available for hourly fees as well as lessons.

In the Village, Jackson arena has an Olympic-size **ice skating** rink. Call 253-6148.

Snowmobiles are available at Nichols Snowmobiles (253-7239) or from Farm Resort (888-3525).

Horse-drawn sleigh rides take place at Edson Hill Manor (253-7371), Stowehof Inn (253-9722), and Topnotch (253-8585).

Snowshoe rentals and guided tours are available from Umiak Outdoor Outfitters, 253-2317.

Ben and Jerry's ice cream factory is just down the road in Waterbury and offers tours that include samples. Winter is not nearly so busy as summer, so it's a good time to take a tour.

Special events include the Stowe Winter Carnival, the oldest winter celebration in the country, normally the second half of January; the Stowe Challenge Cross-Country Races in February; and a Sugar Slalom race with sugar on snow at the finish line for skiers and watchers and the traditional Stowe Snow Beach Party, both in April.

Getting there and getting around

Getting there: Driving time to Stowe from Boston is nearly four hours; from Montreal, 2.5 hours. The resort is a few miles north of Waterbury off Exit 10 of I-89.

Numerous flights arrive at the Burlington airport, which is 45 minutes from Stowe. All major rental car companies have offices at the airport and most hotels have a transfer service from the airport. You can make transfer arrangements when you make your hotel reservations.

For skiers from Washington, Philadelphia or New York, the perfect prelude to the New England charm of Stowe is a romantic trip aboard Amtrak's Montrealer. This is like stepping back into an Agatha Christie novel, with comfortable private berths, helpful attendants to bring cocktails to your room, and the incomparable sensation of watching the moonlit landscape of New England whirl past your window to the lonely call of the train's whistle. The train arrives in Waterbury (15 miles from Stowe) early in the morning in plenty of time for a full day of skiing. Dinner and breakfast are included in the price, which will vary depending on place of origin. Reservations required.

Getting around: You can manage without a car, but we recommend one. The Town Trolley ($1 per single ride; $5 for a week-long pass) is fine for short jaunts, but a slow way to get to the mountain if you're staying in town. Also, it doesn't operate at night.

Information/reservations

For the Stowe Area Association, call (800) 247-8693 (24-STOWE). Representatives can take care of almost everything, including airfare.

For slopeside accommodations at the Stowe Mountain Resort, call (800) 253-4764 (253-4SKI).

Round-the-clock snow conditions: call 253-2222.

Address and phone: Stowe Mountain Resort, Stowe, VT 05672; 253-3000.

Local telephone area code is 802.

Stratton Mountain, Vermont

Manchester is the quintessential Vermont town gone chic. A Vermont farmer arriving here would think he was in some Disney caricature of what Vermont *should* be. Tourists love it—outlets everywhere, gift shops, craft shops, antique shops, Orvis fly fishing on the Battenkill River, steepled churches, manorial hotels, charming country inns, gourmet dining. And it's all very upscale for the most part. Finding a place for a family with young children to stay can be problematic; you'll be relegated for the most part to motelish lodging or condominiums—forget the quaint inns. Weekend traffic is atrocious.

Stratton is an Alpinesque condo village at the base of the lifts that is, village-wise, to Vermont what Vail is to Colorado. Evening activity consists of hopping between a few bars, three hotels, and the upscale shopping arcades, often while wearing a fur coat.

Where to ski

This also is a cruising mountain. The upper mountain has some steeps for advanced intermediates. Upper Lift Line to Lower Lift Line is made for big giant-slalom turns. Black Bear, Polar Bear, Grizzly Bear and Upper Tamarack—all served by the Grizzly double chair—are narrow runs in fine New England tradition with good vertical. Upper Kidderbrook to Freefall provides another good advanced cruise. Upper Standard starts steep but mellows at the bottom.

The double-diamond trails are steep, with big bumps that short skiers may have a hard time seeing over. Upper Spruce is the easiest of the double-diamond trails.

The lower mountain and Sun Bowl are strictly for those who want to look good—very good. Stratton does its best to ensure that if a skier forgets to uplift in a turn he will still have a chance to get around.

Stratton Facts

Base elevation: 1,872; **Summit elevation:** 3,875; **Vertical drop:** 2,003 feet
Number and types of lifts: 14–1 twelve-passenger gondola, 4 quad chairs
1 triple chair, 6 double chairs, 2 surface lifts
Acreage: 480 skiable acres **Snowmaking:** 58 percent
Uphill capacity: 20,020 skiers per hour **Bed base:** 8,000

Last season, Stratton opened a Ski Learning Park with 10 gentle trails served by five lifts, including two new surface lifts. It includes a terrain garden, where bumps and rolls are sculpted by the mountain staff, so beginners can practice their balance and independent leg action *before* they encounter bumps sculpted by hundreds of other skiers' skis.

Mountain rating

Stratton is one of America's best ego-inflating dual ski areas. Excellent grooming on the mostly mellow terrain makes it even easier. Experts can find some good challenges, but don't expect to be pushed.

Cross-country

The Manchester area offers an excellent series of trails through the surrounding hills.

Hildene (362-1788) is in Manchester Village with 15 km. of trails winding through the pine-covered estate of Robert Todd Lincoln.

Nordic Inn (824-6444), just east of Peru, has trails that wander into the Green Mountain National Forest.

The Stratton Ski Touring Center (297-4061) is located at the Sun Bowl and has 20 km. of tracked cross-country trails and 50 km. of backcountry skiing. Lessons and guided tours (including a moonlight trek) are available.

Viking Ski Touring Center (824-3933) in Londonderry provides 40 km. of groomed trails through woods and open fields.

Porc Trails (824-3933) are a series of ungroomed trails maintained by the West River Outing Club of Londonderry. If you intend to use them, make sure someone knows where you are and when you intend to return: the trails are not patrolled daily. Call for directions and parking locations.

Snowboarding

Boarding is allowed lessons and rentals are offered. However, Stratton was one of the pioneers in this high-growth branch of the ski industry. Burton Snowboards, one of the earliest manufacturers, is headquartered in Manchester Center, and Stratton was one of the first major ski areas to allow the sport. Burton's founder, Jake Burton Carpenter, grew up skiing there. Stratton has a halfpipe and excellent instruction.

Lift tickets (93/94 prices)

	Adult	Child (7-12)
One day	$41	$26
Three days	$105 ($35/day)	$69 ($23/day)
Five days	$165 ($33/day)	$105 ($21/day)

These are weekend rates—midweek rates are lower. Other multiday rates are also available. Children younger than 7 ski free. At Stratton, skiers aged 62-69 ski for $31 on weekends; $26 midweek; skiers 70 and older ski for $16 any day.

Ski school (93/94 prices)

Group lessons cost $22 and last an hour and 45 minutes. Ten sessions cost $180 and 20 sessions cost $300. The multi-lesson books are transferable, making them perfect for families. **Private lessons** cost $55 an hour, with additional skiers $20. Additional hours are discounted.

Children have the Big Cub and the Little Cub programs, both with lunch and two lessons for $55. Big Cub is for children 7-12, while Little Cub is for children 3 to 6 .

NASTAR races cost $4 for adults and $3 for children younger than 19. A self-timed race course costs $1 a run or $8 for ten runs.

Accommodations

For **Stratton Reservations** call (800) 843-6867. This toll-free number also handles several properties off the mountain and in Manchester as well.

The **Village Lodge** is smack in the middle of Stratton and is the premier property for location—walk out your door and you are a hundred yards from the gondola. The Village Lodge, with rooms decorated in subdued hotel colors, has no amenities such as pool, dining room, or lounge; for those, take the shuttle to its larger sister hotel, the **Stratton Mountain Inn** in the center of the village with a spa, dining areas, lounges and a variety of rooms . A personal favorite is **The Birkenhaus,** which still has its old-world flavor with excellent service and European-style attention to making you comfortable. This is a small hostelry with the best food on the mountain. The **Liftline Lodge** provides Stratton's most economical lodging on the mountain and sprawls over several wings and buildings.

The **Mountain Villas** is a collection of condos suitable for families. Stratton Reservations has plenty of condos all within easy reach of the slopes. NOTE: The prices on these properties are significantly lower when you buy a Stratton Mountain package. Children younger than 6 stay and ski free anytime. Children 12 and younger stay free in the same room with their parents.

Manchester/Manchester Center

Manchester is filled with many tiny bed-and-breakfast establishments and New England hotels in the Currier and Ives tradition. Most discourage children, but if you brought children to these antique-filled houses, you would be a wreck before the trip was over.

Some of the best properties in the region are the **Wilberton Inn** (362-2500 or 800-648-4944) which is a classic, fashionable address; the **Equinox** (362-4700 or 800-362-4747, reservations only) grand, impressive and expensive (but surprisingly reasonable if you get a package deal); **The Inn at Manchester** (362-1793) a quaint, smaller country inn with 19 rooms; and **The Palmer House** (362-3600), an unpretentious hotel in Manchester Center with comfortable, spacious country decor, four-poster beds, hot tub and sauna, built around a courtyard.

Though it's a few miles out of Manchester Center in the opposite direction of the two ski areas, **Barrows House** in Dorset (867-4455, 800-639-1620) is a good choice for anyone who seeks serene lodging. It is a beautifully restored 200-year-old country inn on expansive grounds, but is still close to Manchester Center's shopping and dining. Barrows House has a first-rate gourmet restaurant that is open to the public for breakfast and dinner, plus a tavern. Innkeepers Linda and Jim McGinnis have midweek lodging-and-meals packages that are quite reasonably priced.

For families, try the **Aspen Motel** (362-2450), **Johnny Seesaws** in Peru (824-5533), and **The Red Sled** on Route 11/30 (362-2161). All are motelish and basic, but you won't have worry about breaking anything.

For **Manchester area central reservations**, call (802) 824-6915.

The closest RV Park is in Dorset on Route 30.

Dining

In Manchester try these less formal, chef-owned eateries— **The Black Swan** (362-3807) which gets two thumbs up from everyone; **The Chantecleer** (362-1616) which is table-side gourmet dining; **Dina's Restaurant** (362-4982) which presents American cuisine in an 18th-century farmhouse.

For family fare in Manchester strike out for the **Sirloin Saloon** (362-2600) with a rustic steakhouse atmosphere and a salad bar to write home about, and where children are readily welcomed. It is popular and mobbed on the weekends. **Laney's Restaurant** (362-4456) has an open kitchen where you can see grilled items being prepared. **Gurry's Restaurant** (362-9878) is burgers and pizza but with specials that are kind to the wallet.

For Mexican and Cajun head into Manchester and try the **Park Bench Cafe** (362-2557). For popular Italian/American meals and pasta try **Garlic John's** (362-9843) which attracts massive crowds.

The best food on Stratton mountain is found in the **Birkenhaus**, which receives rave reviews from virtually everyone. The other on-mountain property that has attained a well-deserved niche in the hearts of the locals and repeat tourists is the **Liftline Lodge** with its special buffets—when lift-line attendants say it's a deal, check it out.

A small restaurant not widely known is **Brush Hill** (896-6100) in West Wardsboro on Route 100, only eight miles away from Stratton Mountain Village. Ask a local how to find the back road to Mt. Snow and take it. When you hit Route 100, turn right and it's a couple of hundred yards on your right. Chef Michael Sylva and his wife Lee have retreated to the woods from big-city restaurants to create their own Green Mountain cuisine. Dining here is by reservation only. Closed Mondays and Tuesdays.

Other top gourmet spots in the vicinity are **The Three O'Clock Inn** (824-6327) in an old restored farmhouse in South Londonderry; **Mistral's at Old Toll Gate** (362-1779) in the center of Manchester; **Barrows House** on Route 30 in Dorset and **The Dorset Inn** (867-5500) also on Route 30 and the oldest continuously operating inn in Vermont. Jackets are preferred in these. Most entrées will run from $15 to $20. The two Dorset restaurants are about a 15-minute drive from Manchester Center in the opposite direction from the ski areas.

For more down-to-earth, out-of-Manchester fare try the **River Cafe** (297-1010) in Bondville with the best ribs in the area. Upstairs at **The Red Fox** (297-2488) in Bondville was recommended by just about every local and regular. **Jamaica House** (874-4400) in Jamaica has great Italian food and a homey bar. Across the street in Jamaica you find the **Brookside Steak House** (874-4271) right on the river with a giant salad bar.

For good simple sit-down food try **Jake's Marketplace Cafe** (824-3811) in Londonderry. **Johnny Seesaw's** (824-5533) in Peru has real Yankee cuisine.

Après-ski/nightlife

In Manchester the hottest pickup scene is at **Park Bench Café** with pitchers of margaritas, or try **Mulligans Bar** in Manchester Village. Once you get started just wander through town, bar to bar, until you find the spot with the evening's action.

At Stratton, when you get off the slopes, après-ski is on the packed deck of the **Bear's Den** with oom-pah-pah bands, or in **Mulligans** serving 50 different types of beer, or **Cafe Applause** in the Stratton Mountain Inn. In the evenings the action continues in Mulligans (with live entertainment on weekends) and the Cafe Applause (great '50s and '60s jukebox if there's no live music) if you are staying on the mountain. Off the mountain, try the **Red Fox** down in Bondville for occasional music and dancing, or the **Jamaica House** for simple bar with TV action.

Child care

The Baby Cub program takes children from 6 weeks through 5 years.

Other activities

Shopping: This is a major non-ski activity here. About 40 factory outlet stores are spread among five shopping centers and several stand-alone stores in Manchester and Manchester Center. Most are brand-name stores you'll find at other factory outlet centers, but a few are rare birds, such as The Down Outlet, Tse Cashmere and Orvis Catalog Outlet Store. These towns also have many boutiques and shops that stock handcrafted, regional gift items; unusual clothing and other things you didn't know you needed until you saw them.

The **Stratton Sports Center** has facilities for indoor tennis, racquetball, indoor pool, hot tubs, saunas, fitness center, tanning salons, and massages.

Getting there and getting around

Getting there: Manchester Center is at the intersection of Routes 7A and 30 in southwestern Vermont. Stratton is on Route 30 about 15 miles east of Manchester. Look for the Stratton Mountain Road from Route 30. If you're heading straight for Stratton from Interstate 91, take Exit 2 at Brattleboro, follow signs to Route 30, then drive 38 miles to Bondville and the Stratton Mountain Road.

The area is about 140 miles from Boston, 235 from New York City and 470 from Washington, D.C.

Getting around: Manchester is about 90 minutes from the Albany, NY airport and requires a car for easy access.

Information/reservations

The main number for information on Stratton Mountain Resort and for mountain lodging reservations is (800) 843-6867. If you want to make lodging arrangements in the Manchester area, 824-6915.

The Stratton Corporation, Stratton Mountain, VT 05155; (802) 297-2200.

Telephone area code is 802.

Sugarbush
Mad River Valley
Vermont

If Vermont is quintessential New England, then the Mad River Valley is a pretty fair candidate for quintessential Vermont. Its two main towns, Waitsfield and Warren, meet the visual requirements of anyone looking for the classic New England country town. Beautiful white and pastel clapboard houses fill the streets, historic buildings have lovingly been restored, and the narrow white-ribbon ski trails of Sugarbush stand out on the pine-green wooded slopes of 3,975-foot Lincoln Peak. Quaint country inns and charming, excellent restaurants abound, yet condos and hearty-fare eating establishments meet the needs of skiers on a budget.

During the 1960s, Sugarbush was dubbed Mascara Mountain for the proliferation of New York models who accompanied influential New Yorkers and Bostonians. Though a bit of that jet-set image lingers today, the resort has been positioning itself in the mainstream skier market by emphasizing its snowmaking ("Mo' Better Snow"), upper-end slopes ("Where Great Skiers Ski") and variety ("A Big Mountain Ski Vacation"). More than any other resort area in Vermont, Sugarbush/Mad River Valley offers something for every level of skier at every level of accommodation luxury.

Where to ski

The skiing is on three separate mountains—Sugarbush South and Sugarbush North, which comprise the Sugarbush ski resort, and separately owned Mad River Glen on Route 17.

Sugarbush Facts

Sugarbush North: Base: 1,535'; Summit: 4,135'; Vertical drop: 2,600 feet
Number and types of lifts: 7—1 quad superchair, 2 quad chairs
2 double chairs, 2 surface lifts
Sugarbush South: Base : 1,575'; Summit: 3,975'; Vertical drop: 2,400 feet
Number and types of lifts: 9—3 triple chairs, 4 double chairs, 2 surface lifts
Acreage: 400 skiable acres Snowmaking: 60 percent
Uphill capacity: 15,018 skiers per hour Bed base: 6,600, (2,200 on mountain)

SUGARBUSH NORTH
Mt. Ellen 4,135'

PANORAMA

BLACK DIAMOND

F.I.S.

RIM RUN

UPPER LOOKIN' GOOD

LOWER RIM RUN

ELBOW

BRAVO

EXTERMINATOR

LWR EXTERMINATOR

SPIN OUT

M

LWR ELBOW

WAY BACK

GLEN HOUSE

ENCORE

WHICH WAY

NORTHSTAR

CRUISER

NORTHWAY

HAMMERHEAD

THE CLIFFS

N

MAINSTREAM

WALT'S TRAIL

NORTHRIDGE EXPRESSWAY

SEMI-TOUGH

INVERNESS

BRAMBLE

LOWER BRAMBLES

VILLAGE RUN

LOWER F.I.S.

CHICKADEE

STRAIGHT SHOT

GRADUATION

EAST ST.

SUGAR RUN

P

J   O

L   +

MOUNTAIN LODGE

K

P

MAP INFORMATION

● Easier	Recreational Racing	
■ More Difficult	Snowboard Half-Pipe	
◆ Most Difficult	Shuttle Bus	
◆◆ Experts Only	Warming Hut	
Snow Making	Slow Skiing Area	
Ski Patrol		

Please remember, trail ratings describe only relative degree of challenge of a particular slope or trail within the Sugarbush trail system. Trail ratings here should not be compared to those found at other ski areas.

Each area provides a different experience. Heading the list of positives is the terrain, which goes from super gentle to super steep, and is well maintained. (Notice we did not say "groomed" —generally both areas groom what needs to be groomed and leave alone what should be left alone.) Topping the negatives list are the plodding lift systems. A local once told us that the lifts had one speed: slow. We would amend that to two speeds: Slow and Awful Slow. But lift lines aren't a problem, so one doesn't much begrudge the extra time spent on the lifts.

That slow lift problem has been addressed at least on Sugarbush North, which has three quads—one high-speed superchair and two fixed-grip lifts. Their installation a few years ago almost doubled the uphill capacity.

Sugarbush South is serviced by nine lifts and has varying terrain. As you face the mountain, the runs to the left are generally the most difficult and those to the right are designed for beginners and lower intermediates. The runs served by Castlerock lifts are very black and no place for timid skiers.

For an intermediate a good start would be to take the Sugar Bravo triple chair, then traverse to the Heaven's Gate triple and the top of the mountain. From here, take Upper Jester, rated blue, (but barely more than a green), then choose from Downspout, Domino, Snowball, Murphy's Glades, or Lower Jester, to complete the run to the base. The most fun for intermediates on this part of the mountain would probably be to use the Sugar Bravo lift and go either right or left to explore the intermediate terrain. Warning: there is a long runout at the bottom of Jester—be ready with your pushing technique.

The far right side of the area is served by the Gate House double chair, then a surface lift, which takes skiers even higher. Here intermediates will have relatively wide runs and good cruising. Beginners will want to stick to this section of the mountain, practicing on Pushover and Easy Rider and then graduating to Slowpoke and Sleeper.

Experts will find plenty of challenge. The entire Castlerock area offers narrow New England-style steeps, and if you are lucky the Castlerock run will occasionally be groomed, making for a heavenly smooth steep. Note that the Castlerock lift is one that qualifies for Awful Slow: even when the resort is nearly empty at midweek the wait can be eight to 10 minutes.

From the top of Heaven's Gate experts can drop down a trio of short steeps directly below the lift or descend Organ Grinder with its tricky double fall line. To the left, experts will find the legendary Stein's Run with its steep, moguled face and a trio of slightly less challenging expert runs.

Sugarbush North is more modern in the sense that it has wide-open cruising runs that a skier won't find at South or at Mad River Glen. The main skiing area is served by the three quad lifts we mentioned. This is primarily an intermediate playground, though the double blacks at the top—F.I.S., Black Diamond, Exterminator and Bravo (the latter a single-diamond)—are among the toughest in New England. North also has more extensive snowmaking than South (76 percent is covered).

On the map, the intermediate runs from the top of the Summit quad chair seem relatively short, but the map is misleading. The Rim Run connecting to Northway and then to either Which Way, Cruiser or North Star comprises one of the classic cruising runs in the United States. The other intermediate section is Inverness, which is served by a quad chair and offers a good training area. Beginners have an excellent area just to the left of the base area with a T-bar and a short double chair.

Mad River Glen is a totally separate ski area and a throwback to earlier ski days. Mad River Glen prides itself on being tough (even the beginner trails here might be graded intermediate at Sugarbush), traditional (it's one of two areas in the nation with a chair lift for solo riders), natural (little snowmaking, combined with plenty of tight tree skiing), daring (can't imagine any other ski area with so much "out-of-bounds" skiing) and homey (skiers with serious tracks to carve have got to love a cafeteria with peanut-butter-and-jelly sandwiches to go).

Experts, real experts, have one goal: the top of the single chair. Yes, the lines do get long—very long. The ski patrol and lift operators scan the line and attempt to weed out beginners and lower intermediates who would have no business at the top. Meanwhile, the real experts happily wait. For them, this is what skiing in the East is all about.

From the top of the single chair, experts can immediately drop down the Chute or the Fall Line, or if they are with a guide or local madman they can venture into the area called Paradise, entered by dropping down an eight-foot waterfall. Real experts: ask around for Octopus's Garden and the 19th and 20th hole. If you look like you know how to ski, a local may direct you there.

The single chair also has plenty of well groomed terrain for the solid intermediate. And guess what? It's not icy. Mad River Glen owner Betsy Pratt let her groomers know in no uncertain terms that this was her mountain, she wanted to ski it, and she didn't want to skate it. So they found a way to scoop and buff the snow, so when the weather cooperates it is surprisingly easy to ski. Antelope and Catamount offer relatively moderate alternate routes down the mountain.

Mad River Glen Facts

Base elevation: 1,637'; Summit elevation: 3,637'; Vertical drop: 2,000 feet.
Number and types of lifts: 4—3 double chairs, 1 single chair.
Acreage: about 95 skiable acres   Snowmaking: 15 percent
Uphill capacity: 3,000 skiers per hour   Bed base: 6,600

At the single chair midstation, tree skiing beckons through the Glades on one side of the lift line and Lynx on the other. More timid souls can traverse on Porcupine and drop down the wide-open Grand Canyon or thread through the narrow Bunny Run.

This brings skiers to the section served by the Sunnyside double chair. Upon reaching the top of this sector, intermediates can turn to the left and drop down Quacky to Porcupine, Grand Canyon and Bunny; or they can go below the lift and to the right down a short series of expert trails, Panther, Partridge, Slalom Hill and Gazelle, most of which empty into Birdland.

Birdland is ostensibly the beginner's area. Granted, there are Duck, Lark, Robin, Wren and Loon on which to train beginners, but there are also more intermediate tight runs like Snail and Periwinkle. If you find yourself going through this area, remember that even though there are green circles at every fork in the trail, real intermediates can have plenty of fun here too. Suffice it to say, if you learn to ski here, nothing will daunt you elsewhere.

One note: At press time, Mad River Glen owner Betsy Pratt was not sure if she would open the ski area this season or not. The plan was to sell the ski area as a not-for-profit corporation through public shares—2,000 of them at $1,650 each. By mid-summer, sales were a little slow. So call ahead before you make a special trip.

Mountain rating

Experts: Head to Mad River Glen, the Castlerock section of Sugarbush South, and the short-but-steep Black Diamond and Upper FIS, plus Exterminator and Bravo at Sugarbush North.

Intermediates and cruise hounds: You'll have the most fun at Sugarbush North. If you're looking for day-long challenge, strike out for Mad River Glen and if you are just entering the intermediate ranks, test Jester and the Gate House area of Sugarbush South.

Beginners have their best area at Sugarbush North, and acceptable sections of Sugarbush South near Gate House. Never-evers should not start at Mad River Glen—take at least a week's worth of lessons first.

Cross-country (94/95 prices)

The Sugarbush Winter Recreation Area, outside the Sugarbush Inn, has 25 km. of prepared trails across from the inn. Trail fees are $12 a day for adults, $8 for children, with reductions for guests staying in Sugarbush Resort properties. Equipment rentals, private lessons and group lessons are available. Other nearby cross-country areas are **The Inn at the Round Barn Farm** with 30 km. of groomed trails, rentals, instruction and snowshoe rentals ($8 trail fee, $4 for inn guests); **Blueberry Lake** with 30 km. of trails ($9 fee); and **Ole's** (near the airport) with 35 km. and the most varied terrain in the area.

Snowboarding

Boarding is allowed everywhere at Sugarbush, but was banned at Mad River Glen during the 93/94 season. Both Sugarbush mountains have halfpipes (the trail map pinpoints their location). South built what it claims is the East's largest snowboard park last season. World Cup riders helped design it, and boarders dubbed the park Fred, an acronym for Radical Extreme Descent, preceded by an expletive deleted.. (Now you know.)

Ski school (93/94 prices)

Sugarbush already had a great ski-school reputation, which should only be enhanced with the recent addition of Paul Brown, former ski school director at Sugarloaf. Brown built Sugarloaf into one of the top instructional programs in the East.

Rates for **group lessons** are $24, with no discounts for juniors or children. **Private lessons** are $45 an hour. An all-day private lesson for one is $225; $310 for two to four skiers. Sugarbush has a **beginner's special**, including the lower lifts, a two-hour lesson and rentals, for $39.

Children are divided into age groups for instruction. The Minibear program takes kids 4-5 years old for a combination of ski school and play activities, the Sugarbear program is for those 6-11, and the Catamount program is for ages 12-16.

The three- or five-day **Centered Skiing Program** is designed to help the intermediate to advanced skier overcome the mental barriers that limit confidence. The three-day cost is $339 per person, which includes 20 hours of instruction, lift ticket, a video to take home and daily continental breakfast. The five-day cost is $499. The program is offered a couple of times each month. Call the ski school at 583-2381, ext. 341 for more details.

Sugarbush also has a women's ski clinic, either two or five days in length, that it schedules several times each season.

Mad River Glen (93/94 rates) has a ski school that, like the area, marches to its own drummer. Mad River offers weekday clinics, and private lessons with a maximum of four skiers per instructor. One-hour one-person rates are $30; additional people cost $15. Mad River has bump clinics on Mondays and Fridays and telemark clinics Tuesday-Thursday. The combined cost of clinic and lift ticket is $30.

Beginner ski packages for first-timers are limited to three people. All-day cost, $45; half-day cost, $35. Packages include lessons, rentals and lift tickets.

Mad River Glen has a program for children 6 to 12 years. Half-day packages cost $25; full-day programs, $40.

NASTAR racing programs are offered throughout the season. When opened, two runs through the timed race course cost $5, with a dollar for each additional run.

Lift tickets (94/95 prices)

Sugarbush

	Adult	Child (7-13) Senior (65-69)
One day	$42	$23
Three days	$114* ($38/day)	$63 ($21/day)
Five days	$170* ($34/day)	$100 ($20/day)

Children 6 and younger and those 70 and older ski free. Sugarbush lowers ticket prices for adults in its Value Season, Nov. 1 through Dec. 16 and April 3 through closing. Prices during that time are $30, one day; $81, three days; $125, five days. Children's and seniors' prices stay the same.

The Ski Vermont's Classics features an interchangeable lift ticket for Stowe, Sugarbush, Smuggler's Notch and Jay Peak. Vermont Classics tickets are available to guests of participating hotels (most are in the Burlington area) and at the ticket windows of the four mountains. Program begins after Christmas and runs through April 1st. For more information on the Vermont Classics Ski Pass, call 863-3489 or any of the ski resorts.

Mad River Glen

	Adult	Junior (6-15) Senior (65-74)
One day	$26	$20
Three days	$74 ($24.66/day)	$56 ($18.66/day)
Five days	$*	$*

Adults pay $30 on holidays. Children 5 and younger will be issued a free ticket when skiing with a paying adult. Skiers 75 and older ski free.

* Skiers who buy a four-day lift ticket get their fifth, sixth and seventh days free.

Accommodations

This area has some of Vermont's finest country inn accommodations, all of which can be booked through Sugarbush Central Reservations, (800) 537-8427. Or call the inns directly.

Topping the list is recently restored **The Inn at the Round Barn Farm** a mile from Route 100 across the wooden bridge on East Warren Road. (Indeed, this rates with the best B&Bs we've seen anywhere in ski country.) The farmhouse has been made into an elegant, spacious, 11-room bed-and-breakfast. It is peaceful and quiet, strictly No Smoking, children discouraged. Room rates for two people including breakfast, range from $95 for a small room with shower and private bath to $175 for the stunning Richardson Room with Vermont-made pencil post king bed, skylights, fireplace, oversized Jacuzzi and steam shower. During the winter, 30 km. of cross-country tracks are outside the door. Call 496-2276.

Tucker Hill Lodge (496-3983 or 800-543-7841), two miles from Sugarbush's lifts, has 22 rooms, each with a choice of breakfast alone or breakfast and a four-course dinner. Prices per day per person start at $124 for the room-and meals deal.

If you like history, you will adore **The Waitsfield Inn** (496-3979 or 800-758-3801), in the center of Waitsfield Village. It started life in the 1820s as a parsonage, was a sleeping-bag dorm for young skiers in the '60s and '70s, and is now a quaintly elegant 12-bedroom B&B. Each of the rooms is named for someone who lived in the house during the 19th century, and a booklet gives short biographies. A highlight is the inn's common area, a charming room built in what was once the stable. The inn is run by Steve and Ruth Lacey, he a droll Brit and she a bouncy Californian. Prices start at $130.

Other B&Bs that we found quite charming were **Lareau Farm Country Inn**, (496-4949) a roomy 14-bedroom inn that is connected to a popular weekend-only restaurant, the American Flatbread Kitchen; and **West Hill House** (496-7162), a four-bedroom (all with private bath) inn that is inexpensive ($85 weekdays; $90 weekends) but beautifully decorated.

The most luxurious full-service hotel property is the **Sugarbush Inn** located on the access road. Ski-and-stay packages start at $67 per person based on double occupancy. Though the inn and its 46 rooms are beautiful, the service was consistently underwhelming during our stay last season. The inn has a 25-km. cross-country trail system, indoor swimming pool, fitness center and saunas.

Another favorite is the **Weathertop Lodge** on Route 17 between Waitsfield and Mad River Glen (496-4909). Rates are about $50 per person weekends, less during the week.

Mad River Barn (496-3310) has spacious rooms and some of the best lodging food in the valley (both in quantity and quality). To stay here is a step into a wonderful 1940s ski lodge.

Families will want to check into the **Madbush Falls Country Lodge** on Route 100 (496-5557) or the **Hyde Away** (496-2322). Both are great spots for children and close to the slopes. The Hyde Away has become the favorite locals' dining hangout on Thursdays for Fish Night.

Of the condominiums in the Village at Sugarbush South, the most luxurious are the **Southface Condominiums** with hot tubs in each unit and a shuttlebus ride from the slopes. **The Snow Creek** condos are ski-in/ski-out, but you have the noise of snow guns at your back window during snowmaking operations. The **Paradise** condos are newer but a good walk from the slopes; however, they have good shuttle service. **The Summit** units are roomy and **Castle Rock** condos are close to the slopes. **Unihab** looks like boxes stacked on one another, and **Middle Earth** condos are 10 minutes from the lifts and small.

Rates range from $126 for a one-bedroom in value season to $635 for a four-bedroom during holiday periods. Guests may use the indoor pool, indoor tennis, racquetball, squash courts, aerobics, Jacuzzi, steam room and Nautilus equipment at the Sugarbush Sports Center for an additional fee. These condos are close to the children's center.

Almost as close to the lifts as Sugarbush Village units is the newly completed **The Bridges Resort and Racquet Club.** This complex has racquetball courts and an indoor pool. Rates: two-bedroom, two-bath units start at $238. Call 583-2922 or (800) 453-2922.

Skiers heading primarily for Mad River Glen should check into the **Battleground** condos, starting at $184 for a two-bedroom unit. Call 496-2288 or (800) 248-2102.

Dining

With more than 40 eating establishments in the valley, this area boasts a very high excellent-restaurant-per-skier ratio. The only other competition in New England is the Mt. Washington Valley in New Hampshire.

The top of the line is **Chez Henri** (583-2600) in Sugarbush Village at the base area of Sugarbush South. The restaurant manages to capture a true French bistro feeling—it is romantic and cozy, with low ceilings and a flickering fire. The owner, Henri Borel, personally greets guests and makes them feel at home. He also supervises the excellent wine selection. Henri features lunch, fondue in the late afternoon, then dinner until 10 p.m. Entrées range from $13.50 to $22.

Sam Rupert's, down a driveway to the left as you approach the Sugarbush parking lot, has developed lots of fans and offers an eclectic menu rivaling any in the area with a good reasonable wine list. Bill Brunell adds real magic to evenings twice a week.

The Common Man has attracted an excellent clientele and a reputation for good food. The atmosphere is great New England baroque barn with crystal chandeliers. Entrées generally range from $12 to $18; 583-2800.

Tucker Hill Lodge on Route 17 between Waitsfield and Mad River Glen has one of the best reputations for dining in the valley. The menu changes every night of the week. Expect to pay between $16 and $24 for entrées. Reservations are suggested; 496-3983. The downstairs lounge at Tucker Hill is called Giorgio's Cafe, which serves Italian meals.

The **Terrace Room** at the Sugarbush Inn is more intimate with similar prices and continental dining. The menu changes daily depending on what foods are in season. The **Grill Down Under** is a more casual dining spot in the Sugarbush Inn and **Knickers** in the clubhouse at the Sugarbush Cross Country Center is enjoyable.

The Bass Tavern on the access road serves tasty, heart-healthy and creative meals ($10-$16) around a giant fireplace.

Mad River Barn Restaurant has a popular Saturday buffet, and dinners Sunday through Friday from 6:30 to 8 p.m. Meals are prepared by chefs from a nearby culinary school, Mary's in Bristol. Another Sugarbush tradition worth the effort is the **Flatbread Kitchen** open only on weekends at the Lareau Far Country Inn. Call 496-4949 to make sure they are serving.

For families out to stretch the budget and still get good fare, number one for good, wholesome food at reasonable prices is the **Hyde Away** on Route 17. Thursday's Fish Night is a big hit with locals. For simple, quick food, try **The Den** on Waitsfield's main street, or **D.W. Pearl's. The Bass Tavern** has excellent heart-healthy fare.

Alas, our favorite breakfast spot, Pitcher Inn, burned down in 1993 and hasn't reopened. Other good spots for morning fare are **D.W. Pearl's,** the **Hyde Away** and **Pepper's Restaurant** at Pepper's Lodge. The Mad River Barn lays out excellent homemade muffins and jams and serves only real maple syrup.

Après-ski/nightlife

Après-ski starts at the base lodges, which seem to do booming business at the bar as the lifts begins to close. Or head to **Chez Henri** where the bar fills up with people quietly drinking beer or wine. The **Hyde Away** is where you will find the locals; the **Blue Tooth** is most popular with tourists. The **Bass Tavern's** happy hour often will get rowdy. One or the other Sugarbush base lodges will usually have a live band for après-ski. On weekends try the **Sugarbush Inn** for a slightly more upscale crowd. If you are coming from Mad River Glen, the only place to stop is the **Mad River Barn.** The bar there looks like an old Vermont bar should look: moose head hanging over the fireplace, hunting scenes on every wall, big couches and stuffed chairs, wood paneling and a choice of bumper pool or shuffleboard.

In the evenings, **Gallagher's** has dancing with a mix of music from rock to country-rock and an interesting crowd. **Mad Mountain Tavern,** across from Gallagher's, has become popular because of live music on weekends. **Chez Henri's** disco attracts an upscale, slightly older group.

Child care

The **Sugarbush Day School and Nursery** was the first child-care facility ever established at a ski resort. It takes children 6 weeks to 3 years. Two emergency medical techs and a registered baby nurse are in residence. Toddlers get a pre-ski program that uses games on and off the snow to introduce skiing.

Hourly rates are $6; with lunch, add $3. Full-day program with lunch is $45.

Mad River Glen has the Cricket Club Nursery for children 18 months to 6 years. Rates run $30 a day for the first child and $25 a day for the second child.

Other activities

Shopping: Waitsfield and Warren have several art galleries, country stores and antiques/collectibles shops that are fun for browsing and buying. Warren Village has the best within-walking-distance collection of shops.

The **Sugarbush Sports Center** and the **Bridges Resort and Racquet Club** have various sports and exercise facilities.

Snowshoe treks are available from the summit of Sugarbush North to Sugarbush South. Call 583-0381.

Sleighrides and skijoring can be arranged at the Vermont Icelandic Horse Farm in Waitsfield. Call 496-7141. Other farms offering sleighrides are the Lareau Country Inn (496-4949) and Whispering Winds Farm in Moretown (496-2819).

Ice skating rinks are at Tucker Hill Lodge, Sugarbush Inn or the Skatium next to Grand Union in Waitsfield.

Mad River Flick (426-4200) has first-run movies, plus something at the concession stand most movie theaters don't offer: beer and wine.

Getting there and around

Getting there: Sugarbush is off Route 100, about 20 miles south of Waterbury. Burlington airport is about an hour away. Amtrak offers train-ski-lodging packages, with daily service from New York, Philadelphia and Washington, D.C. For information, call (800) 237-7547 for packages; (800) 872-7245 for train only.

Getting around: Sugarbush has four free shuttles: the Village shuttle, which connects several lodging properties with Sugarbush South; the Parking Lot Jitney, which circles each area's parking lot; the Intermountain Shuttle, which connects South and North; and the Fun Shuttle, which connects lodging at Sugarbush South with Waitsfield's downtown. The first two work fine. The intermountain shuttle runs once per hour during the week; once per half hour on weekends. Get to the stop early. The nightly Fun Shuttle also runs once per hour from 6 p.m. to 12:30 a.m. For a one-time visit to town it's okay, but for more frequent visits, bring or rent a car.

You will need a car to get to Mad River Glen.

Information/reservations

Sugarbush Central Reservations will arrange all phases of your trip: (800) 537-8427 (53-SUGAR).

Snow phone: for Sugarbush call 583-7669; for Mad River Glen call 496-2001 or in VT 800-696-2001.

For **Mad River Glen** information call 496-3551.

The local telephone area code is 802.

Alyeska, Alaska

Alyeska, 40 miles southeast of Anchorage, is an unusual ski resort: the mountain rises from sea level to 3,939 feet, and 2,850 feet of its vertical is skiable. The lower half of the mountain is forested and the upper portion is above the tree line. The base altitude is only 270 feet above sea level, the lowest of any major ski area in the world. This, coupled with upper-mountain snow accumulations reaching 750 inches a season, can make for rare conditions: on a mid-April visit there was still 20 feet of snow on the upper mountain and the temperature at the top of the lifts was just 30 degrees.

Images of Alaska tend toward ice, sled dogs, igloos and pipeline construction in subzero weather. Anchorage reality is much different. Warm Pacific currents cause winter temperatures to average 10 to 30 degrees Fahrenheit. But plenty of snow does fall, and with the mountains dropping right into the sea, the avalanches along the road skirting the edge of Turnagain Arm are normal. Snow control cannons trigger slides over the road, and a drive to Alyeska can take you through more than a half dozen cleared avalanches.

Until very recently, the resort's facilities were Spartan—no large hotels, no extensive shopping facilities or restaurants, and lifts that did the job but were becoming outdated.

Change began in 1991 with a $70 million expansion program that is coming to fruition this season. Within the last two years the resort has opened a 60-passenger tram transporting skiers more than a mile from the base to mid-mountain, a high-speed quad, a new beginner chair lift, a day lodge and an on-mountain restaurant. In August, 1994, the final major component came on line: the 307-room luxury Alyeska Prince Hotel, which replaces the only other lodging, the 27-room Nugget Inn, which closed when the Prince opened.

Alyeska Facts
Base elevation: *270';* **Summit elevation:** *3,160';* **Vertical drop:** *2,850 feet*
Number and types of lifts: *9–1 60-passenger tram, 1 quad superchair, 2 quad chairs, 3 double chairs, and 2 surface lifts*
Acreage: *480 skiable acres* **Snowmaking:** *none*
Uphill capacity: *9,450+ skiers per hour.*

You will find most Alaskans surprisingly open and chatty; be prepared to tell and hear some good stories. It's hard for Alaskans to stay in touch with family members in the Lower 48, so they'll chat freely with visitors.

Where to ski

The superchair Spirit of Alyeska carries skiers 1,411 vertical feet to the top of the lift-serviced terrain, which is at the base of the Alyeska Glacier. Up here it's wide-open, above-treeline skiing. The entire 2,500 feet of vertical is skiable in one continuous run, with intermediate to super-expert pitch depending on your choice of route.

Alyeska also has a unique combination of open bowl skiing and trails through the trees directly under Chairs 1 and 4. Beginners will stick to the area served by Chair 3 and the surface lifts. Intermediates can take the new quad chair, drop into the bowl and ski whatever they can see. It doesn't take much judgment to figure out whether you are getting in over your head, and this bowl gives you plenty of room to traverse out of trouble. The bowl funnels into Waterfall and ends on Cabbage Patch before reaching the base area.

For intermediates taking the Spirit Quad to the top of the resort, it's best to follow the Mitey Mite: swing left when you get off the chair. This takes you past the Skyride snack bar, and back to the Quad by three intermediate routes, or tip down South Face (very steep and ungroomed).

From the Quad, experts can go right and drop down Gail's Gully or Prospector and take a gully left or right of Eagle Rock, then back to the Quad. Experts willing to work can take the High Traverse from the Quad, arcing through The Shadows between Mt. Alyeska and Max's Mountain, dropping down through new snow and open steeps; or continue over the ridge to find good steeps and a short section of gladed skiing on Max's Mountain (when opened by the Patrol—it's avalanche-prone until March).

Mountain rating

Alyeska has a small beginner area, but we wouldn't suggest this as a place to learn to ski unless you're athletic.

Intermediates will have a field day, especially with the wide-open bowl skiing and spectacular views from the top of the Quad. Experts have some good drops but the real challenge of Alyeska is the tremendous variety of terrain and snow conditions from top to bottom. Snow may be groomed, cut up or untouched. Often there is powder at the top moistening to mashed potatoes at the bottom.

Cross-country

The Nordic Skiing Association designed and prepared the 10-km. Winner Creek trail, which leaves from Alyeska's base and wanders through woods, across meadows and up and down gentle hills. The trail is not groomed. You can also skinny-ski around nearby Moose Meadow area—locals will point you there; it's not marked.

There are hundreds of kilometers of groomed cross-country trails in Anchorage at Kincaid, Russian Jack and Hillside Parks. The Chugach State Park hillside trails are easily accessible (with a 4-wheel-drive) wilderness areas. There's a Nordic resort at Hatcher Pass (an hour and a half north of downtown Anchorage) and more cross-country trails at Sheep Mountain Lodge, 50 miles north of Palmer.

Ski school (93/94 prices)

You will meet some very interesting people teaching skiing. The half-dozen full-timers, all PSIA-certified, build houses, drive boats and catch salmon in the summer. Part-timers might be pharmacists, lawyers, pilots, mothers, purchasing agents, or firefighters.

Ski school adult **group lessons** (age 11 and up) are at 10:45 a.m. and 2:30 p.m. Adult group lessons cost $35. Juniors 11-13 and seniors 60+ pay $25. Special **beginner programs** combine beginner lift, lesson and rentals for $35; $99 for three consecutive days.

Private lessons are $40 an hour, $20 for extra students.

Alyeska has snowboard and telemark lessons, but you will need to contact the ski school ahead of time, because these lessons are not regularly scheduled.

Alyeska has a weekend **children's program** for ages 4-10 with 2-hour lesson, or full-day program including cafeteria lunch with the instructor. It is often overbooked, so always try to make reservations (783-2222).

The **Challenge Alaska Adaptive Ski School**, a chapter of National Handicapped Sports, provides skiing for the disabled with support from Alyeska Resort. All disabilities, all ages, by reservation only. A skier with a disability, and ski buddy, may purchase discount lift tickets and rent adaptive ski equipment. Open Tuesday-Sunday, usually December 15 to April 15. Challenge Alaska has information on local wheelchair-accessible accommodations and amenities. Call: Challenge Alaska, Box 110065, Anchorage AK 99511-0065, fax (907) 561-6142.

Alyeska Ski School phone: 783-2222.

Lift tickets (94/95 prices)

	Adult	Child (8-12) Senior (60+)
One day	$29	$17
Two days	$54 ($27/day)	$32 ($16/day)
Three days	$79 ($26.33/day)	$47 ($15.66/day)

Though these prices seem a bit low for a resort, keep in mind that Alaskan winter days are shorter than they are farther south. Here, the lifts don't start running until mid-morning (about 10:30 a.m.). Children 7 and younger ski for $7. Students with ID pay $23 for day tickets. Night skiing on 19 trails runs Thursdays through Saturdays 4:30-9:30 from January through March, plus November and December holiday periods: Adults—$14, children and seniors—$12.

Child care

Here, Alyeska has a problem. Little Bears Playhouse day-care center is near the resort (783-2116), but it is normally full with local children. The staff may recommend other babysitters who live in the valley.

Accommodations

The only accommodations at the base of the resort are in the resort's new, 307-room **Alyeska Prince Hotel** and privately owned condominiums which may be rented through management agencies.

The Prince's rates are $160-$260 per night. Call (800) 880-3880 for reservations.

About 50 condominium units are managed by two firms, **Vista Alyeska Accommodations**, Box 1029, Girdwood AK 99587 (30 units), 783-2010, fax 783-2011. A condo sleeping six costs $175-$250 a night, a condo sleeping four costs $125 to $200 depending on amenities. Some have fireplaces, whirlpools, hot tubs and wet bars. Fireplace use is not restricted by air quality regulations.

Alyeska has a few bed-and-breakfasts. See Anchorage Visitors Guide B&B section under "Alyeska" alphabetic listings.

The larger bed base is in Anchorage, a 35- to 55-minute drive depending on weather. Major hotels include the Regal Alaskan, Hotel Captain Cook, Hilton, Holiday Inn, Sheraton and Westmark. There are many smaller hotels and motels, and hundreds of bed-and-breakfast rooms (some with spectacular views) available through the B&B reservation services. See the free Visitors Guide, available throughout the area.

Dining

Alaska is casual about dress, and you'll see suits and long gowns in the same dining room with blue jeans. Skiwear is always acceptable. These are some of our favorites; see the Visitors Guide for more selections.

The Alyeska Prince Hotel has four restaurants. The **Pond Cafe**, the largest with seating for 164, serves breakfast, lunch and dinner with a California-Italian menu. **Prince Court** concentrates on seafood in a casual setting, but is open for dinner only Fridays through Mondays. The **Takanawa Sushi**

Bar and the **Katsura Teppanyaki Room** are open for dinner five nights a week, but seat just 14 and 18 diners, respectively. There are several on-mountain eateries as well, including the **Seven Glaciers Restaurant and Lounge**, which is at the second level of the Glacier Terminal at 2,300 feet. (Reservations: 754-2237).

Alyeska & vicinity: Perhaps the best restaurant in the area is the **Double Musky Inn**, a mile from the lifts on Crow Creek Road. It's mind-boggling to find great Cajun food in Alaska. Entrées from $18 to $30. No reservations, opens at 5 p.m.

Turnagain House, a white-tablecloth restaurant looking out on Turnagain Arm halfway to Anchorage, has a reputation for fine seafood and other dishes with excellent service. Entrées $15 to $30. Reservations.

Chair 5, casual, less expensive, offers prime rib, halibut and a tasty, very spicy chicken jalapeño. Girdwood business district next to the Post Office.

The Bake Shop at the resort boardwalk has killer soups, energy-filled buttered sticky buns with fruit filling, and sandwiches. Walk in, meals $5-$9. Lots of locals, ski instructors and patrollers here.

The Girdwood Griddle in the business district has some of the best homestyle breakfasts at modest prices.

Edelweiss, a three-minute walk from the resort base, has German cooking at modest prices.

Anchorage: For those with deep pockets and taste for the best, call the **Marx Brothers Cafe**, for inventive continental cuisine and impeccable service in a cozy frame-house setting which reminds us of a small New England inn. Reservations required. Most entrées $20-$30.

Likewise, the **Corsair**, with continental cuisine offered by owner Hans Kruger. The style is elegant—expect to spend the whole evening.

For Northern Italian, **Romano's** in midtown has a strong local following; no reservations. **Little Italy** in South Anchorage, closer to Alyeska, also is packed with locals, reservations taken and occasionally needed. Moderately priced, entrées $11-$21.

Also moderately priced with fresh seafood specials daily are **Simon & Seafort's Saloon & Grill** (livelier) and **Elevation 92** (quieter), around the corner from each other downtown. Also try **Jens' Restaurant & Gallery** and **Europa Cafe** in midtown. Seemingly a hole in the wall, **Club Paris** is an intimate downtown steak house.

For great views, especially at cocktail time, try the top-floor **Crow's Nest** at the Hotel Captain Cook, or **Top of the World** in the Hilton. **Josephine's** in the Sheraton also has a view, but is open only for Sunday brunch. Reservations; bring $$$ if dining.

Many Japanese have settled in Anchorage, and good moderately priced restaurants such as **Akaihana**, **Tempura Kitchen**, **Daruma**, **Kumagoro**, **Shogun**, **Yamatoya** and **Ichiban** are the result. All offer tempura, sukiyaki and other cooked dishes as well as sushi and sashimi. **Thai Cuisine** has— surprise—Thai cuisine. There are good Chinese establishments and a few Korean.

Families should head to **Sourdough Mining Co.** (great ribs, corn fritters) **Gwennie's Old Alaska Restaurant** (breakfasts, sandwiches, historic photos), **Hogg Brothers** (wow omelets for working people), **Red Robin**, the **Royal Fork**, **Peggy's**, **Lucky Wishbone** (the best fried chicken), and **Arctic Roadrunner** (super burgers).

For margaritas and Mexican cooking: **La Mex**, **Garcia's**, **El Patio**, **Mexico in Alaska**. Nice places, not great cuisine.

Après-ski/nightlife

The **Aurora Bar and Lounge** in the Alyeska Prince Hotel has a moderately lively atmosphere in the bar, where skiers can watch sports on TV. The lounge is quieter, with a rock fireplace and comfortable sofas and chairs. For immediate après-ski, head to the **Daylodge Don's Bar** for Don's Ramos Fizz.

The **Double Musky** and **Chair 5** also have taverns. On the drive into Anchorage, the **Bird House** is a legendary sunk-in-the ground log building. Try a drink, an incredibly hot pickle, and some conversation while trying to sit up straight. Bring a business card: you'll find out why. Look for the "Bar" sign and bird head on the building.

Anchorage has a highly developed nightlife and cultural scene, a legacy of the pipeline days, the long winter nights, and generous doses of oil patch money.

For theater, opera, drama and movies, buy the local newspaper (Daily News). There's a Friday morning entertainment tabloid that's very helpful. You'll be surprised at the visiting artists and productions at the Alaska Center for the Performing Arts downtown, or the University of Alaska in midtown.

Mr. Whitekeys' Fly By Night Club puts on a zany, hilarious show called (depending on the season) Christmas in Spenard, Springtime in Spenard, or Whale Fat Follies. Call 279-7726 for reservations. This may be the only bar in the world where you can order Spam with champagne, or Spam nachos. After the show, there's dancing to the Spamtones. Mr. Whitekeys, the owner, sponsored a climber eating a can of Spam on the summit of Mt. McKinley.

For loud rock and dancing try **Chilkoot Charlie's**, "where we cheat the other guy and pass the savings on to you," or **Midnight Express**. For quieter dancing and a slightly older clientele try **Legends** at the Sheraton, **Whale's Tail** at the Hotel

Captain Cook, or the lounge at the Golden Lion Best Western. For country music head to **Last Frontier South**.

Other activities

For a **dogsled** trip, run by Bob Crockett's Chugach Express Dog Sled Tours, call 783-0887 for reservations; last-minute calls don't work. Trips and prices range from 30 minutes to 3 hours, $20 to $50+ per person.

The variety of other activities is staggering. Of course, Anchorage has many fine shops where you can buy native crafts, plus items from around the world, thanks to Anchorage's position as a stop on long-distance international flights. This city of 250,000 is the business, cultural, transportation and, to some extent, government center of the state. Use your Anchorage Visitors Guide, buy a newspaper, ask locals on the chair lift for their favorite things.

Getting there and getting around

Getting there: Alyeska is 45 miles south of downtown Anchorage. Get on Gambell Street south, which becomes the Seward Highway, Route 1, along Turnagain Arm. This spectacular drive is one of the best parts of the skiing experience at Alyeska, and if you see cars parked by the road near Falls Creek, stop—the drivers are watching Dall sheep. Toward spring you may see bald eagles as the fish return.

Getting around: If you choose to stay at an Anchorage hotel, Alaska Sightseeing runs regularly scheduled transportation to the resort. Ask at the hotel desk. Otherwise, you'll need a car. If you are driving on mountain roads, or on back roads in Girdwood, get a 4-wheel-drive vehicle. Locals do.

Information/reservations

Alyeska Resort, Box 249, Girdwood AK 99587; 783-2222, snow conditions tape 783-2121, fax 783-2814. Hotel reservations: (800) 880-3880.

The source for community information is the **Anchorage Convention & Visitors Bureau,** 1600 A St. #200, Anchorage AK 99501. Phone the main office 276-4118, fax 278-5559, for a copy of the encyclopedic Anchorage Visitors Guide. Request First Class Mail.

Questions and details: phone ACVB's Log Cabin Visitor Center (274-3531) or drop in at 4th and F downtown. There's also an Airport Visitor Center in the baggage claim area.

The local telephone area code is 907.

Mid-Atlantic Resorts

Blue Knob, Claysburg PA, (814) 239-5111
7 lifts, 21 trails, 1,100 vertical feet

This mountain is in a part of Pennsylvania that gets more natural snow than the Poconos. The mountain has the lodge at the top, like Snowshoe. You'll find the beginner areas at the top as well; toward the bottom the pitch becomes steeper. The resort is 150 miles from Philadelphia and 100 miles east of Pittsburgh. Take the Bedford exit off the turnpike, then follow Rte. 220 north to Pavia and follow the signs.

Camelback, Tannersville PA, (717) 629-1661
12 lifts, 30 trails, 800 vertical feet

This is the busiest Poconos resort. All trails are blanketed with manmade snow. For the 1994-95 season the Pocono Mountains largest ski area, Camelback, is adding nearly $3 million in on-mountain improvements. Camelback is cutting three new trails (one top to bottom expert) and building the first detachable high speed quad in the Poconos. Camelback promises that the new terrain and lift will virtually eliminate the area's notorious lift lines. This barely qualifies as a destination resort, with only 250 townhouses located at the base. A 150-room hotel, The Chateau, overlooks the trail network. The resort is an easy 100-mile drive from New York City or Philadelphia—if at all possible, avoid it on weekends.

Whitetail, Mercersburg PA, (717) 328-9400
4 lifts, 17 trails, 995 vertical feet

This is the newest Pennsylvania resort, in fact the newest major resort to be built in the nation in more than 10 years. The owners have spent $20 million on startup costs, installing three quads (including one high-speed detachable), building a beautiful Deer Valley-inspired base facility and trying to give Eastern skiers an upscale ski experience. In addition to having 100 percent snowmaking covering its 100 acres of trail, a children's center and 4,000 per hour skier capacity, it's just two hours from the White House.

Elk Ski Area, Union Dale PA, (717) 679-2611
5 lifts, 17 trails, 1,000 vertical feet
This is, for Pennsylvania, a tough skier's mountain. The slopes are good for advanced skiers and solid intermediates who want some practice. Even the beginner trails are difficult. There is no real "resort area," but the region has about 50 hotels. Elk is in the northeast corner of Pennsylvania near Scranton.

Seven Springs, Champion PA, (814) 352-7777
18 lifts, 30 trails, 970 vertical feet
Hidden Valley, Somerset PA, (814) 443-6454
8 lifts, 16 trails, 610 vertical feet
These resorts are about three and a half hours from Baltimore and Washington and an hour from Pittsburgh. Seven Springs has the best base facilities and Hidden Valley offers quieter surroundings. Trails at these two resorts will keep beginners and intermediates happy for a day or so. Seven Springs has the more difficult trails.

Snowshoe, Snowshoe WV, (304) 572-5252
7 lifts, 33 trails, 1,500 vertical feet
Snowshoe sits atop Cheat Mountain, topping off an inverted resort: the facilities are at the summit. Snowshoe's altitude of 4,800 feet is higher than Stowe or Killington. The area often gets 200 inches of snow and has extensive snowmaking. This is the most elaborate and extensive resort in the South. The main problem is access: this resort is difficult to reach, at the end of a 10-mile car path, but once there, every skier can enjoy the mountain. Last year Snowshoe replaced the triple lift on Ball Hooter with a new quad. For the 1994-95 season, the lodge will be refurbished.

Silver Creek, Slatyfork, WV, (304) 572-4000; (800) 523-6329
4 lifts, 14 trails; 663 vertical feet
Snowshoe bought nearby Silver Creek Resort during the 1992-93 season adding, a terrific family area to its holdings. Several miles down the mountain from Snowshoe (connected by shuttle bus) Silver Creek is less crowded, and the slopes are wider and better designed than at Snowshoe. The downside is the skiing is less challenging. One lift ticket is good at both areas.

Canaan Valley, Davis, WV, (304) 866-4121
21 trails, 3 lifts; 850 vertical feet
A long time favorite ski area for Washington skiers, Canaan (pronounced Kuh - NAAN) Valley ski area is located in a pristine wilderness area. Deer stroll in front of the park hotel. There is terrific cross country-skiing nearby in the Dolly Sods and along

mountain gorges. The alpine skiing is good with a variety of terrain for all levels. New for the 1994-95 season, Canaan Valley is building a new base facility.

Timberline Four Seasons Resort, Davis, WV (304) 866-4801
17 trails - 2 chairs, 1 T-bar; 1,084 vertical

This area was one of the first in the country to welcome snowboarders. It is a small family area, boasting a two-mile long beginner's run. Usually uncrowded compared to next-door Canaan, and many of the skiers are resort property owners. Canaan Valley and Timberline do not cooperate with interchangeable lift tickets.

Wintergreen, Wintergreen VA (804) 325-2200
5 lifts, 10 trails; 1,003 vertical feet

Wintergreen is located less than an hour south of Charlottesville along the famed Skyline Drive. While natural snow is limited, the manmade variety is religiously pumped out day and night. The lodge is rather upscale with boutiques and antiques. Most skiing is mellow, but The Highlands offers a thousand feet of bumps with limited crowds, thanks to good control by the ski patrol.

Wisp, McHenry, Maryland - (301) 387-4911
5 chairs, 3 surface lifts; 23 trails on 80 acres; 610 vertical feet

Located above scenic Deep Creek Lake, Wisp is the closest thing below the Mason-Dixon Line to skiing Lake Tahoe. A solid family ski area with terrain for all levels; intermediates will especially enjoy cruising on the backside of the mountain.

Midwestern Resorts

The biggest Midwestern ski areas may not have the great verticals of mountains to the east and west, but they have enough terrain, fine facilities, and uphill capacity to tune anyone up for bigger adventures. The following are the best Midwestern ski destinations. Expect lift tickets to be between $25 and $30 everywhere except Michigan's Lower Peninsula, where weekend tickets will be in the mid-$30s. All the resorts offer midweek price incentives and stay-and-ski packages.

Michigan's Lower Peninsula:

Boyne Highlands and Boyne Mountain,
Harbor Springs and Boyne Falls MI (800) 462-6963 (GO-BOYNE)
55 trails; 520 vertical feet

The Mountain and **The Highlands** are about 30 minutes apart and exchange lift tickets. The Mountain's steep chutes and mogul fields are among the best in the region; Hemlock has long been the standard-bearer for Midwestern steep. The Mountain has the nation's only high-speed six-seat chair. The Highlands is a Michigan classic, with wide sweeping bowls and New England-style trails that slice through the woods. The Highlands added more beginner terrain and a new chair last season to complement its more demanding runs. Each resort has an uphill capacity of around 22,000 skiers per hour (tops in the Midwest). Boyne's snowmaking capabilities are legendary. Boyne Mountain routinely stays open on weekends through April.

Nubs Nob is just across the valley from the Highlands. Nubs offers the best trio of advanced slopes in the Lower Peninsula. Recent additions of intermediate and beginner terrain help round out the variety. It's the locals' choice, and one of the top day-trip areas in the Lower Peninsula. It has no lodgings.

Sugar Loaf, Cedar MI (616) 228-5461; (800) 748-0117
20 trails, 500 vertical feet

One of the most scenic resorts in the Lower Peninsula, the backdrop of Lake Michigan's blue-gray waters and the Manitou Islands offshore make it hard to keep your eyes on the slopes. A well-rounded area, The Loaf boasts some great steep with Awful-Awful and Manitou (Michigan's only FIS-sanctioned racing hill), and cruisers like Devil's Elbow and Sugar 'n' Spice. Gambling packages are offered at the Leelanau Sands Casino.

Crystal Mountain, Thompsonville MI (616) 378-2911
22 trails, 375 vertical feet
    This skis much bigger than its 375-foot vertical. It's a great family area that offers solid intermediate slopes and lots of lower-level trails. As evidence of its appeal, Crystal ranks annually among the top 10 resorts nationally for NASTAR participants. It has a variety of lodging and a fitness center with pool.

Shanty Creek/Schuss Mountain, Ballaire MI
(616) 533-8621; (800) 348-4440; 30 trails, 450 vertical feet
    This resort offers a nice weekend retreat. These two separate areas about five miles apart are now operated as one with interchangeable lift tickets. Shanty has the nicest lodging, but Schuss has the better skiing—a good skier will get bored quickly at Shanty.

Michigan's Upper Peninsula

This is a rugged land of dense forests, long winters, deep snows and a collection of ski areas called Big Snow Country. The region receives over 200 inches of snowfall annually. About a six- to seven-hour drive from Chicago, its center is Ironwood. These areas have enough variety to keep skiers happy for a weekend or a midweek trip.

Indianhead Mountain, Wakefield, MI
(906) 229-5181; (800) 346-3426 (3-INDIAN)
18 trails, 638 vertical feet
    Indianhead runs are wide boulevards. It's an intermediate's dream—long, smooth runs—but they all look the same. The skier who likes a good challenge may get bored here but it is a great family area. The lodge and compact ski area sit atop the mountain. Runs fan out into the deep forests below, but all the lifts funnel back to the lodge on top.

Blackjack, Bessemer, MI (906) 229-5115; (800) 848-1125
16 trails, 465 vertical feet
    Blackjack appeals to intermediate and advanced skiers, befitting its brawny lumberjack image. They will enjoy busting down some of the wide bump runs or exploring the many narrow chutes and trails that fork off the boulevards. The Black River meanders through the valley—very picturesque.

Big Powderhorn Mountain, Bessemer, MI
(906) 932-4838; (800) 222-3131; 23 trails, 600 vertical feet
    This area offers a good variety of trails and the most uphill capacity in the immediate area (9,600 per hour). It has tree-lined trails, open bowls, rambling runs and narrow chutes to explore, plus the most slopeside lodging, restaurants and après-ski activity in the area.

Whitecap Mountain, Montreal, WI (715) 561-2227
32 trails, 400 vertical feet

Whitecap has had a facelift in recent years. Several new shops and a conference center have been added to the day lodge, but the expansion still preserves the Old-World charm. The most interesting mix of trails in the area drops down three peaks in every direction. It's the one place in the Midwest where a trail map comes in handy. Located in the Pekonee Mountains, it's in sight of Lake Superior on a clear day.

Porcupine Mountain, Ontonagon, MI (906) 885-5275
14 trails; 600 vertical feet

About 45 minutes north of Indianhead, Porcupine offers some of the most stunning Lake Superior views. It's almost perched on the shoreline, and the lake is in evidence on every run. Being state-owned, it offers the best lift rates in the area.

Minnesota

Blessed with superb ski terrain and consistently cold temperatures, northern Minnesota has some of the best snow conditions east of the Rockies, and the northwoods scenery is spectacular. What's here? Three excellent ski areas with big vertical drops (for the Midwest)—Giants Ridge, 550 feet; Spirit Mountain, 700 feet; and Lutsen, 800 feet. They are around Duluth and within an hour or so of each other.

Lutsen, Lutsen, MN (218) 663-7281
27 trails; 800 vertical feet

About an hour north of Duluth, Lutsen is the closest thing to true mountain skiing in the area. It has the only gondola in the Midwest. It will remind you of a New England ski area—three mountain peaks, long rock-ribbed trails flanked by birch and pine, and tight headwalls. Moose Mountain offers some great cruisers and breathtaking views of Lake Superior. The Mountain Inn and Village offers first-class slopeside lodging.

Spirit Mountain, Duluth, MN (800) 642-6377
20 trails; 700 vertical feet

Spirit Mountain has good vertical, long runs, snowy winters and great views of Duluth and the harbor perched on the Superior shoreline. The skiing is long on intermediate and beginner runs, without much variation in pitch and few twists and turns. A high-speed covered quad services the beginner trails—nice on cold days. An expert won't find challenge here.

Giant's Ridge, Biwabik, MN (218) 865-4143
19 trails; 500 vertical feet

About an hour's drive northwest of Duluth, this area is not as crowded as the other two. The trails soar off the crest and are varied in pitch, with a headwall here, a bowl there. The day lodge is first class, and so is the cross-country skiing.

Wisconsin

The skiing here has a certain ruggedness that you won't find in Michigan's Lower Peninsula. It's full of rocky outcroppings—spared the effect of the glaciers that spread over the upper Midwest some 10,000 years ago. It doesn't receive the natural lake-effect snow that Michigan gets, but the areas do an adequate job of snowmaking.

Devil's Head, Merrimac, WI (800) 338-4579 (DEVILSX)
21 trails; 500 vertical feet
In the beautiful Baraboo Bluffs overlooking the Wisconsin River Valley, this area has excellent beginner and intermediate skiing. One of the beginner runs is nearly two miles long. Its drawbacks are little advanced terrain and not much terrain variation. It is a full-service resort with a country-club atmosphere. Weekend crowds can be huge.

Located just down the road is **Cascade** with 460 vertical feet and a wide variety of skiing. It's straightforward skiing, with solid cruising and hefty faces for the bumps. It has more uphill capacity than Devil's Head (14,000 per hour), but weekend lines can still be long. These two resorts, located just three hours from Chicago, together are consistently rated the top day-trip destination in the Midwest.

Rib Mountain, Wausau, WI (715) 845-2846
13 trails; 624 vertical feet
Rib is the most European-feeling setting in the Midwest with the city nestled at the base of the mountain. It offers no-frills skiing with wide, western-like slopes. The narrow chutes off the Rib will entice advanced skiers. Lodging is available in the city.

Mt. La Crosse, La Crosse, WI (800) 426-3665
17 trails; 516 vertical feet
Skiers will find most of this area's runs are cut through rocky bluffs containing headwalls and chutes. It sits high atop a rugged bluff overlooking the Mississippi River. It has the only true double-black slope in the Midwest—Damnation.

Iowa and Illinois

A couple of good areas located in the tri-state corner are **Chestnut Mountain** (800-397-1320) near Galena, IL and **Sundown** (800-397-6676) near Dubuque, IA. They sit about 30 miles apart on bluffs overlooking the Mississippi River. Both have a 475-foot vertical and offer a good variety for all abilities. Their biggest drawback is lack of natural snow, but they do a good job with snowmaking.

Part of the charm of this area is that you can stay in and explore the historic river ports of Galena and Dubuque. Both have quaint B&Bs and country inns offering ski packages (800-747-9377). Riverboat gambling is a popular après-ski activity.

Canadian Resorts

Canada is a great destination for a ski vacation. Generally, the giant mountains and vast snowfields are in the West, while the narrow trails and quaint ski towns are in the East, just as they are in the U.S. But a Canadian ski vacation also has some very attractive differences. Some examples:

• Some of Canada's leading ski areas are in national parks. Banff and Jasper National Parks have four ski areas within their boundaries. The scenery is magnificent and wildlife sightings (elk, moose, bighorn sheep, etc.) are common.

• You can stay in an opulent, historic hotel, even if you're on a budget. The Canadian Pacific hotel chain includes several grand hotels built to accommodate late 19th- and early 20th-century luxury rail travel. Some refer to them as winter Snow Castles. During summer, they are jammed with tourists willing to pay premium prices. In the winter, prices plummet. Enjoy strolling through the expansive lobbies and pretend that you're skiing on trust-fund money or lottery winnings. The Canadian Pacific Snow Castles are detailed in the following chapters.

• Americans get the benefits of a foreign ski vacation without the jet lag. This isn't everyone's cup of tea, but we think it's fun to have multicolored money in our wallets instead of greenbacks, to calculate the exchange rate (especially when it's in our favor), to present our passports at the airport and, in the case of a Québec vacation, try to communicate in another language.

Prices are in Canadian dollars, which, at press time, was about $1.38 Canadian dollars for each U.S. dollar. Unless noted, prices do not include the G.S.T., Canada's Goods and Services Tax of 7 percent. Foreign tourists can get a G.S.T. refund for goods they take out of the country and on hotel rooms they pay for themselves (but not on rooms prepaid through a travel agent). You can't get refunds for meals or services such as transportation or lift tickets. Most hotels have refund forms.

Canada can be as cold as you've heard, or warmer than you imagined. We've skied in windbreakers in January, and huddled into fleece neck-warmers during a sudden April snowstorm. The best advice is to be prepared clothing-wise.

Travelers from the United States should bring a passport if they have one. Crossing the border is much easier and quicker with one than without, particularly when traveling by air.

Lake Louise Ski Area
Banff Region, Canada

Lake Louise Ski Area is Canada's largest, comprising two mountains and four faces. Fifty runs have names, but there are lots of acres with no names: 65 percent below tree line for snowy days when you want to stay more protected, 35 percent for clear days when you feel you can see into Alaska.

The expansiveness, together with the efficient lift system, allows skiers to get to the far reaches of the mountain quickly—if you can't get out of the base area on one of its three lifts in ten minutes, you get your ticket price refunded. To date, no one has claimed it.

Where to ski

The three front-side lifts and the gondola give access to mostly beginner and intermediate terrain; more confident intermediates take Top of the World to access the Back Bowls, Larch Area and the Summit Platter, three separate areas each having their special appeals.

About the Platter: first off, realize that it used to be a T-bar until they decided the steepness demanded concentration, not conversation, so it's one up at a time now. The skiing here is nicely moguled, wide and above treeline—almost all black diamonds with a touch of blue.

Either from the Platter or Top of the World Chair, you can dip down into the Back Bowls, especially in the morning because it will be in the sun. Most of the advanced skiing is found here in Paradise Bowl, but there are intermediate ways down as well.

Or if you'd rather, you can use The Ski Out for a spell and explore the sister mountain, Lipalian, and the Larch Area runs, some for all levels of skiers. There's great tree skiing directly under the lift between Larch and Bobcat runs. From the top of the

---

Lake Louise Facts
Base elevation: 5,400'; **Summit elevation:** 8,650'; **Vertical drop:** 3,250 feet.
Number and types of lifts: 11–2 quad superchairs, 1 quad chair, 2 triple chairs, 3 double chairs, 3 surface lifts
Acreage: 4,000 skiable acres **Snowmaking:** 40 percent
Uphill capacity: 23,955 skiers per hour **Bed base:** 2,500 within 10 minutes

Larch Chair, you'll see that some powder freaks have hiked up to the 8,900-foot summit to leave tracks down Elevator Shaft Chute, between two rock outcroppings, a bit out-of-bounds but skiable.

For a more modest thrill in a less traveled area, exit left off Larch Chair, then stay right and high on a gladed traverse until you find a deep powder bowl under Elevator Shaft. Called Rock Garden, it's not labeled on the map but it's in bounds, a hidden playground of loops and swoops, moguls and Cadillac-sized rocks. Albertans have renamed the spot Dances With Rocks.

For beginners, start on the Sunny T-Bar; it's the area used by instructors for beginner classes. Then progress to the Friendly Giant for your first big mountain experience on Wiwaxy, a two-and-a-half-mile cruiser. Next step is Eagle Chair to try Pika, long and meandering around the back, or Deer Run and Eagle Meadows down the front.

Intermediates should not miss Meadowlark on the front or Gully from Top of the World, but they will find routes suited to them on all faces.

If you want sun all day, you can stay on the front, which faces south—rare for ski slopes, but this is far enough north that it keeps its snow until mid-May and is covered with snowmaking. If you want sun all day *and* want to ski the whole area, go to the Back Bowls in the morning, ski Larch midday and end up on the Front Face.

And if this is too much to remember, take advantage of the free daily guided tours by Friends of Louise. A crew of volunteers, the Friends guide skiers of all levels around this vast mountain. Tours leave at 9:30 a.m., 10 a.m. and 1 p.m. at Whiskyjack Lodge.

Mountain rating

A key factor in Louise's 60 years of skiing history is that skiers of all abilities have terrain suited to their skill level from all lifts except the Summit Platter. This makes it nice for groups of varying ability levels who want to ride together on the lifts.

Cross-country

Lake Louise has about 60 miles of groomed trails and access to hundreds of miles of backcountry trails. The ungroomed, well-marked trail to Skoki Lodge, a rustic log cabin (meaning no electricity, no plumbing, wood-burning stove), begins just above Temple Lodge at the ski area and heads up the valley and over Boulder Pass, seven miles one way. If you're not up for skiing so far into the wilderness, follow the gentle Shoreline Trail starting in front of Chateau Lake Louise, an easy mile and a half one way. Skiing *on* Lake Louise is not recommended.

A complex 13-mile network called Pipestone Loops is accessed four miles west of the Lake Louise Overpass on the Trans-Canada Highway. Although all are marked beginner, some are suitable for the intermediate.

There are probably half a dozen other trails in the area comprising a total of 50 miles of groomed touring. Rental shops, especially the one in Chateau Lake Louise that also rents clothing, can furnish trail maps.

Before setting out on any of the trails, check trail conditions at a park warden's office or by phoning 762-4256. Be aware that trail classification is done by healthy Canadians in good shape.

Snowboarding

Yes, everywhere on the mountain. There's a highly visible halfpipe right under Friendly Giant, the express chair on the Front Face. Snowboard rentals and lessons are available.

Ski school (93/94 prices in Cdn$)

Group lessons (1.75 hours in the morning, two hours in the afternoon) begin at 10:15 a.m. and 1 p.m. for $22. **Private lessons** are $50 per hour, reduced to $32 if taken at 9 a.m. or 3 p.m. Extra skiers, $16 each.

Beginner's Special is a $32 one-day package including a 1.75-hour lesson, equipment rental, beginner area lift ticket and a half-price discount on the next full-day all-area lift ticket. "You'll be skiing by the end of the day or we'll teach you again the next day free." Arrive well before lesson to pick up equipment.

The **Kinderski** program, ages 3-6, provides supervised day care, one ski lesson and indoor and outdoor play at beginning and end of day. Cost is $27.

In the **Kids Ski** program, children are guided around the mountain with instruction along the way for $19 for the morning; $33 for full day. Children's lift ticket, $10, must be purchased additionally. Optional lunch is $5.

The **Club Ski Program** operates at Lake Louise, Sunshine and Mt. Norquay. Groups of similar interest and expertise ski together with the same instructor for four hours a day at each of the three areas. This allows for maximum improvement through continuity and lets you make new skiing friends, learn the best runs at each resort for your particular ability level, and cut into lift lines. A three-day program costs $134. A similar children's Club Ski program is $104.

Lift tickets (93/94 prices in Cdn$ including GST)

	Adult	Child (6-12)
One day	$39.50	$10
Three days	$120 ($40/day)	$42 ($14/day)
Five days	$200 ($40/day)	$70 ($14/day)

Students 13-25 with ID and seniors 65 and older ski for $35. Children younger than 6 ski free. Multiday rates listed here are for the Tri-Area Pass, valid here, at Mystic Ridge/Norquay and Sunshine Village. The pass also includes bus transportation from hotels to the ski areas and other benefits.

Accommodations (Prices Cdn$)

Two quite different properties are the supreme lodgings in the area, **Chateau Lake Louise** and **Post Hotel**.

The Chateau is lodging in the grand manner of the old railway hotels. Skiers get a break: since summer is high season, winter rates are a fraction of the summer prices—$95-$160 for what those poor fools who don't ski pay $145-$295 for in summer. Some 500 guest rooms, several restaurants, 32 shops, in-hotel Nordic ski center, ski clothing rental, masseuse, and complimentary ski bus service make this century-old Lady of the Lake right up to date for skiers. Reservations (800) 441-1414.

The Post Hotel is a cozy, beautifully furnished 93-room log lodge with great views on all sides and fireplaces in 38 of the rooms, two of which are lovely riverside cabins with heated slate floors. Newly expanded and thoroughly renovated, it's personal, quiet, with the warmth and elegance provided by Swiss innkeepers. The buffet breakfast is a board of tasty delights (including cinnamon-baked apple rings, yum!) for $12 right on the way to the slopes. Except for Christmas, rates are in the $105-$225 range. Five minutes from the lifts; free shuttle. (800) 661-1586.

Lake Louise Inn is a moderately priced family hotel with a noisy bar. $85-$145. (800) 661-9237.

Deer Lodge, near the Chateau, is the antithesis of the Chateau: No phones, no television, rustic, but great rooftop hot tub. Old but well kept up. $110-$130. (800) 661-1595.

The Canadian Hostel Association opened hostel accommodations next to the Lake Louise Inn.

Dining (prices Cdn$)

In the **Chateau**, the most elegant dining room is the **Edelweiss**, serving such entrées as salmon and duckling for $15-$20. The most popular restaurant is the Walliser Stube Wine Bar serving Swiss cuisine such as raclette and fondue. It's romantic and dark with a cherrywood bar, and winds around the lower level of the hotel with great views out tall windows. **The Poppy Room** is a family restaurant, cheery and light, the only one open for breakfast in winter. Entrées $12-$16, sandwiches $7-$9. **Glacier Saloon** has a western theme, with steak sandwiches, finger food and salads.

The Post Hotel is generally recognized as serving the finest cuisine in Lake Louise and is well known throughout Alberta. Continental, in the Swiss tradition. Go here on special occasion.

Deer Lodge has homemade breads, patés, fish, veal and beef dishes as well as innovative specials and pastries.

Lake Louise Lodge is a good spot for families, often serving a hearty Italian buffet.

Après-ski/nightlife

Lake Louise has ten licensed bars, several of them in the Chateau. **The Glacier Saloon** has a lively atmosphere and dancing. For a quieter time, the **Walliser Stube** has a warm feel, and serves cappuccinos and the chain's traditional blueberry tea (actually Earl Grey tea with Grand Marnier and Amaretto). In the Lake Louise Inn, **The Saddle Lounge** is quiet and **Charlie II's** is noisy. In the Post Hotel the **Outpost** has a pub atmosphere and the **Beehive** in the Samson Mall is quiet.

Child care (prices Cdn$)

Chocolate Moose Park serves children 18 days to 12 years with a variety of ski and play programs including a hot lunch. Infants under 19 months require reservations. Babies' care cost is $21 per day or $4 per hour, $3.75 per hour for toddlers. Day care for kids 3-6 is $3.50 per hour.

Other activities

Skating, snowshoeing, tobogganing, fishing, sleigh rides and great shopping are some of the other activities you'll find during the winter in Banff/Lake Louise.

Getting there and getting around

Getting there: Lake Louise Village is 115 miles west of Calgary and 36 miles west of Banff. Direct or one-stop flights connect Calgary with most major cities via seven airlines.

Getting around: Regular bus service is available from the airport direct to most hotels and the Lake Louise ski shuttle is free and operates from most hotels to the base of the ski lifts. Buy the Tri-Area ski pass and your bus transportation is included.

Information/reservations

Central reservations and information, call (403) 256-8473.

Skiing Louise, Ltd. (Box 5, Lake Louise, Alberta T0L 1E0), (403) 522-3555.

Mystic Ridge/Norquay
Banff Region Canada

Norquay has been softening up its image in the past few years. Once known as a small but tough ski area, it now is mid-sized and not quite so tough as before, thanks to 70 additional acres of intermediate terrain added a few years ago.

Some things remain the same, however. Mystic Ridge/Norquay, as it is known at this time, still has those mogul plunges right down its face, bump ribbons which seem to hang right over the main street in Banff. Mystic Ridge/Norquay still is the closest resort to Banff, only four miles away. And it still has the most spectacular view of Banff and the Bow Valley from the North American chair, a lift scrambling up those bump ribbons. If the prospect of the run down puts your heart in your throat, you can ride back in the lift. Many do.

Where to ski

Lone Pine is the name of that double-black mogul belt stretching up a 35-degree pitch. It's where the photos are taken, where the intrepid launch themselves with a hope and a prayer, and where lunchers at Norquay and Cascade Lodges watch their every move. Each year the area has a contest to see who can make the most consecutive runs in seven hours (Club 35,000) on this 412-meter, skeleton-jarring wall. Both men and women have done more than 20 trips, which says a lot for local physical fitness.

From the base the area retains its appearance as a haven for mogul maniacs. But the terrain unseen from the base on the Mystic Express Quad, mainly intermediate, is groomed well. Three runs there, Excalibur (a black), Illusion and Knight Flight (blues) are partially groomed, leaving skiers a choice of packed snow or powder. Also, there are several fall lines for each run.

Mystic Ridge/Norquay Facts
Base elevation: 5,350'; **Summit elevation:** 7,000'; **Vertical drop:** 1,650 feet
Number of lifts: 5–1 quad superchair, 1 quad chair, 2 double chairs, 1 surface lifts
Snowmaking: 90 percent of skiable terrain
Total acreage by trails: 162 acres skiable terrain
Uphill capacity: 6,300 per hour **Bed Base:** 10,000 in Banff

The management asserts, "there is still a lot of adventure skiing in our area." They don't want their expansion to dilute anything for the skier who loves expert drops. For example, the two blacks on Mystic Express—Black Magic and Ka-Poof—are groomed regularly, whereas the blacks off North American are rarely groomed. Another appeal for the adventure seeker is a chute on Ski Norquay called Valley of the Ten, a narrow drainage perfect for avalanches and elevator skiers. To get to it, skiers at the top of North American chair drop off (correct terminology) to the left into a drop-out (accurate again) called Gun Run, the steepest thing on the mountain.

For first-time visitors up Norquay—the peak, not the resort— the easiest way down, still a black, is Memorial Bowl. It's so steep they have stock fences staggered at the top of Memorial Bowl to force people to do wide traverses getting into it. "We think that's damn nice of us," they say. They also say in more serious tones, "You'd better be ready for North America chair."

To ski smart, take the high intermediate from Mystic or Spirit back into the main base area on Speculation. The most popular run off Spirit, Abracadabra, also tends to ice up because of its high traffic, but the resort is taking steps to limit the skiers.

Skiers wanting to stay in the sun all day have a challenge. Since at midday none of Mystic gets sun except the front two runs, Black Magic and Ka-Poof, both blacks, they'd better learn to ski bumps.

Mountain rating

Whereas the Old Norquay had 50 percent expert runs and 35 percent beginner, with the intermediates squished in between, Mystic Ridge/Norquay claims 11 percent beginner, 45 percent intermediate, 28 percent advanced and 16 percent expert. What is considered advanced in the U.S. is often intermediate here.

Intermediates will find their neck of the woods on the two new quads, Mystic Express and Spirit. What's left for beginners is to poke around the base.

Cross-country

See Sunshine section for Banff area trails.

Snowboarding

The North American Snowboarding Championships were held here in 1988, so MR/N is a great supporter of the sport. Clinics are $25; $20 if you rent a board here.

Ski school (94/95 prices in Cdn$ plus GST)

Learn-to-Ski packages for beginners are $30 for a 90-minute group lesson, lift ticket and equipment. Adult **group lessons** are $22 for a two-hour lesson. Children pay $17.

Private lessons are $35 per hour for adults, each additional person is $10 per hour and $15 for two. Before 10 a.m. or after 2:30 p.m., a private lesson is $29.

MR/N participates in Club Ski, a three-day program of lessons with the same instructor and group, but skiing one day each at three resorts. See Lake Louise ticket section for specifics.

Lift tickets (94/95 prices in Cdn$ with GST)

	Adult	Child (6-12)
One day	$29.90	$13
Three days	$120 ($40/day)	$42 ($14/day)
Five days	$200 ($40/day)	$70 ($14/day)

Adult rates include night skiing on Wednesday. Night skiing only, 4 to 9 p.m. is $15. Students 13-25 and seniors 55 and older ski for $23 per day. Children 5 and younger ski free. Multiday rates listed here are for the Tri-Area Lift Pass, which is valid at MR/N, Lake Louise and Sunshine Village. The pass includes bus transportation between hotels and the ski areas. When used here, it also includes $7 in other MR/N services.

Dining and accommodations

MR/N has lunch facilities. For evening dining and all lodging, Banff has a good selection of both. See the Sunshine Village chapter for details.

Child care

Children aged 19 months to 6 years are taken on a drop-in basis for $5 per hour per child, daily 9 a.m. to 4 p.m. Additional options include plans for lunch and combination snow play and ski instruction. Children have a mini-mountain all to themselves for snow play.

Getting there and getting around

Mystic Ridge/Norquay is the closest major ski area to the town of Banff, ten minutes away. Free shuttles pick up skiers at 11 Banff hotels and the bus depot, as well as from the four Lake Louise hotels via the bus depot in Banff.

Information/reservations

For more information, write Mystic Ridge/Norquay—Box 1258, Banff, Alberta T0L 0C0, or phone (403) 762-4421. Calgary Snowphone is (403) 221-8259.

Groups of 50 or more can rent MR/N any night except Wednesdays. They have private use of the ski hill and a buffet dinner for Cdn$35 per person, and can add activities such as a disk jockey, karaoke, a casino and fun races.

Sunshine Village
Banff Region, Canada

The Great Divide Chair charges up the incline of a typical Canadian Rockies dip slope called Lookout Mountain, a tilted wedge with rocky cliffs on all sides. At the top, nearly 9,000 feet above sea level, you will have crossed into British Columbia. All around are snowy peaks and somewhere near your ski tips is the Great Continental Divide itself. If you throw a snowball over your right shoulder, it will melt and find its way to the Pacific. Over your left, it will become one with the Atlantic, occasion for one snowflake to say to another, "There but for fortune go you or I. Adieu." Scenery like this encourages such musings on fate and the cosmic wonders of North American geology.

It also encourages you to point your tips down and let that other cosmic force, gravity, take over. The dip slope is wide, with an infinite number of ways down, some smooth, others more moguled, all exhilarating. In part, it must be the removed, top-of-the-world feeling that causes such abandon.

After all, you got here by an unusual route: up a narrow canyon in a six-person gondola from the parking lot, around a sharp left turn ("No way!" you say as you board. "Gondolas don't turn." But there are more things in heaven and earth, Horatio, than are dreamt of in your ski fantasies—this one turns!) and then fifteen more minutes up another drainage, and *then* you're at what feels like a ski area base village. You can ski down all the way to the bottom, but it's here at the Village that the play really starts, around a lodge, rental shop, general store, restaurant and the highest on-hill accommodation in the Rockies. From here, a half dozen lifts and tows take off in all directions. Most people never ski all the way down until the end of the day; some not until the end of their vacation.

Sunshine Village Facts
Base elevation: 5,440'; **Summit elevation:** 8,954'; **Vertical drop:** 3,514 feet
Number of lifts: 12—1 gondola, 1 quad superchair, 1 triple chair,
4 double chairs, 5 surface lifts
Snowmaking: none **Total acreage by trails:** 960 acres skiable terrain
Uphill capacity: 17,600 per hour **Bed Base:** 10,000 in Banff

The longest ski season in the region, sometimes even into June, and the most snow (360 inches as opposed to 120 and 140 at the other areas) are Sunshine's strong points. Its reputation is based on its dramatic views—if the weather's clear. Sunshine is family-oriented; with such a centralized on-mountain village no one can get lost, yet people can spread out to play wherever the terrain suits them. The quieter, more remote on-mountain living experience suits some, while Sunshine's location 15 minutes from Banff makes town life after hours accessible.

And Banff is a gem of a town, not just a fabricated purpose-built village, but a real community with real people, real stores instead of boutiques and galleries, a handful of museums with a history to fill them, and an Edwardian manor growing out of the trees—the Banff Springs Hotel.

Where to ski

Most of the lifts splay out in several directions from the on-mountain village at the top of the gondola, which is more for morning transport than for ski-trail access during the day. Two lifts, the Wheeler double chair and the Fireweed T-bar, are down-mountain from the other lifts and permit skiers to enjoy the varied runs under the gondola.

You'll find the most exhilarating skiing on the Great Divide Chair. Take Angel Express to get to it. Intermediates should first try the new run down the face of Angel, called Ecstasy—just to get ready for the high country.

From the top of Angel Express, it's wide open, above-tree-line skiing, with views of the Great Divide. Blues working up to blacks will find a bonanza there.

The most challenging route from the Great Divide is far to the right toward the Tee-Pee Town chair as you head down. Don't forget there's a cliff edge. The appeal in getting as far out along the cliff edge as you dare is of course virgin snow, less trafficked. If you stay on the edge, you have to dip down a drop innocuously called The Shoulder. It's the only thing on the mountain labeled a black which should be a double black. To avoid it, turn left and you'll negotiate only blacks, and find some great tree skiing.

Mogul runs can be found off the Tee-Pee Town Chair. If that's mild for you, take the WaWa T-bar on the opposite side of the Village up to a ridge with a left-hand dropoff called Paris Basin. It doesn't even look like a run, but they ski it. Used to be that if you got to the top and decided against it, you'd have a long traverse and a lot of poling. A new cat trail has made this traverse much easier.

Come to think of it, poling is something to watch out for in other places at Sunshine—most notably at several spots on Highway One, familiarly dubbed Tuck 'n' Pole by locals—if you don't tuck, you pole. Be sure to look far ahead coming off the

Great Divide when you're headed back toward Strawberry Chair or you'll get caught on an up-slope.

The three-mile run at the end of the day from the Village down to the parking lot is a long luscious trip for beginners and a lovely end-of-day cruiser for intermediates. Advanced skiers can play on the occasional drops to the left, but they're short and eventually rejoin the ski-out.

To find powder just after a storm, head immediately to ByeBye Bowl (left, facing down off the Divide), but it gets blown off quickly. The day after a storm, try Paris Basin. To stay in the sun, ski Standish Face in the morning and Lookout Mountain (Great Divide) in the afternoon. A ski tour takes off from the upper gondola terminal at 9:50 a.m. and 12:50 p.m. daily.

Mountain rating

With a whopping 60 percent of Sunshine's terrain marked intermediate, this a cruiser's mountain. The remaining 40 percent is divided evenly between beginner and expert.

One run loved by snowboarders and early intermediates is Dell Valley, a natural halfpipe where the g-forces will have you swooping up one side of a gorge, then turning to gain momentum on the down-slope to swoosh up the other side—just like the skateboarders.

Cross-country

There are some lovely easy loops along the Bow River. Take Banff Avenue to the end of Spray Avenue, or turn left and cross the river. Trails wind through the whole area.

Banff Springs Golf Course Clubhouse offers ski and skate rentals, plus group and private lessons. Maps and information on more challenging trails are available at the Clubhouse.

Snowboarding

Snowboarders are welcomed and rentals can be had at Sunshine for $25 a day, $20 half day. One snowboarding instruc-tor is certified. Private lessons with him are $40 an hour, $70 for two hours, $100 for three hours, with an additional $15 for extra shredders.

Ski school (93/94 prices in Cdn$ plus GST)

Sunshine en courages the traditional **Ski Week,** an on-mountain week-long stay, by providing appealing packages including classes with the same instructor for the whole time. Groups can be divided by ability level or by family, and the pack-age includes evening activities as well. For two people, five-night, six-day packages range from $598 to $798, depending on time of season and room.

Group lessons are $20. A never-ever package includes a longer lesson (two hours and a half), rental equipment and lift ticket for $43. Short Turn Clinic or lessons for moguls and steeps are $25.

Private lessons are $43 per hour (plus $16 for an additional person), $75 for two hours (plus $21 for additional person), and $107 for three hours ($32 for extra person).

Instruction for **children** comes in two packages. The Wee Angels is for 3-5 year olds just venturing onto the slopes; boots and skis are included with a lesson from 1 to 2:30 p.m. for $10. The Young Developers (aka Little Devils) is for 6-12 year olds just starting or well on their way. The price of $38 for full day includes lunch, $22 half day, $65 for two days.

Lift tickets (93/94 prices in Cdn$ with GST)

	Adult	Child (6-12)
One day	$38	$10
Three days	$100 ($33.33/day)	$30 ($10/day)
Five days	$149 ($29.80/day)	$50 ($10/day)

Students with ID ski for $33. Skiers 65 and older ski for $30. Children 5 and younger ski free. Other multiday tickets are available.

Sunshine participates in Club Ski, a program of consecutive lessons with the same instructor and group, but skiing at three resorts. Lift line privilege is a big appeal. See Lake Louise ticket section for specifics.

Accommodations (prices in Cdn$ plus GST)

Banff National Park is most popular during the summer, which means that lodging prices are a relative bargain in winter. Rooms can be found for as little as $50, and even the premier locations are within most budgets. Unless otherwise noted, lodging prices listed here are $70 to $150 per night.

The Sunshine Inn, on the mountain at the top of the gondola, is the only lodging in Banff National Park with ski-in/ski-out convenience. By staying here, powder hounds can get in a couple of runs before the other skiers arrive. Rooms range from $80 per person (low season) or $110 (regular season) to suites from $105 (low season) to $195 (regular). All nightly rates include two days of skiing, and lessons are complimentary for stays of five or more nights. Children 6-12 are $15 a day, which covers lodging and lifts. Meals are optional and are $38.50 daily for adults and $25 for children for three meals. One room has a kitchenette. (800) 661-1676.

All other lodging is in Banff. The **Banff Springs Hotel**, which was built over a 40-year period starting in 1888, is the region's architectural jewel. A $50 million restoration has returned the baronial Canadian Pacific Railway Hotel to its Old World Scottish charm. This is the great classic brick monolith you've seen in many photos, the cinnamon-colored walls and steep roofs rising nine stories out of the evergreens with dramatic peaks behind it and not another building to be seen. About 2,000 people a night can stay here. Its public areas are expansive, designed for turn-of-the-century mingling—we're talking a ballroom for 16,000. Ski season is the off season and the rates plummet to a third of summer prices. (800) 441-1414 in the U.S. and Canada.

Banff Park Lodge and Conference Center, which hosts many cultural activities, is an expanse of cedar buildings in a wooded area two blocks from downtown. (800) 661-9266.

The Cascade Wing of the Mount Royal Hotel, formerly known as the Cascade Inn, gets a fair amount of street noise from Banff Avenue but has an exceptionally good restaurant.

The Inns of Banff Park, a modern, multi-level lodge with balconies in most rooms, is a 15-minute walk from downtown. On-site ski rentals and repairs. (800) 661-1272.

High Country Inn on Banff Avenue is one of the least expensive places to stay.

For information about other lodging, contact **Banff Reservations**, Box 1628, Alberta T0L 0C0 (403-762-5561).

Dining

At Sunshine Village, the **Eagle's Nest Dining room** in the Sunshine Inn offers fine dining such as lobster and filet mignon. **The Chimney Corner,** the inn's fireplace lounge, serves a sit-down lunch of croissants, soups, salads, pastas, ribs and steak sandwiches. **Trapper Bill's** serves burgers. **Day Lodge Cafeteria** serves chili, stew, soup and pizza, and its deli will make sandwiches to order.

At the Banff Springs, you have 16 restaurants to choose from. **The Samurai** serves Japanese cuisine including Shabu-Shabu, a healthy fondue broth. **The Pavilion** serves Italian dinners and **Grapes** is the wine bar, originally the writing room. It only seats 26 and is a one-man restaurant, a cozy corner in the cavernous hotel serving fondues, soups, and salads; wine tasting, too. **Downstairs,** a 24-hour deli, packs picnics.

In the town of Banff, the **Bow View** is warmly personal, the **Ticino** is a long-standing reliable establishment serving Italian and Swiss cuisine. **La Fontaine Dining Room** in the Cascade Hotel has good food in lovely furnishings. **The Bistro** has a varied menu with pastas and salads.

Après-ski/nightlife

The Happy Bus shuttles skiers to night spots around Banff until midnight for $1.50. **The Mt. Royal** has a lively bar for après-ski. Next door is **The Rose and Crown**, an English-style pub with draught ale and darts. **Bumper's Loft Lounge** has a casual crowd, with live entertainment and ski movies. **Joshua's Pub** has Old Banff atmosphere, good food and Calgary's Big Rock ale on tap. Country & Western fans will find the live entertainment at **Wild Bill's** on Banff Avenue to their liking.

At the Banff Springs Conference Center, **Whiskey Creek** is a hopping bar, attracting locals and tourists. In the Hotel proper, the **Rob Roy Room** has dining and dancing and the **Rundle Lounge** is a lounge with quiet music for hotel guests. At the **Waldhaus** at Banff Springs Golf Course, Happy Hans and Lauren, on accordion and trumpet, get everybody singing.

Child care

Kids Kampus Day Care is for children 19 months to 6 years. Available 8:30 a.m. to 4:30 p.m. for $5 per hour, plus $4 for lunch, to a maximum of $30 per day. Reservations recommended; call (403) 762-6560.

Other activities

Shopping: The Banff Springs Hotel has nearly 50 shops, many of which have unusual items such as regional handicrafts. Shoppers also will find other places to browse in town.

Around the Banff Springs Hotel, **tobogganing, skating,** and **sleigh rides** are part of the tradition. The Mountain Mushers provides **dog sledding,** 678-5742. The rink is lit for night skating until 9 p.m. Toboggans are available at the Waldhaus.

Three museums of note: **Whyte Museum** of the Canadian Rockies, for historic and contemporary art and historic homes; The **Luxton Museum,** for Plains Indians history and the **Natural History Museum** for local geology.

Getting there and getting around

Getting there: Calgary Airport is served by major airlines. Banff is 130 miles west of Calgary on the Trans-Canada Highway (#1), an hour and a half drive. The Sunshine exit is five miles west of Banff; then five more miles to the gondola base parking area.

Getting around: It is possible to ski Banff and Lake Louise without a rental car by using Happy Bus shuttles ($1.50 a ride) in the area and Pacific Western Transportation (403-762-4558) or Brewster Transportation (403-762-6700) for regularly scheduled buses between the airport, Banff, and the ski areas. If you plan to do a lot of exploring, it's best to rent or bring a car.

Information/reservations

Sunshine Village, Box 1510, Banff, Alberta T0L 0C0; phone (403) 762-6500, or (800) 661-1676 in the U.S. or Canada for Sunshine Inn reservations. For information about other lodgings, contact Banff Reservations, Box 1628, Alberta T0L 0C0 (403-762-5561).

All prices are in Canadian dollars. (At press time, one U.S. dollar was worth $1.38 Canadian.) Unless noted, the local area code is 403.

Marmot Basin
Jasper, Alberta, Canada

Jasper is a winter vacation spot in the fullest sense of the word, with loads to do aside from skiing. The largest of the Canadian Rockies National Parks, Jasper is studded with lakes, threaded by cross-country trails, and has spectacular drives such as the Icefields Parkway. Even though Jasper is overloaded with tourists in the summer, it's delightfully uncrowded in the winter. Consequently, relatively few people outside Alberta know much about Jasper's Alpine ski area, Marmot Basin.

Being in a national park, Marmot Basin has developed slowly, a feature to its advantage today, for it still has a hidden feel, this far into the northland and separated from the hustle of Banff by a three-hour panoramic drive. It's far enough north, and far enough from a major airport (three hours from Edmonton) that people aren't here by mistake. They come for the scenery, the remoteness, the wonder of a herd of elk outside one's chalet, the call of Canadian geese swooping over Lac Beauvert in the spring while the ski area still has winter snow.

They call Marmot Basin "The Big Friendly," and indeed it aims to be skier conscious, with a good host program and convenient services.

The townsite of Jasper sprang up from a tent city in 1911, when the Grand Trunk Pacific Railway was laying steel up the Athabasca River Valley toward Yellowhead Pass, and its growth was rather helter-skelter. Hugging the Athabasca River and nestled against the train station, the town is relatively nondescript, consisting of clapboard cottages, a steepled Lutheran church, stone houses and lodgings with no single architectural scheme. It has a Great Plains small-town feel rather than a resort atmosphere—it's human, without a shred of glitz.

Marmot Basin Facts
Base elevation: 5,640'; **Summit elevation:** 7,940'; **Vertical drop:** 2,300 feet
Number and types of lifts: 7—1 quad superchair, 1 triple chair,
3 double chairs, 2 surface lifts.
Acreage: 1,000 acres **Percent of snowmaking:** 1 percent
Uphill capacity: 10,080 skiers per hour **Bed base:** 5,500

Where to ski

Two peaks, a handful of bowls and a wide ridge constitute the ski area. The lower peak, Caribou Ridge, which takes two chair lifts to get to, is only 7,525 feet high. "We let the scenery, not the elevation, take your breath away," locals say. Even so, it climbs above the tree line, a notably low topographical feature determined by the last Ice Age. Marmot has the best glade skiing in the Canadian Rockies, and much of it is off the triple chair and Kiefer T-bar which service Caribou Ridge. Directly below are black mogul runs, negotiable by a strong intermediate when groomed (an event that takes place every Friday) but off to the right as you face downhill, advanced skiers can play in the trees in a black area misnamed Milk Run. Don't let the title fool you.

By staying high to the right, skiers can take another lift, Knob Chair, to gain 500 more vertical feet on Marmot Peak. Here the lift doesn't climb to the summit, but that doesn't stop hardy Canadians from hiking up, as their tracks on upper slopes testify. It's all Alpine bowls up here, and it feels like Switzerland. Even intermediates can negotiate The Knob by a sinuous route down, but experts will want to drop into the fine powder in Dupres Bowl, a true scooped-out hollow, outrageously large, with Dupres Chute dividing it from Charlie's Bowl, a depression even steeper and farther away that stays untracked longer. Here's where knowing skiers head for. It should be a double black; try telling that to Canadians. The most horrendous bump runs are just to the right of the Knob Chair—Knob Bowl and Knob Hill.

Stay high and even farther to the right from The Knob facing down. Here experts have an entirely different playground all to themselves—a ridge wide enough that some parts are treeless, like Thunder Bowl, others gladed, like Chalet Slope. Here, powder lasts the longest, be cause it takes you three lifts to get there.

Intermediates and beginners will have the most fun on the lower mountain, where trees provide shelter from the sometimes fierce winds that block visibility on the naked summit.

Mountain Magic Tours are available and free daily, morning and afternoon. Tours leave from the Lower Chalet; check with Guest Services for times.

The area's one high-speed quad, Eagle Express, serves as the primary access chair to the upper-mountain lifts. That makes it a wait sometimes; don't come back to the base during peak loading times, like mornings before 9:30. There's rarely a wait on Caribou Chair on the lower mountain far to the right. It has terrain for all abilities and also will get you to the upper-mountain lifts. You can reach it directly by driving past the main lodge and heading for the farthest parking lot.

Mountain rating

Skiers of different levels can ride the same lifts, a factor which makes Marmot good family skiing. The terrain is nearly evenly divided, with 35 percent beginner, 35 percent intermediate and 30 percent expert. Beginners have expansive mountain access, with 1,100 vertical feet on Eagle Express after they master terrain from the Red T-bar. They can even head up to Caribou Ridge for an above-tree line thrill where a high, wide trail, Basin Run, takes them safely back to the lower slopes.

Cross-country

This is prime ski touring country, and even if you've only done downhill, you'll want to try it. The scenery's guaranteed to draw you into the sport.

Jasper Park Lodge trails, nearly 16 miles, are unparalleled for beauty and variety—lake shores, Alpine meadows and forests. They're gentle, groomed and easily accessible. The easiest is Cavell, a three-mile lope with the elk. The perimeter loop samples a little of everything the Jasper Park Lodge trails offer.

Near Jasper Townsite, a good beginner trail is Whistlers Campground Loop, short of three miles, level and lit for night skiing. Pyramid Bench Trail, rated easy, overlooks the Athabasca River Valley. Patricia Lake Circle, three and a half miles and rated easy, provides several stunning views of Mt. Edith Cavell, the region's most prominent and dramatically sloped peak.

Trail maps are available in most lodgings. Guided cross-country excursions on weekends in February and March are offered by Parks Canada. Call 852-6146.

A full day's ski over Maccarib Pass from the Marmot Basin Road on the north shore of Amethyst Lake leads skiers to Tonquin Valley Lodge and hearty, home-cooked meals and welcome beds. Contact Tonquin Valley Ski Tours, Box 550, Jasper, Alberta T0L 1E0; (403) 852-3909.

Snowboarding

Snowboarding has come to stay at Marmot. The Inside Edge Snowboard Cup is held in the spring and the area has a halfpipe. Lessons and rentals are available.

Ski school (94/95 prices in Cdn$ including GST)

Adult **group lessons** are $20 for two hours. Never-ever lessons which include lift pass and equipment cost $34 throughout the season.

Lessons for **children** 4 years and up are $15.

Ski Improvement Weeks include five two-hour sessions, Monday to Friday, video, a fun race and a Jasper Night Out. Adults are $87. Children 6-12 are $62.

Private lessons are $38 for an hour, $150 all day. Additional skiers, $15 each per hour. **Specialty clinics** (moguls, racing, powder) may be requested for $20 per person with a minimum group of three.

Lift tickets (94/95 prices in Cdn$ including GST)

	Adult	Junior (6-12)
One day	$34	$14
Three days	$102 ($34/day)	$42 ($14/day)
Five days	$170 ($34/day)	$56 ($11.20/day)

Youth/student prices (ages 13-25) are $28 for a full day, but college-age students must be full time and present a valid student ID. Seniors aged 65 and older ski for $20 per day, and like the juniors, they get their fifth skiing day free. Children younger than 6 ski free.

Accommodations

Although **Jasper Park Lodge** is now part of the Canadian Pacific Hotels, it's not in the style of a baronial manor like two others in the region. Rather, it's a grouping of traditional log cabins from the 1920s and new cedar chalets with spacious modern suites. All buildings are connected by a pathway along Lac Beauvert to the main building, which is like a Canadian hunting lodge. Elk graze the meadows and golf course and the haunting call of Canadian geese will tell you for sure where you are. Open in winter only since 1988, it's a relative newcomer in Canadian Rockies winter lodgings. Rates start under $100 prior to Christmas, and rise toward $200-per-night for large suites in peak periods. Nordic and downhill ski packages are available; write Jasper Park Lodge, Box 40, Jasper, Alberta T0E 1E0, or call 852-3301 or (800) 441-1414. On the grounds, **Milligan Manor** is a newly restored eight-bedroom deluxe cabin overlooking the fairway and its resident elk herd.

All other lodging is in Jasper Townsite. **The Astoria** is a small hotel of character with elegantly renovated guest rooms 852-3351. **Chateau Jasper** has suites renting for $180-$250. Indoor pool and whirlpool, dining room, cocktail lounge and heated underground parking; (800) 661-9323. **The Athabasca Hotel**, one of Jasper's original lodgings, is close to the bus and VIA RAIL station. Rooms are $48-75; suites $170-$185; 852-3536. **Marmot Lodge** has rooms with kitchens and fireplaces; indoor pool, sauna and whirlpool on the premises. No charge for children under 12. Rooms range from $50 to $135; (800) 661-6521. **Pyramid Lake Bungalows** has skating and cross-country trails at your doorstep. Located five miles from the Townsite, it has a lovely view, private whirlpools, kitchenettes and fireplaces, as well as a restaurant on the premises. Bungalows range from $50 to $120; 852-3536.

An RV park is located 12 miles from the ski area.

Dining

At Jasper Lake Lodge, the **Beauvert Dining Room** over-looks the lake, is expansive, able to seat 800, but the **Edith Cavell** is the flagship restaurant, with white-glove tableside service, mahogany and silver, and a harpist playing. French veal and shrimp in a pastry are specialties. **The Moose's Nook**, open only until New Year's, serves Arctic char (a landlocked salmon), buffalo and elk (domestic game), pheasant and duck. For breakfast, **The Meadows** features wholesome food in a country setting; food service continues all day.

In town, **Villa Caruso** (852-3920) serves steaks, prime rib, barbecued ribs, seafood and Italian dishes. Live music, beautiful view; make reservations. **The Palisades** (852-5222) serves barbecue chicken and ribs under an atrium roof in a refined atmosphere of wingback chairs by the fireplace. The **Amethyst Dining Room** (852-3394) serves light and healthy cuisine (beef, local fish) in an up-tempo, casually elegant restaurant. Breakfast features omelets and a skier's buffet. **Mamma Teresa Ristorante** in Athabasca Hotel serves traditional Italian cooking in informal surroundings. A lovely buffet brunch on Sunday can be had at the Chateau Jasper's **Le Beauvallon Dining Room** (852-5644). Make reservations.

Mountain Foods Cafe, (852-4050) a sit-down or take-out restaurant, has affordable prices for its deli items. Pizza is at **Jasper Pizza Place** (852-3225), Greek cuisine at **L & W Restaurant** (852-4114), Japanese entrées and sushi bar at **Tokyo Tom's** (852-3780).

On the slopes, Marmot Basin has two food service areas. Upstairs in the Lower Chalet, **Country Kitchen** features pasta, sandwich bar and the local tradition, Marmot Basin Edible Soup Bowl—a delicious, hearty novelty. **Paradise Chalet**, mid-mountain, has a cafe and lounge. On busy days, lunch before 11:45 or after 1:15.

Après-ski/nightlife

Jasper is not known for rocking nightlife, but many of the in-town hotels have lounges. The **Atha-B Club** in Athabasca Hotel has the liveliest dancing in town; it also has **O'Shea's,** an Irish pub. **Echoes Lounge** in Marmot Lodge has nightly entertainment. Jasper Park Lodge's **Tent City** nightclub recalls the history of the area.

Child care

Little Rascals, the indoor nursery, serves children 19 months through 5 years. It's $3.75 an hour, with supervision during the lunch hour, but lunch is an extra cost. Reservations: 852-3816.

Other activities

Heliskiing in Valemount, British Columbia, 56 miles away along a scenic drive, is available mid-February to mid-April. Contact Robson HeliMagic at (604) 566-4700 for reservations, information, and car rental to the pickup site, an hour from town.

Valemount Snowmobile Tours operates three-hour tours in the high backcountry, stopping at a warm-up cabin. From January through mid-April, rates are $115 for one, $140 for two. Call 852-3301, Ext. 6110.

Canyon Crawls is the ominous name of guided Maligne Canyon Tours where visitors walk 1.2 miles through a 6-20 foot wide gorge on the frozen river, with naturally sculpted ice falls on both sides. Insulated hiking boots and traction sandals provided. It takes about three hours, but it's one of those once-in-a-lifetime activities that you'll brag about afterward. Only available in January and February.

Sleigh rides are available at Jasper Park Lodge for $10 an hour; 852-3301, Ext. 6052. Skating, too.

A drive on the **Icefields Parkway** (Highway 93) is a spectacle not to be missed. The highway winds through lodgepole and spruce forests, craggy peaks with crenellations on one side and deep slopes on the other, and along the Athabasca River, to the breathtaking Columbia Icefields nosing down into the valley.

A great time to visit is during the **Jasper in January festival,** which will be Jan. 14-29, 1995. Lift tickets at Marmot Basin are discounted for adults and youth ($23 per day), and hotels mark down rooms as much as 30 percent off already low winter prices. And the town throws in fireworks, snow sculpture contests, a parade and lots of other fun activities.

If you fly into Edmonton, spend some time there and tour the **West Edmonton Mall,** the second largest shopping mall in the world. Part shopping center, part amusement park, it covers 48 city blocks, has more than 800 stores and services, and includes (among other attractions) a good-sized indoor amusement park with a gut-wrenching, triple-loop roller coaster called Mindbender; a dolphin show, an 18-hole miniature golf course, an ice skating rink, and an indoor water park with enormous water slides, a giant wave pool and beach, and 85-degree temperatures. If you can swing the bucks, stay at the adjoining Fantasyland Hotel, where every floor is decorated in a theme such as Hollywood, Canadian Pacific Railway, Roman, Polynesian, etc. A night in one of the theme suites is a decadent indulgence and adventure you'll probably remember for a while.

Getting there and getting around

Getting there: Four major carriers fly into the closest city, Edmonton: Delta, American, America West and Northwest.

Private planes land at Hinton, a town just east of the park boundary.

From Edmonton, Jasper is 270 miles west on Highway 16, a three-hour ride. By prearrangement, Jasper Park Lodge will send in a van for groups, even of four to five, for a price of $15 to $20 each, depending on the size of the group. The ski area is 12 miles south of Jasper via Highway 93, 93A and Marmot Basic Road.

VIA RAIL operates service to Jasper from Toronto and Vancouver, on its newly restored '50s-style art deco train, the Canadian. U.S. travel agents have more information. Greyhound operates daily service from Edmonton and Vancouver; 421-4211. Brewster Transportation operates the Banff-Jasper Ski Bus and the Marmot Basin Bus Service from Jasper; 852-3332. The Edmonton Journal Ski Bus operates day return trips to Marmot Basin from Edmonton; 448-1188.

Getting around: A car is best here. The ski area is a few miles from the town and lodging.

Information/reservations

For ski area information, write **Marmot Basin Ski-Lifts**, Box 1300, Jasper, Alberta T0E 1E0; 852-3816.

Jasper Park Chamber of Commerce, Box 98, Jasper, Alberta, T0E 1E0 (852-3858) will provide information on activities outside Marmot Basin. There is no central reservations number.

All prices are in Canadian dollars (at press time, one U.S. dollar was worth about $1.38 Canadian).

Local telephone area code is 403.

Red Mountain
British Columbia, Canada

Rossland, British Columbia, is gaining a reputation as the town where skiers stop for a day or two and never leave. Kiwis, Aussies and Europeans, plus a lot of Canadians, stay in the small Kootenay town to ski the big peaks of Red Mountain Ski Resort.

Nancy Greene trained on Red, and went on to win Olympic gold in 1968. Kerrin Lee-Gartner, also from Rossland, did the same in 1992. In fact, Red Mountain has contributed more skiers (27) to Olympic and World Cup competition than any other mountain in North America.

Until 1989, the mountain was owned and operated by a community ski club. Its casualness is appealing. Even today maps don't show boundaries, and skiers still explore the territory. Winter temperature at Red Mountain averages 20 degrees Fahrenheit, and typical season snowfall is 300 inches.

Where to ski

The twin peaks, Red and Granite, tower over Rossland from only two miles away, yet Granite's beginner trail is nearly five miles long. The reason is because trails and woods can be skied on all 360 degrees of the mountain.

Less of Red is available to skiers, but locals know a trail down the backside that leads to downtown Rossland. The trail has probably been there since the 1890s, when early miners skied Red Mountain. The first Canadian downhill championships were held on Red in 1897. It was 50 more years before the first chair lift was built. Even today, Red has just one chair, a double. That's all it needs. Granite has two chairs, a double in front and a triple in back, and a T-bar in front of the lodge. Not many lifts, but they will take you anywhere you could want to go.

Thousands of acres of woods are dotted with private cabins, and 30 marked trails. There's no point in deciding on a favorite

---

Red Mountain Facts
Base elevation: 3,888′ **Summit elevation:** Red: 5,205′ Granite: 6,699′
Vertical drop: 2,811 feet
Number and types of lifts: 4 - 1 triple chair, 2 double chairs, 1 surface lift.
Acreage: Hundreds (ski area had no specific count) **Snowmaking:** None
Uphill capacity: 4,000 skiers per hour **Bed base:** 260 rooms within 8 miles

run through the woods, because you may never find it again—skiers who have worked at the resort for years still find new routes. An instructor told of discovering a narrow line next to a downed tree whose branches were recently cut. He figured a skier had cut his own trail during the summer and was unable to find it again. Neither could the instructor.

Skiers are advised to double up in the woods. A free guide service is available to newcomers, and it's smart to take the tour. Even half the named runs are treed. But beginners needn't fear—there's plenty for them too, from every chair. On Red, Dale's Trail winds gently around like a logging road, and Little Red Run is served by the T-bar. On Granite, South Side Road winds from the Paradise side to the base, and Long Squaw and Easy Street combine for a gentle five-mile run.

Mountain rating

The runs are classified as 20 percent beginner, 35 percent intermediate and 45 percent advanced—lots of advanced terrain.

Cross-country (94/95 prices in Cdn$)

The **Blackjack Cross Country Ski Club** is across the road from Red Mountain Resort. It has 40 km. of tracks, most double-tracked with a skating lane. The trails wind through hemlock stands, past frozen beaver ponds, through open fields and some racing loops with steep ups and downs. Trail tickets, actually day memberships, cost $5, with a maximum family fee of $10.

For backcountry touring, skiers can buy a one-use-only lift ticket ($7) to gain access to 30 square miles from the top of **Granite Mountain.** It's smart to check with the ski patrol first regarding snow conditions.

Free cross-country skiing on tracks set after every snowfall is available 25 km. north of Rossland (on Highway 3B) in **Nancy Greene Provincial Park.** Trails are maintained by the Castlegar Nordic Ski Club. High Country Sports, at the base of Red Mountain, offers rentals and instruction.

Snowboarding

Red Mountain snowboard instruction methods have never failed to get beginners navigating gentle slopes within an hour. Riding the T-bar is tricky, but it's a good test of balance.

Red Mountain appeals to freeriders, because of the abundance of woods. A lot of the turns are tight, though; beginners ought to stay on the open slopes.

Ski school (94/95 prices in Cdn$)

Red Mountain Ski School is where many of Canada's ski instructors train and earn their ratings: CSIA Levels 1 through 4. The school also teaches coaches and snowboard instructors. **Instructor's courses** are available for CSIA Levels 1 ($190), 2

($435) and 3 ($435). In addition, Coaches Levels 1 and 2 Courses, and Snowboard Level 1 Instructor's courses are offered.

There's some serious teaching going on Red Mountain, and its high caliber is to the benefit of regular skiers. One-hour **private lessons,** by appointment only, cost $39 for one hour ($15 per additional person); discounts for additional hours.   On Tuesdays and Thursdays a buddy can join your lesson free. Two-hour **group clinics** are $25 for ages 7 and older.

Children's lessons are for ages 3 1/2 to 6. A two-hour lesson with hot chocolate break is $29; and all-day lessons and care is $40 per day or $102 for three days.

The **Starter Pack** is a good program for first timers. It includes a 90-minute lesson, rental equipment and T-bar lift ticket, and is $28.50 for ages 7-15 and $33.50 age 16 and older.

Specialty clinics are available through the sponsorship of Rossland businesses. A beginner snowboard package (lifts, lesson, rental) is $49.95 for ages 9 and older. Telemark lessons, on request, cost $96 for four hours, plus $49 for each additional person. Secret Stash explores the Red Mountain's hidden trails. Skiers go with a pro and pay $10 per hour each, minimum three skiers.

Lift tickets (94/95 prices in Cdn$)

	Adult	Child (7-12)
One day	$35	$20
Three days	$95 ($31.66/day)	$54 ($18/day)
Five days	$149 ($29.80/day)	$85 ($17/day)

Skiers 65 and older pay $23 full day, $62 for three days, $98 for five days. Students aged 13-18 or with ID ski for $30 full day, $81 for three days, $128 for five days. Children 6 and younger ski free.

Accommodations

Red Mountain itself operates Central Reservations, and can book all travel, lodging and ski packages and arrangements. Its international toll–free number is (800) 663-0105.

The 67-room **Uplander Hotel** in downtown Rossland sets the standards for lodging and dining, and like every place else in town is five minutes from the slopes. Prices for a double room and lift tickets are $66 -$80 per person, plus 15 percent in taxes.

At the ski area is the **Red Shutter Inn**, with overnight prices starting at $51 including breakfast and taxes.

Three-bedroom cabins (ski in, walk up) cost $115 at the **Red Mountain Cabins & Motel**. The **Ram's Head Inn** is the place first-time visitors plan to try next time. It's a short walk from the lifts and is No Smoking, a new trend in Canada. Ski week packages start at $450. A double room is $190, with lift tickets.

In residential Rossland, the **Heritage Hill Inn** has rooms for $85 for two people, including breakfast but not lift tickets.

Dining

Sourdough Alley is the Red Mountain cafeteria, with the Rafter's Lounge upstairs specializing in pizzas and Mexican food. Soups, stews and sandwiches are at the **Paradise Lodge**, on the backside of Granite Mountain.

In town, the **Uplander** offers the widest array of food for serious diners. Its chef has been written up in big-city newspapers. She specializes in French, but her steaks and seafood keep 'em coming back.

In town try the **Flying Steamshovel Inn**, **Rockingham's Restaurant** (30 appetizers alone), and **Rossland Pizza** for Greek, Italian and pizza.

Après-ski/nightlife

In a town this size (4,000), the action is where you and your friends get together. The biggest party of the year is the Winter Carnival for three days near the end of January, and 1995 will be the 98th annual celebration, with skating parties, a snow sculpture contest, dances, etc. A peak experience is to stand on a downtown roof and watch the city parade go by, several times.

For Rossland pubs and lounges try the **Onlywell Pub**, **Rockingham's Restaurant** and **Powder Keg** at the Uplander.

Child care

No infant or toddler care. Ski instruction starts at age 3 1/2 and is detailed in the Ski School section.

Other activities

Shopping: Rossland has a small collection of unusual shops along Columbia Avenue, the main street.

Paragliding in tandem with a pro patroller is offered off the tops of Red ($35) and Granite ($60) on certain weekdays. **Ice skating,** with rentals, is at the Rossland Arena. **Heli-touring** the Red Mountain area costs $290 for up to six people.

Getting there and getting around

Getting there: Red Mountain is ten miles from the Canada-U.S. border, 125 miles north of Spokane. The airport in Castlegar, 20 miles north, is served by Air B.C. from Vancouver (90-minute flight) and Calgary. Shuttles and rental cars are available.

Getting around: Though it's possible to fly in and stay at a place that will shuttle you to and from the slopes, we recommend a car for off-slope exploring.

Information/reservations

One call can do it all: (800) 663-0105. The local telephone area code is 604, and all prices are in Canadian dollars. (At press time, one U.S. dollar was worth $1.38 Canadian.)

Whistler/Blackcomb
British Columbia, Canada

Whistler/Blackcomb has emerged as one of the most popular ski resorts in North America; in most ski magazine surveys, it alternates the number-one position with Vail. There are several reasons for this: Whistler (the name by which most folks refer to this two-mountain resort) has twin mountains with the largest vertical drop on the continent (more than 5,000 feet for each), tremendous bowl skiing, runs that wind down the mountainside seemingly forever—and to top it all off, a marvelous base village filled with lodging, restaurants and nightclubs, all within walking distance (cars are banned from Whistler Village center).

Generally, Whistler gets rave reviews, but the two drawbacks that come up most often in skier word-of-mouth are often made to sound worse than they are. One is Whistler's weather. Located relatively close to the Pacific Ocean at a low base altitude just over 2,000 feet, Whistler gets driving rain and blinding fog at times. Lift riders sometimes pass through three weather systems on their way to the top, at 7,500 feet. It can be snowing or raining in Whistler village, sunny on top and perhaps fog in the middle. But sunny days are frequent, especially later in the season. And on those days, skiing conditions here are just awesome. Horrendous lift lines are sometimes another problem, but in reality, the line looks longer than the actual wait, thanks to high-speed lifts at both ski areas.

Let's not forget, having considered the few drawbacks, that plenty of skiers adore Whistler/Blackcomb. This is one of the

---

Whistler Facts
Base elevation: 2,140'; **Summit elevation:** 7,160'; **Vertical drop:** 5,020 feet
Number of lifts: 11–1 10-passenger gondola, 3 quad superchairs, 3 triple chairs, 2 double chairs, 2 surface lifts **Snowmaking:** 7 percent
Acreage: 3,657 skiable trail acres **Uphill capacity:** 22,295 per hour **Bed Base:** 8,000+

Blackcomb Facts
Base elevation: 2,214'; **Summit elevation:** 7,494'; **Vertical drop:** 5,280 feet
Number of lifts: 13–1 8-passenger gondola, 6 quad superchairs, 3 triples, 3 surface lifts **Snowmaking:** 28 percent **Acreage:** 3,341 skiable trail acres
Uphill capacity: 27,112 per hour **Bed Base:** 8,000+

most international of ski resorts, attracting skiers from Australia, Asia, Europe, Latin America and the eastern regions of the U.S. and Canada.

The twin mountains of Whistler and Blackcomb, which rise above Whistler Village, are separately owned and managed. They are a bit like Siamese twins. Joined at their bases, but distinct individuals, they fight like crazy over the skier population of the Pacific Northwest, but to the rest of the world they act as a single cooperative unit, knowing that tourists will ski both.

Whistler Mountain opened for skiing in 1966, 12 years before the village itself was built. Bowls, chutes, woods and trans-mountain runs were the standard. It was tough-guy stuff for the skiers of that day. Blackcomb Mountain opened in 1980, its ski run design reflecting the thinking that skiers preferred gentle fall-line skiing. Over the years, Blackcomb has added wilder terrain and Whistler has built gentle fall-line runs. Those who ski both frequently can tell the subtle differences, but to the occasional visitor, the two mountains seem quite similar, especially now that Blackcomb has installed a gondola.

Whistler Village is definitely European-style, specifically built to house, feed and amuse tourists. It was never a town that grew into a resort; just the opposite. In fact, the housing shortage causes many of the workers to live in Pemberton or Squamish. Those who live in Whistler use the same facilities as the visitors—75 restaurants and bars, and more than 100 shops. More than 2,700 rooms are in condos, B&Bs, lodges and hotels.

And now a new part of the village, Whistler North, expands the entertainment and shopping possibilities. Local residents overwhelmingly favor the new IGA grocery store. Fewer appreciate the McDonald's with its underground drive-through ordering system, but McD's mini-pizzas are welcome chow if you're in a rush to the Vancouver airport. The two villages are a five-minute walk apart. They form two points of a triangle, with Blackcomb's base area the third.

Where to ski

Ski both mountains; part of the appeal is to stand on one summit or ridge and look across the steep Fitzsimmons Valley at the runs of the other—to chart out where to go or gloat over where you've been. Both mountains offer complimentary tours in the morning and afternoon, and they may be the best way for first-timers to learn their way around the slopes. Tours usually leave from the Roundhouse on Whistler and the Rendezvous on Blackcomb at 10:30 a.m. and 1:30 p.m.

Once you are up and out of the village area, the skiers spread out and there are few long lines except at the Peak Chair on Whistler and the Seventh Heaven superchair at the top of Blackcomb. On Blackcomb, head instead to the Crystal Ridge and Glacier Express chairs. From the Express, both glacier T-bars and easily accessible.

At Whistler, it's a good idea to start at the ten-person gondola, Whistler Express, and take a speedy ride up 3,800 vertical feet to Roundhouse Station. Ascending over so much terrain, you'll think you're at the summit, but one glance out the gondola building reveals a series of five giant bowls above the treeline. These spread out from left to right: Symphony Bowl, Harmony Bowl, Glacier Bowl, Whistler Bowl and West Bowl (plus the unseen Bagel Bowl, far to the right edge of the ski boundary), all served by the Peak Chair.

Expert skiers will pause just long enough to enjoy the view and then take Peak Chair to the 7,160-foot summit, turning left along the ridge to drop into Glacier Bowl. Or they'll do the wide mogul apron, Shale Slope, in upper Whistler Bowl, rest awhile at the ridge and then have another go below Whistler Glacier. There are no marked runs here—it's wide open. Be creative and let fly. Expert skiing off this summit is in West Bowl, but there are two intermediate ways down. One, Highway 86, is to the right of West Bowl, keeping to the ridge around Bagel Bowl instead of dropping in. The other is Burnt Stew, arguably the most scenic on the mountain. It goes high and wide off to the left of Harmony Bowl, sometimes flattening out into a bit of a trudge. Reached by a long cat track looping behind the bowls, this is one of the great classic runs of North America because of its Alpine views dominated by the imposing Black Tusk peak.

If you want to know what skiing a distance of five miles feels like, take the Alpine T-bar from Roundhouse Station and turn right to find the bronze plaque identifying Franz's Run, one of the longest ski trails in North America. The run turns and pitches and rolls and goes forever. Intermediates love it.

The World Cup course (the men will be at Whistler Feb. 25-26, 1995) is a good challenge run for advanced intermediates. It starts at the top of the Orange Chair and goes a long, long way to the Whistler Creek Base Area.

Beginners won't be able to experience the upper bowls, but will find numerous easier routes down from the Roundhouse, which is, after all, more than 3,800 feet above the village.

Don't forget, there's another whole mountain. Fitzsimmons Chair at the village gives access from the Whistler Gondola area to Blackcomb. Blackcomb's new 8-passenger sit-down gondola, Excalibur, is just to the left of Whistler Mountain's 10-passenger lift (in which four skiers have to stand). A new high-speed quad at the top of the gondola will connect skiers to Blackcomb's glacier skiing at the summit.

Another fast way up Blackcomb Mountain is on the speedy Wizard Express, a sleek quad with an aerodynamic Plexiglas windscreen that also keeps out the rain, which can be a menace at the 2,200-foot base area. At the top of the lift, 2,230 feet higher, you're still not halfway up the mountain. Hop on Solar Coaster, adjacent to Wizard Express unloading area, for another 2,000 feet. Here at Rendezvous Restaurant are numerous routes down for all abilities.

To get into the wide-open above-treeline territory, take Expressway, a lazy beginner's traverse, to Seventh Heaven Express. That lift takes you to Mile High summit, where a free guided exploration of this upper terrain for intermediate and advanced skiers is available daily at 11 a.m. During the uphill ride, off to the right, you'll see the blacks of Xhiggy's Meadow. But once at the Mile High summit, the routes off the backside into Horstman and Blackcomb Glaciers give the feeling of being hundreds of miles into the wilderness. You can also reach these glaciers by taking the Glacier Express, which starts at the bottom of the Jersey Cream chair. While going down the spine off the backside of Horstman, keep to the left and peer over the cornice into the double-black-diamond chutes. Just seeing the abyss—or seeing someone hurl himself into it—gives quite a rush.

The best-known of these severe, narrow chutes is Saudan Couloir, named for Sylvain Saudan, a European extreme skier. The entry requires a leap of faith and skill. Unbelievable though it may be, once a year Blackcomb hosts a race down Saudan Couloir. Nearby is Cougar Chute, also a double black.

One of the most difficult chutes on the mountain is Pakalolo, which is very narrow and steep with rock walls on either side. "You don't want to miss a turn," a local says. Another, called Blowhole, drops from the trail leading to the Blackcomb Glacier from the Horstman Glacier.

A surprise for Blackcomb beginners is a sinuous run called Green Line. The run takes off from the upper terminal of Seventh Heaven Express and follows the natural contours of the mountain from top to bottom on trails groomed daily. It's a thrilling way for beginners to do big-mountain skiing, but getting down, down, down may take all day. Another easy way down from the Hut is the Crystal Traverse run. It winds down below the glaciers, becomes the Crystal Road, passes the Glacier Creek Lodge before joining Green Line two-thirds down the mountain.

Intermediates will especially love the runs off the Jersey Cream chair. They are wide and as smooth as the name implies.

Mountain rating

This resort has plenty of terrain for all levels of skiers. When you ask locals which mountain they prefer, you get mixed responses. Even super experts have reasons for enjoying both, and intermediates will have a field day on either set of slopes. Beginners can have fun, especially because they can get down from the summit (and it's always fun to be able to get to the top), but the terrain for never-evers is only so-so. Other destination resorts of this size usually have a large, gentle, isolated learning area easily accessible at the base. Neither mountain has this.

Cross-country

Nordic skiing is available on the municipal **Lost Lake Trail**, 22 km. of double-tracked trails with a skating lane. Trails are well marked, and start a quarter-mile from the village. Trail passes are Cdn$6, but skiing is free after 4 p.m. At night, a 4-km. stretch of trail is lit until 11 p.m. The Chateau Whistler Clubhouse, on the golf course, is a great rest stop, as is the log hut at Lost Lake. Call 932-6436 for conditions or information.

Most avid cross-country skiers take **BC Rail** to the Cariboo and the 100 Mile House. For information, contact BC Rail Passenger Services, Box 8770, Vancouver, B.C. V6B 4X6, or call 984-5426 or Great Escape Vacations at (800) 663-2515.

Snowboarding

Whistler Mountain picked four areas to sculpt for freeriders, gladerunners, waveheads and tricksters. It's a unique concession to snowboarders' needs, well ahead of the usual ski-area halfpipe. Beginner group lessons for all ages cost Cdn$33 for two and a half hours. Add another $33 for lift ticket and board/boot rental. Adult weekend camps (average age getting closer to 40) are available for $236, which includes breakfast, snacks, coaching, lift tickets and equipment.

Blackcomb Mountain, home of five-time world snowboarding champion Craig Kelly's summer snowboard camps, has a big halfpipe near the top of the Catskinner Chair. The mountain attracts mostly freeriders. First-timer lessons for $60, including Magic Chair lift ticket, board and boots, assure linked turns within 90 minutes.

Ski school (93/94 prices in Cdn$ plus GST)

Each mountain has its own ski school, as well as a dual-mountain ski school/ski host program called Ski Esprit, three or four days that combine guiding and instruction on both mountains. It costs $160 for three days and $195 for four.

At Whistler, the rate for a two-hour **group lesson** (10:30 a.m. or 1 p.m.) is $40, $65 for a private one-hour lesson and $115 for a two-hour private lesson. First-time skiers pay $46 for a two-and-a-half-hour lesson, rentals and lift ticket. At Blackcomb, the rate for an hour-and-a-half group lesson is $34. Private lessons are $67 for one hour, $155 for three hours. First-time skiers are offered a three-day, all-inclusive package for $148.

Both mountains offer **adult workshops** in parallel skiing, bumps, powder and racing. A two-and-a-half hour course is $40. At Whistler, Stephanie Sloan's Women Only ski and snowboard programs are offered six times a season. They stress self-motivation, fitness and nutrition. Three-day programs are $185, plus $99 for a lift ticket; four-day programs are $240, plus $132 for a lift ticket. At Blackcomb, the Ladies Unlimited program for intermediate or advanced skiers is $160 for a two-day session, $195 for a three-day session, plus lift tickets.

Ski Scamps is the children's instructional program at Whistler. Wee Scamps (2-4 years) $48, provides lunch, snacks and skis. At Blackcomb, **Kids Kamp** operates Wee Wizards for 2 to 3 year olds for $50, including lunch and ski equipment rental. Super Kids for 4 to 12 year olds, Mini Masters for 7 to 10 year olds, and Super Stars for 10 to 13 year olds are all $36.50 a day, with half days and multidays available. All children's lessons are from 9 a.m. to 3:30 p.m., except weekends and holidays when they begin at 8:30 a.m.

Lift tickets (93/94 prices in Cdn $ plus GST)

	Adult	Child (7-12)
One day	$44*	$19*
Three days	$132 ($44/day)	$63 ($21/day)
Five days	$205 ($41/day)	$92 ($18.40/day)

Though each mountain has its own pricing, the dual-mountain lift ticket (listed here in the multiday rates) is the only one that makes sense for destination skiers. The asterisked one-day price is for Blackcomb; Whistler's one-day rate is $2 less for adults and $1 less for children.

Teens (13-18) ski for $36 at Blackcomb and $33 at Whistler, while ages 65 and older ski for $32 at Blackcomb and $30 at Whistler. Children 6 and younger ski free.

Those who drive to Whistler can save about $5 per lift ticket by purchasing them at grocery stores in Squamish, a town about 25 miles south of the resort. Save-on-Foods (turn left at McDonald's) offers Whistler tickets, no grocery purchase required. Three miles north on Highway 99, Super-Valu sells Blackcomb tickets.

Accommodations (Prices in Cdn $)

Chateau Whistler is one of the jewels in the crown of impressive French chateau-style Canadian Pacific Hotels (owners of Chateau Lake Louise and Banff Springs Hotel) with 350 rooms in 13 stories, an expansive sun deck stretching below the high turrets, several restaurants, night club and extensive health club. Rates: $150-$950. Call (800) 441-1414.

Other than the Chateau, the largest deluxe lodging is **Delta Mountain Inn**, with 300 rooms, 30 percent of which are kitchen-equipped suites. Hotel rooms are $129-$235, studios are $159-$310, and a one-bedroom suite is $295-$380.

The **Glacier Lodge** is decorated in pale plush. One-bedroom condominiums are $175-$370; two-bedroom, $235-$410. Lodge rooms are $95-$155. The **Nancy Greene Lodge**, operated by the

Canada - Whistler/Blackcomb 463

1968 Olympic gold medal winner, has 140 rooms from $79 to $225. Cozy common areas around the fireplaces give a European feel. Families who don't mind a slightly longer walk to the village center may find the large two-bedroom condominiums at **Tantalus Lodge** suitable for $155-$299.

The **Fairways Hotel, Hearthstone Lodge** and **Listel Hotel** would be considered moderate, offering rooms for $79-$450 (the latter price for a two-bedroom condo in high season). More medium-priced units are available at **Mountainside Lodge,** mini-kitchenette studios for $85-$180.

The **Westbrook Whistler** is right at the village base area, between the Whistler and Blackcomb gondolas. Rates range from $79 for a room to $280 for a two-bedroom condo.

The least expensive accommodations are outside the village at **Shoestring Lodge** offering dorm beds for $20 per night and twin or queen rooms for $70-$80. **Whistler Resort and Club** has rooms for $80-$99 a night. There are three dormitories, **BCIT Lodge, Fireside Lodge** and **UBC Lodge** with beds for $12-$19 a person. Twenty minutes north of Whistler, on Highway 99, **Pemberton Hotel** (894-6313) has $20 rooms, per person.

Whistler also has upscale B&Bs, owned and operated by families and sharing a central living area. These are located in residential areas and usually have no more than six rooms. Most have private baths. Rates vary from $55 to $180 and include breakfast. Ask for those with BC Accommodations approval.

Durlacher Hof is the genuine B&B article for skiers wanting an Austrian lodging experience. At the door, you swap your boots for boiled-wool slippers. Each of the seven rooms has its own bath and extra-long beds. Visiting celebrity chefs prepare dinner on the weekends. Room rates are $85-$180.

Central reservations: 932-4222; (800) 944-7853.

Dining

For years locals have said the **Rimrock Cafe and Oyster Bar** (932-5565) in Highland Lodge is the best restaurant in town. It is not in the village center but in Whistler Creek, a short ride away. Well-prepared seafood, especially lobster and poached British Columbia salmon, is complemented by an extensive wine list. **Les Deux Gros** (932-4611) is another favorite of diners who want the best in French fare. It's located about a mile south of Whistler in Twin Lakes Village.

Val d'Isère (932-4666) located in the heart of Whistler Village features fine French cuisine. Umberto Menghi, a flamboyant Italian chef whose TV cooking show is popular in Canada, is well known for his restaurants in Vancouver and three in Whistler—**Trattoria Di Umberto** (932-5858), **Settebello's** (932-3000) and **Il Caminetto Di Umberto** (932-4442). Continental cuisine is featured. Umberto's main man for

16 years, Mario Enero, broke off in January of 1993 and opened his own **La Rua** (932-5011). His food thinking is ahead of what most diners are ready for, so he holds back a bit to the enrichment of the selections: charred rare tuna, spicy prawns, notorious polenta, tagliattelli, and BC deer loin. **Araxi** (932-4540), on the village square, serves Mediterranean dinners, imaginative pastas and pizza rusticas for $13.50 to $21.50.

At **Timberline** (932-5211) the quality meals are consistent and imaginative. The sunflower baked salmon with sweet pepper sauce is a favorite. **Wainright's** (938-1921) in the Nancy Greene Lodge serves excellent meals and extensive buffet breakfasts at mid-range prices as does **Evergreens** (932-7346) in the Delta Mountain Lodge. **The Keg** (932-5151) has good steaks and other basic American-type cooking.

On the Blackcomb side top dining spots are the **Wildflower** (938-2033) in the Chateau Whistler, **La Fiesta-Hot Rock Café** (938-2040) serving Mediterranean and Mexican cuisine (with excellent paella and heavy on the tapas), **Monk's Grill** (932-9677) at the Wizard Lift base with great lunches, and **Monk's** (932-2779) in the Chamois building, for dinner with piano.

At the streetside entrance to the Le Chamois building is a new Thai restaurant, **Thai One On** (932-4822). The menu is big, so ask if you're not sure. The Pak Tua Gai, peanut sauce on a bed of spinach with chicken, is a fine entrée for $8.95.

With more Japanese skiers than any other North American resort, Whistler also has excellent Japanese restaurants: **Sushi Village** (932-3330) and **Irori** (923-2221). For steaks cooked Japanese steakhouse-style, it's **Teppan Village** (932-2223). **Nanbantei Yakitori** of Tokyo (and Hong Kong, Singapore and San Francisco) recently opened in Whistler North and is recommended by residents.

Moderate-priced dining is also available. **Jimmy D's Roadhouse** (932-4451) across from the conference center has affordable steaks, chicken and pasta. For light dinners and creative lunches, **Zueski's** is situated conveniently at the Whistler gondola base. **Peter's Underground** (932-4811) is a family self-service restaurant serving large portions.

A short walk from the village area along Fitzsimmons Creek in the Fitzsimmons Lodge, **The Border Cantina** (932-3373) serves decent Mexican fare for *poco dinero*.

Good food is served on the mountains, too. The best on each are **The Raven's Nest**, at the top of the Quicksilver Express chair on Whistler Mountain, and **Christine's** in the back of the Rendezvous Lodge on Blackcomb (reservations are a good idea here; 938-7437). Eager skiers can board Whistler's gondola at 7:30 a.m. for a $8.95 (lift ticket extra) buffet breakfast and first rights to the ski runs. Whistler also offers **Moonlight Dine & Ski** four times per season, on full-moon nights only. Call 932-3434 for dates and cost.

Après-ski/nightlife

Après-ski spills out onto the snow from **Longhorn Pub** at Whistler Village gondola base and **Merlin's** at Blackcomb. Both are of the beer-and-nachos variety with lively music. **Citta** in the center of Whistler Village is also a good après-ski spot.

For a quieter environment at the Whistler base area, **Nancy Greene's Piano Bar** from 3 to 6:30 p.m. hosts specialty coffees and guitar and piano music to help create a warm, gentle atmosphere. Creative aperitifs are mixed at **Planter's Lounge.** On the Blackcomb side, **The Mallard Bar** in the Chateau Whistler provides quiet piano music après-ski.

Later in the evening, the reggae and rock at **Buffalo Bill's** starts at 9 p.m. and gets wailing by 10. Another disco is the **Savage Beagle,** and behind the Savage Beagle you'll find **Tommy Africa's** with a young crowd at the pool tables. The locals seem to congregate at **Garfinkle's** which has beer by the pitcher, TVs on almost every wall and a well-used dance floor.

Child care

The only community licensed preschool, **Dandelion Day Care,** charges $22 for a full day and $15 for a half day for children ages 3-5. Call 932-1119.

Other activities

Shopping opportunities are numerous in Whistler Village. The pedestrian-only streets are perfect for window-shopping.

Dog-sledding takes off on trails through an ancient cedar grove. After the ride, you're served lunch in the Cougar Lake Facility, a small log cabin in the woods. Call 932-4086.

Heli-skiing is offered by Tyax Heli-Skiing (932-7007), Whistler Heli-Skiing (932-4105), Western Canada Heli-Sports (938-1700) or Mountain Heli-Sports (932-3512). The same companies have **scenic flights,** as does Whistler Air (932-6615), which also features the option of landing on a glacier.

Hundred of miles of Whistler logging roads are accessible for **snowmobiling** from Highway 99. Whistler Snowmobile Guided Tours has three-hour guided tours several times a day, and two evening rides. A favorite is the Ancient Cedars tour up Cougar Mountain to a cedar grove, with a snack in a backcountry cabin on the return loop.

Covered tennis courts are at the Delta Mountain Inn, **ice skating** and drop-in **hockey** take place at Meadow Park Arena (938-7275) a few miles north of the village and **snowshoe** treks are offered by Canadian Snowshoeing Services (932-7877). **Sleigh rides** are offered by the Whistler Outdoor Experience Company (932-3389).

The **Whistler Activity and Information Centre** provides information on these or other activities, as well as book reservations. Call 932-2394.

Getting there and getting around

Getting there: Canadian Airlines and Air Canada fly to Vancouver. The most scenic way to travel the 75 miles north to Whistler is to board **BC Rail's** passenger trains, which have schedules designed to accommodate skiers. Trains leave North Vancouver at 7 a.m. daily, arriving at 9:34 a.m. They depart Whistler at 6:10 p.m. and return to North Vancouver at 8:35 p.m. Fare is $13 for adults, $6.50 for children younger than 12, one way. Taxis go from the airport to the train station and a bus picks up train passengers at several downtown locations.

Also, **Perimeter Transportation** leaves directly from the Vancouver Airport and goes to Whistler six times a day, with the last bus leaving at 11 p.m. Fare is $26.75 one way. Reservations are required. Call 261-2299.

Maverick Coach Lines operates from the downtown Vancouver bus depot at the corner of Dunsmuir and Georgia, and charges $13 one way. Call 255-1171. **Airport Express** shuttle will get you to the bus depot; call 255-1171. Skiers staying in Vancouver can hop the Blackcomb Ski Bus (622-8051) between 6 and 7 a.m. at various downtown hotels, ski all day and be back in Vancouver by 6 p.m., for $59 plus seven percent GST.

Allow plenty of time in the Vancouver Airport, both arriving and leaving, for customs declarations and currency exchange.

Getting around: Forget the car. You'll never use it while you're staying at Whistler Village.

Information/reservations

For specific information about each mountain, contact **Whistler Mountain Ski Corp.**, Box 67, Whistler, B.C. V0N 1B0; Call 932-3434 or 685-0521. Blackcomb: **Blackcomb Mountain,** Box 98, Whistler, B.C. V0N 1B0; 687-1032 or 935-3141.

For general information about the Whistler area, contact **Whistler Resort Association**, 4010 Whistler Way, Whistler, B.C. V0N 1B4; 932-3928 or toll-free in the U.S. (800) 944-7853.

Unless otherwise noted, all telephone area codes are 604 and all prices are in Canadian dollars. (At press time, one U.S. dollar was worth $1.38 Canadian.)

Québec Region
Canada

The closest thing to France in North America is the Canadian province of Québec. This section of Canada still speaks French as its primary language, maintains many of the French traditions and has managed to create a cuisine and way of life that still blend the rustic adventure of the New World and the sensibilities of Europe.

Québec offers more than a simple peek into a North American France. Here you can find some excellent skiing which, combined with the cities, the menus and the countryside, provides a vacation experience you'll remember long after the winter weather warms into summer.

Though much has been written about the French push for language purity in this region, the fact of the matter is that English is spoken virtually everywhere. French is still the *official* language and all signs are written in French, but at the resorts and in the cities, the natives are very friendly (at least to English-speakers from south of the border) and are more than willing to help make your vacation here enjoyable.

Québec City

Any visit to this province means a stop in Québec City with the historic, towering Château Frontenac on Place d'Armes surrounded by narrow cobblestone streets lined with boutiques and bistros. Between the *antiquitiés* and *galeries* you'll find delightful *patisseries* and *cafés* where you can enjoy a pleasant *gâteau avec café au lait*. Québec's version of Restaurant Row is rue St-Louis. For the latest in tourist kitsch souvenirs, walk down rue du Tresor. The nearby Ursuline Convent and Museum provides in sight into convent life of the 1600s and 1700s.

Below the Château Frontenac is the lower town. A short funicular will take you from the hotel to the oldest street in North America, **rue de Petit-Champlain**, running beside the towering town walls. The 1688 **church of Notre-Dame** still provides worship services as well as sightseeing. Stop in at the **Maison Chevalier**, a restored 18th-century house, and the **Place Royal**, once the heart of New France. The **Musée de Civilisation** showcases Québec history, art and culture.

Winter Carnival takes place annually around the end of February. It lasts ten days and always includes two weekends. If you are skiing at Mont-Sainte-Anne during that time you are in luck. The festival features parades, ice sculptures and music, with plenty of drinking and dancing—just imagine a Mardi Gras in the snow.

The main tourist office is at 60 rue d'Auteuil, just north of Grande Allée. A second tourist office is on Place d'Armes which deals with destinations in other parts of the province. Down in the Place Royal area, near the river, is another tourist office at 215 rue de Marché-Finlay in the Lower Town.

Montréal

This cosmopolitan center is the third largest French-speaking city in the world. Here the New World blends perfectly with the Old. Soaring skyscrapers stand side by side with Art Deco edifices but Vieux-Montréal, the center of government and commerce, still reminds visitors of the grand old days. Visit the Quai Jacques Cartier to see the evolving waterfront development—it now has art galleries, a flea market and a crafts center. See the **Place d'Armes**, sight of Indian battles. Stop in at the neo-Gothic **Notre-Dame Basilica** opened in 1829. The **Montréal History Center** in the old fire hall on Place d'Youville provides a historic overview to the city.

Make sure to walk down **rue St-Denis** for its Latin Quarter appeal and wander down the pedestrian **rue Prince Arthur** for the latest in shopping.

Winter is the perfect time to visit *la ville souterraine*, or underground city, which accesses more than 1,000 shops, hundreds of restaurants and bars, ten shopping plazas, six hotels and two train stations—all without stepping out into the cold weather.

For winter browsing there are plenty of museums (most closed on Mondays)—the Musée des Beaux Arts, the city's main art museum, the Contemporary Art Gallery, the Centre for Architecture, the McCord Museum, Saidye Bronfman Museum and the Château Dufresne Museum of Decorative Arts.

The main Montréal tourist office is at 1001 rue Square Dorchester. Other offices are at 174 rue Notre-Dame Est in Old Montréal and at the airport.

The ski resorts
Mont-Sainte-Anne

This is the town ski slope for Québec, only 20 miles east of the city. It has 2,050 vertical feet of skiing rising from the St. Lawrence River. The mountain has some of the most advanced lifts and ski pass systems in North America. The capacity of this lift system is an amazing 18,000 skiers per hour, so it's rare to find lift lines even on weekends, when Québec seems to come en masse to ski.

The views down to the river are spectacular. The skiing on more than 50 trails is perfect for virtually every level of skier. Naturally, hot experts will complain, but they do almost everywhere. The lift system includes bubble-topped high-speed quads and an eight-person gondola. Snowmaking blankets almost 90 percent of the terrain. *And* the computerized lift ticket system allows you to ski for a full week, full day, half day, a couple of hours, or any other combination you can dream up.

The Children's Center located at the base of the mountain offers day care for children aged 12 months and older. A Kinderski school takes learners from 3 to 6 years of age.

Parc du Mont-Sainte-Anne, P.O. Box 400, Beaupré (Québec) G0A 1E0; (418) 827-4561, reservations: (800) 463-1568.

Tremblant

This Laurentian resort located 85 miles north of Montréal was recently purchased by the same folks who own Blackcomb Mountain in British Columbia. Since then, $53 million has been put into bringing this resort back to its former status as an elegant ski resort. New facilities include a pedestrian village with ski-in/ski-out lodging, shops and restaurants; snowmaking; new lifts; new trails; and a new mountain-top restaurant, *Le Grand Manitou.*

Today the resort has 2,131 vertical feet of skiing with a very New England narrow-trail feel. Though most of the mountain's slopes are just right for families and casual skiers, advanced and expert skiers will find new steeps, such as Zig Zag and Vertige on the South Side, and Dynamite on the North Side—all of which were new in 93/94, and all of which are covered by snowmaking. Snowmaking now blankets 37 of the 57 trails, about triple what snowmaking was two years ago. Five new lifts in the past two seasons—three of them high-speed quads—have increased lift capacity to 18,800 skiers per hour. If you haven't skied Tremblant in a while, it's time to visit once more.

Tremblant, 3005, chemin Principal, Mont-Tremblant (Québec) J0T 1Z0; (819) 681-2000, reservations: (800) 461-8711.

Gray Rocks

Gray Rocks, a 75-mile drive north of Montréal on Highway 117, is a mouse compared to Tremblant and Mont-Sainte-Anne—it has 620 feet of vertical and four chair lifts. But this tiny resort has carved a big slice of the student skier market: the success of this Learn-to-Ski-Week concept is overwhelming, with more than 140,000 lessons given in this resort every season. Some ski writers claim this is a kinder, gentler resort, but lessons are not only for the timid first-time skiers. Here, skiers of every level are faced with a challenging week of perfecting technique.

Part of the success is the activity off the slopes. Where off-piste might mean deep powder at some resorts, at Gray Rocks it means good times. A week at Gray Rocks has been compared to a week-long party cruise with snow. Families are mixed with families. Singles are matched with other singles—*Glamour* rates this one of the best single-man hunting grounds in North America. Groups eat together, sharing stories of the day's lesson and then the après-ski starts with creative alternatives to disco such as moonlight cross-country skiing, snow rafting races, lumberjack contests (and he's O.K.), beer fests, fashion shows, and pool parties.

Ski week prices range from Cdn$552 to Cdn$750 based on double occupancy in a standard room, with superior rooms running about 15 percent more. A special Thanksgiving weekend ski school is also available.

Gray Rocks, P.O. Box 1000, St. Jovite (Québec) J0T 2H0; (819) 425-2771, reservations (800) 567-6767.

Cross-country

Cross-country skiing is excellent throughout this province. Near Parc du Mont-Sainte-Anne there is a network of 214 km. of marked and groomed trails including 100 km. reserved for skating. Terrain mix leans toward the difficult, but with plenty of kilometers for beginners and intermediates. You'll find heated cabins along the trails, a wilderness lodge with lessons as well as room and board, a chalet with cafeteria, ski school and other amenities plus a skating rink and toboggan run.

The region between Montréal and Tremblant claims 23 cross-country centers with more than 1,000 km. of trails. These trails connect inns, villages and other ski areas, making them well-suited for ski touring. Starting about 40 miles north of Montréal, try one of these major cross-country areas: Morin-Heights (150 km.), l'Estérel (95 km.), Far Hills (100 km.), Mont-Tremblant Park (160 km.), and Gray Rocks (90 km.).